D1737850

FROM SEA TO SHINING SEA

A HISTORY OF THE UNITED STATES

FROM SEA TO SHINING SEA

A HISTORY OF THE UNITED STATES

Bernard A. Weisberger   *Third Edition*

Webster Division, McGraw-Hill Book Company

New York   St. Louis   San Francisco   Auckland   Bogotá   Düsseldorf
Johannesburg   London   Madrid   Mexico   Montreal   New Delhi
Panama   Paris   São Paulo   Singapore   Sydney   Tokyo   Toronto

The United States Today

State Capitals and Major Metropolitan Centers shown on map:

Augusta, Montpelier, VT, N.H., Concord, Boston, Rochester, Albany, MASS., NEW YORK, Buffalo, Providence, R.I., Hartford, CONN., Newark, New York, Green Bay, MICHIGAN, Milwaukee, Lansing, Detroit, Cleveland, PENNSYLVANIA, Trenton, Madison, Chicago, Toledo, Pittsburgh, Harrisburg, Philadelphia, N.J., OHIO, Baltimore, Dover, Columbus, Annapolis, DEL., ILLINOIS, INDIANA, Washington D.C., MD., Springfield, Indianapolis, Cincinnati, W. VA., St. Louis, Louisville, Frankfort, Charleston, Richmond, VIRGINIA, Norfolk, KENTUCKY, Raleigh, Nashville, NORTH CAROLINA, TENNESSEE, Memphis, Columbia, SOUTH CAROLINA, Birmingham, Atlanta, MISSISSIPPI, ALABAMA, GEORGIA, Jackson, Montgomery, Jacksonville, Mobile, Tallahassee, Baton Rouge, New Orleans, FLORIDA, Tampa, Miami, MAINE

★ State Capitals
● Major Metropolitan Centers
 Extended Urban Areas

State	Admission Date	Population 1970 Census	Population 1980 Census
Alabama	1819	3,373,006	3,863,698
Alaska	1959	294,607	400,331
Arizona	1912	1,752,122	2,714,013
Arkansas	1836	1,886,210	2,280,687
California	1850	19,715,490	23,510,372
Colorado	1876	2,178,176	2,877,726
Connecticut	1788	2,987,950	3,096,951
Delaware	1787	542,979	594,779
Florida	1845	6,671,162	9,579,495
Georgia	1788	4,492,038	5,396,425
Hawaii	1959	748,575	964,624
Idaho	1890	698,275	943,629
Illinois	1818	10,977,908	11,321,350
Indiana	1816	5,143,422	5,454,154
Iowa	1846	2,789,893	2,908,797
Kansas	1861	2,222,173	2,355,536
Kentucky	1792	3,160,555	3,642,143
Louisiana	1812	3,564,310	4,194,299
Maine	1820	977,260	1,123,560
Maryland	1788	3,874,642	4,193,378
Massachusetts	1788	5,630,224	5,728,288
Michigan	1837	8,778,187	9,236,891
Minnesota	1858	3,767,975	4,068,856
Mississippi	1817	2,158,872	2,503,250
Missouri	1821	4,636,247	4,901,678
Montana	1889	682,133	783,674
Nebraska	1876	1,468,101	1,564,727
Nevada	1864	481,893	800,312
New Hampshire	1788	722,753	919,114
New Jersey	1787	7,084,992	7,335,808
New Mexico	1912	998,257	1,290,551
New York	1788	17,979,712	17,557,288
North Carolina	1789	4,961,832	5,846,159
North Dakota	1889	610,648	652,437
Ohio	1803	10,542,030	10,758,421
Oklahoma	1907	2,498,378	2,998,124
Oregon	1859	2,056,171	2,617,444
Pennsylvania	1787	11,669,565	11,824,561
Rhode Island	1790	922,461	945,761
South Carolina	1788	2,522,881	3,067,061
South Dakota	1889	661,406	687,643
Tennessee	1796	3,838,777	4,539,834
Texas	1845	10,989,123	14,152,339
Utah	1896	1,060,631	1,454,630
Vermont	1791	437,744	511,299
Virginia	1788	4,543,249	5,321,521
Washington	1889	3,352,892	4,109,634
West Virginia	1863	1,701,913	1,928,524
Wisconsin	1848	4,366,766	4,689,055
Wyoming	1890	328,591	468,909

Bernard A. Weisberger

Dr. Weisberger received his Ph.D. in history from the University of Chicago. He has taught at Wayne State, the University of Chicago and Rochester, and Columbia and Stanford Universities. He presently is at Vassar College.

CONSULTANTS

Dr. John W. Blassingame
Department of History, Yale University

Gerald Hardcastle
Department of Social Studies
Nathan Hale High School, Seattle, Washington

Peter P. Carlin
Superintendant, Continuing Education
and Special Projects Cleveland Public Schools

Arthur H. Rumpf
Curriculum Specialist, Social Studies Milwaukee Public Schools

Anne Dawson Falzone
Social Studies Writer, New York

Editorial Development: Rosalyn Kelley, Marlena Baraf, Robert Nirkind
Editing and Styling: Naomi Russell Onco, Patricia McCormick
Designer: Tracy Glasner
Additional Photo Research: Alan Forman
Production Supervisor: Angela Kardovich

Library of Congress Cataloging in Publication Data

Weisberger, Bernard
  From Sea to Shining Sea

  Rev. ed. of: The impact of our past.
  Includes Index
  Summary: A history of our country which may be used as a full year course. Includes the constitution and a list of presidents.
  1. United States—History. [1. United States—History] I. Title.
E 178.1. W 4 1982   973   81–1513
ISBN 0-07-069099-5   AACR2

Contents

UNIT 1
Peopling the Americas

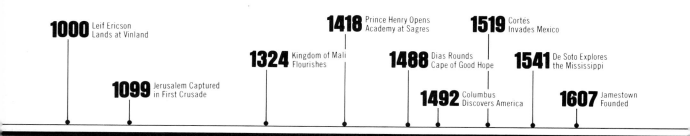

1000 Leif Ericson Lands at Vinland

1099 Jerusalem Captured in First Crusade

1324 Kingdom of Mali Flourishes

1418 Prince Henry Opens Academy at Sagres

1488 Dias Rounds Cape of Good Hope

1492 Columbus Discovers America

1519 Cortés Invades Mexico

1541 De Soto Explores the Mississippi

1607 Jamestown Founded

CHAPTER 1
The First Americans

CHAPTER 2
The Coming of the Europeans

CHAPTER 3
Slavery Comes to the Americas

CHAPTER 4
Colonial America

American history is the story of the coming together of many different peoples—sometimes in harmony and sometimes in bloodshed. When Columbus planted Spain's flag on an island in the Caribbean,

1613 Tobacco First Sent to England from Virginia

1619 First Blacks Land at Jamestown

1664 English Capture New Amsterdam

1619 First Meeting of Virginia Burgesses

1723 Benjamin Franklin Arrives in Philadelphia

there were already some 20 million people living in the Americas. Incorrectly called "Indians" by Columbus, these people had developed many remarkable societies and civilizations. You will study these societies in Chapter 1.

After Columbus and other early European explorers brought the news of new lands back to Europe, a period of migration began. White Europeans came to the Americas in search of riches, freedom, and opportunity. Black Africans were forcibly brought in chains.

The way Americans have viewed their past has been greatly influenced by the group they are descended from. And their past begins with Indian, African, and European peoples. Chapter 1 explores the American Indian heritage. Chapter 2 concentrates on the European part of the story. Chapter 3 focuses on the African part. Finally, Chapter 4 describes the colonial society that White and Black Americans had built along the east coast of North America by 1750.

CHAPTER 1
The First Americans

The United States is made up of people who are always on the move, people who crowd the subways, airways, and highways. Its history begins with human beings in motion, restlessly seeking food, warmth, safety, and a place to rear their young. All animals do this. But, as far as we know, only people dream of better lives. In the Americas, people from all over the world who dream of a better life have been meeting and mingling for thousands of years.

"Thousands of years" may sound like a mistake to you, if you think that American history begins with Columbus discovering the New World in 1492. Actually, the Indians who were here when Columbus arrived were the first people of "America."

For a moment, think of the earth as a spaceship moving endlessly through space. Many families of people live on board, in "rooms" separated by green forests, wrinkled brown mountains, and blue oceans. If you were in another spaceship, looking through openings in the cloud curtain, you would see earthlings moving about the icy chambers near the poles and through the warm gardens at the equator. If you had a time machine that squeezed thousands of years into seconds, you would see streams of humanity migrating over the globe like columns of ants.

More than 25,000 years ago, such a column of people began to move from Siberia, in Asia. These people crossed a land bridge to Alaska and then headed southward. Glaciers still covered much of North America. When the glaciers finally melted, the level of the ocean rose enough to cover this land bridge. These first migrations took many centuries to spread across North and South America. As the people flowed southward, they left their bones, crude tools,

READING GUIDE

1. **How did the contrasting environments of North and South America influence the First American civilizations that developed?**
2. **What type of political organizations developed in the Aztec and Incan societies?**
3. **How did the First North Americans make use of nature's gifts?**

Portrait of Strutting Pigeon, wife of White Cloud, by George Catlin.

weapons, and household utensils in various places. Gradually, the earth covered these things. Scientists have dug down and found some of this ancient litter. Using special instruments to determine the age of these remnants, they found that people had reached southern South America about 8000 years ago.

1. The Continents They Found

societies
groups of people living together and bound by the same way of life

environments
surrounding conditions that influence a community's cultural development

Southwest Indians file past giant cacti that flourish in the sun-baked desert.

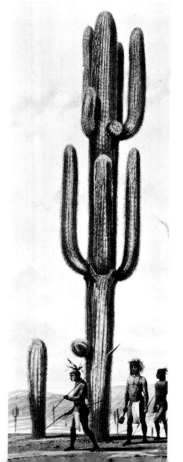

The map on the opposite page shows at a glance the migration of these First Americans. Actually, the whole march probably took thousands of years. Compare that to the 200 years since the American Revolution or even to the 500 years since Columbus. You will see that those of you whose ancestors come from Europe or Africa are newcomers in the Western Hemisphere.

Columbus called the people he found in the Americas "Indians." He did so because he thought he had arrived in the East Indies. He also thought of these people as one group. In 1492, Columbus and other Europeans were unaware that there were millions of First Americans, divided into hundreds of nations and tribal **societies.** They were spread over two continents, occupying nearly half the land surface of the earth.

Just as the Indian peoples of the Americas differed, so did the physical environments in which they lived. The two continents of North and South America offer many contrasting **environments.** Towering mountains run down the entire length of the western parts of both continents. In North America, there are great, almost treeless plains. They are between the Rocky Mountains in the west and the Appalachians in the east. However, the northeastern part of North America was once solid forest. And parts of North and South America are deserts. These deserts are shut off from rain-bearing clouds by mountain walls. By contrast, in large areas of South and Central America, jungle foliage multiplies under daily rains.

The many different kinds of natural settings in the Americas can be illustrated by matching some extremes. The Pacific Coast of Colombia, in South America, is one of the world's wettest places. More than 254 centimeters (100 inches) of rain fall there every year. Chile's Atacama Desert is one of the driest places in the world. Rainfall there is barely measurable. The Andes Mountains of Chile house some of the world's highest towns, more than three miles above sea level. Idaho, in the United States, has the deepest gorge, Hells Canyon, which cuts 2401.6 meters (7900 feet) into the earth. In the town of Churchill, in Canada, the temperature is below freezing six months of the year. In Maracaibo, Venezuela, the average daily temperature is 32°C (90°F) in January and 34°C (94°F) in August. The first peoples of the Americas learned to survive not only in icebound lands but also in climates that threatened to bake them. They had to develop tools and

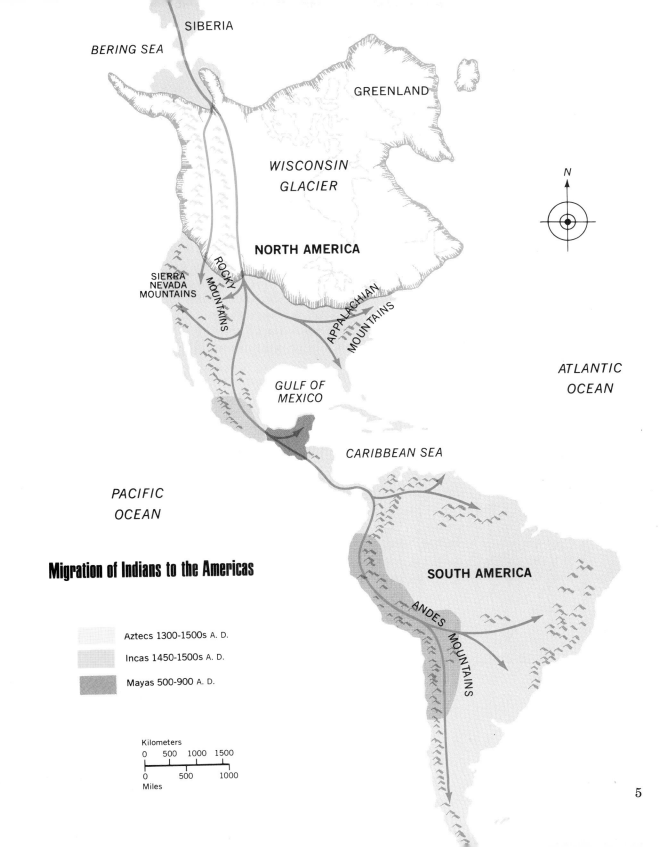

SIBERIA

BERING SEA

GREENLAND

WISCONSIN
GLACIER

NORTH AMERICA

N

SIERRA
NEVADA
MOUNTAINS

ROCKY
MOUNTAINS

APPALACHIAN
MOUNTAINS

ATLANTIC
OCEAN

GULF OF
MEXICO

CARIBBEAN SEA

PACIFIC
OCEAN

Migration of Indians to the Americas

SOUTH AMERICA

ANDES
MOUNTAINS

Aztecs 1300-1500s A. D.

Incas 1450-1500s A. D.

Mayas 500-900 A. D.

Kilometers
0   500   1000 1500

0   500   1000
Miles

5

skills in order to feed themselves on high, dry plateaus as well as in steep canyons.

America's First Cultures

It is no wonder, then, that the First Americans had so many different **cultures**. If people, such as the Kiowas, live on prairies and depend on the buffalo hunt for food, then that tribe will need good hunters. Their small children will be taught how to be swift and clever. But other people, such as the Hopi, may live in the hot desert, growing corn and beans. They may put the greatest emphasis on priests who can bring necessary rain by prayer. Their children may learn that sacred dances are more important than skinning a carcass. They may be praised for making a good hoe or water pot.

Among the First Americans, there were many different ways of making a living. There were also different ways of playing, worshiping, raising a family, and establishing common rules. But, however great the differences among the peoples of mountains, deserts, and jungles, there were some important likenesses as well. All First Americans recognized that they were part of the world of nature. Whether the animals they saw around them were seals or sea gulls or alligators or jaguars, the Indians believed that beasts and people were meant to share the earth. They hunted animals for food. They used the skins and bones of animals for their own clothing and dwellings. They cut trees and plants from the earth or dug holes in it to plant crops. But they thought of the animals as their kin and considered the earth as a caretaker.

The First Americans believed that animals had great powers. For example, birds could soar into the skies where the gods made thunder and lightning. Fish could live in water while human beings could not. Belief in the power of animals is not surprising. We still say a person is as "sly as a fox," "wise as a serpent," or "fierce as a lion." People often thought they could acquire these qualities from the animals. They would wear the skins of the animals or paint their pictures on the tepee or on robes or shields.

All First American cultures shared the belief that people, spirits, and animals were related. This explains another custom common to all the known First American cultures. They did not believe in the private ownership of land. The sun, air, water, plants, and beasts were spirits or were made by the gods. No one person could own them. In the 1800s, an American Indian had a horse which escaped into a White family's pasture. The family complained that the animal had eaten their grass. The American Indian replied, "Did you make the grass grow?"

One tribe or nation might fight another for a hunting ground or a fertile valley. But it was the tribe, not the individual, that made the

cultures
ways of living

Communication in early American Indian civilizations was often by hand signals. Here, the question "Who are you?" is answered "Pantu."

claim. And, the tribe did not own the land. The people only used the land with the permission of the spirits who ruled the world.

When Europeans first came to the New World, they thought the beliefs and ways of the First Americans were "barbarous" and "savage." Nothing could have been farther from the truth. First American societies were far from primitive. They had highly developed *civilizations*. A civilization arises when a community has developed beyond the simple struggle to stay alive. At this stage of growth, more complicated governments and religions develop. People create impressive monuments, celebrating their civilization's way of life. These monuments may be public buildings, shrines, or other scientific and engineering feats, like highways. Monuments may also take the form of works of art and historical records.

A Mandan, helped by sled-pulling dogs, crosses the frozen Missouri River.

Questions for Discussion
1. Define *societies, environments, culture.*
2. What makes a group of people a civilization?
3. How does a culture differ from a civilization?

2. Three Early Civilizations of the Americas

economy
a system of production and distribution of goods

When Peru was conquered by Spaniards in 1532, it was occupied by people who were called by the same name as their ruler, the Inca. Incan civilization had already made great strides in the important task of developing an **economy**. Most people were farmers, not hunters. They learned to grow various foods which are still eaten today. These foods include white potatoes, sweet potatoes, beans, tomatoes, peanuts, and several kinds of corn. They learned not only to preserve the seeds and plant them each growing season but also to breed different varieties of the same plant. This was a tremendous step forward in establishing a civilization. In their constant search for food, a hunting tribe must follow the game animals. But farming people can stay in one place and build a civilization. If they move, they can take their food supply with them and build again.

South American Indians paddle a canoe down the Amazon River past a steaming jungle.

The Economy and Government of the Incas
The Incas faced the problem of farming on steep slopes of the Andes Mountains. They solved this problem by cutting terraces, or steps, into the hillsides. They covered these terraces with soil patiently carried in baskets up narrow paths. They laid down grooved stones from which precious rainwater gurgled into irrigation ditches. They enriched the soil by mixing it with carefully collected *guano*, the droppings of birds and bats. With skillfully braided nets, they took fish from the seas and lakes. Food was shared by all, and extra food was held in storehouses to supply people in times of famine.

The Incas also learned to breed and tame animals such as the llama, a sure-footed relative of the camel. They used the llama as a pack animal to help farm large tracts and to carry harvests from field to storehouse. The Incas also domesticated the alpaca, which furnished coarse wool for the common people. They also hunted wild beasts. The *guanaco* was valued for its meat. The *vicuña* furnished especially fine wool for the garments of the rich.

Planting and harvesting were important ceremonial acts. Nobles with golden spades often began the work, just as our governors and mayors sometimes turn the first shovelful of earth on the site of a new dam or tunnel. The Incan people were fine farmers. A Spanish traveler wrote that whenever they settled a new spot of ground, soon "it caused great happiness to see it."

Commerce was highly developed. The Incas navigated along the coast to trade their goods. The Incan **political system** also greatly impressed one of the conquering Spaniards. In 1532, the Incas controlled an **empire**. The Spaniard admired the Incan skill in ruling this empire, "parts of which were rugged and covered with forests, parts mountainous, with snowy peaks and ridges, parts consisting of deserts of sand," and all of it lived in by people with "varying languages, laws, and religions." To hold the empire together peacefully, political power was centered firmly in the Lord Inca.

The Lord Inca divided the empire into four parts. Each part was ruled by a noble. Under these nobles were other nobles, each responsible for a set number of commoners. The duties of the nobles included yearly visits to villages to make a careful count of their people, animals, and crops. Therefore, the Lord Inca could determine, quickly, how many people he could rely on to work in the fields and to fight in a war. He was able to find out how much grain, gold, and other goods he might expect in *tribute* (forced payment).

Fine, wide, dry roads with high stone walls ran through the empire. Llamas could move quickly along them with baskets full of tribute to support the government. Soldiers could also travel quickly along them to keep order.

The cities where Lord Inca kept his palaces and storehouses became centers of public affairs and business. Thus, the Incan political system was one force that helped create an *urban* (city-centered) civilization.

The Incan nobles had great power and position. They showed their high rank by wearing fine robes and golden earplugs, which were disks pushed through holes in the earlobe. The Spaniards laughed at how the ornaments stretched the flesh. They called the Incan nobles

On the opposite page, Incan fishermen cast their nets and lines from balsa-log rafts.

Citizens carrying the mummified remains of the Lord Inca.

political system
the way of ruling

empire
a large area that includes a number of different territories ruled by a single authority

Only nobles could carry the golden litter of the Lord Inca.

Three aspects of Incan life. Top: Incan masons are building a wall. Middle: Women hoe a field. Bottom: Incan nobles break the earth in a spring-planting ceremony.

orejones ("big ears"), and greedily eyed the gold. The nobles were privileged and petted. But they were also expected to work as hard as any official or soldier.

Above them all stood the Lord Inca himself. He was supposed to be the descendant of Inti, god of the blazing, life-giving sun. When he traveled, proud nobles willingly carried his litter. A parasol shielded him from the sun. And his own magnificence was hidden from commoners by gold curtains embroidered with blazing serpents, moons, and other symbols. Only a favored few saw him face to face.

Aztec Society

The Aztecs lived in central Mexico. They had a very structured civilization, which reached its peak around the thirteenth century. Their highly developed social structure contributed to the greatness of the empire.

The ruling family and all their relatives made up the highest group of society. The Emperor was chosen from the royal family, but he did not have to be the son of the previous ruler. The Aztecs chose the best-qualified male member of the royal family. Members of the royal family were expected to serve as good examples for others to follow. If they failed, they were severely punished.

The nobility made up the next level of society. A person had to earn the right to be a noble by performing an outstanding service. Neither the rank nor its privileges could be passed on to the children of nobles. Members of these upper classes were punished more harshly than members of the lower classes for the same failings.

One way to enter the nobility was through outstanding military service. Most soldiers came from the lower class. By taking prisoners or killing a certain number of the enemy, the soldiers earned the right to wear certain adornments. If the soldier were particularly successful, he would be admitted to the noble class. Members of the priesthood could also rise to the nobility. Though most did not, some still achieved a great deal of power and status.

A third group in society was the *pochteca*, or merchant class. Members of this group were large-scale traders. They would undertake long journeys, often through unfriendly territory, to exchange finished goods for raw materials. Because of their travels and knowledge of language, these merchants sometimes served as spies for the Aztecs. They were not required to serve in the military.

Artisans also had a privileged position in Aztec society. Like the pochteca, they did not have to do agricultural work or to serve in the military. Usually, the entire family would work at a craft. The children learned the skills, so that occupations were often passed down in the same families.

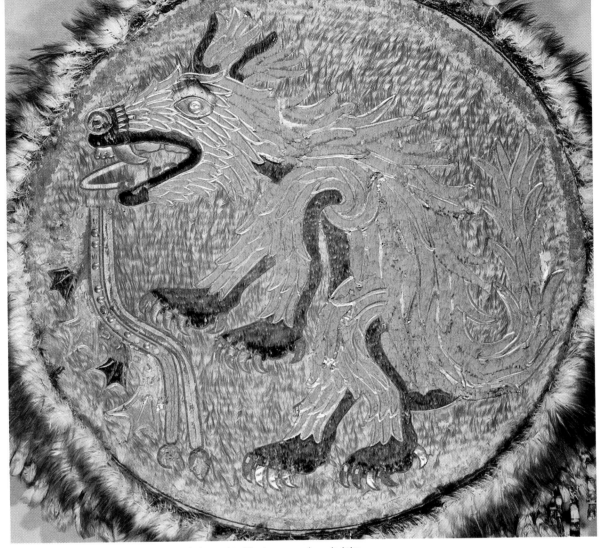

The elaborate feather shield above once belonged to Montezuma, who ruled the Aztecs during the Spanish invasion.

The laborers below bring grain to a government storage house.

Generally, agricultural workers were the lowest class of free people. Some workers owned their own property. Agricultural workers were required to give military service. This was not always a burden, since outstanding military service sometimes led to a higher class position.

Slaves made up the lowest class of people in Aztec society. People were not born into this class. They became slaves in a number of ways. Some were prisoners of war. Others became slaves as a punishment for crimes. A third group agreed to become slaves, because they either were unable to pay their debts or were unable to provide for themselves. The slave owner provided food, clothing, and shelter. A

Above: Mayan warriors.

Below: Aztec gold pieces. From top to bottom: an earplug, a monkey-head pin, an owl's head, and a lip plug.

slave was not obligated to serve in the military. There was little stigma attached to being a slave. Slaves could buy their freedom and could marry free persons. Children of slaves were born free.

Children in Aztec society were required to attend school. The children of the upper classes, and an occasional youngster from the lower classes, attended the schools run by scholarly priests. Among the subjects taught were religion, astronomy, philosophy, and history. Students were subjected to strict discipline, fasting, and sacrifice. The purpose of schooling for upper-class children was to prepare them for high government offices or for roles as priests or priestesses.

Most children of the lower classes went to a different kind of school. In these schools, boys were required to provide manual labor on community projects. Military training was of major importance. Every boy of the lower class was expected to become a warrior. Girls were trained to become managers of the house and family. Intellectual achievement, such as reading and writing, was not required of these children as it was of children from the upper classes.

The Art and Music of the Aztecs

The works of art created by a civilization tell us many things about it. They reveal the state of its *technology* (the ability to apply knowledge to useful purposes). Can its people weave cloth? Can they make dyes? Can they refine metal and file and hammer it into shape? Can they mold and bake clay into pottery? Works of art tell us what a society thinks is beautiful and what it values or cares most about. Because artists sometimes portray everyday scenes in their sculptures and drawings, they show us what daily life was like at the time. We can then tell what was carried on a hunt, how people wore their hair, and what kinds of pets children had.

The Aztecs were an Indian people who had dominated much of Mexico for nearly a century before the Europeans arrived. Their civilization was intricate and powerful. Their art shows that they could also lavish care on simple objects and make them beautiful. They were able to dye their jars and their woven cotton garments with brilliant colors made from herbs, berries, and bark. Around the borders of their clothes and around their pottery ran clever designs of repeated lines, zigzags, and squares.

They were skillful at making small gold ceremonial objects, such as breast pins and earplugs. On these objects, they reproduced the likenesses of animals.

Aztec artists took advantage of nature's own brilliant plumage. They produced striking effects by weaving feathers into cloth. They also fastened bits of colored stone and shell to objects created from wood.

The Mayan temple of Kukulkan in Mexico.

Mayan warriors in ceremonial dress.

Like adornment, music was an important part of ceremonial services. Mournful pieces were played on a variety of flutes, whistles, trumpets, conch shells, and drums. Since there was no written form of music, musicians were responsible for memorizing many different pieces. These musicians were highly regarded because of their place in religious services, but they also had great responsibilities. Since music was thought to soothe the gods, a note played wrong was thought to make them angry. Thus, a musical error could carry a severe penalty.

The Mayan Religion

The Mayas lived in parts of present-day Guatemala, Belize, and Mexico. The great age of the Mayan civilization lasted about 600 years and ended around 900 A.D. When Europe was in the period called the Dark Ages, Mayan priests were studying astronomy. Mayan artists were carving fantastic designs in stone, and Mayan workers were building great temples that resembled pyramids. The Mayas had developed a calendar and a very advanced numerical system.

Religion played a large role in the daily lives of the Mayas. The Mayan gods were both good and bad. They controlled life, death, storms, earthquakes, fire, and harvests. The chief Mayan crop was **maize** (corn), and the plant itself was worshiped as a god. The god associated with the sun was supposed to have a good influence on medicine, books, and writing. The god of death was pictured as a fleshless figure surrounded by animals such as an owl or a dog, each of which had an evil significance. It was believed that in heaven, no one worked, and everyone was guaranteed that all good things would be plentiful forever. In Mitnal, the Mayan hell, there was no food or warmth and no end to suffering.

This turquoise-and-shell ornament represented one of the Aztec gods.

maize
Indian corn

13

A Mayan battle scene, from the Temple at Bonampak in Mexico.

Hunters often disguised themselves in deerskins, complete with antlers.

Only the priest-rulers knew the gods' needs. They told the people what they must do to satisfy the gods. Priests ordered huge religious centers—some as large as a modern city—to be built in honor of the gods. Only priests lived in these cities. The Mayan people visited the cities to attend rituals held there. If the priests predicted bad times, the Mayas cut themselves and collected the blood in bark saucers. They presented this gift to the gods. If the evil prophecy did not change, sometimes the priests called for a human sacrifice. During the great age of the Mayas, human sacrifice was not common. However, as the Mayas became more warlike, the practice increased. Human sacrifice reached a peak at Chichen Itza, Mexico, around 1200 A.D.

Questions for Discussion

1. Define *economy*, *political system*, *empire*, *urban*.
2. How did the Incas use nature to build their civilization?
3. What system did Incan rulers use to govern?
4. What does a civilization's art tell us about its technology? Its values? Its daily life?
5. What was the role of the pochteca in the Aztec society?

The First Americans north of Mexico did not build civilizations as beautiful as those built by the Incas, Aztecs, or Mayas. However, they did develop many remarkable abilities, one of which was to use what nature provided, thoroughly and without waste. Nature provided tools, clothing, food, and medicine. When Whites first came to live in the wilderness, they learned that the only way to survive was to imitate the ways of the First Americans.

Since the First Americans lived in close touch with nature, they were affected by the climate, **topography**, and location of the land they lived on. Though there were many basic similarities in the societies, culture, and worship, each nation developed some of its own characteristics.

The Economy of the First North Americans

Nations in the Southeast, such as the Creek, Choctaw, Powhatan, Chickasaw, Alabama, and Cherokee, had the advantages of living in an area that had a warm climate and long growing season. Their economy was based on agriculture. They supplemented crops of corn, squash, and wild rice with wild berries, nuts, game, and fish. With a strong agricultural base and plentiful game, the southeastern nations developed villages of well-built houses and ceremonial centers. Food was usually plentiful, so the people could remain settled in one place.

The land from the Atlantic coast to the Great Lakes was referred to as the Northeastern Woodlands. The culture of each tribe was affected by its location in this widely differing area.

The Nanticoke, Delaware, and Montauk lived on the fertile coastal plains. They raised corn, hunted game, and fished. The northern

3. The First North Americans

topography
the physical or natural features of an area

The drawings on this page show different ways in which regional tribes provided for themselves. Below: Florida women plant seed while the men, using fishbone hoes, prepare the ground. Below Left: a Northeastern Indian roasts fish on a wooden grill.

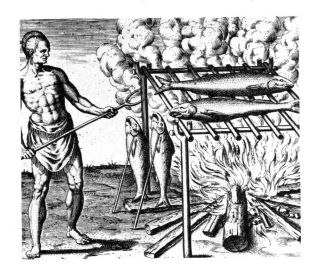

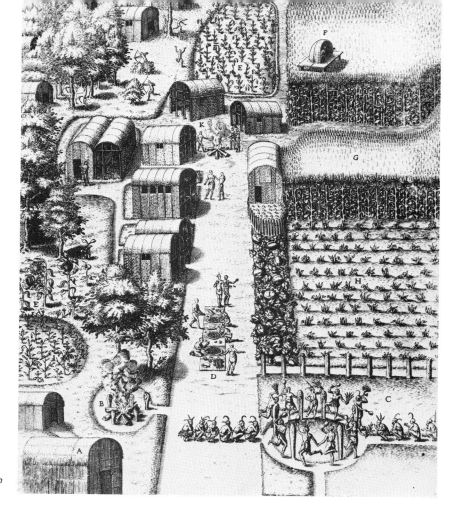

The Indian village of Secotan, North Carolina, as it looked in the 1500s.

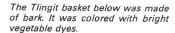

The Tlingit basket below was made of bark. It was colored with bright vegetable dyes.

Iroquoian tribes lived inland and obtained most of their food from farming. They were able to settle in large communities and build sturdy houses for shelter. These settlements lasted about twenty years. When the soil became worn and the supply of wood became scarce, the people would move on. The Iroquoian tribes of the Northeastern Woodland depended mainly on hunting to get animal hides for clothing and trading. In contrast, the Penobscot and Abnaki in northern Maine lived in a much harsher climate and on less fertile land. They were seminomadic. Since the soil could not support agriculture, they had to wander about in search of food. Moose was the staple of their diet and beaver the source of their clothing.

On the northern plains, the First Americans were also seminomadic. The Pawnees, for instance, planted the corn, squash, and beans in the spring. But in summer and early fall, they hunted buffalo. Then they moved from their sod-covered log dwellings to tepees or wickiups. The *tepees* were made of three poles lashed together in the form of a tripod and covered with skins. The *wickiup* was usually a dome-shaped dwelling made of saplings and brush. The advantage of these dwellings was the ease with which they could be disassembled and reassembled.

Nations of the Southern Great Plains, such as the Comanches and Kiowas, were nomadic people who relied mainly on the buffalo for their survival. Hence, these people packed up and followed the buffalo as they moved. However, all nations of the Great Plains made remarkable use of the buffalo. They nourished themselves with buffalo meat and used the horns to make tools and jewelry. Buffalo hide, cut into strips, provided snowshoes and harnesses, and in larger pieces, tepees and covering for shields. Buffalo teeth made decorations and magic charms, and the buffalo's shaggy coat provided caps, footwear, and robes. Even the stomach of the buffalo was used to store water!

In the Pacific Northwest, plentiful supplies of salmon and other fish provided food for the American Indians. Just as farming and hunting supplied the backbone of the economy of the Kickapoos, Chippewas, Sauk and Fox of the Central Prairies, the salmon was the basis for the wealth of the Tlingits, Haidus, and Kwaki'utls of the Pacific Northwest.

Natural materials were used by all American Indians. The bark of trees, stretched over poles, furnished housing for forest dwellers. Fishnets were made of twisted vines or bark strips. The ribs of a canoe might be springy saplings; its skin consisted of pieces of birch bark sewn together with strips of animal sinew. The canoe was

Garments like the Tlingit shirt above were woven from goat hair over a base of cedar bark. Their complicated designs indicated the wearer's ancestry.

Left: A form of lacrosse played by members of a First American tribe.

Below: This flying frog was once part of a war helmet worn by the Tsimshian tribe.

17

Early North American Indian Tribes

ATLANTIC OCEAN

PACIFIC OCEAN

GULF OF MEXICO

Montagnois
Miemac
Malecite
Abnaki
Mahican
Massachusett
Pequot
Shinnecock
Delaware
Nanticoke
Algonkin
Iroquois
Huron
Erie
Powhatan
Wyandotte
Pamunkey
Susquehanna
Tuscarora
Manahoac
Cusabo
Tutelo
Catawba
Utina
Cherokee
Yuchi
Yamasee
Seminole
Calusa

Cree
Chippewa
Ottawa
Potawatomi
Winnebago
Menominee
Fox
Miami
Sauk
Iowa
Illinois
Shawnee
Chickasaw
Creek
Dakota
Missouri
Osage
Choctaw
Natchez
Ponca
Omaha
Quapaw
Caddo
Biloxi
Oto
Kansa
Wichita
Atakapa

Salishan
Kutenai
Blackfeet
Flathead
Assiniboin
Atsina
Hidatsa
Yakima
Palouse
Mandan
Chinook
Cayuse
Nez Percé
Bannock
Sutaio
Crow
Arikara
Suislaw
Klamath
Modoc
Shoshoni
Nootka
Shasta
Maidu
Pomo
Washo
Cheyenne
Pawnee
Comanche
Waco
Tonkawa
Miwok
Ute
Arapaho
Kiowa
Kanankawa
Costanoan
Salinan
Navaho
Hopi
Zuñi
Apache
Pueblos
Concho
Lagunero
Coahuiltecan
Tamaulipec
Cahuilla
Yuma
Papago
Pima
Mohave
Yurok

waterproofed with sticky tree gum. Spear and arrow shafts were of wood. Points were of sharpened bone or stone. Deerskin furnished leggings and moccasins, which were decorated with porcupine quills or birds' feathers. Dishes were made out of hollowed pieces of wood.

The First Americans lived without the convenience of easily replaced manufactured goods. It is hard to imagine their lives in our age of plastics and throwaway packages. They suffered hunger, cold, and disease, in blizzards and droughts. Yet, as long as nature provided, they needed no outside help.

The Political Life of the First Americans

The political life of the First Americans was extremely varied. As with their lifestyle, political life was governed by the forces of nature. Political organization depended on a stable population. For this reason, areas with harsh climate and scarce resources—areas unable to support many people easily—had little political organization. In areas such as the Artic, lower California, and the Great Basin in Nevada and Utah, the extended family became the largest political and social unit.

In less harsh areas, such as the Subarctic, Northwest coast, California, and the Southwest, there was a more complex political organization. Leadership of families or clans was often based on heredity. The leader of the clan was usually the person with the most prestige, which in turn might be based on wealth or ability.

Political organization, which included control over an extended family and allowed for varieties of rank, was most common among the nations of the plains, the prairies, and the East Coast. A wide variety of political systems existed. But the words to describe them came from the vocabularies of Europeans and did not always exactly fit the First Americans' ideas of what they were doing.

The least common system was a *monarchy*—rule by a single leader. Monarchies did exist among the nations of the Southeast. The hereditary ruler for the Natchez was called the Great Sun, who had absolute control over his subjects. He was served by everyone in the group and had his own personal servants and slaves.

An *aristocracy* was a political system where the nobles of the tribe held the real power, even though there was one recognized leader. Among the Pawnee, each village had a hereditary chief. He was succeeded by his eldest son, if that son were capable. If not, the chief's council would select another close male relative. The hereditary chief selected the members of the council from among the best warriors, and together they would make decisions. The council could outweigh the hereditary chief. In some cases, the priests could override the council's decisions.

The picture above tells a tale much like the Biblical story of Jonah being swallowed by the whale. In this case, a salmon has swallowed an Indian.

A Plains Indian tribe holds a council meeting.

democracy
rule by common consent

Some tribes practiced a form of **democracy** that allowed both men and women to have their say. When peoples from different tribes met, the councils were usually conducted in a democratic manner.

When the Sioux or Iowa tribes, for example, held a treaty council, the men sat in a circle to show that all of them were equal. The leaders were supposedly the bravest as well as the smartest tribal elders. However, an ambitious young man could become a leader by fighting well or by performing some clever act.

A person's first loyalty was to the tribe. Villagers lived together and shared the toil of planting and harvesting as a group. Hunting tribes pursued the game together and shared the kill. If times were lean, all went hungry. If the gods gave many fat bucks or bear, everyone was completely stuffed. War parties marched as a unit, though in battle, braves tended to fight for booty and trophies as individuals. Quarrels within the tribe were often settled by councils. If one Cheyenne murdered another, for instance, the elders might exile him or else force him to present gifts to his victim's family to make up for the crime. The Pueblos, who lived literally on top of each other in "apartment houses" of sunbaked brick, dealt with an unruly member by refusing to speak to him until he gave in.

The Iroquois created a complex political system. They were actually a *confederacy* (league) of five nations—the Mohawks, Senecas, Oneidas, Onondagas, and Cayugas. Each nation had its leaders, called "sachems." Some leaders inherited their role and some were chosen for their ability. A council of fifty sachems, representing all five nations, met to make war and peace and to settle matters common to all league members. This council bears a resemblance to the United States Congress, which is perhaps not entirely accidental. Some of the Americans who wrote our Constitution were familiar with the League of the Iroquois.

Games and Recreation

Games and athletic events were another important part of the life of the First Americans. Recreation provided a necessary break from the rigorous routine of survival. For children, the activities also provided a training ground for skills needed as adults. Children's games were often imitations of adult activities.

For adults, games of chance were among the most popular. One game was a variation of the pea-and-shell game. Someone would put a stone under a moccasin and then switch several moccasins around. While one group was trying to keep track of the stone, their opponents would be singing and waving their arms to distract them. Sometimes, a whole community would challenge another community, and the game would go on all night.

Hand games were also very popular. Simple and elaborate variations of "which-hand-is-it-in" were played for hours and at every opportunity. Some people would risk anything they owned on the outcome.

A popular ball game played among North American inhabitants was a form of lacrosse. This game often involved sixty to one hundred stick-wielding players. Northern tribes, like the Iroquois, used one stick to play the game. Southern tribes, like the Choctaws, used two sticks. In their desire to get the ball to the end of the field, many players would run over other players. It was not uncommon for participants to be hurt or even killed. In fact, the game was taken so seriously by some tribes that sons were assigned to a team at birth. A person's first son was assigned to one team and the next son to the other team. They would then play on their own team for the rest of their lives. It was not mere coincidence that the game prepared young men for war. In cultures that wasted nothing, even games had a purpose.

Religion and the Indians of the Southwest

Religion among the First Americans was mixed with magic, medicine, and the daily life of the tribe. Religion taught Indian people how to live together and helped them to please the spirits. In the American Southwest, the Zuni and Hopi believed that kindly spirits visited the tribe for six months each year as messengers of the gods. During this time, the entire tribe took part in elaborate ceremonies which featured dances, songs, poetry, and beautiful *regalia* (tribal dress). Priests, wearing masks that represented the different spirits, could relay the people's needs to the gods. It was hoped that the gods would be pleased by the ceremony and bring rain or cure a disease. Even though many of the ceremonies lasted for nine days, with one ceremony following another, the worshipers usually remained calm

The buffalo-hide painting below shows an Apache ceremony celebrating the coming of age of young women. The young women dance with older women of the tribe around the ceremonial fire.

21

A LEAGUE OF NATIONS

The Iroquois Confederacy call themselves the "Hau de no sau nee." "Hau de no sau nee" means League of Six Nations. Originally, though, the Iroquois Confederacy was composed of only five nations, and was referred to as the League of Five Nations.

The Iroquois are First Americans who lived in the Northeastern Woodland region of the United States for about twelve thousand years before the Europeans came to this country. They were especially concentrated in the New York area. To Europeans, the Iroquois were known as the "People of the Longhouse" because they lived in long, wooden dwellings.

The Iroquois inhabited an area that was fertile and rich in river valleys, forests, deep lakes, and clear streams. They hunted, fished, and farmed. They also gathered wild foods such as fruits and nuts and stored crops such as maize and beans.

There was no one nation called the Iroquois, but rather several related tribal groups that belonged to the Iroquois. Five main nations were Mohawk, Seneca, Oneida, Onandaga, and Cayuga. These five nations often fought among themselves and raided each other's villages.

Hiawatha and Dekanawida were two men who thought of a way to end the feud among the Iroquois nations. They had thought and dreamed of an everlasting peace among the five nations. Hiawatha, who was mistakenly thought to be a Chippewa by the writer Longfellow, was a Mohawk, who lived between 1522 and 1575. Dekanawida was a Huron who lived with the Mohawks. They wanted a peace that was founded on equality and brotherhood among all Indians.

Hiawatha and Dekanawida not only wanted a league established to bring peace among the nations. They also wanted political and military unity.

Hiawatha worked hard trying to get each nation to join. He went from nation to nation to tell them of the plan. As a result of his work, the Iroquois Confederacy or League of Five Nations came into existence in 1570.

The Iroquois Confederacy was governed by a constitution. The constitution contains (1) recognition of freedom of speech, rights of women to participate in government; (2) the concept of separation of powers in government; (3) checks and balances among the powers within the government.

Under the Iroquois Confederacy, the council was the only legitimate body authorized to conduct land transactions. Chiefs were nominated by women and then elected by the whole village. All five nations in the Confederacy elected a representative. In times of need, food, clothing, and shelter were shared. The political and economic ideals of the Confederacy were learned by the colonists as a result of contact with the Iroquois people. Many of the ideals were written into the Constitution of the United States.

The Confederacy became the League of Six Nations when, in 1713, the Tuscaroras were forced to leave their homeland and sought the protection of the Iroquois Confederacy.

If Hiawatha and Dekanawida were alive today, they would be pleased. For the everlasting peace they dreamed of and worked so hard for has survived into the twentieth century. To this day, the League of Six Nations exists.

Plains warriors file off to battle, shields in hand.

and orderly. Modesty and seriousness were highly valued, and it was believed the spirits would punish anyone involved in conflict or violence.

Folk tales explaining the nature of the universe and its people were an important part of tribal religious ceremonies. All tribes had marvelous legends about this. Some thought that the earth was carried on the back of a great turtle; some that the starry Milky Way was the backbone of the sky; some that certain plants, like prairie grass, were the hair of gods who lived underground. Whatever the legend, it provided an answer to the questions: Where am I? What kind of universe do I live in?

Some southwestern tribes believed that certain individuals, called *shamans*, were in direct contact with the spiritual world. In some tribes, shamans were medicine men who applied herbs that cured disease. The Navaho shaman presided over curing ceremonies by singing sacred songs, handling holy objects, and making paintings with colored sand, pollen, crushed flowers, and minerals. The purpose of the ceremony was to restore the patient's harmony with nature, as

23

Pueblo people perform the Green Corn Dance in front of a pueblo dwelling in New Mexico.

Below: a sea-monster mask used in ceremonies by the Kwakiutl people of Alaska.

well as to cure the disease. Shamans from other tribes conducted ceremonies to guarantee good hunts, plentiful harvests, or success in war.

Some ceremonies were individual, but some were tribal. The whole tribe might have a three-day feast when boys reached fighting age or girls became old enough to bear children. They were celebrating because the tribe's life would surely go on. This practice might be compared to a school graduation in a small town, with several days of parties, concerts, dances, dinners, and worship services for everyone.

Imagination, closeness to nature, strong tribal feeling, and great ingenuity marked the various Indian cultures of the Americas. These First Americans left their names on the land. They placed many foods on our table and many words in our language. Their history is found in our history books. But in 1492, they were about to lose their position, their land, and in many cases, their culture. When the Europeans arrived, the tragic story of the First Americans began.

The First Americans were not able to maintain their own way of life against the invading Whites. The new settlers disrupted the established order, and in time, the survival of the original inhabitants was in danger. Just how many First Americans perished is the subject of controversy. In recent years, the estimates of *anthropologists* (those who study human culture and its development) have been adjusted upward. In the area between the Rio Grande and the Arctic Circle, perhaps as many as 12,500,000 people lived. By 1850, there were probably fewer than 500,000 First Americans left.

Questions for Discussion
1. Define *aristocracy, confederacy, monarchy, topography*.
2. What effect did nature have on the economy and political systems of the First Americans?
3. Why did the First Americans feel such strong loyalties toward their tribes? How did they express this loyalty?
4. Why was there such a close relationship between nature and religion in the First American cultures of the Southwest?

Chapter 1 Review

Summary Questions for Discussion

1. Why did Europeans refer to all the people they found in North and South America as "Indians"?
2. Explain how a culture is affected by the environment in which it exists.
3. What early civilization occupied Peru? What type of economy did it have? Why is the economy significant for the development of a civilization?
4. Describe the political system used by the Lord Inca to control his empire.
5. How does art reveal the state of a society's technology? its values? its everyday life?
6. What was the role and significance of music in the Aztec civilization?
7. Describe the role of religion in the daily life of the Mayas. What was the privileged position of the priest-rulers?
8. Give four specific examples to show how the First Americans used nature and their surroundings to provide for themselves. How was the political life of First Americans affected by nature?
9. What role did games and athletic events play in the life of the First Americans?
10. What were some of the contributions to our culture made by the First Americans?

Word Study

Fill in each blank in the sentences that follow with the term below that is most appropriate.

anthropologists   monarchy   societies   confederacy   empire
environments   maize   pochteca   democracy   technology
cultures

1. Groups of people living together who are bound by the same way of life are called _____.
2. A system of government where rule is by common consent is called a _____.
3. The types of civilizations that developed in the Americas were influenced by the surroundings or _____.
4. The Incan civilization was able to control a large territorial area known as an _____.
5. The form of government where a single ruler holds all power is called a _____.
6. The Iroquois created a complex political system called a _____, which was actually a league of nations.
7. The merchant class in the Aztec civilization was called the _____.
8. The ability to apply knowledge to useful purposes is called _____.
9. The chief crop of the Mayans was _____.
10. The people who study human cultures and their development are _____.

Using Your Skills

1. What do the pictures on pages 15, 16, and 17 tell you about the First Americans' economy and ability to deal with nature?
3. What does the Aztec art on pages 10 and 11 tell us about the Aztec economy and technology?

25

The Coming of the Europeans

We have seen how, over thousands of years, the Indian peoples of North and South America had built different cultures and impressive civilizations. Now we shall examine how, in a matter of about 250 years, Europeans found and claimed these great continents and began to destroy or subdue the Indian societies in their path.

To Whites, 1492 is a date of discovery, new beginnings, and promise. To First Americans, it marks the beginning of the end of an age of independence. Europeans found and claimed North and South America and began to destroy or subdue the Indian peoples and societies which stood in their paths. By 1542, the Aztec and Incan empires were destroyed. By 1642, France, Spain, Portugal, England, and Holland had claims to great portions of the Americas and had set up colonies along the coasts. By 1742, one French-Canadian explorer, Pierre de La Vérendrye, had pierced the wilderness of the interior and perhaps reached the Rocky Mountains.

Why did the Aztec and the Incan empires collapse? An important reason for the defeat of the First Americans by the European invaders was the superior weapons of the Europeans, which came as a result of a "knowledge explosion" that began around the year 1100. Within a few hundred years, this sudden burst of knowledge gave Europeans gunpowder, the printing press, and many scientific discoveries. The new age bred curiosity and an appetite for products from strange lands. It sent Europeans out in ships to explore the world and to plant European *institutions* (customs and organizations) in the midst of already existing societies.

READING GUIDE

1. **What developments in Europe made it possible to begin the age of exploration?**
2. **How did Spain rule its New World empire?**
3. **What conditions had to be met before England could become involved in the race for land in the New World?**

European explorers sailed in Spanish galleons, huge three-masted ships.

1. The Age of Discovery

Sea serpents were one of the fears of sixteenth century sailors.

First, Europeans had to conquer their fear of the unknown. In about the year 1100, many Europeans saw no sharp line between real and imaginary places. They thought that the Garden of Eden was somewhere on the map and that there were countries of people with one eye or no heads. They did know for certain that land or sea travel was terribly dangerous. On land, robbers as well as murderers awaited the luckless traveler. At sea, there were pirates, storms, fog, and cruel rocks that could tear the bottom out of a ship.

Ignorance encouraged people to make up legends and tales about the perils that they feared. They believed in seagoing serpents, unicorns, and dragonlike creatures who crunched and swallowed men and ships.

It was a brave sailor indeed who would venture out of sight of land when such horrors lay in wait for him. Before exploration could begin, organized, factual knowledge had to replace such nightmares.

Ships also had to be designed that could survive the many dangers of the open Atlantic and carry enough men and provisions for long voyages. In the generally calm Mediterranean, oars could be used to row long, slender galleys. But such vessels would be smashed to bits in rough water. Also, these vessels needed so many rowers and sailors that they were only useful on short journeys. If they had ventured into the open sea, the ships soon would have been lost. Little was yet known about navigation. In short, there was no advanced technology for discovery. Instruments such as the compass, mechanical clock, or

The scientific studies of the 1500s led to new navigation instruments and improvements in ships. However, little was known about the sea itself. These horrifying monsters attacking a ship appeared in an atlas published in the mid 1500s.

Italian cities controlled the increasing trade from Africa and Asia. These cities grew rich distributing the products throughout Europe. European countries sometimes went to war to control these wealthy centers of trade. In this 1464 picture, victorious warships tow a defeated fleet into the Bay of Naples.

cross-staff (instrument used to measure heavenly bodies) would have allowed for more scientific navigation.

However, despite this lack of a more advanced technology, the Norse, from what is now Norway, built ships that reached Iceland and Greenland in the Atlantic by 1000 A.D. In that year, Leif Ericson, a Norseman, landed on the North American coast, probably in northern Newfoundland. Leif Ericson called this land "Vinland" because he saw grapevines. But the Norse did not explore inland. Nor were they able to maintain **colonists** there. In time, Ericson's discovery was almost forgotten, even by the people who lived in Western Europe.

colonists
permanent settlers from another land

A Great Change Begins in Europe

By 1100, Europe was beginning to change. Before that time, life was tied to the soil and to time-tested, always repeated ways. Working as patiently as their plodding oxen, peasants tilled the same plot for generations.

During the Middle Ages, there had always been a **barter economy**—my knife for your coat; my chicken for that pair of shoes you made. But around the year 1100, the longing for more goods encouraged traders to travel longer distances and to make more complicated exchanges. Wool cloth from France was exchanged for fur from Russia. Swords from Spain were exchanged for salted fish from the shores of the Baltic Sea, far to the north. For such enterprises, money, loans, and, in time, banks were needed. Thus, a **market economy** slowly began to take shape.

barter economy
an economic system based on the swapping of goods for goods

market economy
an economic system in which people work for wages and pay for goods with money

29

During the Middle Ages, more and more people were able to buy products from distant lands. This illuminated manuscript shows the kinds of booths that sprang up in the trading centers of those times. At such booths, people might buy exotic cloths or spices or simply get a shave.

revolution
a sudden, major change

centralized government
a government whose power is brought together under one central authority

As a result, adventurous merchants from many lands began to trade at great fairs. Because of these fairs, centers of trade began to develop. These centers eventually grew into cities. Life was still crude, but it was no longer static. In northern Germany, many of these cities joined together to form the *Hanse*—a confederation. This powerful league of trading cities carried on extensive commerce with other European countries, including England, Flanders, and Italy. The Hanse reigned supreme over most northern trading until the Atlantic Ocean became a more important trade route than the Baltic Sea.

Other forces for change were at work as well. Between 1095 and 1291, there were a number of European expeditions to Palestine for the purpose of winning back the Holy Land from the Muslims. Although these Crusades failed in the long run to win back the biblical lands, they did help to turn the Mediterranean Sea into an avenue for European commerce. The Crusaders met with Arab traders whose camel saddlebags were loaded with spices, silks, gold, and jewels. These items had been brought thousands of miles by land and sea from Africa and Asia. Soon, trade with these merchants thrived. Much of it was handled by the merchants of Italian cities such as Florence, Venice, Genoa, and Naples, places which became bustling and beautiful.

The development of the printing press in 1454 was an important factor in spreading knowledge of a wider world. The writings of earlier geographers, such as Claudius Ptolemy and Marinus of Tyre, and the romantic tales of Marco Polo's thirteenth-century travels, became widely available for the first time. Marco Polo's adventures in China and India indicated that these places could be reached by ship. His tales of wealth and luxuries helped shape people's aspirations.

Trade with the Orient and within Europe itself, plus the increasing knowledge of life in other areas, aroused people to demand more of life. They began to dream ambitiously, and they began to dare the unknown. Consequently, Europe underwent a **revolution**, which, in turn, provided an important reason for overseas exploration.

Portugal Discovers a Route to the East

A political change occurred as well. In England, France, Spain, and Portugal—four countries with at least one face turned toward the Atlantic Ocean—strong kings came to power between 1100 and 1500. They replaced the old, patchwork rule of quarreling feudal lords with the beginnings of strong, **centralized government**. By 1492, the provinces of Aragon and Castile in Spain were united by the marriage of Ferdinand and Isabella, and the last Muslim-held territory in Spain was regained. Portugal had won its independence from Castile in the

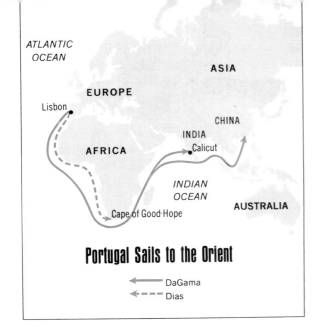

Portugal Sails to the Orient

← DaGama
←--- Dias

A Flemish engraver pictured many of the European explorers of the New World in a book published in 1590. Here he portrays First Americans greeting Columbus on Hispaniola.

twelfth century and was developing an interest in trade. The rulers of these two countries provided money, ships, weapons, and encouragement for exploration.

But in order to explore the world over the horizon, scientific information had to be gathered to replace existing fears and hunches. One of the pioneers of the modern age was a Portuguese prince named Henry the Navigator. About 1418, Henry established an academy at Sagres, Portugal, overlooking the sea. Portugal was close to Africa, and its leaders were interested in the ivory, gold, pepper, and slaves that might be found there. Henry also believed that following the coastline of Africa might eventually lead to India and its riches. India was to the Portuguese what the moon was to us before the first men landed there. Prince Henry's base at Sagres was their Cape Kennedy.

At Sagres, Henry gathered astronomers, geographers, and mathematicians who patiently studied scholarly books and "pumped" for information every sea captain who had voyaged southward. This information was turned into charts and improved ships and instruments of navigation. Henry gave all of this knowledge to captains, who then probed down the west coast of Africa toward the equator and beyond.

Henry died in 1460, but his work went on. In 1488, the Portuguese explorer Bartholomeu Dias, blown off his course by a storm, found land to the west instead of to the east. He had actually "turned the corner" of the continent and discovered the Cape of Good Hope. Meanwhile, the Portuguese were prospering on the trade in ivory, gold, and slaves in the Gulf of Guinea.

Prince Henry of Portugal, sometimes called "father of the modern world."

31

Now the road to India was almost open. In 1497, Vasco da Gama left Lisbon. He rounded the Cape, went up the eastern coast of Africa, and then, pointing straight for the rising morning sun, made for Calicut in India.

Da Gama's voyage was not profitable. Yet once he arrived in Asia by water with his ships and guns, the world began to change. Europe, though composed of small nations, was on its way to five centuries of world domination. For instance, by 1549, Portuguese vessels had sailed as far as Japan. By then, Portugal owned trading posts and territory in Africa, India, and China. In addition, other major European countries wasted no time in seeking equally fine rewards.

Columbus Discovers the New World

The sailors who flew other countries' colors from their mastheads also profited from Portuguese experience and research. One such navigator was Christopher Columbus.

In his day, geographers believed that all the earth's land was divided among Europe, Asia, and Africa. They simply did not know that the Americas were part of the world, and neither did Columbus. What is more, he died in 1506 still believing that he had found a part of Asia. By then, a navigator named Amerigo Vespucci knew better and said so. That is why mapmakers agreed to use Vespucci's first name and call the new land mass "America." But to say that Columbus did not know what he had discovered is not to take credit away from him. In fact, Columbus began a new era in the history of the world.

Born in 1451 to a weaver in Genoa, Italy, Christopher Columbus went to sea as a young man and settled down sometime before 1480 in Lisbon, Portugal. Lisbon was a sailors' and traders' town. There was exciting talk about opening sea routes to the Indies. The more Columbus read and argued, the more certain he became that it would be better to take the direct western course to Asia than to continue the long search for a route around Africa to the east. In 1484, he asked the king of Portugal for ships, guns, a crew, and supplies to prove his theory. The king turned the matter over to a committee of experts, who said that Columbus was "a big talker." In a sense, he was. He judged the distance from Europe to Japan to be about one fourth of what it actually was. The Portuguese turned him down, as did King Ferdinand and Queen Isabella of neighboring Spain.

But Columbus was persistent. In 1492, after eight years of pleading by Columbus, Ferdinand finally gave in. He was persuaded not only by Queen Isabella but by his own royal treasurer, who thought it was a good gamble.

With his three tiny ships, Columbus sailed from Spain on August 3, 1492. A grim two months followed. The supplies of salted meat, hard

The Portuguese established one of the most far-flung empires the world had seen. They were also the first Westerners to reach the Japanese islands. Here, in the early 1600s, priests and officials greet Portuguese officers wearing pegged pantaloons.

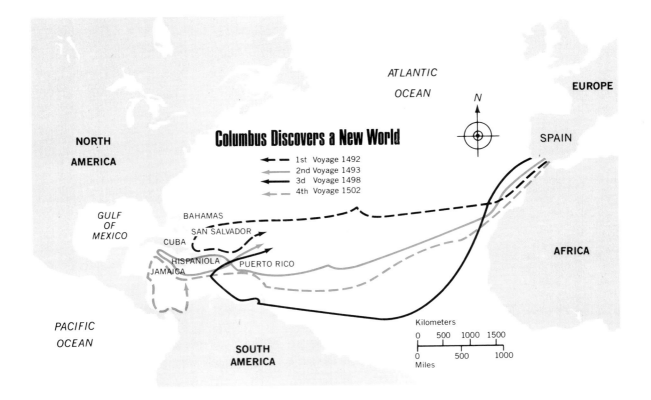

Columbus Discovers a New World

- ◀— — — 1st Voyage 1492
- ◀——— 2nd Voyage 1493
- ◀——— 3d Voyage 1498
- ◀— — — 4th Voyage 1502

ATLANTIC OCEAN

EUROPE

N

NORTH AMERICA

SPAIN

GULF OF MEXICO

BAHAMAS

SAN SALVADOR

CUBA

HISPANIOLA

PUERTO RICO

JAMAICA

AFRICA

PACIFIC OCEAN

SOUTH AMERICA

Kilometers
0   500   1000 1500
0   500   1000
Miles

bread, dried peas, and wine ran dangerously low. The sailors grew mutinous and threatened to make the captain turn back. Finally, in the early morning of October 12, land was sighted. The next day at dawn, Columbus stepped ashore at the Caribbean island which is today called Watlings Island.

Taino Indians came out in their canoes. Columbus found them a friendly folk, who "invite you to share anything they possess." He observed that "fifty Spaniards could **subjugate** this entire people." This was a warning of what was to come. Columbus sailed on to Hispaniola, left the crew of the *Santa María* behind, and returned to Spain with the *Niña* and the *Pinta*. He and his crew were received as heroes. Within six months, Columbus set out with seventeen ships filled with people anxious to become rich in the New World. Columbus left them on Hispaniola. He then went on to explore other Caribbean islands. When he returned to the settlement, he found that the expectations of easy money had soured and that there was widespread discontent and rebellion. Columbus tried to bring things under control. Then he left his brother in charge and set sail for Spain.

By the time Columbus arrived in the New World on his third journey, a revolt was in progress against his brother's government. To

subjugate
to force to submit to control or servitude

A portrait of Christopher Columbus.

33

serfs
Persons bound to their master's land and transferred with it to a new owner

calm the Spanish settlers, Columbus allowed them to have land grants and gave them permission to use the inhabitants of the land for labor. Though Columbus did not want to make **serfs** of the Indians, he had to give in to the demands of the Spanish settlers. Unfortunately, this action set the pattern for future Spanish efforts to encourage settlement and agriculture in the colonies. Forced labor and the introduction of diseases to which the Indian people had no immunity caused the death of most of the conquered Indians within fifty years.

Columbus made one more journey in his fruitless search for an all-water route to India. He died penniless and ignored, never realizing that he had established the base of Spain's colonial empire.

Questions for Discussion

1. Define *colonist, barter economy, market economy.*
2. What changes led to the age of discovery and exploration?
3. Why were the Portuguese the leaders in the age of exploration?
4. Why was the New World named "America"?
5. Why were Columbus's accomplishments important?

2. Spain Conquers an Empire in the New World

This engraving shows Balboa accepting tribute in gold from the people of Panama.

The world would never be the same again, for the discovery of the Americas began a new era in history. The first sign of this was the speed with which the Spanish rushed to possess what Columbus had found for them. By 1519, Spaniards had conquered parts of Cuba and Hispaniola, Panama and Yucatán, and other tropical regions near the Isthmus of Panama, where the two Americas pinch in and join each other. The magnet that attracted Spain's explorer-conquerers was gold, which Columbus had seen islanders wearing as jewelry.

Juan Ponce de León was one of the earliest adventurers to tire of mining and agriculture on Hispaniola and set out to explore and conquer. Ponce de León's search for a mythical fountain of youth led him through the Gulf of Mexico, until he landed on the coast of Florida. When Ponce de León returned to Hispaniola with neither gold nor renewed youth, other adventurers were already trying their own luck.

One of these explorers was Vasco de Balboa. In Panama, he heard from an Indian about a land to the south where gold was plentiful. Aflame with excitement, Balboa pushed through jungles, swamps, and over mountains. He found not only gold but also the Pacific Ocean, which helped to convince Europeans that they had actually discovered a new continent and not just a part of Asia.

In Cuba, another young Spanish soldier, Hernando Cortés, listened to tales of the fabled empire of the Aztecs. In 1519, with 11 ships, 600 men, and 16 horses, Cortés landed on the Mexican coast and boldly marched his tiny army to the great Aztec city of Tenochtitlán,

Left: In 1798, the Spanish founded San Luis Rey de Francia, a mission in southern California.

Right: In 1695, the nobles of Mexico City greet a new viceroy.

today called Mexico City. On the way, Cortés' cavalry routed Indian armies who were enemies of the Aztecs. Cortés was helped not only by the use of firearms and enemies of the Aztecs, but by the Aztec religious belief. The Aztecs, including the Emperor Montezuma II, believed that the Spaniards were gods who had returned to the Aztec people after a long absence. Cortés demanded an audience, a face-to-face talk with Montezuma. When the proud ruler appeared, Cortés had him seized and made a prisoner. The Aztecs tried to drive the Spanish out but were soundly defeated in battle. Cortés then ordered Montezuma slain. The land of Mexico became New Spain. Cortés had established himself as a *conquistador*—which in Spanish means "one who conquers."

Thus, the Aztec nation in Tenochtitlán fell to Spain in 1521. Ten years later, Francisco Pizarro set out with 180 soldiers, including 27 mounted men, to find the wealth of the Incas. He finally reached Cajamarca, home of the Lord Inca. Four thousand of the best Incan warriors stood in ranks around the Lord Inca. Pizarro and his men were a tiny island of shining armor in a sea of Incan power. Behind the armor, Pizarro's men hid their guns. A Spanish priest offered the Lord Inca a prayer book and told him that he must accept Christianity as the true faith. The Lord Inca proudly and confidently flipped the book into the dust. Then, at a signal from Pizarro, the Spaniards opened fire. Two thousand Incas were slaughtered. The Lord Inca was captured and agreed to become a Christian. Nevertheless, he was strangled to death.

Peru became a part of the Spanish empire in the New World, which included large parts of South and Central America and, later, North America. Incan golden ornaments were melted down into bars and sent in wallowing treasure fleets back to the royal treasury in Madrid.

This picture represents Cortés invading Mexico.

missionaries
people sent to do religious or charitable work in a foreign country or territory

The Incan priests and nobles became simply "Indians," all alike in the Spanish eye. Incan peasants and warriors toiled in the fields and in the mines for the glory of a distant foreign ruler. Incan temples were plundered and replaced with the churches of the invaders.

The conquistadors believed that their victories over the powerful Incan nation were signs of God's approval. They thought of the wealth of the conquered lands as a feast spread for them to enjoy. They saw no reason to respect the customs of the defeated Incas. These conquistadors did not think of themselves as robbers. Rather, they saw themselves as the most civilized people on earth. In this spirit of conquest and plunder, Spain pushed its new empire into the heart of North, as well as South and Central, America. By 1609, its flag flew over Santa Fe, in today's New Mexico. In the 1700s, its explorers and **missionaries** carried the flag of Spain and the teachings of the Catholic Church as far north as San Francisco.

How Spain Ruled Its New World Empire

Spanish rulers could not hope to fill great valleys and deserts, some big enough to swallow up all of Spain, with settlers. Nor could they enforce tight control over Indian tribes and nations scattered over miles of almost impassable mountains. So the political system they developed was based on the creation of little centers of influence and authority. In the attempts to control the Indians, the missions were especially important. Missions were points of settlement built around a church. The officials of the Catholic Church in Spain took the work of converting the American Indians seriously. In the New World, different members of religious orders became as important to the empire as soldiers and governors.

These were the first missionaries in the New World. With forced Indian labor, missionaries planted gardens and built storehouses, hospitals, chapels, and stately homes. The mission buildings were often grouped around an open plaza or square, as in Spain. They were built of common native materials such as stone and clay. These missions were bits of Spain in an American setting. The crucifix in the chapel, before which the Indians were forced to kneel, was Spanish. Yet the pottery jugs that held the Communion wine were as Indian as the cornmeal cakes served at the friars' tables. The American land always put its mark on the Europeans who tried to repeat their own way of life there.

A few settlers in Spanish North America spread out from these centers to establish ranches. For the owners, cattle and grain were the gold and silver of the New World. Guarded by only a few soldiers in **presidios** and lightly ruled by officials from the **pueblos**, many Spaniards made America their permanent home.

presidios
military garrisons
pueblos
small towns

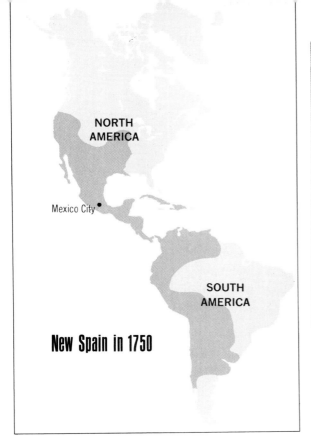

New Spain in 1750

Pizarro conquered Peru easily after his men slaughtered most of the Incan leaders at Cajamarca.

The center of Spain's sprawling new empire was Mexico City. In contrast to a thinly populated place like California, the capital of Mexico City was crowded with the stately homes of bishops, generals, and officials, all served by the local population. Coaches clattered by, and people in European finery chitchatted. Behind the imposing official buildings were market stalls and ordinary homes. By 1539, this city had a printing press and by 1551, a university. Here was a largely European city where, only a few years earlier, the Aztecs had worshiped the sun and their emperor.

Only Spain was destined to find such a rich land ready to be subdued. Almost another century went by before any other European country successfully established another permanent settlement in the New World. In that century, Europe was slowly losing its medieval characteristics. These changes would affect the nature of the settlers to come and the character of the settlements.

Questions for Discussion

1. Define *conquistador, missionary.*
2. What role did missionaries play in the New World?

FERDINAND MAGELLAN

For sheer courage and persistence in the face of odds, few stories match the accounts of the heroes of the great age of exploration. In tiny ships, with only primitive tools for navigation, these courageous people sailed unknown seas. For months and even years, they were out of touch with all civilization. By comparison, modern astronauts, even hundreds of thousands of miles in space, are tracked, monitored every second, and protected against disaster by many scientific "backup" systems to save them if things go wrong. This is not to deny the courage of the people who explore space, but to remind ourselves of what bravery was necessary to discover a New World.

Consider Ferdinand Magellan, for instance—or Fernando de Magallanes, as the Spanish called him. Portuguese-born, he served Portugal's king in India and Africa. He then offered to lead an expedition to the Moluccas—islands rich in spices, in what is now Indonesia—by sailing westward from Europe. Portugal turned him down, but the king of Spain was willing to try. Magellan sailed from a Spanish port on September 20, 1519, with five ships and 265 men. They sailed on a southwesterly course. By the end of that year, they were off the coast of South America, exploring every river mouth for a way through to the Pacific. Two of the ships were wrecked, and some of Magellan's impatient officers mutinied. Nevertheless, he got enough support from others to put the uprising down, killing some men in the process and executing others afterwards. Other men died of sickness in the harsh winter climate as they neared the southern tip of the Americas. Not until Magellan had been gone thirteen months did he discover a *strait*, or passage through, which now carries his name.

The three remaining ships took almost three months sailing across the Pacific. Food ran out and the starving men caught and ate the rats aboard their vessels. They took off the leather wrappings around rigging (used to prevent fraying of the ropes wherever two of them crossed) and chewed on them to suck out whatever juice might be left in the dried animal hides. For fresh water, they wrung rain and morning dew out of extra canvas sails spread on the dirty decks.

Finally, they reached the Philippine Islands. They got food from the people they found there. But Magellan involved himself in a local tribal quarrel and was killed in a battle. The expedition moved on. One ship was now so rotten and creaky that it was abandoned. Two ships finally made it to the Moluccas and loaded spices. One of these turned back, hoping to get as far as Panama before it fell apart. But this ship was wrecked. Only four sailors survived the wreck and were eventually able to get to Spain. The last ship, the *Victoria*, limped home to Spain and got there on September 6, 1522, with eighteen men. It was a superb feat of navigation, proving once and for all by actual experience that the world was round and that the Americas were not connected to the Asian mainland. It cost four ships, three years, and over 240 lives, including that of the commander.

3. What attracted Spanish explorers to the New World?
4. How did the work of the missionaries differ from the work of the conquistadors?

3. England, France, and Holland Enter the Race for Empire

Spanish success in the New World stirred the envy of other European kings. It was worth sending out expeditions to see if a land like that of the Incas, ready to **pillage**, lay beyond the sunset. There was another reason, too. At first, no one knew the exact shape and size of America. It might be as thin as a serpent; it might be a chain of islands. As Columbus had dreamed, somewhere it might have an opening through which vessels could sail westward and stock up on China silk, Calcutta ivory, and Sumatra pepper. The search for the Northwest Passage began. It went on until mapmakers finally realized the full width of the American continent. Many died in search of the impossible. Actually, there is a water passage across the top of North America, but it is always closed by ice. Only powerful icebreakers or submarines can get through.

pillage
to loot or plunder

First England and then France and Holland joined the race to explore and to establish claims in North America. As you look at the map on page 47, you will see that, although each expedition has its own story, some things stand out that were shared by them all.

Exploration was confined mainly to the shorelines of the continent. All the explorers from John Cabot to Jacques Cartier followed a pattern. They would find an inviting river or bay and sail up it until there was no further passage. Where the bays cut deeply into the continent, explorers like Henry Hudson were able to explore farther. The risks were terrible—North Atlantic storms, icebergs, and angry Indian people.

But the efforts of the explorers were not wasted. They mapped and named most of the North American coastline, claiming vast areas for the European kings who had sent them. Their reports made the English, French, and Dutch realize that there were valuable prizes in America other than gold and the Northwest Passage—prizes such as fish, lumber, furs, and land. By 1600, farsighted planners and merchants were thinking of setting up permanent settlements. The age of exploration was about to give way to the age of colonization.

The title page from a 1609 book promoting settlement of Virginia.

In 1607, after the failure of an earlier effort, the English established a lasting colony at Jamestown, Virginia. In 1608, also following unsuccessful attempts, by the French, to settle elsewhere in the New World, Quebec was founded. Quebec became the capital of French Canada. In 1624, a Dutch post was set up at Fort Orange, now Albany, New York. Within seventeen years, three new contestants had entered the North American colonial game. Its prize was a vast land empire. How did the entrants of this contest differ?

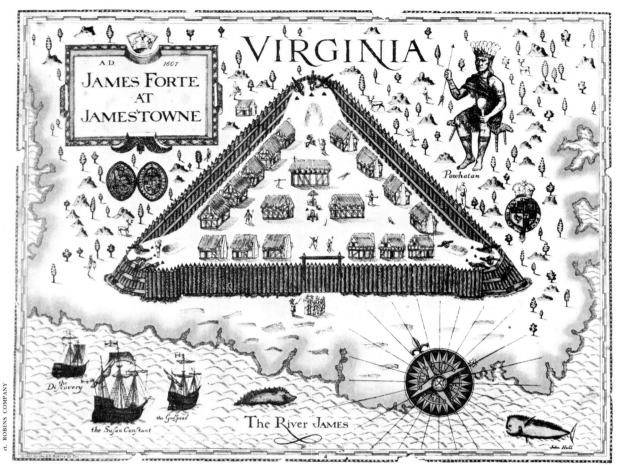

A drawing of the Jamestown area in 1607. The ships at left—the Discovery, the Godspeed, and the Susan Constant—brought colonists from England.

inflation
an increase in the cost of goods and services without an increase in production, leading to a decrease in buying power

dissenters
people who oppose generally accepted practices

The First English Colonies

England had to become a well-established power in order to become involved in the race for the land and the wealth in the New World. Spain had been a leading power in the sixteenth century, but the reign of Queen Elizabeth I strengthened England. The defeat of the *Spanish Armada*, Spain's navy, by the English in 1588 contributed to England's control of the seas and Spain's diminishing power.

The silver and gold that flooded into Spain from the conquests of Mexico and Peru found its way into the pockets of the merchants in England and elsewhere on the Continent. While **inflation** was robbing some Europeans of a chance for survival, it was enriching the merchants whose wealth was in products that were constantly increasing in value. These economic changes along with growing numbers of religious **dissenters** provided the money and the desire for people to establish colonies in the New World.

40

JOHN SMITH: A YARN SPINNER OR NOT?

Of all the fascinating people on the American scene, one of the liveliest was John Smith, who helped to found the Jamestown colony in Virginia. He was also influential in encouraging English settlement in what later became Massachusetts. He was quarrelsome, brave, curious, and enthusiastic. He was either a man of marvellous luck and skill, or one of history's most inventive tellers of tall tales.

Smith wrote a book about his adventures in which he told of leaving his native England as a young man to serve as a soldier of fortune in a Hungarian-Turkish war. He said that he fought three single combats with famous Turkish warriors and won them all. As a result, he was given prizes and honors by the Prince of Hungary. Smith was later captured by Turkish soldiers and sent to Constantinople as a "present"—a slave—for the wife of the Turkish ruler, or Pasha. This woman, Tragabigzanda, fell in love with him. To save him from the Pasha's jealousy, Tragabigzanda sent him to her brother who lived far off in Russia. There he was enslaved again. But he managed to escape and wandered all the way across Europe, making his living by fighting or begging, depending on which was called for at the time. All of this happened before he was 25 years old.

Smith joined the group sent out by the London Company to plant a settlement in Virginia. He was part of a council which was supposed to run affairs. However, he couldn't get along with the others. So instead, Smith chose to go off with a few men on exploring trips. It was on one of these trips that he was captured by American Indians. They were about to bash his head in, Smith said, when he was saved by the plea of King Powhatan's daughter, Pocahontas (then a girl of about thirteen). When Smith got to Jamestown, his old enemies were in control of things. *They* sentenced him to hang. But, at the last minute, a ship with new orders arrived from England, and he was saved. Later he was made chief of the colony, got into more scrapes, and finally went home.

Actually, Smith's bosses in England wanted the settlers to look for gold. It was Smith who thought that the real wealth of Virginia was in the soil. He said the Company should send out good, hard-working people to plant, fish, hunt, and get a good living from the marvellous bounty that Nature set out in America.

Smith became interested in the fishing and fur trade of New England and made one trip there. While in New England, he wrote a book promoting it very enthusiastically. On a second trip there, he was captured by pirates, spent months at sea, and finally was set ashore in France. From there he went to England. He never did get back to the New World, whose animals and plants and people absolutely fascinated him. But John Smith continued to write good advice for colonists—and many stories of his own travels and doings, which may or may not be 100 percent accurate.

Early attempts at settlement were doomed, because the search for gold was the main reason for the effort. England was not strong enough to challenge Spain's supremacy in the West Indies and the southern lands of Northern America. However, the writings of several people spurred settlement for other reasons. Thomas More's *Utopia* encouraged those who felt that somewhere in the world a better life could be fashioned. The Reverend Richard Hakluyt's *Navigations, Voyages, Traffiques and Discoveries of the English Nation* promoted the idea of establishing an overseas empire that would make England self-sufficient. Whether visionary or practical, in the seventeenth century, the motivations existed for a different style of invasion of the New World.

The English colony at Jamestown was the first of these successful ventures. It began as a company-owned outpost. King James I of England gave a group of stockholders called the Virginia Company the right to settle and to do business on "his" American soil. King James had claimed the land as a result of John Cabot's voyage, in return for a share of the profits. The first stockholders envisioned a fort and storehouse, built by workers brought over in three ships. The colonists would go out to discover gold, trade with the Indian people, and even cultivate silkworms. Jewelers, goldsmiths, and weavers would work in the town, preparing the goods to ship home. Food would be grown on company-owned land.

Not one of these dreams worked out. For the first five years, the colonists not only found no gold, but starved and died of a variety of diseases. The strong leadership of John Smith was a major factor in the group's survival. Finally, the company decided that the way to survive was to divide the land among the settlers, who, in turn, were urged to farm it. Such farming became profitable after 1613, when a shipload of tobacco was sent back to England. King James called it a "stinking weed," but tobacco became very popular in Europe and was the colony's most profitable crop.

Tobacco made a great difference in colonizing style. Settlers who were lured to seek "most Excellent fruites by Planting," were more likely to become permanent residents.

This pattern of settlement existed also in the next English colony, in Massachusetts. The Pilgrims who landed at Plymouth in 1620 were members of a small, close-knit community, seeking to practice their religion in a way that was forbidden in England. In a few years, they were followed by less radical members of the Church of England, called Puritans, who set up the Massachusetts Bay Colony around Boston. These settlers thought the Church in England no longer followed God's plan. But in the New World, both church and community would.

Trappers, such as the one below, spent most of the year hunting beaver in the wilderness near Hudson Bay.

This picture of Edward Winslow is the only authentic portrait we have of a Mayflower Pilgrim. He posed for the portrait while visiting England in 1651.

A nineteenth-century artist portrayed Pilgrims walking to church, carrying their guns and Bibles.

France's River Empire

Unlike the town-dwelling New Englanders or the Virginia planters, the French developed a lightly inhabited string of settlements along a lengthy chain of rivers and lakes. These settlements were to the north and to the west of the English colonies. Like the English, the French had failed in their attempts to place a permanent colony in the New World in the sixteenth century. It was not until the English had already settled at Jamestown in 1607 that Henry IV sent Samuel de Champlain to try again to establish a permanent French colony. Founded in 1608, Quebec became the base for further colonization and exploration.

Progress in the early days of French settlement was slow and hard. The French nobility and merchant investors wanted quick profits from the fur trade. They did not want to plow profits back into the maintenance and development of the settlements. Therefore, in order for the colony to survive, Champlain had to make compromises that proved costly later on. In return for the use of land that was rich with furs and for access to waterways that were necessary for transportation and exploration, Champlain helped the Algonquins and the Hurons in their wars with the Iroquois' League of the Five

After 1621, the Dutch West India Company had a monopoly on all the trade between Holland and the entire coast of the Americas. The company's flag became a familiar sight in the ports of the New World.

43

Nations. As a result, the Iroquois later allied themselves with the English in the final struggle that developed for control of the eastern half of the Northern Hemisphere.

Many of the French who came to the New World were explorers and adventurers. They moved inland in search of more furs and the Northwest Passage. They found that by using the Indian canoes, they could move up the St. Lawrence river, into the Great Lakes, then down the rivers flowing into the Mississippi River. By 1634, Jean Nicolet had reached present-day Wisconsin. By 1673, two French travelers, Jacques Marquette and Louis Joliet, had traveled down the Mississippi as far as modern Arkansas. They turned back at that point, convinced that the Mississippi emptied into the Gulf of Mexico and not the Pacific Ocean. Nine years later, Robert de La Salle reached the place where the Mississippi empties into the Gulf, near present-day New Orleans. His exploration formed the basis of France's claim to the Louisiana Territory.

The French colonies suffered from a shortage of farmers and skilled workers. Unlike England, France did not allow religious dissenters to settle freely in North America. Nor did they encourage settlement by promising land and self-rule. French companies were unwilling to do what the Virginia Company had done at first—send more ships and fresh supplies when the first colonies were almost wiped out by disease, hunger, and Indian attack. Frenchmen with a vision of empire like Champlain and La Salle pleaded for the king to support them and reap glory, but in vain.

What kept "New France" going was the profit in the fisheries and, above all, the wealth from trading in beaver pelts. Although there were some farmers, the characteristic French settler was the trapper. With snowshoes, rifle, and pouch, the trapper was superb at living in the cold wilderness. He went ever farther inland in search of new places for his traps, meeting with Indian people to whom he would give blankets and kettles in exchange for skins. In many ways, he was like the Indians among whom he dwelt and often married—a nomad.

La Salle and his party, which included American Indians, cross frozen Lake Michigan. They entered the ice-clogged Mississippi River in February 1682 and reached the river's mouth two months later.

The Dutch Build New Amsterdam

An important American city was begun in 1626 by the Dutch. Naturally, we think of New Amsterdam, later called New York, as a jewel that the Dutch government should have treasured for its future value. Actually, it was only a minor holding to them. From 1621, the Dutch West India Company had controlled the territory that the Dutch claimed as a result of Henry Hudson's 1609 voyage up the river named for him. As a company, it was more interested in the promising sugar trade with Dutch outposts in the Caribbean and South America than in developing a colony in New Amsterdam.

Fishery workers clean and dry cod-fish before shipping them to Europe. After being cleaned in the shed, at the left, the fish were dried on the beach or on the rack, at the right.

Yet, from the start, New Amsterdam was an unusual colonial town. It had a fine harbor. Sailing ships came down the Hudson River from Fort Orange (present-day Albany) loaded with furs from the north and with grain from the Dutch farms along the river's banks. At New Amsterdam, the ships' cargoes were transferred to seagoing vessels. Wharves and warehouses soon sprang up along the harbor. Dutch tidiness and orderliness did not permit the town to grow in a sloppy manner. Streets were neatly laid out, the rows of houses precisely lined up, the fort built at the foot of the island, and the wall built across it to bar any invasion from the Indians in that area.

Because it was such a good port, the city became home to many travelers. It had an international flavor. A visitor in 1643 could claim to hear eighteen languages spoken from passersby in the streets. And because the Dutch had just come out of a long religious struggle with Spain in 1624, they adopted a policy of allowing people to be free to practice their own religion in the New World.

Though the Dutch did expand into New Jersey, Delaware, and Long Island, New Amsterdam remained the center of their American colony. But during a war between Holland and England in 1664, an English fleet captured the city. Angrily, its last Dutch governor, Peter Stuyvesant, surrendered it.

Exploration Inland and Claims to a Continent

In the 1500s, French, Dutch, and English explorers only touched the edges of the continent. By 1742, Europeans had explored much of the interior.

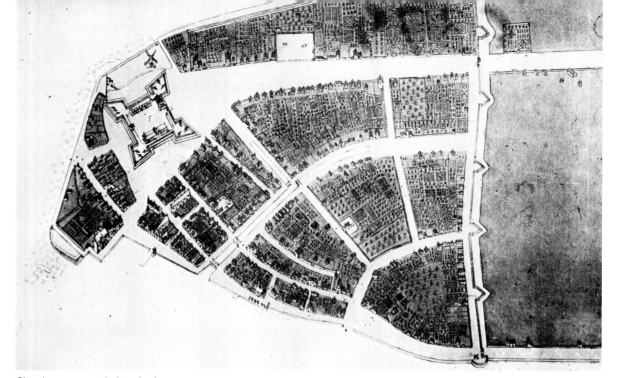

City planners commissioned a drawing of New Amsterdam in 1660 because they could not find house sites for new arrivals. After studying the drawing, the directors of the Dutch West India Company concluded that "... too great spaces are as yet without buildings... where the houses... are surrounded by excessively large plots and gardens."

The Spanish had begun this work. In 1528, a would-be conquistador named Panfilo de Narvaez was shipwrecked on the Texas coast of the Gulf of Mexico. One of his officers, Alvar Nunez, Cabeza de Vaca, his Black companion, Estevanico, and two other men survived. For eight years they wandered across northern Mexico, living among the Indian people. Finally, they came upon a Spanish outpost. The Spaniards were astonished to hear these ragged, bearded "savages" speak their own language. When Cabeza de Vaca and Estevanico finally convinced their listeners that they were Narvaez' men, they were taken to Culiacán, on the Pacific. They became the first explorers to cross the continent north of the Isthmus of Panama.

Gold fever continued to lure Spanish explorers like Hernando de Soto. In 1539, he landed in Florida. For the next three years, he pushed northward and westward (as far as present-day Oklahoma) in search of legendary cities of gold. Finally, he came to a river as wide as an ocean harbor. The Indians called it the Mississippi. For De Soto, it became his grave. De Soto's men were afraid that the Indians would attack if they knew that the Spanish leader had died of illness and exhaustion like an ordinary mortal. So they told the Indians that De Soto had gone to heaven to talk with the gods there. Then, in the middle of the night, they rowed out to midstream and threw the weighted body into the water.

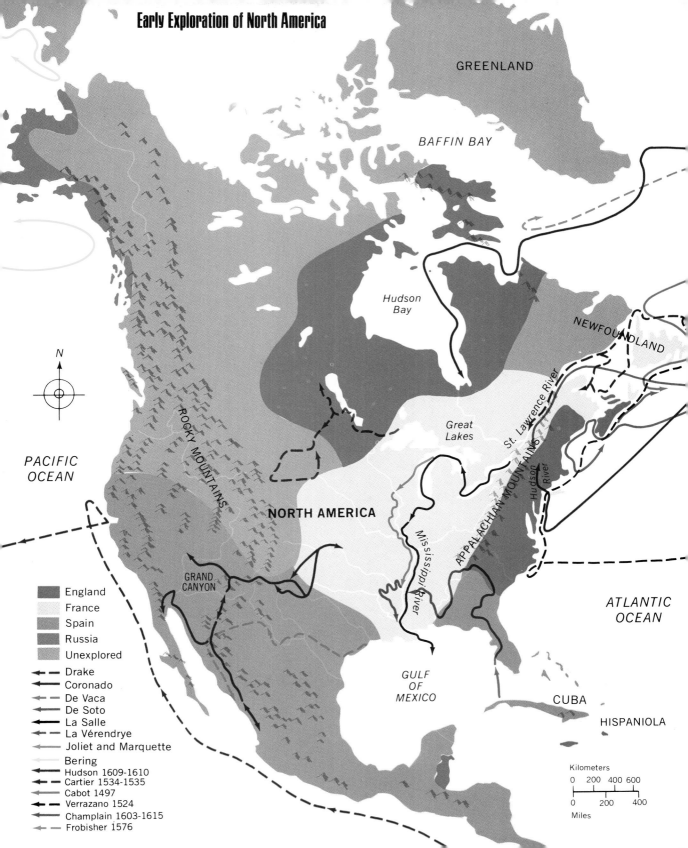

Early Exploration of North America

GREENLAND

BAFFIN BAY

Hudson Bay

NEWFOUNDLAND

Great Lakes

St. Lawrence River

ROCKY MOUNTAINS

APPALACHIAN MOUNTAINS

Hudson River

PACIFIC OCEAN

N

NORTH AMERICA

GRAND CANYON

Mississippi River

ATLANTIC OCEAN

GULF OF MEXICO

CUBA

HISPANIOLA

England
France
Spain
Russia
Unexplored
Drake
Coronado
De Vaca
De Soto
La Salle
La Vérendrye
Joliet and Marquette
Bering
Hudson 1609-1610
Cartier 1534-1535
Cabot 1497
Verrazano 1524
Champlain 1603-1615
Frobisher 1576

Kilometers
0 200 400 600

0 200 400
Miles

About the same time, another Spaniard, Francisco de Coronado, spent several years searching for the fabled golden cities. He saw buffalo and stood at the edge of the Grand Canyon. He also rode over the territory that later became the states of Arizona, New Mexico, Texas, Kansas, and Colorado. These very same territories would one day produce millions of dollars worth of oil, wheat, and cattle. But his eyes, sweeping the endless prairie grass, could not see the wealth beneath. So, he gave up in despair.

The French made the greatest strides into the center of the North American continent. Père Jacques Marquette and Louis Joliet went south from Lake Michigan, despite tales of "horrible monsters which devoured men and canoes together."

Robert de La Salle, following on their trail, reached the Mississippi's mouth, where he claimed for King Louis XIV of France all "nations, minerals, fisheries, and rivers" in the region drained by the Mississippi. Since the rivers that finally flow into the Gulf begin as far east as North Carolina and as far west as Montana, he was including almost two-thirds of the future United States as part of "Louisiana."

Fifty years after La Salle, another French explorer, Pierre de La Vérendrye, headed westward from Lake Superior. In eleven years of searching, he got as far as present-day Montana and probably saw the Rocky Mountains. Had he gone only a little farther, he would have found rivers flowing westward to the Pacific Coast.

Over a century before Verendrye, Sir Francis Drake, an Englishman, in his round-the-world voyage, had cruised along the California coast as far north as present-day San Francisco.

In 1741, Vitus Bering explored much of the west coast of Alaska, which he claimed for Russia.

Thus, by 1742, the broad outlines of North America were known, and because of these explorations, huge territories had been claimed by England, France, and Spain. The French and Spanish had conquered and were ruling large empires. The English had gone farthest in planting compact, enduring settlements.

But Europeans were not to be the only people to change the history of the Americas. People from another continent were also to become part of the American story. They came from Africa—as prisoners.

Questions for Discussion
1. Define *dissenter.*
2. Why was the Northwest Passage important to early explorers?
3. How did the early efforts of the English, French, and Dutch to colonize North America differ?
4. In what ways were the colonization efforts similar?

Chapter 2 Review

Summary Questions for Discussion

1. What were some fears Europeans had to get rid of in order to begin the age of discovery?
2. Who were the first people to successfully venture out into the Atlantic?
3. Why did the market economy begin to replace the barter economy?
4. Why was the Hanse a significant league?
5. What effect did the Crusades have on medieval trade?
6. What effect did the development of the printing press have on the world?
7. Identify Prince Henry the Navigator, Bartholomeu Dias, and Vasco da Gama.
8. What nation finally financed Columbus's voyages?
9. How did Columbus's actions in dealing with the American Indians set a pattern for future Spanish settlement?
10. What areas were conquered by the Spanish?
11. Who were Juan Ponce de León, Vasco de Balboa, Hernando Cortés, and Francisco Pizarro?
12. Why did the Pilgrims and Puritans settle in Massachusetts?
13. Why were the early days of French settlement slow and hard?
14. What resulted from Champlain's aid to the Algonquin and Huron?
15. Describe the colony of New Amsterdam, and show how it reflected Dutch values.

Word Study

In the sentences that follow, fill in each blank with the term below that is most appropriate.

colonies	barter economy	Hanse
conquistadors	market economy	missionaries
dissenters	presidios	inflation

1. In a _____ people work for wages and pay for goods with money.
2. Cities in Northern Germany joined together in leagues called the _____.
3. Many Europeans came to America to establish _____, permanent settlements.
4. The Spanish _____ came to conquer and pillage wealth.
5. Religious and charitable work was done by the _____.
6. Those who oppose generally accepted practices are called _____.
7. An economic system based on swapping goods for goods is called a _____.
8. The military garrisons that were established by the Spanish were called _____.

Using Your Skills

1. Using the map on page 31, explain why Portugal would be one of the first countries to send out explorers. Why did Dias and Da Gama follow the routes they did?
2. Using the map on page 33, can you find a clue as to why Columbus refused to believe that he had not found the Indies?
3. Referring to the map on page 47, name some major North American rivers and mountain ranges that European explorers had discovered by 1742.
4. What do the pictures in the chapter tell you about the economic life of the colonists?

CHAPTER 3

Slavery Comes to the Americas

There are some White Americans who proudly trace their ancestors back to the English who helped to found Jamestown. There are Black men and women who would have been able to trace their ancestors back to the Africans who also helped found Jamestown. However, no records were kept of all the children of the twenty Black Africans dropped off at Jamestown by a Dutch ship in 1619. That was only twelve years after Virginia was founded. Those twenty Blacks were the pioneers among Americans of African descent. Today, Americans of African descent number more than twenty million.

The part that Black men and women have played in the shaping of America is too often forgotten. Most Black people spent their first three centuries in the New World in slavery. And slaves helped build this country. But why did the Europeans who landed in the New World prefer Africans as slaves? Those who planted colonies in America found that thousands of laborers were needed in the mines and on the plantations that grew sugar, cotton, tobacco, and indigo. European farm workers were slow to settle in a strange, dangerous, and demanding new continent. Some American Indians were enslaved as laborers, but this practice proved largely unsuccessful. American Indians could easily escape in their native land. As fate would have it, powerful, armed Europe discovered America and Africa at about the same time. The Portuguese captains who touched on the shores of West Africa during the 1400s found that Black slaves were cheap and easy to come by. Therefore, they became one answer to the labor problem in America.

READING GUIDE

1. **What was Africa below the Sahara Desert like before the beginning of the European slave trade?**
2. **What prompted the growth of the slave trade?**
3. **How did North American slavery differ from South American slavery?**

A sixteenth-century bronze head from Benin, Nigeria.

1. The African Heritage

The map of Africa (see page 53) gives you some idea of the variety and richness of ancient African civilizations. Egypt, with its great pyramids, temples, and works of art, was a powerful state thousands of years before Christianity began. South of Egypt, on the Nile River, was the kingdom of Kush. Its thriving trade in iron products centered around the capital city of Meroe. In the fourth century A.D., Kush was overcome and largely destroyed by the people of Axum. Axum, then, became the capital of a new Christian state, Ethiopia.

These lands are less important to American history, however, than those to the west. Even in the days of the Roman Empire, the southwestern part of Africa was cut off from Europe by the burning sands of the Sahara Desert. Between 640 and 710 A.D., Arabs conquered all North Africa from Cairo to Fez. The Arab world became yet another barrier between Europe and *sub-Saharan* (south of the Sahara) Africa.

Therefore, the Europeans did not know that this part of Africa was a land of rolling hills, green grasses, and gentle rains. Nor did they know of its many varied peoples—Kru, Ashanti, Fanti, Ewe, Yoruba, Ibo, and many others. Africans are no more alike than are Europeans—Italians, Swedes, and the Irish. Europeans knew nothing of the great kingdoms in West Africa. Despite differences in language and culture, the people in these kingdoms were united and their cities prospered. These kingdoms existed long before Europe's own age of growth began around 1100.

In West Africa, three great empires—Ghana, Mali, and Songhai— rose and fell along the banks of the Niger River between about 500 and 1600 A.D. Ghana was a flourishing trade center from 700 to 1100 A.D. Its caravans, carrying gold, salt, copper, and slaves, traded with the Arab ports on the Mediterranean coast and with the great trading kingdoms of East Africa on the Red Sea.

These kingdoms had powerful armies and treasuries full of gold. An Arab traveler in Ghana in 1076 told of its king, who could put 200,000 soldiers into the field and who, when he received his people, was surrounded by princes with gold plaited into their hair. In 1324, the emperor Mansa Musa of Mali made a pilgrimage to Mecca in Arabia and gave 90 camel-loads of gold to people along the way.

However, late in the eleventh century, Berber warriors attacked Ghana. And by the twelfth century, very little was left of the once prosperous country. Mali began to decline around the fourteenth century.

By the fifteenth century, Songhai was an important center of learning and trade. The University of Timbuktu produced many highly educated people, such as doctors and scholars. The respect for learning

This drawing first appeared in an early 1800s book by Frederic Shoberl. Shoberl pictured many skilled West African craftsworkers in his book. Here, a goldsmith practices his craft.

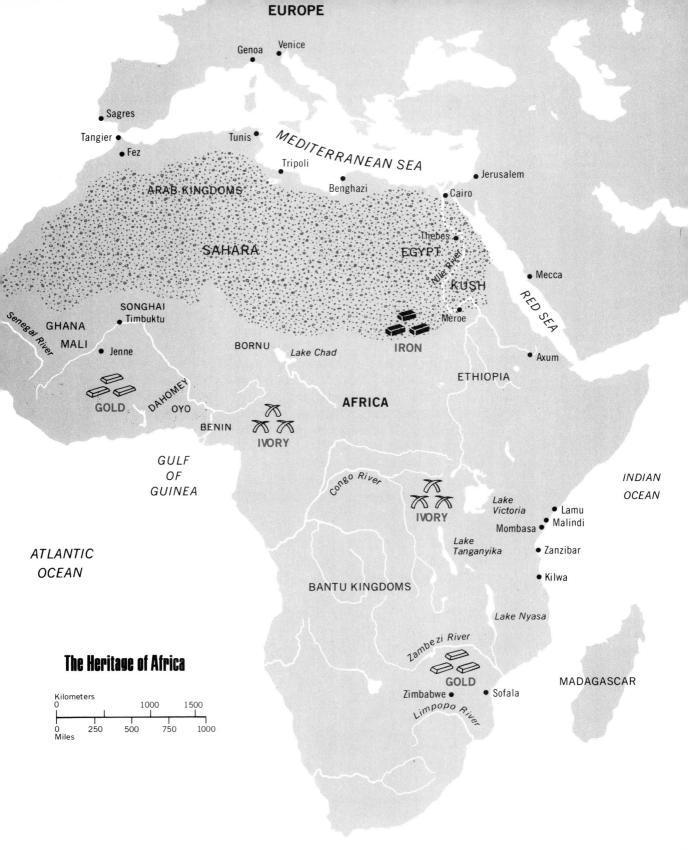

EUROPE

Genoa
Venice

Sagres

Tangier
Fez

Tunis

MEDITERRANEAN SEA

Tripoli

Benghazi

Jerusalem

Cairo

ARAB KINGDOMS

SAHARA

EGYPT

Thebes

Nile River

KUSH

Mecca

RED SEA

SONGHAI
Timbuktu

GHANA

MALI

Jenne

BORNU

Lake Chad

Meroe

IRON

Axum

ETHIOPIA

Senegal River

GOLD

DAHOMEY

OYO

BENIN

IVORY

AFRICA

GULF
OF
GUINEA

Congo River

IVORY

Lake
Victoria

Lamu
Malindi

Mombasa

Zanzibar

Lake
Tanganyika

ATLANTIC
OCEAN

INDIAN
OCEAN

Kilwa

BANTU KINGDOMS

Lake Nyasa

The Heritage of Africa

Zambezi River

GOLD

MADAGASCAR

Zimbabwe

Sofala

Kilometers
0   1000   1500

Limpopo River

0   250   500   750   1000
Miles

was so great that the book-trading business became quite profitable.

South and west of the Niger, along the Gulf of Guinea, were smaller kingdoms such as Benin, Oyo, and Dahomey. On the east coast of Africa were great trading centers such as Mombasa and Zanzibar. In the south of Africa, in the area of the Congo, Zambezi, and Limpopo Rivers, were powerful Bantu kingdoms.

Economy and Government of West Africa

The peoples of West Africa were farmers who grew millet and other crops. They raised cattle in the fields around their villages. The West Africans also mined and refined gold. They manufactured iron farm tools and weapons. In addition, they made ceremonial and artistic objects out of bronze, an alloy of copper and tin. One of the few Europeans who visited a West African village reported that he saw men and women "weave cotton, work in leather, and *fabricate* (make) iron."

The peoples of these villages traded their ivory, iron, gold, cattle, and cloth for salt, medicines, books, and jewels. These other goods came from the north and from the ports along the Red Sea and Indian Ocean. In spite of these contacts with the outside world, the desert to the north and the heavy forest along the coast to the south protected the West Africans from invasion and discouraged travel. Thus, they developed a close-knit pattern of life. Each village was almost a complete little world. Its people belonged to the same tribe. They lived in groups consisting of *extended families*—grandparents, parents, children, adopted children, grandchildren, some aunts, uncles, and cousins, and servants—usually all in adjoining houses. Many such families formed a clan. Wise men and women of the clans made decisions about sharing work, taking part in ceremonies, getting

This painting of the emperor of Mali appeared in a fourteenth-century atlas of the known world.

Another Frederic Shoberl drawing. Here, a man weaves cotton.

54

This Fulani town and plantation were located in the country of Bondu between the Senegal and Gambia rivers.

married, and other events in growing up and growing old. Like feudal Europe, African society did not change greatly from generation to generation.

The political systems of West Africa differed from people to people. For example, the king of Dahomey appointed the headmen of his villages, chose his own heir from among his sons, and named all the royal officers. However, other kings had less power. Sometimes, their officials could only come from certain aristocratic families. These officials could be chosen by the eldest members of those families, including the women. Among some peoples, the king was chosen by a council of village chiefs. The council shared the king's power and could also *depose* (remove) him if they were displeased. For example, if the council of the ruler of Yorubaland sent the lord an ostrich egg, it was a sign that he was supposed to kill himself.

Kings had important religious and ceremonial roles, however. They were especially honored when they used their magical powers to please gods and ancestral spirits. But it is important to know that kings did not own their peoples or even their lands. They had to divide honors with craftspeople, priests, and village nobles, who owed their **status** not to royal favor, but to custom and family.

The kings were representatives for their peoples. As representatives, they were the ones who met with outsiders with whom they dealt in trade or fought in war. The West Africans had a mixture of monarchy, aristocracy, and democracy in the political arrangements of their differing clans. The limited powers of the king, the strong influence of religious leaders, and the position of well-born families are factors that have led historians to compare fifteenth century West Africa with medieval Europe.

The Heritage of West African Art

Some of our knowledge of West African culture comes from works of art. These works continue to influence craftspeople and to inspire artists the world over. Only certain families were allowed to train their children to become craftspeople such as blacksmiths, wood sculptors, or brass casters. Those who had mastered a particular skill made up a privileged group and enjoyed a special position in the society.

The objects created by African artists almost always had a religious meaning. This is true of most so-called primitive art. Primitive artists, like modern cartoonists, often twisted things out of their real shape or size to make a point. But African sculptors sometimes chose to portray objects realistically.

status
rank or social position in the eyes of others

A king rides his horse through a village on the West African coast, accompanied by servants and followers.

56

African culture, history, and tradition has been passed on, generation to generation through works of art, such as this bronze horn blower from Benin, Nigeria.

African expression took other forms as well. Olaudah Equiano, a West African boy who was enslaved around 1750 and later learned to write English, said that he came from "a nation of dancers, musicians, and poets." Africans excelled in the use of drums, flutes, horns, xylophones, and other instruments. Music and dance are still part of religious worship for some Americans, who not only sing hymns and listen to choirs but also perform folk masses and rock 'n' roll plays of biblical stories. For most West Africans, songs and dances were an expression of their religion, traditions, and history.

1. Define *extended family*, *depose*, *status*.
2. Why was there so little contact between Europeans and Africans before the middle of the fifteenth century?
3. How did the societies of Black Africa differ in the ways they governed themselves?
4. How does a study of the art of Black African societies help us to learn about their cultures?
5. How did African societies carry on trade with each other and with outsiders? How do they hand down their customs and traditions from one generation to the next?

2. The Slave Trade

The coming of Arab slave caravans and European slave ships disrupted the West African societies. A kind of slavery had existed among the clans, just as some form of *compulsory* (forced) labor existed all over the world from ancient times.

West African slaves were peoples who had to perform work for whoever owned them. They would neither leave their owners' service, nor receive payment, except food and shelter. Their status was below that of free people. They, however, often worked no harder than and

An African village is overwhelmed by slave traders who have been supplied with guns by Europeans.

lived as well as their masters. They could have families of their own. They were given important responsibilities. In many ways, they were probably better off than European peasants.

People became slaves in various ways that did not brand them as naturally inferior. The population of the west coast of Africa was divided into many small, independent tribes. Warfare among these tribes led to the taking of prisoners of war. Other people became slaves as a result of hard times, which forced them to sell themselves to pay all they owed. Still, others were criminals, sentenced to become the king's slaves instead of serving out prison terms. Slaves could be sold or given away, and African rulers did give slaves as gifts.

Beginning around 900 A.D., Arab traders developed a growing trade in slaves. They carried the slaves northward across the desert to the Mediterranean coast. That was how some sub-Saharan Africans found their way to Europe before the mid-fifteenth century.

When Europeans first appeared on the Guinea coast, offering iron, firearms, beads, mirrors, cloth, and *cowry shells* (a seashell used for money in African trade) in exchange for slaves, African chiefs were glad to deal with them. They did not know that the Europeans' demands would be so great, so long-lasting. They did not realize that the Europeans would take away millions of men and women.

At first, the trade was simple. A captain would land and talk with a local chief or ruler. After some presents were given, the chief would round up a few people who were already slaves and hand them over.

Up until the early seventeenth century, the demand for slaves was limited. Prior to that time, many European ships traded on the Guinea coast for gold and elephant tusks and never took on any slaves at all.

But gradually, as settlements in the New World expanded and the need for labor grew, the slave trade became more organized. Sugar cane, cotton, and tobacco were responsible for major increases in the demand for labor. European countries like Portugal, England, and Holland set up special companies to trade in slaves. These companies built permanent bases or forts on the coast by agreement with the Africans, not by conquest. African chiefs began to send raiding parties into neighboring villages, sometimes their own villages, to round up potential slaves. No effort was made to separate villagers already enslaved from those who were free. Men, women, and children were hustled away from their homes in a sudden, devastating surprise attack. Those who resisted were killed. The rest were yoked neck-to-neck and driven without mercy along the trails southward to the coast.

These slave trains were called *coffles*. As the demand for slaves grew, the source of slaves went further and further inland. Hundreds of suffering captives were rounded up from as far inland as 500 miles. They were then taken to the coast in coffles that extended for miles.

A brass sculpture of the head of a young boy, created by a member of the Dogon tribe in Mali.

59

Some of the captives tried to kill themselves to find relief from their sorrows and pain. If they did not succeed, they were beaten in order to discourage others from trying the same escape. Slaves who became too weak to continue were beaten, killed, or left to the mercy of the wild animals and the environment.

Once at the fort on the coast, the terrified captives were kept in special pens. Their jailers were either European or African. Slave-ship crews and captains bargained with these agents, offering a certain amount of cloth, iron, or rum for each captive. Once an agreement was reached, the captain of the slave ship, perhaps along with a doctor, examined the Africans rounded up for shipment. Those selected were branded with the buyer's mark and kept in captivity until a full shipload of captives was gathered. The sick or injured who had not been chosen were left to die.

The Middle Passage to the New World

Then came the worst part, *the Middle Passage*. That was the term used for the voyage to the Americas. Up to the time they boarded the ship, the slaves were at least in familiar territory. Now, chained hand and foot, they were thrown into huge canoes, manned by Kru tribesmen. The slaves were then taken out to the ships anchored offshore. Some tried to throw themselves overboard or strangle themselves with their chains. But they were finally forced into the hold of the ship. Since the purpose of the slave ship was to pack in as much "cargo" as possible, the Blacks were forced to lie on the rough decks crowded next to each other, with no room to sit up. In good weather, the slaves were brought up on deck during the day, in chains, and fed beans or cooked cereal or sweet potatoes and water. During storms, however, they lay packed below decks for days on end, wallowing in their own filth. The suffocating stench of a slave ship could be smelled by other vessels miles away. Disease swept through

Part of a slave train on route to a coastal fort. From this fort, slaves were sold or traded and forced onto ships bound for the Americas.

Above: Traders packed slaves as tightly as possible. Men, women, and children were forced to lie with their backs on the deck. Often, men were chained together to prevent a revolt.

the slave decks, often killing as many as half the slaves before the four to five weeks' voyage ended.

The Africans did not take this brutal treatment without resistance. But they were always under armed guard, first by their African captors and then by White sailors. The slave Olaudah Equiano believed that the "horrible monsters with long hair" were going to eat him. In the slave pens ashore and on the ships, there were attempts to murder the guards and to escape. Written records tell of 55 mutinies between 1699 and 1845 and refer to at least 100 others.

Occasionally, they were successful. In 1839, slaves aboard the schooner *Amistad* murdered the officers during the voyage from one Cuban port to another. They were led by a captive named Cinque. Cinque was the son of an African ruler. After many adventures, the slaves finally succeeded in returning to Africa.

For the most part, though, the hardest-battling slaves who revolted were shot, or beaten helpless, or killed themselves in despair.

The slave trade brought out the worst in captains and crews. A slave ship captain, John Newton, who later entered the clergy, explained that the slave trade "gradually brings a numbness upon the heart" and makes those involved in it "too indifferent to the sufferings of their fellow creatures." For this and other reasons, it was not easy to get seamen to sign up for duty on slave ships. Wages were higher than for many other trades, but many sailors signed up when they were drunk or because they were trying to escape the law. Others were just in desperate need of a job or were unaware of what they were getting themselves into. The seamen were treated almost as badly as the slaves. The ship's captain knew that he would be paid for each slave that he delivered alive, but he would have to pay a year's wages to each sailor who returned alive. Unscrupulous captains saw to it that few crewmen returned to Liverpool or Bristol to collect their wages.

Slave trading was so profitable that it lasted for almost four centuries. The Congress of the United States passed laws forbidding

Slave-ship doctors examine captured Africans (above) and recommend the healthiest for purchase (below).

the African slave trade after 1808. However, smugglers continued to bring in slaves until slavery was abolished at the end of the Civil War. According to some estimates, 15 million Africans were brought as slaves to the Americas.

Questions for Discussion
1. Define *cowry shells*, *coffles*.
2. Describe the slave trade that took place in Africa before and after Whites came.
3. How was the slave trade an example of how one people can be inhumane to another people?
4. Why was the slave trade "big business" for so long?

3. Slavery in the Americas

In July 1839, a group of 54 Africans seized their Spanish slave ship and killed the captain. Led by an African named Cinque, they sailed the ship to Long Island. There, they were arrested, and the case eventually reached the United States Supreme Court. John Quincy Adams defended them and won their freedom. The Africans raised money for their passage home with public appearances and returned to their native country in 1841.

For many of the slaves, New World life began in the West Indies. By 1815, Spanish colonists were importing 10,000 slaves a year to these islands. Thousands were needed on the sugar, indigo, and various other plantations owned by French, Dutch, British, and Spanish settlers in the Caribbean islands. Thousands of other slaves were *seasoned* there before being sent to the mainland of North or South America. Seasoning meant accustoming the slaves to plantation work. Slaves often worked from sunup to sundown cutting, hauling, crushing, and then boiling sugar cane. Women, even those caring for infants whom they carried on their backs, had the same tasks as men. Like men, they were beaten if they did not work fast enough. Food consisted of poor grades of fish, plus a little cornmeal or other grain. No wonder almost one-third of the slaves died while being "seasoned."

The treatment of slaves varied from one colony to another. In South America, for example, the Black slave's fate was softened a little. To begin with, the powerful officials of the Spanish church insisted that slaves be baptized as Catholics and allowed lawful marriage. Slave families could not be broken up by sale, which happened later in the English colonies. In the Caribbean colonies

Slaves for the Caribbean region were imported by French, Dutch, British, and Spanish settlers to work on plantations, such as the one above.

White women were scarce so some early White settlers married Black or Indian women. A Latin American population of many strains—European, Indian, African—emerged. Gradually, hatred among the races lessened. On the whole, though, most New World planters did not marry outside their race. Because they were occupied with their money and racial fears, they tended to be less than fair-minded.

Thus, it was not unusual for African slaves to be treated brutally in Portuguese and Spanish mainland colonies and treated more humanely in Caribbean colonies. In the Caribbean colonies, slaves often had a good chance of becoming citizens. Although they did revolt now and then, the bitterness between Black servants and White masters was not as extreme as it was in other places where slaves were thought of as less than human.

Revolt in Haiti

The French colony of Haiti provided one example of how much cruelty slavery could breed. Haiti is the western half of the island of Hispaniola. In 1697, Spain gave up that half to France after a war. The French sugar planters were especially harsh. They intended to make money quickly and return home. They had no interest in seeing that an island population thrived. Nor did the king in Paris ever think of Haiti's Blacks as subjects for whom he had much responsibility. The planters also became concerned when the slaves outnumbered them by as many as twenty to one.

maroon
a fugitive Black slave of the West Indies and Guinea in the seventeenth and eighteenth centuries or a descendant of such a slave

Pierre Toussaint L'Ouverture was the first Black man to lead a successful revolt in the New World. By 1801, he had reorganized the government on the island of Hispaniola. The next year, Napoleon sent troops to recapture Haiti and Santo Domingo. Toussaint was betrayed and taken prisoner to France, where he died in 1803. His followers defeated the French and proclaimed independence in 1804.

prejudice
an opinion or judgment formed without knowledge of the facts

indentured servant
a servant bound by a legal contract and required to work for one master for a fixed term of years

All these forces added up to rule by terror. Overseers were allowed to overwork Haitian slaves. Planters found that it was cheaper to replace those who died with new imports from Africa than to take good care of the living. *Black codes* (special laws for Blacks) clamped an iron grip on the slaves. They could not meet, carry weapons, strike or insult Whites, or move off the plantations without permission. Every means of self-defense was kept from them. The punishments included whipping; branding; cutting off noses, fingers, and ears; and breaking bones. Thousands of runaways hid in Haiti's jungles and hills. **Maroons** often numbered a thousand men and women. Within a few years after the first Blacks were brought to Haiti in 1510, these maroons waged constant attacks against the planters.

In 1791, Blacks led by a slave named Toussaint L'Ouverture arose in a bloody revolt, killing their masters and burning the homes of French colonials. For a time, Toussaint allied his forces with the Spanish, who controlled the eastern end of the island, called Santo Domingo. When the British landed in Haiti to support the Spanish, it appeared that France might lose the entire island. Then the government in Paris offered freedom to all Blacks who would help in defeating Spain and England. Toussaint accepted the offer, was made a general, and led the Black forces to victory. By 1801, he was the head of a practically independent island.

In 1802, Napoleon sent 20,000 French troops to reestablish his control in Haiti and Santo Domingo. Napoleon tried to regain control in Haiti by inviting Toussaint to visit him in France. Once Toussaint was in France, he was captured and imprisoned. Nevertheless, other Haitian Blacks continued to fight. Napoleon's troops were finally beaten. On January 1, 1804, Haitians proclaimed the independence of the New World's first Black nation. This victory of slaves over White masters alarmed slave owners in America and sparked many new laws that were designed to keep slaves in line. Even these laws did not give slave owners peace of mind. A European visitor to the South in 1856 reported that planters never went to bed without loaded guns within reach.

Slavery in Britain's North American Colonies

Slavery in the English colonies was closely tied to racial **prejudice**. When the first twenty Africans were landed in Virginia in 1619, it was apparently not certain that they would be slaves. Many White laborers came to the colony as **indentured servants**. At first, it seemed that Africans would be treated in the same way. After a time, they would be given land and freedom. Some won these rewards. However, as time went on, the rules for Black and White servants became different. Only "Christians" could bear arms, according to a Maryland

law of 1648. Africans were not considered Christians at that time.
Only Whites could meet in groups after dark, said another Maryland
law. When a White servant ran away in Virginia, his or her
punishment was to serve a little longer. But when a Black man named
John Punch did so in 1640, he was made to serve his master for the rest
of his life. By 1661, a law was passed in Virginia that indicated that a
Black's time of indenture did not expire. In the following year, a law
was passed that stated that a child would be slave or free depending on
the status of its mother. In time, marriage between Blacks and Whites
was forbidden by law. Gradually, in most colonies, the institution of
slavery became more rigidly fixed in the economy and society. It
became harder for Blacks, slave or free, to obtain the opportunities
that were available to Whites, indentured or free.

By 1700, almost all incoming Africans were sold as slaves at
auctions after the "cargo" had been advertised in posters. Following
the examples of Virginia and Maryland, slavery soon spread to the
Carolinas. Four of the proprietors of the colony were members of the
Royal Africa Company, which was responsible for the slave trade. In
1663, the proprietors offered settlers twenty acres for each Black male
slave and ten acres for each Black female slave brought into the colony
in the first year. Similar encouragement was offered for importation of
slaves in later years. Georgia, after forbidding slavery for the first
seventeen years, finally gave in to the pressure from the settlers and
began to allow slavery in 1750. Growers of tobacco, rice, and indigo in
the Southern colonies came to believe they could not do without
African labor.

In the 1700s, the treatment of slaves on the Southern plantation
depended much on the master. Most slaves were field hands. Most of
the time, they put in grueling days of outdoor work with nothing to

In this picture, French soldiers who tried to put down the revolt of Haitian Blacks are hanged.

look forward to at sunset except another such day. The difference between slavery in Spanish America and in the American South was that there was no church or strong central government to protect slaves from their masters. The Black slaves were like pieces of movable property with no right to families or anything else of their own. They could not sell their labor for the highest wage as free laborers could. Nor were they protected by the laws that protected free people. Governments in the English colonies were under strong local influence. In the South, that meant letting the planters do what they liked with their slaves.

Slavery was not limited to the Southern colonies, although Blacks were in less demand in the Northern settlements. The Dutch had used slaves on the larger Hudson Valley plantations. But their slave code was not elaborate, and many slaves were *manumitted* (freed). When the British took control of the Dutch colony, slavery was promoted. Yet slavery was never very successful in the Middle Colonies. There, the economy was based on commerce and small-scale farming. In some areas, there were objections to slavery, based on moral grounds. The Quakers in Pennsylvania passed laws and regulations that led to the elimination of slavery in that colony.

Though the number of slaves in the middle colonies was never as great as in the Southern colonies, settlers in New England also benefited from the slave trade. Northern merchants in the New England area prospered from the slave trade. Yankee clippers competed with ships out of Bristol and Liverpool for slaves from the Guinea coast. Wealth gained from the slave trade contributed to the industrial expansion of the New England colonies.

Yet, even as the colonies were prospering from the slave trade and slave labor, the arguments in favor of slavery were weakening. Planters were learning that the so-called pagan Africans could learn as quickly as any European. A Captain Matthews of Virginia boasted in 1649 of the forty Blacks who practiced trades in his house. Free Blacks and slaves worked on plantations, and, a century after that, in towns as coachmen, barbers, waiters, cooks, carpenters, blacksmiths, shoemakers, and in many other skilled occupations.

As the number of slaves increased, the White owners took steps to curb the danger of rebellion. Runaways were severely punished. Black codes not only dealt cruelly with those who resisted White authority but also forbade slaves to gather together. Immigrants to America from other lands could keep many of their customs, worship in their familiar tongue, and gradually grow accustomed to a new style of life as they let go of their past. The Africans, however, were forbidden to gather with their own people to share a common past. Their language, customs, and often self-esteem were ripped from them.

This detail from a nineteenth-century drawing shows a slave pulling a heavy barrel along a city street.

A few masters tried to convert the Blacks to Christianity. Since religious gatherings were the only kind allowed to Blacks, churches came to be important centers of Black life in America. Black preachers often assumed leadership roles in Black communities. But colonial governments, especially in the South where slaves were numerous, never were pleased with the efforts to convert Africans to Christianity. They discouraged masters who tried to educate slaves, especially by teaching them to read. Southern colonial governments were not happy with owners who overcame fear and set their slaves free. It was felt that free Blacks, Christian Blacks, and Blacks who could read would disprove the argument that Blacks could not care for themselves and needed supervision. In addition, Blacks who could read and freed Blacks would only inspire other Blacks to revolt.

Indeed, that is just what the slaves did. Slavery was always weakened by the goodwill of some Whites and the courage and love of freedom that some Blacks experienced. Slaves were never happy, as slaveholders liked to believe. From the beginning, there was rebellion. In Virginia, as early as 1663, a plan for revolt was uncovered before it could be carried out. South Carolina was the scene of three serious rebellions in 1739. In New York, there was a revolt in 1712, in which

THE GOING PRICE FOR EARLY SLAVES—IN SMOKE

Slavery only came to the colonies gradually. We know little about the exact details. For example, we do not know who "John Punch" was. He was described only as "a negro," who was captured in 1640 with two other runaway indentured servants, who happened to be White. Indentured servants had to serve for a fixed number of years. The punishment for the white escapees was to add time to their servitude. Poor Punch was sentenced to serve his master for the rest of his life, something that never happened to a White man. So, we can assume that his sin was not in doing something especially wrong, but in just being Black.

As lifetime service for Blacks became common practice, a curious thing happened. Indentured servants could be willed, sold, or given away. A servant for life was obviously more valuable than one whose contract— similar to that of a professional athlete—had only a short time to run. A lot more work could be extracted from Blacks, so they fetched a higher price. In early Virginia and Maryland, this price was measured in pounds of tobacco. Money was almost unavailable in those colonies so tobacco became a means of exchange. Black women were most valuable of all, because their children would become slaves.

The records show it clearly. In 1643, one Virginian's will listed eight White servants worth 400 to 1100 pounds of tobacco each. But an "antient"—very old—Black man and an eight-year-old "Negro" girl brought 2000 pounds each. In 1645, two Black women and a Black boy fetched a whopping 5500 pounds of valuable tobacco. In 1648, a court listed the value of seven servants in an estate. In that list was a White woman and a White man with three years yet to serve, and a White man with six years to go. They were valued at 1000 or 1300 pounds of tobacco. But "Emaniell," and "Mingo," two Black servants, brought 2000 pounds each. No time limit was mentioned for their contracts. They were slaves and would prove more expensive to future buyers.

slaves killed nine Whites. These revolts were but a few of many. All were put down. Dozens of Blacks were hanged, burned alive, and tortured. Laws to control free Blacks were made even stricter.

The first United States census in 1790 counted more than 750,000 Blacks in the total population of nearly 4,000,000. Of the Blacks, almost 700,000 were slaves. Slavery had become a way of life in the new nation. The brutality of slavery shocked some of the country's best minds. For example, Thomas Jefferson, author of the Declaration of Independence and a slave owner himself, was worried. "I tremble for my country," he once wrote, "when I reflect that God is just." He had cause for alarm. Slavery in America would neither continue nor end without further bloodshed and brutality. Nor would the damages be limited to America.

Effects of the Slave Trade on Africa

Modern historians and archaeologists are just beginning to piece together the results of the slave trade on African history and on

African descendants. Some historians believe that the effects of the slave trade were widespread.

With the exception of a few private sales, slave owners bought slaves at public auctions. Blacks became little more than goods to be sold or traded to the highest bidder.

When Europeans first made contact with Africa in the fifteenth century, differences existed in their cultures, but the Europeans and Africans treated each other as equals. However, it was not long before Europeans realized what wealth could be gained from the slave trade. The result was that the relationship between Europeans and Africans changed.

The slave trade disrupted the existing cultures and economies of the West African people. Power and wealth shifted to merchants and slave traders. This shift disrupted the importance of the traditional leaders in African society. In a letter to the King of Portugal soon after the Portuguese began to take slaves in Africa, Dom Affonso, King of the Congo, wrote that the Portuguese merchants and agents "have traded and given away goods in such abundance that many of our **vassals**, who used to obey us, no longer do so because they are now richer than we ourselves. This is all doing great harm not only to the service of God, but to the security and peace of our kingdom as well." The King of Portugal ignored Dom Affonso's request to put an end to the slave trade.

vassals
subject peoples

The poster below advertises the auction of a cargo of slaves just arrived from the Guinea Coast.

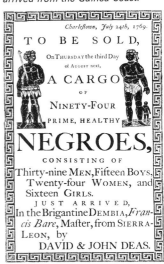

Economic progress was also upset by the slave trade. African traders were able to obtain consumer goods in exchange for human "cargo." As a result there was little need to expand the already existing industries, such as textiles and mining. In some instances, the competition from imports wiped out West African industries. The demand for goods spurred on the Industrial Revolution in Europe and America. However, it did nothing for African development. The wealth that came to the Guinea coast was not used as capital to develop industry. Rather, merchants paraded themselves in all their wealth.

Arab traders force slaves across the Sahara during a sandstorm. The picture was drawn by an Englishman who tried to cross the desert in 1818.

Rulers used their wealth to maintain armies and to win territories and followers. Both of these practices stifled the development of industry and were of no long-term benefit to Africa.

The social, political, and economic effects of the slave trade seem to be far-reaching. The Africans with whom most Europeans and Americans came in contact were slaves. In order to justify slavery, myths of Black inferiority developed. Respect for Africa as an equal partner decreased. When the slave trade ended, Europeans spread a colonial empire in Africa. Even at the beginning of this century, the African continent was still contributing to the wealth of the rest of the world, while getting little in return.

Questions for Discussion

1. Define *black codes, maroons, manumitted, vassals, prejudice.*
2. For what kinds of work was slave labor found to be most profitable in the Americas?
3. Why did the slaves have to be "seasoned"?
4. What was the attitude of the Spanish and Portuguese toward the slaves?
5. Why did Toussaint L'Ouverture's rebellion against French rule in Haiti make Whites elsewhere more fearful of Blacks?
6. In the English colonies, what was the effect of the "Black codes" on the culture of slaves?
7. What effect did the slave trade have on the economies of the West African people?

Chapter 3 Review

Summary Questions for Discussion

1. When and where were the first Black slaves brought to America?
2. Why did Europeans enslave Black Africans?
3. Why did Europeans have a very limited •knowledge of Africa?
4. List examples of the wealth and power of the early West African empires of Ghana, Mali, and Songhai.
5. What were the roles of the wise men and women of the clans?
6. How does West Africa around 1400 compare with medieval Europe?
7. What position did artists and artisans hold in West African society? What was the main theme of the art?
8. Describe the economy of West Africa.
9. How did Africans from the sub-Sahara find their way to Europe before the mid-fifteenth century?
10. How did West Africans become slaves?
11. Why was the Middle Passage considered the ''worst part'' of the slave trade?
12. Why did so many slaves die in the process of seasoning?
13. Why was slavery less popular in the Northern than in the Southern colonies?
14. Why did churches become important centers of Black life in America?
15. How did the slave trade affect (a) the power of the traditional leaders in African society, (b) the political progress, and (c) the economic progress?

Word Study

Fill in each blank in the sentences that follow with the term below that is most appropriate.

cowry shells   Black codes   indentured servants   status   depose

manumitted   prejudice   coffles   maroons

1. Europeans offered firearms, beads, cloth, and _____ in exchange for slaves.
2. The people herded together in slave trains were called _____.
3. The social position or _____ of slaves was below that of free people.
4. These runaways hoped to organize and _____ the people who were holding them.
5. In Haiti, many slaves became _____ or runaways and hid in the jungles.
6. Special laws for Blacks were called _____.
7. Many years would pass before the slaves were freed or _____.
8. Many White laborers came to America as _____ under contract for a fixed number of years.

Using Your Skills

1. Study the map of Africa on page 53. Name three major rivers of Africa. Which one was fairly well known to Europeans before 1500? Why?
2. If the pictures in this chapter were the only evidence that was available to you about slavery, what might be a possible theory about the relationship between slavery and violence? Why?
3. What do the pictures in the chapter tell you about West African society? art? economy?
4. The pictures on pages 65 and 66 show the Haitian slave revolt. What effect would the pictures have upon slave owners? and slaves?

CHAPTER 4
Colonial America

In the first 150 years after England started a colony in Virginia, English settlements multiplied rapidly. Little outposts originally facing starvation grew into thriving communities. While the French and Spanish empires spread over millions of acres, England's colonists were mostly settled in a compact ribbon of territory, about 80 kilometers (50 miles) wide, running down the Atlantic Coast. There, in the valleys with many rivers flowing to the sea, the pioneers gathered the wealth of the soil and the forest. They built towns and started a new way of life.

In this new land, the roles that people were accustomed to playing changed. Those people who might have been servants or worked on someone else's land in England often found themselves landowners and masters in America. Women developed new independence in America, though in most of the colonies they had few legal rights and could not own property. Women were a vital part of the economy of the new colonies. In many ways, they were freer than they would be for another 200 years.

As colonial settlements grew, the society that developed became more varied and complex. A society that has grown bigger than a single settlement gives rise to many special occupations and *classes* (groups of people who share a role or position in the society). Towns sprang up with traders, teachers, workers, doctors, and other specialists. By 1750, the colonists made a living in many ways. They grew grain, tobacco, and indigo; combed the forests for furs and for

READING GUIDE

1. **How did the beliefs of the Puritans affect life in New England?**
2. **What accounted for the growth of tolerance in the Middle Colonies?**
3. **How did the plantation economy affect life in the South?**
4. **In what ways did life become more democratic during colonial times?**

This engraving shows central Philadelphia in the 1700s.

timber to build houses and ships; fished for cod and for whale. Colonists gathered in cities and linked these cities with *post roads* that cut through the woods and the farmlands. Post roads were built for mail carriers. These roads extended from what is now Portland, Maine, to St. Augustine, Florida. The colonists also built a chain of forts along the edge of the wilderness. Throughout the thirteen colonies, people, goods, and ideas mingled in an American setting.

1. New England: A Shipping Economy

To New England's first settlers, God was everywhere, always watching over His own. Richard Mather, the Puritan minister, described in his journal the stormy voyage from England to Massachusetts in 1635. Every fair day was because of "the goodness of our God" and every gale a sign of "His overruling providence." A Puritan's whole life was built around religion. Hence, it was important to the Puritans that a public school system be set up so that Satan could not keep people "from knowledge of the Scriptures." In these public schools, even the youngest Puritans learned the alphabet from a *primer* (first reader) that referred to a Bible story or from a story that made a religious point. Even before the 1647 law that legalized public schools was passed, a college called Harvard had been founded and a printing press had been set up. The Puritans were more educated than any other colonists. Much of the literature from that era has been preserved, including the poetry of Anne Bradstreet and the theological and philosophical works of Jonathan Edwards.

Ministers were the real leaders in a community. They believed their purpose was to work God's will on earth. It was unthinkable that anyone should not belong to a church. The Puritan believed that the church was a place where people could help each other become more holy. Thus, the political system was a *theocracy*—rule by religious leaders.

In the words of the Puritan leader John Winthrop, Christians were meant to "bear one another's burdens." This meant that "the care of the public must hold sway over all private interests." Individuals did not casually choose their own farms and house lots. Instead, the governments of New England colonies laid out neatly surveyed townships. A central square, on which cattle grazed in the early days, became the "common." The land surrounding the common was divided into individual plots and was then assigned. Some of these lots were reserved for public buildings, such as schools.

Land was generally distributed by the leaders according to need and talent. The expansion of the settlement was encouraged by 93 square-kilometer (36 square-mile) grants of land to groups who wanted to forge out on their own. By the 1700s, new immigrants had to

A page from a 1767 New England primer that taught the alphabet.

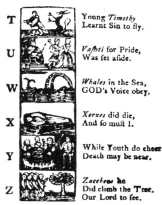

T	Young *Timothy* Learnt Sin to fly.
U	*Vashti* for Pride, Was set aside.
W	*Whales* in the Sea, GOD's Voice obey.
X	*Xerxes* did die, And so must I.
Y	While *Youth* do cheer Death may be near.
Z	*Zaccheus* he Did climb the Tree, Our Lord to see.

FORT OSWEGO

FORT NIAGARA

FORT DETROIT

FORT SANDUSKY

FORT DUQUESNE

FORT MASSAC

FORT CUMBERLAND

Albany

Falmouth (Portland)

Portsmouth

Boston

Newport

New London

New York

Philadelphia

Baltimore

PROCLAMATION LINE 1763

Williamsburg

Norfolk

Edenton

New Bern

FORT AUGUSTA

Charleston

Savannah

St. Augustine

Colonial America in 1750

AGRICULTURE AND TRAPPING:

cattle and grain

tobacco

rice and indigo

furs and skins

SEA INDUSTRIES:

🐟 fishing

🐋 whaling

FOREST INDUSTRIES:

△ lumber and timber

⊥⊥ shipbuilding

⊞ naval stores

GENERAL INDUSTRIES:

ironworks

rum distilleries

Post Roads

Kilometers
0   100   200   300

0   50   100   150   200
Miles

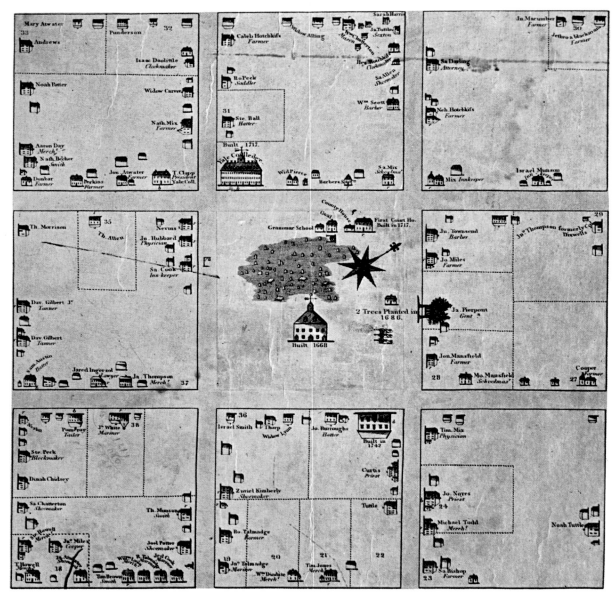

The layout of New Haven, Connecticut, was typical of most New England towns. The map above includes the names and occupations of the residents.

buy land from the descendants of the early settlers or go further west, expanding the frontier.

These new settlers also set up their towns using the gridiron pattern, which became the standard for American towns and cities. In fact, 93 square-kilometer (36 square-mile) measure for townships was used later by the United States government for surveying public lands. And, by the end of the eighteenth century, it was the pattern for the settlement of the Northwest Territory.

Threats to Puritan Control

In early New England, church leaders kept tight control over social as well as religious life. Such strict control proved to be hard on dissenters like Roger Williams, who openly disagreed with church leaders. An early believer in civil liberties, Roger Williams questioned certain aspects of Puritan life in Massachusetts. He believed that religion and government should remain separate. The government should have no authority over religious services. Williams also denied the right of the King to give the colonists land that belonged to the original inhabitants of America.

Williams' attacks on religious and civil authority caused concern among the Puritan leaders. They controlled the General Court and the Massachusetts legislature. Eventually, the General Court ordered that Williams be returned to England. He fled to what later became known as Rhode Island, where he purchased land from the American Indians. His colony developed into one that allowed representative government and separation of church and state. He treated the Indian people fairly and granted a measure of toleration for Jews and Catholics in his colony.

Shortly after Roger Williams left Massachusetts, Anne Hutchinson, another dissenter, fled. She had questioned the authority of the religious leaders and was banished by the General Court. She and her followers founded Portsmouth, Rhode Island. Further quarrels caused her to move to Long Island, New York. In 1643, Anne Hutchinson and her family were killed in an Indian raid.

As the New England Puritans prospered, it became harder for the religious leaders to maintain total control. The Puritans found that they had to resort to drastic methods in an effort to discourage other religious beliefs from filtering into Massachusetts. For instance, in Boston, three Quaker missionaries were hanged.

The decline of the absolute power of the Puritan leaders was further affected by the Salem witch hunts. In the spring of 1692, several young people in Salem, Massachusetts, became interested in the writings of a Puritan leader. The Puritan was Cotton Mather, and his writings were on the subject of witchcraft. A group of girls accused a servant of being a witch. In turn, she was frightened into accusing others. By the time the episode was over, nineteen men and women were hanged for witchcraft. When the accusations began to include prominent leaders, the officials brought an end to the trials. In the end, the accusers admitted their mistakes. However, the moral leadership of Puritanism was discredited.

In the 1740s, a revival of interest in religion was stirred up by a number of clergymen throughout the colonies. They included the theologian Jonathan Edwards and a traveling Calvinist preacher from

Anne Hutchinson led a stormy life. After banishment from Massachusetts, she and her followers founded Portsmouth, Rhode Island. Further quarrels caused her to move to Long Island, where she and her family were killed in an Indian raid.

piety
devotion to religious duties

England, George Whitefield. Followers of these men called themselves "New Lights." The New Lights urged a return to **piety** and rigorous religious practices. Critics of the revivalists, the "Old Lights," held that a show of religious enthusiasm was not a sure sign of true faith. Instead of uniting congregations to a common purpose, the revival inspired the development of new congregations. As a result, the unity of religious thought, so important to the early Puritans, was lost. Like other colonies, Massachusetts and Connecticut became the sites of many different religious practices.

The Decline of the American Indians

Difficulties between the American Indians and the settlers developed because of several factors. Many New England settlers paid the American Indians for land. But the Indian people did not put the same meaning on the land transactions as the settlers did.

Settlers not only purchased land for their present use, they also bought land for their future needs. The land they bought for the future was not used. And often, the settlers resold the land. American Indians, on the other hand, believed that land could not be owned. They felt that land belonged to all people and should be used by all. Therefore, if the settlers were not putting the land to use, they had no right to hold it.

This ship's carpenter was one of many employed in the growing New England shipbuilding industries.

Trading between the settlers and the Indian people was more successful. However, its effects on American Indian culture were harmful. In the early years when game was plentiful, the American Indians could supply the traders' demands for animal pelts. In return, the American Indians received many metal tools and guns, which they favored. When the supply of animals was depleted, the American Indians' standard of living also suffered.

A certain tenseness between the Indian people and settlers was always present. Some settlers were fearful, and some American Indians were resentful. In one incident, the Pequots, the most powerful tribe in New England, reacted to a raid on one of their villages by attacking two English settlements. In a gesture of retaliation, settlers attacked a Pequot village in 1637. The New Englanders killed nearly 400 of the Pequots and tracked down the rest to be sold into slavery.

The Puritans tried for a time to convert American Indians to Christianity. Unlike the French and Spanish missionaries who had the financial support of their governments, the Puritans did not. Instead, they depended on the voluntary contributions of wealthy Puritans in England. Even though certain things were accomplished, the money was hardly enough to sustain an all-out effort. John Eliot, a missionary, established "praying Indian" towns. These towns were an attempt to provide Christian Indians with a community of fellow believers and to adapt them to a lifestyle similar to the settlers. It is estimated that there were over a thousand Indians who became Christians in Massachusetts.

These efforts were resented by those American Indians who wanted to stem the tide of change. These people were traditional people who believed that their culture and traditional ways of life were being destroyed. During 1675 and 1676, King Philip, a Wampanoag, led his people in a major uprising against the Puritans. About a thousand settlers were killed before the uprising collapsed from lack of supplies. King Philip was killed, and his wife and son were sold into slavery in the West Indies. The Indians became more embittered. As a result, they allied themselves with the French in later conflicts between English and French settlers.

The Triangular Trade

Puritan elders believed that God meant His world to be used and improved. Hard work became a form of worship. So New Englanders, or "Yankees," as they came to be called, worked earnestly. They farmed their rocky soil and reaped generous harvests from the forest

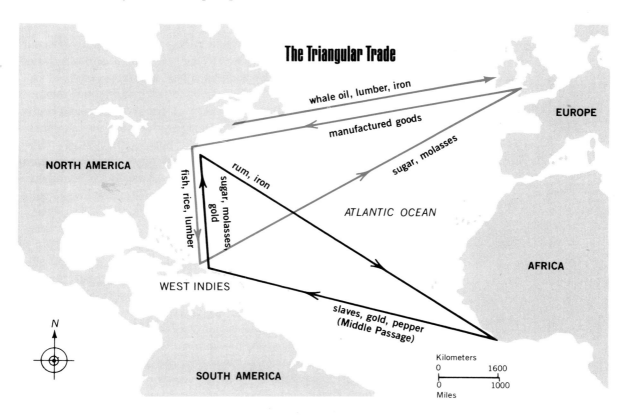

The Triangular Trade

and sea. The wilderness contained fur, but its trees also furnished fine timbers for ships. As early as 1631, a tiny vessel named *Blessing of the Bay* was launched in Boston. One hundred years later, Yankee-built ships manned by Yankee sailors were familiar sights in the ports of the West Indies, Europe, and Africa.

New England skippers might leave Boston or Providence with a load of lumber, salted fish, horses, and furs. They would head south, stopping at other colonial ports to take on tobacco and rice. Then they would put in at a West Indian island and unload the horses, the lumber to build the planters' houses and mills, and the fish and rice to feed the slaves. In exchange, the captains would receive sugar and currency. They would then sail east across the Atlantic Ocean. The vessels would, perhaps, stop in Spain to add wine and lemons to the cargo. The next stop would be London, where the sugar, wines, and fruit were sold. Finally, the Yankee vessel would return home, full of furniture, clothing, glass, tools, and ironware.

In 1757, an American artist named John Copley painted this portrait of James Tilley, a very successful New England merchant.

You will note (see map on page 79) that there was a triangle of trade. Its three points were the New England colonies, the Caribbean islands, and England. Another, sinister, triangle existed as well. The New Englanders bought molasses, a by-product of refined sugar cane, in the West Indies. After distilling the molasses in New England, they sailed to the African coast. There the New Englanders traded the rum for slaves. Then they would sail back to West Indian ports and exchange the slaves for molasses. With this second batch of molasses, the New Englanders sailed back to New England. Later, New England became a center of opposition against drinking and slavery. However, its early fortunes rested partly on rum and the slave trade.

As Yankee merchants and sailors gathered in the profits of these trades, many changes took place. Codfish and pine planks became as important in the once-Puritan world as psalms and farms. People from Boston, Providence, and Salem helped to link three continents separated by the Atlantic Ocean. The isolation of America was finally broken.

Boston: City of Commerce

By 1760, when Boston was about 130 years old, it had a population of over 15,000. No longer was it a small Puritan wilderness community. Religion was still important in the life of the city. But the masts of the many ships at the wharves also showed that Boston was now a city that depended on commerce.

The city's merchants were honored citizens. They dressed well, dined well, and lived in elegant homes.

However, Boston was not all business and commerce. Its citizens included royal officials and the ministers who preached in handsome

This 1764 watercolor of Boston shows the harbor crowded with ships.

brick churches in the heart of town. There was also a middle class that made its living by special skills. Paul Revere was one such person. The son of a French immigrant, he made fine silver bowls, pitchers, tongs, and other objects in his shop. Another special-skilled person was John Adams. He went to Harvard College and then returned home to practice law.

There were many other people, men and women, free Whites and indentured servants, free Blacks and slaves, who did get their hands dirty for a living. They were waiters at the inn; grooms for horses; apprentices to tailors, butchers, shoemakers. There were people who did odd jobs for grocers, cabinetmakers, stonemasons, and bricklayers. There were also sailors between voyages and workers at the shipyards.

Questions for Discussion

1. Define *piety, theocracy.*
2. Why were ministers in colonial New England such highly respected people?
3. How did the religious ideas of the Puritans affect their patterns of life?
4. What threats to Puritan control developed in the Massachusetts colony? How were they dealt with?
5. Why was a return to piety viewed as a possible solution to the problems of the Massachusetts colony?
6. How did the Puritan attitude toward work result in the triangle trade?
7. How did life in colonial Boston differ from life in an early Puritan village?

2. The Middle Colonies: America's First Breadbasket

In 1650, a Dutch official wrote that "New Netherland" was "the handsomest and pleasantest country that man can behold," with "grass as high as a man's knees" to feed cattle and "all sorts of fresh ponds, brooks, and rivers." Much of the soil of the Middle Colonies— New York, New Jersey, Pennsylvania, Delaware, and parts of Maryland—was level and rich. Once settlers cleared an area of trees, they found it easy to grow corn, wheat, rye, oats, and flax—from which linen is made. In the early period of settlement, pioneers could feed their families with plentiful game and with limitless fish. Later, when the land was developed, the settlers cultivated orchards and raised pigs and chickens to make up for the wild deer and turkeys that the pioneers had killed off or driven away.

The Middle Colonies became America's first farm heartland. Unlike the Old World, land was not hard to get. A farm could be rented from a rich English or Dutch settler who had been given a large estate by the government in return for bringing in settlers. Or a poor person could work as an indentured servant for seven years. At the end of that time, some colonies would give this person 20.2 hectares (50 acres). By 1750, however, these opportunities were almost entirely closed to Blacks who had been indentured servants.

On this plentiful land, the White colonists built a comfortable way of life. On farms, Europeans who settled in The Middle Colonies learned to use everything nature provided. They ground their own wheat to make flour, and baked bread on their own hearths. They butchered their own hogs and cattle. What meat they did not eat right away, they salted for future use. The colonists made clothing from

These two drawings were done by an amateur artist from York, Pennsylvania. A local farm woman (below) skillfully slaughters a hog. A York tavern-keeper (below right) fries sweet potatoes.

sheep's wool or from linen. The members of the household prepared the flax fibers, spun them into thread, and wove the cloth. Then they dyed it with bark or berry juices, cut it, and sewed it. The settlers put the hides of cows, sheep, and pigs to good use as well. Once the animal had been skinned, the hides were converted into leather by a local tanner. Then the local craftspeople cut, sewed, and glued the leather to make shoes, boots, gloves, leather shirts, and leggings.

Everyone worked hard, including the children. The work yielded a reward that landless European peasants could not expect: a chance to be property owners and the opportunity for a better life.

Working hard left little time for recreation. Settlers often found some time in a necessary activity. For example, men hunted and fished, and women attended quilting parties. Children enjoyed playing ball and tenpins and using stilts and swings. In winter, popular pastimes were ice skating and sleighing—two activities introduced by the Dutch in New Amsterdam.

The pioneer settlers in the Middle Colonies needed little from the outside world. At first, the settlers were forced to buy iron and glass from Great Britain. But when the Middle Colonies were allowed to manufacture them, theirs were as good as Great Britain's. However, the farm folk did appreciate imported luxuries such as coffee, tea, sugar, books, china dishes, and lace caps. For the most part, though, these early American communities were **self-sufficient**. This self-sufficiency gave the pioneers a sense of independence which influenced the colonists' beliefs about the role of government and the rights of individuals.

A Moravian foot-washing ceremony in the Middle Colonies.

self-sufficient
able to provide for oneself without the help of others; independent

Religious Diversity Welcomed

The Middle Colonies, especially Pennsylvania, differed from the New England Colonies in a way other than the richness of the farmland. These colonies were not founded by tiny groups of people who discouraged outsiders as the first Puritans in Massachusetts did. Instead, they prospered by attracting many newcomers of different faiths. Moreover, William Penn, who founded Pennsylvania in 1681, had a special reason to be friendly to newcomers who were independent-minded in religious matters. Penn himself was a Quaker. The Quakers believed in simplicity of dress, speech, and worship. They also believed that each person should be guided by the "inner light" of conscience. Because they objected to all interference by the government in religious matters, they were terribly persecuted, not only in England but in Massachusetts as well.

Europeans were attracted to Pennsylvania. It was a place of good land and peace. And it was a place without whipping posts or gallows

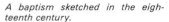

A baptism sketched in the eighteenth century.

83

Colonial Pennsylvania welcomed a number of religious groups. In this picture, a Quaker speaks his conscience as others listen.

proprietary colony
a colony that is formed when a ruler gives a large tract of land to a family or person. These people, called proprietors, have governing power over the lands.

for religious minorities. Thousands of Germans from the Rhine Valley, which was torn by wars and church quarrels, emigrated to Penn's paradise. They first came in 1683 and founded a suburb of Philadelphia which is still called *Germantown*. By 1760, Germans made up one-third of the colony's population. The *Pennsylvania Dutch* got their name from a mistaken pronunciation of the German word *Deutsch*, meaning German. The Germans who came to Pennsylvania were divided into many religious groups, such as Lutherans, Moravians, Schwenkfelders, Dunkards, and Mennonites.

After 1700, a number of Presbyterians from northern Ireland began to settle in the Middle Colonies as well. Some European Jews were also attracted by the religious freedom and economic opportunities of New York and Philadelphia.

English Catholics, as well as many Protestants, settled in Maryland. This colony was founded as a **proprietary colony** under a grant given to Cecil Calvert, Lord Baltimore, in 1632. Calvert hoped to establish a haven for English Catholics. In 1649, the Maryland legislature passed an Act of Toleration, which granted religious freedom to any Christian people.

Ben Franklin's Philadelphia

Philadelphia was the center of the Quaker's world. Just as Boston grew beyond a Puritan village, Philadelphia became something bigger than a Quaker reformer's model city. Its special style is shown in the life of its leading citizen, Benjamin Franklin.

Young Ben Franklin, born in 1706, worked for his brother James, a Boston printer. However, when Ben was sixteen, he set out to make his own fortune and headed for Philadelphia. There he became a printer and, eventually, the owner of his own paper, *The Pennsylvania Gazette*.

The *Gazette*, like other colonial newspapers, not only printed reports of wars, accidents, disasters, political quarrels, births, and deaths. Through its advertisements, it also told of what was happening in the world of business. The person who put out the town's gazette also printed laws, sermons, and *almanacs*—volumes full of information about the weather, tides, and other things useful to sailors and planters. But publishing the *Gazette* and other materials was only one of Franklin's activities. Franklin sold the latest books imported from Europe. In addition, he soon became involved in buying and selling land and goods. In this way, he became wealthy enough to spend most of his time doing the things he liked.

Among his hobbies was science. Franklin's most famous experiment, in which he proved that lightning was electricity by flying a kite on a wire in a storm and drawing a spark from a key at the wire's end, is probably familiar to you. But Franklin also liked to use his scientific knowledge to develop useful gadgets such as the Franklin stove. This heated a room much better than an open fireplace.

Benjamin Franklin was also a great organizer of city services, such as improved street cleaning and a new street-lighting system. He was responsible for setting up a police force, a school that became the University of Pennsylvania, a city hospital, and a circulating library. He served as a deputy postmaster, as a member of the Pennsylvania legislature, and as the colony's agent in London.

Even before the American Revolution, Franklin was showing that the colonies could produce outstanding thinkers. He was a practical American, as eager to be of use in this world as the Puritans were to prepare for the next. But Franklin needed a city to challenge his talents, and Philadelphia's diversity and growing urban needs provided this challenge.

Questions for Discussion

1. Define *self-sufficient*.
2. How did the Middle Atlantic Colonies differ from the New England colonies?

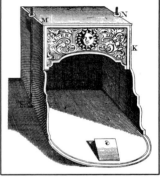

Benjamin Franklin (below) first published his Pennsylvania Gazette *in 1729. His scientific inventions included the stove above.*

3. How did William Penn's policies encourage immigration to Pennsylvania?

4. Why would Benjamin Franklin be considered an outstanding thinker?

3. The South: A Plantation Economy

staple crops
farm foods grown or produced in a particular region and necessary for its livelihood

This water color was sketched near Fredericksburg, Virginia, and is called "An overseer doing his duty."

Southward from Pennsylvania was the area of the **staple crops**. The most important product was tobacco, with rice running a close second. Both crops required hard labor by large groups of workers. The tobacco plantation was a kind of agricultural factory. Part of the plantation grew food for the work force. But most of the plantation was devoted to producing the leaves that Europeans enjoyed smoking.

These "factories," like the farming communities of the Middle Colonies, were self-sufficient. The plants were grown, cured, put in barrels, and loaded on ships right at the planter's own riverside wharves. In various buildings on the estate, slaves worked as carpenters, blacksmiths, coopers or barrelmakers, shoemakers, tanners, and butchers. One Virginia planter, George Mason, even had Black spinners, weavers, knitters, and a distiller who made "every fall a good deal of apple, peach and persimmon brandy" from the plantation orchards.

The planter rarely saw, or needed, much cash. The tobacco was shipped to a *factor*, or agent, in London. The factor sold the tobacco and used the money to buy goods as the planter instructed him— books, ball gowns, dolls for the children, hymnbooks, a coach for the whole family. The plantation owner was often in debt to the factor if tobacco prices fell. Usually, the solution was to borrow more money to buy more land, thus hoping to grow more tobacco and eventually catch up. So, being in debt was often a part of the planter's way of life.

Like the New England town and the Middle Colony farm, the plantation was a small world of its own. However, where the center of authority in the township was the minister, on the plantation it was the master who ruled Blacks and Whites alike. Of course, not all Southerners owned large estates. In fact, only a very few did. But the aristocratic holder of many acres set the tone that the ambitious often tried to imitate. It was the planter's social importance that provided great political influence. That importance rested partly on the ownership of slaves.

In the world of slavery, both Whites and Blacks had very definite social ranks. Among Southern Whites, the overseer, who actually supervised slaves, had a very low status. Somewhat above the overseer was the person who owned land but no slaves. The highest on the social ladder was the class of planters who owned slaves but did not work with them in the fields.

Planters lived well on Virginia plantations that often covered thousands of acres. The plantation pictured here included a great house, slave cabins, barns, warehouses, a water mill, and a dock for ships.

Responsible owners were supposed to be caretakers of the slaves. They had to settle disputes among the slaves, like judges. If they chose, owners furnished slaves with religious instruction and led prayer meetings. The owner was also supposed to doctor sick slaves. Because owners supervised all buildings, roads, and drainage ditches on the plantation, they also had to be fairly good architects and engineers. Only a tiny number of plantation owners played all these parts wisely and well. Unfortunately, they were expected to be responsible for many people in ways that nobody is today.

As for slaves, the closer they got to the owner's family, the more dignity they gained, at least in the eyes of Southern Whites. The hard-working field hands were usually dressed in tattered garb. They were issued just two outfits a year. Their diets consisted of cornmeal, fat pork, and molasses. They were forced to live in dirt-floored cabins. And they were often thought of as two-legged animals. On the other hand, skilled workers led somewhat different lives. House servants such as the waiter, the cook, or the nursemaid were also considered to

South Carolina slaves enjoy a rare moment of relaxation—possibly preparing for a wedding. Why do you suppose that pictures like this one were popular among the defenders of slavery?

be skilled workers. These slaves were better dressed and sometimes had a chance to become better educated.

Whatever their status, the life of plantation slaves was limited. Contact outside the plantation was not permitted. Social life and entertainment were furnished by the slaves themselves. Blacks expressed their feelings about their life and work through songs and dances.

It is important to remember that slavery represented a long and brutal episode in our history. The system was a terrible one. Only a limited number of slaves were able to earn money and to buy their freedom. However, this depended on the master. And there were many different kinds of masters. Some were brutes who beat their slaves. But there were also men like George Washington who met their responsibilities well and freed their slaves. Whites and Blacks built the South together. The lives of slaves and masters were mingled so much that Black and White Southern history cannot be separated.

Charleston: City of Southern Charm

The South's most important and beautiful city was Charleston, South Carolina. Its waterfront was lined with fine brick houses. Cities were less important in the South, where there was less commerce and industry than in the Northern colonies. But Charleston attracted those people who conducted the trade in rice, indigo, and slaves for much of the South.

Charleston's social tone was set by Carolina planters. The growing season on rice plantations was hot and damp. Mosquitoes and fevers were abundant. Hence, typical Carolina landowners would build townhouses in Charleston and live out the unhealthy months there with their families.

Charlestonians tended to imitate French, Spanish, and Dutch West Indian sugar planters, as well as English country gentry. They enjoyed elegant clothing, fine furniture, and good food. The Charlestonians of wealth did not give up English styles altogether. They hunted the fox with hound and horn in costumes whose styles were borrowed from England. They might send their sons to London to study law. In religion, they were likely to be proud members of the government-supported Church of England.

It is a mistake to think that all Carolinians lived in this leisurely fashion. There were urban Charlestonians in the business of selling cloth or ships' supplies, who were as sober as Quakers. In fact, sometimes they were Quakers. In the backwoods of the Carolinas, there were hard-working new immigrants from northern Ireland. These people wore homespun clothes and scorned "aristocratic folderol." They believed that only a Methodist, Baptist, or Presbyterian was a true Christian. But the landowning gentry were the people looked up to and copied.

Slaves who worked as house servants usually received better treatment from their owners than the field hands. Here, a Black nurse looks after the son of a wealthy Virginian.

Questions for Discussion

1. Define *factor, staple crops*.
2. How did the South's staple crops promote the growth of plantations?
3. Why did plantation owners need little cash to conduct their business?
4. How did the plantation influence the social status of the owner?
5. Why were the owners of large plantations in the South politically important?

4. Education in the Colonies

In the early years of the colonies, schools were established to teach children how to read so that they could study the Bible. The main purpose of higher education was the training of ministers. As a result, boys usually had more opportunity than girls to further their education. Some girls did not even attend regular school. They went to the home of a widow or other respectable woman for instruction in reading, needlework, and other skills necessary for running a house.

Children in New England had the best opportunity for at least an elementary education. Towns of fifty householders were required to hire a teacher. But even then, literacy was not universal. As the colonies expanded westward, families were farther from the towns. If they could, parents taught their own children or hired a schoolmaster who traveled from home to home.

An Englishman painted this view of Charleston, South Carolina, from across the Cooper River.

In the larger communities and cities, like Boston, more advanced schooling was provided. Grammar schools taught Latin, which was necessary for college admission. In Massachusetts, the Puritans established the first of several colleges in the colonies.

In the 1650s, a college for American Indians was built at Harvard. Its purpose was to train American Indians to serve as ministers among their own people. The plan, like a similar one at the College of William and Mary, was a failure. But at Harvard, John Eliot, a missionary to the American Indians, published a translation of the Bible in the Algonquin language.

By contrast, the German inhabitants of Pennsylvania showed the least interest in formal education. Suspicious of too much outside influence that might weaken their culture, they felt that their children were educated enough if they could read the German Bible.

On the other hand, the Quakers in Pennsylvania had a very practical approach to education. They wanted to eliminate illiteracy and provide everyone—rich and poor alike—with a trade. This emphasis on practical education led to the establishment of trade schools in Philadelphia. These schools taught navigation, bookkeeping, surveying, and needlework. Study in foreign languages was also popular because of foreign trade and commerce in the city.

At first, education in academic subjects was scanty in the colonies, particularly for girls. The idea of schools supported by tax money was known only in New England. Even these colonial schools were not totally free. Parents of students were expected to supply firewood for the stoves. If they did not, their children could freeze. True public education did not come about until the early nineteenth century.

However, education in a particular trade was widespread. Boys of every class and girls of poorer families had to learn a trade. Eventually, they were all expected to go out to work. Young men and some young women learned a trade by way of *apprenticeship*.

PHILLIS WHEATLEY

Phillis Wheatley (1753-1784) was the first Black woman poet in America. She was enslaved and transported by John Wheatley, a prosperous Boston tailor to be a house servant for his wife. In the Wheatley house, Phillis Wheatley learned to read English and Latin. She became versed in Greek mythology, ancient history, and the contemporary English poets.

Phillis Wheatley wrote her first verses when she was 13 years of age. Her poems were religious in tone, and were often about death. Her first work, "An Elegiac Poem on the Death of that Celebrated Divine, . . . George Whitefield," was published in 1770. In 1773, Phillis Wheatley accompanied her employers to London where she published her first bound volume of verses: *Poems on Various Subjects, Religious and Moral, By Phillis Wheatley, Negro Servant to Mr. John Wheatley of Boston, in New England*. After returning to Boston in 1774, Phillis Wheatley published several poems, including an address to George Washington.

When the Wheatleys died a few years later, Phillis Wheatley became a free woman. She then married John Peters, a free Black, in 1778. After several years of poor health and poverty, Phillis Wheatley died in 1784.

Memoirs and Poems of Phillis Wheatley (1834) and *The Letters of Phillis Wheatley, The Negro Slave-Poet of Boston* (1864) were published after her death.

The system of apprenticeship was an ancient method of passing skills on to the younger generation. In the colonies, the relationship between the teacher and the pupil was regulated by the Statute of Artificers. This regulation dated back to 1563 in Elizabethan England. Although the time of service established by a contract varied, it was usually between three and seven years. During this time, the apprentice was to serve the teacher loyally, protect property, and keep trade secrets. In return for the labor, the apprentice received food, clothing, lodging, education in the trade, and some limited time free for schooling.

The life of an apprentice was often hard. Sometimes, young children of six or seven were bound out by their parents. Other older apprentices voluntarily made a contract so that they would learn a trade. Still others were orphans, who were bound out by the town. Apprentices were not always able to get the trade they wanted. For example, Benjamin Franklin wanted to be a cutler. And had he succeeded in getting himself bound out to a knifemaker instead of a printer, the history of the era might have taken a different turn.

Government in the Colonies

From the beginning, it was assumed that the colonies would be ruled by people with the most power, as in England. A mighty proprietor of a colony, such as Maryland's Lord Baltimore, would rule

THE AMERICAN COLONIES

Colony	Year Founded	Leader	Reasons Settled
New England Colonies: Massachusetts Bay: Plymouth	1620	William Bradford	Religious freedom
Rhode Island Providence	1636	Roger Williams	Religious freedom
Connecticut Hartford	1636	Thomas Hooker	Agriculture
New Hampshire Exeter	1638	John Wheelwright	Expansion
Middle Colonies: New York: (originally New Netherland) New Amsterdam	1626	Peter Minuit— Dutch Duke of York— English	Trade
New Jersey: scattered settlements	1664	Lord Berkeley Sir George Carteret	Trade and Agriculture
Delaware:	1638	Peter Minuit (who left Dutch West India Company and went into Swedish service)	Trade and agriculture
Pennsylvania: Philadelphia	1682	William Penn	Religious freedom agriculture
Southern Colonies: Virginia: Jamestown	1607	John Smith	Trade and agriculture
Maryland: St. Mary's	1633	George Calvert	Religious freedom agriculture
North Carolina: Albermarle Colony	1653	Group of proprietors	Agriculture
South Carolina: Charleston	1663	Group of proprietors	Trade and agriculture
Georgia: Savannah	1732	James Oglethorpe	Agriculture; protection from Spanish Florida; place for debtors of England to serve prison terms

his people, like a feudal baron. A business organization like the Virginia Company would manage its "plant" in the New World as any other employer would.

But these plans did not take into account that, with plenty of free land for the taking, New World settlers could easily become "gentlemen landowners." In Virginia in 1618, the Virginia Company established "head rights." Under this system, persons who paid their own passage to America were given fifty acres of land for themselves and for each member of their group. They would also receive an additional fifty acres for anyone else whose passage they paid for in the future. These enterprising settlers were not easily made to pay rent to proprietors. Nor were they willing to obey the orders of English company officials. These officials were people who shared neither their dangers not their problems. Soon these settlers demanded—and got—a "say" in affairs.

In Virginia in 1619, the Virginia Company called a meeting of *burgesses*, representatives of landholders, from around Jamestown. These burgesses did not gather once and go home, as was intended. Instead, they announced that they would meet each year and act as a lawmaking assembly. Though the laws they passed had to be approved by the Company in England, the House of Burgesses was the earliest representative lawmaking body in America. When Virginia became a **royal colony** in 1624, it still maintained some of the progress it had made toward self-government.

In Massachusetts in 1634, settlers insisted on choosing delegates to a "General Court." Like the House of Burgesses in Virginia, the General Court also became a *legislature* (lawmaking assembly) and helped to govern the colony. The companies and proprietors had to go along with these demands, because they needed newcomers to make their settlements prosper.

Considering the differences in colonial life, it is rather surprising that after a century and a half most of the colonies had similar patterns of government. By 1760, every colony had a legislature of some kind. The legislatures were chosen by those White males who owned land or property. All the colonies but one had a governor appointed by the king or the proprietor. The governor was an important figure, to be sure. He was responsible for enforcing royal regulations and controlling foreign trade, manufacturing, and money. He declared war, conducted negotiations with the American Indians, gave out royal lands, and sat as the colony's chief judge. He selected a council of rich and often well-known colonial leaders to share his great power.

The governor's power was far from total, for it was the legislatures that raised the tax money to run the government. The legisla-

William Byrd II, a Virginia aristocrat, was a member of the House of Burgesses.

royal colony
a colony ruled by the monarchs and ministers of another country

Cecil Calvert, the second Lord Baltimore, posed with his grandson Cecil holding a map of Maryland. Calvert was the first proprietor of Maryland and ruled for 43 years.

tures voted on how this money should be spent, including how much the governor should be paid. They were also responsible for establishing schools, roads, and criminal laws. They were responsible for every kind of social regulation from marriage laws to setting *curfews*, or rules ordering people off the streets after a certain hour.

The members of these legislatures had many arguments among themselves. Planters, merchants, city folk, westerners out on the frontier, and members of different faiths quarreled at times. Many of their disagreements arose from the uneven and rapid growth of the colonies. Pioneers in the newer, western sections wanted good roads, better defenses, more money for what they produced, cheap land, and freedom of choice in religious matters. Lawmakers from older, settled areas were unwilling to share power or raise taxes to meet such needs. They disliked the rough representatives of the raw, new districts. But most colonial legislators were from a class of hard-working businesspeople, professional people, and farmers who felt that they could make their own future by managing their own property. Long after the Americans rebelled against England, a veteran of the Revolution was asked to give his reason for the rebellion. "Young man," he said, "we had always governed ourselves and we meant to go on doing so. That was all."

Questions for Discussion
1. Define *apprenticeship, legislature.*
2. How did the education of boys and girls differ in the colonies?
3. What was the role of the early legislatures in the colonies?
4. How were the people governed in the English colonies of North America?

Chapter 4 Review

Summary Questions for Discussion

1. Give examples to show the place of God in the life and activities of New England's first settlers.
2. Why was a theocracy the natural political system for the Puritans?
3. Describe the pattern in which land was distributed and towns established.
4. What were Roger Williams's beliefs on religion and government? How did he run his colony of Rhode Island?
5. Why did Anne Hutchinson flee Massachusetts?
6. Show how each of the following contributed to the decline of the absolute power of the Puritan leaders: (a) prosperity, (b) persecution of the Quakers, (c) Salem witch hunts, and (d) the expansion of the colonies.
7. What resulted from the actions of Jonathan Edwards and George Whitefield?
8. What difficulties developed with the American Indians over land, trading, and religion?
9. Why was Boston considered a City of Commerce by 1760?
10. Why were the Middle Colonies considered America's first farm heartland?
11. By what means did one acquire land in colonial America?
12. Why were early American communities considered self-sufficient?
13. What do Quakers believe? How did William Penn's beliefs influence the establishment of Pennsylvania?
14. What was the Maryland Act of Toleration of 1649?
15. How did the attitude toward education affect the actions of the following: Puritans, John Eliot, German inhabitants of Pennsylvania, and Quakers.

Word Study

Fill in each blank in the sentences that follow with the term below that is most appropriate.

apprenticeship	piety	factors	royal colony
classes	pioneers	legislature	self-sufficient

1. Colonial America was settled by individuals called _____.
2. Many colonies were able to be economically independent or _____.
3. People who acted as agents for plantation owners were called _____.
4. The lawmaking body of a colony was its _____.
5. Virginia was a _____, which meant that it was ruled by England's monarchs through ministries.
6. A system of _____ was used to train individuals in various crafts.
7. A social hierarchy developed in the colonies, and people in similar positions were grouped into _____.

Using Your Skills

1. By 1750, what were the five largest cities in the English colonies in America? Check your list against the map on page 75. List the major products you would expect to flow into and out of these five cities.
2. Examine the map on page 79. Why were there two triangles of trade? Who profited at each point? How were the economies of the colonies of the North and South interrelated as a result of the triangles of trade?

Unit 1 Review

Summary

The history of America is the story of the movement of various peoples. The American Indians came slowly over a period of centuries. The earliest Europeans came in search of adventure and wealth. Others came to escape religious persecution. The Africans came by force to serve as slaves on the plantations of the New World.

When the Europeans arrived, they found many differing cultures and civilizations. The Incas of Peru and the Aztecs of Mexico were among the highly developed groups. The societies of the North American Indians were most memorable for their skill at making use of Nature's gifts.

The tide of European immigration picked up around the seventeenth century as the lures of God, Glory, and Gold beckoned more fiercely. By 1750, a colonial society had taken shape along the New World's coast. It was influenced by American Indians, Europeans, and Africans.

Summary Questions

1. What might be some of the reasons why the American Indians moved from Asia to the Americas?

2. How did different groups of American Indians adapt to the extremes of the climate and landscape of the Americas?

3. How were the values of the American Indians expressed in their cultures? in their art? in their religion? in their government?

4. What events in Europe between 1100 and 1490 made possible the discovery and exploration of the New World?

5. Why were Europeans able to discover, explore, and lay a firm claim to so much of the Americas, despite the existence of American Indian societies?

6. Compare the motives of Spain, England, France, and Holland in establishing claims to the New World.

7. Why were the English attempts to colonize North America more successful than those of the French?

8. Describe the role of each of the following in the history of the slave trade: Arab traders, European traders, African chiefs, captains of the slave ships, the triangular trade.

9. What effect did the slave trade have on the history of Europe? Africa? America?

10. Explain the difference between a slave and an indentured servant.

11. Describe the role of geography in the establishment of the economic lives of the colonies: (a) New England as a shipping economy, (b) the Middle Colonies as America's first Breadbasket, and (c) the South as a Plantation Economy.

12. How did the class structure that developed in each group of colonies differ? How did these differences affect the way of life in each area?

Developing Your Vocabulary

Choose the correct term to complete the following sentences.

1. European institutions were (brought to, removed from) the areas of colonization.

2. Colonies were established in order to (strengthen, weaken) the mother country.

3. An economic system in which people exchange goods is known as a (barter economy, market economy).

4. A sudden or major change is known as a (revolution, reform).

5. Cortés and Pizarro were examples of Spanish (conquistadors, missionaries).

6. People who oppose accepted religious practices are known as (dissenters, missionaries).

7. People sent to do religious work in a foreign country are known as (missionaries, fanatics).

8. During an inflation, prices (rise, fall) and money becomes worth (more, less).

9. To pillage is to (build up, destroy) an area.

10. A staple crop is one that is (necessary, unnecessary) for the livelihood of a region.

11. Dissatisfied people would have the desire to (install, depose) an ineffective leader.

12. The training period for a trade is known as (an apprenticeship, inflation).

13. Black codes upheld the principle of (equal, unequal) status for Blacks.

14. Extended families (do, do not) include grandparents, aunts, and uncles.

15. Slave trains were called (coffles, maroons).

16. People who explore uncharted areas are known as (pioneers, dissenters).

17. A government run by a few religious leaders is known as a (monarchy, theocracy).

18. The way in which members of a society manage production and distribution of goods is known as its (government, economy).

19. A state ruled by a hereditary, privileged class is called a(n) (confederacy, aristocracy).

20. A person is (subjugated, manumitted) when he or she is set free.

Developing Your Skills

Dramatizing

1. Write an account, from the point of view of a North American Indian, on the initial contact with European explorers.

2. Describe the change in your personality as you are captured by a group of strange peoples, torn away from your relatives and friends, carried to a land across the sea, and then put in a position of lifelong slavery.

Classifying

3. Prepare a table summarizing the events of discovery and exploration. Use the following headings:
Date   Individual   Country of Origin
Area of Exploration   Motive

4. List important events in colonial history that serve as milestones for our present political system.

Special Activities

1. Investigate the life of a person of similar age and background as you in colonial America. Where would you be living? What would you be doing? How similar or different was this person's life to your own?

2. Read an account of a slave that traces his or her capture in Africa through to the experiences in America. Report to the class. (Possible Reference—Alex Haley's *Roots*)

UNIT
2
The Birth of a Nation

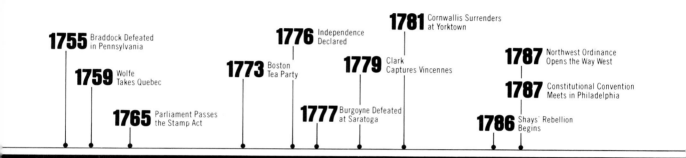

1755 Braddock Defeated in Pennsylvania

1759 Wolfe Takes Quebec

1765 Parliament Passes the Stamp Act

1773 Boston Tea Party

1776 Independence Declared

1777 Burgoyne Defeated at Saratoga

1779 Clark Captures Vincennes

1781 Cornwallis Surrenders at Yorktown

1787 Northwest Ordinance Opens the Way West

1787 Constitutional Convention Meets in Philadelphia

1786 Shays' Rebellion Begins

CHAPTER 5
The Road to Revolution

CHAPTER 6
Waging War

CHAPTER 7
Winning the War for Independence

CHAPTER 8
The Challenge of Independence

CHAPTER 9
Framing a New Government

CHAPTER 10
First Steps of a New Nation

What is the meaning of the American Revolution? Our study of
Unit II begins with this question. Chapter 5 deals with one of the

1789 Washington Inaugurated First President

1803 Jefferson Purchases Louisiana

1814 The British Burn Washington D.C.

events that quickened the coming of the Revolution. This event was a war between Britain and France in which the colonies played a major role. After this war, the colonies began to believe more and more in their ability and right to govern themselves.

Chapters 6 and 7 describe how the United States won its independence from Britain in a war that lasted from 1776 to 1783—the longest war the United States has ever fought. Chapters 8 and 9 present an account of how the nation came to grips with the problem of governing itself in a way that was almost as revolutionary as the Revolution itself. These chapters first examine how the Constitution came to be the nation's fundamental law. Then, they focus on the basic ideas of the Constitution—ideas by which Americans have ruled themselves for nearly two centuries.

Chapter 10 discusses how the infant government withstood the test of internal conflict. The new nation faced serious problems. Among them was the problem of how to find some balance between the use of personal freedoms and the needs of the nation in a time of national danger.

CHAPTER 5
The Road to Revolution

In July of 1776, a political revolution was beginning. Thirteen English colonies had proclaimed their freedom. Thus, they began the modern age of political revolution. In this case, it was a revolt by colonial peoples living in a region controlled by a distant nation.

Revolutions do not happen overnight, even though the actual change in government may seem to take place quickly. Before 1776, there were twelve years during which Great Britain and its colonies walked the road to war. Those years saw rising tempers and heard angry voices. They saw legal and peaceful protests finally turn into armed revolt.

Arguments between the colonists and Great Britain appeared to be about small problems, such as a few pennies in taxes on a pound of tea or on a newspaper. But the roots of conflict ran deeper, involving such questions as: Who shall rule? Who shall choose rulers? How do different groups in a nation share the costs and advantages of government fairly? When may a person or even a society resist the lawful government? How should local governments, like those of cities or states, share power with a central government, which controls a nation or an empire? And finally, when political changes are necessary, what methods work best to bring them about?

Questions like these are not answered all at once or for all time. The leaders who made the American Revolution had to struggle with them long after the last gunshot faded away. So long as Americans continue to ask these basic questions and to pursue the ideals of liberty, human rights, and justice, the ideas behind the American Revolution will remain alive.

READING GUIDE

1. **In a war between France and Britain for control of North America, why did the Americans feel that a French victory would threaten their future?**
2. **Why do people revolt against their government?**
3. **Why does a dispute sometimes result in violence, even though neither side really wants it?**

New York rebels topple a gilded statue of King George III.

1. Britain and France Fight for Mastery of North America

Only fifteen years before the American Revolution began, the people of the thirteen colonies were willingly fighting and dying for King George of England. In 1760, the long battle between France and England to control the eastern half of North America ended. The French were defeated, though the actual peace treaty was not signed until 1763 in Paris. The flag of France had been planted in Quebec at the beginning of the 1600s. At about the same time, the flag of England had been planted in Jamestown. The rivalry between the two nations broke into war in 1689. Until 1763, they fought with each other for control of North America. Their conflict was really one long war fought in several episodes on many continents.

THE EARLY WORLD WAR
1689–1763

European War	American Colonial War
War of the League of Augsburg (1689–1697)	King William's War (1689–1697) English v. French Iroquois v. French
War of the Spanish Succession (1702–1713)	Queen Anne's War (1702–1713) Abenakis v. English colonists French and Abenakis v. English colonists French and Indians v. English
War of the Austrian Succession (1740–1748)	King George's War (1744–1748) English v. French French and Indians v. English
Seven Years' War (1756–1763)	French and Indian War (1754–1763) French and Indians v. English

North American Colonies 1689–1763

Unexplored

Russian after 1763

British

British after 1763 (once French)

British after 1763 (once Spanish)

Spanish

Spanish after 1763 (once French)

An American Indian fighting with a British resident of Deerfield, Connecticut.

America Becomes Part of a World War

Each stage of the struggle between France and England involved colonists and Europeans thousands of miles from Paris and London. Some of the fighters included American Indians and colonists who died in the forests and in the pioneer settlements of a distant continent. But the battles of France and England in North America were part of a world war involving other European powers as well. Like France and England, some of these other powers had colonies in Africa and Asia.

The Deerfield Massacre was but one example of what the long war meant to the English colonists. It took place in 1704 during the second round of fighting known as Queen Anne's War. Some 50 Frenchmen and 200 American Indians swept into and burned the little town of Deerfield in the Connecticut valley. They killed many of the townspeople and carried the rest off as prisoners. The colonists grew angry and more determined than ever to oust their French enemies. They also became more loyal to Britain as they became more dependent on the British army for protection.

Most American Indian tribes—with the exception of the Iroquois—sided with the French. The French colonial system had stressed the establishment of trading posts rather than permanent settlements. Few tribes were forced from their land, and many benefited from the trade. On the other hand, the English, after initial friendly contact, had begun to push the tribes westward. Many American Indians saw the war as a chance to "get back" at the English for 150 years of dishonest and brutal treatment.

The French and Indian War

After an indecisive third round, known as King George's War (1744–1748), France and England headed into a final bloody contest known as the French and Indian War. The fighting began when the French built Fort Duquesne, where Pittsburgh stands today. To do this in 1754, they had to drive off a small force of Virginia **militiamen.** The force was commanded by a lieutenant colonel named George Washington, who was a planter in peacetime.

militiamen
citizens who serve as soldiers in an emergency

Why was a Virginia landowner involved with soldiers in what is now western Pennsylvania? The reason was that Washington and other Virginians believed the future lay in the rich, unsettled lands of the West. Virginia's original charter gave the colony all the territory between the Great Lakes and the Ohio River. So Washington was there to maintain the claim of England's king and Virginia's colonists.

General Braddock and his troops march in stiff formation toward Fort Duquesne.

The French jumped this claim, but not without good reason. The Ohio River, which begins at Fort Duquesne, is a great water route to the Mississippi Valley. If the French controlled it, they might someday link their settlements on the Gulf of St. Lawrence and the Gulf of Mexico. They would then dominate the heart of North America. England's colonies would remain cramped along the coast (see map on p. 102). England decided that the French colonists must be removed.

In 1755, Britain sent an expedition to take Fort Duquesne. The commander, General Edward Braddock, was a veteran fighter trained for European warfare. He was willing to have about 500 colonial troops under Lieutenant Colonel Washington join his thousand red-coated regulars. After all, England and the colonists had a common interest in taking Fort Duquesne. But he was unwilling to listen to uniformed Virginia or Pennsylvania farmers when they told him how to fight in the wilderness.

Braddock marched his men in close ranks to the beat of fife and drum, along the trail that had been cut through the dark tangle of forest. A few miles from the fort, French and Indian soldiers swooped down on his great, slow, snakelike column and began to fire from the cover of trees. Washington and other colonial officers begged Braddock's permission to have the British fight like the American Indians or the experienced backwoodsmen. That is, they wanted to fight in small groups and take full advantage of the protection of trees and rocks. Instead, Braddock insisted that they remain in column, firing away blindly while bullets from unseen enemies cut them down. In the end, Braddock was killed. More than half of his troops became casualties, and the shattered task force retreated.

For the next four years, the war went badly for the English. But in 1759, the tide turned. William Pitt, the energetic English Prime Minister, sent a slender, red-haired general named James Wolfe to take Quebec. It was a big assignment for a man of 32. Quebec was the heart and brain of the long French river "empire." If that city were taken, New France would be destroyed.

Quebec looked unconquerable. It was perched on high cliffs overlooking the St. Lawrence River. But Wolfe had himself rowed along the bank, and his keen eye picked out a tiny, unguarded path winding its way to the top. On the night of September 12, 1759, whaleboats drifted ashore and unloaded troops. These forces struggled up the trail amid whispered commands and curses. By dawn, some 3000 English soldiers were drawn up on level ground outside the city. The able, but surprised, French commander, Marquis de Montcalm, had to fight. The battle was fought European-style: Long rows of infantrymen crashed out volleys through the smoke, then reloaded and advanced in a line. When the smoke cleared, both

The French and American Indians ambush the British. General Braddock, mortally wounded, is falling from his horse.

The death of General James Wolfe,
as painted by Benjamin West.

Generals Wolfe and Montcalm had been killed. However, the British
had won. Quebec surrendered. The next year saw the fall of all
remaining French strongholds in Canada. By the terms of the treaty
signed in 1763, France gave Canada to Great Britain. At the same
time, France gave Louisiana to Spain.

There were many meanings to the end of France's Canadian
adventure. First, the British had become masters of North America,
but at a huge financial loss. Second, American colonists had gained
valuable experience in fighting with and against professional European troops. Finally, the fear of France, which drove the English
colonists closer to Britain for many years, was gone. These three
factors would now combine to create a pattern of trouble for England.

Questions for Discussion

1. Define *militiamen*.
2. How did the French and English colonial systems differ in purpose?
3. How did this difference affect the American Indian's attitudes?
4. What common interest did the Americans and the British have in
   driving the French out of North America?
5. Why did the British want to capture Fort Duquesne and Quebec?

2. The Making of a Revolution

The government in London quickly moved to clean up the
wreckage of the war and pay its huge costs. One of the first steps in this
move was a 1763 ruling to forbid settlement west of a "Proclamation

MERCANTILISM

Mercantilism was an economic system that existed in Europe from the 1500s to the 1700s. Under this system, European powers molded their colonies' economy to fit their own trading needs. In this manner, they hoped to become wealthier and more powerful than their rivals.

In England, Parliament passed the Navigation Acts during the 1600s and 1700s to strengthen its economic control of the thirteen colonies. As a result of these acts, the colonies were forced to trade only with English. This meant that trade was confined to the British empire. All European products being shipped to the colonies had to be routed through England before crossing the Atlantic. Other laws limited colonial manufacturing because the British wanted the colonists to depend largely on them for manufactured goods.

A series of acts passed during the 1600s and 1700s were designed to prevent colonial competition with British industries and to encourage the colonists to export goods needed by Great Britain. The British granted certain trading favors and rewards to such exporters.

The Acts of Trade and Navigation were the heart of the old colonial system (1660-1673), which saw the colonies as part of a great economic, rather than a political unit.

During the early years of mercantilism, there was not much opposition because the laws were not strictly enforced. There was no major governing body to enforce the laws. Those assigned by Parliament to enforce the Acts were either incompetent or lacked means of forcing the colonists to obey. Others were corrupt. Evasion of the laws was rampant, and smuggling was a common profession in the colonies. When England finally decided to tighten administration of the laws, the colonists began their resistance.

Many historians feel that the American Revolution was the result of one capitalistic economy trying to impose its interest on another.

Line" running down the Allegheny Mountains (map, page 5). The proclamation would hold back pioneers until an American Indian policy could be worked out. This seemed especially necessary after an Ottawa chief named Pontiac united many tribes in a 1763 rebellion. It took a year to subdue the rebellion. Even though a policy with the American Indians would have made peaceful settlement in the new areas more likely, the measure angered the colonists.

Next, London tightened up the machinery for collecting **duties**. However, worst of all was an act proposed in 1765 by Britain's Prime Minister, George Grenville, for raising **revenue**. This act required that newspapers, legal documents, licenses, and business forms could only be printed on paper with special stamps. In Grenville's eyes, this act, called the Stamp Act, was only fair. For the colonies would be paying for their own past and future defense.

But the Stamp Act looked vastly different across 3000 miles of ocean. The colonists recognized London's right to regulate boundary affairs by proclamation lines. In addition, they also coped with the

duties
import taxes

revenue
government income

Sugar Act of 1764, which regulated foreign trade by placing duties on molasses. But the Stamp Act was a direct tax. As Virginians, Pennsylvanians, and New Yorkers saw it, such a tax could be levied only by their assemblies, to which they themselves sent elected delegates, not by British Parliament. As a simple slogan explained, "No taxation without representation." Colonial legislatures protested the new law bitterly. They claimed, as loyal English people, the rights for which the English had fought in an earlier era.

Protest did not stop there. The year 1765 saw the beginning of new forms of colonial resistance. There was cooperation among the colonies as delegates met in a Stamp Act Congress, which passed resolutions of protest. There was economic pressure. Hundreds of merchants agreed to **boycott** British goods until the hated law was rejected. There was **propaganda**. Mobs broke into warehouses and burned the stamps stored there. Faced by this increasing protest, the British Parliament promptly **repealed** the Stamp Act.

The Boston Massacre

Parliament ended the Stamp Act because it could not be enforced. But some members of Parliament made sure that the colonists understood that London was still boss. A Declaratory Act was passed in 1766, stating that Parliament had a right to make laws for the whole empire, "in all cases whatsoever." The next year, Britain's chief financial minister, Charles Townshend, placed new taxes on imported paint, glass, paper, and tea in a series of laws known as the Townshend Acts.

Once more, boycott agreements, protest meetings, and newspaper editorials cried out in rage against this "tyranny." Once more, too, government officials—and pro-British "loyal" colonists who believed that even unpopular laws ought to be obeyed—were threatened with mob action. In Boston, the threats seemed disturbing enough for Britain to bring in troops. The British argued that the life of no one—rich or poor, pro-Yankee or pro-British—was safe without law and order. But Bostonians felt that the red-coated soldiers were the enemy, no matter what they did or did not do.

This feeling led to a number of street brawls between the troops and Bostonian sailors and workers. Usually, after some spitting, shoving, name-calling, and a few arrests, these fights broke up. But on the night of March 5, 1770, a squad of British soldiers was faced with a crowd that was hooting and throwing snowballs and rocks. Trying to cool things down a British captain said something that sounded like "Fire!" The furious "lobsterbacks" blasted shots directly into the crowd, killing five Boston men.

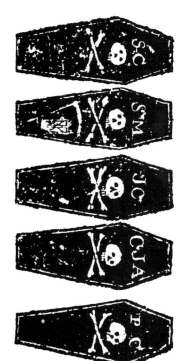

Colonists reacted sharply to the Stamp Act. A 1765 magazine carried the propaganda above.

This engraving by Paul Revere shows the British firing upon unarmed colonists in the "Boston Massacre."

No matter who had started the fight, this was a dreadful moment. Angry talk had been replaced by bullets. Men had died. The colonists now had **martyrs** and could claim that "unarm'd, defenseless and innocent citizens" had been slaughtered in what they called the "Boston Massacre."

martyrs
those who sacrifice their lives for the sake of a principle in which they strongly believe

Makers of a Revolution

Many colonists who had been lukewarm in their support of the *Patriot*—anti-British—side were now shocked and joined the protestors. This process did not happen accidentally. Rather, it was encouraged by careful planning and hard work.

To arouse people to armed action with an emotional appeal takes organization and skill. In the thirteen colonies, there were some very able **radicals**. For example, Patrick Henry, who was discussed in Chapter 4, had a gift for great phrases. In Virginia's assembly, he made a speech against the Stamp Act of 1765, comparing George III to past tyrants. When some other member gasped "Treason!" Henry snapped, "If this be treason, make the most of it!" Ten years later, when urging the Virginians to raise a militia and prepare to fight Britain if need be, he said, "Give me liberty—or give me death!" Long after they had forgotten exactly what his speech was about, Patrick Henry's battle cries could still make people's blood boil.

radicals
those who believe in and work for revolutionary changes

109

Radicals like Patrick Henry spoke out against British colonial rule and then demanded revolution.

THE ROAD TO REVOLUTION

Writs of Assistance, 1760
Enabled the British to search American colonial homes without stating so in advance.

Revenue Act (Sugar Act), 1764
Enabled the British to increase duties on colonial goods; banned certain colonial imports.

Currency Act, 1764
Ended issues of currency in the American colonies.

Quartering Act, 1765
Colonists were required to house British troops in their homes, inns, and other unoccupied dwellings.

Stamp Act, 1765
British placed taxes on newspapers, almanacs, pamphlets, legal documents, licenses, and other items made of paper.

Declaratory Act, 1766
Gave Parliament authority to make laws binding the American colonists.

Townshend Acts, 1767
Taxes were placed on glass, lead, paper, tea. The acts also provided for efficient collection of these taxes.

Protection for Customs Officials, 1768
Armed escorts assigned to tax collectors.

Tea Act, 1773
Taxes on British teas going to America were removed. Americans still had to pay import taxes.

Coercive Acts (Intolerable Acts), 1774
Ships were prohibited from loading and unloading in Boston's harbor.

Boston's Samuel Adams was no spellbinder with words. But, he was a fine organizer, Adams was a guiding spirit of the Boston chapter of the Sons of Liberty. The Sons of Liberty was a group of Patriots in various colonies who organized parades and rallies to condemn the Stamp Act, the Townshend taxes, and other British "villainies." Adams also founded a political discussion club in Boston—where most of the discussion was anti-British. He founded a newspaper to tell readers how wicked it was for the House of Commons "at 3000 miles distance" to rule American colonists who would soon outnumber Britain's population. Adams was also a founder of the Massachusetts Committee of Correspondence. Each colony's committee exchanged information and plans with committees in the other colonies. The Committees of Correspondence drew the colonies together and kept the pot of resistance boiling.

Another radical, Thomas Paine, did not arrive in America until 1774, on the eve of war. He had been unable to earn a living in England as a government worker, corset maker, grocer, or teacher. But in America, he was the man to put the argument for independence in the hard-hitting language of *Common Sense.*

Debate in England

Radicals like Sam Adams and Patrick Henry were always opposed in the colonies by **moderates** who believed that peace could be worked out under British rule. This rule had lasted for more than a century and a half. Moderates believed that there was no need for a **confrontation** involving force between both parties. Only the radicals who called themselves Patriots desired that. The colonies had thrived under Britain's flag. True, they were not represented in Parliament. But neither were most English people, since only wealthy property owners could vote. Better to let nonviolent boycotts and appeals to the king's generosity do their work. Wild talk about rights and resistance only stirred up trouble.

Some members of England's Parliament took the same moderate view. A number of them spoke for the British merchants who were badly hurt by the loss of their colonial buyers of cloth, hardware, shoes, and other manufactured goods. Some friends of the American colonists agreed with their American "cousins" in places like Philadephia that governments ought to have very little power over people's lives and property.

In 1775, one other line of pro-American argument was put forth in a Parliamentary speech by Edmund Burke, a famous British writer of the day. He called for **conciliation** with the colonists. The colonists had prospered for many years without much attention from Parlia-

moderates
those who believe in and work for slow, orderly change

confrontation
head-on meeting

conciliation
an effort to bring about good will

Some people in England saw the struggle with the colonies as harmful to the Empire. A cartoon that appeared early in 1776 shows the government ministers killing the American goose that laid the Empire's golden eggs.

111

ment, he said. Their prosperity enabled them to enrich the whole empire with their trade. They took care of their local affairs ably, including taxation. "Obedience is what makes government," said Burke, and the colonists obeyed their assemblies. If the royal ministers were foolish enough to force the colonists to obey London, they would only breed hatred. The British would be killing the American goose that laid golden eggs.

Calls for conciliation did not win widespread favor. The king and the men he chose for top jobs believed that they had either unlimited power over the colonies or none at all. This "either-or" attitude resulted in a **polarization** of opinion. "Blows must decide," said George III.

polarization
movement away from moderate positions to two conflicting extreme positions

In 1770, the British repealed the Townshend Acts. However, they kept the tax on tea to prove that they still had the right of taxation. Then, in 1773, they proposed that only the British East India Company be allowed to sell tea in America. Such an act would ruin American importers. As Patriot pamphlets pointed out, this was proof of Parliament's bad intentions. The Patriots felt that sterner measures should be taken against the British. New boycott agreements were signed. The spirit of violence was at work as well.

At New York and Philadelphia, the Patriots forced ships loaded with the hated tea to turn back. But the ships were allowed by order of the royal governor to tie up at Boston wharves. The Sons of Liberty had an answer to that. On the night of December 16, 1773, a group of men disguised as American Indians with tomahawks marched boldly aboard the three tea ships. They hauled out the chests of tea, smashed them open, and poured the contents into the harbor. This "Boston Tea Party" was in open defiance of the laws of Parliament and the king.

London recognized the challenge. This was not peaceful dissent but lawless destruction of property. So Parliament passed a set of laws designed to punish Massachusetts. The colonists often referred to them as the "Intolerable Acts." Massachusetts was deprived of self-government. And, after June 1, 1774, the port of Boston was to be closed to all ships until the tea was paid for. The choice became one of submission or starvation.

The other colonies suddenly found themselves united in Boston's defense. If one colonial "child" could be punished, so could all the "children." The message seemed to be "Join or Die," as Ben Franklin's slogan put it. Shipments of food were sent into Boston by land. In addition, a call went out to delegates from all the colonies for a meeting in Philadelphia in September to discuss ways of resistance.

Two years after the Boston Massacre, colonial leaders were still using the event to stir up anti-British feelings. Here, Americans are asked to remember the horrible massacre and the five men who were murdered.

AMERICANS!
BEAR IN REMEMBRANCE
The HORRID MASSACRE!
Perpetrated in King-ſtreet, Boston,
New-England,
On the Evening of March the Fifth, 1770.
When FIVE of your fellow countrymen,
Gray, Maverick, Caldwell, Attucks,
and Carr,
Lay wallowing in their Gore!
Being baſely, and moſt inhumanly
MURDERED!

Paul Revere engraved this version of Ben Franklin's famous cartoon which first appeared in the Pennsylvania Gazette *in 1754.*

JOIN OR DIE

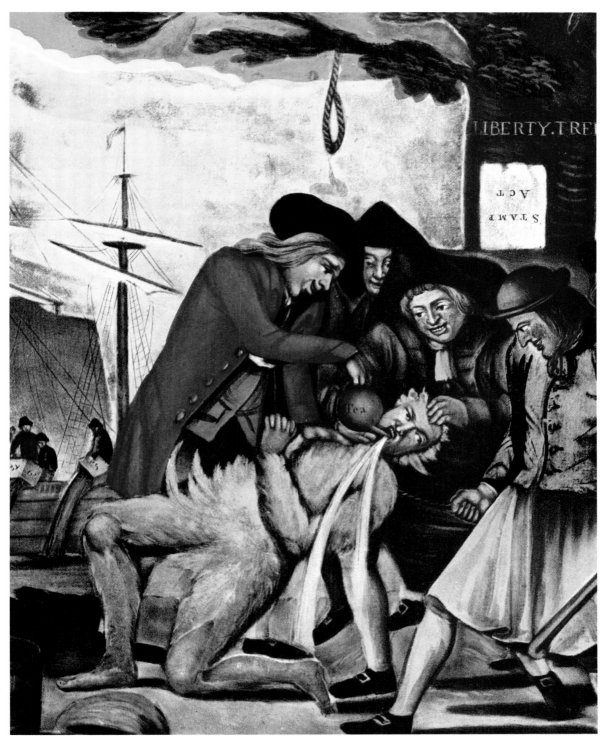

A British tax collector who has been tarred and feathered is given a dose of boiling tea by followers of Samuel Adams.

This First Continental Congress moved the colonies closer to war. The delegates adopted a new boycott agreement, urged the colonies to raise militia to protect themselves, and insisted that they would never submit to what they called the "unlawful" taxes of Parliament. Virginia's Patrick Henry expressed the delegates' feelings: "I am not a Virginian," he said, "but an American." The Congress was not yet a government, but an American nation was slowly emerging.

Questions for Discussion
1. Define *duties, revenue, boycott, propaganda, radical, moderate, confrontation.*
2. How did the colonists use boycott and propaganda to get the Parliament to repeal unwanted acts?
3. Explain why the moderates lost out to the radicals in the disputes between England and the colonies.
4. What is meant by "no taxation without representation"?

3. The Shot Heard Round the World

Resistance in America and stiff-necked policies in England had turned a movement for self-government within the British Empire into a drive toward separation. As late as the spring of 1775, few colonies were talking of independence. But each week brought events that left little room for compromise. People were becoming captives of their own actions.

At the time, General Thomas Gage was commanding British troops in Boston. He was deeply concerned about the little groups of colonial militia who were drilling in nearby towns so that they could be ready for action at a minute's notice. In April, he planned an unpleasant surprise for these "minutemen." He would march a body of troops into Concord, seventeen miles away. The "provincials" were supposed to have some arms stored there. In a quick, surprise move, he would seize these arms. It would not be war. Instead, it would be like a police raid to pick up illegal guns, catching the colonists off balance and warning them that the British would allow no more rebellious acts.

Gage did not count on the excellent ability of the Bostonians to get wind of his plans. When his raiding party gathered in the chilly predawn darkness of April 19, Paul Revere and William Dawes had already slipped out of town and were riding the roads to Concord and nearby Lexington to warn the minutemen.

When the advance guard of the 700-man task force of redcoats got to Lexington on the way to Concord, they found about 40 American minutemen lined up. No one is quite sure what happened next. The American captain, John Parker, was a veteran soldier who did not want to fight against such odds. The British commander, Major John

In this engraving by militiaman Amos Doolittle, the redcoats open fire on retreating minutemen at Lexington.

Pitcairn, was under orders to avoid a fight if possible. As the British line moved forward and the nervous but determined minutemen refused to fall back, someone fired a shot. The redcoats were edgy, as well. A volley crashed out from their ranks and probably from the Americans at the same moment. When the smoke had cleared, the minutemen were falling back—eight of them lying dead on the ground.

This was the real thing. Death, now an umpire in the dispute between parent country and colonies, had a profitable April day. The British then pushed on to Concord. But Dr. Samuel Prescott had reached the town to warn them of the redcoats' approach. Men from the surrounding towns hurried to Concord, and by the time the British arrived, the Americans were three to four hundred strong. The British destroyed some supplies in the town. But a skirmish at North Bridge, in which two Americans and three British died, convinced them that it was time to return to Boston.

Word of the engagements had spread fast. Now companies of militia were pouring in from every village within a few hours' march. The orderly British retreat turned into a disaster when these "country bumpkins" from Massachusetts farms, firing from behind houses, stone walls, and haystacks, attacked the seasoned troops. In a "furnass of musquetry," the British almost fled back to base. Seventy-three men were killed, and nearly three times as many wounded.

The importance of that day was enormous. The word spread that again the British had shot down the Americans, but this time the Americans shot back. These battles reassured Americans that they could handle the British.

Soon companies from all over New England poured into the area around Boston. In May, one American outfit even captured the great northern fort at Ticonderoga on Lake Champlain from the small, surprised British garrison. Massachusetts began to feed, equip, and drill the country boys who were coming into camp. They were now becoming an army instead of a collection of part-time fighters.

By the time the Second Continental Congress met in May, war was the primary issue. Moderates still urged, and eventually got, a final petition to the king. But the members still went about planning for a Continental Army to support New England's forces. The job was made harder because Congress had no idea of how much authority it had. The delegates were representatives of communities that were rapidly becoming excolonies, but were not yet states as you know them today. One certain fact existed: The door to peace was nearly closed.

The Battle of Bunker Hill Brings War Closer

War became inevitable on June 17, 1775, at the Battle of Bunker Hill. This was a high point near Charlestown, a village just across the bay from Boston. The Americans had moved out the night before to fortify it. If they could get cannon up its slopes, they could easily bombard the British ships and soldiers below. But the British knew this and could not allow it. So, that morning, more that 2000 British troops were rowed across the bay and lined up in neat scarlet ranks for a charge against the little fortification that the Americans had built. This happened not on Bunker Hill but on Breed's Hill, next to it. While this took place, the British fleet bombarded Charlestown and destroyed it.

In midafternoon, the British lines advanced up the slope, drums thundering, bayonets gleaming in the sun. They came within a few yards of the breastworks behind which stood the Americans. The Americans were dressed in everyday clothes and carried weapons of every kind and size. These weapons included old captured French muskets, hunting guns, pistols, even weapons made in local black-

Sympathy for the revolution was aroused by leaflets such as the above.

116

PAUL REVERE

Little Known Facts about Paul Revere's Ride

Stories, poems, and cartoons have probably told you about Paul Revere galloping through the night to warn the minutemen of Lexington and Concord that the British were coming. Basically, that is what happened—but some of the sidelights and highlights make it an even better story.

First of all, Paul's ride was only one night's work in a long, busy, and useful lifetime. When the Revolution started, he was the best-known maker of fine silver items—teapots, spoons, cups, jewelry—in Boston. Some of his works are museum pieces. During the war, Paul Revere served as a Colonel of Artillery. After the war was over, he went into the business of making copper. He became the founder of what is now one of the largest copper companies in the United States—Revere Copperware.

Secondly, he had already ridden out on April 16—two days before the famous ride—to warn the Patriots at Concord that the British were planning a raid, and that they had better hide their guns and powder. The trip on the 18th was simply to alert them that the British were, now, actually on the way. And the famous lanterns hung in a Boston church steeple were not signals *to* Paul Revere, as Longfellow's poem says. *He* put them there to let the Patriots know that the British were crossing the Charles River in boats. The lanterns would tell the story if he could not get through.

However, he *did not* get all the way through, but did reach Lexington on a borrowed horse. And he did alert the minutemen along the way, just as the poem says. But there, Revere stopped for a short time. He was then joined by another messenger, William Dawes, and a young doctor, Samuel

Prescott, who had been out late courting. The three of them started out for Concord after midnight. A British patrol stopped them. Dawes and Prescott got away. Revere was captured and detained for a couple of hours, and then let go. He continued his journey, but this time on foot because the British had "drafted" his horse.

There is a final part of the story that is only a legend, but is worth telling. Revere started his trip by boat—going from Boston, across the Charles River's wide mouth, to what was then called Charlestown. He had with him two friends who helped him row across. But there was a British ship in the river. Noting the British ship, Revere and his friends realized they needed something to wrap around the oars to muffle the squeaking in the *oarlocks*—the little stirrups that held the oars in place. Otherwise, they could not slip silently by the ship. So they returned to the shore. The story goes that one of Revere's friends ran to his sweetheart's window, whistled her awake, and whispered a few words. Down fluttered a flannel petticoat "still warm," which did the job of wrapping the oars.

Above: Before the Battle of Bunker Hill in May, 1775, Ethan Allen and his men seized Fort Ticonderoga on Lake Champlain.

smiths' shops. At a word of command, a crashing fire exploded from the muzzles. The British were mowed down by the hundreds. Some companies were cut to eight or nine men. The British straggled down the hill to lick their wounds. Gamely, they tried again. But another assault was shattered. Finally, a third attack was successful. Out of ammunition, the Yankees retreated and lost the battle. Yet, once again, the provincials had shown themselves able to stand up to England's best-trained and bravest soldiers. One of the Americans on the hill was Salem Poor, a Black man whose bravery was commended by his officers. In fact, some 5000 Black Americans served in the first American army during the Revolutionary War.

Bunker Hill was a full-fledged battle between organized forces, including ships of war. A town had been leveled. There was no longer any doubt on either side that a long, costly struggle was ahead. In preparation, Congress had given command of the American army to the respected, experienced Virginia soldier, George Washington.

Questions for Discussion

1. Define *minutemen.*
2. Why are the actions at Lexington and Concord considered "The Shot Heard Round the World"?
3. How did the Second Continental Congress prepare for war?
4. What factors made war inevitable?

Chapter 5 Review

Summary Questions for Discussion

1. What prompted the war between the English and French from 1689—1763?
2. What was the effect of the Deerfield Massacre on the English colonists?
3. Why did most American Indian tribes side with the French during the fighting?
4. What resulted from the construction of Fort Duquesne by the French?
5. What was the effect of General Edward Braddock's leadership?
6. State three results of the ending of the French Canadian empire.
7. What was the purpose of the Proclamation Line?
8. What was the purpose of the Stamp Act of 1765? What were the colonists' reactions?
9. Why is the "Boston Massacre" a significant event on the road to revolution?
10. What did each of the following men contribute to the revolutionary cause: Patrick Henry, Samuel Adams, Thomas Paine?
11. Explain the differences in the stands taken by the radicals and moderates in the colonies.
12. Who was Edmund Burke? Why did he call for conciliation with the colonists?
13. What caused the "Boston Tea Party"? How did Parliament react?
14. How did the other colonies react to the "Intolerable Acts"? How did the First Continental Congress react?
15. What was the purpose of General Thomas Gage's planned surprise on the minutemen? What was the significance in American history of the battles of Lexington and Concord?

Word Study

Fill in each blank in the sentences that follow with the term below that is most appropriate.

militiamen	patriots	repealed	radicals	duties
propaganda	conciliation	confrontation	revenue	boycott

1. Great Britain, in an attempt to increase _____, began to impose more import taxes or _____ on the colonists.
2. The angry colonists employed various means to get these taxes removed or _____.
3. Two methods used were _____ and _____.
4. The colonists' defiant actions produced a _____ with Great Britain.
5. More extreme colonists were called _____.
6. The colonists had taken up arms in previous times as _____ or citizens serving as soldiers in an emergency.
7. Although the British considered their actions rebellious, the colonists considered themselves _____.

Using Your Skills

1. Choose three visuals in this chapter, and explain how they could be used as propaganda by the Patriots.
2. How do the pictures show that British military techniques and strategies were not suitable for fighting in the colonies?
3. Explain how the picture on page 111 illustrates Edmund Burke's position in 1775.
4. From the map on page 102, tell why the territory lost by France in 1763 was considered by the American colonists to be of great importance to their future.
5. Construct a time line of important events from 1763–1775.

CHAPTER 6
Waging War

As commander of the Revolutionary forces, George Washington had one quality needed for a successful revolution—exceptional leadership. Washington was not superhuman. In peacetime, he loved hunts and dancing parties as much as any other Virginia gentleman. In war, he was no genius. He made many battlefield mistakes. He did not win so much respect from his generals that they always obeyed him. And, he did not always keep his temper with officers who fumbled in their tasks. Also, he quarreled with Congress when it refused his requests.

Yet, Washington had two qualities that blazed like lighthouses of hope in the war's darkest days. He was unselfish and steady. Everyone knew that he would never use his position to seek power, praise, wealth, or other prizes that tempt even the best of people. When the British seemed unbeatable, Washington never thought of surrendering. He was in the war to win independence for his country.

In any society, one job of a leader is to show those qualities that the society most admires. In self-governing, hardworking, eighteenth-century America, this ideal figure was a man of property, common sense, and dedication to public service. Washington was neither sage nor saint. But he was courageous and level-headed. Because the colonies knew this, they were willing to follow him.

Fortunately, the colonies had many gifted leaders. In the Continental Congress sat two future Presidents, John Adams and Thomas Jefferson. The members also included Benjamin Franklin and dozens of others who would one day be governors, senators, judges, and makers of constitutions. America had one basic ingredient for success in a revolution—leadership.

READING GUIDE

1. **How did the pamphleteers prepare the people for the idea of independence?**
2. **How did the Declaration of Independence change the nature of the war?**
3. **In war, what are some of the advantages and disadvantages of being on the defensive? Of being on the offensive?**

George Washington surveys the battlefield at Trenton, New Jersey.

I. The Pamphlet War

Abigail Adams actively encouraged pamphleteering against the British.

Mercy Otis Warren ridiculed the British in her writing. She was an influential propagandist of the Revolutionary War.

Before the war with bullets began, the war of words was waged. Nearly 200 printing presses existed in the colonies. Between 1763 and 1783, two thousand political pamphlets came off the presses. These were small, inexpensive books that were written to stir up, inspire, and influence the public. In the early days, the pamphleteers focused on local issues and controversies. But by 1765, they were dealing with broader issues. They often touched on problems that concerned all the colonies and launched a flurry of opposing views.

Publication of a series of pamphlets would bring a writer into the public eye. Those who wrote often and wrote well gained fame and recognition for their work. For example, Samuel Adams was known for his radical works. And James Otis of Massachusetts earned a reputation as an "eagle-eyed politician." He was one of the earliest writers to foresee what course the colonies might take. In 1765 he wrote, "Revolutions have been. They may be again." Seeds of the revolution and the Constitution could be found in his writing. Otis's career as a political writer, however, ended abruptly. He was beaten by a group of Tories and his health was badly weakened.

Meanwhile, his sister, Mercy Otis Warren, took up the cause. She wrote plays, poems, and broadsides ridiculing British authorities. When the British prevented her plays from being performed, she had her works distributed in pamphlet form. Characters like Brigadier Hateall and Sparrow Spendall crowded the pages with caricatures of British faults. She also wrote the *History of the Rise, Progress and Termination of the Revolution* (1805).

Mercy Otis Warren was encouraged to write by her friends Abigail and John Adams. They saw the value of Warren's witty writing to the colonial cause. John Adams himself wrote many pamphlets that kept the questions of law and liberty before the people.

One of the most moderate and influential writers was John Dickinson, whose career spanned forty years. His *Letters from a Farmer in Pennsylvania* were a response to the Townshend Acts. He explained that it was not enough for a government to be fair and reasonable. Instead, a government must be limited so that it could never be anything but that.

As the conflict with Britain heightened, the pamphleteers took firmer stands on their positions. Some more traditional writers claimed that there was a natural aristocracy that was meant to rule. People were born to obey. More moderate Tories, such as Samuel Seabury and Joseph Galloway, argued for more reasonable ideas. Seabury offered a reform program. Galloway developed a plan for a federal union of the colonies and Britain.

But the time was not ripe for moderate views by either side. By 1775, pamphlets urging independence were gaining followers. Yet,

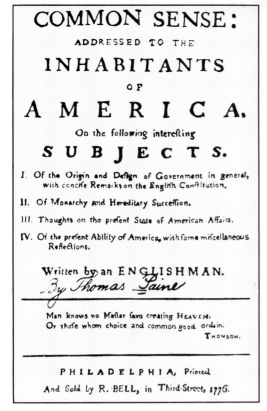

COMMON SENSE:

ADDRESSED TO THE

INHABITANTS

OF

AMERICA,

On the following interesting

SUBJECTS.

I. Of the Origin and Design of Government in general,
with concise Remarks on the English Constitution.

II. Of Monarchy and Hereditary Succession.

III. Thoughts on the present State of American Affairs.

IV. Of the present Ability of America, with some miscellaneous
Reflections.

Written by an ENGLISHMAN.

By Thomas Paine

Man knows no Master save creating HEAVEN,
Or those whom choice and common good ordain.
THONSON.

PHILADELPHIA, Printed
And Sold by R. BELL, in Third-Street, 1776.

Thomas Paine, author of Common Sense, advocated the immediate declaration of independence from Britain on both practical and ideological grounds.

even after Lexington and Concord, many people knew only whom they were fighting against but not what they were fighting for.

Common Sense

To have the strength to endure the suffering of war, the people needed a cause greater than the quarrels over a tax on tea or stamps. The early enthusiasm for the revolution might have died out as wounds, hunger, and death set in. By January 1776, some people were urging Congress to give the Patriots a cause worth dying for. They wanted to take the giant step of declaring the colonies independent.

So said Thomas Paine in the pamphlet *Common Sense*. Paine was not a long-time colonist. He was an Englishman who had come to America in 1774. He settled in Philadelphia where he contributed to the *Pennsylvania Magazine*. On January 9, 1776, he published his anonymous pamphlet, *Common Sense*, in support of independence.

Paine struck the right note at the right time. He wrote in a manner that was easily understood by all. *Common Sense* included straightforward arguments against the most common objections to independence. Paine wrote that the Americans "owed nothing to the king of England or to any king." Of all types of government, monarchy was the worst. He openly attacked George III. Paine said that while some king may deserve honor, this does not guarantee that all the descendants of that person should also rule. Paine wrote that an honest man was worth more than all the "crowned ruffians of Europe."

To those who believed that America benefited by its connection with Great Britain, Paine offered this argument: "I answer roundly, that America would have flourished as much, and probably more, had no European power taken notice of her. The commerce by which she hath enriched herself are the necessaries of life, and will always have a market while eating is the custom in Europe." Nor was Great Britain's protection of any value. Great Britain "did not protect us from our enemies on our account, but from her enemies on her account."

Paine challenged those who favored *reconciliation*—the settling of differences—with Great Britain to come up with a single advantage. He claimed it was folly to have to send a petition 4828 kilometers (3000 miles) away and wait months for a response. He argued that it was ridiculous for an island the size of Britain to rule a continent as vast and far away as America.

Effects of *Common Sense*

In its first three months, *Common Sense* sold 120,000 copies. Since there were about 3.5 million White inhabitants, including children and people who could not read, this means that up to one literate American in every three owned the pamphlet. Today that is comparable to the impact of a television program reaching 50 million sets. The pamphlet attained total sales of 500,000. Based on the widespread sales, Congress concluded that public opinion favored independence. Throughout the colonies, newspapers reviewed the pamphlet and printed editorials and letters about it. The idea of independence went from just being thought about to being openly discussed.

By the spring of 1776, the movement toward independence gathered strength. Congress began to react accordingly. In February, it authorized **privateers**. Congress also called for an **embargo** on exports to Britain and the British West Indies. In March, an **envoy**, Silas Deane, was sent to France to petition for aid. Deane was to tell the French that independence was likely. In April, American ports were opened to trade with all countries except Britain.

At the same time, other changes were taking place. In each of the colonies, people favoring independence were gaining control of the legislatures. In Massachusetts, the town meetings voted in favor of independence. Shortly thereafter, South Carolina and North Carolina gave their delegates to the Continental Congress permission to favor independence. In May, Congress advised the states to form independent state governments. In June, Richard Henry Lee, a delegate from Virginia, introduced a resolution calling for independence. A commit-

privateers
an armed private ship authorized to cruise against the commerce or warships of an enemy

embargo
a legal stoppage on trade by one country toward another

envoy
a person chosen to represent one government in its dealings with another

124

tee was chosen to write a "declaration" explaining the call for independence. The resolution was adopted on July 2. The declaration was approved on July 4, 1776, and signed by the members in August.

Questions for Discussion
1. Define *reconciliation*, *privateers*, *embargo*, and *envoy*.
2. What role did the pamphleteers play prior to the Revolutionary War? Who might be their counterparts today?
3. Why can it be said that Thomas Paine, in *Common Sense*, "struck the right note at the right time"?

Red-headed, thirty-three year old Thomas Jefferson, a Virginia lawyer, planter, and gifted thinker, actually wrote the Declaration of Independence. He was chosen for the job by his fellow committee members, because they knew he was a first-rate writer. They wanted the Declaration to appeal to people's emotions as well as to present a sound legal argument. And Jefferson did both brilliantly.

Jefferson wrote the Declaration of Independence to explain to the colonists and to the world why the colonies were separating themselves from Britain. In some ways, the fate of the new country was in his hands. There were still many Americans who were not committed

2. The Declaration of Independence

DECLARATION OF INDEPENDENCE

When in the Course of human events, it becomes necessary for one people to dissolve the political bands which have connected them with another, and to assume among the Powers of the earth, the separate and equal station to which the Laws of Nature and of Nature's God entitle them, a decent respect to the opinions of mankind requires that they should declare the causes which impel them to the separation.

We hold these truths to be self-evident, that all men are created equal, that they are endowed by their Creator with certain unalienable Rights, that among these are Life, Liberty and the pursuit of Happiness. That to secure these rights, Governments are instituted among Men, deriving their just powers from the consent of the governed, That whenever any Form of Government becomes destructive of these ends, it is the Right of the People to alter or to abolish it, and to institute new Government, laying its foundation on such principles and organizing its powers in such form, as to them shall seem most likely to effect their Safety and Happiness. Prudence, indeed, will dictate that Governments long established should not be changed for light and transient causes; and accordingly all experience hath shown, that mankind are more disposed to suffer, while evils are sufferable, than to right themselves by abolishing the forms to which they are accustomed. But when a long train of abuses and usurpations, pursuing invariably the same Object evinces a design to reduce them under absolute Despotism, it is their right, it is their duty, to throw off such Government, and to provide new

Guards for their future security. —Such has been the patient sufferance of these Colonies; and such is now the necessity which constrains them to alter their former Systems of Government. The history of the present King of Great Britain is a history of repeated injuries and usurpations, all having in direct object the establishment of an absolute Tyranny over these States. To prove this, let Facts be submitted to a candid world.

He has refused his Assent to Laws, the most wholesome and necessary for the public good.

He has forbidden his Governors to pass Laws of immediate and pressing importance, unless suspended in their operation till his Assent should be obtained; and when so suspended, he has utterly neglected to attend to them.

He has refused to pass other Laws for the accommodation of large districts of people, unless those people would relinquish the right of Representation in the Legislature, a right inestimable to them and formidable to tyrants only.

He has called together legislative bodies at places unusual, uncomfortable, and distant from the depository of their Public Records, for the sole purpose of fatiguing them into compliance with his measures.

He has dissolved Representative Houses repeatedly, for opposing with manly firmness his invasions on the rights of the people.

He has refused for a long time, after such dissolutions, to cause others to be elected; whereby the Legislative Powers, incapable of Annihilation, have returned to the People at large for their exercise; the State remaining in the mean time exposed to all the dangers of invasion from without and convulsions within.

He has endeavoured to prevent the population of these States; for that purpose obstructing the Laws of Naturalization of Foreigners; refusing to pass others to encourage their migration hither, and raising the conditions of new Appropriations of Lands.

He has obstructed the Administration of Justice, by refusing his Assent to Laws for establishing Judiciary Powers.

He has made Judges dependent on his Will alone, for the tenure of their offices, and the amount and payment of their salaries.

He has erected a multitude of New Offices, and sent hither swarms of Officers to harass our People, and eat out their substance.

He has kept among us, in times of peace, Standing Armies without the Consent of our legislature.

He has affected to render the Military independent of and superior to the Civil Power.

He has combined with others to subject us to a jurisdiction foreign to our constitution, and unacknowledged by our laws; giving his Assent to their acts of pretended legislation:

For quartering large bodies of armed troops among us:

For protecting them, by a mock Trial, from Punishment for any Murders which they should commit on the Inhabitants of these States:

For cutting off our Trade with all parts of the world:

For imposing taxes on us without our Consent:

For depriving us in many cases, of the benefits of Trial by Jury:

For transporting us beyond Seas to be tried for pretended offences:

For abolishing the free System of English Laws in a neighbouring Province, establishing therein an Arbitrary government, and enlarging its Boundaries so as to render it at once an example and fit instrument for introducing the same absolute rule into these Colonies:

For taking away our Charters, abolishing our most valuable Laws, and altering fundamentally the Forms of our Governments:

For suspending our own Legislature, and declaring themselves invested with Power to legislate for us in all cases whatsoever.

He has abdicated Government here, by declaring us out of his Protection and waging War against us.

He has plundered our seas, ravaged our Coasts, burnt our towns, and destroyed the lives of our people.

He is at this time transporting large armies of foreign mercenaries to compleat the works of death, desolation and tyranny, already begun with circumstances of Cruelty & perfidy scarcely paralleled in the most barbarous ages, and totally unworthy the Head of a civilized nation.

He has constrained our fellow Citizens taken Captive on the high Seas to bear Arms against their Country, to become the executioners of their friends and Brethren, or to fall themselves by their Hands.

He has excited domestic insurrections amongst us, and has endeavoured to bring on the inhabitants of our frontiers, the merciless Indian Savages, whose known rule of warfare, is an undistinguished destruction of all ages, sexes and conditions.

In every stage of these Oppressions We have Petitioned for Redress in the most humble terms: Our repeated Petitions have been answered only by repeated injury. A Prince, whose character is thus marked by every act which may define a Tyrant, is unfit to be the ruler of a free People.

Nor have We been wanting in attention to our British brethren. We have warned them from time to time of attempts by their legislature to extend an unwarrantable jurisdiction over us. We have reminded them of the circumstances of our emigration and settlement here. We have appealed to their native justice and magnanimity, and we have conjured them by the ties of our common kindred to disavow these usurpations, which, would inevitably interrupt our connections and correspondence. They too have been deaf to the voice of justice and of consanguinity. We must, therefore, acquiesce in the necessity, which denounces our Separation, and hold them, as we hold the rest of mankind, Enemies in War, in Peace Friends.

We, therefore, the Representatives of the United States of America, in General Congress, Assembled, appealing to the Supreme Judge of the world for the rectitude of our intentions, do, in the Name, and by Authority of the good People of these Colonies, solemnly publish and declare, That these United Colonies are, and of Right ought to be Free and Independent States; that they are Absolved from all Allegiance to the British Crown, and that all political connection between them and the State of Great Britain, is and ought to be totally dissolved; and that as Free and Independent States, they have full Power to levy War, conclude Peace, contract Alliances, establish Commerce, and to do all other Acts and Things which Independent States may of right do. And for the support of this Declaration, with a firm reliance on the Protection of Divine Providence, we mutually pledge to each other our Lives, our Fortunes and our sacred Honor.

The signing of the Declaration of Independence on July 4, 1776.

to either independence or reconciliation with Britain. So, this was the last major opportunity to win people over to the cause of independence. Jefferson also had to convince European monarchs that the colonies were worthy of their help. In particular, the American Patriots hoped for assistance from France and Spain. These countries were Britain's traditional rivals. But the kings were unlikely to help rebellious subjects overthrow the rule of another monarch. What the European powers gained in trade with Britain's colonies might well be lost if their own subjects were inspired to revolt.

Thomas Jefferson divided the Declaration of Independence into four parts. The first part, the Preamble, explained why the Declaration was written. It served as an appeal to the people of America and Europe.

The New Theory of Government

In the second part of the Declaration, Jefferson drew heavily from the writing of John Locke, a seventeenth-century English philosopher. Locke wrote in *Two Treatises of Government* that the task of government was to protect people's rights better than they could for themselves. People, in effect, made a deal with their rulers. The people (the governed) would obey the rules of the government as long as the government protected their rights. However, the government would lose its right to rule when it no longer fulfilled its part of the bargain. This idea was called a "compact theory of government." It meant that government was based on an agreement between those who were ruled and those who ruled.

Jefferson portrayed the relationship between the colonies and the king as a voluntary one. He based his arguments on Locke's compact theory of government. Jefferson also wrote that all men were created politically equal. He said that people had certain rights that could not be denied them. These rights were natural rights. Among them were life, liberty, and the pursuit of happiness. Governments obtained their right to rule from the consent of the governed. In return, governments owed people the protection of certain rights. When rulers interfered with the rights of their subjects, the rulers should be replaced. This should not be done for unimportant or temporary reasons. Jefferson wrote that people would endure what was bearable rather than overthrow a government. But when the wrongs were too great, there was no other choice.

Breaking the Ties

Jefferson and Congress claimed that the right of self-government was a natural right. It was not granted simply because the colonists were British citizens. It was a right all people had. The colonies had freely chosen to adopt British law and to honor the British monarch. The third section of the Declaration points out how the king no longer served the needs of the people. Therefore, based on the people's natural right of self-government, they could withdraw their voluntary support. The Declaration of Independence did not condemn monarchies in general. Jefferson directed his attack at one king in particular, George III. The Patriots did not want to offend the other rulers who might come to their aid.

As you have seen, Jefferson's ideas were not original. What made the Declaration so outstanding was that theory was now being put into practice. The colonies now had an *ideology*, a set of principles, to fight for. They were fighting for the right to establish a government as they saw fit. It was a great experiment and the beginning of a new age. The world in 1776 could not imagine how quickly and how far the influence of the American Revolution would spread.

Many colonists remained loyal to England. As pictured above, a Tory was often strung up.

Declaring War

The fourth section of the document declared the independence of the colonies. They were now "Free and Independent States . . . . They have full Power to levy War, conclude Peace, contract Alliances, establish Commerce and do all other Acts and Things which Indepen-

The Liberty Bell, rung in Philadelphia on Independence Day, July 4, 1776.

dent States may of right do." This part of the Declaration served a practical purpose. It was a message aimed at foreign powers. It showed the willingness of the "Independent States" to form alliances for help with European countries and to establish trade with them.

There is a certain contradiction in the fact that Jefferson held slaves while he wrote of liberty. However, people often describe a perfect world worth struggling for without being perfect themselves. In time, Jefferson's words would inspire those who wished to end slavery.

Division on the Home Front

Once the Declaration of Independence was approved by Congress, the colonists were divided. The Patriots' position was strengthened. The Tories, who were pro-British, were now considered guilty of treason. The actual number of people who remained loyal to the king is subject to dispute. At one time, John Adams claimed that one-third of the colonists were Patriots, one-third were Tories, and one-third were neutral. Others claim that as few as 10 percent were active rebels. whereas up to 50 percent were neutral. Certainly, many people remained loyal to the king but kept that fact hidden.

There were Tories in every colony. They were members of every class of society and members of nearly every family. Benjamin Franklin's son was a Tory, but his son's son was a Patriot. There were Tories even among such well-known revolutionary families as the Otises of Massachusetts.

People were Tories for many reasons, both honorable and selfish. Some were connected with great families that had been honored by the king. Some were making a good profit supplying the British armies. Some doubted that the Patriots would ever be able to control the radicals who had burned stamps and dumped tea. Some, like the Scottish backwoods settlers in North Carolina, simply disliked the revolutionary leaders. They became Tories in order to settle old

INDEPENDENCE DAY

On July 2, 1776, the Second Continental Congress took the step of declaring the colonies to be "Free and Independent States." The date, wrote John Adams, was one that ought to be celebrated with "pomp and parade, with shows, games, sports, guns, bells, bonfires and illuminations (fireworks), from one end of this continent to the other, from this time forward forevermore." July 4, the day the Congress officially approved the final wording of the Declaration of Independence, actually became our day of celebration. Because Adams had served with Thomas Jefferson on a committee to write the Declaration, the meaning of the American Revolution was very clear to him.

A fire on September 21, 1776, raged through New York City and destroyed over 1000 buildings. The British accused Americans of starting it and captured some suspects. The suspects were strung up by their heels or bayoneted and then thrown into the flames.

scores with the coastal landowners who supported Congress. And some felt that loyalty to the Crown should not be given only as a reward for good behavior: "My king, right or wrong" was their view.

In no single colony were the Tories strong enough to take control on their own. But they did help the British troops. Thousands fought on the side of the king. They were particularly active in North and South Carolina and New York. Their impact in Virginia, Maryland, Connecticut, and Massachusetts was small. These colonies were the older ones, with a stronger tradition of self-government. The Tories never seemed to muster the strength and influence equal to their numbers in the population. They were not as well organized throughout the colonies as the Patriots were. Nor did they have a strong ideology or dynamic leadership.

Unity is always hard to achieve. In wartime, it is almost impossible without violence. Because people are killed in battle, others feel ready to kill anyone they think disloyal. The Patriots looked upon

The Continental Army was reinforced by volunteers. These volunteers had to be ready "in a minute" in times of emergency. In this picture, a "minuteman" readies himself for battle.

the Tories as traitors. They expected to fight the British soldiers, but not their fellow colonists. As a result, the Patriots reacted strongly against the Tories. When the Tories were captured, they were apt to be treated more harshly than the British regulars. State legislatures seized and then sold Tory property. Mobs threatened known Tories. In extreme cases, some were even tarred and feathered or put to death. About 80,000 Tories fled to Canada, the British West Indies, and Britain.

In return, Patriots received harsh treatment at the hands of the British troops who considered the Patriots to be traitors to the king. Many Patriots died in prison ships anchored off the coast.

Questions for Discussion

1. Why was the Declaration of Independence in 1776 such an important document at home and abroad? Is it still as significant today?
2. What effect did the division on the home front have on the war and the people involved?

3. Howe Drives Washington Out of New York

While the war of words was still being waged, the war with guns went on. In the summer of 1776, the Americans were doing better in propaganda than in battle. In June, the war shifted southward when the British left Boston by sea and moved against New York City. This city was not easy to defend because it was on Manhattan Island. The British fleet controlled the surrounding waters. Still, Washington could not give it up without a fight. Late in August, while British ships massed in the harbor, Washington, under the cover of bad weather, moved part of his troops across the East River to modern-day Brooklyn on Long Island.

This move proved to be a big mistake. Britain's General William Howe landed 15,000 troops and attacked at once. The Americans still lacked the experience and skill to stand up indefinitely to waves of red-coated British troops and their green-clad, German-speaking, Hessian **mercenaries**. By August 28, Washington's forces were battered and weak. The redcoats were a powerful enemy. The Americans badly needed new supplies and men, but reinforcements were stranded on the other side of the river—and enemy warships could blast anything that moved.

However, sometimes an army of amateurs has advantages. Among Washington's men were two regiments from the fishing towns of Salem and Marblehead in Massachusetts. On a pitch-dark, rainy night, these salty "soldiers" laid down their muskets and manned the oars of a collection of small boats gathered from wharves along the river. Working through the night, they rowed back and forth, bringing the army to safety on the Manhattan shore.

Still the American forces were far from complete safety. Ahead of them, they had a long march northward on Manhattan Island. If General Howe had pursued them immediately, the war might have ended then and there. But the British, particularly General Howe and his brother Admiral Howe, felt that the Americans' defeat at Brooklyn Heights might cause Congress to discuss peace. At Admiral Howe's request, Congress sent envoys to talk with him. Benjamin Franklin, John Adams, and Edward Rutledge met with Admiral Howe. But they

A rendering of life along the waterfront in old New York.

133

Mary Ludwig Hays, nicknamed Molly Pitcher because she brought water to soldiers at the Battle of Monmouth, was an American hero of the Revolutionary War. When her husband was wounded, she took his place at the cannon.

found no resolution for their differences. Lord Howe had no authority to recognize the independence of the colonies, and the Americans would accept nothing less.

Meanwhile, General Howe was gathering supplies for an assault on Manhattan if that were necessary. He was confident that the Continental Army would be wiped out at the next serious encounter.

Fortunately for the Patriots' cause, Howe waited two weeks from the time that he defeated Washington's forces on Long Island until he started his determined pursuit. This delay gave Washington time to regroup his troops and begin his retreat. Between September and November, Washington fought several battles as he moved northward. Each one bought the Continental Army a little time. But the British were driving on. As they advanced, they captured carelessly guarded American forts full of men and supplies.

One of the most critical losses occurred at Fort Washington, on the Hudson River, across from New Jersey. Washington trusted General Greene's judgment that the fort could be held against superior British strategy and power. It was in this battle that Margaret Corbin became one of the first women to take an active part in the fighting. After her husband was struck down, she took his place at the cannon and fired until she was seriously wounded. Later, she was assigned to the Invalid Regiment at West Point and retired on a pension. After Fort Washington, it was evident that the Americans needed more than bravery—they needed experienced officers and troops.

Meanwhile, a fleet of British ships carrying 2500 trained and equipped soldiers arrived in New York. Sir Henry Clinton had tried unsuccessfully to take Charleston. He sailed to New York in time to let General Cornwallis, who was with him, set out with General Howe in pursuit of Washington. With fresh troops and plenty of supplies, the British were confident. By December, Washington was hiding out in Pennsylvania with what he called, "the wretched remains of a broken army." Washington had seen 5000 of his men taken prisoner. *Morale*—the will to win—was nearly shattered.

Washington Counterattacks at Trenton and Princeton

Now was the time for the person Tom Paine called a *sunshine patriot*—someone who only supports a winner—to give up. The American soldiers shivered around the campfires, without shoes, blankets, or winter uniforms. Washington wrote that the "cry of want

As part of his strategy to isolate New England, General Howe evacuated his troops from Boston to later regroup in New York.

BETSY ROSS

The American Flag Elizabeth (Betsy) Griscom Ross, maker of the first American flag, was born on January 1, 1752, in Philadelphia. Educated and raised under strict Quaker traditions, Ross was disowned by her parents when she married John Ross, an Episcopalian, on November 4, 1773. At the onset of the Revolution, John Ross died after being fatally injured in a gunpowder explosion. Betsy Ross then assumed the responsibility of managing her late husband's upholstery business.

It was reported that Betsy Ross was secretly visited by George Washington and Robert Morris in early June of 1776. The result of this meeting was the making of the nation's first flag fashioned after a sketch done by Washington. Betsy Ross is the first official flagmaker of whom the government has any record.

Ross' business remained very profitable over the years. She continued to run it until she was 75 years old. Her daughter, Clarissa Wilson, took over and carried on the business until 1857. Betsy Ross died in 1836.

(lack) of Provisions" came to him from everywhere. Sickness struck down hundreds. Volunteer soldiers were deserting the army at an alarming rate.

It was then that George Washington showed his greatness. He knew he was in danger. Like a hunted fox, he was almost in the jaws of the hounds. But what if the fox suddenly startled everyone by turning around and tearing the throat out of the closest enemy? On the night of December 25, during a driving snowstorm, Washington ferried his men across the ice-choked Delaware River and marched them along the New Jersey shore to Trenton. There, three Hessian regiments were sleeping off a Christmas drunk, convinced that neither man nor beast would stir in such bitter weather. Out of the sleety dawn, the ragged but game Americans suddenly attacked. Within two hours, the Hessian commander had been killed and 900 of his men taken prisoner. And the Americans were hauling captured supplies back to the boats.

Washington could not afford to be content with his victory at Trenton. General Howe was likely to order General Cornwallis to strike a blow when Washington was least prepared. In a short time, Washington's army would practically break up as the soldiers returned

Washington reviews his ragged "rebel" army at Valley Forge.

home when their enlistments were over. In an emotional appeal, Washington addressed his troops. He asked them to remain for another six weeks. Three thousand men agreed to remain. General Washington recrossed the Delaware and reestablished the army at Trenton. He needed to capture British supplies and to be victorious in order to maintain the fighting will of the Patriots.

When Cornwallis learned of Washington's move, the British general decided to use his superior force to pin the American forces against the river and destroy them. Cornwallis moved to Trenton, within a mile of Washington's troops. In a clever move, Washington deceived Cornwallis. While the British slept, the Americans muffled the wheels of their cannons with strips of cloth, left decoys in camp, and marched toward Princeton. Gaining distance on them, Washington's troops were able to defeat forces headed to reinforce Cornwallis. The Americans, burdened with captured supplies, left Princeton. They again eluded Cornwallis's larger force, which fell back to protect supplies at New Brunswick. Then both armies went into winter quarters. In those days, guns and wagons could move on the rough dirt roads only after winter snows and spring thaws were over.

This brilliant counterattack when things were darkest forced the British to plan yet a third year in their attempts to crush the rebels. It also gave the colonists courage and thus restored their morale.

The Crucial Year

Then came a decisive year—mid-1777 to mid-1778. Late in July of 1777, the British moved an expedition by water and land against

137

Top: In October 1777, Benedict Arnold, riding the white horse, leads a charge during the crucial battle at Saratoga. Inset: Portrait of General John Burgoyne.

strategy
an overall plan

Philadelphia. In hot summer and hazy autumn, they beat Washington's men in several battles, occupied Philadelphia, and chased the Continental Congress to York, Pennsylvania. In December, the "rebel" army went into winter camp at nearby Valley Forge.

Despite hunger and subzero weather, Washington continued to drill his hard-pressed, unfortunate troops. Washington's army was ill-fed, not because Pennsylvania's farms produced no beef and cider, but because there was a shortage of wagons for delivery. Also, state governments lagged in furnishing their assigned shares of medicine, clothes, and blankets. And many merchants refused to accept the paper money issued by Congress. But a third straight winter of American survival proved to the British that the rebels could not be starved out. Besides, at Valley Forge, Washington already had news of a stunning American victory that occurred the autumn before. Washington knew that this victory would soon turn the tide.

In June of 1777, a British army was gathered in Canada under "Gentlemen Johnny" Burgoyne, a poetry-writing, party-loving British general who had a great **strategy** to end the war. He would move down from Canada along Lake George and Lake Champlain to the Hudson River. At Albany, he would meet redcoats sent north from New York by General Howe. Then, a wall of British bayonets would split the colonies in two.

But Burgoyne was fighting inland, where geography worked in favor of the Americans. Burgoyne's columns of British and Hessians thrashed through the upstate New York wilderness in the hot weather. They were slowed to a crawl by their heavy guns and wagons. New England, anxious not to be cut off, sent militiamen who swarmed around Burgoyne like "birds of prey," as one of his men noted. Against orders, Burgoyne's American Indian partners killed settlers and roused the countryside further against him. Worse, General Howe never sent the promised help from New York City. Instead, he had decided to leave there to take Philadelphia.

By October, after suffering two stunning defeats against American generals like Benedict Arnold, Burgoyne's army was surrounded at Saratoga. Four days later, Burgoyne surrendered his entire force. The Americans had not only stopped a third British campaign but captured a whole royal army! Only a year later, one of America's heroes at Saratoga, General Arnold, turned traitor and aided the British.

Thus, a third phase of the war began. By 1778, the British had shown that they could capture almost any American port city. They could win battles in the open field. Their control of the sea—like

Northeast Campaigns 1775–1778

Benedict Arnold, a colonel in the American army who later turned traitor and aided the British army.

139

control of the air today—gave them power to move freely. But they could not move far inland to destroy American farms and break popular resistance. Therefore, after 1778, it became clear that the Patriots could not win by fighting on the settled strip of coastline. There, the British armies could win European-style battles. They had to move deeper inland.

The Balance of Power

There were several reasons why the British assumed that the rebellion in the colonies would be short-lived. Britain had the strongest navy in the world. The British navy expected to be able to cut off supplies to the colonies and to control every port. The British could move their troops and supplies and maintain communication by sea. The British army was well equipped, well disciplined, and fully trained. There was no comparison between it and the ragtag forces that made up the Continental Army. The British could afford to pay for mercenaries to fill their ranks. They also expected to be able to tap a vast resource of American colonials loyal to the king.

On paper, the war appeared nearly won. As the years dragged on, the British must have realized that they had made some grave miscalculations. Early in the war, the British had easy victories along the coast.

However, when the fighting moved inland, the Patriots' advantages became more apparent. The Tories were not so eager to help the British, because they knew that they would be at the mercy of the Patriots when the British moved on. The officers and men of the Continental Army had gained their experience in the French and Indian Wars. They were also more familiar with the terrain. Instead of engaging the British in major battles, when possible, they would pick away at the redcoats from under cover. With their superior guns and experience in hunting to survive, the Americans engaged in an early type of **guerrilla warfare.**

The British depended on the Hessian troops too much. Fighting for money and not for a cause, the mercenaries lacked the drive that the Patriots had. The major miscalculations may have been that the British underestimated the quality of American leadership as well as the strong desire of the Americans to win.

Deborah Sampson joins the army dressed as a man. She fought in several battles. Her identity was discovered when, after being wounded, she was put in a Philadelphia hospital.

guerrilla warfare
irregular warfare by independent bands. Often involves hit-and-run tactics.

Questions for Discussion

1. Define *mercenaries, strategy, sunshine patriot.*
2. What are the disadvantages of using mercenary soldiers?
3. Why is mid-1777 to mid-1778 considered a decisive year?
4. How did British plans of action differ from the American plans?

Chapter 6 Review

Summary Questions for Discussion

1. What qualities made George Washington an exceptional leader for the colonies?
2. What was the purpose of the political pamphlets written from 1763 to 1783?
3. Identify each of the following: Samuel Adams, Mercy Otis Warren, John Dickinson, and Samuel Seabury.
4. In your own words, state Thomas Paine's arguments in *Common Sense* against (a) the king of England, and (b) continued connection with Britain.
5. Why was Thomas Jefferson chosen to write the Declaration of Independence?
6. What is contained in the Preamble to the Declaration of Independence?
7. Explain Locke's compact theory of government.
8. How did Jefferson apply Locke's theories specifically to the colonies?
9. What was the purpose of the fourth section of the document?
10. Explain why some people remained loyal to Britain.
11. Give examples to show that "in the summer of 1776 the Americans were doing better in propaganda than in battles."
12. Describe the winter of 1777–1778 at Valley Forge.
13. How was General Burgoyne's strategy thwarted?
14. Why did the British assume that the rebellion in the colonies would be short-lived?
15. What advantages did the Patriots have over the British?

Word Study

Fill in each blank in the sentences that follow with the term below that is most appropriate.

monarchy   privateers   envoys   embargo   warfare
mercenaries   strategy   morale   guerrilla

1. The colonists needed a plan or _____ to successfully overthrow the government of George III.
2. By his own steadfastness, Washington helped improve the _____ of his soldiers.
3. Exports were halted by an _____.
4. _____ were authorized to cruise against British commerce.
5. The colonists were not professionally trained, as were the hired soldiers or _____ used by the British.
6. However, on familiar terrain, colonial soldiers engaged in a type of _____.
7. Realizing that foreign help was necessary, colonists sent representatives or _____ to other countries to seek aid.

Using Your Skills

1. Look at the map "Northeast Campaigns 1775–1778" on page 139. In 1776, why were the British troops pulled out of Boston? What was the general strategy in Howe's move against New York in the same year? What was General Burgoyne's strategy in pushing south from Canada in 1777? In each case, why did the strategy fail to work?
2. Read the Preamble to the Declaration of Independence on page 125 and in your own words, explain its meaning.
3. In the Declaration of Independence, Thomas Jefferson lists the grievances against George III. Wherever you can, note for each grievance the specific act to which the Americans objected. (See text of Declaration on pages 125 to 127.)

CHAPTER 7

Winning the War for Independence

In 1778, no one seemed to realize that Britain had already made the errors that would cost that country victory. From the very beginning of the difficulties with the colonies, King George III had adopted a hard line. Even before independence was declared, he labeled the rebels as traitors. This action further strengthened the resolve of the Americans to free themselves from Great Britain. It also helped unify the revolutionaries, who might otherwise have fought among themselves.

The British did not start the war with an all-out effort to win. Instead, their leaders hoped that there was still a chance for reconciliation. As a result, the British did not seem to use their full power. They could have sacked most of the coastal cities with their superior naval forces, but they did not. Instead, they left the ports open for privateering and merchant shipping. As you saw in Chapter 6, on two occasions in 1776, General Howe failed to follow up his battle advantage thus allowing Washington's forces to slip away. These initial failures had far-reaching consequences. By failing to crush the revolution in these early days, the British left the way open for Washington to build and maintain the Continental Army. It also gave the Americans time to seek and obtain foreign aid.

The British tried to reassert control over the colonies at a time when they had almost no friends in Europe. Thus, the British were stretching their men, materials, and ships over a wide area. Nations like France, who alone could not have taken Britain on, were now able to take advantage of the situation.

READING GUIDE

1. **How did the participation of the French turn the tide of the war?**
2. **Why were the British unable to hold onto the southern territory they had gained?**
3. **Why did many people consider the Treaty of Peace a generous settlement?**

The surrender of Lord Cornwallis at Yorktown, by painter John Turnbull.

1. The Tide Turns

The first great sign of change came as a result of the victory at Saratoga, when France and the United States signed a treaty of **alliance.** In February 1778, the Americans gained the open support of mighty France.

King Louis XVI of France did not join the fight because he loved liberty or the Americans. He simply wanted to get back at England for France's losses in the French and Indian War. The Count de Vergennes directed the king's foreign affairs. Vergennes feared that the British defeat at Saratoga would affect King George III's attitude toward the colonies. The British might now be willing to offer the Americans all the concessions that they had been unwilling to grant them before. For these practical reasons, the French acted quickly to assist the Americans.

The French decision may have come just in the nick of time. In fact, the British king was considering giving in to almost every American demand, short of independence. The colonies were to be offered freedom from Parliamentary taxation and unwanted British military presence. All acts of Parliament to which the colonists objected would be revoked, even limitations on trade with other nations. All the concessions would be guaranteed by treaties. However, all these concessions would have made no difference, since at this point, nothing short of independence would have been acceptable to the Congress. The die was now cast for a worldwide conflict.

To the Americans, France's entry into combat was a godsend. As the ally of a great power, Congress could now borrow money more easily. In addition, Washington would soon get trained French troops and, even more importantly, the French navy, to help him. Spain and the Netherlands were soon drawn into the fight against Britain. Even Catherine II of Russia became involved in protecting the rights of

Poland's Thaddeus Kosciusko gave the Patriot army invaluable instruction in military engineering.

Western Campaign 1778-1779

America

Prussia's Friedrich von Steuben, who trained the American army during the winter at Valley Forge.

Above: France's Marquis de Lafayette in 1781.

neutral traders against the British navy. Now, England could no longer give full attention to America.

Besides seeking troops from France, Congress also authorized its foreign agents to get help from foreign military experts. There were so many Europeans willing to serve that Congress finally restricted acceptance to those who were superior leaders and who could speak English. France's Marquis de Lafayette was 20 when he volunteered to serve without pay. He and Thaddeus Kosciusko of Poland believed that young people everywhere could share in the endless struggle for liberty by joining the colonists' rebellion. The worldwide appeal of Thomas Jefferson's words were beginning to be realized.

For a lifelong officer like the Prussian Baron Friedrich von Steuben, opportunity was probably as important as democratic ideals. At Valley Forge, he began to teach Washington's officers and troops the many things he knew about military *hygiene*, or cleanliness and disease prevention. He offered another vital element of revolutionary success—training, drilling, organization, and discipline.

The War in the West

The American Revolution was not limited to the original thirteen colonies. At the outbreak, a scattering of settlers lived west of the Appalachians. Most of these settlers came from Virginia, Pennsylvania, and North Carolina. They included both Patriots and Tories. Many of the Patriot settlers who took an active part in the fighting were

A modern painting shows British Lieutenant Colonel Henry Hamilton surrendering at Vincennes to George Rogers Clark.

Virginians. They had both personal and patriotic reasons for seeking the defeat of the British.

Virginia had long claimed large areas of valuable western land. British policy threatened these claims. To add to this, prior to the Revolution, Pennsylvania traders sought support from British leaders to establish a new colony. They wanted to establish the colony on land that Virginia claimed south of the Ohio River. By the Quebec Act of 1774, Britain put control of land north and west of the Ohio River under authority of the governor of Canada. By virtue of its colonial charter, Virginia also claimed this land. If the British won the Revolution, control of the disputed territory would surely be lost to the Virginians. However, if the Americans won the Revolution, but lost control of the land west of the Appalachians, the new nation might be hemmed in by powerful neighbors, such as Britain, France, and Spain.

The Patriots also feared that during the war, the American Indians would ally themselves with the British. There was already a struggle between the expansionist frontier settlers and the American Indians, who resented the imposition on their lifestyle and the taking of their lands. Most American Indian tribes did indeed ally themselves with the British because of this threat. If the British had had the full support of all the tribes in the area, their chances for driving the settlers back east of the Appalachians would have been greater. However, things did not work out that way. Instead of supporting the British, some tribes—Mohicans, Oneidas, Tuscaroras, and Catawbas—sided with the Patriots.

The battles between the British forces and the Americans were most often brief encounters. There was brutality and retaliation on both sides. With few supplies and limited forces, neither side in a battle found it easy to take and hold territory. It was not until June of 1778 that the Americans were able to make significant military progress.

At that time, a band of about 200 western riflemen crowded onto rafts in the Ohio River. They were starting one of the most important expeditions of the war. One of Virginia's militia officers, Colonel George Rogers Clark, believed that he could enforce Virginia's claim to western land by capturing British posts in the old Ohio country.

Clark performed his mission brilliantly. He floated and marched to the Mississippi and captured some settlements in Illinois. Then, he doubled back toward a British fort at Vincennes, in present-day Indiana. By then, it was February 1779. Melting snows had turned the whole area into a swamp. After slogging the last few miles through water that sometimes reached shoulder-height, Clark boldly attacked. In so doing, he forced the surrender of the British commander.

This astonishing feat broke the British hold on the area between the Alleghenies and the Mississippi. When the time came to write the peace treaty, American negotiators claimed that territory and set the new nation's flag one-third of the way to the Pacific.

The War at Sea

No less important to the war's outcome were American and French victories at sea. The tiny American navy played no real part in winning the war. From the very beginning, the navy was beset with many problems. Congress did not have the money available to outfit enough ships to challenge the British navy. This was not surprising. At that time, no nation had a navy strong enough to rival the British navy. The American navy was also plagued by a shortage of cannons, naval supplies, and willing sailors.

Despite these limitations, the Continental Navy did interfere with some British shipping. The Americans were more successful off the coast of Europe, because the British navy fairly well controlled the American coast. Captain Gustavus Conyngham operated out of French and Spanish ports, while both countries were still neutral. His ships, aptly named the *Surprise* and the *Revenge*, did enough damage to British shipping to cause the British to howl in protest. At one point, the British even threatened to seize France's shipping fleet if the French did not take measures to stop the Americans.

It was not until after the French entered the war that another famous captain arrived on the scene. John Paul Jones was able to enjoy the aid of the French as he set out to harass British shipping. The most

In the Continental Navy's most famous action, John Paul Jones and the Bonhomme Richard *defeated the British* Serapis *after a three-hour battle.*

Captain Conyngham

In this chapter, you have been introduced to Gustavus Conyngham, a forgotten American hero of the Revolutionary navy, such as it was. He is worth a closer look. For one thing, he was an Irishman by birth. He did not come to the colonies until 1763, at the age of nineteen. In September of 1775, he sailed from Philadelphia in the brig *Charming Peggy*, intending to bring it back to the Americans loaded with military supplies, which he would buy in Holland. However, the British influenced the Dutch to prevent the sailing, leaving Conyngham stranded in Europe. He went to Paris, where he got a commission from the American officials there, and sailed off on the successful cruises mentioned. His victories became widely known. In fact, in Paris, a cartoon of him was circulated, showing him as a gigantic pirate, with pistols in his belt and a sword in hand, labeled the terror of the English.

Unfortunately, the "terror" was captured by the English in 1779 and sent off to one of their prisons. At first he was in irons, sometimes in solitary confinement, and always badly fed. But his spirit remained strong. Twice he tried to escape, and the third time, he succeeded by digging his way out—in his words, "committing treason through his Majesty's earth."

His luck finally ran out. He went to London, found friends and money, reached Holland, and finally got on a homeward bound ship. Unfortunately, that ship was captured. He was returned to the jail from which he had escaped until the end of the war.

When it was over, he petitioned Congress for compensation for his services. Congress, forgetful of his past contributions to victory, said no. Conyngham also failed in an attempt to reenter the navy. He spent the rest of his life as a merchant marine skipper and trader. He lived to take part in preparations to defend Philadelphia from a British attack that never came during the War of 1812.

famous of his battles was against the British ship, *Serapis*. The *Serapis* was larger, swifter, and better equipped than Jones's ship, the *Bonhomme Richard*. The *Serapis* was part of the British Baltic fleet. John Paul Jones came upon it as the *Serapis* was returning home with a cargo of naval supplies—the lifeblood of the Royal Navy. With great skill and some luck, John Paul Jones was able to outmaneuver the British ship and overcome its advantages.

Yet, the greatest American damage to British shipping was done by privateers. These lightly armed, fast, privately owned ships destroyed millions of dollars' worth of British shipping. Tempted by the possibility of prize money from the sale of captured vessels, sailors were more willing to sign up on privateers. More than 2000 ships sailed with commissions from the state and Continental governments.

Unfortunately, privateering may have actually weakened the American cause. Privateering drew thousands of sailors who might

British and French ships battle in March 1781.

have served in the Continental Navy. Privateers were not subject to an overall plan of action or joint ventures. Had all the power of the privateers been directed under a unified command, the Continental Navy might have been effective.

At sea, the French navy bore the brunt of the fighting, most of which took place far from the colonial coastline. These sea fights were formal, savage affairs in which long lines of rocking wooden ships, yardarm to yardarm, pounded each other to splinters. Although many of these grisly, slaughtering matches ended in a draw, French naval power proved to be decisive in the final American·victory.

The War in the South

In 1778, the British decided to shift the war into the South. There, the last acts of the war were played out. During 1780 and 1781, war swept cruelly through backwoods communities. Those years made the reputation of commanders who specialized in hit-and-run tactics.

At first, the British strategy of cutting away the southern half of the new nation—just as Burgoyne's campaign was supposed to slice off New England—seemed to work.

In December 1778, the British launched an attack on Savannah, Georgia. They greatly outnumbered and quickly crushed the American militia. With the help of British troops from Florida, the triumphant forces then took Sunbury and Augusta once more. Georgia thus came under the control of the British king.

In early April 1780, Sir Henry Clinton was able to take Charleston from General Benjamin Lincoln. The assault was the first major British attempt to regain control of South Carolina. Clinton, with support from the British navy, was able to lock up the Continental Army in Charleston. By mid-April, a supply depot nearby was taken.

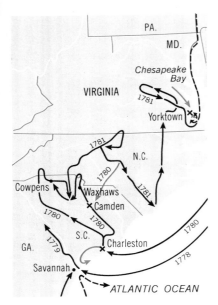

Southern Campaigns 1778–1781

← British
← American
←--- French

By early May, Lincoln's army of 5000 troops surrendered. This proved to be the largest American defeat of the war. Clinton placed Lord Charles Cornwallis in command and sailed for New York. With the strategic points under control, the British began to ravage the countryside in hopes of scaring the colonists into giving in. They burned and sacked towns at will.

Congress appointed General Horatio Gates to command the army in the South. Gates was both inexperienced in commanding a moving campaign and overanxious to enlarge his reputation. At the end of July 1780, he decided that he would lead a march on Camden, South Carolina. He did not realize the poor physical condition of the men under his command. Nor did he take into consideration the difficult terrain of the route he chose. When the Continental forces arrived at Camden on August 16, they were too exhausted and sick to fight. General Gates escaped, but most of his army did not. Two days later, another American force, commanded by Thomas Sumter, was overtaken at Fishing Creek, North Carolina. Now, the way for the British invasion of North Carolina was open. It appeared as though nothing could stop the wrap-up of the South.

The war in the South focused attention on the role that Blacks played in the Revolution. The British reminded Blacks that their masters, though fighting for "liberty," were still slave owners. In 1779, the British promised freedom to Blacks who would join their side. An unknown number of slaves ran away from their masters to do so.

The Americans also turned gradually toward enlisting slaves and free Blacks. Congress discouraged it at first, anxious to keep guns out of Black hands. But by the middle of the war, manpower was scarce. So, several states on their own enrolled Blacks—free and slave—in their ranks.

Of the 5000 Blacks who served, some were freed as a reward for service. Others became free when their Tory owners fled. So, although not planned as such, the Revolution encouraged the end of slavery.

The Patriots Fight Back

By October 1780, the steady stream of bad news from the Carolinas took a turn for the better. A force of local mountaineers from the Carolinas, Virginia, western Tennessee, and Kentucky overran a force of Tories at King's Mountain in North Carolina. The execution of some Tories by the Patriot forces discouraged active support of the British by other Tories.

The defeat of the British also caused General Cornwallis to reconsider his plans to hold North Carolina. The British believed that that region was full of people who would be moved to aid the

"Swamp Fox" Francis Marion (on horseback, second from left) and some of his highly successful guerrilla troops take a raft across the Pee Dee River in South Carolina.

pro-British side. However, the great Tory uprising did not take place. In fact, the success of the mountaineers against the British altered the face of the war in the South. Cornwallis abandoned Charlotte, North Carolina, and withdrew to South Carolina.

In addition, the American success at King's Mountain encouraged more Patriots to strike out at the British. Sumter, who had been defeated at Fishing Creek, was back with a large group of followers. General Francis Marion, known as the "Swamp Fox," led a ragtag group of Patriots who used guerrilla warfare with devastating effectiveness. They would appear suddenly, hit hard at a British wagon train or supply post, then run and hide as the flames lit the sky. Secretly moving through the swamp, Marion's guerrillas kept a far larger British force off balance. At times, hit-and-run tactics can enable a small and weak force to outfight superior numbers.

Guerrilla warfare, however, made any American a suspicious character to British officers. It also made any Tory a potential threat to the American forces. Houses were set aflame, young boys dragged to prison, crops destroyed, and farm animals and slaves carried away. Starvation, disease, massacre, and grief were the fate of many innocent Southerners.

In May 1780, British troops swept through the Waxhaws, a wooded frontier region on the border of North and South Carolina. Shortly after witnessing the massacre, thirteen-year-old Andrew Jackson (center, foreground) joined the Patriot army

Greene Replaces Gates

On the day of the American success at King's Mountain, another important event occurred. General Gates, whose lack of wisdom had endangered the American forces, was replaced by General Nathaniel Greene. Greene had a fine reputation. After reviewing the troops now under his command in the South, Greene wrote Washington of their "wretched and distressing" condition. Yet, he was able to raise their spirits and obtain enough supplies to revive their effectiveness. He described his tactics in these words: "We fight, get beat, rise, and fight again."

Greene had few regular forces and thus depended heavily on local militia. However, he had an excellent corps of officers on whom he could depend. To protect North Carolina, Greene divided his forces, putting half under Brigadier Daniel Morgan. Morgan covered the west side of the route that Cornwallis would be taking from South Carolina. Greene covered the east side himself. Cornwallis sent Colonel Banastre Tarleton, who had been very successful in South Carolina, against the western flank. To Cornwallis's surprise and dismay, Tarleton was defeated by Morgan's troops. Morgan and Greene then outmarched Cornwallis and rejoined one another in Virginia.

From Virginia, the Americans circled back and met Cornwallis's force at Guilford Courthouse, North Carolina. Here, the British won the battle. Yet, the costs were high. The British withdrew to the coast to get reinforcements from the sea. And Greene continued to harass the British. Eventually, the British lost all but the coast of South Carolina.

Cornwallis's forces had been reduced from 3000 to 1700 strong. In order to be active again, he united with a force of nearly 5000 troops in Virginia. Shortly after his arrival in Virginia, Sir Henry Clinton ordered Cornwallis to build a naval base along Chesapeake Bay. Cornwallis issued picks and shovels to his men, and they began their work at Yorktown.

Questions for Discussion

1. Define *hygiene* and *alliance*.
2. What help did the Americans receive from foreign countries? What motivated the foreigners?
3. How did the war in the West differ from the war in the South?
4. What heroic actions were displayed during the war in the West? At sea? In the South?

2. Victory at Yorktown and the Treaty of Peace

In the summer of 1781, drums rattled across New York and New England. Washington's forces had long been keeping an eye on the British in New York. His veterans were now joined by many French regiments under Count Jean Rochambeau. Exciting news came from the South. Lord Cornwallis and his army were in Virginia, at Yorktown, with a river at their backs. At the same time, Francois de Grasse, French admiral, was in the West Indies with a large fleet. If he could come up into the bay, he might be able to defeat Cornwallis and free the South.

The plan depended on the French and Americans getting down to the coast of Virginia quickly. So knapsacks were packed, loved ones

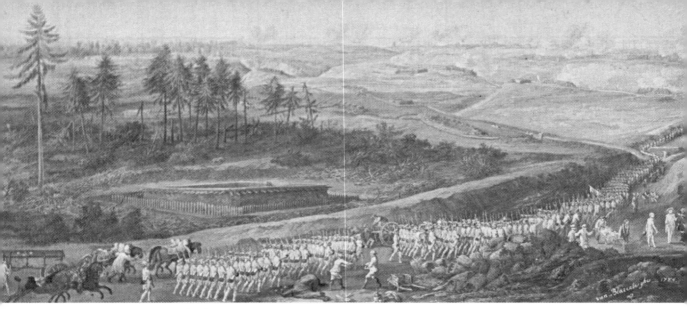

French regiments march into battle to support American troops at Yorktown. Louis Van Blarenberghe, a Frenchman who was at Yorktown for the surrender, was the painter.

kissed, and goodbyes said in both French and English. By land and water, Washington's and Rochambeau's troops hurried southward to their destiny.

The climax actually came at sea on September 5, 1781. It was then that France's Admiral Count de Grasse fought off a British fleet under Admiral Thomas Graves. Sea power did its work. For a few weeks, the French and Americans could successfully close in on an English general whose lines of supply and retreat were cut off by French warships.

On October 17, as more than 15,000 French and American beseigers moved steadily closer, Lord Cornwallis asked for terms of surrender. Two days later, for the second time in four years, an entire British army marched out to lay down its arms. They passed between ranks of smiling Frenchmen, some remembering Quebec, and Americans, many with memories of the bad autumn of 1776.

The Battle of Yorktown did more than free the South. It actually marked the end of the war. Yet, on first hearing the news of the American victory, King George III was still unwilling to have peace with American independence. However, the reality of the situation could not be denied. England had fought for almost seven years to subdue its angry colonists and make them help pay the cost of driving France from Canada. Now England was deeper in debt than ever, bogged down in a world war, and pushed partway out of the Ohio country. It was time to face facts, swallow pride, and admit defeat. There were no more campaigns. The British musicians had chosen an appropriate tune to play as their men paraded out at Yorktown—"The World Turned Upside Down."

Cornwallis surrenders at Yorktown.

The Treaty of Peace

During the war years, American envoys to Europe had learned one lesson well—the workings of European diplomacy. They began to realize that, like Britain, their own ally, France, and France's ally, Spain, were out for their own good. France wanted to humble Britain and take revenge for its defeat in the French and Indian War. Spain wanted the return of Gibraltar, at the entrance to the Mediterranean Sea. And, if American interest had to be sacrificed to obtain these ends, so be it.

The new nation benefited from having able ministers. John Jay, John Adams, and Benjamin Franklin were the primary negotiators of the peace settlement. It was John Jay who had held out for a recognition of independence as the first step in any peace negotiations. The British minister had sought to postpone independence by suggesting a close alliance, common citizenship, or some federal form of government.

By 1782, the first draft of the treaty was ready. The concession of independence was a tremendous diplomatic victory for the American envoys. France had hoped that independence would be delayed in order to keep the Americans at war. Spain hoped to settle the question of Gibraltar before American independence was secured. But the Americans held firm. They wanted the British out of America before the Continental Army completely fell apart.

The treaty declared the United States free and independent. It established the boundaries of the new country. East of the Mississippi, the boundaries were approximately what they are today—but without Florida, southern Louisiana, Mississippi, and Alabama. The United

States would have free navigation on the Mississippi River. The British army would withdraw. The United States conceded that Congress would not impede the collection of debts by Tories. Also, the states agreed that they would cease confiscating Tory property and would not prosecute Tories as traitors. John Adams was able to secure American fishing rights off the Newfoundland coast.

Until the British defeat at Yorktown, the Americans could not have expected such generous peace terms. Peace and independence would probably have been offered only on the condition that each nation would keep what it had. This possibility would have left Spain in control of both sides of the Mississippi River and the land bordering the Gulf of Mexico. Britain would have acquired the main seaports from New York to Savannah and controlled some of the land west of the Appalachians in the Ohio country.

The Americans were well satisfied with the terms. The French minister was not surprised by Britain's generosity. He wrote to an associate that the "English buy peace rather than make it." The American envoys had secretly negotiated the treaty with Great Britain. This was in direct violation of the terms of the Franco-American alliance agreement. Through his spy network, the French foreign minister had remained informed of the wheelings and dealings that were going on behind his back.

When All Was Said and Done

Wars do not end at the exact moment when guns stop firing. A humorist once said peace was "an interval of cheating between two periods of fighting." That statement is a bit harsh. A famous German general once put it another way, when he wrote that war was an extension or continuation of **diplomacy**. Diplomacy exists because independent nations have interests that are sometimes in conflict, just as people living in a crowded, busy house have arguments over space, quiet, and the use of strategic places like bathrooms and kitchens. Nations try to solve their disputes by political and economic pressures and by bargaining, just as individuals do. A war is a confession that these peaceful means have failed.

Though the American Revolution ended in 1783, the fighting had not. Attempts to start a new political system and to unify the thirteen colonies went on in the making of the Constitution. The quarrels between Americans and the British over territories and other economic matters such as trade went on as well. Yet, America was now a separate nation and could use full diplomatic and military power to gain important goals.

The American flag flew over the Allegheny Mountains and up to the banks of the Mississippi River. However, the British remained in

diplomacy
the art of conducting relations between nations

Lake of the Woods

Lake Superior

BRITISH CANADA

MAINE
(MASS.)

Lake Michigan

Lake Huron

Lake Ontario

N.H.

NEW YORK

MASS.

Lake Erie

CONN.

R.I.

PENNSYLVANIA

N.J.

DEL.

MD.

Ohio River

VIRGINIA

ATLANTIC
OCEAN

SPANISH
LOUISIANA

NORTH CAROLINA

Mississippi River

SOUTH CAROLINA

GEORGIA

The United States in 1783

British forts

Fur trade with Indians

Fishing rights

Trading between New England and
West Indies

Spanish influence

State boundaries

Territory of the U.S.—November 30, 1782

New Orleans

SPANISH FLORIDA

0   50   100   150   200   250 Miles

GULF OF MEXICO

Ben Franklin is received at the Versailles Palace in France.

forts at Niagara, Detroit, and other places. Their agents still offered blankets, rum, and hopes of restored power to the American Indians in return for furs. Yankee skippers still were entangled with British regulations governing trade with the West Indies. And Yankee fishermen still needed to determine the actual boundaries between the fishing waters off Maine and Canada. Patriots and Tories had each suffered property losses, and the American and British governments each tried to win payments for war damages.

However, not all the trouble spots involved England. Spain was to become a problem on the southern border of the United States. The British had given Florida to Spain in the 1783 treaty. As the owners of Louisiana since 1763, the Spanish also held New Orleans, which was the natural port connecting the Mississippi with the Atlantic. Clearly, as Americans moved westward, they would use the Mississippi as their outlet to the world. They would never again allow another nation to control that river's mouth. Settling disputes that arose from expansion made the tasks of American diplomats difficult. But for nations, as for people, trouble is a sign of life.

Questions for Discussion

1. Define *diplomacy*.
2. What was the significance of the Battle of Yorktown?
3. What issues between the British and Americans were left unresolved by the Revolution? Why were they likely to be diplomatic sore-spots?
4. Why was control of the mouth of the Mississippi so important to the United States?

Chapter 7 Review

Summary Questions for Discussion

1. What concessions were being considered by King George III when the French decided to aid the Americans?
2. Why did the French aid the Americans?
3. Identify each of the following individuals: Marquis de Lafayette, Thaddeus Kosciusko, Friedrich von Steuben.
4. Explain why Virginians had both "personal and patriotic reasons" for seeking the defeat of the British.
5. Why was the position taken by the American Indians a significant factor in the course of the Revolution?
6. What contribution did the American navy make to the war effort?
7. Identify each of the following: Captain Gustavus Conyngham, John Paul Jones.
8. Who were the privateers? What motivated their actions? How did they weaken the American cause?
9. What role was played by the French navy?
10. What factors worked against the Americans in the Carolinas?
11. What techniques were employed by General Francis Marion and his forces?
12. What strategies did General Nathaniel Greene employ against the British? What were the results?
13. How did the coordination of American and French actions result in the British defeat at Yorktown in 1781?
14. To the British, why was Yorktown "The World Turned Upside Down?"
15. During the war, what did the Americans learn about European diplomacy?
16. Who were the primary American negotiators of the peace settlement?
17. What were the provisions of the peace treaty?
18. How did the French react to the treaty?
19. What problems remained between the British and the Americans after 1783?
20. What problems did the new nation have with Spain after the Revolution?

Word Study

Fill in each blank in the sentences that follow with the term below that is most appropriate.

alliance   diplomacy   strategy

1. After the British defeat at Saratoga, France entered into an open _____ with the United States.
2. War proved that peaceful resolution of disputes of _____ had failed between the colonists and Great Britain.

Using Your Skills

1. What pictures in this chapter would provide evidence *against* the following generalization? The Americans won the Revolutionary War with little difficulty and little help from foreigners or foreign countries.
2. Refer to the map of the war in the South, 1778–1781, on page 150. Why did the British shift the war to the South in 1778? What did Cornwallis believe was the advantage of his position at Yorktown in 1781? Why did it turn out to be a disadvantage, rather than an advantage?
3. Looking at the map "The United States in 1783" on page 157, list the areas of dispute that could have developed after the peace treaty of 1783.
4. Make a time line of the military events of the Revolutionary War, from 1775 to 1781.

CHAPTER 8
The Challenge of Independence

When the war was over in 1783, there was no general agreement among Americans either to form a single nation or to establish a particular kind of government.

In a sense, cooperating to win the war had been easy. The Patriots knew only too well the value of Ben Franklin's famous statement that if they did not all hang together, they would all hang separately.

In peacetime, however, cooperation did not come as easily. Without the threat of war it was harder to smooth over the existing differences between big states and small ones. Conflict also existed between states with many slaves and states with few, states with western lands and states without them. Even states whose people lived mostly by the profits of seafaring and states whose wealth came largely from plantations found themselves at odds with one another.

The First Continental Congress of 1774 was a gathering of delegates from widely separated colonies, which thought of themselves practically as independent little nations. The next year, the colonies formed a temporary wartime government. In 1776, they declared their independence of Britain. By 1781, all the states had adopted an agreement, the Articles of Confederation, which put this wartime government on a permanent footing.

Though the Articles of Confederation created a "United States of America," each state kept its "sovereignty, freedom and independence," much like a member of the United Nations today. Six years later, what we now know as the Constitutional Convention was held. It began merely as a meeting of representatives sent by their states to undo some troublesome kinks in the Articles. In those thirteen years between 1774 and 1787, Americans advanced toward a strong national government, step by uncertain step.

READING GUIDE

1. **How did the new state governments reflect democratic ideas?**
2. **Why was it difficult to establish a new central government?**
3. **What were the problems under the Confederation?**

An American politician presents his point of view to the people.

1. The New State Governments

Two months before the proclamation of the Declaration of Independence, the Second Continental Congress advised the states to form new governments. The colonies, soon to be independent, had to be changed into self-governing states. Eleven of the thirteen states drew up new constitutions. Connecticut and Rhode Island kept their colonial charters and removed all references to the Crown.

The formation of these new governments reflected how American life differed from European life. James Madison wrote how the world admired the way in which free governments were established in America. It was unusual to see citizens freely debating about a form of government and selecting responsible people to put that government into effect.

The new Americans were not just Europeans in a different setting. Life in the colonies altered people's expectations. Those state representatives who drew up the new constitutions had strong roots in the past. They were influenced by British tradition, such as the Magna Carta and the Bill of Rights of 1689, as well as their American colonial experience. The Americans hoped to design a government that had all the good points of the British government. Naturally, they wanted safeguards to prevent the misunderstandings that had led to their differences with Britain. Americans were also influenced by the writings of Montesquieu, a famous French writer who believed in the separation of power among three branches of government—executive, legislative, and judicial.

An important purpose in establishing new documents was to secure those rights that the colonists felt George III had violated. The typical state constitution included a written bill of rights that listed a variety of liberties. The government could not infringe on these liberties for any reason. Among the freedoms that were protected were those of speech, assembly, and petition. The constitutions also included rights that the British had already gained—the right to moderate bail, to humane punishment, to a speedy trial before a jury of one's peers, and to a writ of *habeas corpus.* Other provisions were based on recent colonial experiences—freedom of the press, freedom of elections, prohibitions against general search warrants, and a standing army.

In keeping with the theory of separation of powers, the writers of most state constitutions provided for a governor with limited powers, a two-house legislature, and a judiciary. In practice, however, the legislature had the most power and the fewest checks on its activities. The new state constitutions left the position of governor almost powerless. In most states, the governor had no power to dissolve the legislature or to veto legislative acts. In many of the states, the governor was elected by the legislature and could be replaced by it. In

habeas corpus
an order requiring that a detained person be brought before a court to decide the legality of his or her detention

fact, constitutional writers in Pennsylvania completely did away with the position. In most states, the judiciary was appointed by the legislature as well.

Not every state was careful about submitting its written constitution to the people for approval. People in Massachusetts, however, were particularly cautious. They were aware of the dangers of allowing the legislature to impose a constitution. If this method were allowed, then some future legislature might change or even abolish the existing one. Massachusetts voters rejected the constitution that was drafted by its legislature. Instead, the towns voted to hold a special constitutional convention (1779). The finished product was then submitted to the people for their approval in 1780. The new nation soon followed Massachusetts in establishing its own lasting constitution.

Separation of Church and State

One of the many democratic changes that took place during the Revolutionary era was the separation of church and state. Prior to that period, most states had *established churches*—churches that were supported by tax money. In New England, it was the Congregational church. In New York and the South, it was the Anglican church. But the ideas of liberty and equality sparked a growing opposition to this union.

In New York and the South, the removal of tax support from the Anglican church began during the war. Without much opposition, the

An example of the grand old churches of New England. This particular church was erected in 1744 and removed in 1811.

constitutions of North Carolina, Georgia, and South Carolina provided for the disestablishment of the Anglican church.

In Virginia, the attack on an established religion occurred after the state constitution was adopted. It was launched by farmers in the back country who objected to paying taxes to support a religion they did not believe in. During the Revolutionary War, wealthy planters had relied heavily on the support of back country farmers to further the cause of independence. As a result of this bond, the planters were willing to listen to the farmers' demands for disestablishment. In 1777, the Virginia legislature repealed the bill requiring tax support of the Anglican church.

In 1786, the Virginia Assembly took a much larger step. The Assembly finally gave in to the reasoning of Thomas Jefferson and to the arguments of James Madison by passing the Virginia Act for Establishing Religious Freedom. This act was a milestone in the quest for true religious freedom. It proclaimed that no person should be forced "to support any religious worship, place, or ministry whatsoever . . . " People's religious beliefs should in no way affect their rights as citizens. This law went further than any others of its day. It became the model for the first amendment to the United States Constitution, which guarantees freedom of religion, speech, assembly, and petition.

The concept of an established church held on more vigorously in New England. There, the Congregationalist clergy were most often Patriots. State support of the Congregationalist church did not end until 1817 in New Hampshire, 1818 in Connecticut, and 1833 in Massachusetts.

The Challenge of Democracy

The gradual separation of church and state was only one of several democratic movements fostered by the Revolution. For example, the ideas of the Revolution made many people more aware of the injustices of slavery. In Massachusetts, slaves brought freedom suits against their masters. In 1781, Quock Walker sued for and won his freedom on the basis that the Massachusetts Constitution declared all persons to be free and equal. This decision virtually ended slavery in Massachusetts. Other New England colonies took similar action. By 1792, abolition societies existed in all states from Massachusetts to Virginia. In spite of the growing antislavery feeling, however, slavery continued in most parts of the country.

During this period, the distribution of land and political power shifted. By the end of the Revolution, the states had taken over lands that were formerly owned by the king, proprietors, and Tories who had fled to Canada. The opening of the West and the availability of the

Tory lands made it easier for the landless classes to own their own property. Land was no longer available only to the wealthy. At the same time, state constitutions lowered the property qualifications for voting. As a result, property ownership and political power were spread over the population. Now, more and more people could have a voice in the government.

Political Reform

As the colonies grew closer to open resistance to Britain, the number and types of people involved in political activities grew. When the colonies belonged to Britain, political power was held by merchants, professional people, and wealthy landowners. But the Revolution had served as a golden opportunity to become politically aware. Mass meetings during the Revolution had allowed thousands of ordinary folks to sample a taste of political action. They had spoken up at meetings, taken part in riots, and joined committees. These people also believed that they had a right to take part in the new government. The state legislatures were made up of delegates from the rural and western-most regions of the states, as well as from the coastal, developed areas. As a result, there were democratic and conservative delegates competing for political control. When the conservative delegates gained control, power tended to remain in the hands of the wealthy. When the democratic forces gained power, other groups got their chance at a slice of the political pie. A contrast of the constitutions adopted by the states of South Carolina, Pennsylvania, and New Jersey will illustrate the results.

Before democratic reforms were instituted, political power was concentrated in the hands of wealthy citizens such as those pictured below. These people are conducting business at a counting house.

165

An example of a colonial New England "saltbox" home. This style of housing had a square frame, two floors and usually an attic.

When the time came for the states to form new governments, South Carolina's Provincial Congress had seventy members available. Apparently, most were from the developed coastal area. The committee they appointed to form the new constitution was made up of wealthy planters, lawyers, and merchants. In order to unite the state against Britain, the committee allowed the new legislature created by the constitution to include delegates from the western portion of the state. Otherwise, the members provided for power to remain in traditional hands. Strict requirements for property ownership determined who could vote and who could run for office. The lower house chose the upper house from among its own members, each of whom served for two years. The two houses selected a council that carried out executive and judicial functions. All officials had to be Protestant. They answered to the legislature, not directly to the people.

In contrast to South Carolina, the farmers, artisans, and small property owners of Pennsylvania had always had more say in their government. They sought a constitution that would expand the democratic features of the government. The convention that drew up the constitution consisted of men with diverse backgrounds.

Pennsylvania's constitution provided for a one-house legislature and no governor. All free taxpayers and their sons who were at least 21 years old elected the legislature annually. Representation for Philadelphia and the counties was in proportion to their taxpaying inhabitants. The sessions of the legislature were usually open to the public. Proceedings and votes were published weekly.

The Pennsylvania constitution provided for a Council of Censors. This council was elected every seven years by the people. It had the power to investigate the actions of the legislature and the Supreme Executive Council. The Council could also call for a convention to amend the constitution.

Unlike South Carolina and Pennsylvania, the New Jersey constitution had a blend of conservative and democratic features. The property qualifications for holding office probably barred 90 percent of the population from eligibility. However, the property qualifications for voting allowed a fairly wide base of political participation. The constitution provided for voting by free Blacks, non-Christians, and women. Compared to the constitutions of other states, New Jersey's was the most democratic in regard to political participation.

Most of the new constitutions contained some form of democratic progress. Yet, there still remained a great deal of ground to cover in order to truly achieve a democratic way of life.

Questions for Discussion

1. How were the new state governments different from the old colonial governments?
2. Why did most state constitutions include a bill of rights and provisions for disestablishment?
3. How democratic were the state constitutions?

2. Formation of the Articles of Confederation

In many ways, the formation of a central government was far more difficult than the establishment of state governments. Many members of the assemblies and conventions that formed the state constitutions had experience with local, colonial government. But they did not have experience in forming a national government, which would require the cooperation and union of the several states.

In 1776, as soon as the Congress began to consider independence, the Continental Congress took steps to set up a constitution for the new nation. John Dickinson headed the committee that wrote the first draft of the Articles of Confederation. This draft was presented to Congress shortly after the Declaration of Independence was ratified.

This first draft provided for the possibility of a strong central government. There were few limitations on the power of Congress and no guarantees of power to the states. Congress was to have power over state boundaries and western lands. It was to have the power to raise an army and a navy, wage war, and make foreign treaties. It could also establish post offices, coin money, and regulate American Indian affairs. Each state was to have one vote.

As members of the Continental Congress began discussing Dickinson's proposals, they realized that it would be difficult to form a strong, central government that would please all the states. Because they had just fought a war to rid themselves of a strong, tyrannical government, the states were very reluctant to give up their newly acquired authority.

A major blow to the development of a strong central government was the amendment proposed by a delegate from North Carolina. He proposed that all **sovereign** power should reside in the states and that Congress would exercise only those powers specifically delegated to it. With Congressional acceptance of this amendment, the chances of the government under the Articles of Confederation evolving into a strong central one were greatly reduced.

The proposal for one vote per state in Congress was accepted. At first, the states with larger populations objected. The small states, however, knew that their vote would be worth less if representation

sovereign
fully independent and self-governing

ARTICLES OF CONFEDERATION

We treat the Constitution with such respect that we often tend to downgrade the Articles of Confederation as a botched job in the making of governments. And yet, there were interesting things about that document, which was the best in the way of a charter that thirteen jealous and warring states could put together in 1777.

For example, did you know that the "United States" had thirteen Presidents before George Washington? The Articles of Confederation provided for a Congress of delegates from each state—as many as the state wished to send. When Congress was not sitting, the business of the United States was to be carried on by a "committee of the whole," meaning thirteen representatives—one from each state. When those thirteen sat down together, they chose one from among their number as "the chair" or "President of the United States." The first person to hold the job was Maryland's John Hanson. This is understandable, since it was Maryland's ratification of the Articles that put them into operation. Of course, he had no power—but he *did* have the title.

And did you know that we almost had a fourteenth state under the Articles, and quite a state at that? The last paragraph of the Articles of Confederation invited Canada to join if it wished. It was thought that the Canadians, too, might be ready to throw off the British yoke. They weren't—but if they had, it is interesting to think what might have followed. Canada would have been by far the greatest "state" in size and the smallest one in population. How would they have voted in the Constitutional Convention? If they had joined, the United States would now extend to the North Pole. The Canadians probably would have subdivided themselves into states. And the United States would have had the state of Quebec, whose official language was French.

However, we were saved all these problems because it did not happen—which shows that sometimes things that do not happen can be as interesting as those that do.

During the Revolutionary War, American folk hero Daniel Boone often led new settlers across the Appalachian mountains and into Kentucky.

was in proportion to population. And those who opposed a strong central government also preferred equal voting rights.

The Articles of Confederation, as drafted by John Dickinson and altered by Congress, were finally accepted by Congress in November 1777. The document was then presented to the states for their ratification. Ratification had to be **unanimous** before the Articles would go into effect. On March 1, 1781, Maryland became the last state to ratify the Articles of Confederation. Maryland had held out, waiting for Virginia to give up its claims to western land. Finally, bowing to the need for an official government, Virginia abandoned the claims.

unanimous
having the agreement and consent of all

Government Under the Articles

The Articles of Confederation were only an agreement of association among the thirteen ex-colonies. Each one, now a sovereign state, furiously guarded its own freedom. Each state had one vote in Congress, regardless of its size or population. Nothing could be done without the consent of two-thirds, or nine, of the states. Furthermore, the Articles could not be changed without the consent of every single state. Above all, Congress could not tax the states. It could ask the states to share the common expenses in proportion to each one's population. But the states had to collect the funds from their own citizens and forward the money, if they chose, to Congress. The people of a state would not pay a cent in taxes directly to the United States. There was no provision for a single *executive* (chief officer) to enforce the laws that Congress made. Nor was there provision for a national court system to decide what was fair or unfair.

The arrangement was perfect for preventing the central government from destroying the individual freedom of the states. However, it left the United States powerless to do many things necessary for a nation to function. The weaknesses would, in time, compel revision of the government.

The Great Land Ordinances of the Confederation

The signing of the Articles of Confederation became possible only when the states that had land claims running deep into the West finally agreed to give them up. These lands became part of the **public domain.** How should this land be given to settlers? Under the colonial system, individuals had been allowed to carve out choice portions wherever they liked, provided they had the royal governor's permission. Such a system made for a wild scramble to get permission and to grab the best plots.

By an *ordinance* (law) of 1785, Congress set up a new plan for the Northwest Territory, consisting of the public domain north of the Ohio River. The public domain was to be surveyed and divided into 15-square-kilometer (6-square-mile) townships. These townships were further divided into square-kilometer (square-mile) sections. Neatly mapped and numbered, such sections were to be sold by the government, at conveniently located offices, to all paying customers. The idea was to have a fair and orderly procession westward. The United States could control land sales by deciding when to open certain areas for sale. The money from land sales would add greatly to the treasury. Additionally, the revenue from one section in every township would be used for public schools.

public domain
land owned by the government that belongs to the community at large

The Ohio Company built a village for new settlers across the Muskingham River from Fort Marmar. This lithograph shows the fort and village as they appeared in 1790.

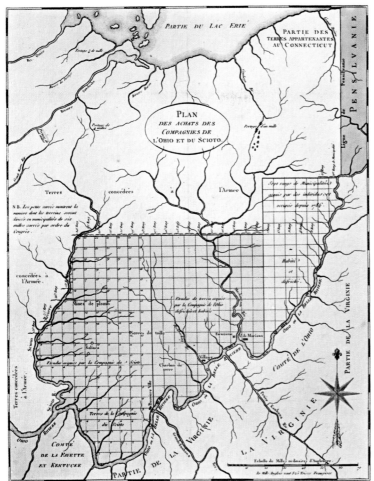

The Northwest Territory

The map on the left shows land areas in the Northwest Territory that were bought by the Ohio and Scioto Companies. The writing is French because the Scioto Company tried to attract settlers from France.

How would settlers in the new lands be governed? After their own unpleasant experience with British attempts to rule them from faraway London, the members of the Confederation Congress knew how hard it would be for them to manage "colonists" deep in the western wilds. So in 1787, they passed another ordinance for the Northwest Territory. Under this ordinance, early settlers would at first be ruled by Congress. This would be followed by a period of limited home rule. When a part of the territory had a population of at least 60,000 free inhabitants, it could become a state and be admitted to the United States. Eventually, five states—Ohio, Illinois, Indiana, Michigan, and Wisconsin—were carved out of this area. This system of gaining statehood was later used for other territories taken or bought by the United States, right up through 1959, when Alaska and Hawaii were admitted as the 49th and 50th states.

These settlers at the Council Bluffs ferry were part of the great American westward expansion.

The Northwest Ordinance was remarkably generous. It told the inhabitants of America's inland "empire" that, as their population grew, they would become equals of the "parent country" on the Atlantic Coast. It guaranteed the basic rights of United States citizens to the territorial residents who were temporarily voteless. The Ordinance even prohibited slavery in the area. Experience was paying off. It was almost as if the former subjects of George III were saying, "This is how you should have treated us!"

Questions for Discussion

1. Define *habeas corpus, sovereign, public domain.*
2. Why were the authors of the Articles of Confederation so fearful of a strong central government? What actions did they take to prevent its development?
3. Why did the states retain sovereignty?
4. How did the land ordinances of the Confederation set up an orderly and efficient system of dealing with the public domain?

The weaknesses of the Articles of Confederation became more apparent after the Revolutionary War. The war was followed by a difficult period of adjustment. The relationship of the states with one another, with the central government, and with foreign powers still had to be determined. One historian called the years between 1783 and 1787 a "critical period" in American history. It was a time in which the states could either fall to squabbling among themselves or bind together in mutual support. Sometimes, the pressures seemed so great that the Americans themselves began to fear that the states would be picked off, one by one, by foreign enemies.

One of the major difficulties facing the new nation was economic disorder. Under the Articles of Confederation, the central government had no power to levy and collect taxes. In most cases, with the exception of New York and Pennsylvania, the state legislatures sent only a fraction of the money requested. This left the Congress constantly short of ready cash. The United States had insufficient money to pay its foreign debts, the war veterans, or even day-to-day expenses.

3. Problems Under the Articles of Confederation

Because furs were in great demand, fur trappers were always among the first settlers in a new territory.

The government was not alone in its financial problems. The whole economy was going through a trying period of readjustment. As British possessions, the colonies had had certain trade benefits. But as part of an independent nation, they no longer enjoyed these benefits. Farmers, planters, and merchants had to find new markets for their products. New industries had to be developed so that the country could stop importing items it could not afford. Had the central government been in control of foreign trade, the states might have been able to protect their industries and get more favorable trading terms. Instead, each of the states was free to make its own arrangement. Britain was able to take advantage of the competition among the states for foreign trade. The free exchange of goods was also hampered among the states. Each state tried to protect its merchants by levying tariffs on goods from other states. This practice made the free exchange of goods difficult and raised prices to buyers.

Currency Problems

Perhaps the most serious economic problems resulted from the lack of a uniform, stable currency. During the war, Congress and each of the thirteen states issued paper money. By the end of the war, however, the paper money was almost worthless. It was backed neither by silver or gold, nor by a government in which the people had great faith. Merchants would not accept the paper money in payment of debts, and the states would not accept it for payment of taxes. This caused serious hardship for debtors. Many farmers did not have the money to pay their debts for land and supplies. The farmers wanted the states to issue paper money again and to declare that the money had to be accepted in payment of debts.

Rhode Island and North Carolina passed laws making the paper money *legal tender*—acceptable for the payment of debts. In Rhode Island, if a merchant refused payment in the paper money, the debtor could bring the payment to the nearest judge. Many merchants and other creditors closed up their businesses and fled the state so that they could not be found and could thus avoid accepting payment.

Shays' Rebellion

Farmers in Massachusetts were very seriously affected by the currency problem. Before the war, they had enjoyed a substantial amount of income as a result of their trade with the British West Indies. When the colonies severed their ties with Great Britain, the farmers lost out on this business. They were now hard pressed to pay their debts and taxes. In Massachusetts, the merchants and owners of businesses controlled the state legislature. They resisted the pressure to print paper money and to declare it legal currency. Under law, that

Three early American coins used as legal tender.

meant that farmers who were unable to pay their debts would lose their farms. But under the leadership of a war veteran, Daniel Shays, numbers of them blocked the steps of courthouses and prevented the judges from deciding their cases. Later, Shays' men attacked a government arsenal in Springfield but were driven away by Massachusetts militia. This caused the uprising to collapse.

However, Shays' Rebellion was a serious matter. Forcible defiance of the law could lead to *anarchy*—a condition in which there is no government at all. Then, life might become a free-for-all, totally lacking in law and order. Some leaders of the Revolution began to see things as the British had in 1774. Where would resistance end? "Are your people mad?" wrote George Washington to a friend in Massachusetts. A British paper crowed that the Yankees, "having overturned the government under which they were born and bred are unwilling to submit to any kind of government."

Foreign Affairs

The central government was too weak to protect the interests of the new nation abroad or at home. British policies hurt American traders. American ships were barred from Canada and the West Indies. Since most traders carried on a triangular trade between Europe, the West Indies, and America, most of the trade between America and Britain had to be carried on British ships. As long as that situation existed, American shipping and shipbuilding interests suffered.

Left: In September 1786, armed protesters led by Daniel Shays appeared at a courthouse in Springfield, Massachusetts. They hoped to stop the court from acting against debtors. Violence was avoided when both sides agreed to disperse, and the court adjourned. Right: In January 1787, Shays and his men returned to Springfield to attack the state arsenal. This time, Massachusetts troops drove them off. Shortly afterward, the rebellion collapsed. However, most of the reforms sought by the protesters soon became law.

Another difficulty in relations with Great Britain was that Britain had failed to fulfill the terms of the peace treaty. Britain had agreed to evacuate the military and fur trading posts in the Northwest Territory. The British claimed that they were not leaving all the posts because the United States had failed to carry out their part of the peace treaty, relating to Tory claims for damages. The British, in fact, did not want to lose control of the valuable fur trade in the territory south of the Canadian border. The British held on to the fur trading posts. The settlers in Canada continued to trade with the American Indians. They provided them with various supplies and guns in exchange for their furs. The American settlers appealed to Congress to do something. But Congress was powerless to help. (See map on page 171.)

Another serious threat to the welfare of the United States was posed by Spain. The Spanish governor of the land that Spain still controlled in the South tried to lure the western settlers into seceding from the United States. In return, he would grant them the right of navigation on the Mississippi and free access to New Orleans. The western settlers needed access to New Orleans as a natural outlet for their exports. It was far easier to ship their goods down the Mississippi than to carry them over the Appalachians and to the East Coast. Some settlers and officials, especially after being bribed, were tempted to take the Spanish up on their offer. When John Jay negotiated a treaty that endangered the settlers' claims to free access, many western settlers were nearly driven into the Spanish trap. But Congress was aware of the problem and refused to ratify the treaty. Negotiations with Spain broke down. Thus, the issue of access to the Mississippi and to New Orleans was not settled until 1795.

Another sign of weakness was the inability of the central government to provide protection for American shipping. American ships were being attacked in the Mediterranean by small nations off the coast of North Africa. The United States had neither the navy nor the diplomatic clout to prevent the piracy. This was one more problem that spurred people to look for a better way to govern themselves.

Questions for Discussion

1. Define *anarchy*, *legal tender*.
2. What were the most serious problems faced by the United States under the Articles of Confederation? Which problem would you attempt to solve first? Why?
3. Why was the currency problem so serious? Whom did it affect the most?
4. Why did Shays' Rebellion make many Americans fearful of anarchy?

Chapter 8 Review

Summary Questions for Discussion

1. When and why did the Second Continental Congress advise the thirteen colonies to form the new governments?
2. What was the influence of each of the following on the creation of the new state governments: (a) the character of American life, (b) British tradition, and (c) the writings of Montesquieu.
3. What is the purpose of the bills of rights? What were some of the new rights listed?
4. How was the theory of separation of powers put into practice?
5. Why was Massachusetts careful to submit its written constitution to the people for approval?
6. What did the Virginia Act for Establishing Religious Freedom state?
7. What effect did the Revolution have on (a) slavery and (b) the distribution of land and political power?
8. Show how the constitutions of South Carolina and New Jersey reflect the backgrounds of the delegates chosen to write them.
9. Why was John Dickinson's original proposal for a constitution altered by the Continental Congress?
10. Concerning the Articles of Confederation:

(a) What was the amendment proposed by a delegate from North Carolina? What were the effects of its passage? (b) Who favored equal voting rights in Congress? Why?
11. What weaknesses existed in the Articles of Confederation?
12. What was the ordinance of 1785 concerning the Northwest Territory?
13. Why was the Ordinance of 1787 considered generous?
14. Why is the period between 1783 and 1787 considered a "critical period" in American history?
15. What were the limitations faced by the central government in each of the following areas and what were the effects? (a) taxes, (b) foreign trade, (c) currency
16. Why did Daniel Shays lead a rebellion in Massachusetts? How was it significant?
17. How did British policies hurt American traders?
18. What aspects of the peace treaty were not fulfilled by the British? What were the effects?
19. What problems did the United States face with Spain?
20. Why were pirates in the Mediterranean a problem?

Word Study

Fill in each blank in the sentences that follow with the term below that is most appropriate.

unanimous	public domain	anarchy	legal tender
sovereign	established churches	ordinance	*habeas corpus*

1. The states wished to retain _____ power.
2. Fearing imprisonment without due cause, they required writs of _____.
3. Seeking separation of church and state, states almost eliminated _____.
4. Laws or _____(s) were passed outlining procedures for dealing with the land owned by all the states together.
5. Some states passed laws that made paper money _____, acceptable for payment of debts.
6. Unless the government maintained control, there was fear of _____.
7. The states ratified the Articles of Confederation by _____ vote.

CHAPTER 9

Forming a New Government

In May 1787, the focus of the young nation once more fell on Philadelphia. There, a group of delegates gathered from all the states except Rhode Island. Their objective was to revise the Articles of Confederation. As they arrived in the city, most of them probably had well-conceived notions of what they thought was wrong with the Articles. However, few of them expected that it would take four months before they would finish what they had set out to do.

Among the delegates were some of the best minds in the country. Yet, not one person could claim that the ideas he brought with him had not been molded and reshaped. The final document, although signed by a majority of the delegates, was probably, in part, a disappointment to them all.

Today, some of those ideas considered by the delegates would seem strange indeed. Alexander Hamilton proposed that the Senate be appointed for life. He sought a strong executive, who would be elected indirectly by the people and would also serve for life. The executive would have a veto that could not be overridden.

Gouverneur Morris favored many of Hamilton's proposals. He wanted the Senate to represent the wealthy. He also wanted new states to enter the Union on an inferior basis with the older states. Morris felt that the "remote wilderness" was not a place for a person to develop political experience.

On the other side of the issues were men such as James Wilson. He wanted broad suffrage. He proposed a legislature and an executive elected by all eligible voters. Benjamin Franklin, in turn, saw no need for an executive at all. He favored government by a one-house legislature, free from checks and balances.

Finally, after months of discussion in the hot, muggy rooms of the State House, the Constitution was written. This document became the foundation for the national and state governments of the United States. The Constitution still serves as a model for representative government throughout the world.

READING GUIDE

1. **Why is compromise so necessary in a democratic nation?**
2. **What are the basic principles of the Constitution?**
3. **How did Washington serve as a unifying symbol?**

George Washington addressing the Constitutional Convention.

Robert Morris (above) and Gouverneur Morris (right) were both Pennsylvania delegates to the Federal Convention in 1787.

1. Making and Ratifying the Constitution

Given time, the Confederation might have been able to solve some of its problems when prosperity returned to the land. But by 1786, thoughtful people in all the states were becoming convinced that basic changes were needed. It was not enough to get the states to pay their requisitions or to stop levying taxes on each other's products or to agree as a group to honor treaties with foreign powers. Something further had to be done.

In a move to improve cooperation among the states in trade and commerce, Virginia called a meeting to be held in Annapolis, Maryland. Only five states attended. However, they made an important decision concerning what should be done about the weaknesses of the Articles of Confederation. The Annapolis Convention made a proposal to Congress that a gathering of delegates be held in Philadelphia the following year. The purpose of that gathering was to consider the "defects" in the Articles of Confederation. The members of the Annapolis Convention thought that more states would heed a request for a meeting if the invitation came from the Congress.

At first, Congress was not at all sure that it wanted to call for a new convention. The members recognized that the government needed improvement. But they differed over how the changes should be made. Some thought that Congress should exercise the power to amend the Articles of Confederation. Others thought that state conventions should be held. Each of these conventions would then select members with the power to work together to change the constitution. Finally, Congress decided to carry out the request of the Annapolis Convention. By doing so, it signaled its own end.

Major General Charles Pinckney (left) was one of South Carolina's representatives at the Federal Convention.

The Delegates

So in May of 1787, a group of representatives chosen by their state legislatures met once more in Philadelphia. This was the Quaker city where the Second Continental Congress had proclaimed America's independence eleven summers before. By any standard, this new gathering was one of able and influential people. The majority were college graduates. Several were members or former members of college faculties. Many were well schooled in history and philosophy. Others were noted lawyers. Almost all had served in state legislatures or Congress. By today's standards, it was a fairly youthful group. The average age of the delegates was forty-two. Five members were under thirty and only four exceeded sixty. At eighty-one years of age, Benjamin Franklin was the oldest.

In all, fifty-five delegates from twelve states took part in the Federal Convention. Among them were some of the outstanding revolutionary figures. George Washington headed the Virginia delegation, which also included James Madison and Edmund Randolph. Alexander Hamilton represented New York. Pennsylvania's delegation included Gouverneur Morris, Robert Morris, and Benjamin Franklin. South Carolina's representatives included a wartime governor, John Rutledge, and General Charles Pinckney. Thomas Jefferson, John Adams, and Thomas Paine did not attend because they were in Europe. Patrick Henry refused to attend because he was a strong supporter of the Articles of Confederation. As he put it, he "smelled a rat." And Samuel Adams was not chosen to attend.

When the delegates assembled, they unanimously chose George

this clause first ?

peachments of Officers of the United States; to all cases of Admiralty and Maritime Jurisdiction; to Controversies between two or more States, (~~between a State and~~) between a State and citizens of another State, between citizens of different States, and between a State or the citizens thereof and foreign States, citizens or subjects. (In cases of Impeachment, cases affecting Ambassadors, other Public Ministers and Consuls, and those in which a State shall be party, ~~this jurisdiction shall be original.~~ *the supreme Court shall have original jurisdiction* In all the other cases beforementioned ~~the jurisdiction shall be appellate,~~ *both as to law and fact* with such exceptions and under such regulations as the Legislature shall make. ~~The Legislature may assign any part of the jurisdiction abovementioned (except the trial of the President of the United States) in the manner and under the limitations which it shall think proper, to such Inferior Courts as it shall constitute from time to time.~~

this clause first ?
the Sect C!

Sect. 4. The trial of all crimes (except in cases of impeachment) shall be by Jury — and such trial shall be held in the State where the said crimes shall have been committed: but when not committed within any State, then the trial shall be at such place or places as the legislature may direct. — The privilege of the writ of Habeas Corpus shall not be suspended: unless where in cases of rebellion or invasion the public safety may require it — *agreed —*

~~Sect. 4. The trial of all criminal offences (except in cases of impeachments) shall be in the State where they shall be committed; and shall be by jury.~~

Sect. 5. Judgment, in cases of Impeachment, shall not extend further than to removal from office, and disqualification to hold and enjoy any office of honour, trust or profit under the United States. But the party convicted shall nevertheless be liable and subject to indictment, trial, judgment and punishment, according to law.

agreed

XII

a remit bip'd credit nor on the treaty make Laws

No State shall coin money; nor grant letters of marque and reprisal; nor enter into any treaty, alliance, or confederation; nor grant any title of nobility.

XIII

agreed.

No State, without the consent of the Legislature of the United States, shall ~~emit bills of credit, make any thing but specie a tender in payment of debts~~ lay imposts or duties on imports; nor keep troops or ships of war in time of peace; nor enter into any agreement or compact with another State, or with any foreign power; nor engage in any war, unless it shall be actually invaded by enemies, or the danger of invasion be so imminent, as not to admit of a delay, until the Legislature of the United States can be consulted.

XIIII

agreed. —

The citizens of each State shall be entitled to all privileges and immunities of citizens in the several States.

XIV

agreed.

Any person charged with treason, felony, or ~~high misdemeanor~~ *other crime* in any State, who shall flee from justice, and shall be found in any other State, shall, on demand of the Executive Power of the State from which he fled, be delivered up and removed to the State having jurisdiction of the offence.

+ If any Person bound to Service or labor in any of the United States, shall escape into another State, he or She shall not be discharged from such service or labor, in consequence of any regulations subsisting in the State to which they escape, but shall be delivered up to the Person justly claiming their service or labor.

Referr'd to the Com of five Aug. 28.

XVI

Full faith ~~shall~~ *further* be given in each State to the acts ~~of the Legislatures, and to the~~ records, and judicial proceedings of ~~the courts and magistrates of~~ every other State; *and the Legislature may by general laws prescribe the manner in which such acts, records, and proceedings, shall be proved and the effect thereof.*

XVII

New States may be admitted by the Legislature into this ~~government~~ — but no New State shall be hereafter formed or erected within the jurisdiction of any of the present States ~~without the consent of~~ the Legislature of such State as well as of the General Legislature.

Nor shall any State be formed by the junction of two or more States, or parts thereof without the consent of the Legislatures of such States as well as of the Legislature of the United States.

~~New States lawfully constituted or established within the limits of the United States may be admitted, by the Legislature, into this government; but to such admission three fourths of the Members present in each House shall be necessary. If a new State shall arise within the limits of any of the present States, the consent of the Legislatures of such States shall be also necessary to its admission.~~

XVII

Washington as the president of the convention. They then adopted rules of procedure. In a move that benefited the small states, each state was granted one vote. Near the beginning of the convention, the members reached another important agreement. They agreed that their real mission was to begin at the beginning and rewrite the Articles entirely. They agreed, also, to keep the proceedings secret, so that they could finish the job free from public pressure. Through four hot summer months, they worked six days a week under the familiar and trusted leadership of George Washington. Not all the delegates stayed the whole time, nor were they all pleased with the results. Only thirty-nine delegates signed the final document. The state of Rhode Island sent no delegates. But a group of influential merchants from that state communicated to the convention that they supported the proceedings.

Since the participants maintained the secrecy to which they were pledged, information about what took place at the convention did not become public until the nineteenth century. This information came primarily from two sources. The secretary of the convention, William Jackson, recorded the votes and resolutions of the delegates. He turned his records over to George Washington. In 1796, Washington gave them to the State Department. These papers and some additional material collected from the delegates were eventually edited by John Quincy Adams and printed by the government in 1818. In addition, James Madison kept painstaking notes of the meetings. Since he never missed a day of the convention, his notes were quite thorough. They were published in 1840, four years after his death. Thus, Madison's notes provide the clearest picture of the nature of the discussions and arguments that took place.

The Great Compromise

The finished Constitution was a set of compromises, and compromises always anger some people. However, compromise was needed, for every delegate was determined to defend the interests of his own state as well as those of the nation. Much of what the large states wanted was included in the Virginia Plan. This plan was presented by Edmund Randolph on May 29. It called for a strong central government consisting of three branches. The legislative branch would have two houses. Membership in both houses was to be based on population. The large states reasoned that the states with the greatest number of taxpayers should have the largest representation. But the small states feared that they would be permanent losers in a lawmaking body that made decisions by counting noses.

On June 15, after two weeks of discussion, William Paterson of New Jersey presented the small-state plan. It called for a weak central

James Wilson, a lawyer and one of the delegates from Pennsylvania, successfully fought for adoption of the Constitution in his home state.

government and a one-house legislature with equal representation. It was based on the theory of state sovereignty.

By the end of June, the convention had decided that the new government should have a two-house legislature. But the question of how many Representatives and Senators each state should have was still not settled. Both the large and the small states were insistent that it should be their way. With everyone so unwilling to give in, it appeared that the success or failure of the whole convention would depend on how this issue was settled.

The delegates appointed a committee of one member from each state to discuss the problem. They decided in favor of a plan offered by the delegates from Connecticut. On July 16, the members of the convention voted on the committee's proposal. They agreed to have a legislature consisting of two chambers—a Senate in which each state was equally represented, and a House of Representatives based on population (Article I, Sections 2 and 3). Slaveholding states wanted their slaves counted toward representation in the House. However, they did not want slaves counted if Congress collected a tax from each state in proportion to its population. The compromise was to count each slave as three-fifths of a person (Article I, Section 2).

So it went, down the line, issue after issue. The slave trade might be prohibited, but not before 1808 (Article I, Section 9). Duties might be placed on imports (Article I, Section 8) to protect Northern manufacturers from foreign competition, but not on exports (Article I, Section 9), which were most important to the Southern states. There were hot tempers in the hot meeting rooms. But problems were

Bottom Left: The Declaration of Independence, the Articles of Confederation, and the United States Constitution were all signed at Independence Hall, Philadelphia, seen here as it appeared in 1778. Bottom Right: Supporters of the Constitution celebrate its ratification in New York with a thirteen-gun salute.

BEN FRANKLIN

Why I Favor the Constitution "I confess that there are several parts of this constitution which I do not at present approve, but I am not sure I shall never approve them; for having lived long, I have experienced many instances of being obliged by better information or fuller consideration to change opinions. . . . It is there that the older I grow, the more apt I am to doubt my own judgement of others.

". . . . I agree to this constitution with all its faults, if they are such, because I think a general government is necessary for us, and there is no form of government but what may be a blessing to the people if well administered, and believe farther that this is likely to be well administered for a course of years, and can only end in despotism (tyran-ny), as other forms have done before it, when the people shall become so corrupted as to need despotic government, being incapable of any other.

"I doubt, too, whether any other convention we can obtain may be able to make a better convention. For when you assemble a number of men to have the advantage of their joint wisdom, you inevitably assemble with those men all their prejudices, their passions, their errors of opinion, their local interests, and their selfish views. From such an assembly can a perfect production be expected?

"Thus, I consent, Sir, to this convention because I expect no better, and because I am not sure that it is not the best. . . ."

settled by debate. After years of trouble, the era of violence was ending. The experienced politicians knew the time to build had come.

The Struggle Over Ratification

As the delegates rode home from Philadelphia, the brilliant autumn countryside that they saw from their coach windows was the scene of lively debate. This was because the delegates had provided that the Constitution be ratified by conventions in the states. Approval must come from the people, the source of power. In meeting houses, taverns, and parlors, in cities and in country towns, the people read hastily printed copies of the Constitution and made preparations for choosing delegates to the ratifying conventions. The *Federalists*—those who supported the Constitution—were soon exchanging verbal shots with the *anti-Federalists*—those who opposed the Constitution.

The anti-Federalists were generally those who saw no benefit and much possible harm in a strong central government. They pointed out that the Constitution as drafted did not protect individual liberties. No limit was put on the taxing powers of Congress. The President, as Commander in Chief of the armies, might use them to make himself a **dictator**. Also, the anti-Federalists feared that the lifetime appointments of Supreme Court justices would make for a judicial aristocracy that would not have to answer to the people.

dictator
a ruler who has total authority without limits or checks by others

Above all, the states that had proudly resisted England's tyranny were reduced to what some thought was second-class status. The Preamble to the Constitution spoke of "We the people" and made no mention of states. States could no longer protect themselves with armies and navies, make their own treaties with American Indians or friendly powers, or coin money if needed (Article I, Section 8). Article VI clearly said that the Constitution was the "Supreme Law of the Land" and that even state judges should obey it, whatever their own state constitutions or laws might say.

To answer all these objections, the Federalists pointed out the urgent need for union. Alexander Hamilton, James Madison, and John Jay published the *Federalist* to explain and defend the proposed Constitution. They stressed the limits and checks on the national government's powers. They agreed that if the Constitution were ratified, they would immediately support constitutional *amendments*, or changes, to guarantee individual liberties. These first ten amendments, known as the Bill of Rights, were ratified in 1791. They appealed to all those who had something to gain from a government that could stand up to foreign powers and promote commerce and prosperity. It was worth taking some risks with a strong government, they said, to gain these ends. All government was a calculated risk in which people traded some liberty in return for protection from disorder.

The Federalists convinced a majority of people. Beginning with Delaware, one after another, the states ratified the Constitution. By June of 1788, nine states had joined—enough to start the new government (Article VII). New York and Virginia, two big, key states whose absence would have been crippling, ratified the Constitution that summer of 1788, after hot debate. In Virginia, two outstanding men opposed one another. Bold Patrick Henry led the fight against the Constitution. And the more reserved James Madison was a leading supporter. Madison's logical arguments, along with proposals for a bill of rights, carried the day for the Federalists. In a very close vote, Virginia's convention ratified the Constitution on June 25. The news was carried to New York as quickly as possible. Thus, the cause of the anti-Federalists was weakened, and Hamilton's gamble to stall New York's vote until the results were known from Virginia, paid off. With barely a vote to spare, New York's convention ratified the Constitution. North Carolina and Rhode Island held out until after the new government was in office.

Of course, hard feelings resulted. In Pennsylvania, for example, Federalist crowds lit a bonfire to celebrate. But enraged anti-Federalists drove them away and "converted the intended joy into mourning" by burning a copy of the Constitution. But the attitude of most anti-Federalists was that of Patrick Henry of Virginia, who said

James Madison, chief promoter of the first ten amendments to the Constitution, known as the Bill of Rights.

he would "patiently wait in expectation of seeing that government changed." The people's willingness to wait and see what the new government actually did was what saved the nation from further turmoil. Trust was the real miracle that occurred at Philadelphia.

Questions for Discussion

1. Define *Federalist, dictator, amendment.*
2. What important compromises were written into the Constitution?
3. Why did the anti-Federalists fear a strong central government?
4. Why did the Federalists stress the urgent need for union?

2. The Basic Principles of the Constitution

The Constitution underwent many changes before it was ready for ratification. Even after the Constitution was ratified, it continued to change. The first changes came by amendment—the passage of the Bill of Rights.

The major states had voted for ratification on the assurance that a bill of rights would be added to the Constitution. The state governments that were formed at the time of the Revolution had written their own bills of rights. Many people considered it a step backward to accept a new central government whose actions were not similarly restrained.

James Madison provided the primary force behind the proposal of a bill of rights by the new Congress. Many members of Congress were anxious to complete matters of commerce and taxation in the first session of Congress. They tried to postpone indefinitely taking up the matter of amendments to the Constitution. However, James Madison would not let the issue drop. In an eloquent address to Congress on June 8, 1789, Madison explained the need for a bill of rights. He also outlined what he thought it should include. After three months of discussion, twelve amendments received the necessary two-thirds vote of the House and the Senate. The proposed amendments then went to the states for ratification. Only ten of the twelve received the required approval of three-quarters of the state legislatures. These ten amendments, known as the Bill of Rights, officially became part of the Constitution on December 15, 1791, after they were ratified by Virginia.

In addition to the Bill of Rights, decisions of the Supreme Court have also changed the Constitution. An early example is the case of *Marbury* v. *Madison* in 1803. Just before President John Adams (the nation's second president) left office, he made several appointments to the federal judiciary. One of these appointees, William Marbury, was confirmed by the Senate, but did not receive his commission before Adams left office. The new Secretary of State, Madison, held up the documents that would have made Marbury's appointment official.

Marbury sued for a Supreme Court writ to force Madison to give him his commission. According to the Judiciary Act of 1789, the Supreme Court had jurisdiction over these matters. Chief Justice Marshall refused to grant the writ. He said that the part of the act on which Marbury based his claim was unconstitutional. Congress cannot pass a law giving the Supreme Court jurisdiction not granted it by the Constitution. Marshall concluded that "a legislative act contrary to the Constitution is not law." He said that the Constitution was the "paramount law," and was to be interpreted by the courts. This power of *judicial review* (the right of the Supreme Court to determine if a law is constitutional) has made the Supreme Court a most important part of the American political system.

Finally, although the Constitution did not provide for certain general practices, custom has made them a part of American political life. For example, the role of political parties in selecting candidates is familiar to most Americans, a practice unforeseen by the framers of the Constitution. The various customs that have developed over the years have been dubbed the "unwritten constitution."

The Constitution has changed with the times. Yet, its basic

THE BILL OF RIGHTS

1st Amendment: (a) Guarantees our right to worship as we please, or not to have a religion if we prefer; (b) guarantees freedom of speech and of the press; (c) guarantees our right to assemble in groups for any peaceful purpose; (d) guarantees our right to petition government officials with our protests or opinions.

2nd Amendment: Protects our right to keep and bear arms.

3rd Amendment: Protects our right not to have to keep soldiers in our homes, except in times of war when laws must be passed if this is to be allowed.

4th Amendment: Limits the conditions under which the police may search our homes and seize evidence and people.

5th Amendment: (a) Protects our right not to have to stand trial for a serious offense unless a grand jury has voted an indictment; (b) protects us from being tried twice for the same crime; (c) protects us from having to testify against ourselves; (d) protects us from losing life, freedom, or property without due process of law; (e) protects us from having property taken away for public use without being paid a fair price for it.

6th Amendment: Guarantees the right to a speedy and public trial with the crime one is accused of well defined.

7th Amendment: Guarantees our right to a jury trial in all disputes about property over $20.

8th Amendment: Protects us from cruel and unusual punishment and from fines and bail charges greater than the crime warrants.

9th Amendment: Gives to the people all rights not specifically mentioned or listed in the Constitution.

10th Amendment: Reserves for the states or the people all rights not given to the federal government.

Many more amendments have been added to the Constitution since the Bill of Rights. These amendments have made it possible for the Constitution to meet the needs of a changing nation.

A commemorative engraving of George Washington. The thirteen linking circles represent the thirteen original colonies. The top circle represents the Federal government.

principles have remained the same. The first of these is *federalism*, a principle of government in which power is distributed between a central authority and a number of territorial units. Federalism in the United States works as follows. The federal government has certain *exclusive powers*—powers held by only one level of government. These powers are spelled out in Article I, Section 8. For instance, the federal government alone may coin money and make treaties. But the Tenth Amendment plainly says that any power not clearly given to the federal government remains with the states or with the people. Therefore, the states also have exclusive powers, such as the right to regulate education and marriage. There are also some *concurrent powers*—powers shared by two governments. Both governments, federal and state, may collect taxes. Both have courts to interpret the laws. In short, the Constitution's answer to the question of whether there should be a single central government or many state governments is "both!"

All was not peaceful, as conflicts between the federal and state governments began to spring up at once. But a second principle of the Constitution is that the courts, rather than the armed forces, settle these disputes. All judges in all courts—state and federal—recognize the Constitution, and laws or treaties made under its authority, as the supreme law of the land. And all officials, in the long run, bow to the rulings of the courts. Only on rare occasions has it been necessary to use force to carry out a court decision. One such exception was the use of federal troops to bring about the court-ordered integration of Central High School in Little Rock, Arkansas, in 1957. And only once, during our Civil War, did the system break down to the point where bayonets and guns replaced judges' opinions in deciding a contest between the nation and the states.

Finally, the powers of the federal government are carefully limited by the Bill of Rights, which specifically forbids the federal government to do certain things—such as establishing an official religion (First Amendment). In addition, as you shall see, the powers of each branch—executive, legislative, and judicial—of the federal government are limited by a system of checks and balances.

The creators of the Constitution were always struggling for a balance between a government strong enough to get things done yet not strong enough to take away individual liberties. One of the reasons they managed so well was that their opinions reflected certain attitudes held by most Americans.

The Powers of the Presidency

Those who met in Philadelphia wanted a strong executive who could and would see that the nation's intentions were carried out. They

George III, crowned King of Great Britain at the age of 22, is shown here in his coronation robes. He typified the kind of chief executive Americans did not want.

wanted a leader. So, they gave the President command of the armed forces and the diplomatic service and the right to choose many federal officials, as well as the heads of executive departments (Article II, Section 2). All of these officials were to be responsible to the President.

At the same time, the checks and balances of the Constitution put many restrictions on the President. Equally important as the Constitutional limits were people's feelings that the President should be someone like themselves. They did not want a regal, pompous figure who ruled from on high like George III. Even so, one anti-Federalist grumbled that the chief executive would be an "elective king."

The first Congress after the Constitution was ratified decided not to address the President by any elegant titles such as "His Elective Highness," a name suggested by Vice-President John Adams. Since Adams was rather roly-poly, one congressman made fun of his idea by suggesting that the Vice President be called "His Rotundity." A simple title suited President George Washington. He was a dignified man, but he cared for neither fancy clothing nor fancy names. The tradition he set was carried further by the third President, Thomas Jefferson, who walked to his own inauguration and, in his slippers, entertained a startled British ambassador in the White House.

The ideal of a President as an ordinary person who puts aside private business to serve the people has lasted to this day. Even though the office is one of the most powerful on Earth, its exercise requires that an individual win the people's loyalty. That is why the President still takes part in such public ceremonies as tossing out the first ball at the season's opening baseball game. Compare this practice to that of the Incan nobles on page 9 of Chapter 1, who used to turn the first shovelful of earth at the planting of the year's crop.

The Extent of Democracy in the Constitution

The Constitution also reflects the competing viewpoints of its makers on the question of how aristocratic or democratic the new government should be. As lawyers and people of property, many of the founders distrusted what they called the "passions" of the "mob," or those who might have nothing to lose from a sudden overthrow of the government. Because the power of the federal government was limited, the power of any voting majority was also limited.

Furthermore, parts of the national government were, and some still are, removed from popular control. Until the Seventeenth Amendment was passed in 1913, Senators were chosen by the state legislatures instead of directly by the people (Article I, Section 3). The President was not, and still is not, directly chosen by the people (Article II, Section I). Instead, the people of each state choose

Presidential electors, who then formally elect the President.

On the other hand, the Constitution had some surprising democratic provisions at a time when monarchy and aristocracy were common practice throughout the world. Representatives had to appeal to the voters for reelection every two years (Article I, Section 2). No property qualifications were required for holding any federal office. No religious test could be imposed on the holders of any such office (Article VI). Persons eligible to vote for members of the lower houses of state legislatures had to be allowed the right to vote for members of the House of Representatives (Article I, Section 2). Some defenders of the Constitution expected that representatives would be chosen not just by the rich, the educated, and the powerful, but also by people from ordinary walks of life.

Another democratic feature, and perhaps the most important, was that the ratification of the Constitution was accomplished by popularly elected state conventions. This method recognized that the power of the government resided in the people and not in any legislature created by a constitution. James Madison said that the difference between a government dependent on legislatures and one dependent on the people is "the true difference between a league, or treaty, and a Constitution."

In the 1780s, a movement toward democracy existed throughout the country. This feeling could be seen in the action of states like Virginia, which established freedom of religion and forbade practices that had tended to restrict land ownership to the rich. Even in the South, people talked of a day when slavery might vanish. Many states considered relaxing laws that imposed harsh punishments for small

An English artist painted this watercolor to poke fun at the "best families" in England on their way to greet the King at the palace.

crimes or threw people in to jail for debts.

This current of democracy was to continue as the young country grew. The feeling of the people was different from other societies, where a hereditary aristocracy or a crowned king governed. Rather, Americans believed what Thomas Jefferson had said—that people might not be angels, but there were no angels in human form fit to govern them. Unlike that of English aristocrats, the power of American politicians, who had to seek votes from the people, was not a matter of privilege.

Both the ideal of a President who leads by example and that of the democratic politician taking his case to his "bosses," the people, were embodied in the Constitution in reaction to the colonists' experience under British rule. The hard-working people of young America had been resentful when tracts of land or public office and honor went to the friends and favorites of royal governors and titled proprietors.

Government as the Servant of the People

Yet, one principle the Americans got directly from the English experience was that the individual enjoyed certain rights that the government was forbidden to take away. This differed from some ancient societies that looked upon the king or chieftain as a god personified who therefore had a god's total power over all subjects. Dictatorships also look upon the individual as far less important than society or its political form, the government.

But eighteenth-century Americans thought of the government as a servant and not as a master of the people. They knew that government

The Constitution provides a system of checks to balance the power among the three branches of government. Above: This 1882 cartoon praised President Chester Arthur's veto of a bill that would have kept Chinese laborers out of the United States for 20 years. Below Right: In 1952 the Supreme Court ruled that President Harry Truman's seizure of the steel mills was unconstitutional. The Court's decision inspired this cartoon.

194

had great powers, with its armies and police officers. Therefore, they made a list of things that the government was firmly forbidden to do with that power. The first ten amendments are quite clear. Congress may make no law limiting the freedom of speech, press, or religion; excessive bail shall not be imposed; no person shall be compelled to be a witness against himself or herself in a criminal case. The Bill of Rights guarantees absolutely the rights of petition and of freedom from unreasonable search and unfounded arrest. It assures speedy jury trials. The Bill of Rights also raises other barriers against a government that might try to break the spirit of its people by cruel punishments, like that being inflicted on the English Quaker at the right. And the Ninth and Tenth Amendments state that this list of prohibitions is not complete. The states and the people keep all rights not expressly given to the central authorities by the Constitution. These rights are called *residual powers*.

The Bill of Rights has been challenged many times, especially in times of war. One challenge came as early as 1798, when Congress passed the Alien and Sedition Acts, severely limiting freedom of speech. Such laws have always been fought and eventually repealed.

The punishment for this seven-teenth-century Englishman is a tongue-branding. The Eighth Amendment forbids cruel and unusual punishments.

Checks and Balances Provided by the Constitution

The Constitution was a kind of written contract between the people and the government, a contract created by the people themselves. As such, it ingeniously divided the power of the federal government among the various branches. Each branch was able to block or slow down the others. The Constitition was a carefully thought-out answer to the ever-present problem: how to trust government enough not to cripple it and so deprive people of its advantages, yet not trust it so much that it enslaves the people.

The system of checks and balances helped to provide the answer to this problem. Congress may pass laws, but a President who thinks the laws unwise or hasty can *veto* (reject) them. Yet, if two-thirds of the members of each house of Congress still support the law, they can override the veto (Article I, Section 7).

The President can appoint people to high offices. But if the Senate thinks the people poorly qualified, it can refuse to *confirm* (approve) them (Article II, Section 2), as has happened many times. The President can order the army and navy into military action without waiting for Congressional approval. However, only Congress has the power to declare war and to provide money for the armed services.

The Constitution also provides that the House of Representatives can **impeach** a President it feels is guilty of serious illegal acts. If the Senate, which would serve as jury in an impeachment trial, votes to

impeach
charge a public offical with misconduct in office

195

convict by a two-thirds majority, the President is removed from office. This provision has been used only once, in 1868 when President Andrew Johnson was impeached and came within one vote of being convicted by the Senate.

The life-appointed justices of the Supreme Court seem to be independent of Congress. Yet Congress can change the number of the judges. The President appoints federal judges, but the choices must be accepted or rejected by the Senate. In addition, Congress has the power to impeach judges. Finally, the Court may declare acts of Congress or of state legislatures unconstitutional but, unlike the executive branch, it has no power to carry out its decisions. In a 1832 case, *Worcester* v. *Georgia*, the Court ruled that Georgia had violated the Constitution in chasing certain American Indians from reservation lands in the state. President Andrew Jackson, who sympathized with Georgia, declared, "(Chief Justice) John Marshall has made his decision. Now let him enforce it." Marshall found he could not, and the American Indians never got their land back.

A portrait of John Marshall, who served for 34 years as the third Chief Justice of the United States Supreme Court.

On the whole, however, the system of checks and balances works. The Constitution the framers wrote was not perfect, but as the aged Benjamin Franklin, a delegate to the Convention, put it, he was astonished to find it "approaching so near to perfection as it does." Franklin thought the new government could be "a blessing to the people if well administered." He asked his fellow delegates, who were dissatisfied with certain notions of the Constitution, to sign anyway and give the document a chance to operate. By and large, the whole country has done the same thing for 200 years, changing this or that provision from time to time. Thus, the government the Constitution created is always in the process of changing.

By June of 1788, twelve years after the colonies had resolved to be independent, Congress was notified that nine states had ratified the Constitution. The United States was at last to be really united. For the first time, the machinery for the American government as it stands today would be put together and operating.

Questions for Discussion
1. Define *federalism, judicial review, veto, confirm, impeach.*
2. Why was the Bill of Rights a necessary addition to the Constitution?
3. What methods have been used to alter the Constitution to meet the needs of changing times?
4. What do we mean when we say that the Constitution, federal law, and treaties together make up "the Supreme Law of the Land"?
5. In what ways did the Constitution reflect experiences of the Americans under British rule?

6. Why were the Ninth and Tenth Amendments included in the Bill of Rights? How did they protect the people? The states?

The work to elect officials began in the states. They would have to choose Senators, Representatives, and Presidential electors. There were few **precedents** to serve as models in choosing the President. However, choosing Senators and Representatives was not much of a problem. The states had plenty of experience in choosing their own representatives to the assemblies and delegates to the many conventions and congresses that had met since the fires of protest were first lit in 1765. The voting was usually done in meetings held in townships and county seats. There was no one election day. The eleven states in the Union were to choose their Senators, Representatives, and electors at various times between October 1788 and the following January. In every state but Pennsylvania, it was necessary to own some property to vote. In Pennsylvania, a voter had only to be a taxpayer.

Each state had its own idea of how to pick Presidential electors. In five states, people voted directly for them. In Massachusetts, the voters chose twice as many as were allowed (that is, twice as many as the state's number of Representatives and Senators). The legislature then cut that list by half. In Georgia, Connecticut, and South Carolina, the legislatures did the choosing. New York never agreed on how it should be done and so cast no votes in the first Presidential election.

The first election was a little disorganized. It was as if some carpenters using unfamiliar tools were trying to put up a building according to a new plan of which there was no clear picture.

However, one thing was quite certain. The one man in the new nation of whom Southerners, Yankees, Quakers, backwoodspeople, city folk, the wealthy, and those who hoped to be wealthy looked to with respect was George Washington. He gave the country its first essential unifying force. The Presidential electors met in their various state capitals. Each voted for two men. The name with the highest total of votes was to become President, and the runner-up Vice President. When the votes were opened and counted by the newly assembled Senate in New York, the nation's first capital, George Washington had received the vote of every one of the sixty-nine electors. New England's John Adams had thirty-four. Washington was truly the hub around which the states were linked. Because of him, federalism became a practice and not just a theory.

precedent
an example from the past; in law, a judicial decision that may be used as a standard in later cases

Washington's Inauguration
Once more, George Washington was called from his plantation at

Mount Vernon to serve his country. Actually, he had little enthusiasm for more years of working hard for others while his own affairs were neglected. He wrote a friend that he felt like "a culprit going to the place of his execution." But duty was duty, and early in April, he set out for New York.

It was a triumphal procession. Crowds turned out at every crossroads town. The bigger cities competed in honoring him. At Baltimore, there was a grand banquet. At Philadelphia, an arch of laurel boughs was put up under which the national hero might ride. And New York outdid itself. George Washington was rowed across the harbor from the New Jersey shore to Manhattan Island in a splendid barge manned by thirteen smartly dressed sailors. Foreign warships at anchor fired salutes. Flags decorated the rigging of merchant ships, and cheers filled the air.

That was April 23, 1789. One week later, as cannon shots boomed and church bells rang, George Washington took the oath of office on the balcony of Federal Hall in Manhattan. Washington always had good sense about how to play his part. He accepted the crowd's cheers, rode in a handsome coach, and was as dignified as any crowned prince when he received callers. Yet, for his inauguration, he wore a plain brown suit of cloth made in Connecticut. He wished to encourage American manufacturing, and setting a personal example seemed a fine way to do it.

Below: An arch of laurel boughs constructed for Washington's triumphal procession to New York. Right: A thirteen-gun salute is fired as the President-elect is ferried across New York Bay.

The painting above shows Washington's second inauguration at Independence Hall, Philadelphia.

John Adams, Vice President under George Washington and the second President of the United States.

Behind him stood Vice President John Adams, who had once defended the soldiers accused of the Boston Massacre and ten years later had helped write the Declaration of Independence. There, too, stood the first Speaker of the House of Representatives, Frederick Mühlenberg, the son of a German immigrant. Together, the three men stood for much in the history of the very young nation. They were making a beginning, and much remained to be done. The world would be watching and learning. "The preservation of the sacred fire of liberty," said Washington in his inaugural speech, was deeply, perhaps finally, "staked on the experiment intrusted in the hands of the American people." They would have to prove whether a nation could be both self-governing and successful.

Questions for Discussion

1. Define *precedent*, *presidential elector*.
2. Why was the choice of Washington for President important?
3. How does the present method of selecting a President differ from the method used in 1789?

Chapter 9 Review

Summary Questions for Discussion

1. What was the purpose of the Annapolis Convention? What were the results?
2. Describe the characteristics of the delegates to the Constitutional Convention.
3. Who was chosen president of the convention?
4. Why were compromises needed at the convention?
5. What was the Virginia plan? What was the small-states plan?
6. What was the Three-Fifths Compromise (Article I, Section 2)?
7. What was the Commerce Compromise (Article I, Sections 8 and 9)?
8. Describe the arguments of the Federalists and anti-Federalists.
9. What is the purpose of a Bill of Rights?
10. Describe the case of *Marbury* v. *Madison* and its results.
11. What is the "unwritten constitution"?
12. What is federalism? What are some of the powers that may be exercised only by the national government? only by state governments? by both the national and state governments?
13. According to the Constitution, what is the role of the courts?
14. What powers were given to the President by the Constitution ?
15. How did the Constitution limit the powers of the voting majority?
16. What provisions of the Constitution were surprisingly democratic for the time in which it was written?
17. List those things that the government was forbidden to do.
18. What are the Ninth and Tenth Amendments?
19. What is a system of checks and balances? List three examples.
20. Describe the election of Washington and Adams.

Word Study

Fill in each blank in the sentences that follow with the term below that is most appropriate.

amendments	exclusive powers	impeach	veto	confirm
judicial review	concurrent powers	dictator	precedents	federalism

1. The powers of the President were limited to prevent him from becoming a _____.
2. If the President were to commit serious illegal acts, the House of Representatives was given the right to _____ him.
3. Certain powers called _____ were limited to one level of government.
4. Some powers called _____ were to be shared by the national and state governments.
5. The principle of government in which power is distributed between central and state governments is known as _____.
6. An example of checks and balances would be the President's power to _____ bills passed by Congress.
7. Another example of checks and balances is the power of the Senate to _____ Presidential appointments.
8. The United States Constitution has been expanded since its creation by _____, such as the first ten, which are called the Bill of Rights.
9. The Supreme Court decision in *Marbury* v. *Madison* set the _____ of giving the Supreme Court the right to determine if a law is constitutional.

CHAPTER 10
First Steps of the New Nation

It took only four months for the Constitutional Convention to draw up a plan of government. Still, the making of a nation takes longer. A nation is a body of people who usually share a territory, a language, an independent political system, and many common beliefs and traditions. The government is only the machinery through which a nation carries out its will. National feeling is often so strong that a nation can be defeated in war and occupied for years, yet will survive in people's hearts and become free again.

The United States became a nation in the middle of an age of *nationalism*—intense loyalty to, and feeling for, one's own nation. In the nineteenth century, struggles for national independence erupted throughout Europe and the Americas. In the twentieth century, the struggle for independence occurred in Asia, Africa, and the Middle East.

The building of an American nation began long before independence was declared in 1776. The use of the English language and the heritage of English traditions acted as one unifying force. Also, the post roads that connected colonial towns helped to make the nation. Every problem shared by all the colonies, such as frontier defense, was another force for nationhood. Fighting side by side against the French, soldiers and sailors from different colonies were creating a nation. And colonial editors protesting together against Parliament were creating a nation, too.

By 1789, there was a United States of America under the Constitution. As Washington said, however, it was an experiment whose success was not certain. Thirty years elapsed, during which the new American nation passed a number of difficult tests. Free elections were held in which two clashing parties exchanged power peaceably.

READING GUIDE

1. **What were some of the developments that helped to keep the United States together?**
2. **How did the development of political parties affect the country?**
3. **How did the War of 1812 affect America's relationship with Europe?**

Philadelphians celebrate the Fourth of July in 1819.

The nation's first leaders, the Federalists, built a sound financial system, gained some respect abroad, and forced a few angry citizens at home to obey the nation's laws. The Federalists' successors, the Democratic-Republicans, doubled the nation's territory and fought a second, short war with Great Britain. By 1819, Americans were able to celebrate Independence Day certain that the young nation could stand on its own.

1. Washington's Presidency

When the delegates to the Federal Convention debated about how much power to give the President, they were influenced by their experiences with King George III. They did not want to grant another leader the type of power that the king had abused. Yet the delegates also assumed that George Washington would be the first President. And their trust in him outweighed their fears.

The Constitution contained a brief outline of the powers of the President. The role itself had to be fashioned by Washington. He knew that what he did and said would establish precedents that would influence the conduct of future Presidents. As a result, he carefully weighed his actions.

One of Washington's first concerns was the correct conduct of the President. If he were too informal and encouraged unlimited public visits, he would never get his work done. He remembered that the leaders under the Articles of Confederation "led lives more like inn keepers than administrators." On the other hand, if he were too

In 1791, the First Bank of the United States was established in Philadelphia.

WASHINGTON'S CABINET

Vice President	John Adams	1789, 1793

Secretary of State
    originally Department of Foreign Affairs
    established as Department of State
    September 15, 1789
	John Jay
	Thomas Jefferson
	Edmund Randolph
	Timothy Pickering
		1789
		1790
		1794
		1795

Secretary of War
    established as Department of War
    August 7, 1789
	Henry Knox
	Timothy Pickering
	James McHenry
		1789
		1795
		1796

Secretary of the Treasury established September 2, 1789	Alexander Hamilton Oliver Wolcott, Jr.	1789 1795

Postmaster General
    established September 22, 1789;
    established as Post Office Department
    May 8, 1795
	Samuel Osgood
	Timothy Pickering
	Joseph Habersham
		1789
		1791
		1795

Attorney General established September 24, 1789	Edmund Randolph William Bradford Charles Lee	1789 1794 1795

separated from the people, he would be accused of being too much like a king. Washington soon found out that he could be himself only in private. At other times, he had to act in such a way as to inspire awe and respect for the office of the Presidency. To do this, he maintained a rather serious, formal attitude. He met with the public only at scheduled times and bowed rather than shook hands. When riding in the city, he traveled in an elaborate yellow coach, pulled by six cream-colored horses and attended by uniformed servants.

Since the Constitution did not spell out the relationship of the President with the other branches of government, this too had to be worked out in practice. One area not clearly defined was the relationship between the President and the Senate. The Senate wanted some control over Presidential appointments. When Washington sent a rather routine list of appointments to the Senate for confirmation, he expected no problems. The Senators surprised him by refusing to confirm a person appointed to a federal position in Georgia. The Senate explained that the two Senators from Georgia objected to the individual. Washington accepted the beginning of the practice of *Senatorial courtesy*. From then on, he consulted with a state's Senators before he made an appointment in that state. To this day, Presidents do the same thing.

Another contest of power arose between the Senate and the President over who should have the power to dismiss officials. Washington wanted the appointees to be responsible to him alone. Since it had the power to confirm appointments, the Senate felt it should also consent to removing appointees. In a very close vote in the

Congress, a bill was passed that implied that the power to remove officials belonged to the President. This power could be exercised without Senate approval.

The Constitution calls for the Senate to give the President advice and consent on treaties. Washington asked for advice from the Senate on an early treaty dealing with American Indians. When the Senators began debating the terms of the treaty, Washington was so displeased that he never asked for the Senate's advice again. He merely sent a negotiated treaty to the Senate for its approval or rejection. As a result, the possibility of the upper House becoming a council to the President faded. The Senate assumed a legislative, or lawmaking role, rather than one of sharing policymaking decisions with the President.

However, a council of advisers did arise from another source. According to the Constitution, the President "may require the Opinion, in writing, of the principal Officer in each of the executive Departments . . . . " In 1789, Congress created three executive departments to aid the President. So, the Department of State was created to help the President with foreign and domestic affairs. The Department of the Treasury was set up to deal with financial matters. And the Department of War handled military matters.

By 1790, Washington began to call on the *Secretaries* (heads of the Executive Departments) for more help. Eventually, these department heads became known as the "Cabinet." The Attorney General's office, created in 1789, became the fourth cabinet office. Washington appointed an Attorney General to handle matters of the law. It was not until 1907 that the Cabinet as it is recognized today became official.

Alexander Hamilton and the Treasury

The task of getting the country into working order was enormous for Washington's Administration. The new government inherited a debt of over $75 million. This was an astonishing amount for the day. The United States owed about $12 million of that amount to foreign nations. The country had almost no sources of income or credit.

For the critically important job of Secretary of the Treasury, Washington chose 34-year-old Alexander Hamilton. Born in the West Indies, Hamilton was the right-hand man of a West Indian merchant by the age of 14. At 19, he was a student at what is now Columbia College, in New York City. During that time, he was involved in radical politics as the author of anti-British pamphlets. At 20, he was an officer in the army and then later became military secretary to General Washington. At 30, he was a brilliant lawyer and a New York delegate to the Constitutional Convention. At 34, Hamilton was a tested political warrior and financial expert.

The first Secretary of the Treasury, Alexander Hamilton, urged Congress to create a national banking system for the United States.

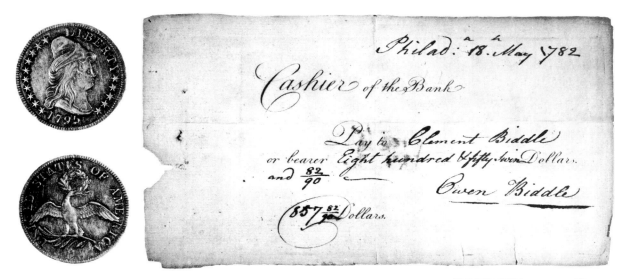

But radical as he was over the question of American independence, Hamilton did not favor total democracy. He distrusted unchecked rule by the "mass of people" and favored a government run by "the rich and well-born." His main desire, however, was for an energetic government. Hamilton hoped for a partnership between elected officials and forward-looking, wealthy merchants and manufacturers. He believed that trade and manufacturing increased employment, encouraged immigration, and so helped farmers by providing a market for farm products.

Hamilton used his role as national money manager to promote these ideas. First, he proposed that the national government pay all its wartime debts with new loans. Hamilton insisted that the United States must pay its debts to other nations in order to have its currency accepted. He saw debt repayment as a way of establishing good credit in case future loans were needed. And he wanted the central government to pay the war debts of the states. He also wanted the government to levy a protective tariff so foreign competition would not destroy new and growing industries. Hamilton believed that these policies would benefit the whole nation. They would increase the states' respect for the central government. In addition, confidence in the American government would be raised abroad. He also hoped to foster a feeling of nationalism among the different interest groups.

There was immediate opposition to some of these plans. Many discharged soldiers, farmers, and merchants who held notes from the wartime government had sold them at a fraction of their face value. Had the new federal government redeemed them at face value, these people would have benefited the most. Since it was usually the rich

Top: The head and tail of a 1795 ten-dollar gold piece and a 1782 bank check—the oldest in the United States. Above: The head and tail of a 1793 copper half-cent piece and a 1789 small change bank note.

who had the money to buy up the notes in the first place, opponents to Hamilton's plan saw it as a plot to help the rich get richer.

In fact, the issue became sectional. Many Southern states, such as Virginia, had already paid or made arrangements to take care of their wartime debts. These states did not want to be taxed to pay Northern debts, most of which belonged to New England. Southern states also felt that Hamilton's tariff proposal would benefit the Northern states. As a matter of fact, Hamilton hoped that his proposals would lead to a wider development of industry throughout the country. His tariff proposal, however, was temporarily rejected.

In spite of this, Hamilton kept the issue alive. In 1790, he was able to get his wishes through compromise. If he agreed to move the nation's capital to the banks of the Potomac River on land donated by Maryland and Virginia, Jefferson would secure enough Southern votes to secure the passage of the bill. On July 10, Philadelphia became the temporary capital until 1800. The funding provision for debt became law on August 4.

The First National Bank

Hamilton also asked Congress to create a special bank to keep the government's money and to control the amount of money local banks could lend. Opponents argued that Congress was not granted this power in the Constitution. But Hamilton disagreed. Article I, Section 8 stated that Congress could make all laws necessary and proper for carrying out its powers. This has been called the "elastic clause." Congress had the power to coin money, collect taxes, and borrow money. If creating a bank was necessary to perform these tasks, then, said Hamilton, the bank was constitutional. If Congress was directed to do a job, it could also create the necessary tools for the job. This use of the elastic clause of Article I, Section 8 gave many anti-Federalists nightmares. They suspected the central government of being too powerful already. And they also feared that the elastic clause would turn into a cord twisted around the necks of the states.

Hamilton skillfully used his political experience to persuade Congress to adopt his program, which included the First Bank of the United States. In 1791, Congress passed a bill that granted a twenty-year charter to the Bank of the United States. The new system would consist of his one large central bank in Philadelphia with branch banks in major cities.

Thus, the country had been rescued from possible bankruptcy. United States coins and paper currency were good anywhere. As a result, such currency served as a very solid symbol of pride in the new nation.

At Fort Cumberland, Maryland, Commander-in-Chief George Washington reviews troops called out to suppress the Whiskey Rebellion.

The Whiskey Rebellion

One of Hamilton's new taxes was an *excise tax* (a tax levied on the production, sale, or consumption of a product within a country) on liquor. This tax was especially hated on the frontier of western Pennsylvania. The settlers there faced a brutal struggle transporting their corn, rye, and wheat by wagon. Roads were swampy in wet weather, dusty in dry weather, and rocky in all seasons. But 24 bushels of grain could be distilled into 2 kegs of whiskey. One keg on each side was a perfect load for a pack horse. The corn walked to market, as the farmers said. Besides, the farmers used the whiskey as both currency and medicine, as well as to celebrate great occasions and to cheer up their hard lives.

Pennsylvania farmers, outraged by the new excise tax on liquor, tar and feather a tax collector.

All over western Pennsylvania, people not only denounced the excise tax collectors but tarred and feathered them. They believed they were doing just what colonial crowds had done to Stamp Act offcials, with as good a reason. In August of 1794, protesters marched into Pittsburgh.

To the Federalists, this protest was Shays' Rebellion all over again. They were determined to prove that the United States was ruled by its laws. So Washington ordered 15,000 militia into service.

But as the army moved westward, the rebellion fizzled out. The rebels were scattered, eventually agreed to the tax, and finally signed

A rustic view of Georgetown, the Potomac River, and Washington, D.C., in 1801.

loyalty oaths to the government. Washington had shown that federal authority would be used when needed.

The suppression of this Whiskey Rebellion was proof of the central government's strength. And, on a little point of land between two branches of the Potomac River, another, more lasting national symbol was being created.

Washington, D.C., Becomes the Nation's Capital

The Constitution gave Congress power to create a district that would become the "seat of Government." In 1790, the lawmakers chose the location for this District of Columbia and looked for an expert to design the new capital city, which was to be called Washington. The President recommended Major Pierre Charles L'Enfant for the job.

L'Enfant was a French-born architect and engineer who believed that the capital should express the spirit of America—wide open like the future, but still anchored to the wisdom of the past. His plan called for a capitol building on a hill and a "presidential palace" facing it at the opposite end of a wide mall, or promenade. There would be wide avenues cutting through the regular checkerboard pattern of streets. Where these diagonal avenues crisscrossed, there would be open spaces. These would be saved for fountains, gardens, statues, and great buildings in the style of ancient Greece and Rome.

As a city planner, L'Enfant was ahead of his time. He was also hot-tempered and demanded more money and more obedience than Congress would stand for. After many quarrels, Congress fired him.

The job of continuing his work fell to a Marylander named Andrew Ellicott, one of three men appointed as surveyors of the District. Ellicott's coworker was a friend and neighbor named Benjamin Banneker, a highly talented Black man. Thus, Banneker was the first Black to receive a Presidential appointment.

Banneker's father was a slave who was later able to buy his freedom and send his son to a private school. Benjamin Banneker's keen mind soon led him beyond the school's program. He taught himself mathematics and astronomy, as well as surveying. After helping to design Washington, he, like Benjamin Franklin, wrote and published almanacs. Banneker sent one almanac to Thomas Jefferson

An engraving of Pierre L'Enfant's plan for Washington, D.C.

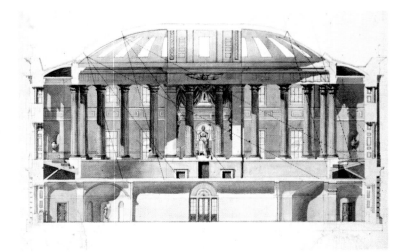

Top: Pierre L'Enfant designed Washington, D.C. Above: Benjamin Banneker surveyed the District of Columbia. Right: Benjamin Latrobe's design for the hall in the south wing of the Capitol.

with a note saying he hoped it would prove that any "narrow prejudices" about Blacks being "brutish" were false.

Slowly, Washington, D.C., was created. Its buildings were the work of some gifted immigrants. The Capitol was designed by William Thornton, born in the West Indies, and Benjamin Latrobe, from England. The President's "palace," the White House, got its basic design from Irish-born James Hoban. Black, White, American-born, and foreign-born, all had a hand in creating the finished product. Thus, the United States was a "nation of nations" from the start.

The New Nation's Foreign Policy

The first Secretary of State was Thomas Jefferson. As author of the Declaration of Independence, he had told the world why Americans planned to free themselves from Britain. Now, he was the President's chief spokesperson for the new nation's foreign policy. He had his hands full almost at once.

Shortly after Washington was inaugurated, a revolution broke out in France. In 1789, the French overthrew the monarchy. Four years later, they beheaded their king, Louis XVI. To Europe's other monarchs, the French Revolution with its democratic ideals was as welcome as the plague. They moved to stamp out the disease before it spread. Austria, England, Spain, and other European nations were soon at war with France. With only a few interruptions, the fighting lasted for twenty-two years and laid many problems on the United States' doorstep.

The first of these problems was what to do about the 1778 alliance that the United States had with France. Did the alliance require the United States to go to war on France's side? Washington was in a spot. It was important to keep the word of the United States—as important as paying debts. But conducting a war would be a disaster for a young nation just getting on its feet. The President asked the advice of his Cabinet. Hamilton argued for tearing up the treaty, now that the king who had approved it was dead. Jefferson said that the treaty was not with the king but with the French nation, which was still very much alive. But he advised that the United States proclaim **neutrality**. Finally, in 1793, Washington issued a Proclamation of Neutrality.

This problem was only the beginning of trouble. Both French and British warships attacked American vessels trading with the other side and seized their cargoes. Being neutral was dangerous. At any time between 1793 and 1812, America might reasonably have gone to war with either the French or the British. But there were special reasons for a fight with the British. They still held the western forts, which they were supposed to have given up in 1783. They refused to allow Yankee vessels to trade with the British West Indies. In turn, the British were angered because some states interfered with the collection of pre-Revolutionary War debts owed by Americans to British merchants.

Tension rose so high that Washington decided to send John Jay, first Chief Justice of the Supreme Court, to negotiate a treaty with Britain. The agreement Jay reached was by no means satisfactory. The British agreed once more to leave the Northwest. However, they did not retreat an inch on their "right" to seize American ships headed for French harbors. They allowed only a tiny trade with British West Indian Islands. And Jay had to promise in return that his government would levy no special taxes on British imports and would pay the prewar debts.

There was a roar of protest at the treaty. Among those attacking the treaty was Jefferson, who had resigned as Secretary of State in 1794. Jay was burned in effigy. However, Washington used his prestige to support the pact, and it was confirmed by the Senate in 1795. If the new nation had gone to war with Britain, it might have been overwhelmed—or perhaps have had to beg help from the French and risk becoming a French puppet. In any case, Washington was eager to keep the nation free of foreign involvements.

About the same time, Thomas Pinckney concluded a far more favorable treaty with Spain. Conflicts with this European country were related to southwestern border disputes, navigation on the Mississippi, and the use of the port of New Orleans.

In 1795, Pinckney obtained some concessions from the Spanish. Spain may have feared a British-American alliance or attacks by American frontier settlers. The Spanish granted Americans unrestricted navigation on the Mississippi and, for at least three years, the use of the port of New Orleans. Spain also agreed to the Florida

neutrality
a policy of not taking sides

An image of Chief Justice John Jay is burned by citizens angry over the treaty he negotiated with England in 1794.

In January 1794, Thomas Jefferson, the first Secretary of State, resigned from office and temporarily retired from public life.

boundary claimed by the Americans. At least for the time being, some international problems were being settled.

Questions for Discussion

1. Define *Senatorial courtesy, Secretaries, excise tax, neutrality.*
2. How did Washington add to the "unwritten constitution"?
3. How did Washington's actions affect the role of the Senate?
4. Why is it important for a government to have a good financial rating? What policies did Hamilton favor to give the nation a good financial rating?
5. Why was the crushing of the Whiskey Rebellion a victory for the national government?
6. How did Washington's administration deal with the problems posed by France, Britain, and Spain?

2. The Growth of Political Parties

Each year, the country moved toward greater unity. Yet, one development seemed to be tearing the United States apart faster than the new government could bring the country together—political parties. Differences of opinion are bound to occur in a free society. The country had divided once on whether to support the Constitution. Soon after 1789, a new split occurred between followers of Jefferson and those of Hamilton.

You have already seen what Hamilton favored in government. Jefferson, who opposed Hamilton, believed in strong local, but not strong federal or central government. He distrusted government efforts to encourage manufacturing and the growth of cities. In Jefferson's mind, only a people living on the fruits of their own land could be truly free. Farmers, he said, were "the chosen people of God." Cities added only as much strength to a nation "as sores do to the human body." If Americans were crowded into cities, they would soon "go to eating one another." Jefferson also welcomed the French Revolution. "A little rebellion, now and then," he wrote in 1787, was a "good thing for any country." To Hamilton, such thoughts were frightening.

Gradually, pro-Hamilton and pro-Jefferson groups formed, first in Congress, then in the country. The Hamiltonians called themselves *Federalists*. They drew their support mainly from the wealthy merchants, bankers, and professionals. These were the people who had benefited most from Hamilton's financial policies. They also favored Britain in the war that developed in Europe between Britain

A 1798 political cartoon shows Federalists and Democratic-Republicans "debating" at Congress Hall in Philadelphia.

and France. New England, which depended heavily on trade and commerce, was mostly Federalist. The Jefferson followers took the name *Democratic-Republicans*. Many of them were farmers, workers, and small merchants. Helped the least by Hamilton's programs, they did not benefit directly from trade with Britain either. They favored France in foreign affairs. The South and West, which were primarily agricultural and expansionist, were generally Democratic-Republicans.

Would the sections be torn apart? In his farewell address, Washington asked Americans to shield themselves from "the jealousies and heartburnings" of party argument. He also urged them not to take sides in foreign wars. Otherwise, there would be "frequent collisions" and even "bloody contests."

Nevertheless, the differences that were developing between these two groups could not be ignored. While Washington was President, the ideas of the Federalists were carried out. After Jefferson resigned as Secretary of State, he felt free to oppose the government. By the time Washington refused to run for a third term, there were two active groups grasping for political power. On the one hand, the Federalists

w. nted to elect another President who would represent their views. So they nominated John Adams for President. On the other hand, the Democratic-Republicans nominated Thomas Jefferson for President.

According to the Constitution, the electors chosen to vote for the President and Vice President were each to cast two votes. The candidate who received a *majority* (one vote more than half of the electors) would become President. The closest runner-up would be Vice President. When the ballots in the 1796 election were counted, John Adams received the most votes. He became President. But Thomas Jefferson received more electoral votes than Thomas Pinckney. For the first and only time in American history, there was a President of one party and a Vice President of another.

The XYZ Affair

After the hotly contested 1796 Presidential election, party spirit still flared. In addition, controversy was stirred up by the growing problems in foreign affairs. France was now under the control of a five-man Directory. Unfriendly toward the United States, the Directory ordered seizures of American ships in the West Indies. The British attacks that prompted the Jay Treaty were child's play compared to the damage done by the French.

The difficulties with France widened the gap between the Federalists and the Democratic-Republicans. The Democratic-Republicans refused to see the change in character of the French government. Meanwhile, the French were trying to surround the United States with French territory. The Canadians in Quebec were urged to break away from Britain and form a republic under French protection. The French were also trying to pressure Spain into turning over the Louisiana and Florida territories to France. (See map on page 221.)

However, Adams did not want to fight a war with France if he could avoid it. He knew that the United States was not prepared to fight. So he decided to send a commission to France in the hopes of improving relations and ending the French seizure of American merchant ships. The French minister, Talleyrand, delayed meeting with the Americans. Instead, he sent three aides who indicated that the French minister would talk to them only if he received a bribe of about $250,000. The Americans refused the terms, and the two envoys returned to the United States.

Adams told Congress that the mission had failed. He ordered preparations for war, including expansion of the army and navy. When members of both parties protested, he told them of the demands of Talleyrand's aides—agents "X," "Y," and "Z." Adams immediately got the support he wanted. Congress voided all treaties with France, and American privateers sought out French vessels.

For a time, the United States and France were involved in an undeclared war. To the disappointment of some Federalists, such as Hamilton, war was not declared. Under Napoleon, the French began to realize the value of American neutrality. In 1800, the two nations signed an agreement that ended the old alliance of 1778 and reestablished commercial relations. John Adams had prevented a war but at the cost of dividing and weakening the Federalist party, many of whom wanted a war with France. At the same time, he had also weakened his chances for reelection.

Conflicts and Coalitions

Adams succeeded in avoiding open warfare with France. Yet he was not tolerant of the pro-French faction in his own country. In 1798, the Federalist Congress passed several acts that were aimed at foreigners who sympathized with Democratic-Republican, pro-French ideas. The Naturalization Act increased the residency requirement for citizenship from five to fourteen years. The **Alien** Act allowed the President, without trial, to jail or **deport** "dangerous" immigrants who had not yet been **naturalized.**

The **Sedition** Act allowed the federal government to arrest and try those who uttered "false, scandalous and malicious" criticism of public officials.

However, the Alien and Sedition Acts were short-lived. Democratic-Republican state legislatures in Virginia and Kentucky passed resolutions stating that such unconstitutional acts were null and void within those states. This doctrine of *nullification* could destroy the unity created by the Constitution. If nullification were allowed, the states could ignore federal law. Both the Alien and Sedition Acts and the Virginia and Kentucky Resolutions seemed to prove that Washington's fears about the country being torn apart by party hatred were well founded.

Still, things were not as bad as they seemed. To begin with, parties began to be a unifying force. A Virginia planter might vote Democratic-Republican because of Jefferson's *agrarian*, pro-farm ideas. But so might an Irish immigrant who only cared that the Democratic-Republicans were opposed to England, Ireland's old enemy. A Rhode Island maker of cotton cloth was likely to vote Federalist because of Hamilton's idea of a protective tariff against foreign textiles. So would a Charleston ship carpenter who believed that the Federalists encouraged commerce. This would mean more ships, therefore creating more work for carpenters.

Party loyalties, therefore, united sections and classes. In a system of two great parties, each one had to unite many groups into a **coalition** in order to win elections. Jefferson, who ran for President in

alien
a foreign immigrant who has not become an American citizen

deport
send out of the country

naturalized
legally made citizens

sedition
the illegal criticism of the government

coalition
a temporary alliance

1800, recognized the danger of disunity. However, the outspokenness of the great Virginian frightened many people. Jefferson was brilliant. He loved the good things of life. And he was hospitable to all kinds of radical ideas. Many Hamiltonians believed that such a man was a tool of the devil. Federalists believed that, if Jefferson were elected, he would sink the navy, dismiss the Senate and the Supreme Court, and perhaps even attack religion and the family.

Power Changes Hands

In the close election of 1800, Jefferson was chosen President. The Federalists had nominated John Adams and Charles Pinckney. The Democratic-Republicans supported Thomas Jefferson and Aaron Burr.

The election contest was bitterly fought along party lines. The Federalists believed that the Democratic-Republicans would make the United States a pawn of the French. In turn, the Democratic-Republicans felt the Federalists would always favor Northeastern commercial interests over the agricultural and trade interests of the rest of the country. But the Federalists were still depending on the wealthy and the property owners for their political strength. They were no longer able to combat the growing political strength of the Democratic-Republicans, who had support among the farmers, workers, and small merchants.

Once more the faults of the electoral system were apparent. Thomas Jefferson and Aaron Burr, both Democratic-Republicans, each received seventy-three electoral votes. So the election was thrown into the House of Representatives, where each state had one vote. The House would decide who would be President and who would be Vice President. On the thirty-sixth ballot, Jefferson emerged the victor. To prevent this situation from occurring again, the Twelfth Amendment to the Constitution was passed in 1804. This Amendment requires separate balloting for President and Vice President.

After the election, the Federalists waited for doomsday. But Jefferson chose to soothe rather than punish his enemies. In his inaugural address, he called for "harmony and affection." Like Washington, he urged an end to "political intolerance." He declared, "We are all Republicans, we are all Federalists." To this he added a statement that finally explained his seeming radicalism. If any citizens wished to dissolve the Union or change the form of government, he said, "Let them stand undisturbed as monuments of the safety with which error of opinion can be tolerated when reason is left free to combat it."

"Mad Tom," as Jefferson was called in cartoons did not always believe in radical schemes. But he was always willing to listen. Whereas the Sedition Act seemed to say that too much free speech

REPUBLICANS

Turn out, turn out and save your Country from ruin !

From an Emperor—from a King—from the iron grasp of a British Tory Faction—an unprincipled banditti of British speculators. The hireling tools and emissaries of his majesty king George the 3d have thronged our city and diffused the poison of principles among us.

DOWN WITH THE TORIES, DOWN WITH THE BRITISH FACTION,

Before they have it in their power to enslave you, and reduce your families to distress by heavy taxation. Republicans want no Tribute-liars—they want no ship Ocean-liars—they want no Rufus King's for Lords —they want no Varick to lord it over them—they want no Jones for senator, who fought with the British against the Americans in time of the war.—But they want in their places such men as

Jefferson & Clinton,

who fought their Country's Battles in the year '76

MAD TOM in A RAGE

Top: This poster is from Jefferson's reelection campaign. Bottom: This Federalist cartoon claims that President Thomas Jefferson is destroying the federal government. However, Jefferson won reelection in 1804.

The frayed banner above commemorates the election of Thomas Jefferson as the third President of the United States.

pulls a society apart, Jefferson argued that only the free discussion of ideas can persuade people to change their laws and rulers peaceably. The peaceful takeover by the Democratic-Republicans was well named "the revolution of 1800." It proved that power could change hands in the United States with no angrier sound than that of pens inking voters' choices on ballots.

Questions for Discussion

1. Define *deport, naturalized, alien, sedition, Democratic-Republican, coalition.*
2. Why did Jefferson's political ideas frighten some Americans in 1800?
3. How did John Adams's handling of foreign affairs with France prevent war but cost him his chance for reelection?
4. How did the Alien and Sedition Acts lead to the passage of the Virginia and Kentucky Resolutions?
5. In what ways did political parties both divide and unite people in the early days of our country?
6. How did the election of 1800 result in the expansion of the Constitution?
7. Why was Jefferson a firm believer in allowing those who disagreed with the government to speak out?

3. The Administrations of Thomas Jefferson

It was fortunate that Jefferson was open-minded. As President, he soon found that men in power must sometimes change their ideas to keep up with events. Jefferson believed in a simple, inexpensive government with "a few plain duties to be performed by a few servants." Yet, in his two terms, the "plain duties" of the administration came to include the fighting of an undeclared foreign war and the making of a treaty doubling the nation's size.

The Louisiana Purchase

In 1800, Napoleon Bonaparte, the powerful dictator of France, forced Spain to give him the Louisiana Territory. Jefferson was worried about New Orleans being in the hands of a strong power. It was vital to keep the Mississippi open for western trade. So in 1803, Jefferson sent agents to try to buy New Orleans from France. When they reached Paris, Napoleon had decided—in part because of the successful Haitian revolt led by Toussaint L'Ouverture—to sell the Louisiana Territory. He surprised the American envoys by offering them the entire territory for $15 million. They accepted his offer.

Weeks later, when the news reached Jefferson by ship, he was in a tight spot. Though Congress had authorized Jefferson to buy New Orleans, neither Congress nor the Constitution had given him the right to buy the entire territory. Jefferson had less of an excuse to buy the Louisiana Territory than Hamilton had had to create a national bank. However, Jefferson's wish to increase the size, power, and security of the new country he helped to create was so strong that he put aside his principles and accepted Napoleon's offer.

In doing so, Jefferson won a rich prize. The Louisiana Territory included parts of a dozen future states and doubled the size of the country. It contained what one day would be portions of the gold and silver mines of the Rockies, the oil and natural gas wells and the ranch

Above: Meriwether Lewis posed for this portrait after returning from his expedition. His ermine-tailed cape is probably the one presented to him by a chief of the Shoshoni. Below: Louisiana Territory explorers Meriweather Lewis; William Clark; Sacajawea, their Shoshoni guide; and others of the exploration party.

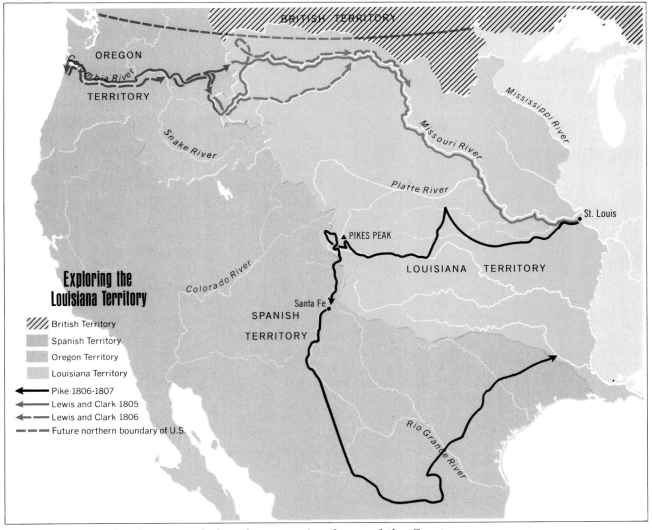

Exploring the
Louisiana Territory

British Territory
Spanish Territory
Oregon Territory
Louisiana Territory
Pike 1806-1807
Lewis and Clark 1805
Lewis and Clark 1806
Future northern boundary of U.S.

BRITISH TERRITORY

OREGON

TERRITORY

Columbia River

Snake River

Colorado River

SPANISH

TERRITORY

Santa Fe

PIKES PEAK

LOUISIANA TERRITORY

Platte River

Missouri River

Mississippi River

St. Louis

Rio Grande River

lands of the Southwest, and the wheat-growing farms of the Great
Plains.

In 1804, Jefferson sent two army officers, Meriwether Lewis and
William Clark, to explore the Louisiana Territory and go beyond it to
the Pacific. They were to learn everything possible about the peoples,
the land, the animals, and the climate. Moreover, they were to collect
types of soil, as modern-day lunar explorers have done.

The two captains set out from St. Louis in May of 1804. The
expedition was a breathtaking, two-and-one-half-year adventure.
After months of terrible perils—hailstorms, attacks by grizzlies,
snakebites, overturned canoes, swarms of mosquitoes, and fevers—
they came down the Columbia River and reached its mouth. On
November 7, 1805, Clark, whose spelling did not compare with his
abilities as an explorer, wrote in his journal: "Ocian in view! O! The
joy!"

Problems at Sea

Jefferson was barely settled in the White House when Tripoli, a small North African state, stirred up trouble. Like other **Barbary States**, Tripoli permitted its armed ships to capture defenseless foreign merchant ships. The only way for European nations and the United States to escape such piracy was to pay protection money.

In the spring of 1801, Tripoli demanded more money. Jefferson angrily refused. So Tripoli declared war. The United States sent its tiny young navy into action and fought a series of sharp battles with the enemy. In 1805, Tripoli finally asked for peace. But piracy from other Barbary States continued until 1815. It is only fair to say that European nations had often looked the other way when the victims of piracy were their enemies. As an emerging power, though, the United States gained prestige by battling Tripoli and by encouraging freedom of the seas.

To Jefferson, a still more serious problem existed. American cargoes were being seized by the British and French. These nations hoped to cut off each other's trade even with neutral nations. When the British navy defeated the French navy at Trafalgar, near Gibraltar, in 1805, Napoleon had to plan a new strategy to stop Britain's trade. He had to take advantage of France's position as the "lion," with strength on land, against Britain's position as the "shark," with strength at sea. So Napoleon issued the Berlin Decree. It forbade trade with Britain by any European nation under French control. It also stated that a ship of any neutral nation trading with Britain would be subject to seizure. However, this was only a "paper" blockade of Britain's ports,

Barbary States
the old North African states of Tripoli, Algiers, Tunis, Morocco

In 1804, Captain Richard Somers sailed his ship, the Intrepid, into a harbor in Tripoli, hoping to destroy Tripoli's fleet. Before he could, the Intrepid blew up, killing Somers and his entire crew.

An American sailor fights off a pirate trying to board a United States ship.

because Napoleon's navy was not strong enough to enforce it. The purpose of the decree was to prevent neutral ships from bringing British goods to ports under France's control. Though France and its allies suffered from these shortages, the British economy was cut off from substantial outlets for its goods.

Britain answered by issuing a series of Orders in Council. These orders forbade other nations from trading with France or its allies. It prohibited trade in any European ports closed to British ships. And it also required neutral vessels to stop at British ports to be searched before going to any open port in Europe.

Not to be outdone, France issued the Milan Decree in 1807. This decree stated that any ship that allowed the British to search it either on the sea or in port would be subject to seizure by the French.

The Orders in Council affected American shipping the most. The British naval superiority enabled the British to put their orders into effect. The French were limited to the coastal waters of Europe. The more adventuresome American merchant vessels considered it a challenge to get around them. Blockade running became quite profitable. As a result, many merchants were attracted to the United States. By 1807, foreign trade reached an all time high. However, this form of trade put the United States in constant conflict with France and Britain.

Still worse was the British practice of **impressment**. British warships would stop American vessels and search them for deserters

impressment
the forcible drafting of American citizens into the Royal Navy

EARLY FOREIGN POLICY

The United States, in its early days, was a weak—though proud—nation. As a nation, it had to deal realistically with situations. One such problem was the frequent capture of American sailors by the navies of the Barbary States. Although by Thomas Jefferson's administration there was enough of a navy to put a stop to this practice, the policy was to buy off the "pirates." In 1797 the United States signed a treaty with Tripoli giving that nation's ruler $40,000 in gold and silver coins, five rings (three with diamonds and one with a sapphire), many yards of good cloth, and $12,000 in Spanish money. The ruler also managed to get four brocade robes out of the deal. In 1805, to ransom some captured American citizens, the United States paid $60,000 to Tripoli.

By the Virtue, Firmness and Patriotism of
JEFFERSON & MADISON,
Our Difficulties with England are settled—our Ships have been preserved, and our Seamen will, hereafter, be respected while sailing under our National Flag.

NEW-YORK, SATURDAY MORNING, APRIL 29, 1809.

IMPORTANT.

By the President of the United States —A Proclamation.
WHEREAS it is provided by the 11th section of the act of Congress, entitled " An " act to interdict the commercial intercourse between the United States and Great Bri-" tain and France, and their dependencies ; and for other purposes,"—and that " in " case either France or Great Britain shall so revoke or modify her edicts as that they " shall cease to violate the neutral commerce of the United States," the President is authorized to declare the same by proclamation, after which the trade suspended by the said act and by an act laving an Embargo, on all ships and vessels in the ports and harbours of

Presidents Thomas Jefferson and James Madison hoped to avoid war with England by enforcing embargoes. This 1809 broadside credits them with success.

from the British fleet. Sailors who could not prove American citizenship were impressed. It was as humiliating as if, for example, today, Soviet soldiers came aboard American passenger planes at European airports and dragged off people whom they accused of being Soviet citizens trying to escape.

In the summer of 1807, trouble broke out when the British ship *Leopard* demanded the right to search the American Frigate *Chesapeake*. They claimed they were searching for deserters from the British navy. When the commander of the *Chesapeake* refused, the British ship opened fire. Three Americans were killed, eighteen wounded, and four taken prisoner. The American cry for war became louder.

Jefferson could not afford to fight the British or the French. But he believed that both countries could not do without American supplies. So Jefferson decided to use economic means to gain respect for America's rights as a neutral nation. One of his plans was the Embargo Act of 1807. This act forbade American ships to leave for foreign ports. The Act was ineffective against Britain and France. But the results were disastrous for the American economy. Warehouses in the United States were jammed with goods. Many merchants remained abroad and continued to trade, using foreign licenses. Others smuggled goods to Canada. Many seafarers fled to the British provinces, while farmers and merchants alike suffered losses. Seagoing New England was the hardest hit and reacted most vigorously. Finally, three days before he left office in 1809, Jefferson ended the embargo against all nations except Britain and France.

Questions for Discussion
1. Define *Barbary States, impressment.*
2. What did Jefferson accomplish by the Louisiana Purchase?
3. Why was the Lewis and Clark expedition so important?

4. What problem was caused by the Barbary States?
5. How did Jefferson respond to the impressment policy?

4. The War of 1812

By 1812, due to Jefferson's bold purchase, the United States was now a nation whose boundaries stretched from the Atlantic to the Rocky Mountains. This was a great change for a former "confederation" of thirteen states. But at sea, America still suffered as a weak neutral, caught between warring France and England.

Jefferson followed Washington's precedent by refusing to run for a third term as President. So in 1808, James Madison of Virginia became his successor.

Madison had served as the Secretary of State under Jefferson for eight years. He wanted to find a peaceful solution to the problems at sea. At the same time, Madison wanted the United States to gain respect.

To attain this respect, a law was passed that forbade American business people to trade with Britain and France. This law was called the Non-Intercourse Act of 1809. But trade with these two nations was what the Americans needed. In 1810, the law expired. And, once again, merchants began the dangerous activity of blockade running.

The drawing below is supposed to show the British advance on Washington, D.C., just before they occupied and burned parts of the city on August 24, 1814. In fact, they faced little opposition, and their advance was not that formal.

The first naval action in the War of 1812 was off New London on June 23. The action involved the H.M. frigate Belvidera, and American frigates President, United States, Congress, Hornet, and the Argus.

Madison then signed a new law which requested that Britain and France do away with their restrictions on American shipping. When either nation agreed, the United States would refuse to do business with the other.

Napoleon recognized the dangers of such a deal. The United States could easily be accused of taking sides with the agreeable nation. So in 1810, France removed its restrictions against American shipping. Despite warnings that Napoleon could not be trusted, Madison issued orders forbidding trade with Great Britain. As feelings of nationalism and pressures for war built up, the country sent a new group of younger Representatives from the frontier states to Congress. These Representatives gained influence in the House when Henry Clay of Kentucky was elected Speaker of the House. Clay was one of a group of Representatives known as the "War Hawks." These were members of Congress, usually from the frontier, who favored war with Britain. Clay used his position as Speaker to appoint other War Hawks to important committees. Thus, Representatives favoring war acquired influence in the House out of proportion to their number.

The War Hawks saw Britain as the logical target in a war to save the nation's "honor." They did not mind that war with Britain would actually ally the United States in a common cause with Napoleon. The western settlers still believed that British bribes caused the conflicts that they had with the American Indians. Along the old Northwest frontier, the Shawnee chief Tecumseh led an uprising to defend his people from the westward flow of White settlers. This uprising was blamed on the British. On the frontier, American politicians cast an eye at lightly defended Canada. Fresh from victories against the American Indians, some western "War Hawks" believed that Canada would be easy pickings.

In New York and New England—the major commercial regions— there was strong opposition to war with Britain. In spite of the restrictions on neutral trade, American shipping was healthy. The Federalists felt that war would benefit expansionism and the West. And they did not trust the government's claim that war against Britain was to protect shipping interests.

Finally, war was declared in June 1812. Madison had been tricked by the French into believing that Napoleon had revoked the Berlin and Milan Decrees. In fact, the French were still seizing American ships.

Madison gave the following reasons for war with Britain: impressment of seamen, interference with American shipping, and incitement of the American Indians. Yet, only a few days earlier, Parliament had revoked the Orders in Council, giving up the policy of interference with American shipping. Many British merchants did not want to lose their profitable trade with the United States. This time British politicians who did not want to kill the goose that laid golden eggs won. But it was too late. War had started. The reaction in the United States was mixed. New Englanders, who depended on trade, greeted the declaration with lowered flags and tolling church bells.

For a time, the war threatened to destroy everything that had been built up by the United States since the end of the Revolution. The War Hawks had foolishly overestimated American power. The little navy fought bravely, and against great odds won several remarkable victories at sea. The forty-four-gun frigate, the *Constitution*, with its copper sheathing, was a worthy match for any British ship. It sank the *Guerriere* and the *Java* and picked up the nickname, *Old Ironsides*. In other combat, on Lake Erie, Captain Oliver Hazard Perry successfully defeated a British squadron near Put-in-Bay. He reported, "We have met the enemy and they are ours." However, that was not often the case. British naval power was overwhelming. And the British struck back with a vengeance. Before long, the American navy was destroyed or bottled up in port.

On the Canadian frontier, matters were also disappointing. The Americans tried to wage a land war with an unprepared army. They planned a three-pronged attack to subdue Canada. They were to invade Canada from three different locations along the Great Lakes. But results were disastrous. General William Hull led his force of 2000 soldiers into the Canadian wilderness. When he heard that a group of British soldiers and American Indians were approaching, he withdrew to Detroit. Eight days later, he surrendered Detroit to a small group of British soldiers without firing a shot. The two other forces fared no better. The attacks at the Niagara River were easily crushed. And the drive north from Plattsburg failed when the militia refused to go onto Canadian soil. This situation was repeated at other locations along the northern frontier, as state militias refused to fight.

There were few victories inland and even fewer along the coast. The British attacked Maine and annexed part of it east of the Penobscot River. British ships were able to bombard coastal towns with hardly any opposition. When Napoleon was defeated in Europe, Britain was able to devote more attention to the war in America. The

THE STAR SPANGLED BANNER

The Star Spangled Banner, written by Francis Scott Key in 1814 and sung to music composed by John Stafford, is the national anthem of the United States.

During the War of 1812, William Beanes was captured by the British and held prisoner aboard a warship in Chesapeake Bay. Francis Scott Key and John S. Skinner received permission from President James Madison to communicate with the British to negotiate Beanes' release. The negotiations were successful. The British agreed to release Beanes. However, the British were about to attack Fort McHenry at the time. So they held all three Americans aboard a prisoner-exchange boat at the rear of the British fleet until the battle ended.

The attack was launched on Tuesday, September 13, 1814, and lasted for almost 24 hours. The three Americans, aware that Fort McHenry lacked defenses, frantically worried all night, not knowing who was winning the battle because of the intense smoke and haze on the battle front. Early the next morning, as the smoke cleared, they saw the American flag still flying atop the fort. Key was so filled with emotion that he began to write, on the spot, words to express his feelings. He wrote most of the words in a few minutes. After their release later on that morning, he returned to Baltimore and finished the other stanzas the same day.

The poem was distributed the next day on handbills and was instantly a favorite among the patriots. *The Star Spangled Banner* was first sung in public by actor Ferdinand Durang in Baltimore, to the tune of "Anacreon in Heaven." In March, 1931, Congress officially approved the song as the national anthem. However, the Army and Navy recognized *The Star Spangled Banner* as the national anthem long before Congress adopted it.

A soldier's wife lends a hand at Fort Niagara.

crowning blow came on August 24, 1814, when a British force sailed up Chesapeake Bay, landed in Maryland, marched on Washington, and burned the nation's new capital. President Madison had just barely escaped. The only American soldiers nearby were Maryland and Virginia militia who had run away the day before after a brief fight. British soldiers amused themselves by sitting in the hall of the House of Representatives, voting to burn the "nest of Yankee democracy," and then doing just that. The White House was put to flames. It seemed as if an army of militia could not save the country. Apparently, a point as low as the dismal days of December 1776 had been reached.

Victory and Triumph at the Peace Table

Yet, after that dark summer week in 1814, things improved steadily. A few weeks later, the British moved northward to attack Baltimore. From the Patapsco River, their fleet pounded Fort McHenry, the key to the city. Despite an all-night bombardment, the Americans held out. Dawn saw their flag still flying. Thus, the British abandoned the attempt, and their northward drive collapsed.

At about the same time as the British failure at Baltimore, another British force invading from Canada was stopped on Lake Champlain. The British, who had little interest in the war to begin with, now moved to end it. They sent envoys to a meeting with American peacemakers at Ghent, in Belgium. On Christmas Eve in 1814, both sides signed a treaty that more or less called the war a draw. It said

The British suffered their worst defeat in the War of 1812 at the Battle of New Orleans. Here, British Major General Sir Edward Pakenham lies dying in the midst of the battle.

nothing about the issues of free trade and sailors' rights. And it left the American boundary with Canada just where it had been before the war. Both sides did agree to negotiate the other existing issues at later dates.

However, the news of peace arrived too late to prevent a major battle and an American victory. Before the Treaty of Ghent was signed, the British had sent a 7500-strong expedition from Jamaica to New Orleans to seize the mouth of the Mississippi. The British landing force of crack troops left their ships below New Orleans and marched westward toward the city. Waiting for them was an American army commanded by a militia general named Andrew Jackson. Jackson's 6000-strong force was made up of several elements. There were those from the frontiers of Tennessee and Kentucky, all dead shots. Others were French-speaking planters from New Orleans, a detachment commanded by the pirate Jean Lafitte, as well as two battalions of free Blacks from New Orleans.

On the misty morning of January 8, 1815, the British troops advanced against the Americans, who were lined up behind a breastwork of cotton bales. Deadly accurate fire killed or wounded 2100 British soldiers. The Americans had only seventy-one casualties. The nation was jubilant. Thereafter, Americans remembered the victories of the war and forgot the defeats. Some even called the conflict "The Second War of Independence."

In the four years immediately after the war, a series of treaties reflected the growing power of the nation. (See the map on page 232.)

DR. THORNTON

The Man Who Did It All Some of you may know that Americans live in an age of specialists, where it may take thirty years to learn, in college, graduate school, and internship, how to be a scientist, an engineer, a doctor, a pharmacist, an accountant, an attorney.

But it was not so in the 1800s. Not that there was not a great deal to know, but a clever and hardworking person could manage to learn several "trades," or at least the basics. A genius like Benjamin Franklin could master many of them and be an artist, a journalist, a diplomat, a businessman, and a scientist.

Benjamin Franklin was not the only genius, however. Take Dr. William Thornton, born in the Virgin Islands in 1759, and educated as a doctor in Edinburgh, Scotland. Dr. Thornton moved to the United States in 1787 and became a citizen, and a good one. In 1789, using just a few reference books, he designed a building for a library in Philadelphia in a prize competition, and won.

Then he joined a man named John Fitch, who was trying to run a boat operated by steam-driven oars on the Delaware River. They made the boat run at 13 kilometers (8 miles) an hour on regular trips. But somehow the idea of this kind of boat never caught on, and it was put away. Later, Robert Fulton claimed credit for the first steam-driven boat.

Then Dr. Thornton entered *another* competition for a design for the new capital building to be raised in Washington, D.C. He won that competition, too. He was then made one of the commissioners of the city. Eventually he moved there to become a fulltime architect, designing rich and ornate houses.

Then President Thomas Jefferson made him superintendent of patents. In 1814, the British had captured Washington, D. C. After capturing it, they began to burn it down. The story is told that the British were about to put the torch to the Patent Office. Seeing this, Thornton, then 55 years old, interrupted. He asked the British officer in charge if he would not be ashamed to destroy a building that had no military value, that was not part of the government of the United States, but a place where the records of human genius were kept. The story goes on that the Britisher agreed, somewhat shamefacedly. The story may not be true, but the Patent Office was not burned.

Dr. Thornton worked at his job as Patent Superintendent until he died in 1828. He also painted, wrote three novels, devised a method of teaching the deaf to speak, and wrote a pamphlet against slavery (though his idea was to ship the slaves back to Africa). He tried to get a national university started in Washington and proposed a Panama canal. He also bought stock in gold mines and sheep ranches. Altogether, he was a very busy American.

In 1817, the British agreed to a treaty, called the Rush-Bagot Agreement, that demilitarized the boundary with Canada. By the Convention of 1818, the British and Americans also agreed that the boundary between the United States and Canada would be at the 49th parallel, from Lake of the Woods to the Rockies. In addition, the United States and Great Britain agreed to share the Oregon Country north of the 42d parallel.

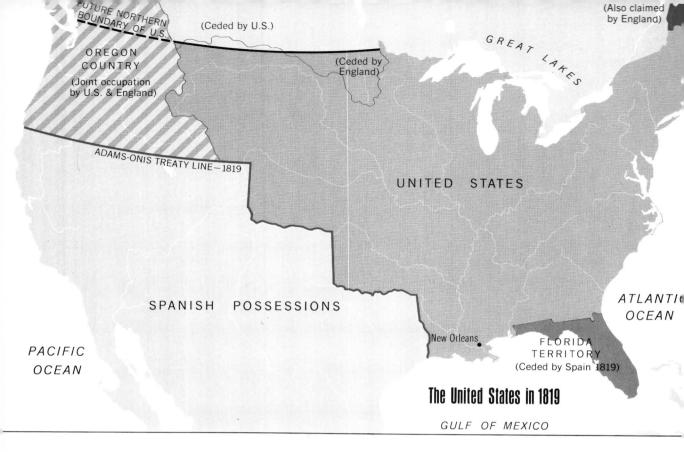

FUTURE NORTHERN BOUNDARY OF U.S.

(Ceded by U.S.)

OREGON COUNTRY
(Joint occupation by U.S. & England)

GREAT LAKES

(Also claimed by England)

(Ceded by England)

ADAMS-ONIS TREATY LINE—1819

UNITED STATES

SPANISH POSSESSIONS

ATLANTIC OCEAN

PACIFIC OCEAN

New Orleans

FLORIDA TERRITORY
(Ceded by Spain 1819)

The United States in 1819

GULF OF MEXICO

In 1819, Secretary of State John Quincy Adams negotiated another treaty, this time with Spain. One part of this Adams-Onis Treaty sold Florida to the United States. The more important part traced out the boundary between Mexico and the Louisiana Territory south of the 42d parallel. These two treaties gave the United States a boundary that ran all the way to the Pacific Ocean. The treaties also marked the end of American involvement in European wars for the next 100 years. The nation was now free to turn away from the Atlantic and concentrate on its vast new lands to the West.

Questions for Discussion

1. Why did the War Hawks get their greatest support in the West?
2. Why is the War of 1812 often referred to as "The Second War of Independence"?
3. Who commanded the American forces at the Battle of New Orleans? Why is the battle sometimes described as an "accidental battle in an accidental war"?
4. How did the treaties negotiated with European powers between 1817 and 1819 end United States involvement in their wars?

Chapter 10 Review

Summary Questions for Discussion

1. What forces helped to unify the colonies into a nation?
2. Describe five precedents established by Washington.
3. Why was the cabinet created?
4. As Secretary of the Treasury, what was Hamilton's financial program? What did he hope to accomplish?
5. What is the "elastic clause" of the Constitution? How did Hamilton use it to justify his bank?
6. Who was involved in the layout and construction of Washington, D.C.?
7. What problems did the French Revolution of 1789 create for Washington? How did he resolve it?
8. Why was John Jay sent to Britain to negotiate a treaty? What were the provisions of this treaty?
9. What areas of conflict existed with Spain? What was agreed upon by the treaty negotiated by Thomas Pinckney?
10. What were Jefferson's views on government?
11. In the election of 1796, how did the United States elect a President and Vice President from two opposing parties?
12. Describe the XYZ affair.
13. How could political parties unite people of different sections of the country?
14. How did the election of 1800 show the faults of the electoral system? What is the Twelfth Amendment that resulted?
15. What motivated Jefferson to purchase the entire Louisiana Territory?
16. Why did Tripoli declare war on the United States? How did the United States gain prestige from this war?
17. What effect did the Embargo Act of 1807 have on the American economy?
18. What reasons did Madison give for war with Britain?
19. What was the character of the treaty signed at Ghent in 1814?
20. What was provided for in the Adams-Onis Treaty?

Word Study

Fill in each blank in the sentences that follow with the term below that is most appropriate.

Senatorial courtesy   naturalized   Democratic-Republican
deport   nullification   nationalism
Sedition   excise tax   agrarian
coalition   Alien   Secretaries
impressment   Federalist

1. The Presidential advisors who make up the Cabinet are called _____.
2. Pro-Hamilton groups called _____ opposed pro-Jefferson forces called _____.
3. Another term for farm-related interests is _____ interests.
4. Each party had to unite many groups into a _____ in order to win elections.
5. Although there was great loyalty or _____ in the country, some issues divided and tested the new nation.
6. At home, a Whiskey Rebellion had resulted from the imposition of an _____.
7. Immigrants who were not yet _____ were often considered dangerous.
8. The _____ Act gave the President the right to arrest immigrants or _____ them.
9. The Virginia and Kentucky Resolutions attempted to establish the principle of _____.
10. The British policy of _____ was a major cause of the War of 1812.

Unit 2 Review

Summary

The American Revolution of 1776 was a political revolution with roots that ran deep and with results that were far-reaching. The failure of legal and peaceful attempts at reconciliation with the mother country resulted in an armed revolt. At first, the colonists sought equal rights as loyal English subjects. At the same time, they did not want laws imposed upon them without having some say in their government. As the British became more stubborn in their stand against self-government, the colonists became more radical. This resulted in the colonists' drive for independence from England.

Before the first shots were fired, the groundwork for independence had already been laid. At home, the pamphleteers, especially Thomas Paine in *Common Sense*, kept the questions of law and liberty alive. Thought finally ended in action with the writing of the Declaration of Independence by Thomas Jefferson. And independence was declared on July 4, 1776. By 1783, the Treaty of Paris was signed. This treaty declared the United States free and independent and established boundaries for the new nation. The problems now were those at home as the new nation entered a very critical period. The question was, "Would the United States survive?"

In 1781, the Articles of Confederation were adopted. The Confederation government lacked power and was unable to function efficiently. Without an executive or judicial branch or means of enforcing laws, the Confederation faced serious problems. Of these, foreign affairs and financial distress were the most prominent. So in May 1787, delegates returned to Philadelphia to revise the Articles. The result was the Constitution of the United States. Through a series of compromises, the delegates finally agreed on a document that has survived the tests of time. The Constitution called for a federal system of government. The national government was divided among three branches, with checks and balances on each. By 1789, the new government was functioning. George Washington was elected its first President. The thirty years that followed served as a test of endurance for the young American nation. What began in the 1760s as a plea by loyal English colonists for "Rights of Englishmen" resulted in the creation of a new nation—a nation that by 1819 had survived severe growing pains.

Summary Questions

1. What were the underlying conflicts or questions at the root of the American Revolution?

2. In what ways did the British use of force against the colonists at Lexington and Concord have a result opposite from the purpose for which it was intended?

3. What part did propaganda play in arousing the colonists to rebel against their lawful government, the British?

4. What were the advantages and disadvantages of the colonists during the Revolution? of the British?

5. What role did foreign nations play during the American Revolution?

6. In what ways was the Treaty of Peace in 1783 a generous settlement? What unsettled problems remained?

7. In the Declaration of Independence, what arguments did Jefferson use to convince his fellow Americans that independence was a just and legal step? Why did he appeal to the "opinions of mankind" rather than simply to the opinions of Americans?

8. What was the purpose of George Rogers

Clark's expedition into the interior of the United States?

9. What were the major weaknesses of the Articles of Confederation?

10. Why was compromise necessary in the creation of the federal Constitution? Why is it an important factor in democratic government?

Developing Your Vocabulary

Choose the correct term to complete the following sentences:

1. Taxes on goods coming into a country are called (duties, excise taxes).

2. A government with a hereditary ruler such as a king or queen is a(n) (monarchy, anarchy).

3. (Federalism, Nationalism) is a feeling of patriotism or love or loyalty toward one's country or ethnic group.

4. Powers held both by the state and federal government are known as (exclusive, concurrent) powers.

5. The Senate has the right to (confirm, impeach) Presidential appointments.

6. The Hessian soldiers hired during the Revolution by the British were known as (mercenaries, privateers).

7. (Moderates, Radicals) are those who use extreme methods to accomplish their ends.

8. A strategy employed by the British on the eve of the War of 1812 was (guerrilla warfare, impressment).

9. An (alien, envoy) is a person chosen to represent one government in its dealings with another.

10. The Supreme Court's ability to judge a law unconstitutional is known as (judicial review, federalism).

Mapping

1. On an outline map of the United States, locate and label:

    a. the original thirteen states

    b. the territory acquired by the Treaty of Paris of 1763.

    c. the boundaries as established by the Treaty of 1783

    d. the Louisiana Purchase

Analyzing and Interpreting

2. For each of the following events, describe the circumstances involved, the results of the event, and its significance in the development of the United States.

    a. Washington's proclamation of Neutrality

    b. The Jay treaty with England

    c. The Pinckney Treaty with Spain

    d. The XYZ Affair

    e. The Alien and Sedition Acts and the Virginia and Kentucky Resolutions

    f. The Louisiana Purchase

    g. The War with Tripoli

    h. The War of 1812

UNIT
3
The United States Expands to the Pacific

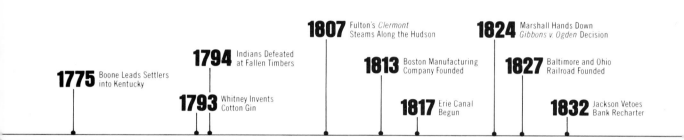

1775 Boone Leads Settlers into Kentucky

1794 Indians Defeated at Fallen Timbers

1793 Whitney Invents Cotton Gin

1807 Fulton's *Clermont* Steams Along the Hudson

1813 Boston Manufacturing Company Founded

1817 Erie Canal Begun

1824 Marshall Hands Down *Gibbons v. Ogden* Decision

1827 Baltimore and Ohio Railroad Founded

1832 Jackson Vetoes Bank Recharter

CHAPTER 11
The Pioneer Spirit

CHAPTER 12
The Beginnings of Industrial America

CHAPTER 13
Westward to the Pacific

Some of the first English settlers in Virginia and Massachusetts felt the magnetic pull of the West almost immediately. In the nineteenth century, Americans felt that same strong urge to explore westward. This opening of the new frontier is the subject of Unit 3. The frontier drew not only settlers, but gold miners, soldiers, and sailors as well. The English novelist Charles Dickens once wrote that an American would probably refuse to enter heaven unless assured of the possibility of moving farther west. What has the frontier meant to Americans? This is the historic question with which we begin the unit.

1846 Oregon Territory
Acquired by Treaty

1837 Panic and
Depression

1848 First Women's Rights
Convention

1836 Texas Wins
Independence

1849 Gold Rush
in California

The three chapters in Unit 3 depict different phases of American expansion in the 1800s. The subjects discussed in Chapter 11 are the life led by frontier settlers, the growth of new states in the Old Northwest and Old Southwest, and the invasion of White settlers into American Indian lands in the Far West. In Chapter 12, there is a description of the rapid changes in transportation and industry that went along with, and sometimes speeded up, the move westward. In Chapter 13, you will learn about the carving of new states and territories in the Far West, out of lands either claimed or owned by other countries. The political and social effects of this first period of American industrial growth are also examined.

Was this burst of expansion a force toward progress? This is the question asked in the final part of the unit.

CHAPTER 11

The Pioneer Spirit

Henry David Thoreau, an American writer living in Concord, Massachusetts, used to take walks to exercise. He noticed that whenever he started out without any destination in mind, he always found himself heading westward. "I must walk toward Oregon," he wrote in 1845, "and not toward Europe." In saying that he was drawn westward, Thoreau was expressing a feeling shared by many other Americans.

The westward movement began with colonial settlements, such as Deerfield, Massachusetts. By 1775, the frontier—the area of farthest westward settlement—was in Kentucky and Tennessee. By 1850, enough Americans were settled in California to demand, and to get, statehood. It took 150 years to reach the Allegheny Mountains, but only 75 years more to reach the Pacific Ocean.

In this great move across the continent, Americans experienced new ways of thinking that are still apparent today. For example, Americans began to believe that growth was a good thing and that the future would always be an improvement on the past. Unfortunately, this belief lead frontier settlers to use up land, grass, timber, and game with little thought that their quantities might one day be limited. Another change in attitude was the respect given to an individual who, without social position or wealth, earned his or her own way by hard work and ability.

The expansion westward was only one part of national growth. In addition, the United States established itself among the community of nations. And the American people developed a strong national pride—"America for the Americans." North and South America would no longer be subject to the whims of European powers.

READING GUIDE

1. **Despite the hardships involved, why have Americans been drawn to the West?**
2. **How were the American Indians forced to make way for the migration of White settlers?**
3. **Why are the pioneers, the mountaineers, and the Western settlers considered American folk heroes?**
4. **How did American foreign affairs make way for American territorial expansion?**

Harvey Dunn's painting captures the spirit of explorer Jedediah Smith.

1. The Lure of the West

The most powerful magnet pulling Americans westward was cheap, undeveloped land. In a new nation of farmers, owning land made people independent. A move to new land meant the opportunity to raise bigger and better crops and to improve one's standard of living. No one who knew how to plow and plant and who was willing to "pull up stakes" had to feel trapped by past failures. A bad yesterday could not spoil the hope of a good tomorrow.

The land, however, was never completely free. The federal government sold land at auctions. But it was always sold in plots of the smallest size and at the lowest price. In 1785, a settler needed at least $640 in cash to buy the smallest-sized farm sold by the government.

Realizing that settlers could not afford the land, Congress lowered the minimum plot size in 1804. By 1820, after several changes in land laws, as little as $100 in cash could buy a family its own farm of 32 hectares (80 acres). Yet, even that sum represented the savings of a year or two of hard work.

Many pioneers, called *squatters*, tried to get free land by clearing a farm without owning it. By doing this, they hoped that, in time, possession would give them *title* (legal ownership). There was always the risk, however, that, after years of bitter effort, the rightful owner would appear and claim the land.

Both the squatters and those who bought their land needed some *capital*—money, tools, and other things necessary for production. Pioneers needed axes, plows, seeds, wagons, horses, oxen, chickens, guns, and ammunition. In this sense the pioneer was a *capitalist*—a person who owns a business and sells a product for profit.

Often, a pioneer bought land from a private company of *land speculators*, those who bought thousands or millions of acres from the government not to farm but to sell for a profit. Though speculators often sold pioneers bad land at high prices, some companies honestly worked to improve their holdings and to attract customers. They did this by building roads, mills, bridges, and other aids to settlement.

When the prices for farming products, like cotton, were high, land prices soared. So farmers and planters borrowed money to buy more land, counting on future income to repay their debts. These land holdings were based on credit. Settlements eventually spread out over a wide area. But they were ill-equipped because they lacked schools and other needed services.

In spite of the problems of starting a frontier farm, millions of Americans found the means to move westward. Often, the same family made many such moves. Most land gave generous harvests. And more land always seemed to be available farther west. As a result, many pioneers did not see the need to care for the soil, save trees, or protect game animals for the future.

Advertisements promised a great future in the West. This 1836 poster promotes a new town site in Illinois.

240

Government and Pioneering

Moving westward was an adventure into the unknown. The first few families to move to a new frontier were intruders in a strange and sometimes harsh world. They had to endure sickness without doctors and hospitals, and disasters without police officers. If important tools broke or food supplies were destroyed, lifesaving replacements were rarely available. Only after a good number of families had settled a new frontier did the beginnings of organized community life appear.

Because they had to depend on themselves, the early Western pioneers became strong individualists. When they needed help, they rarely looked beyond their few neighbors. They were apt to be impatient with the government, which seemed far away, hard to reach, and run by people who did not understand their problems.

Yet, for certain key needs, such as transportation and defense, the Western pioneer relied more on government than most Americans. When the early settlers had finally harvested the first crop of corn or fattened the hogs, they still faced the problem of getting produce to market. A nearby river was helpful because it was easy to float goods downstream on rafts or in flatboats. However, land transportation was very poor. Rain turned "back-country" roads into mudholes. New settlers badly needed level, well-drained highways. And they needed bridges and canals. The demand for these "internal improvements," as they were then called, was basic to Western life. Only the national government had the capital to undertake these **public works.**

public works
works constructed for public use or enjoyment, especially when financed and owned by the government (for example, schools and highways)

241

Pennsylvania settlers hold a community "Flax-Scutching Bee." Frontier folk made an enjoyable social event out of the dull chore of beating flax to separate the valuable linen fibers from the woody pulp.

Daniel Boone's love of the frontier became legendary. This engraving was made from a portrait painted when Boone was 85.

Certain political leaders sought to provide the needs of the frontier settlers. At the end of the War of 1812, President Madison called for the development of a system of roads and canals that would connect the frontier with the eastern coast. One of the features of Henry Clay's "American System" (Chapter 12), which included a call for a protective tariff and a national bank, was public works at federal expense. Clay of Kentucky and John Calhoun of South Carolina persuaded Congress to appropriate money to build a "national pike." The Cumberland, or National, Road reached from the upper Potomac River to Wheeling on the Ohio River. This road was later extended across Ohio and Indiana into Illinois. As each section of the road was completed, it was turned over to the state in which it was located. (See map, page 245.) President Madison had doubts about the constitutionality of internal improvements at federal expense. When Calhoun's Bonus Bill for further improvements reached Madison's desk, the President vetoed it. After that, expansion of transportation became the responsibility of the states and private industry.

The settlers depended heavily on the federal army to move the American Indians off their tribal land. From colonial days on, Westerners demanded that lawmaking bodies located in the East spend money on forts and troops in American Indian country. Each westward step of the frontier was accomplished not only by self-reliance, but also by the efforts of an active federal government.

Questions for Discussion

1. Define *squatter, title, capital, capitalist, land speculator.*
2. What was the relationship of the squatter to the development of the American frontier?
3. How did the frontier experience make people self-reliant?

The first stage of westward migration broke through the barrier of the Allegheny Mountains about 1760. After 1765, settlers on their way West could get as far as Pittsburgh on roads that had been cut by the British armies during the French and Indian War. From Pittsburgh, they could float down the Ohio. An inviting gateway through the southern part of the Allegheny Mountains was Cumberland Gap. (See map on page 245.) Through it passed the people of the future state of Kentucky. Many of these settlers were led by the remarkable Daniel Boone.

Boone was born near Reading, Pennsylvania, in 1734. He did not have much formal schooling. However, by the age of 12, he was an experienced hunter and traveler in the wilderness. When he was in his teens, his family moved to North Carolina. Soon afterward, he participated in the French and Indian War. Then, Boone settled down in North Carolina to farm. Each winter, he left home with traps and gun to spend months in the lonely forests, where he felt most comfortable.

In 1775, a group of land speculators, the Transylvania Company, hired Boone to lead a party of settlers into Kentucky. Boone led the families through Cumberland Gap. Once in Kentucky, he directed them in building a fort. These families were to become the future customers of the Transylvania Company.

To defend their invaded hunting grounds, the American Indians frequently attacked the pioneers. Kentucky soon became known as "the dark and bloody ground." Along with other leaders, Boone held the settlements together. His admiring neighbors elected him to posts such as legislator, sheriff, and colonel of militia. But he had a longing to move on. In 1788, he pushed northward into present-day West Virginia, and then to Missouri where, in 1820, he died.

Boone was later glorified because he was a new type of national hero. A good, brave, uneducated man, Boone won respect for his courage and his skills in leading "civilized" Easterners into the wilds of the West.

By the end of the Revolution, settlements had been planted in Kentucky and Tennessee. In both places, pioneers met, elected officials, and challenged the authority of Virginia and North Carolina to govern them. The "colonists" of the Allegheny Mountains succeeded in getting Kentucky admitted as a state in 1792, and Tennessee in 1796.

Settling the Old Northwest and the South

The next big thrust of pioneers westward, from about 1800 to 1850, settled the region of rolling hills and prairie between the Allegheny Mountains and the Mississippi River.

2. Expanding the Frontier

In March 1775, Daniel Boone led the first large party of settlers through the Cumberland Gap and then northwest to the Kentucky River.

At Boonesborough, Kentucky, they built this small but important frontier outpost.

In this painting, General "Mad Anthony" Wayne leads his troops against his American Indian opponents in the Battle of Fallen Timbers.

An American Indian approaches two American army officers at the signing of the Treaty of Greenville.

This was the West contained in the original boundaries of 1783. Each advance of the Whites meant the continued loss of the land and freedom of the American Indians.

In the summer of 1789, war with the American Indians broke out in the Northwest Territory. This war began for two reasons. First, there were many "border incidents" between American Indian and White hunting parties. In addition, the British were encouraging the American Indians to form a confederacy of tribes north of the Ohio River and to resist the American advance. At first, it seemed that the Indians might be successful. In 1790, they ambushed and defeated a small party of Americans led by General Josiah Harmar. A year later, they defeated a force led by General Arthur St. Clair and killed some 630 Americans.

Washington then called on another wartime general to subdue the Northwest. Like most American generals of his time, "Mad Anthony" Wayne was a successful civilian-turned-soldier. He had been a tanner and then a surveyor in Pennsylvania before the Revolution. After that, he served as a Congressman and then became a southern planter. He spent a year carefully drilling his recruits. Then he marched into American Indian country and let word spread that he would attack on a certain day in August 1794. The Indians fell into the trap. Wayne knew that the braves fasted before a battle. So he sat for three days waiting while the American Indians grew hungrier each hour. Finally, when many of them had given up and left their camp in search of food, he attacked. In a few hours, the Indians were defeated.

This Battle of Fallen Timbers had a powerful impact. The British, who were supposed to be neutral, no longer dared to aid the American Indians openly. Therefore, the chiefs realized that they could not hope to stop the Americans, who would raise new armies and keep coming. So, in 1795, at General Wayne's command, they signed the Treaty of Greenville, giving up their hunting lands in present-day southeastern Indiana and southern Ohio. White settlers realized that the new national government would use force to open the old Northwest for them and subdue American Indian resistance.

Florida became the site of further conflict between the desires of American settlers and American Indian claims. In 1814, the Seminole branch of the Creeks gave up territory in Georgia in a treaty with the United States government. The Seminoles and runaway slaves then used Spanish Florida as a base of operation against settlers in Georgia. The Seminoles were encouraged by two British traders, who suggested that the Treaty of Ghent voided the American treaty with the American Indians.

In 1817 after several settlers were scalped, President Monroe sent Andrew Jackson to subdue the Seminoles. Jackson not only attacked

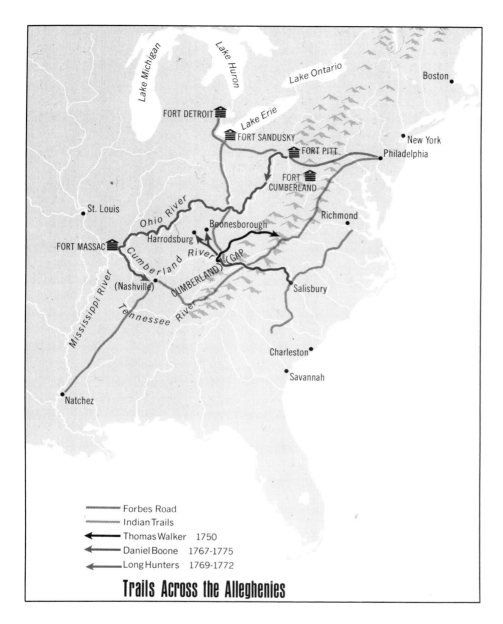

Trails Across the Alleghenies

Map legend:
- Forbes Road
- Indian Trails
- Thomas Walker 1750
- Daniel Boone 1767-1775
- Long Hunters 1769-1772

Map labels: Lake Michigan, Lake Huron, Lake Ontario, Boston, FORT DETROIT, Lake Erie, FORT SANDUSKY, FORT PITT, New York, Philadelphia, FORT CUMBERLAND, St. Louis, Ohio River, Boonesborough, Richmond, Harrodsburg, Cumberland River, FORT MASSAC, CUMBERLAND (GAP), Mississippi River, (Nashville), Salisbury, Tennessee River, Charleston, Savannah, Natchez

the Seminoles on the American side of the border, but he also swept into Florida.

Jackson beat back the Seminoles. He captured, tried, and executed the two British traders. He also took over several Spanish forts. In answer to the criticism that he broke international law, Jackson claimed that the Spanish could not police their own territory. All the members of Monroe's Cabinet, except John Quincy Adams, agreed with the President that Jackson had overstepped his authority.

245

In 1835, Seminoles attacked this blockhouse in Florida.

Chief Osceola of the Seminoles. Osceola led his people in a fight to keep their land in Florida.

Adams claimed that Spain had an obligaton to control the settlers in its territory. If Spain could not do so, then it should give up the territory. Spain had withdrawn troops from Florida to send them to Latin America to crush revolts in the Spanish colonies. The Spanish government realized that it might be wiser to negotiate a treaty with the United States before Florida was seized. In 1819—in return for the United States' promise to pay $5 million in claims against Spain by United States citizens—Spain ceded Florida to the United States. At the same time, Spain also gave up its claim to the Oregon country to the United States and defined the Mexican boundary.

Community Living on the Frontier

Now, thousands of settlers flocked into the new territories. There were enough to make Ohio a state in 1803, followed by Indiana in 1816, and Illinois in 1818. For each pioneer family, the westward move meant the individual experience of pulling up roots. Yet, there was always a group aspect to frontier living.

Log-cabin settlers were far removed from civilization, but they still had a sense of unity. Since they were isolated, they depended heavily on other nearby pioneers for help in emergencies. Besides, the basic human need for companionship was bound to bring people together. Many tasks were shared. When it was time to put up a cabin, for example, neighbors might unite to roll and lift the heavy logs, eat the food prepared, and refresh themselves with cider and whiskey.

Another event that unified the settlers was the camp meeting. Thousands of pioneers believed in a genuine, burning hell to which they would likely go if they did not get God's help in repenting their

Carl Bodmer, a Swiss artist who toured the United States from 1832 to 1834, painted this view of a farm on the Illinois prairie during the winter.

wickedness and changing their ways. At outdoor gatherings, preachers in buckskin shouted at sinners to turn away from evil. The listeners often twisted and squirmed in fear or leaped and sang for joy.

A strange combination of frontier forces worked to form the American character. There was a democratic spirit evident in the plain speech and dress of the settlers. Any attempt to put on airs was certain to be resented. Yet, in this classless society, an individual who did not share the common outlook on any subject was viewed with suspicion. For example, a young man who did not want to fight American Indians or become wealthy was not likely to be popular. Nor was a young woman who doubted the authority of preachers or thought that girls should be well educated. Individual pioneers were heavily influenced by majority opinion, because the need for community closeness was overpowering.

The Southwestern Cotton Frontier

So many wagons crowded the roads into the old Northwest after 1815 that one foreigner wrote, "The old America seems to be breaking up and moving westward." The same movement was going on south of the Ohio River. Its driving force was cheap land. However, the westward movement received much help from a device invented by one Yankee, Eli Whitney.

Eli Whitney was born in 1765 to a well-off Massachusetts farmer. Since boyhood, he had loved to tinker. Before he was out of his teens, he had run a successful nail-manufacturing business. At the age of 23, he entered Yale College as a freshman, even though he was older than

Eli Whitney, inventor of the cotton gin, as painted by Samuel Morse.

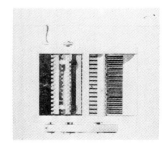

One of Eli Whitney's drawings for the first cotton gin.

Slave labor and the cotton gin brought wealth to the South in the 1800s.

most seniors. Upon graduating in 1792, he went south. While he was a guest on a Georgia plantation, he heard local landowners say that England's growing textile industry needed raw cotton so badly that cotton could become a more profitable crop for the South than tobacco, rice, or indigo. But the only kind of cotton that grew easily in the South had stubborn, clinging seeds in it. The cotton was so difficult to clean that a hardworking slave could clean only a pound or so a day. If someone could design a machine to do the job more quickly, the South would have another important cash crop.

Within ten days, Whitney designed a model for a cotton gin and, by April 1793, had perfected the device. Now a slave could grind out 50 pounds of cotton fiber a day. Soon, water-powered cotton gins cleaned millions of pounds and made cotton the king of Southern crops. As a result, Southerners swarmed across the southern Appalachian Mountains in search of good cotton lands. A North Carolina planter wrote, "The Alabama fever rages here with great violence and has carried off vast numbers of our citizens." Enough were "carried off" to make Mississippi a state in 1817, followed by Alabama in 1819.

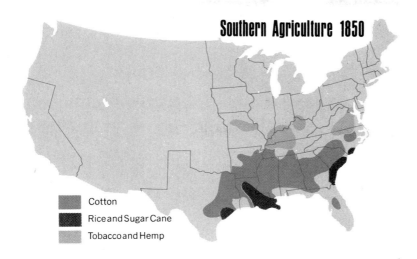

Southern Agriculture 1850

- ■ Cotton
- ■ Rice and Sugar Cane
- ■ Tobacco and Hemp

The Southwest, too, was a frontier. Its large planters were not old, settled, aristocratic families. Rather, they were newcomers on their way up in the world. The best lands and biggest plantations were in river valleys. However, in the hills thousands of hardworking small farmers dwelt, eager for cheap land and internal improvements.

But this cotton frontier differed in one all-important way. It expanded the area in which slave labor could be used. By 1820, the South was booming, and it was no more ready to give up slavery than New England would have been ready to give up seafaring.

A New Indian Policy

The usual way of dealing with American Indian tribes was to sign treaties with them at meetings. The American Indians would gather for several days of pipe-smoking, exchanging of gifts, and drinking of whiskey. American officials encouraged this practice to confuse the American Indians' judgment. The Indians would then often trade more of their hunting lands for money and supplies. Surrounded by soldiers, the chiefs had little choice. If such "diplomatic" tactics failed, there was always the army or the militia.

As the line of settlement swept toward the Mississippi, the government devised a new American Indian policy. Encouraged by President Monroe, Congress set up the Bureau of Indian Affairs in 1824. The Bureau pursued a policy of removal. All the nation's Indians were to give up their old lands and move west of the Mississippi to the Great Plains. And their new lands would be guaranteed to them forever. The hope was that once a "permanent Indian frontier" was set up, clashes between Whites and Indians would end.

However, this seemingly generous offer had drawbacks. On the Great Plains, which extended to the Rocky Mountains, there were almost no trees and little rainfall. In 1825, almost all Americans

In August 1825, a number of Indian tribes and representatives of the United States government attended this Grand Council at Prairie du Chien, Wisconsin. Within 25 years, nearly all the tribes represented there had ceded their hunting lands to the United States government.

In about 1837, the Georgia militia attacked a Creek village.

believed Whites could not survive on what was at that time called the "Great American Desert." But Congress assumed that because some Indians survived on the Plains, all Indians could.

The American Indians from the East knew better and therefore resisted resettlement as long as possible. President John Q. Adams was sympathetic to their plight. He tried to maintain a decent policy of American Indian relations. In 1825, he revoked an unfair treaty that had been made with the Creeks in Georgia. In 1826, 404,700 million hectares (1 million acres) of good cotton land were restored to them. But Adams was unable to overcome the resistance of the governor of Georgia without resorting to the use of federal troops. Finally, lacking the support of Congress, Adams was forced to back down.

This process of Indian removal was cruel. Southern Indians of five tribes—Choctaw, Creek, Chickasaw, Cherokee, and Seminole—had long been adapted to White ways. The Cherokees, for example, had become farmers in North Carolina and Georgia and owned thousands of cattle. This tribe also owned slaves, gristmills, sawmills, cotton gins, and looms. They had a written language, a school system, and a newspaper. In 1827, they even organized a self-governing state, the Cherokee Republic.

However, Georgia speculators and settlers were eager to get their hands on Cherokee land. President Jackson refused to protect the Indians, even though Georgia defied federal court orders in dealing with the Cherokees. This threat by the state of Georgia to the power of the federal government went unheeded. Jackson felt that Indian rights should not interfere with White settlement. Eventually, the Cherokees were forced to sign agreements to give up their lands. They were driven west, to the new Indian Territory. Many Cherokees lost their lives along a route that became known as the "Trail of Tears."

Some of the Indian tribes, however, did put up a strong fight. Chief Black Hawk of the Sauk and Fox tried to regain his tribal land. His people were unable to survive west of the Mississippi, where they were in conflict with the Sioux. When the hungry remainder of his people crossed the Mississippi into Illinois, they were driven into the Wisconsin wilderness and massacred.

The Seminoles also put up a last-ditch effort to keep their land in Florida. The majority of the Seminoles refused to honor an unjust treaty made in 1832. Led by their brave chief Osceola, they eluded the United States Army for years. In fact, some of their descendants still live in the Everglades.

The era of Indian resettlement was marked by corruption and dishonesty on the part of federal officials. Little of what was promised to the Indians was delivered into the right hands. Thousands of

Robert Lindeux's "The Trail of Tears" shows the Cherokees' forced exodus from their native Georgian land.

Indians died of disease and starvation when they were forced to travel during the winter. In 1832, a cholera epidemic killed many. Others died of starvation when they arrived in their new land because they did not have the money to buy the tools necessary for planting and harvesting. And in 1889, even the Indian Territory was taken by the Whites and renamed Oklahoma.

Questions for Discussion
1. Why could the Cumberland Gap be considered a gateway to the West?
2. What was Daniel Boone's role in expansion of the West?
3. How did community living on the frontier work to form the American character?
4. How did the cotton gin promote Western settlement?
5. What was the government's policy toward the American Indians?

3. Discovering the Far West

Many pioneers had settled on the grassy prairies in Illinois and Indiana, east of the Mississippi. These lands were well-watered, easy to farm, and not far from wooded areas. When White settlers moved beyond the Mississippi to the edge of the Great Plains, they halted before this challenge of a new environment. They did this because distances were huge. Streams to travel on were rare. The farther one moved toward the Rocky Mountains, the drier the soil became. And the Indians there were determined to keep their land. Mounted on

In 1847, H.G. Hine painted this view of the untamed prairie.

their wild ponies, these Indians were faster, tougher foes than the forest Indians.

Yet, beyond those mountains and the deserts of the Southwest lay a Pacific Coast region with rich soil. Beginning around 1840, some settlers began to find ways across plain and mountain to this new promised land. On these journeys, they met the Plains Indians— Sioux, Blackfeet, Cheyennes, Arapahos, Apaches, Kiowas, Comanches, and others. These people lived in the last areas of the United States to be overrun by Whites.

The Plains Indians depended on the buffalo for their existence. As discussed in Chapter 1, the hides, horns, and bones of the buffalo enabled Plains Indians to flourish in a treeless world.

Curiously, the Spaniards had something to do with prolonging the existence of the Plains Indians. The Spanish explorers introduced the horse into North America. Some of their horses escaped and multiplied into herds of magnificent wild horses. Sometime after 1720, the Plains Indians learned to capture and ride them. Then they were able to hunt the buffalo with far more ease and success than on foot. When some Indians were able to replace bows and arrows with firearms, hunting became even easier.

The Kiowa, Sioux, Cheyenne, Arapaho, and other Plains tribes became mounted, *nomadic* (wandering) Indians instead of settled villagers raising corn and beans. A wonderful, buffalo-based Plains Indian culture grew up. The combining of the Whites' horse and gun with the Indians' skill in pursuing and using the buffalo produced a new kind of Indian culture. It flourished only 150 years before the pioneers moved in and destroyed it.

For Plains Indians, killing buffalo was not done for sport. A successful buffalo hunt meant food and clothing. Jacob Alfred Miller's "Yell of Triumph" captures the spirit of a buffalo hunt.

Mountain People Explore the Far West

The first White probings into the Plains and mountain world, however, were made by those who were themselves ill at ease in settled surroundings. These were the mountain people who worked for the fur-trapping companies. By the 1820s, they were pursuing the beaver and other fur-bearing animals all the way to the Rocky Mountains.

Trappers like Jedediah Smith or Jim Beckwourth or Jim Bridger were men who could live alone in a wilderness different from the one Daniel Boone had known. They could wander over thousands of square miles of mountain and desert. They could find their way from place to place as easily as city dwellers find their way from home to office. They disappeared alone into mountain country each fall and spent the winter trapping and living with the Indians. They could read animal tracks and other hunting clues with the skill of the Indians. They decorated

Trapper Jim Bridger was the first White known to have visited the Great Salt Lake.

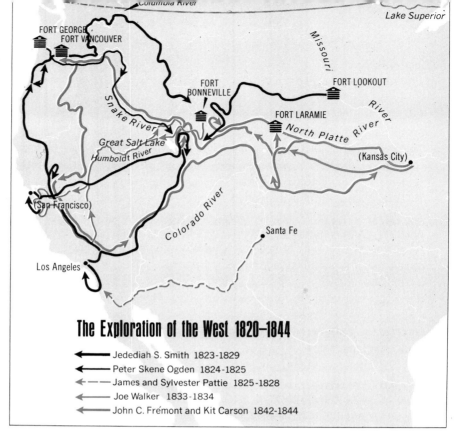

The Exploration of the West 1820-1844

←——— Jedediah S. Smith 1823-1829
←——— Peter Skene Ogden 1824-1825
←– – – James and Sylvester Pattie 1825-1828
←——— Joe Walker 1833-1834
←——— John C. Frémont and Kit Carson 1842-1844

James Beckwourth, one of the first trappers and explorers in the West.

their clothing with feathers and shells and used Indian charms, spells, and herbs to "make medicine" when they were sick. These mountain people survived terrible hardships—blizzards, near-starvation, and ghastly wounds from battles with people or wild animals.

JAMES PIERSON BECKWOURTH

Mountainman and Scout James Pierson Beckwourth was a famous mountainman and Indian scout who discovered the pass named for him in the Sierra Nevadas of California. He is also credited with being a founder of Pueblo, Colorado.

Beckwourth (also Beckwith) was born in Virginia on April 26, 1798. As a young adult, he migrated to the Far West. Soon thereafter, in the 1820s, he joined several expeditions under the leadership of fur trader William H. Ashley. Beckwourth was later befriended by the Crow Indians and spent the next six years living with them and learning their ways. It was through the

Crows that Beckwourth acquired the skills that gave him the reputation of being one of the finest Indian scouts on record.

Beckwourth participated in the Mexican War by joining the forces of Stephen Kearney in California in 1846. After the Mexican War ended, Beckwourth lived in California, Missouri, and Colorado. He later took part in the Cheyenne War of 1864, again being of invaluable service as a scout. Afterwards he settled near Denver, where he died around 1867. James Beckwourth's autobiography, *The Life and Adventures of James P. Beckwourth*, was published in 1856 and reissued in 1931.

.In springtime, they appeared at trappers' meeting points where fur buyers and sellers met. They unloaded their peltry, ate and drank until content, and then were off again. These settlers were truly free.

They opened the way for organized parties of people attempting to conquer the wilderness. In 1824, Jedediah Smith pioneered a route through South Pass in Wyoming. South Pass became a key gateway on the Oregon Trail. Three years later, he made the first overland trip to California. Peter Skene Ogden, a Canadian competing with American fur trappers in the disputed Oregon Country, explored the north side of the Great Salt Lake. In 1828, Sylvester Pattie and his son James found their way from Santa Fe to San Diego, only to be thrown into jail by the Mexican governor there. In July 1833, Joe Walker left Fort Bonneville. He followed the Humboldt River, crossed the Sierra Nevadas, and arrived in San Francisco, California.

Soon the trails of the mountain people were crisscrossing the Far West. In 1842, the federal government showed its increasing interest in the West by sending an expedition under Lieutenant John C. Frémont and his trapper-guide, Kit Carson, to explore the central Rocky Mountains.

Frémont's published account of his second visit to the West did much to increase America's interest in California. He stressed the vast trading and farming potential. He also revealed the weak hold the disorganized Mexican government had over the region.

Kit Carson won nationwide fame as the guide for three highly publicized expeditions to the West led by John C. Frémont.

Settlers moving west camp along the Laramie River in Wyoming.

The Settling of the Far West

The trails found by the mountain people were soon put to use by traders and immigrants. In 1824, business people in Missouri began to send yearly caravans to Santa Fe, then a part of Mexico. These long strings of wagons brought textiles, tools, and hardware from the United States. In exchange, they got silver, mules, and furs from Mexico. By 1846, bawling oxen and their drivers cursing in fluent English became common sounds in the southern Rocky Mountains.

Missionaries also came with the early wave of settlers in the Oregon Country. In 1834, Jason Lee founded a mission and school to serve the Flatheads. Two years later, Marcus and Narcissa Whitman went to Oregon to bring their medicine and religious beliefs to the American Indians. Catholic missionaries also came. Father Jean de Smet, a Jesuit, established the Sacre Coeur Mission.

In 1836, Captain Benjamin Bonneville led the first wagon trains through the South Pass of the Oregon Trail. Jason Lee returned to the East in 1836 to encourage additional settlers. His supporters began publishing *The Oregonian and Indian Advocate*. Soon, news of the rich soil, timberlands, flashing streams, and many furs convinced thousands of Easterners to head West.

Americans were also heading for California in ships. Merchant ships from New England were sailing around Cape Horn, at South America's southern tip, and beating their way northward to the California coast. There they swapped manufactured goods for cowhides, which they took back to shoemaking factories in New England. Visitors to California aboard these ships brought back glowing reports of the climate and fertile soil of this Mexican province.

It did not matter much to them that California was a province of Mexico and that the United States still shared Oregon with the British. As Americans, they believed that it was their right to go anywhere on the continent if opportunity beckoned.

By the summer of 1846, wagon trains were beginning to cross the great Western regions. Large parties of families, wagons loaded with household goods, left Independence, Missouri, in the spring. With a whole lot of luck, they crossed the Plains and mountains and had their animals grazing on the banks of western rivers before the autumn snows fell. The overland trail was long and dangerous. Now, however, entire families were making the trek that only a few mountain trappers had braved five and ten years earlier.

The Mormons

In 1846, the Mormons became one of the largest groups to journey westward. The Mormon religion was founded in the 1820s by Joseph Smith of Palmyra, New York. Smith said that the angel Moroni had

One of the sights seen by settlers moving to Oregon was Mount Hood, viewed here from the Columbia River.

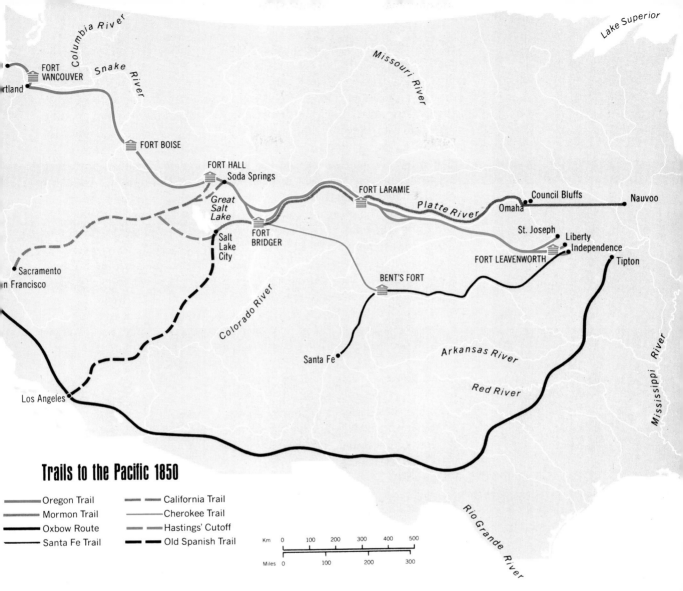

Trails to the Pacific 1850

Oregon Trail	California Trail		
Mormon Trail	Cherokee Trail		
Oxbow Route	Hastings' Cutoff		
Santa Fe Trail	Old Spanish Trail		

Km 0 100 200 300 400 500

Miles 0 100 200 300

given him a revelation. And this revelation led him to discover several golden tablets inscribed with symbols. Smith translated these symbols into the *Book of Mormon* in 1830.

The Mormon Church picked up a huge following. Converts lived as far away as Denmark and Scotland. Smith and his followers tried to establish settlements based on their religious beliefs in New York, Ohio, Illinois, and Missouri.

But everywhere the Mormons went, they met with distrust. People misunderstood their beliefs and resented them. In Independence, Missouri, the frontier settlers thought that the Mormons were against slavery, because they had come from the Northeast. So the newcomers had to move on, even though Joseph Smith was strongly opposed to freeing the slaves.

The Mormons then settled in Nauvoo, Illinois. There they prospered for a time. But when Smith announced that he had had another revelation instructing him to establish *polygamy* (the practice of having several wives) among his group, hostility began once again. As a result of all the distrust that people had for the Mormons, Smith and his brother were arrested and thrown in jail. On June 27, 1844, an unruly mob dragged Smith and his brother from the jail and shot them to death. So the Mormons were forced to move again.

Under the determined leadership of Brigham Young, the Mormons crossed the plains north of the Platte River. In 1847, they settled in the region of the Great Salt Lake in Mexican territory. Young succeeded in establishing a closely ruled *theocratic society*, a society governed by officials who are believed to be guided by God.

Once in Utah, the Mormons took dry desert land and made it blossom. Their settlement was so wealthy that it became a major stop-off point for travelers going West, especially during the gold rush.

Questions for Discussion

1. Define *theocratic society*. How did the Mormons' experiences lead to the development of this type of settlement?
2. What prevented the Plains Indians from becoming farmers?
3. How did the mountain people prepare the way for the coming of White settlers to the Far West?
4. Why was the Pacific Coast settled before the Great Plains?

4. Breaking Away from European Conflicts

Although the United States saw itself as separate from Europe since 1776, it could not help being affected by European affairs. Even before America's involvement in the War of 1812, American rights as a neutral were violated by England and France. Napoleon's dealings had directed the United States toward war with England. When the Treaty of Ghent brought the War of 1812 to a close, conflicts over territory and influence still had to be settled to prevent constant threats of renewed hostilities.

On the Great Lakes, two opposing navies still faced one another. Having flung back an American attempt to overrun their territory, the Canadians were anxious to protect their borders from their American neighbors. Great Britain was planning to build more ships to patrol the Great Lakes. President Madison could have begun an expensive arms race. Instead, he instructed John Quincy Adams, his minister to England, to propose a mutual *disarmament* (the limitation on a country's arms) of the Great Lakes. The British had a number of reasons for agreeing to the offer. First, it would be far easier for the United States than Britain to maintain a fleet there. Also, a British fleet, tied up in the Great Lakes, would be of no advantage to the British on the high seas.

Thus, in 1817, the Americans and the British approved the Rush-Bagot Agreement. This agreement called for strict limitations on the size and number of armed vessels that each nation could keep on the Great Lakes. This was one small step toward mutual trust. In 1871, the disarmament of the entire United States-Canadian border was provided for in the Treaty of Washington.

The Convention of 1818 between the United States and Britain cleared up some other possible difficulties. The Americans were given the right to fish off the coast of Newfoundland. And the border between Canada and the United States was set at the 49th parallel from the Lake of the Woods to the Rocky Mountains. The Convention did not settle the Oregon border, but it did allow for joint occupation of the Oregon Country. In 1842, the Webster-Ashburton Treaty settled the boundary from Maine to the Lake of the Woods. In 1846, the 49th parallel boundary was extended from the Rocky Mountains to the Pacific Ocean.

The Monroe Doctrine

When the United States became a nation, Europeans had already been colonizing the Western Hemisphere for almost 300 years. Spain,

The American merchant ship, the Planter, repulsing an attack by a French national privateer in July 1799.

France, Portugal, Holland, and England had helped themselves freely to gold, silver, fish, furs, timber, and the rich lands of both North and South America. They had fought frequently over these riches. And it seemed likely that they would go on doing so. In that case, it was probable that the new little republic would soon be crushed by the continuing rivalry of European giants in the New World.

From the beginning, though, some American politicians worked to avoid this fate. They dreamed of a day when the United States would be too strong to be threatened. Fortunately, history worked on their side. From 1792 to 1815, Europe's major powers were busy with problems of war and revolution at home. During that time, revolutionary ideas reached the peoples of the Spanish colonies in Latin America. They, too, took up arms—as the thirteen English colonies had—and declared themselves independent nations.

In 1821, Secretary of State John Quincy Adams felt pleased. The breakaway of Spain's New World colonies had reduced the threat that he feared most—European armies ready to attack the United States from European possessions close to its borders. Moreover, with Spanish trade restrictions lifted, United States merchants were finding good customers in Latin America. In 1822, the United States began to recognize the independence of Latin American republics.

By 1823, however, clouds had gathered on Adams' horizon. In 1815, the monarchs of Prussia, Russia and Austria formed a "Holy Alliance" for putting down revolutions—especially democratic revolutions—everywhere. In 1821, the Russian czar suddenly claimed that Alaska extended southward to the 51st parallel. This line conflicted with British and American claims to the Oregon Territory. The Russians were also extending trading posts south along the coast, to a point just north of San Francisco. Foreign vessels were not allowed within 161 kilometers (100 miles) of the coast. Now, Russian expansionism was conflicting with American interests.

Moreover, there was talk of Spain attempting to win back its South American colonies with France's help. Was a new round of European expansion in the Americas about to begin?

Yet, Adams did have one piece of comforting information. In order for Spain to reconquer its colonies, Great Britain, mistress of the seas, would have to remain neutral. But Great Britain had no wish to see its old enemy, Spain, regain power or to allow any other European nation to grow dangerously strong by taking American lands.

Knowing this, Adams and President James Monroe drew up a statement. This statement became known as the Monroe Doctrine. In a message to Congress in December 1823, Monroe declared that the United States did not wish to see Europeans spread their political system to the Western Hemisphere by interfering with governments

that had already declared their independence. While the United States recognized the right of European countries to keep their remaining American colonies, the Americas were no longer "subjects for future colonization by any European power."

Monroe did not make threats. Nor did he claim that the United States should be supreme in the Americas. Rather, in 1823, Adams and Monroe were more concerned with the security of the United States. The Monroe Doctrine was probably not responsible for the fact that Russia did not press its Alaskan claims or that Spain did not try to regain its lost colonies. Nevertheless, such a declaration was bold and revolutionary. It proposed a new policy, barring the mighty countries of Europe from any new imperial adventures in the Americas.

This cartoon appeared in an American magazine more than 75 years after the signing of the Monroe Doctrine and after the inauguration of Theodore Roosevelt in 1901. It foretold the tough-minded interpretation Roosevelt was to give the Doctrine.

CANADA

ATLANTIC OCEAN

UNITED STATES, 1776

GULF OF MEXICO

CUBA

HAITI, 1804

SANTO DOMINGO, 1821

PUERTO RICO

MEXICO, 1821

BR. HONDURAS

GUATEMALA, 1821

HONDURAS, 1821

EL SALVADOR, 1821

NICARAGUA, 1821

COSTA RICA, 1821

PANAMA, 1821

COLOMBIA, 1819

ECUADOR, 1822

CARIBBEAN SEA

VENEZUELA, 1811

GUIANAS

PACIFIC OCEAN

PERU, 1824

BOLIVIA, 1825

PARAGUAY, 1811

CHILE, 1818

ARGENTINA, 1816

BRAZIL, 1822

URUGUAY, 1825

The Monroe Doctrine

—— Protected under the Monroe Doctrine, 1823

☐ Liberated

▨ Under foreign control

1776 Years stand for date of independence

Kilometers
0   1000

0   500
Miles

Questions for Discussion

1. Why was it necessary to negotiate further treaties with the Europeans after 1812?

2. What is *disarmament*? How was it applied in the Rush-Bagot Agreement and the Treaty of Washington?

3. Why was the United States pleased about the Latin American countries breaking away from Spain?

4. What was the purpose of the Holy Alliance? How did Russian expansionism conflict with American interest after 1821?

5. What prompted the writing of the Monroe Doctrine? What was the main thrust of the Doctrine?

Chapter 11 Review

Summary Questions for Discussion

1. Where was the frontier in 1775? in 1850?
2. What lured Americans westward?
3. What barrier stood in the path of westward expansion?
4. What new states resulted from the early movements west?
5. Why did war break out with the American Indians in the Northwest Territory in 1789?
6. What impact did the Battle of Fallen Timbers have on people's minds?
7. What aspects of the American character were developed on the frontier?
8. What effects did Eli Whitney's cotton gin have on settlement of the frontier? on slavery?
9. What was the policy toward American Indians after 1824? What were the drawbacks of this new policy?
10. What were the effects of the American Indian removal on their population?
11. What role did the mountain people play in opening the frontier?
12. Identify Jedediah Smith, Peter Skene Ogden, Sylvester Pattie, Joe Walker, Lieutenant John C. Frémont, and Kit Carson.
13. What areas of possible conflict were resolved by each of the following: Rush-Bagot Agreement (1817), Treaty of Washington (1871), Convention of 1818, the Webster-Ashburton Treaty of 1842?
14. Why was the United States pleased with the independence of the Latin American countries?
15. What was the Monroe Doctrine? What were its effects?

Word Study

Fill in each blank in the sentences that follow with the term below that is most appropriate.

squatters   title   capital   capitalist
land speculators   public works   theocratic

1. To acquire the legal ownership to land, or _____, pioneers employed various means.
2. In order to purchase land, a person needed _____.
3. Some people, known as _____, tried to get land free by clearing and farming it, then claiming possession.
4. Others bought their land from _____ who had bought thousands of acres from the government to sell at a profit.
5. Bridges, canals, roads, and other internal improvements that are undertaken by the government are called _____.
6. The Mormons set up a _____ or church-centered society.

Using Your Skills

1. Refer to the map "Trails Across the Alleghenies." What means of transportation and routes were used by settlers moving west?
2. Examine the map "Southern Agriculture 1850." What is the relationship of each of the following to the information presented on this map: the cotton gin, slavery, westward expansion?
3. Compare the map "The Exploration of the West 1820–1844" (page 254) to "Trails to the Pacific 1850" (page 257). What do the maps reveal about the relationship between exploration and settlement? Why did so many trails come together around the Great Salt Lake?
4. What do the pictures in this chapter tell you about the government's policy toward the American Indians during the first half of the nineteenth century?

CHAPTER 12
The Beginnings of Industrial America

Part of Mark Twain's novel *Huckleberry Finn* tells of how Jim, a runaway slave, and Huck float down the Mississippi on a raft in search of freedom. The time is the 1840s. One very dark night, they hear the pounding of a steamboat engine. At first, the steamboat looks like "a black cloud with rows of glow-worms around it." Then, "all of a sudden," says Huck, "she bulged out, big and scary, with a long row of wide-open furnace doors shining like red-hot teeth and her monstrous bows and guards hanging right over us." As one historian has noted, the age of steam-powered machines burst upon the people of the United States like that steamboat—suddenly, powerfully, and sometimes destructively.

By 1800, technology had begun to change American life. The cotton gin, created in 1793, proved how one invention could change the life of a whole region. It strengthened slavery, increased the pressure to move the American Indians westward, and quickly brought new Southern states into the Union. And after 1800, a whole group of inventions began to redirect the energies of the entire country.

Steam power, first developed for industrial purposes in England in the late 1700s, was now used for transportation. It soon began to overcome the problems of long-distance travel in the rugged interior of the continent.

READING GUIDE

1. How did the changes in transportation affect the settlement and the development of resources in the West?
2. How did the rise of industry affect society?
3. Why did industrialization spur the need for reform?
4. Why might a growth in literature accompany major economic and social change in a society?
5. How did democratic reforms make way for the election of Jackson?
6. Why is the "Age of Jackson" sometimes called "the age of the common man?"

Steamboats belching smoke crowd a New Orleans levee in 1853.

Some families spent their entire lives on the Erie Canal in boats, such as the one pictured here.

1. An Expanding Transportation System

The toughest engineering problem on the Erie Canal was how to get the canal over a rocky cliff at present-day Lockport. A double set of locks solved the problem.

The first major step in the development of a national transportation system was the building of canals. A canal is nothing more than a constructed ditch, filled with water, connecting two bodies of water. It is not dangerous, which is the greatest advantage. Canal transportation did not present the hazards that other land and sea transportation did. In the nineteenth century, patient horses or mules could tow a clumsy-looking, heavily loaded towboat at a steady 8 kilometers (5 miles) an hour for hundreds of miles without danger or great expense.

A few canals were built in the United States as early as the 1790s. In 1817, work was begun on the most famous one, the Erie Canal in New York. It was built to connect the Hudson River at Albany with Lake Erie at Buffalo. Such a canal would provide a water "highway" through the mountain barrier between East and West.

The father of the Erie Canal was De Witt Clinton, the governor of New York State. Clinton was an early *booster*, that is, a promoter, of the existing glories and future greatness of his state. He tirelessly tried to influence lawmakers, a process known as *lobbying*, to vote money for building the canal. His opponents scoffed at "Clinton's Ditch" as an impractical idea. It would have to run for more than 563 kilometers (350 miles) through country which was still mostly wilderness. Opponents claimed that the cost of construction would be huge and that the canal would never earn much in return. But Clinton fought hard for his project and won public opinion for his side. Finally, New York State gave Clinton the money he needed.

The canal took eight years to complete. Hundreds of workers felled trees, hauled away stumps, and blasted through solid rock to build the canal and its towpath and bridges. Locks were constructed to raise and lower boats over steep hills. Many laborers, including a large number of Irish immigrants, died from disease and accidents on the job. But in October 1825, a triumphant Clinton boarded a canal boat at Buffalo. He cruised down to New York City, where he poured a barrel of Lake Erie water into the ocean. The Great Lakes and the Atlantic Ocean were now joined. Now, thousands of families took this safe water route westward to new homes. And millions of tons of freight moved along the Erie Canal. So much money came pouring in from tolls that a canal-building boom swept the country.

The Steamboat and the River Town

Many people had thought about using steam to power ships from the time that workable, moveable steam engines first appeared. Yet, an invention can only succeed when the time for it is ripe. In 1787, a forgotten American named John Fitch built an awkward-looking steamboat and ran it on the Delaware River. However, Fitch had to find talented people to help him. He needed engineers to help him build more and better boats, promoters to interest people in their use, and investors to put up money and organize steamboat lines. And he also needed politicians who would get state governments to help. Lacking these supporters, Fitch eventually had to give up the idea of being a steamboat operator.

By 1807, conditions had changed enough to favor the building of a successful steamboat. A New York business person and political leader, Robert Livingston, believed that a steamboat line on the Hudson River would prove profitable. So, he turned to his friend Robert Fulton to build a vessel for him. Fulton was an all-around inventor who had even built a submarine with a crude periscope. Fulton designed a small ship called the *Clermont*. In 1807, it thrashed from New York City, upriver to Albany, then back to New York, at a speed of 8 kilometers (5 miles) an hour.

Robert Fulton drew this self-portrait on his plans for the Nautilus, a submarine he designed for the French in 1801.

In 1848, steamboats traveling the Ohio River often stopped at Cincinnati.

ROBERT FULTON

Sometimes, a country is not aware of how lucky it is. Take the case of England in its war against France. England owes a great deal to the stupidity of Napoleon, who missed a chance to sink the British navy during a war between the two countries. This happened because Napoleon would not listen to an American with an idea.

This American was Robert Fulton, a Pennsylvania lad with a genius for drawing and for creating mechanical gadgets. After making a living for a while as a gunsmith, draftsman, portrait painter, and jack-of-all-trades, he went abroad to London for health reasons. While there, Fulton invented machines for spinning flax, twisting rope, sawing marble, and digging canals more rapidly. (He also invented a device for pulling canal boats up and down hills.) Fulton designed iron bridges as well. And he played with the idea of putting a steam engine into a boat.

Then he had what seemed to be a terrific idea. If he could devise a "submarine torpedo"—something that could fire a charge of gunpowder under water—and carry it to the hull of a ship, he would well have the most powerful naval weapon on Earth. The French, strangled by a British blockade, could use such a gadget. So Fulton went to Paris. There he worked, from 1797 to 1800, on a "plunging boat." This boat could submerge to 8 meters (25 feet), keep three crew members alive with tanks of compressed air, and push a "torpedo" against a ship's under-

water bulge, thus blowing it up. Napoleon was interested. The boat worked in tests, and Napoleon offered Fulton a large sum if his *Nautilus*—named for a shellfish—could overtake and blow up a British ship. However, Fulton could not bring it off and Napoleon dropped the idea.

Meanwhile, the British got wind of what was going on and invited Fulton to try his gadget against the French. He got as far as the French harbor of Boulogne. But his torpedoes failed to detonate at the crucial moment. The next year, he blew up an English ship for practice, but it proved to be too late. The British by now had lost interest. The United States was not interested. Fulton did keep Americans informed, but they could not see any use of a torpedo for *their* navy.

Fulton then returned to the United States and resumed his efforts to power a boat with a steam engine. Finally, he ran the little *Clermont* from New York to Albany on August 17, 1807. (Five weeks earlier, he had blown up a ship in New York harbor with his torpedo, just to show he could do it!) The *Clermont* made the trip—at about 8 kilometers (5 miles) an hour upstream. Fulton got the credit, which he did not deserve, for inventing the steamboat. Until he died in 1815, he kept toying with his underwater artillery. The world waited a century for the submarine.

---

monopoly
a business arrangement in which business people control entire areas of an industry or the exclusive right to sell a product

Merchants were now ready to take advantage of a vessel that traveled upstream, independent of wind conditions. Livingston and Fulton established a corporation to run steamboats on the Hudson River. They got the state of New York to grant them a **monopoly**. Soon Livingston and Fulton were prospering.

Livingston and Fulton also encouraged an engineer named Nicholas Roosevelt to build a steamboat at Pittsburgh. In 1811, this steamboat traveled down to New Orleans. By the 1830s, hundreds of riverboats were cruising the Ohio and Mississippi Rivers and their **tributaries**. Their decks were packed with barrels of pork, bales of cotton, crates of liquor, textiles, machinery, and other items for trade and with passengers, as well. River cities like Pittsburgh, Cincinnati, Louisville, St. Louis, and New Orleans began to grow and prosper.

The Early Days of Railroading

The "iron horse" now came puffing and snorting onto the American scene. Both English and American inventors had developed workable locomotives by 1825. In the United States, the first railroad promoters were the business people in the growing cities. They wanted a transportation system that would bring farm produce from the nearby countryside to their warehouses. The system would then carry the manufactured goods they sold back to the farmers. Between 1828 and 1835, the merchants of Baltimore, Boston, Charleston, New York, and Philadelphia had sponsored short rail lines.

Between 1830 and 1850, the railroad-building boom overtook the canal boom. In 1830, there were 2055 kilometers (1277 miles) of canals and only 117 kilometers (73 miles) of railroad tracks. But by 1850, there were 5950 kilometers (3698 miles) of canals and 14,286 kilometers (8879 miles) of rails. The next ten years saw a huge growth of railroads, which marked the end of the canal-building boom (see map on page 271).

In those early days of railroading, many locomotives were painted and decorated like American Indian religious objects. The locomotives were like gods to the Americans: stronger than any animal, swifter than the wind, and tirelessly on the move.

However, not everyone was delighted. The early locomotives filled the air with smoke, set fires with showers of sparks, frightened horses, and killed people in accidents.

MOTHERS LOOK OUT FOR YOUR CHILDREN!
ARTISANS, MECHANICS, CITIZENS!
When you leave your family in health must you be hurried home to mourn a
DREADFUL CASUALITY!
PHILADELPHIANS, your RIGHTS are being invaded! regardless of your interests, or the LIVES OF YOUR LITTLE ONES. THE CAMDEN AND AMBOY, with the assistance of other companies without a Charter, and in VIOLATION OF LAW, as decreed by your Courts, are laying a
LOCOMOTIVE RAIL ROAD!
Through your most Beautiful Streets, to the RUIN of your TRADE, annihilation of your RIGHTS, and regardless of your PROSPERITY and COMFORT. Will you permit this? or do you consent to be a
SUBURB OF NEW YORK !!
Rails are now being laid on BROAD STREET to CONNECT the TRENTON RAIL ROAD with the WILMINGTON and BALTIMORE ROAD, under the pretence of constructing a City Passenger Railway from the Navy Yard to Fairmount! This is done under the auspices of the CAMDEN AND AMBOY MONOPOLY!
RALLY PEOPLE in the Majesty of your Strength and forbid THIS
OUTRAGE!
Railroad Development faced This Propaganda 100 years ago.

Many Americans were horrified by creeping industrialism and warned of future disasters. This poster attacks railroads as an outrage and a threat to the health of the citizens of Philadelphia.

A Transportation Network for the Nation

Although some Americans fought progress, the canals, steamboat lines, and railroads gradually formed a network that unified the country.

The Constitution had joined all the areas of the United States in a common political system. That meant that a passenger or load of freight from a point inland, such as Cincinnati, could go about 1609 kilometers (1000 miles) to New Orleans or New York without a change of currency or a language barrier. However, the transportation system was a slow one. As late as 1815, the trip from Cincinnati to New York took nearly two months.

By 1852, however, the Cincinnati-New York time by rail was a week or even less. Steamboats made the river journey from Cincinnati

Just as the railroad promoted indus-trialization, factories sometimes fi-nanced new rail lines and the devel-opment of new engines. In 1856, a New Hampshire manufacturing company, seen in the background of this painting, built this large wood-burning engine.

to New Orleans in about the same time. Between 1815 and 1860, railroads had reduced by 95 percent the cost of sending freight overland.

High-speed transportation gave the United States east of the Mississippi the kind of economic unity that the Constitution provided politically. By 1860, the linking of numerous short rail lines created a single, national market. Now the crops of the South and West fed and clothed the industrial Northeast. In exchange, manufactured goods were sped to the farms, ranches, and plantations of the West and the South. Each section of the country was becoming more specialized in what it produced and more dependent on other parts of the country for those goods it did not produce. The net result was a national economy that was *interdependent* (with parts dependent on each other).

This national transportation system opened up new opportunities for everyone. Thousands of people were encouraged to move West and start new farms. Others were encouraged to go into the manufacturing or trading of goods. Young America was moving faster and getting bigger, richer, and busier.

Questions for Discussion

1. Define *lobbying, monopoly, tributaries*.
2. How did the Erie Canal promote western settlement?
3. Why did Robert Fulton succeed in doing what John Fitch had failed to do?
4. Describe how the railroads were like gods to the Americans?
5. How did the development of a national transportation system foster the development of a national interdependent economic system?

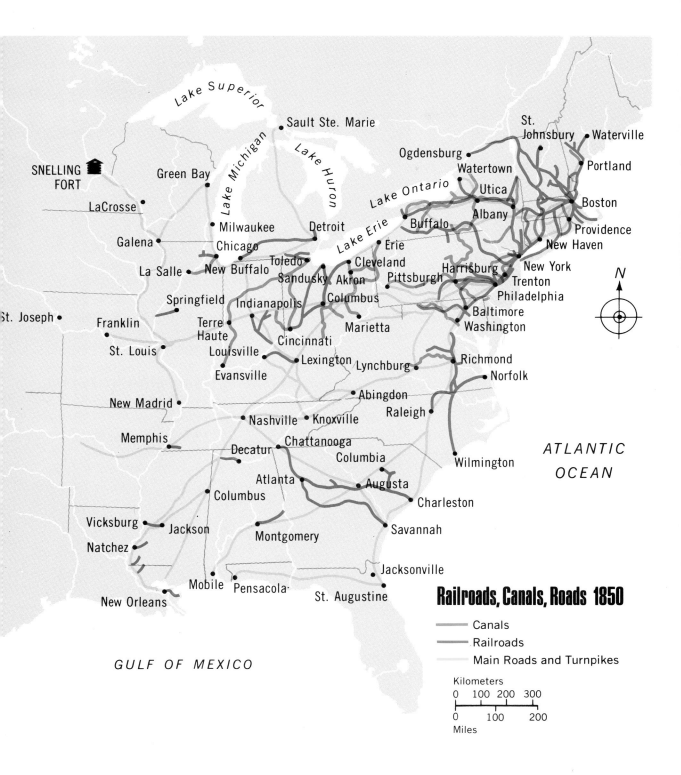

Lake Superior

Lake Michigan

Lake Huron

SNELLING FORT

Sault Ste. Marie

St. Johnsbury • Waterville
Ogdensburg
Watertown
Portland

Green Bay

Lake Ontario

Utica
Boston
Providence

LaCrosse

Milwaukee
Detroit
Lake Erie
Buffalo
Albany

Galena

Chicago

Erie
New Haven

La Salle
New Buffalo
Toledo
Cleveland
Sandusky Akron
Pittsburgh
Harrisburg
New York
Trenton
Philadelphia

Springfield
Indianapolis
Columbus
Baltimore
Washington

St. Joseph •

Franklin
Terre Haute
Marietta

St. Louis
Louisville
Cincinnati
Lexington
Lynchburg
Richmond

Evansville
Norfolk

New Madrid
Abingdon
Raleigh

Nashville • Knoxville

Memphis

Decatur Chattanooga
Columbia
Wilmington

Atlanta
Augusta
Columbus
Charleston

Vicksburg
Jackson
Montgomery
Savannah

Natchez

Mobile Pensacola·
Jacksonville

New Orleans
St. Augustine

ATLANTIC
OCEAN

GULF OF MEXICO

N

Railroads, Canals, Roads 1850

— Canals
— Railroads
— Main Roads and Turnpikes

Kilometers
0   100 200 300

0   100   200
Miles

271

2. The Rise of Industry

Above: At the time of his death in 1862, Samuel Colt was America's best-known and wealthiest inventor. Below: A drawing made for a British patent on a multishot pistol.

The transportation revolution was only one part of the industrial revolution. At the beginning of this great change, a French visitor to the United States wrote of how people, by turning "each drop of water into a reservoir of steam," could change the world. He predicted that one day, "a small part of the human race" could "produce all the material comforts" needed by the rest.

At the heart of the industrial revolution was the new technique of *mass production*. First, inventors created machines with tireless iron arms and fingers that multiplied human effort. These were sewing machines, power looms, and countless others. Many such machines were then placed in a single location—the factory. The final product in a factory was made one part at a time, each part by a different machine. And these machines were so precise that the completed article—whether it was a locomotive or a pocket watch—could be put together from or repaired with these interchangeable parts. Lastly, the machines could be set up so that the final product would be put together as it moved from one person to the next, in an assembly line.

In the 1790s, the United States began to develop the elements of mass production when spinning and weaving machines were introduced in Rhode Island. At first, these machines were run by water power. However, by the 1820s, the steam engine was rapidly replacing the paddle wheel as the source of industrial power. Shortly before the War of 1812, Eli Whitney, inventor of the cotton gin, began to make

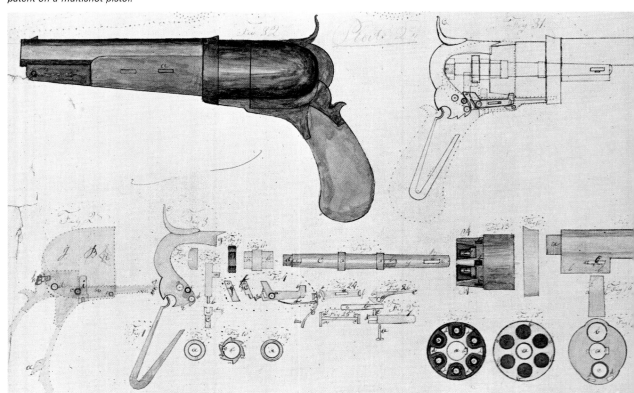

Young women operating power looms in a New England textile factory.

rifles with interchangeable parts. Inspectors for his biggest customer, the United States government, were amazed when workers put together finished guns from piles of barrels, locks, triggers, and guards. Later, the first assembly lines were set up.

One of the pioneers of the assembly-line method of production was Samuel Colt. In the 1840s, Colt sold his fast-firing revolvers to the Texas Rangers. They found Colt's invention to be a deadly weapon in fighting the mounted Comanches. The Comanches could fire a deadly shower of arrows while White enemies fumbled with old-fashioned muzzle loaders. By 1848, Colt had built his own gun factory in Hartford, Connecticut.

The Factory Workers—A New Class

When factories first began to appear in New England, their owners faced a shortage of workers. It was hard to find people willing to trade the sea or the farm for factory labor. Besides, many rural Yankees agreed with Virginia's Thomas Jefferson that industrial workers were bound to be overworked and underpaid, and that they would quickly become paupers and criminals. Some New England manufacturers came up with a plan to disprove these gloomy predictions.

The Boston Manufacturing Company opened a textile factory at

This factory was one of many to open in New England during the dawn of the Industrial Age.

In this detail from a woodcut by Winslow Homer, two workers are leaving a New England factory.

Waltham, Massachusetts, in 1814. Its workers were mostly young women, daughters of farmers in the area around Boston. The young women were expected to live in boarding houses, which the company built near the factory. In these boarding houses, the workers were supervised by older women. The boarders had regular hours for rising, eating, visiting, and church-going. The stern discipline provided by these boarding houses helped the young women's parents overcome their fears of letting their daughters live away from home.

At first, young women welcomed factory work. They saw it as an opportunity to earn some money. And they expected to marry and leave the factory within a couple of years. Hard work and strict rules were a familiar part of life on the farms from which they came. At least in the factory and boarding houses, many of them felt that they had company.

The mills, however, kept salaries very low and the workers were forbidden to discuss their complaints, even among themselves. In some factories, the employers required a signed promise that the employees would not organize into labor unions. If the employees organized anyway, the result was a loss of pay. Since many factories paid wages only two to four times a year, this penalty was very harsh.

Conditions in the factories became worse when the economy was bad. Workers were laid off and others were expected to do more to keep their jobs. In addition, mill owners increased working hours, cut down meal times, and speeded-up the machines. These experiences in the textile industry helped keep women in the forefront of a growing labor movement, in spite of the hardships that resulted from their participation.

Labor and Economic Reform

The labor movement got off to a rocky start. Any combination or alliance to improve wages or working conditions was usually declared illegal by the courts. But court decisions and employer reactions did not stop the laborers from organizing.

From 1827 to 1832, unions sought a wide range of reforms. In addition to improved working conditions, they fought for free public education and the abolition of child labor and imprisonment for debt. In 1827, the Mechanics Union in Philadelphia was leading the struggle for a ten-hour day. By the mid-1830s, skilled workers in most Eastern cities had won their demand "to have sufficient time in each day for the cultivation of their mind and for self-improvement." In 1840, President Martin Van Buren ordered a ten-hour day for all government workers. And in 1842, in the case of *Commonwealth* v. *Hunt*, the Massachusetts Supreme Court ruled that labor unions had the right to exist in Massachusetts.

In Lowell, Massachusetts, women textile workers went on strike to protest a wage cut in 1834. Locked out of the company-owned boarding houses, they were starved into giving up. Yet, they inspired others. In 1844, six women workers organized the Lowell Female Labor Reform Association. Their goal was a ten-hour day. Within the year, the organization had 600 members. One of its founders, Sarah Bagley, began publication of the *Voice of Industry*, directed at the problems of workers. However, conditions did not improve. By the end of the 1840s, women who were able to leave the factories did so. Their places were taken by the stream of immigrants coming into the country from Britain, Ireland, and French Canada. These immigrants depended on the new industrial system for survival.

Immigrants Enter the Scene

In the 1830s and 1840s, tens of thousands of immigrants poured into the United States. By the 1850s, one person out of ten was foreign-born. Of these, almost half were Irish. The rest were mainly of British, German, and French Canadian origin.

The invention of the steamship had an indirect influence on the huge numbers of immigrants coming to America. Since only the rich could afford steamship passage from Europe, the owners of sailing ships had to hustle for the business of the poor. There were so many Europeans wanting to come to America that the sailing ship owners could afford to charge low fares. In fact, it cost a mere ten dollars to come to America from Ireland.

Conditions in their native countries caused many to seek new lives in America. In Ireland, many people had been tenants on British-owned farms. A terrible blight on the potato crop in 1845 caused a famine that lasted for several years. People were faced with the need to leave the land or die of hunger. In other areas of Europe, particularly Germany, there was political unrest. Thousands fled when attempts to improve their lives failed.

New York's population grew each day with the arrival of immigrants like the Irish family in this drawing.

The immigrants' destinations were often governed by their pocketbooks. The poorer immigrants, many of whom were Irish, settled in the slum sections of cities like New York, Boston, Cincinnati, and New Orleans. Immigrants who were able to afford farms took off for the Midwest. In some midwestern communities, Germans and Scandinavians actually outnumbered the people who were born in America.

The new settlers were not always welcomed. People had fears that their way of life would be disrupted. Also, many of the immigrants were Catholics. They were coming into a predominantly Protestant nation. Many of the immigrants were willing—or at least felt compelled—to work for less money than American workers. They competed for jobs with the White American workers and free Blacks. Labor leaders felt that immigrants placed more strain on the unsteady labor-union movement.

Resentment against the newcomers increased as their ranks swelled. *Nativism*, the dislike of anything foreign, became an organized movement. Groups like the Order of the Star Spangled Banner were formed as people convinced themselves that the foreigners were inferior and dangerous.

In 1843, a new political party based on nativism developed. The *Know-Nothings*, as they were called, favored extending the period for naturalization and barring immigrants from holding public office. The Know-Nothings had a strong influence on politics in the Eastern states until their split in 1855.

Questions for Discussion

1. Define *mass production, nativism*.
2. Why was the development of interchangeable parts and the assembly line an important step in the industrialization of the United States?
3. Why did New England textile factory owners tend to hire young women instead of men? What difficulties did these women experience at the mills?
4. What areas of reform were the concerns of the labor movement?
5. How was the influx of immigrants into the United States directly related to the industrial revolution?

3. An Age of Reform

The tremendous changes caused by the industrial revolution led many citizens to think about how to reform American society. The Constitution promised everyone—even though "everyone" was narrowly defined—the "Blessings of Liberty." The machine age promised abundance. And Americans had faith in the power of education to make these dreams come true. Workers felt that widespread education would prevent a "monopoly of talent" on the part of the rich and powerful. Religious leaders, such as Lyman Beecher, thought that a population that read the Bible would preserve morality and republican government. Many citizens felt that schools would spread a feeling of nationalism and that a well-informed electorate would preserve democracy. Education was also seen as a means of "Americanizing" the immigrants. Until the 1830s, however, education in America was largely dependent on the interest of parents and their ability to pay. While White American males in New England enjoyed a comparatively high rate of literacy, education was generally found lacking in quantity and quality everywhere.

THE BAREFOOT BOY.

Blessings on thee, little man,
Barefoot boy, with cheek of tan

A page from McGuffey's Eclectic Readers.

The idea of government-supported public schools met with some success. In the Old Northwest, the idea was incorporated into the Northwest Ordinance in 1785. However, it was not until 1825 that it was put into effect. In Pennsylvania, early attempts to provide free public school education met with stiff opposition. People felt that the government should provide schooling only for the children of the poor. In most areas, people who ran private or religious schools joined ranks with the other opponents of free education. However, by 1850, the principle of a free elementary school education was generally accepted everywhere. Even then, education was by no means universal. For a variety of reasons, many people chose not to take advantage of it or were barred because of race or sex.

As interest was growing for public education, more attention was being paid to teacher training. Each of the states began to require some proof of a teacher's ability and character. In 1839, Massachusetts established a state-supported teacher training school.

Massachusetts was a leader in other educational reforms as well, largely due to the work of Horace Mann. A successful lawyer and politician, Horace Mann gave up his position in the Massachusetts state legislature to become the first secretary of the newly formed state Board of Education. In his twelve years in that post, Mann did much to increase the quality of education in the state. He increased the length of the school term, improved the quality and number of schools, and increased teacher-training and salaries.

In Connecticut, Henry Barnard was a leader of the free-school movement. He improved government supervision, urged better teaching methods, and established school libraries. From 1845 to 1849, he served as commissioner of education in Rhode Island and brought similar improvements to its school system. In 1855, he began to edit the *American Journal of Education*, which was a gathering of information about education, history, and philosophy.

In 1828, Noah Webster published *An American Dictionary of the English Language*. He simplified the spelling of many British words and defined 12,000 words that were not found in any other dictionary. This work and his *Elementary Spelling Book* both promoted uniform spelling and pronunciation. Webster's books did much to promote a national "American" language.

William Holmes McGuffey's work promoted a common base of knowledge. He published the *Eclectic Readers*, which sold 122 million copies. They were the first six textbooks that most students in the country used. The readers included selections from American and British authors. The material was chosen to teach some object lesson in morality or patriotism. For example, one essay was entitled "God Bless the Industrious."

Horace Mann, a leader in educational reforms in Massachusetts.

A page from McGuffey's Eclectic Readers *spelling textbook.*

The bloomer was a trouser outfit for women giving them greater freedom of movement. Popularized by Amelia Jenks Bloomer, it was a serious contribution to the "women's rights" cause and a forerunner of the pantsuit.

feminists
women actively involved in promoting the political, economical, and social equality of the sexes

suffrage
the right to vote

Though most Southern states prohibited education of slaves, education for free Blacks in the North did develop. However, with a few exceptions in Massachusetts and New York, it was segregated.

After a very slow beginning in the 1820s, higher education finally became available for Blacks and women. Lincoln University in Pennsylvania and Wilberforce in Ohio were two colleges established for Blacks. Though most higher education was also segregated, Blacks won admission to Oberlin, Dartmouth, and Western Reserve Colleges. Oberlin also admitted women. In 1862, an Oberlin graduate, Mary Jane Patterson, became the first Black woman to earn a college degree. She went on to become the principal of a high school for Black students in Washington, D.C. And in 1837, Mary Lyon founded Mount Holyoke College in Massachusetts, the first permanent women's college. Some state universities in the West also admitted women.

Samuel Gridley Howe fostered practical education for the handicapped. He founded and headed the New England Asylum for the Blind. Laura Bridgman, one of his students, was the first blind and deaf person to be successfully educated.

Humanitarian Reform

Humanitarianism, the belief that all people are entitled to have better lives, was the underlying force behind other kinds of reform. It aimed to improve the position of large groups of people who were the victims of social, political, and economic injustice. A drive to abolish slavery, which you will study later, was the most powerful such movement. Another was the effort to better the condition of women.

In free America, women could not vote, hold certain jobs, or even own property. Even wealthy women were confined to the home and to a limited education in "polite" accomplishments, such as drawing and piano-playing. In the 1830s and 1840s, a few bold **feminists** attacked these injustices. Amelia Bloomer used her newspaper, *The Lily*, to press for women's rights. She is remembered most for recommending a new clothing style—a divided skirt gathered at each ankle. These *bloomers*, as they came to be called, freed women from heavy, trailing skirts and let them move around actively. In 1848, Elizabeth Cady Stanton and Lucretia Mott held a "Women's Rights Convention" at Seneca Falls, New York. The convention issued a document that quoted the opening of the Declaration of Independence word for word, except to say that "all men and women are created equal." Although Stanton and Susan B. Anthony devoted their lives to building a movement for women's **suffrage**, it was not until 1920 that American women were guaranteed the right to vote.

Dorothea Lynde Dix began a career as a reformer after visiting a jail in East Cambridge, Massachusetts. She was disturbed to find the mentally ill confined with the criminal prisoners. After being ignored by the Massachusetts legislature, she set out to document the horrors inflicted on the mentally ill in state institutions, poorhouses, and jails. After she presented her overwhelming evidence to the legislature, the lawmakers began to act. Laws were passed to improve the treatment of the mentally ill and of prisoners. Dix continued her work in other states, and her reforms even spread to Europe.

Idealistic Reforms

Some reformers withdrew and chose to live apart in little communities, where like-minded people could show others how to live the good life. These tiny **utopias** generally did not last long. In 1825, Robert Owen, an English reformer, started a colony in New Harmony, Indiana. Owen wanted to replace capitalistic competition with planned cooperation. Other utopias worked on different plans. One of the most famous was Brook Farm, begun in 1841 near Boston, Massachusetts. There, some of the smartest men and women of New England ran a farm where land ownership and work were shared by all. In 1848, in Oneida, New York, John Humphrey Noyes founded the most radical utopia. Oneida Colony replaced family life with a system in which each member was considered married to all the other members. Though the Oneida Colony was very successful, it dropped its more radical ideas thirty years later.

There were also reforms aimed at raising the moral tone of all society. Reformers wanted to get people to change habits that they thought were bad. The move for *temperance*—prohibition or strict control over the drinking of liquor—was one of these.

Questions for Discussion

1. Define *humanitarianism, temperance, utopia.*
2. What one objective was shared by all who sought reform?
3. What foundations of American education were laid in the early nineteenth century?
4. How did humanitarianism affect all other areas of reform?

The growth of literature in America paralleled the development of education. The first half of the nineteenth century saw the beginnings of a national literature. American writers were now competing with the easily available works of popular British authors.

Washington Irving was the first American author to win acclaim at home as well as abroad. His *History of New York* was an amusing account of the early Dutch. And the *Sketch Book* introduced the characters of Ichabod Crane and Rip Van Winkle into American literature.

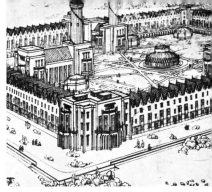

This drawing was the architect's grand design for New Harmony. In fact, the utopian community never got beyond the log-cabin stage.

utopia
a name for an imaginary land with a perfect society, or a place with ideal social conditions

Social reformer and militant feminist Elizabeth Cady Stanton.

4. Literary Nationalism

Washington Irving, the first American to achieve an international reputation as a man of letters. He made writing a full-time profession.

poll tax
a tax people are required to pay in order to vote

One could see the influence of the frontier on American letters in the writings of James Fenimore Cooper. His famous "Leather-stocking Tales" included *The Pioneers*, *The Last of the Mohicans*, and *The Deerslayer*. A strong defender of democracy, he also wrote *The American Democrat*, a political essay.

The writers of New England dominated the literary scene. They included Henry Wadsworth Longfellow, James Russell Lowell, Oliver Wendell Holmes, Herman Melville, Nathaniel Hawthorne, and John Greenleaf Whittier. Two of the most famous were Ralph Waldo Emerson and Henry David Thoreau.

Emerson, a Unitarian minister, gave up the pulpit to write and lecture. He encouraged individualism, self-improvement, and self-reliance. And he lectured against the excessive search for wealth and fame.

Emerson also believed in the ability of people to grasp the truth. He preached that they must be free of hatred and prejudice. Only when individuals were free themselves would democracy work.

Emerson influenced his friend, Henry David Thoreau, who lived near him in Concord, Massachusetts. Thoreau took Emerson's criticism one step further. Thoreau distrusted the new industrialzed American society. He wrote *Walden*, a narrative of his experience while living alone in a self-built hut for two years. In *Walden*, he deplored the "lives of quiet desperation" that people live because they are too busy earning a living to enjoy life. But Thoreau did not recommend his way of living for everyone. Instead, he advocated that people would find their own way in searching for the simple life.

Thoreau was truly angered by the fact that the United States government fought a war against Mexico in 1845, allowed slavery to continue to exist, and did little to discourage the mistreatment of American Indians. In protest, he refused to pay his **poll tax** and was placed in jail. In "Civil Disobedience," he wrote, "Under a government which imprisons any unjustly, the true place for a just man is also a prison . . . where the State places those who are not with her, but against her . . . ." Thoreau's ideas lived on for generations and are still popular today.

Questions for Discussion

1. How did American literature of the early nineteenth century reflect the mood of the nation?
2. How do the thoughts expressed by the early nineteenth-century American authors apply to the world of today?

5. The Democratic Surge

In the era leading up to the election of Andrew Jackson as President in 1828, there were many changes in American life. At the same time that social and economic upheavals were occurring, the political system was undergoing major changes.

When the Constitution was ratified in 1788, there were many obstacles to the universal exercise of self-government. For example, property ownership or tax-paying qualifications for voting existed in every state. In some states, like Rhode Island, the requirements were so rigid that more than one-half the adult White male population was denied the *franchise* (right to vote). And even those people who had the right to vote had no say about who the candidate would be. *Caucuses*, or meetings of members of local and national legislatures, picked those who would run. Even Presidential electors were chosen by the state legislatures and not by popular election. As a result, except for occasional hotly contested local elections, interest and participation in elections was low.

Increased Interest in Politics

However, within a span of twenty-five years, most of this changed. One reason for the increased interest in politics was the change in political parties. Following the War of 1812, the first of the two-party systems faded. New England, the stronghold of the Federalists, failed to support the war. At the Hartford Convention in 1814, the members even suggested *secession*, or withdrawing from the Union. When the war was over, people forgot the defeats and remembered only the victories. As a result, the Federalists were more or less in disgrace and lost much of their political power. In the surge

An 1824 painting of the capitol of the United States at Washington, D.C.

Henry Clay was one of four candidates for President in 1824. Because no candidate had a clear majority of electoral votes, the decision was left to the House of Representatives, and Clay was eliminated.

disenfranchise
to deprive of the right to vote

of nationalism that followed the war, the Republicans adopted many of the Federalists' ideas and acquired many more followers.

In 1816, the Federalists nominated their last Presidential candidate, Rufus King. But he was easily defeated by James Monroe. In 1820, Monroe won reelection, receiving all but one electoral vote. People called this period "an era of good feelings." In reality, it was the lull before the storm. Four years later, four candidates, all Republicans, were battling it out for the Presidency. And two new parties were destined to rise out of the dust of the Republican Party.

What had actually happened? For one thing, the caucus system had broken up. The public was beginning to resent a system that kept the power of nomination in the hands of a select group. Secondly, Monroe was the last of the powerful Virginia politicians who had a nationwide following. And he had no clear-cut successor. Thirdly, sectional interests were making it impossible for the Democratic-Republicans to smooth over their differences and present a unified front.

By the time sharp differences in opinion began to spark political interest, many more people were eligible to vote. In 1791, when Vermont was admitted as a state, its constitution had eliminated both property and tax qualifications for voting. Kentucky, New Jersey, Maryland, and Connecticut soon followed Vermont's lead and changed their constitutions. Between 1810 and 1820, six frontier states that had no property qualifications for voting were admitted. Within ten years, most Southern states had also made similar changes.

There were other movements under way for a more democratic system as well. By 1832, Presidential candidates were no longer chosen by caucuses. The new political parties that arose after the failure of the Republican Party adopted the national nominating convention. Property qualifications for governor were dropped. And state judges and Presidential electors were popularly elected.

At the same time, there were other, less praiseworthy changes taking place. Many of the same laws that increased suffrage for White men took the right to vote away from others. In 1806, New Jersey annulled the right of women to vote. Free Blacks, who had enjoyed the right to vote in northern New England, New York, Pennsylvania, Tennessee, and North Carolina in 1820, were restricted by 1837. Blacks retained the right to vote only in New England, north of Connecticut. They were **disenfranchised** in all of the states admitted to the Union between 1819 and the Civil War. They were not even allowed to live in some Western states. And in the other states, Blacks were forced by discrimination and economic need to accept the lowest paying jobs and the poorest living conditions.

It may seem overly generous to consider the United States a

democratic nation in the early 1800s. Yet the free, White male adult in the United States had more say in his government than his counterpart in any other nation of the world at that time.

Election of 1824

During the campaign of 1824, four candidates were scrambling for the White House. William Crawford, the Secretary of Treasury, was nominated by the Congressional caucus. Andrew Jackson had the support of the Tennessee legislature. John Quincy Adams, the Secretary of State, was the choice of New England. Henry Clay, Speaker of the House, was nominated by the legislatures of Kentucky, Louisiana, Missouri, and Ohio.

The smallest political differences existed between Clay and Adams, who both supported a program of internal improvements at government expense, a high protective tariff, and a national bank. Clay hoped that such a program would bind the sections of the country together in a common interest. The tariff would help the development of Eastern industry. The West and South would provide raw materials for that industry and a market for its finished goods. Good transporta-

A popular view of Andrew Jackson as a dynamic military hero.

When the election of 1824 was thrown into the House of Representatives, John Quincy Adams emerged as the 6th President of the United States.

patronage
the power to make appointments to government jobs on a basis other than just merit

Jackson Forever!
The Hero of Two Wars and of Orleans!
The Man of the People!
HE WHO COULD NOT BARTER NOR BARGAIN FOR THE
PRESIDENCY!
Who, although "A Military Chieftain," valued the purity of Elections and of the Electors, MORE than the Office of PRESIDENT itself! Although the greatest in the gift of his countrymen, and the highest in point of dignity of any in the world,
BECAUSE
It should be derived from the
PEOPLE!
No Gag Laws! No Black Cockades! No Reign of Terror! No Standing Army or Navy Officers, when under the pay of Government, to browbeat, or
KNOCK DOWN
Old Revolutionary Characters, or our Representatives while in the discharge of their duty. To the Polls then, and vote for those who will support
OLD HICKORY
AND THE ELECTORAL LAW.

An 1828 campaign poster promoting Andrew Jackson for President.

tion, built at federal expense, would help the West and South get their produce to the marketplace cheaply. And a strong national bank would provide the financial security for all of this to take place smoothly.

Jackson did not have a clear-cut program. When asked, he said he was for a fair tariff. His opinion on internal improvements was unknown. Jackson's campaign was based on his popularity as a colorful, military figure. William Crawford did not figure heavily in the campaign because of ill health.

When the votes were counted, no candidate had a majority of the electoral votes. For the second time in United States history, the election was thrown into the House of Representatives. Clay was eliminated immediately because he was not one of the top three. He then gave his support to Adams whose interests were most like his own. Thus, Adams became the sixth President of the United States, having received only about one-third of the popular vote.

Adams's Administration

"Bargain and corruption" was the cry of Jackson's supporters when Adams appointed Clay Secretary of State. This was only one of many issues that cast a shadow on Adams's administration. Sorely lacking in leadership qualities, Adams had a difficult Presidency. He saw his office as one of great scope and power. And he felt that the federal government was at fault if it did not use all the power available to it "for the benefit of the people themselves."

But with all his talk of power, Adams did not use appointments and **patronage** to line up allies. He felt that a qualified person should have a position, even if that person was his political enemy. This high-minded attitude was praiseworthy. However, it left his enemies in a position to win support for Jackson and to defy the President's wishes.

So, for four years, Adams waged an uphill battle. His programs for a national university, a revised patent system, a scientific observatory, and federally funded roads and canals were all defeated. In 1826, Jackson's supporters were swept into the House of Representatives. And Congress defeated the most worthwhile proposals Adams offered. By crippling Adams's Administration, Jackson's supporters cleared the way for Jackson's victory in 1828.

Questions for Discussion
1. Define *franchise, caucus, disenfranchised, patronage.*
2. What was the "era of good feeling"?
3. What role did sectional interest play in the election of 1824?
4. How did John Quincy Adams hurt his political career by not using patronage?

The 1830s are sometimes called the Age of Jackson. For some people, Andrew Jackson, President from 1829 to 1837, seemed to embody the individualistic, get-ahead spirit of the nation. In years when steamboat and factory whistles shrieked, "Hurry up! Succeed!" he showed, by example, how to do it.

Jackson was born in the Carolina backwoods. He had no formal schooling. Yet, in frontier Tennessee, natural ability made him a landowner and a success in business. His only legal training was in "reading law"—a kind of on-the-job training—in the office of a lawyer. Yet, when his neighbors elected him a judge, he never doubted his ability to decide cases justly. His only training for combat was in the duels brought on by his hot temper. But as a general, he soundly defeated both the Creeks and the British troops.

Plain people admired this powerhouse, this self-made man. And they wanted him to be President. In 1828, the "common man" finally elected the uncommon "Old Hickory" to the White House. He was the first President since Washington without a college education, Cabinet experience, or diplomatic service. He was also the first President who could claim to be elected by popular vote. By 1828, Presidential electors were chosen by the people in nearly every state.

Jackson's actions in office were as bold as the man himself. He approved of a house-cleaning of the federal government. And he replaced many old-time government officials with his followers. Jackson thought that this *spoils system* was democracy in action. The spoils system was named from a Jackson supporter's remark, "to the

6. The Age of Jackson

This portrait of Andrew Jackson was often carried in campaign parades.

Jackson offered slices of this 1400-pound cheese to voters at a reception.

victor belong the spoils." He called it "rotation in office." Everyone, said Jackson, could perform the few, simple duties of government. Therefore, as many people as possible should be given a chance. This would give the people control over the administration of government.

Jackson also used the veto power freely when he thought that a measure was not in the public interest. He did not restrict himself, as some thought he should, to the veto of bills that he thought unconstitutional.

South Carolina and the Tariff

A major issue of Jackson's Presidency was the question of *nullification*, the right of a state to refuse to obey a federal law. During Jackson's Administration, the fight over the tariff issue foreshadowed a more serious sectional conflict yet to come.

In 1816, the first protective tariff was passed to protect industry. When that happened, South Carolina saw its wealth decline as the Northeastern states prospered. South Carolinians blamed the federal government. They did not see that the land-destroying cotton economy was largely responsible for their ills. When the tariff was raised in 1824 and again in 1828, a wail of protest arose in the South.

In response to the 1828 "tariff of abominations," the South Carolina legislature approved a document called the South Carolina Exposition. Secretly authored by Vice-President Calhoun, it offered arguments to justify the nullification of the tariff. Calhoun claimed that the nation was composed of thirteen sovereign states. Each state had the right to judge when the federal government had gone beyond its authority. This doctrine of states' rights aroused deep feelings in the country.

In a Congressional debate that started as a competition between the South and North for Western votes, the issue of states' rights burst into the open. A Connecticut Senator introduced a resolution to cut down on public land sales in order to discourage factory workers from going West. South Carolina's Senator Robert Hayne attacked this idea, hoping to win popularity with Westerners who wanted to see the population of their section keep on growing.

However, Hayne took the argument beyond that point. He stated that the national government had no right whatever to harm the interests of one section for the benefit of another. When it did so, Hayne claimed that the Union, the federal government, threatened liberty. And the states must stop a too powerful federal government from taking away their sovereignty. The Constitution did not create one nation, he insisted. It was a compact, or agreement, among states, to be observed only when it served their best interests. Hayne's speech was in strong defense of states' rights.

Jackson's opposition to nullification is depicted in this painting, as is his great support among the people.

Daniel Webster, Senator from Massachusetts, replied eloquently. He strongly defended American nationalism. The American people were one. And the nation as a whole was their creation. Its success was the best way of winning freedom for all. The Union had made growth and prosperity possible. Therefore, it should not be destroyed by local jealousies and roadblocks. He closed his speech with a famous passage. Webster prayed that, when he looked at the sun for the last time in his life, he would not see it "shining on the broken and dishonored fragments of a once glorious Union," but on an American flag with "not a stripe erased or polluted, nor a single star obscured." That flag should carry the sentiment "dear to every true American heart—Liberty and Union, now and forever, one and inseparable."

Now that the issue was out in the open, President Jackson was faced with defending the Union or defending states' rights. Calhoun, his Vice-President, counted Jackson on the side of states' rights. At a dinner party at the White House in April 1830, a series of toasts were offered. Jackson revealed his true feelings: "Our Union—it must be preserved." Calhoun replied: "The Union—next to our liberty, the most dear. May we always remember that it can only be preserved by distributing equally the benefits and burdens of the Union."

This cartoon appeared when, in 1833, Andrew Jackson began removing federal deposits from the Second Bank of the United States.

Nullification and the Force Act

In the next two years, the gap between Jackson and Calhoun widened. Calhoun resigned the Vice-Presidency and returned to South Carolina to fight a new tariff instituted in 1832. South Carolina's response to the Tariff of 1832 was an Ordinance of Nullification, based on Calhoun's theory of states' rights. Jackson, calling the action of South Carolina one of treason, asked Congress to pass the Force Act. This bill would give him authority to use federal forces to collect tariffs if South Carolina would not. Meanwhile, Henry Clay sponsored a new tariff that would gradually lower the rates to the 1816 level. Finally, South Carolina accepted the new tariff, thus avoiding a showdown.

Jackson's War Against the Bank

Another important event during this period was Jackson's war on the Second Bank of the United States. The industrial revolution had created some difficult political questions. Should the government play an even larger part in making economic decisions than it already did? Some believed that a democratic government must, for example, help make decisions about wages and the number of hours a laborer could be made to work by an employer. Others insisted that any such enlargement of government's power was a threat to freedom. These

An 1832 anti-Jackson pamphlet critical of "King" Jackson's actions against the Eastern banks.

people wanted the economy to run without government intervention. This policy is known by its French name, *laissez faire*, which means "let alone."

One special area of economic life affecting all the others was *credit*—the power to borrow money. In the growing nation, farmers and business people alike borrowed regularly to buy land or to start a shop, factory, or railroad. Banks lent them this money and charged a price for it, called *interest*. The money lent by banks was not gold or silver. Rather, the money consisted of paper "bank notes," which carried the bank's promise to pay the borrower on demand. Those people who for some reason were prevented from getting credit could not start new enterprises unless they were very rich.

In 1816, Congress had chartered the Second Bank of the United States. Like Hamilton's First Bank of the United States, it was a private bank. However, the bank was allowed to collect and hold government money. Like all banks, it made loans from its deposits. The Second Bank of the United States was the country's biggest financial agent. Throughout the country smaller banks often turned to it for loans. By granting or refusing such requests, the Second Bank had strong control over credit. Some thought that such a restraining hand was useful. Too much easy borrowing could cause trouble if people were unable to pay their debts.

The first director of the bank had allowed easy credit. In the period before 1819, most people were able to meet their payments because of the easy money policy of the national bank. However, because of its policy of easy credit, the bank came to the brink of financial disaster.

In 1818, a new director decided to place the Second Bank on a sound financial footing. He wanted to put an end to the dangerous policy of borrowing for land speculation. The directors of the bank instructed the branch banks not to renew mortgages. They also demanded that the state banks redeem their own bank notes in gold, silver, or national bank notes. However, many state banks were unable to do so and had to close their doors.

At the same time, there was an economic downturn in Europe. The market for American farm products and manufactured goods decreased. European creditors began to demand quicker payment of debts, since they faced a financial crisis themselves. A panic set in during 1819, when many people found themselves without enough income to pay their debts. Many Eastern industrialists closed their factories. And many farmers and planters lost their land. Despite the several causes for these hard times, many people blamed the bank's directors. Together, these sentiments paved the way for the war on the bank.

Since only five of the twenty-five directors were chosen by the President, Jackson felt that a few bankers from the East had a death grip on the nation's economic growth. By then, the strong-willed Nicholas Biddle had taken over as the third director of the bank. He tried to ease the impact of the crisis by expanding credit temporarily. But it still angered Jackson that Nicholas Biddle, the bank's very wealthy director, could reward friendly bankers with loans and deny them to outsiders. So when a bill to renew the charter of the national bank came to him in 1832, he vetoed it in a message that blasted the bank's power. Biddle struck back with a bitter propaganda campaign to defeat Jackson for reelection. But Jackson's power struck like a thunderbolt. "The Bank," he said, "is trying to kill me, but I will kill it." In the end, the people reelected Jackson, and the Second Bank of the United States was dead.

After Jackson's war on the bank, many workers admired Old Hickory for his victory over big business. And because the bank could no longer limit credit, many small merchants also approved of what Jackson had done. They now believed that he stood for equal opportunity for all investors, not merely for the rich. They pictured him as a dashing hero on a prancing horse, while his enemies pictured him as "King Andrew." By 1836, Jacksonians had organized a new national party that called itself Democratic. In 1836, anti-Jacksonians had also formed a new party. They named it after those English people who had battled against royal power. Thus, the Whig party was born.

John Marshall

While Jackson was reducing federal control over business, Chief Justice John Marshall was further extending the freedom of business. Marshall, a Virginian and a Federalist, sat as Chief Justice of the Supreme Court from 1801 to 1835. In a series of decisions, he declared unconstitutional the laws which many states had passed for regulating corporations. Since there was little federal regulation of business at this time, the result was to leave business free to do almost anything it wanted.

In the case of *Fletcher* v. *Peck* of 1810, the state of Georgia wanted to undo a contract that granted land rights near the Yazoo River to certain people. The basis of the objection to the contract was that the sale of the land was corrupt and benefited speculators. The Marshall Court protected the property interests of the people claiming the land because the Court felt that to do otherwise would damage the binding effect of a contract.

Another case that supported contractual obligations against interference by the state was the case of *Dartmouth* v. *Woodward*. The New Hampshire legislature wanted to abolish the charter of

Although he had no prior judicial experience, John Marshall was a most influential Chief Justice. During his 34 years in office, he established that the Supreme Court had the power to determine whether or not a law was constitutional.

Dartmouth College and put it under state control. Marshall's Court decided that a charter granted to a corporation was not subject to the whim of a state. Later when the courts began to recognize the police powers of the states, the effects of these decisions on unlimited business activities were checked.

In other decisions, Marshall did a great deal to expand the power of the federal government at the expense of the states. The case of *McCulloch* v. *Maryland* (1819) defined the doctrine of implied powers. The state of Maryland taxed the bank notes of the Baltimore branch of the Second Bank of the United States. The bank refused to pay. And the Maryland courts upheld the state. So the bank appealed to the Supreme Court. In Marshall's decision, he held that the power of the federal government came from the people, not from the states. Although the power to charter corporations is not directly given to Congress by the Constitution, it is implied. That is, Congress has the right to use any legal means to carry out the powers given to it by the Constitution. This is the so-called elastic clause of the Constitution (Article I, Section 8). The states may not interfere with these functions by taxing or restricting them in any way.

Another blow to states' rights was the decision in the case of *Gibbons* v. *Ogden*. Robert Fulton and Robert Livingston sold their state-approved monopoly of ferry traffic between New York and New Jersey to Ogden. When Gibbons set up a competing ferry line under a federal coasting license, Ogden tried to stop him. In the resulting battle, Marshall declared that the monopoly granted by New York was in conflict with the right of Congress to regulate interstate trade.

As industrialization and transportation expanded, these interpretations of the Constitution opened the way for many new developments. The federal government gained control over things sent through pipelines, wires, and over airwaves. It established a system for payments to the very poor, the disabled, and the retired. These and many other uses of federal power were not foreseen when Marshall made his far-reaching decisions.

Questions for Discussion

1. Define *spoils system, nullification, laissez-faire, interest.*
2. Why did Jackson defend the spoils system?
3. Why is a bureaucracy necessary in a democracy?
4. How did nullification lead to a conflict over states' rights?
5. Why did many business people, as well as farmers and laborers, approve of Jackson's veto of the bill renewing the national Bank's charter?
6. How did the decisions of John Marshall expand the power of the federal government?

Chapter 12 Review

Summary Questions for Discussion

1. Why did De Witt Clinton favor construction of the Erie Canal? What were the advantages of a canal?
2. How did the steamboat help to open up the interior of the United States?
3. Why did the railroad replace the canal as the most important means of internal transportation?
4. What difficulties were faced by early labor organizations?
5. What role did Horace Mann play in improving the quality of education in Massachusetts?
6. What advances were made in education for women, Black people, and the handicapped?
7. What was the role of each of the following in the development of rights for women: Amelia Bloomer, Elizabeth Cady Stanton, Lucretia Mott, Susan B. Anthony?
8. What factors brought the "era of good feeling" to an end?
9. What arguments were used by Senator Robert Hayne in defense of states' rights?
10. How did the Second Bank of the United States control credit in the West and South?

Word Study

Fill in each blank in the sentences that follow with the term below that is most appropriate.

mass production	monopoly	caucuses	nativism
humanitarianism	lobbying	patronage	nullification
disenfranchised	interest	spoils system	laissez-faire

1. Businesses prospered as interchangeable parts and the assembly line became part of the technique of _____.
2. Some business people controlled entire areas of an industry in a business arrangement known as a _____.
3. A government policy of noninterference in business is called _____.
4. Banks grew in number and depositors received _____ on their deposits.
5. _____ or the dislike of anything foreign increased with the influx of immigrants who took jobs in the factories.
6. The belief that all people were entitled to have better lives, also called _____,
   was the theme of many reformers.
7. The _____ or meetings held to choose political candidates had limited representation.
8. The goal of political reformers was to give the vote to the _____.
9. People were sometimes appointed to government positions because they were friends of a leader. This is called the _____ or _____.
10. Opposition to the federal government's growing powers was met by states' righters, who called for a policy of _____, giving states the right to declare federal laws null and void.

Using Your Skills

1. How would you use the pictures and maps in this chapter to disprove the following generalization: "Between 1800 and 1860, life in America underwent no important changes."
2. Examine the map and pictures in the chapter. How did improvements in transportation affect the economic activities of some American cities and towns?
3. Describe how the pictures and cartoons in the chapter show the different attitudes of the Americans toward Andrew Jackson.

CHAPTER 13
Westward to the Pacific

In May 1846, Senator Thomas Hart Benton, of Missouri, gave a speech on the subject of Oregon. In those days, people came to the visitors' gallery in the Senate to listen to good speakers. Senator Benton did not disappoint them. With great style, he spoke about Oregon, then not part of the United States, becoming a state. "The vans of the Caucasian race now top the Rocky Mountains," he said, "and spread down to the shores of the Pacific. In a few years a great population will grow up there." Benton thought that, in time, such growth would improve the condition of Asia. American civilization would surge westward across the sea and change the entire world.

Senator Benton expressed a feeling held by millions of Americans. In the words of a magazine editor, the feeling was one of "our manifest destiny to overspread the continent." The belief that America's expansion was part of God's plan for a better world was also expressed by a young poet, Walt Whitman, when he wrote that from "Democracy, with its manly heart and its lion strength," would spring "the great FUTURE of this Western World!" This spirit led thousands of people to give up their settled lives in the East and move across the continent. They traveled in boats, in wagon trains, on horseback, or by foot. They often saw themselves as agents of progress, sweeping westward as part of a divine plan.

This booming confidence that the American eagle should stretch its wings from the Atlantic to the Pacific Ocean was exciting. Yet, it was rather hard on others who happened to stand in the way. These people included the American Indians, the Mexicans, and those from England, who manned the outposts of the British Empire in Canada

READING GUIDE

1. **Why did the movement of Americans to the West so often lead to conflict with other peoples?**
2. **What part did the army play in the nation's expansion westward?**
3. **What opportunities did expansion offer to a person with money to invest?**

The lure of California has made it the most populous state in the Union.

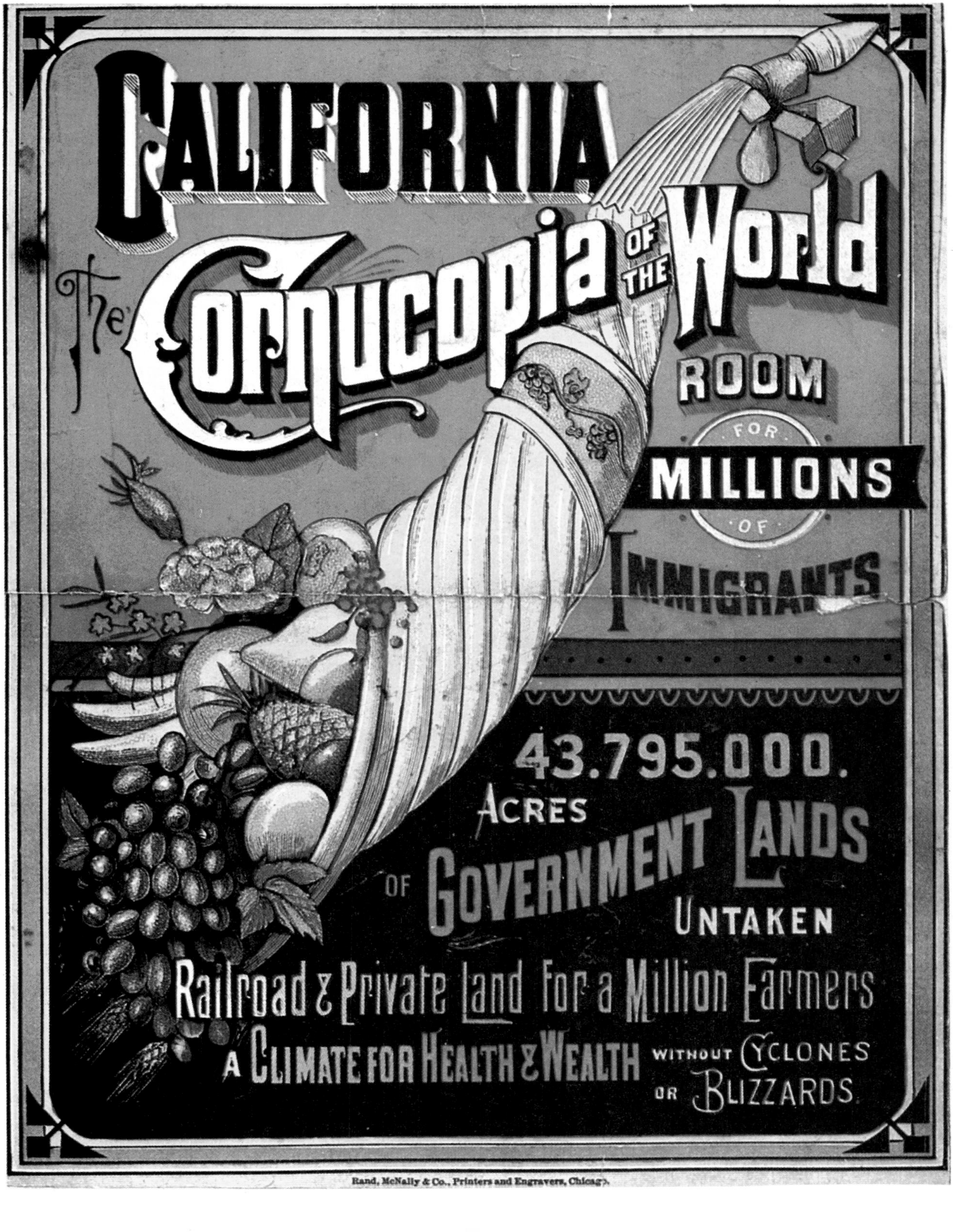

CALIFORNIA

The Cornucopia of the World

ROOM FOR MILLIONS OF IMMIGRANTS

43.795.000. ACRES of GOVERNMENT LANDS UNTAKEN

Railroad & Private Land for a Million Farmers

A CLIMATE FOR HEALTH & WEALTH WITHOUT CYCLONES OR BLIZZARDS.

Rand, McNally & Co., Printers and Engravers, Chicago.

and Oregon. But the American dream of Manifest Destiny was a natural result of the optimism created by the events up to 1845—invention, economic growth, success in diplomacy, and especially expansion westward.

1. The Lone Star State

Westward expansion was not a process that stopped at boundary lines. After 1820, the first large overflow of Americans into foreign territory surged into the Mexican province of Texas. By this time, Mexico had won its independence after a long struggle. The first large group of American settlers in Texas was headed by Stephen F. Austin, the son of a restless Connecticut Yankee. In 1796, his father, Moses Austin, moved to the Far West and operated a lead mine in modern Missouri, then owned by the Spanish. In 1820, he asked Mexican authorities for permission to settle 300 American families in the northeastern province of Texas. But before he was given approval, Moses died. So Stephen, rather than his pioneer father, led the settlers into the promised land.

The Mexican government thought it had made a good bargain. Mexico wanted additional settlers in Texas for the same reasons that colonial promoters in Virginia or Pennsylvania had wanted to find new settlers for their lands—the settlers would cultivate the soil, pay taxes, and keep the American Indians in check.

Texas had a lot to offer people like Austin. Cattle-ranching could be highly profitable on the grasslands of the rich plains. Those who succeeded became great landowners, living in comfortable *ranchos*. In time, the booming cotton frontier was perhaps an even more secure way to quick wealth.

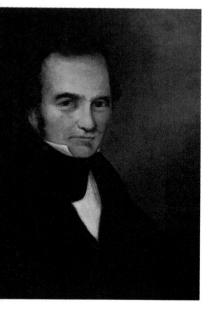

Stephen F. Austin led the first large group of American settlers into Texas. In 1822, he established the first legal settlement there.

Austin's little colony prospered. The Mexicans were encouraged to invite other Americans to become land agents or *empresarios*, who received large grants of land and were responsible for colonizing them. By 1830, Texas presented a strange picture. Its Spanish-speaking settlers had given it a Hispanic flavor. However, some 20,000 American "immigrants" made Texas a typical southwestern frontier, full of land speculators and pioneers with ambitious plans.

Could the Mexicans govern these hardy, adventurous, aggressive newcomers? It seemed so at first. One Texan wrote to a friend, praising the liberty that the Mexican constitution of 1824 promised them. Yet trouble was brewing.

Texans Fight at the Alamo

At heart, the American settlers did not think of themselves as bound by Mexican laws. For example, although most of them were Protestants, they were supposed to adopt the Catholic faith. However, few of them did. As one Texan wrote, "There is no such thing as attending church, since no religion except the Roman Catholic is

The Siege of the Alamo. A large Mexican army was held off for more than a month by 187 Texans. When the garrison fell, all 187 men were killed, including Davy Crockett, pictured here.

tolerated, and we have no priests among us." There was also a disagreement involving slavery. Mexico had outlawed slavery. However, under pressure from American settlers, slavery was allowed to exist in Texas.

Even though Stephen Austin sincerely urged all Texans to respect Mexican laws, few had much respect for the government in Mexico City. They thought Mexico was inexperienced in self-government. Only its generals and rich people had any power. And these two groups were jealous of each other. In addition, revolutions brought frequent changes in rulers.

The American settlers began to resent their treatment by the Mexicans. Although welcomed at first, they became subjected to imprisonment and to denial of those rights they had enjoyed in the United States.

autonomy
the right or power of self-government

In 1833, the Texas settlers asked Mexico for a constitutional change to give their province more **autonomy**. The Mexicans did not like this any better than the American government would have liked a request by some states of the Union to go back to the Articles of Confederation. So they refused. In 1835, the Mexican president, Antonio de Santa Anna, withdrew many of the rights Texans enjoyed and sent troops to frighten them. The struggle had now grown to the point where fighting broke out. In October 1835, the Texans and Mexican troops clashed.

A convention of settlers was scheduled to meet on March 1, 1836. Five days earlier, Santa Anna, marching into Texas with a large army, had surrounded some 187 Americans in the Alamo, a former mission in San Antonio. On March 2, Texas declared itself independent from Mexico. But on March 6, the Mexicans blasted their way through the Alamo's walls and killed every one of the overwhelmed, but still battling, American forces. The American defenders at the Battle of the Alamo included Jim Bowie, Davy Crockett, and the commanding officer, Colonel William Travis. The Texans now had a battle cry in their struggle for independence—"Remember the Alamo!"

Texas Wins Its Independence

By 1835, many American volunteers had come to Texas to help the settlers fight Mexico. One of them, Sam Houston, was to become the George Washington of Texas. Houston was an unusual American. As a young man, he entered the army and fought against the Creek Indians under Andrew Jackson. Like his good friend Jackson, he settled in Tennessee. There, he became a landowner, a congressman, and finally governor of the state. Unlike Jackson, Houston was not an Indian hater. In 1829, after suddenly resigning his office for mysterious

personal reasons, he went to live among the Cherokees. He was actually adopted into their tribe.

Sam Houston arrived in Texas in 1835. Because of his military experience, he was given command of the tiny Texas army. After the Alamo fell—he had been against making a stand there—he took a position on the western bank of the San Jacinto River, near Galveston Bay, in April 1836. The pursuing Mexicans were overconfident. They made camp without proper guards. Like the Hessians at Trenton, they were amazed when their "beaten" foes suddenly attacked them, shouting like demons and shooting cannon loaded with bits of broken horseshoes—the only ammunition they had. In a few hours, the Texas forces defeated the Mexicans. Though wounded, Houston personally accepted Santa Anna's surrender.

The Mexican government did not officially recognize the independence of Texas. However, after the Battle of San Jacinto, Mexico gave up any serious efforts to reconquer its lost province. For nine years, Texas was an independent nation under a new flag with a single star. The "Lone Star Republic" received diplomatic recognition from the United States, France, and England. And thousands of new settlers

After the Battle of San Jacinto in April 1836, Sam Houston, lying wounded, accepts the surrender of Santa Anna. The Mexican commander also signed a treaty with Houston recognizing the Republic of Texas. Although the Mexican government rejected the treaty, Texas functioned as an independent nation for nine years.

Austin, seen here as it looked in 1840, served as the capital of Texas.

from the United States helped to swell the prosperity of growing little towns such as Austin, the nation's capital. Here, merchants trading in cotton and cattle began to develop those urban characteristics that in time would give the southwestern frontier its own thriving cities.

Sam Houston became the Republic's first president. Despite the new nation's successful start, Houston wanted and expected a union with the United States. However, until 1845, American political problems delayed the marriage of the two republics.

annexation
the incorporation of a territory within the domain of another state or country

Those in favor of **annexation** feared the growing friendship between Texas and two European powers—Britain and France. The Southern states were particularly disturbed by the rumor that the British planned to use their influence to abolish slavery in Texas.

The Northern states expressed opposition to annexation. The admission of Texas would give the slave interests more say in Congress. There was also concern that annexation would involve the United States in a war with Mexico.

Questions for Discussion
1. Define *ranchos, empresarios, autonomy, annexation.*
2. What natural resources attracted the first American settlers to Texas?
3. Why did Texans begin to demand more autonomy?
4. How did American settlement in Texas promote the development of urban centers?
5. How did the question of annexation of Texas divide the country?

In 1844, the feelings of expansionists began to be expressed in politics. At the same time, another controversy arose over the issue of slavery. A growing number of Americans were opposed to the further spread of slavery. And when it came to the question of Texas, antislavery and expansionist attitudes clashed. Annexing that "nation" would add a huge new slave state to the Union—perhaps more if Texas chose to be cut up into several states. Some antislavery leaders even charged that in 1835 President Andrew Jackson, a Southerner and a slaveholder, had encouraged Southerner Sam Houston to revolt, steal Texas from Mexico, and then bring Texas into the United States as a slave state.

The 1844 Presidential election offered a test of public opinion on the issue of slavery. By 1844, the old Federalist and Republican parties had disappeared. Now the two major parties were called Whigs and Democrats. The most likely Presidential candidates were Henry Clay of Kentucky, a Whig, and Martin Van Buren of New York, a Democrat. Both were eager to avoid battles over slavery, which would tend to split the nation. Van Buren was also convinced that the Mexicans would declare war on the United States if Texas was annexed. So both he and Clay opposed annexing Texas.

The result was dramatic. When Van Buren refused to support annexation, the nominating convention of his own party refused to select him. He held onto the support of New York and New England. But he had lost the support of the Southern states and Andrew Jackson, who was still a leader of the Democrats. Instead, the Democratic Party chose James K. Polk, a determined expansionist, who favored taking Texas. Polk also wanted the United States to acquire California and to take over the rich Oregon country.

Patriotic feelings ran high in the election. But Polk won in a close vote over Clay. He believed that his victory at the polls meant that the nation supported his views on expansion. However, public opinion in a democracy is not always entirely clear. Was the vote for Polk a vote for more slave territory? Did Americans want new lands without caring much whether acquiring such lands would complicate the slavery question? Americans were in favor of expansion. But were they neutral or perhaps opposed to slavery?

Polk Settles the Oregon Question

Actually, Polk's earliest expansionist move, which concerned Oregon, did not involve the issue of slave territory at all. In 1845, he announced to Great Britain that the United States would not renew the joint occupation agreement of 1818. This might mean that the United States would insist on taking all of Oregon. At that time, the boundaries of Oregon ran from the 42nd parallel, the northern

2. War with Mexico

Two political banners from the 1844 Presidential election. Top: Democratic candidates James K. Polk and Alexander J. Dallas. Bottom: Whig Party candidate Henry Clay.

A cowboy throws a young bull during a roundup in Mexico.

boundary of California, to beyond the 54th parallel, along the southern tip of Alaska. Oregon then extended from the Rocky Mountains to the Pacific Ocean. While the British thought the situation over, Polk let it be known that he would compromise on a boundary at the 49th parallel. That would give the United States the area already settled by several thousand American families. Since the British knew that they could hardly defend faraway Oregon in a war with these Yankees, they quickly looked for a compromise. And by June of 1846, Polk had bluffed his way into getting most of Oregon without a fight.

Conflict with Mexico

In March of 1845, just before Polk's inauguration, President Tyler put before Congress a joint resolution calling for approval of annexation of Texas. His attempt to get the Senate to ratify a treaty had failed months before. However, his new plan worked. A joint resolution needed only a simple majority vote to pass. A treaty required a two-thirds majority in the Senate. With a vote of 27 to 25 in the Senate and 132 to 76 in the House, Congress voted to annex the Republic of Texas and make it the "Lone Star State." Mexico believed this to be a hostile act. And the Mexican ambassador stormed out of Washington.

The conflict over the annexation was not the only problem between the United States and Mexico that carried over into Polk's administration. Mexico also argued that Texas was smaller than the Americans claimed. Its southern boundary was not the Rio Grande River, but rather, the Nueces River further north. In addition, Mexico had stopped payment on debts owed to Americans whose property was destroyed during the many revolutions and civil wars in that country. However, Polk was aware that the Mexican government was practically bankrupt and could not make the payments. And, to add to the problem, Polk showed an obvious interest in acquiring California, which Mexico wanted to keep.

The events in Texas gave the United States a chance to take California by force. In May 1845, Polk ordered General Zachary Taylor to be ready to defend Texas if invaded by Mexico. Then Polk tried to settle matters peacefully. Mexico hinted that they would be willing to negotiate the boundary issue.

So Polk sent an envoy, John Slidell, to Mexico to discuss the debt, the boundary, and the purchase of New Mexico and California. The United States was to assume the debts owed to the Americans. In return, Mexico was to recognize the Rio Grande as the southern boundary of Texas. Slidell was also instructed to offer the Mexican government $5 million for New Mexico and at least $25 million for California. However, when news of the full extent of Slidell's mission leaked out, the Mexican government refused even to meet with him.

In answer, Polk ordered United States troops in Texas to advance as far as the Rio Grande and seize the disputed region. On April 25, 1846, Mexican soldiers and a party of American cavalry clashed. Several Americans were killed. When this news reached Washington, it gave Polk an excuse for a fight. War "exists by the act of Mexico," he told Congress. And Congress promptly declared war. Now "Manifest Destiny" marched in uniform, with bugles blowing.

War with Mexico—The First Phase

The Mexican War was a strange conflict. For one thing, it was the nation's first war fought entirely on foreign soil. And its prizes were territories that were hundreds of miles away from settled America. To capture them, whole armies would have to move over empty country where even mountain people had sometimes gone hungry. The tiny American army of 1846 had to enroll thousands of untrained volunteers. They depended on these volunteers to meet the challenges of the war.

In the end, the United States actually accomplished its goal. The first planned step of the war was the occupation of northern Mexico. General Zachary Taylor was chosen to lead a force westward from the Rio Grande. Known to his troops as "Old Rough and Ready," Taylor was a veteran of frontier service. He usually wore an unkempt uniform and a straw hat. And he slouched in the saddle on his horse, "Old Whitey." Yet, there was nothing messy about the way his soldiers

General Zachary Taylor grew to be a national hero from his victories over the Mexican army. His popularity led him to become the 12th President of the United States.

fought. In May of 1846, they met the Mexicans in two sharp fights at Palo Alto and Resaca de la Palma. In both battles, American sharpshooting skill and use of artillery proved too much for the Mexicans. Taylor pushed onward, occupied Monterrey, and then Saltillo. By the end of 1846, his forces were deep in Mexico.

At about the same time, Captain Frémont was in California presumably on an exploring expedition. When he learned of the impending war with Mexico, he encouraged the California settlers who wished to rid themselves of Mexican rule to do so. Frémont later claimed that he had secret orders from Polk to aid the Americans in California should they decide to rebel, as the Texans had done. In what became known as the "Bear Flag Revolt," some Americans attacked Sonoma and proclaimed the "Republic of California" in June 1846. Their flag had a white background with the name of the republic, a bear, and a star painted on it. Shortly thereafter, Commodore Sloat took control of Monterey, raised the United States flag, and declared California part of the United States.

Meanwhile, an expedition of some 1600 men, under General Stephen W. Kearny, left Fort Leavenworth, Kansas, bound west. Day after day, they rolled through the Southwest, battling thirst, heat, and dust. They kept their eyes open for hostile American Indians and Mexican armies. In six weeks, Kearny reached and fought at Santa Fe, where the Mexicans surrendered without a fight. Then he pushed on to the Pacific Ocean, where he overcame the Mexican forces at San Pasqual in southern California. By January 1847, his forces were in command of Los Angeles. Forces led by Frémont and Commodore Robert Stockton, who had replaced the ailing Sloat, finally won control of California for the United States.

In February 1847, the Mexicans tried to turn the tide by furiously attacking Taylor's outnumbered forces at Buena Vista. But on Washington's birthday, the Americans beat them off in a bloody engagement. The opening phase of the war was now over.

War with Mexico—The Second Phase

The second part of the war was a six-month campaign, in 1847, to force Mexico to sue for peace by capturing Mexico City, its capital. Only with Americans in "the halls of Montezuma" would the Mexicans sign a treaty formally giving up the provinces they had lost to the United States army. General Winfield Scott, an able but vain officer, nicknamed "Old Fuss and Feathers," was in command. "Old Rough and Ready" General Taylor was ordered to stay on the defensive while Scott won this final glory. Since both generals were Whigs, President Polk did not want either one to shine too brightly in contrast to the Democrats. However, it was a lost cause. Both ended up running for

The Mexican War 1846–1848

the Presidency as Whigs. Taylor won in 1848 and Scott lost four years later.

With about 10,000 troops, Scott sailed south to Veracruz on the Gulf of Mexico. By the end of March 1847, his troops had taken the city. Now, step by step, they began to march inland on a long, upward climb. The little army included many young officers trained at West Point, the national military academy. They were proving the value of their training and getting experience that they would use on both sides in the Civil War a few years later. Ulysses S. Grant and Robert E. Lee were among these officers. Mile after mile, they and their regiments of American farm boys marched. They prodded horses and mules over the twisting mountain roads to conquer lands once known to Cortés's Spaniards.

In September, Scott's army reached Mexico City. The Mexicans fought back gallantly. On September 13, American Marines stormed the National Palace, a key defensive point. One week later, the Stars and Stripes flew over Mexico City. Santa Anna gathered his forces for one last attack, only to be finally defeated in October. Both sides now waited for the negotiations that would end the war.

At home, the reaction to the war was mixed. The war was popular in the South and West. Settlers from these areas provided 49,000 volunteers, compared to only 13,000 from the original thirteen states.

However, among Northerners, there had been bitter opposition to the war. An Ohio member of Congress had said that, if he were a Mexican, he would welcome the Americans "with bloody hands to hospitable graves." This meant that he would happily kill the invaders and then bury them. A member of Congress from Illinois, Abraham

Americans storm Chapultepec Castle, in Mexico City, bravely defended by young cadets.

Lincoln, unsuccessfully called for an investigation to see if President Polk had lied about the Mexican attack of April 1846, which had started the fighting.

Cause and Effects

Abraham Lincoln was one of many people who questioned the justice of the Mexican War. Many historians then and now have tried to identify the reasons and assign the blame. This task is not without problems. Like any study of history, it is limited by the information available and the skill of the historian.

Among the suggestions made were that the war was encouraged by the slaveholding states. Not only did they want the land, they also wanted the additional representatives in Congress. This interpretation was encouraged by the abolitionists.

Others lay the blame on the expansionist frontier settlers. The 1844 election platform called for the "re-annexation of Texas and the re-occupation of Oregon." Polk was a Westerner and Western votes gave him the Presidency. Though the idea of Manifest Destiny was a national one, Westerners seemed to be its greatest supporters. Polk did the most to associate Manifest Destiny with the Monroe Doctrine.

Another point of view claims that the fault lay with New England's commercial interests. The movement westward is seen as a means of obtaining Pacific ports. These ports would then form the basis for a profitable Oriental trade. The war over Texas is then seen merely as a trick to obtain California.

Some historians blame Mexico's weakness. They feel that the political unrest in the country encouraged anti-American sentiment. Not to be outdone in patriotism, opposing leaders would rally support against the United States. Some Mexican leaders believed that they would better their own positions by waging a successful war against the United States. These leaders thought that victory was assured by Mexican military superiority, aid from Britain, and opposition to the war in the United States. Therefore, the Mexicans had no intention of settling the Texas boundary question peaceably.

Whatever the cause, the war put a strain on Mexican-American relations for decades. And the loss of territory greatly lessened Mexico's opportunity to become a world power.

The Treaty of Guadalupe Hidalgo

The Treaty of Guadalupe Hidalgo, signed in February of 1848, was a triumph for the United States. It gave the nation the Mexican provinces of Upper California and New Mexico, as the map on page 306 shows. These included four future Southwestern states. For these lands, the United States paid Mexico $15 million. To this day, some Americans consider this payment to be "conscience money" for a bad deed. Others believed such expansion was both right and part of the nation's Manifest Destiny.

By taking the Oregon Territory and California, and by clearing up the dispute over Texas by war, the incredible Polk gained vast parts of the West in just one term of office. Only a little territory remained to be added. In 1853, the government was planning to build one or more railroads to the Pacific. One possible route was along the south bank of the Gila River, the boundary set by the 1848 treaty. James Gadsden was sent to Mexico to purchase the little strip that bears his name, for another $10 million. The Gadsden Purchase completed United States expansion into North American territory that was *contiguous*—or touching its existing boundaries. The next steps of expansion would lead into the Pacific Ocean and the Caribbean Sea.

Only sixty years separated the ratification of the Constitution from the Treaty of Guadalupe Hidalgo. Most Americans thought that this speedy expansion was a sign of God's pleasure with the United States. They were given further cause for this view by an amazing coincidence. Nine days before the treaty was signed, gold was discovered in the American River valley in California.

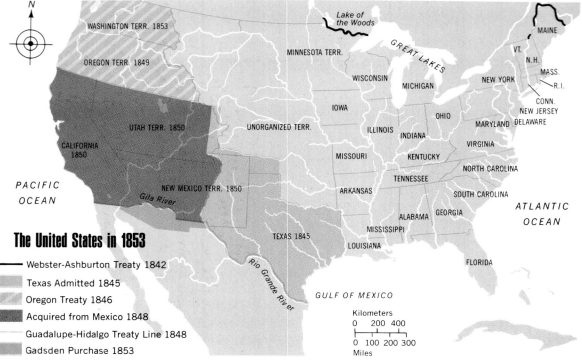

The United States in 1853

— Webster-Ashburton Treaty 1842

Texas Admitted 1845

Oregon Treaty 1846

Acquired from Mexico 1848

Guadalupe-Hidalgo Treaty Line 1848

Gadsden Purchase 1853

Advertisements like this were common during the clipper-ship boom in the 1850s.

3. The Fulfillment of Manifest Destiny

This meant that California and some parts of the other newly won territories would be settled almost overnight. Soon gold-hungry pioneers swarmed westward in droves. As a result, many problems had to be faced. One problem especially was the future of slavery. In any case, the many issues had to be dealt with before the country had much time to think about them. Such sudden growth was exciting, but it also proved to be deeply upsetting.

Questions for Discussion

1. Why did antislavery and expansionist attitudes clash over the question of annexing Texas?
2. How did the principle of Manifest Destiny apply to the American acquisition of Texas?
3. How did events in Texas give the United States a chance to take California by force?
4. Why was there opposition in the United States to the Mexican War?
5. What differing opinions are held concerning the cause of the war with Mexico?

James Marshall was a mechanic from New Jersey. It was he who, on January 24, 1848, discovered bright nuggets of gold at the bottom of a California stream, thereby changing the history of the West. At the time, he was building a sawmill for John A. Sutter. A Swiss citizen, Sutter was an immigrant to California. His ranch, in what is now

San Francisco harbor bustled with activity due to westward expansion.

This lone prospector was one of many to come to California hoping to find gold.

Sacramento, was a welcome resting place for American overland travelers arriving in California after six hard months on the trail. Although Marshall and Sutter both tried to keep the news of the gold strike secret, it rapidly leaked out to the world. By December 1848, President Polk was mentioning California gold discoveries in his annual message to Congress. As 1849 dawned, people began to pour into the region. In that year alone, perhaps 40,000 arrived. Gold was as great a magnet to these people as it had been to the Spaniards three centuries earlier. It seemed as if Coronado's fabled cities had been found at last.

What made the gold fields especially luring was that many people believed it took little organized effort or capital to become rich. The basic tool could be one as simple as a wash basin. The individual prospector scooped up some earth, poured water over it, and sloshed it around to wash dissolved soil away from the heavy particles of gold, which sank to the bottom. Soon people used this same method on a larger scale by shoveling earth into wooden boxes. This washing, or

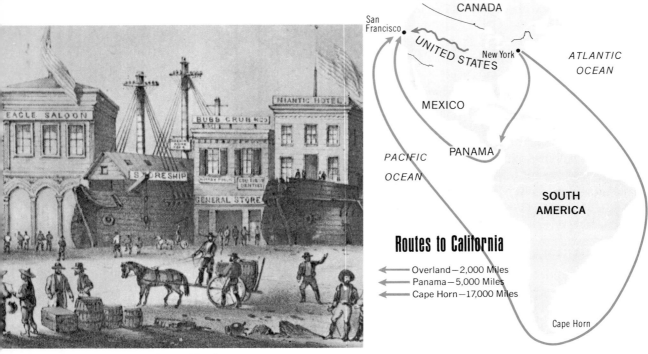

This picture shows the wealth of activity surrounding the city of San Francisco in the 1850s.

Routes to California

← Overland—2,000 Miles
← Panama—5,000 Miles
← Cape Horn—17,000 Miles

placer-mining process, could make people rich very quickly, even if they had started empty-handed. And many Americans came to believe that it was the Manifest Destiny of the United States to shower wealth on its citizens.

From every American county and many foreign lands, people flocked to California. Free Blacks were attracted because California had declared itself a free state. Soon ships lay deserted and rotting in San Francisco Bay as their crews fled into the hills to hunt for gold. The gold seekers gathered in camps where, like the frontier settlers before them, they set up informal governments that made their own rules. Among the rules set up were strict provisions for honoring the claim to exclusive mining rights on a piece of gold-bearing ground of the miner who found it first. Yet, no one ever honored poor John Sutter's claim. These camps dealt out quick, harsh punishments, including *lynching* (executing without a trial). And government by **vigilantes** became a part of the gold-rush experience.

vigilantes
unofficial police who also act as self-appointed judges and jurors

Questions for Discussion

1. Define *lynching, vigilante*. How did they relate to the gold-rush experience?
2. Why did so many Americans believe that the gold fields of California offered a quick and easy way to become wealthy?

Chapter 13 Review

Summary Questions for Discussion

1. Why did Senator Thomas Hart Benton believe that American settlement of Oregon would in time improve the condition of Asia?
2. What is "Manifest Destiny"?
3. What role did Stephen F. Austin play in the settlement of Texas? Why did the Mexican government think it had made a good bargain with the Austins? What were the advantages for the Austins?
4. What was the attitude of the American settlers toward Mexican government?
5. How did the Mexican government react to the demands of the American settlers for autonomy?
6. Why did the Alamo become the symbol for Texas independence?
7. Why is Sam Houston considered the "George Washington" of Texas?
8. How did the question of the annexation of Texas influence the election of 1844?
9. How did Oregon become part of the United States without a war with England?
10. Outline the steps that resulted in war with Mexico.
11. Describe the role of each of the following in the Mexican War: General Zachary Taylor, Captain Frémont, Commodore Sloat, General Stephen W. Kearny, Commodore Robert Stockton.
12. What was the goal of the second phase of the Mexican War?
13. On whom do historians place the blame for the war? Why?
14. What were the effects of the Mexican War on Mexico? On the United States?
15. How was the California gold rush related to the American idea of Manifest Destiny?

Word Study

Fill in each blank in the sentences that follow with the term below that is most appropriate.

ranchos	vigilantes	empresarios
lynching	autonomy	annexation

1. A great deal of territory was added to the United States by the process of _____.
2. Many Americans in Texas had been land agents, or _____.
3. Some large landowners who succeeded in Texas lived on _____.
4. Wanting self-government or _____, American settlers revolted against Mexico.
5. Law and order was often in the hands of self-appointed police officials or _____ who employed harsh punishments.

Using Your Skills

1. Study the map, "The United States in 1853," on page 306 and then answer these questions:
   a. Why were territories organized in the Far West before they were organized in the Midwest? What were obstacles to settlement in the "Unorganized Territory"?
   b. What states were eventually formed from the land acquired from Mexico as a result of the Mexican War? What states were formed from the Washington and Oregon Territories?
2. Which pictures in the chapter give you an idea of what lured settlers westward?
3. How do the pictures about the Mexican War represent the American point of view? Would these same pictures be used in a textbook in Mexico? Why?

UNIT 3 REVIEW

Summary

"Go West Young Man" has been a characteristic cry of Americans. Although the "West" or the frontier has referred to different places during the course of America's history, it has had a magnetic pull not only for settlers, but for gold miners, soldiers, and sailors as well. Yet, the frontier has also been a mixed blessing.

Cheap undeveloped land attracted pioneers. Despite fear of the unknown, settlers had crossed the Allegheny Mountains. And they had established settlements in Kentucky and Tennessee by the end of the Revolution. From 1800 to 1850, the Northwest Territory was the scene of westward migration. The invention of the cotton gin by Eli Whitney made the South and Southwest sections of the country profitable for settlement. Around 1840, settlers headed for the Far West along the Pacific Coast in search of fertile land.

With the movement westward, there was a need to link the old with the new. In transportation, a canal-building boom swept the country. Steam-powered vessels on American and international waterways allowed travel upstream, independent of wind conditions. On land, steam-powered locomotives completed the transportation boom, which helped unify the country. This transportation network could carry the products that were the result of America's industrial revolution. Mass production and interchangeable parts increased production and profits.

The changes in industry also had social, economic, and political effects. Women's rights, immigration, education, temperance, and slavery were just a few areas subject to examination.

During this era, the American political system underwent major changes. Interest in politics increased. And reforms extended popular participation in government.

Americans believed that expansion to the West was part of God's plan for a better world—their Manifest Destiny.

Through war with Mexico and treaties with other foreign nations, the United States extended its borders from "sea to shining sea."

Summary Questions

1. What factors combined to make the extension of the nation's boundaries to the Pacific Ocean a fairly quick movement?

2. Was environment as important in shaping the pioneers' way of life as it was in shaping the American Indian's way of life? Explain.

3. In this unit, you have read that Americans had a mental image of the ideal frontier hero. How did their picture of the American Indian differ from that of the frontier hero?

4. In what ways did industrialization before the Civil War change people's lives?

5. Why did the era of canal-building in the United States end at approximately the same time that the age of railroads began?

6. How were improvements in transportation both a cause and a result of the rapid settlement of the West?

7. What industries in the United States made use of mass production, interchangeable parts, and assembly lines in the first half of the nineteenth century?

8. Cite six ways in which political democracy grew during the Age of Jackson.

9. What was John Marshall's role in strengthening the central government? What was his contribution to the growth of big business?

10. What made many Americans confident that Manifest Destiny was right?

Developing Your Vocabulary

1. A theocratic society is one that is built around (religion, economics).

2. Public works are usually undertaken by (individuals, the government).

3. A person who claimed possession of land based on the fact that he or she cleared and settled it is known as a (squatter, capitalist).

4. People who purchased large tracts of land from the government in order to sell them for profit were (squatters, land speculators).

5. (Monopoly, *Laissez-faire*) is the idea that government should in no way regulate business.

6. To (franchise, disenfranchise) people is to give them the vote.

7. (Humanitarianism, Nativism) is the belief that all people are entitled to have better lives.

8. The money that banks pay you for the use of your money is known as (credit, interest).

9. The use of the assembly line and interchangeable parts is part of (the domestic system, mass production).

10. (Nullification, lobbying) is the policy that calls for the right of states to ignore federal laws.

Developing Your Skills

Drawing conclusions

1. Sectional alliances began to develop over the domestic issues of internal improvements, the Bank of the United States, the factory system, and the expansion of slavery. Is there a firm pattern of sectional alliances that can be distinguished by 1824? Describe.

Comparing and applying information

2. Compare some of the nineteenth-century efforts to reform and create utopian societies with similar efforts today. What are the similarities? What are the differences?

Dramatizing

3. Choose a domestic or foreign issue and invent a dialogue between Andrew Jackson and the present President of the United States.

Interpreting information

4. Draw a cartoon representing one of the following policies described in the Unit:
a. American Indian policy
b. Monroe Doctrine
c. Jackson and the "spoils system"
d. Manifest Destiny

Special Activities

1. Report to the class on the various ways of nominating Presidential candidates—state legislatures, caucuses, conventions, primaries. Indicate which one you feel is most democratic.

2. Investigate how the position of women in American society changed during the first half of the nineteenth century. Consider the influence of (a) the expansion westward, (b) new ideas of democracy, (c) the factory system, and (d) the reform movement. Present your findings to the class.

3. Draw your impression of what the Battle of the Alamo looked like. Present it to the class, stating your sources for your interpretation.

4. Choose one of the following subjects. Research and present your findings to the class. Define the issue, explain the historical solution, and suggest alternatives: The United States and (a) Latin-American relations and the Monroe Doctrine, or (b) Canadian relations and the Rush-Bagot agreement, or (c) American Indian treaties and policies.

UNIT
4
A Nation Divided

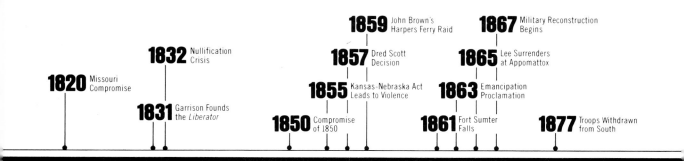

1820 Missouri Compromise

1831 Garrison Founds the *Liberator*

1832 Nullification Crisis

1850 Compromise of 1850

1855 Kansas-Nebraska Act Leads to Violence

1857 Dred Scott Decision

1859 John Brown's Harpers Ferry Raid

1861 Fort Sumter Falls

1863 Emancipation Proclamation

1865 Lee Surrenders at Appomattox

1867 Military Reconstruction Begins

1877 Troops Withdrawn from South

CHAPTER 14
The Coming of the Civil War

CHAPTER 15
The Civil War

CHAPTER 16
The Reconstruction Period

The uniting of thirteen separate governments into one nation in 1776 was one of the most important and favorable turning points in the history of the United States. The splitting of the nation into two parts from 1861 to 1865 was no less important. This period was marked by bitterness and destruction. Now, more than 100 years after the Civil War, its tragic effects are still felt throughout our nation.

Some of the regional differences and disputes are described in Chapter 14. At the same time that forces were at work to drive the Northern, Southern, and Western sections of the country apart, other forces were at work to unite them.

In Chapter 15, there is a discussion of the actual fighting, which scarred farms and forests and stained the land with the blood of young soldiers. Attention is also given to the economic and political struggles that took place behind the lines.

The process of bringing the Confederate states back into the Union and the attempts of a wounded nation to heal itself, are discussed in Chapter 16. The chapter also focuses on the struggle of Blacks to gain dignity as United States citizens. The story of this period is full of a new kind of conflict—a conflict too often between races, a conflict as yet unresolved.

CHAPTER 14

The Coming of the Civil War

*Mine eyes have seen the glory of the coming of
the Lord;
He is trampling out the vintage where the
grapes of wrath are stored.*

These are the opening words of the "Battle Hymn of the Republic," a song of the Civil War. In 1861, when the South seceded from the Union, the American success story ended. Until then, despite some hard times, such as the depression of 1837, there had been growth, prosperity, and progress in the country. Then in 1861, war between the North and the South tore the nation apart. It took four years and 600,000 young people's lives to reunite the nation—and to put an end to slavery.

Why did war occur? The generation that fought in the Civil War had simple answers to this question. Some Northerners thought that it was God's judgment on the land for the sin of slavery. Many other Northerners denied such an idea. For them, the war was fought only to save the *Union* (the nation acting as a whole) from the efforts of those "traitors" who wished to destroy it. On the other hand, Southerners believed that the war grew out of Northern violations of the South's constitutional rights. In their eyes, the South was resisting in 1861 a wrongful government just as their forefathers had done in 1776.

Later generations gave other reasons for the conflict. Some historians say that the war was inevitable because of the different social outlooks between North and South. These differences dated back to the differences between colonial Massachusetts and colonial Virginia. Other historians believe that the causes were rooted in the economic conflict between the industrial North and the agricultural South. And still others lay the blame on the impatience of both sides. Neither the North nor the South was willing to wait and let time settle their differences.

READING GUIDE

1. **How did the sections of the country differ?**
2. **Why did slavery divide the country?**
3. **Why is compromise often a part of making laws?**
4. **Why did compromise fail to permanently solve the conflict?**
5. **What were the events that led to open warfare?**

A larger-than-life portrait of abolitionist John Brown.

1. Sectional Patterns

At times, the same forces that seemed to knit the nation together were also helping to divide it. In all parts of the United States, rapid growth was common. However, different sections of the nation changed in different ways. By 1830, each of the three sections of the United States—Northeast, South, and West—had a different basic economy. As a result, each also had a widely different social and cultural life. In population and area, these sections were as large as most European countries. And Americans often felt more devoted to the section in which they lived than to the nation. So, from 1830 to 1860, the United States became more of a federation of sections—a federation not foreseen in the Constitution.

The Northeast Becomes More Urban and Industrial

The first such great section was the Northeast. It included the New England states, New York, New Jersey, and Pennsylvania. In 1830, the Northeast had a population of about 5.5 million. In 1860, after thirty years of industrial boom, the figure had risen to over 10.5 million. Hundreds of thousands of Northeasterners worked in the factories that manufactured boots, shoes, textiles, clocks, guns, sewing machines, and other goods.

New York has long been a crowded center of trade and commerce. In the 1850s, the boundaries to New York City were limited to Manhattan Island (below center). Brooklyn (lower right) was a separate city and Queens (upper right) a growing village across the East River.

The booming factories of the Northeast attracted a large part of a growing number of immigrants. Between 1820 and 1860, over 5 million newcomers arrived in America. Most of them were from Ireland, Scotland, England, Germany, and the Scandinavian countries. Though many went westward to frontier communities, thousands settled in factory towns and big cities.

To the ports of Boston, New York, and Philadelphia came ships loaded with cotton, silk, tea, gold, and grain. As a result of the Treaty of Wang Hya in 1844, five Chinese ports were open to American ships. In 1854, Commodore Matthew Perry opened Japan to American trade. And in 1856, Siam (now Thailand), improved trade opportunities for Americans. Industrialization in Europe led to a better system of money exchange and lower tariffs on farm goods. In time, the American merchant fleet became the largest in the world.

Owners of large plantations in the South lived in grandeur in mansions such as the one pictured above.

The South Falls Behind

The South presented a strikingly different picture. The South grew sugar, rice, and tobacco as well as cotton. The upper Southern states of Missouri, Kentucky, Delaware, and Maryland produced more mules, horses, corn, and hemp than cotton. Yet people still thought of the South as made up of large cotton plantations. They imagined each plantation being worked by hundreds of slaves. This was in spite of the fact that in 1860, fewer than 50,000 White Southerners out of 5 million owned more than twenty slaves. And Southerners themselves acted as if the typical pattern of living was on a great plantation— where a world of grace and charm, free from the problems and pressures of city life, existed. According to this ideal view of the old South, kindly masters took care of slaves who were never thrown out of work by industrial panics, such as the one in 1837.

However, the reality was not much like the plantation ideal. Many Southerners owned small farms, which they worked with the aid of their families and perhaps a few slaves. Their "plantation houses" were slightly improved log cabins. And they were actually plain and poorly educated people. They often envied their great slave-owning neighbors, whom they generally voted into office.

The Southern slaves were far from carefree. Most of them were shabbily dressed field workers. Their usual diet of corn bread and fat meat did not give them much strength for hard, dusk-to-dawn outdoor work. In their windowless and over-crowded huts, sickness was common. And good medical care was rare.

The whole South paid a price for the cotton boom. Most of the money saved out of profits went into land and slaves. Also, the slave labor force bought very few goods. So, Southern merchants had little reason to stock up on low-cost clothes and goods for a large market.

Master and slaves worshipping together on a South Carolina plantation before the Civil War.

Thus, the South had little industry, few large cities, and few jobs to attract immigrants. As a result, governments of Southern states had few tax dollars to spend on schools and other improvements. Although the South fed raw cotton to the mills of a fast-growing modern world, they reaped few benefits.

The Booming West Grows Closer to the Northeast

The West was a kind of "balance wheel" between the other, older sections. Like the South, it was mostly agricultural, and profitably so. In 1859, Western states of the old Northwest Territory, plus newer

As traffic along the Mississippi River increased, St. Louis grew in size. However, a railroad on the far river bank was to tie St. Louis to the North rather than to the South and shatter the South's hopes for a strong link to markets in the West.

states like Iowa and Minnesota, grew a good part of the 830 million bushels of corn and 172 million bushels of wheat harvested in the United States. With the help of new inventions such as the mechanical reaper, the West was becoming the breadbasket of the nation. It was also the nation's butcher shop. The West raised many of the 32 million hogs and 15 million cattle on American farms and ranches.

Like the Northeast, the West became home to many different peoples. The Ohio Valley was settled in good part by the same kind of Southerners who brought their axes and camp meetings to the mountains of Kentucky. But after the Erie Canal opened, the area around the Great Lakes became filled with New Englanders and New Yorkers. Immigrants from Europe also moved toward the untouched, cheap lands of the new states. By 1860, Missouri, Illinois, and Wisconsin had very large German populations. Wisconsin and Minnesota attracted Scandinavians to work in the lumber industry. So many loggers were Swedish that a saw was called a "Swedish fiddle."

However, unlike the South, the West did not depend only on farming for its wealth. Industry moved westward, too. In cities on the banks of the great Western rivers, factories rose to pack meat, distill whiskey, make rope from locally grown hemp, and build steamboats and farm machinery. By 1860, St. Louis was already a well-developed

The tariff question was the subject of bitter sectional debate for a number of years. The southern viewpoint—that the North was growing rich while the South suffered the consequences—was presented in this 1832 cartoon.

city with newspapers, lecture halls, theaters, and handsome buildings. And so was Cincinnati. Even "upstart" Chicago, not chartered until the mid-1830s, was humming with activity by 1860. The city's lakeside wharves and rail depots were already beginning to make it what the famous poet Carl Sandburg much later called "hog butcher," "stacker of wheat," and "freight handler" to the world.

A large part of the West's produce was still going downriver to New Orleans in 1860. But more and more shipments went by railroad to Eastern cities. On the eve of the Civil War, this growing link between the West and the Northeast created an important change in the political line-up of each section.

The Politics of Sectionalism

The main job of politicians from 1830 on was to arrange peaceful bargains among these three sections in order to preserve the nation. Each section had many **pressure groups**. But in each, the basic economic pattern always made one group dominant.

In the Northeast, after 1815, manufacturers spoke with the loudest voice. Successful Northeastern politicians had to pay close attention to the needs of investors in industry. The well-being of the entire area depended on busy factories. The strongest demand of the manufacturers was for a tariff on imports to protect the items that they made. Such a tax on imported goods was purposely high. Its aim was not to raise revenue but to make it unprofitable for foreigners to sell products in the United States that would compete with American manufactured goods.

In the South, the cotton-growing slaveholders were the politicians. And they were outraged by the tariff. As they saw it, the Southern cotton crop, when sold abroad, earned money that could then be spent on low-cost British and European goods. Instead, the tariff forced Southerners and other farming Americans to buy Yankee goods with higher price tags. Southern politicians claimed that the tariff forced the South to **subsidize** Northern industry.

In the West, the most outstanding needs were for cheap land and for government help to improve transportation. Therefore, politicians who hoped to win the West tried to include these demands in a *legislative package*, or group of laws, which would also appeal to other sections. The political leaders who wanted a national victory for their party then had to win Congressional support for their proposals.

As long as the sections stayed roughly equal in wealth and population but with economic differences, government by "horse-swapping" could go on. Compromise was possible on the basis of sharing the wealth of an expanding economy—that is, some for you and some for me.

pressure groups
interest groups organized to influence public and especially governmental policy

subsidize
to give financial help to

320

However, through the 1830s and 1840s, dangerous things were happening. The Northeast and the West were outracing the South in growth and population. As a result, Southerners were losing the sense of security that comes from dealing as an equal. Also, slavery was becoming a political issue. Unlike other sectional issues, slavery was not just a dollars-and-cents matter. It dealt with Black and White, right and wrong, and the basic values by which people live. When slavery became a battleground between the sections, the "game" of sectional bargaining was played for blood.

Questions for Discussion
1. Define *pressure groups, subsidize.*
2. How did rapid economic growth tend to unite the country in some ways and divide it in others?
3. How did the industrial revolution change the economy of the North?
4. Why did the cotton boom not result in widespread Southern industrial and urban development?

In the Senate on January 26, 1830, Daniel Webster delivered his celebrated reply to Robert Hayne. It stirred up a tremendous emotional reaction on behalf of the Union.

2. Slavery Divides the Nation

In 1820, a number of antislavery societies existed in both the North and the South. Their members believed that slavery was an evil that would pass away slowly as the world grew wiser and right-thinking masters freed their servants. One person who thought this way was Benjamin Lundy, a Quaker abolitionist. He published a newspaper, the *Genius of Universal Emancipation.* Lundy urged people to give up their slaves.

Lundy also supported the American Colonization Society. This society established the colony of Liberia on the coast of Africa. The members of this society tried to raise enough money to buy slaves and to settle them and other free Blacks in Liberia. Lundy knew that even **emancipated** Blacks suffered greatly from discrimination in the United States.

However, the relocation program was not very successful. Many Blacks did not want to go. Another reason for the failure was that the Society could not afford to buy enough slaves to make any real difference. By 1831, fewer than 2000 slaves had been sent to Liberia.

emancipated
to be freed from authority or influence; especially to be freed from slavery

Abolitionists Seek an End to Slavery
Around 1830, a new spirit guided those who were against slavery. The idea of *gradualism*, that slow change is best, was rejected. The new antislavery leaders felt that gradualism was failing. Besides, slavery was a sin—and sin must be cut out of national life immediately. As time went on, this spirit grew. It was aided by such best-selling antislavery books as Harriet Beecher Stowe's 1852 novel, *Uncle Tom's Cabin.*

Abolitionist William Lloyd Garrison once protested slavery by burning a copy of the Constitution at a Fourth of July celebration.

abolitionists
people who worked to do away with slavery forever

An escaped slave, Harriet Tubman made 19 trips back into the South, rescuing 300 people from slavery.

In addition to this feeling, there was a new willingness among Whites in the movement to fight. One of the best known White antislavery advocates was William Lloyd Garrison. Originally, he was an editor of Lundy's paper. But in 1831, he began publication of his own antislavery newspaper, *The Liberator*. On the issue of slavery, he said, "I will not excuse—I will not retreat a single inch—AND I WILL BE HEARD."

Garrison was not content with just freedom for slaves. He was also a stirring advocate of equal rights for Blacks and women. His uncompromising attitude and militancy frightened and angered many Northerners and Southerners.

However, some leaders did take up the cause and pursue it in their own way. For example, Theodore Weld patiently organized the activities of **abolitionists** in the Northeast. He trained at least seventy followers in revival-meeting techniques. He and his disciples converted thousands in the North to the antislavery cause. And, these feelings were to be reinforced by authors such as John Greenleaf Whittier, Ralph Waldo Emerson, Henry David Thoreau, and Walt Whitman.

A third force was also at work behind the new movement for immediate abolition after 1830. There was a stirring among Black Americans—both the approximately 320,000 free Blacks and the two million slaves. David Walker, a Black small-businessman in Boston, spoke for many free Blacks in 1829, when he published a little volume known as *Walker's Appeal*. To White Americans, he cried out, "We must and shall be free, I say, in spite of you." To enslaved Blacks, he urged resistance and escape. He called for an end to fear, because "the God of justice and of armies will surely go before you." About a thousand slaves a year did "protest" against slavery by running away. Later, some who were educated became speakers and writers in the antislavery cause. Together, the Reverend Samuel Cornish and John Russwurm, an early Black editor, published the newspaper, *Freedom's Journal*. And Sojourner Truth, an exslave, spoke out impressively for the rights of Blacks and women.

Others, like Harriet Tubman, helped Southern slaves escape to freedom. One of the most famous exslave abolitionists was Frederick Douglass. Born in 1817, he managed to learn to read and write even though he was a slave. In 1838, he escaped. After bitter months of supporting himself by doing odd jobs, he joined the antislavery movement as a lecturer for the American Anti-Slavery Society. He was a powerful speaker and writer. In Rochester, New York, he established a newspaper, the *North Star*, a kind of Black readers' *Liberator*. Douglass's writings and speeches soon won him widespread fame.

SOJOURNER TRUTH

"That man over there says that women need to be helped into carriages, and lifted over ditches, and to have the best place everywhere. Nobody ever helps me into carriages, or over mud puddles, or gives me any best place!

"And ain't I a woman? Look at me, look at my arm! I have ploughed, and planted, and gathered into barns, and no man could head me! And ain't I a woman? I could work as much and eat as much as a man—when I could get it—and bear the lash as well! And ain't I a woman? I have borne thirteen children, and seen most of them sold off to slavery. When I cried out with my mother's grief, none but Jesus heard me. And ain't I a woman?"

The woman making this impassioned speech for women's rights was Isabella Baumfree, better known as Sojourner Truth.

Born into slavery, Isabella Baumfree was freed from her servitude by the New York State Emancipation Act of 1827. Soon afterwards, she assumed the name Sojourner Truth, explaining that her mission in life was to travel across the United States and spread "the truth."

A gifted public speaker, Sojourner Truth became a leading spokesperson for the abolitionist cause before, and during, the Civil War. When the war came, she raised money to buy gifts for the soldiers, and even went into the army camps herself to deliver the gifts. She also helped Blacks who had escaped to the North, finding them shelter and jobs.

After the war, Sojourner Truth continued to travel and speak out against society's injustices. Because she saw a parallel between the issues of women's rights and slavery, she lectured frequently and passionately on both issues.

Although Sojourner Truth lived to be 105, she was never to realize one of her lifelong dreams: "I must sojourn once to the ballot box before I die."

As the antislavery argument gained in fierceness, violence flamed. In 1831, in Southhampton, Virginia, Nat Turner, a slave preacher, led a revolt. Turner said that his revolt was the result of a direct commandment to him from God. Some fifty White and one hundred Black people were killed before Turner and his followers were hanged.

While the rage against slavery grew, so did the feelings of its defenders. Even in the North, Whites who feared and hated both Black and White opponents of slavery broke up abolitionist meetings, tarred and feathered abolitionist speakers, and burned the offices of abolitionist newspapers.

The South Defends Slavery

Southerners were hurt and bewildered by all that was going on. Most of them were respectable, hard-working, Bible-reading Americans. Two-thirds of them did not even own slaves. Abolitionist papers painted them as being lazy—a terrible sin at that time—living, or hoping to live, off the labor of others. They were branded as enemies of progress and accused of sins that ran from drunkenness to the sale of their own illegitimate Black children.

Active as a lecturer and editor of the abolitionist newspaper, the North Star, Frederick Douglass was a great force against slavery and for women's suffrage.

323

A common defense of slavery appears in these 1841 cartoons. Left: The slaves are happy, while the owners look after their welfare. Right: Factory workers starve during hard times, while the factory owner ignores their plight.

Southerners defended slavery in several ways. One was a simple constitutional argument. The Constitution permitted slavery. Those states that allowed it ought not to be criticized, since the Constitution was an agreement among states with different customs.

Southerners also insisted that Blacks were unable to govern themselves without White help. Yet they felt that if Blacks were set free and given the privileges of Whites—including the vote—the Blacks would then be in the majority in some Southern communities. They would then rule their White neighbors. Almost no Northerner was willing to accept such a fate. Why force it on the South?

A third Southern argument for slavery was simply that slaves were needed to grow cotton profitably. Southerners also pointed out that they had made a huge investment in slaves. They even argued that slavery was a good thing for slaves. The slaves, they said, did not suffer from the uncertainty of the industrial, capitalistic system. White workers were hired at the lowest possible wages, then fired, and allowed to starve in hard times. On the other hand, in the agricultural South, individuals owned labor and looked after it in return for service.

White supremacy
the control of political, social, and economic life by Whites only

However, in defending slavery and **White supremacy,** White Southerners were driven further and further from democratic ways. Southern postmasters opened the mails and burned abolitionist newspapers. Southern Congressmen tried to "gag" Congress by blocking debate on antislavery petitions. Such actions tended to prove abolitionist charges that slavery was a threat to freedom in the entire nation. The South stood alone in challenging the official national belief in liberty for all. A few abolitionists, equally alone, argued in favor of ending a union that included slaveholders.

Questions for Discussion

1. Define *gradualism* and *abolitionists*.
2. Identify William Lloyd Garrison, David Walker, Sojourner Truth.
3. What arguments did the South make in defense of slavery?

3. The Search for a Compromise

The job of the politician was to arrange agreements through compromise among groups and sections. The aim of the reformer was to create a just, perhaps a perfect, society. Hence, the issue of slavery brought politicians and reformers onto a collision course. Yet the federal government was not able to deal directly with slavery. Under the Constitution, it had no control over slavery. However, whenever the question of slavery in the territories arose, the national government became involved. There, its power was clear. The first great clash in Congress on the subject came in 1820. It had the alarming urgency, as described by the aging Thomas Jefferson, of "a firebell in the night."

When Missouri asked Congress for statehood, New York Representative James Tallmadge, Jr. proposed that before being admitted, the would-be state should bar the entry of any new slaves and gradually free those already there. A bitter debate followed throughout much of 1819. Could Congress ban the creation of future slave states so that the South would eventually become a minority in the Senate? Could Congress tell a Southern slaveholder, "If you want to settle in Missouri, you must give up your slaves. You cannot move freely in this country with your special 'property'?"

Opponents of the Tallmadge plan answered all such questions with a ringing "No!" Tallmadge supporters urged Southerners to think twice. Many Southerners agreed that slavery was a curse and a burden. Let them "plant not its seeds in this uncorrupt soil."

The Missouri Compromise of 1820

A compromise was finally reached. Its chief arranger was the popular, persuasive Henry Clay. Clay won votes to admit Missouri as a slave state. At the same time, Maine, New England's last frontier, was to be admitted as a free state to keep a balance in the Senate. A line was drawn across the Louisiana Purchase territory at 36° 30' north latitude. Though Missouri, which lay north of the line, might keep slavery, it should be banned "forever" in the rest of the area north of 36° 30' (see map on page 326).

Clay's argument was that compromise was the price of Union. "All government," he said, "is founded upon the principle of mutual concession (giving in). Let him who elevates himself above humanity . . . say . . . I never will compromise." But slavery haters only saw that evil had been given the green light to spread westward. "We had

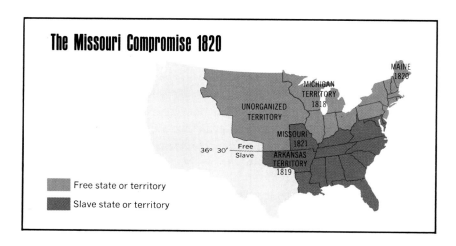

The Missouri Compromise 1820

MAINE 1820

MICHIGAN TERRITORY 1818

UNORGANIZED TERRITORY

MISSOURI 1821

36° 30' — Free / Slave

ARKANSAS TERRITORY 1819

Free state or territory

Slave state or territory

it in our power to stop the progress of slavery," said one abolitionist sadly, "and we chose to let it go on."

Through twenty years of national growth, the Missouri Compromise of 1820 stood firm. Yet the debate over slavery became more heated. The struggle strengthened as the South began to see its political power diminish. As the industrial states grew in population, the percentage of seats held by the South in the House lessened. So it was becoming more important to the South to add new slave states and to keep a balance of power in the Senate.

How long could the compromise of adding one free state for every slave state continue? In 1836 and 1837, Arkansas and Michigan were paired in this manner. In 1845 and 1846, Florida and Texas entered the Union as slave states. These slave states were offset in 1846 and 1848 by the admission of the free states of Iowa and Wisconsin. However, the Mexican War forced the nation to face the question of balance once more in the new territories taken from Mexico.

Slave or Free States

The Mexican War had hardly begun when David Wilmot, a Democratic representative from Pennsylvania, made a proposal to Congress. He wanted an amendment to an appropriations bill to read that "neither slavery nor involuntary servitude shall ever exist" in any land taken from Mexico. However, Wilmot's amendment was defeated in Congress.

President Polk had his own ideas about how the territory would be settled. He proposed to extend the line of the Missouri Compromise. But this suggestion was also defeated.

John Calhoun held an extreme view. He argued that the government of the United States had no right to prohibit slavery in any territory. The territories, he said, belonged to all the states together, and not to the federal government. Since slaves were property, they could be taken anywhere. So it was the duty of the government to protect the "property" rights of the slave owners.

A fourth position on slavery in the territories was the doctrine of "squatters' sovereignty" or "popular sovereignty." According to Senators Lewis Cass of Michigan and Stephen Douglas of Illinois, the people should decide for themselves whether they wanted to allow or forbid slavery. These two men argued that communities were the best judges of their own interests.

The Election of 1848

Both political parties were determined to avoid the issue of slavery during the election of 1848. The Democrats nominated Lewis Cass. They proposed a platform that ignored the slavery issue. With talk of "party harmony," the Whigs nominated General Zachary Taylor. His political views were so unknown that he could be presented as "all things to all men."

Neither party thought that their antislavery factions would bolt the major parties and hold their own convention. Calling themselves the Free Soilers, these dissatisfied abolitionists had as their slogan, "Free soil, Free speech, Free labor, and Free men." They chose Martin Van Buren as their candidate because he was opposed to the annexation of Texas.

In the end, Zachary Taylor was elected. Van Buren had no widespread appeal and failed to carry any state. But the Free Soilers picked up enough seats in Congress to hold the balance of power between the Democrats and the Whigs. Now the South was convinced more than ever that they were losing the political battle. In 1849, when California asked to enter the Union with a constitution barring slavery, some Southerners threatened to leave the Union.

Compromise of 1850

Sectional tensions crackled in the newly elected House. When the representatives assembled in December 1849, it took them sixty-three ballots to choose a Speaker and to get down to business. President Polk had left office before the Congress had been able to agree on the admission of California. But this question had to be resolved soon. The California gold rush had pumped over 100,000 people into the territory still under military rule. This number was far more than the minimum needed for statehood.

Congress also faced the conflict between Texas, a slave state, and the unorganized territory of New Mexico over land both claimed. Free states wanted to limit the size of Texas and slave states wanted proposals for New Mexico to include the right to own slaves.

In addition, there was the question of a strong fugitive slave law. In 1842, the Supreme Court had ruled that state officials were not

John C. Calhoun stirred many passionate debates in Congress prior to the Civil War. His major argument was that the federal government had no right to prohibit slavery in any territory.

327

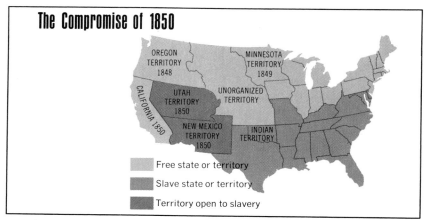

The Compromise of 1850

OREGON TERRITORY 1848

MINNESOTA TERRITORY 1849

CALIFORNIA 1850

UTAH TERRITORY 1850

UNORGANIZED TERRITORY

NEW MEXICO TERRITORY 1850

INDIAN TERRITORY

Free state or territory

Slave state or territory

Territory open to slavery

required to help federal officials capture and return runaway slaves. The Southern states wanted a law that would reverse that policy.

President Taylor hoped to avoid conflict. He asked Congress to keep from "exciting topics of sectional character." However, by this time, tempers in Congress were frayed. Fist fights and threats with deadly weapons were common. So Taylor proposed that California draw up its own constitution. The people should decide for themselves whether California was to be a slave state or free state. But the South could not accept this. In 1849, there were fifteen slave states and fifteen free states. If that balance were destroyed, it would never be regained. And political power would be concentrated in the hands of the free states.

When the issue of admission reached the floor of Congress, three aging political veterans opened the debate. They were men who were still willing to compromise to save the Union. John C. Calhoun, near death, listened while a younger Senator read his speech. This Senator said that the South was a minority in the Union now. The constitution had not created a nation in which a majority had unlimited power. Minority rights were supposed to be recognized. So the North must give the South its due and stop stirring up the slavery question. If not, the Union was as good as ended.

Clay offered a new compromise. California would be a free state. Territorial governments would be organized for Utah and New Mexico with nothing said about slavery one way or the other. That would postpone the question until these states were ready for statehood. In the District of Columbia, slaves could be kept, but not bought or sold. But Northerners must agree to a very strict Fugitive Slave Act, which would force officials of the federal and of all state governments to make vigorous efforts to catch runaway slaves.

On March 7, 1850, Daniel Webster stood up in Congress to defend Clay's plan. Geography would doom slavery, Webster pointed out. Cotton could never grow in the deserts and craggy mountains of the

Far West. And slavery would not go where it was not profitable. Let nature, not battlefields, have the final judgment.

For many weeks, a hotly contested battle was waged in Congress. On one side were the secessionists, such as Jefferson Davis of Mississippi, Robert Barnwell Rhett of South Carolina, and Louis T. Wigfall of Texas. On the other side were the abolitionists and free soilers, like William Seward of New York and Charles Sumner of Massachusetts.

Finally, the compromise measures, as suggested by Clay, were passed. Talk of Southern **secession** died down. The firebell had rung a second time, and the alarm had been answered. But the coals were still smoldering.

secession
the act of withdrawing from the union

The Interlude

At first, people rejoiced at the news of the compromise. They were eager for sectional peace and willing to close their eyes to the impending crisis.

For four years, economic prosperity helped keep the sections satisfied. In the early 1850s, the South prospered when cotton production and prices rose. The industry of the Northeast was expanding. Thousands of immigrants who shunned the South helped provide the labor force to meet the growing demands for manufactured goods. Railroads expanded into all sections of the country. Westerners were able to get their products to Eastern markets. Even the Southern railway network was greatly extended. But the South still could not keep pace with the expansion of the rest of the country.

In 1852, Franklin Pierce was elected President on the Democratic ticket. The Southern Whigs abandoned the antislavery Northern Whigs and voted with the Democrats. This struck a damaging blow to a political party system based on national rather than sectional issues.

Daniel Webster helped cool talk of Southern secession by defending Henry Clay's compromise on California statehood and the Fugitive Slave Act.

Questions for Discussion

1. Why would Thomas Jefferson call the Missouri Compromise, "a firebell in the night"?
2. What were the terms of the Missouri Compromise?
3. How did the Mexican War cause conflicts over the question of slavery?
4. What was the Compromise of 1850?

It was only a matter of time before the fabric of the compromise began to shred. Northern states were doing their best to ignore or to interfere with the operation of the Fugitive Slave Act. In 1852, the publication of *Uncle Tom's Cabin* aroused strong antislavery sentiments. In 1854, the American ministers to Britain, Spain, and France

4. Compromise Fails—the Kansas–Nebraska Act

issued the "Ostend Manifesto," calling for the seizure of Cuba if Spain refused to sell it. Northerners saw this as a plot to increase slave territory at any cost. And so the nation began a sudden rush away from the spirit of compromise.

Stephen A. Douglas, the Democratic Senator from Illinois, introduced a bill to organize territorial governments for Kansas and Nebraska. As a believer in Western expansion and a speculator in Western lands, he hoped to encourage settlement in the West. He also wanted to be able to compete against the South for a central route through the nation for the proposed transcontinental railroad. So to get votes for his bill from Southern Senators, Douglas agreed to a section repealing the Missouri Compromise. There should be no rules against slavery. Instead, the territorial legislatures, elected by the settlers to govern until statehood, should decide whether or not to admit slaves.

Douglas believed that this idea of *popular sovereignty*—letting the local people decide—was a fair one. But hundreds of thousands of Northerners cried out that the South had gone back on its word.

As far as the North was concerned, the Fugitive Slave Law was dead. The day after the Kansas-Nebraska Act was passed, it took a battalion of United States artillery, four platoons of marines, and a sheriff's posse to escort one fugitive, Anthony Burns, to the South. It cost the government $40,000. Burns was the last fugitive returned from Massachusetts.

The Whig Party, which had been beaten so badly in 1852, had almost disappeared. But ex-Whigs, Free Soilers, and angry Northern Democrats joined in "anti-Nebraska" organizations. The groups soon merged into a new party that took the name Republican and strongly opposed the extension of slavery.

After the Kansas-Nebraska Act was passed, Kansas itself became the scene of a conflict between proslavery and "free state" antislavery pioneers. The New England Emigrant Aid Company and other antislavery organizations paid for antislavery settlers to migrate to Kansas. Henry Ward Beecher, a well-known preacher, recommended that the settlers be given rifles to defend themselves. Guns, not Bibles, would be more useful against slavery. So "Beecher's Bibles" were sent to the new Kansans. Meanwhile, in the elections for a territorial legislature, thousands of proslavery people from neighboring Missouri crossed the border and voted illegally. Free-state settlers boycotted this body and formed a government of their own. And armed parties from both sides began raiding each other's homes and settlements. At least 200 settlers lost their lives in a bitter guerrilla war. Federal troops attempted to preserve order, but the situation remained tense.

This poster for Harriet Beecher Stowe's Uncle Tom's Cabin *was published in 1859, two years before the outbreak of the Civil War.*

Free-staters formed an anti-slavery legislature in Kansas in opposition to a pro-slavery counterpart, but troops dispersed it to prevent violence.

New Parties and Realignments

In 1854, the Democratic Party became a victim of the sectional strife that broke up the Whig Party. Some of the Democrats, particularly from the Northeast, flocked to the American, or Know-Nothing Party. Formed in opposition to Catholic immigrants, this party tried to use the issue of immigration to turn the nation's attention away from slavery. Abraham Lincoln opposed the American Party. He believed that if it got control, the country would no longer consider all people equal. The American Party would exclude Catholics, Blacks, and foreigners.

However, the American Party could not remain a refuge for those trying to avoid the slavery issue. In 1855, the party voted to support the Kansas-Nebraska Act. They nominated Millard Fillmore for the Presidency. The Northern members then joined the ranks of the emerging Republican party. As was the American Party's desire, Southern members of the Republican Party sided with the Democrats.

In 1856, the Republican Party held its first national nominating convention at Philadelphia. They nominated John Frémont for president. He campaigned on the slogan, "Free soil, free speech, and Frémont." The Democrats nominated James Buchanan of Pennsylvania. And the issue of the election was "Bleeding Kansas."

Buchanan won. He took all the Southern states and all but one of the border states. Sectionalism was so complete that out of the 1.3 million votes Frémont received, only 1200 came from slave states.

The Dred Scott Decision

Two days after Buchanan's inauguration on March 4, 1857, the antislavery forces received a staggering blow. Supreme Court Chief Justice Roger B. Taney announced a seven-to-two majority decision in the case of *Scott* v. *Sandford*. Dred Scott was a Missouri slave. His former owner had once taken him into Minnesota, north of the 36° 30' line. Later, Scott became the property of an abolitionist, who let him sue for his freedom on the grounds that his stay on free soil ended his slave status. This "test case" backfired. The Court held that Scott, because he was a slave, could not be a citizen of Missouri, nor of the United States. As a result, he could sue neither in either state nor in a federal court. If the justices had stopped there, the impact of the decision would have been minimal. However, they did not. The Court went on to declare that slaves were property. Under the terms of the Constitution, no state could deprive a person of "property without due process of law." When the Constitution was adopted, Taney said, Blacks "had no rights which the white man was bound (by law) to respect." This meant that Congress could not exclude slavery from the territories. The Missouri Compromise was finally defeated.

Supreme Court Chief Justice Roger B. Taney (below) ruled that, as a slave, Dred Scott (above) had no rights as an American citizen.

Questions for Discussion

1. Define *popular sovereignty*.
2. How did the Kansas-Nebraska Act destroy earlier compromises that had been made?
3. Why did the decision reached by Chief Justice Taney in *Scott* v. *Sanford* mean that the Missouri Compromise was dead?

5. The Rush Toward War

In the last few years of peace, certain questions of human rights and governmental power were raised. The first of these was whether or not the United States should remain neutral on the moral question of slavery. In the fall of 1858 in Illinois, the issue was presented clearly in a series of debates between Abraham Lincoln and Stephen A. Douglas. At that time, each was his party's choice for Senator.

The Lincoln-Douglas Debates

Both Douglas, the Democrat, and Lincoln, the Republican, were products of the frontier. Douglas had migrated from Vermont to Illinois and had become a lawyer. Lincoln had come from Kentucky and had followed the same calling. And both men were popular with their neighbors.

Lincoln and Douglas both believed that friends of liberty all over the world looked to the Union as a model of democratic government. They also believed in national expansion and in progress through hard work. And they agreed on a politics of compromise. But where these two middle-aged, middle-class, White, Western lawyers differed was on the issue of what America should do about slavery.

Imagine that you are attending their last debate in Alton, Illinois, on October 15, 1858. Both men are tired and their clothes rumpled from travel. Four or five thousand spectators have come by boat and rail from as far away as Springfield and St. Louis. People are waving banners, bands are playing, and picnic lunches are being enjoyed. In Illinois in 1858, politics is a form of recreation.

Douglas speaks first. He follows a line of thinking he has used in earlier debates. First, he argues that each community must decide its institutions for itself. " . . . In my opinion this government can endure forever, divided into free and slave States as our fathers made it, each State having the right to prohibit, abolish, or sustain slavery just as it pleases." Then he goes on to a theme popular in this southern Illinois community—White supremacy. It is true, says Douglas, that the whole nation claims to believe in the Declaration of Independence, which holds all men to be created equal and, thus, seems to bar slavery. But, he adds, the Declaration "had no reference to negroes at all . . . . They were speaking of white men." Basic humanity requires giving Blacks some privileges. However, each state and territory should answer for itself what these privileges should be. Then, amid cheers, he sits down.

Then Lincoln rises and begins speaking in his high-pitched voice. He must speak carefully. Douglas had insisted that Lincoln is at heart an abolitionist and a believer in Black equality. This charge will lose him votes. So Lincoln repeats, in different words, what he has said in earlier speeches. At Springfield, he has said, "The negro is not our equal in color—perhaps not in many other respects; still, in the right to put into his mouth the bread that his own hands have earned, he is the equal of every other man, white or black." At Charleston, Illinois, he has gone as far as he will go to appeal to prejudice: "I am not nor ever have been in favor of making voters or jurors of negroes, nor of qualifying them to hold office, nor to intermarry with white people." But, he argues, he can feel this way and still hate the institution of slavery.

Lincoln denies that the founders of the nation expected the United States to remain half slave and half free. The founders thought that slavery was dying. So they avoided the use of the word slave in the Constitution. They voted to make the Northwest Territory free. All that the Republicans want, the tall lanky man continues, is to keep slavery from growing. Then it will die out naturally, as it did in the North just after the Revolution.

The nation, Lincoln says, cannot simply leave the issue of slavery to the choice of White communities in the territories. He stresses that

In his debates with Stephen Douglas, Lincoln contended that the issue of slavery could not be left to each state, but must be faced by the nation as a whole.

333

the issue must be faced by the whole nation. On the one hand are the rights of humanity, and on the other, "the spirit that says, 'You work and toil and earn bread and I'll eat it.'" Whether such a statement comes from a tyrannical king or "from one race of men as an apology for (defense of) enslaving another, it is the same tyrannical principle." Lincoln finally sits down to cheers and music.

Lincoln lost the election. But he did make a reputation for himself, which led to the Republican Presidential nomination two years later. The question he raised still lives: Can a society survive without all its members being treated equally?

John Brown's Raid at Harpers Ferry

In 1859, an even more agonizing question arose. Can a society be purified by violent means? True, the American Revolution had been violent. But its leaders did not hate all English people—only the actions of certain rulers. Nor did they believe that they were directly following God's orders. In 1859, John Brown did think of himself as God's officer, with power and duty to punish sinners. And he also believed that the crimes of his guilty land had to be washed away with blood.

By October 1859, Brown had hit on a plan. He would gather a small troop, descend on a border region, and forcefully free a few slaves. Then they would retreat to a mountain hideout and form a free state. And both Black and White haters of slavery would realize that the time was ripe to strike for freedom. He believed that one push would trigger an uprising and bring slavery crashing down in ruins.

On October 16, 1859, Brown and some twenty men, including five free Blacks, moved into Harpers Ferry, Virginia (now West Virginia). They seized the government arsenal there from a few surprised workers. Then they went out into the countryside and gathered a few slaves and some White prisoners. They finally returned to the arsenal and—did nothing! Hoping for a slave revolt, Brown waited while federal and state troops poured into the town. But he was wounded and captured along with eleven of his followers. Ten were killed, including Brown's two sons. After a quick trial for treason, Brown was hanged by the state of Virginia in a public ceremony.

The raid was a total failure. However, Brown's raid had touched the deepest fears of Southern Whites. Had Brown not tried to raise the Blacks to murder them in bed? Southerners demanded to know if the North supported Brown. Few Northerners actually did. Few would have agreed with spokespeople such as Henry David Thoreau, who called Brown "the bravest and humanest man in all the country." Most Americans in the North felt that slavery was lawful, if not just, and that law must be respected.

Stephen A. Douglas, known as the "Little Giant," championed the cause of states' rights in his celebrated debates with Lincoln.

But Southerners panicked. In 1860, hundreds of thousands of them believed that all Republicans—"Black Republicans," as they called them—were secretly in favor of deeds such as Brown's revolt. If the Republicans won the election, the South would no longer be safe in the Union. Therefore, the South must secede.

In the spring of 1860, the Democratic Party, one of the last parties to have both Northern and Southern supporters, split into two parts. One part followed Douglas and nominated him for President. The other, more actively proslavery, chose John Breckinridge. The Republicans nominated Lincoln. A fourth party of neutralists, the Constitutional Union Party, was also formed. When the four-way contest was over, Abraham Lincoln led with just under 40 percent of the popular vote but with a majority in the Electoral College.

The South Secedes

Promptly, South Carolina seceded, followed within four months by six other deep-South states. Without any fighting, these states took over most federal forts and other properties within their boundaries. But in South Carolina's Charleston Harbor, Fort Sumter still remained in government hands.

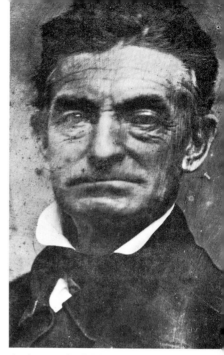

A photograph of John Brown three years before the Harpers Ferry Raid.

One final, basic issue now had to be faced. The seceded states organized themselves as the Confederate States of America, with their capital in Montgomery, Alabama. They elected former Mississippi Senator Jefferson Davis as their President. Now, what should Abraham Lincoln do about the secession of seven states when he took office on March 4, 1861?

Lincoln's problem was a difficult one. If he simply left the Confederate States alone, he would be admitting that the Union was dissolved. But his argument against secession was that the Union was not just an agreement among sovereign states but also an agreement among the people of those states. The people could dissolve the Union but the states could not. Yet, Lincoln could not easily force the Confederates back into loyalty. The slave-holding states that had not seceded as of March 4, 1861, declared that the Union must be voluntary.

In his inaugural address, Lincoln tried to steer a middle course between threats and surrender. He said he would try to hold on to federal property in the seceded states. But he would not try to deliver the mails or collect customs duties by force. He appealed to the secessionists to return voluntarily to the Union. If they felt threatened as a minority, they should stay in the Union and convince others of the rightness of their cause. Thus, they would become a majority.

Jefferson Davis, the elected President of the Confederate States of America.

If secessionists forced their views on other states, that would lead to tyranny. If they broke up the Union, that was a step toward

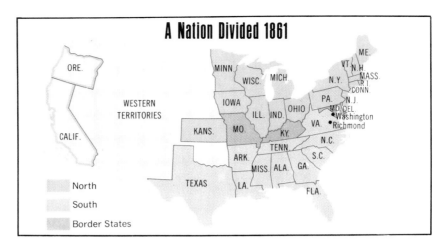

A Nation Divided 1861

North
South
Border States

anarchy. To both the secessionists and the abolitionists, Lincoln's message was "Wait!" "Why should there not be a patient confidence in the ultimate justice of the people? Is there any better or equal hope in the world?" It was clear that Lincoln wanted neither anarchy nor tyranny.

However, for many Americans the time had passed for listening to reason. South Carolinians continued to resent the federal force at Fort Sumter. They felt that the national flag flying within sight of Charleston belonged to a "foreign power." And South Carolina warned that any attempt to bring fresh troops or supplies into the fort would be resisted.

Finally, food began to run low. Lincoln had to give up the fort or send provisions to the troops. He chose the latter course, informing the South Carolina authorities that he was sending only bread, not bullets. But it was too late. On April 12 at 4:30 A.M., Confederate cannons around the harbor opened non-stop bombardment that lasted thirty-four hours. Fort Sumter had to surrender to the Confederates. Confederates had fired on the national flag. Lincoln believed that there was no choice but to meet force with force. Therefore, he called for 75,000 volunteers. The dreaded Civil War had begun, and God had "loosed the fateful lightning of His terrible, swift sword."

Questions for Discussion

1. What were the views of both Lincoln and Douglas on the question of White supremacy?
2. What did Lincoln say was the attitude of the Republican Party toward slavery?
3. How did John Brown's raid help to move the nation toward the Civil War?
4. In his inaugural address, how did Lincoln attempt to bring the South back into the Union?

Chapter 14 Review

Summary Questions for Discussion

1. According to historians, what were the causes of the Civil War?
2. After 1830, what pressure group became the strongest political voice in the Northeast? in the South? in the West?
3. Why did the antislavery advocates of the 1830s reject gradualism?
4. How did the defenders of slavery react to the abolitionists?
5. Why was the South's defense of slavery and their belief in White supremacy undemocratic?
6. When Missouri applied for statehood, what was the proposal given by Representative James Tallmadge?
7. What were the terms of the Missouri Compromise reached in 1820 by Henry Clay?
8. Describe the four positions taken on the subject of what to do with the territory acquired from the Mexican War.
9. How did prosperity in the early 1850s satisfy the various sections of the country?
10. How did the North view the Ostend Manifesto?
11. Why did Senator Stephen A. Douglas introduce the Kansas-Nebraska Act?
12. What were the effects of the Kansas-Nebraska Act in Kansas?
13. How did sectional differences lead to new political parties and party alignments?
14. What was the decision in the Supreme Court case of *Scott* v. *Sandford?*
15. In what ways was Lincoln's inaugural address a middle road between threat and surrender?

Word Study

Fill in each blank in the sentences that follow with the term below that is most appropriate.

pressure groups   subsidize   popular sovereignty
Union   White supremacy   gradualism
secession   abolitionists

1. Civil War was to come when the _____ or nation acting as a whole became sectionally divided.
2. Some groups believed in _____ or control of political, social, and economic life by Whites only.
3. Bitter feelings grew as one section did not want to _____ or give financial help to another.
4. In Congress, _____ from the various sections pushed for their views.
5. Some reformers sought _____ or slow change with regard to slavery.
6. Stephen A. Douglas proposed the idea of _____ or letting the people choose.
7. By 1860, the Southern states had opted for _____ or withdrawal from the Union.

Using Your Skills

1. How do the pictures in this chapter show the sectional differences that existed in the United States in the first half of the nineteenth century?
2. How does the picture on page 331 portray "Bleeding Kansas"? Who are the troops controlling?
3. Compare the two maps, "The Compromise of 1850" (page 328) and "A Nation Divided" (page 336). What states were added to the Union between the time of the Compromise of 1850 and the outbreak of the Civil War? Were any of these states slave states? Why?

CHAPTER 15

The Civil War

It was July 4, 1861, the first Independence Day after the start of the Civil War. Celebrations of the Glorious Fourth were missing their usual enthusiasm. At that moment, the North and South were completing their preparations for the fighting that would begin within a few weeks. In a message to Congress, Lincoln tried to brace Americans by telling them why their fathers and husbands and sons were going to war against their fellow Americans. His message can be summarized in six words, which were read to the Congress: "This is essentially a people's contest."

However, the Confederates were equally convinced that their cause was just and of worldwide importance. In explaining the war to the Confederate Congress, President Jefferson Davis said that it stemmed from unjust Northern attacks on slavery, which had raised Blacks "from brutal savagery into docile [tame], intelligent, and civilized agricultural laborers." The South had to secede, said Davis, to "avoid the dangers with which they were openly menaced." It was a matter of free people defending their rights.

Black Americans did not believe that the coming war was only a quarrel among Whites. Their own futures were at stake as well. Many free Blacks felt like Levin Tilmon of New York, who wrote Lincoln four days before Fort Sumter was fired upon: "If your Honor wishes colored volunteers, you have only to signify [say so]." As for the slaves, they could not speak out. But a Charleston lady noticed that when war talk crackled at Charleston dinner tables, the Black servants "make no sign. Are they . . . stupid, or wiser than we are: silent, and strong, biding their time?"

READING GUIDE

1. **Why is the Civil War often called the first truly modern war?**
2. **What factors determine victory in war?**
3. **Why is there often dissent during war?**

The "Repulse of Pickett's Charge," after a painting by Thur de Thulstrup.

1. Trial by Arms

With her husband, Julia Ward Howe co-edited the antislavery paper, The Commonwealth. *The couple also gave aid to John Brown's often violent campaigns against slavery.*

The first year of war was one of arming, organizing, and finding out how great a struggle the war would be. All over the North and South, recruits joined volunteer companies raised in their home towns. The new civilian soldiers elected local community leaders as their lieutenants and captains and marched alongside their neighbors and friends. At first discipline was slack. War seemed like a big camp-out. Many companies even had their own dashing-looking uniforms.

Time quickly changed all this. The companies were organized into regiments of about one thousand men. These regiments were attached to corps, divisions, and armies. The recruits marched or rode to training camps far from home. There tough new colonels and generals taught them that army life meant drill, camp cleanups, marches, and guard duty. The volunteers soon learned that war also meant loneliness and sickness. Finally, the volunteers engaged in combat, suffered wounds, and sometimes died.

In July 1861, about 35,000 raw Union recruits who had gathered around Washington, D.C., bravely started out to seize Richmond, the Confederate capital, about 90 miles away. On July 21 at Bull Run, Virginia, a short distance from Washington, they met a somewhat smaller and equally untrained Confederate force. After a long day of bitter fighting, the sudden arrival of Confederate reinforcements turned the tide. The Union forces broke into panic and almost ran back to the shadow of the Capitol. Congressmen and others who had ridden out with picnic baskets to watch the "show" were caught in the rout. Hopes of ending the rebellion before autumn were left on the battlefield along with the dead.

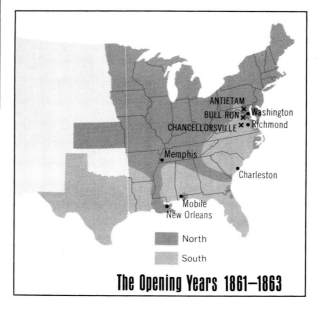

The Opening Years 1861–1863

The first major Civil War battle was a confused, bloody fight between two green armies at Bull Run. However, this 1889 romantic painting features dashing cavalrymen and soldiers dying bravely and painlessly.

In the East, each side maneuvered to capture the other side's capital city. These campaigns in Virginia attracted the greatest share of the public's attention. But the more important theater of the Civil War was probably in the West, the heartland from which most Southern supplies had to come. From the start, the Federal armies did well in this region. In June of 1861, the area which is now West Virginia was occupied by Federal troops. In February of 1862, one

Union spearhead went deep into central Tennessee. In April, a joint land and sea expedition seized New Orleans and moved up the Mississippi to a point just below Vicksburg (see map on page 350). Another force moved down the Mississippi and captured Memphis in June.

Lee Attacks the North

In the East, the rebels seemed to be winning the opening rounds. General George B. McClellan took charge of the Army of the Potomac, the Union force based in and around Washington. His real talent was not in combat but in planning campaigns, training troops, and building a smoothly working system of **logistics**.

In March of 1862, McClellan put most of his army on transports and sailed them down to a peninsula between two Virginia rivers—the York and the James. With this safe seaborne supply line behind him, he began a cautious advance toward Richmond. His opponent, General Robert E. Lee, was a native Virginian, a professional soldier, and an enemy of secession. When Virginia seceded, he resigned from the United States Army saying that he was unwilling to fight against "my relatives, my children, my home."

Lee was as daring as McClellan was cautious. In late June, when McClellan was at last on the outskirts of Richmond, Lee attacked him in a series of actions known as the Seven Days' Battles. The Union army was so badly beaten that it withdrew all the way back to the Washington area. So the war entered a second full year. Not only was victory for the North not in sight, but Lee was attacking boldly.

Aided by his brilliant second-in-command, General Thomas J. ("Stonewall") Jackson, Lee staged an invasion of the North. His Army of Northern Virginia beat the Union troops a second time on the field of Bull Run and then swung into Maryland. The war-weary troops enjoyed the corn, fruit, and poultry of fertile farms at harvest season. But death gathered the biggest crop on September 17. On that date, the two armies met in the Battle of Antietam. After a day of short-range firing at each other in orchards and cornfields, about 11,000 troops were killed or wounded on each side. Lee's losses were almost a quarter of his force. Thus, he was forced to give up his attack and retire into Virginia. This Union victory ended the first Confederate drive northward. But, the price of victory was tragically high.

logistics
the bringing together of soldiers, weapons, and supplies at the right time and place

General George B. McClellan commanded Union forces until Lincoln removed him in November 1862 for being "overcautious." Two years later he was the Democratic nominee for President.

Questions for Discussion

1. Define *logistics*.
2. In the first year of war, how did one become an officer in the volunteer army?
3. Where were most battles fought during the early years of the war?

Above: A young private from Georgia killed at Malvern Hill during the Peninsula campaign.

Left: Southerners lay dead in a cornfield after the Battle of Antietam in September 1862.

2. The Economics and Politics of War

At the opening of the war, people thought that one side would be beaten in a great battle or two, and then surrender. But the Civil War would be won by steady pressure, overpowering material superiority, and a slow breaking-down of the enemy's will and strength. The South, the weaker side, might win battlefield victories. However, the North could survive defeat and fight back with more troops and guns. Each month, war brought a greater reliance on new inventions, such as ironclad warships, the railroad, and the military telegraph. And the North could make more use of these.

The Booming North

Lincoln's half of the nation entered the war with tremendous advantages—about 22 million people to 5 million Southern Whites, over two-thirds of the country's miles of railroad, and most of its ships, banks, and factories. These advantages grew greater with every year of the war. And a heavy influx of immigrants kept the supply of workers and soldiers plentiful.

The West was in a tremendous spurt of growth. For example, one day in the 1860s, a judge in Nebraska counted 400 westward-bound

As a result of the Union blockade, the harbor in Charleston, South Carolina, was crowded with stranded ships and rotting cotton.

hoarding
piling up stocks far beyond immediate needs
profiteering
charging very high prices for items that are scarce

blockade
the use of ships or soldiers to keep an area from getting or sending supplies

wagons at a river crossing. Encouraged by the demands of war, farm production soared. The gold mines of California and the silver mines of Nevada were breaking records for output. In Michigan and Minnesota, lumberjacks cut down tall trees by the thousands. And around Oil Creek, Pennsylvania, where profitable wells were first drilled in 1859, the war years were prosperous.

In the East, factories busily turned out the equipment needed for Union armed forces—rifles, pistols, cannon, gunpowder, telegraph wire, pontoon bridges, uniforms, shoes, canned foods, ships, locomotives, rails, engines, and spare parts. The agricultural South could not match this power. Yet the South had counted on the fact that its soldiers were more accustomed to the outdoor life. They were more adept at using arms. And they were defending familiar terrain.

The Blockaded South

The war brought the North into the modern world with giant steps. At the same time, it drove the South deeper into poverty. Each month of the war, more Southern bridges, steamboats, and railroad lines were destroyed. Moreover, the Union occupation of the upper South early in the war took from the Confederacy valuable areas. These regions produced horses, cattle, and foodstuffs. Prices soon began to climb. Farmers refused to accept payment for their crops in Confederate paper money. Food dealers began **hoarding** and **profiteering**. In cities, proud sons and daughters of the South, famed before the war for their hospitality, stood in line to buy precious flour and meat.

The South had counted on the sale of its cotton to European nations to earn enough gold to carry on the war and to prop up the Confederate economy. But each month, the Northern **blockade** of warships shutting off Southern ports grew tighter. Soon bales of unsold cotton piled up on Southern wharves. King Cotton could not save the Confederacy. A few fast blockade-running vessels got out with some cotton and brought back small cargoes of munitions, medicines, and other vital supplies. But these were like an eyedropper of water to a man dying of thirst.

Southerners grew ever more desperate. After a family's crops had been taken by either army, its slaves had run away, and its able-bodied men had all gone, there was little to do except move to some new place where friends or relatives might help. White Southerners now tasted something few Americans had known—frustration and defeat. They tended to blame the Yankees and to overlook the part that Southern leadership had played in bringing on the war. A future harvest of intense sectional hate was planted as the costly war continued.

Lincoln Issues the Emancipation Proclamation

The war aim of most Northerners was only to restore the Union. Therefore, Lincoln did not want to advance very far in front of public opinion by emancipating, or setting free, the slaves, particularly when he was trying to keep the four slaveholding states of Kentucky, Maryland, Delaware, and Missouri in the Union. "My paramount [main] object in this struggle is to save the Union," he wrote, "and is not either to save or to destroy slavery."

Yet the war itself doomed slavery. When Southern soldiers left for the front, slave-catching patrols stopped operating. When Union troops took over a region, local courts no longer sat to enforce the laws controlling "human property." And most important, thousands of slaves ran away to Union lines, where they found work cooking, washing, driving wagons, and generally being useful.

Lincoln was aware that slaves were a great help to the Southern war effort and that freed slaves could be equally useful to the North. It was this line of reasoning that finally caused him to act.

Using his power as commander-in-chief of the armed forces, Lincoln issued the Emancipation Proclamation on January 1, 1863. It stated that from that date on, all slaves in areas of rebellion would be forever free. Of course, the slaves in those areas were not really freed

A BLACK SOLDIER WRITES HOME

This letter was written by Frederick Douglass's son, a soldier in the Civil War.

My Dear Amelia:

I have been in two fights, and am unhurt. I am about to go in another I believe tonight. Our men fought well on both occasions. The last was desperate. We charged that terrible battery on Morris island known as Fort Wagner, and were repulsed. . . . De Forest of your city is wounded, George Washington is missing, Jacob Carter is missing, Charles Reason wounded, Charles Whiting, Charles Creamer all wounded.

I escaped unhurt from amidst that perfect hail of shot and shell. It was terrible. I need not particularize, the papers will give a better [account] than I have time to give. My thoughts are with you often, you are as dear as ever, be good to remember it as I no doubt you will. As I said before we are on the eve of another fight and I am very busy and have just snatched a moment to write you. I must necessarily be brief. Should I fall in the next fight killed or wounded I hope I fall with my face to the foe.

This regiment has established its reputation as a fighting regiment, not a man flinched, though it was a trying time. Men fell all around me. A shell would explode and clear a space of twenty feet. Our men would close up again, but it was no use, we had to retreat, which was a very hazardous undertaking. How I got out of that fight alive I cannot tell, but I am here.

My Dear girl I hope again to see you. I must bid you farewell should I be killed. Remember if I die I die in a good cause. I wish we had a hundred thousand colored troops we would put an end to this war.

Good Bye to all. Your own loving—Write soon—

Lewis

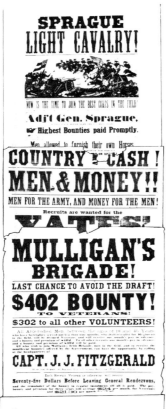

Ads calling for volunteers to the Union army.

until Union armies gained control of the invaded South. After the war, the Thirteenth Amendment to the Constitution was adopted which freed the slaves in the Union states. Lincoln's opponents raged that he had illegally punished individual Southerners, whether guilty of rebellion or not, by taking away their property. But throughout the North and South, Blacks and sympathetic Whites rejoiced at the end of more than 200 years of slavery. War had finally cut a bloody path through the tangled legal problem of emancipation.

Meanwhile, Blacks did not sit with folded hands while Whites argued about them. From the start of the war, freeborn Blacks and ex-slaves asked for the right to be enrolled in the Union army. Many Northerners objected. They believed either that the Blacks would not fight or that, if they went South with guns in hand, they would take revenge on the Whites in John Brown's fashion. Both of these beliefs were false. The proof came when the needs for more troops finally outweighed prejudice in 1862. So Black regiments were formed and sent into action.

From their first exposure to combat in October 1862, Blacks earned the admiration of many White officers, such as one who wrote that they fought "with a coolness and bravery that would have done credit to veteran soldiers."

Recruitment, Resistance, and Riot

Not all Northerners flocked to the colors. Many families, especially in the border areas of Maryland, Missouri, southern Ohio, Indiana, and Illinois, resented the war. Some had relatives in the Confederate armies. Many of them disliked Blacks and "Black Republicans." Coming from poorer and less urbanized parts of their states, they were not influenced by the Republican argument that slavery stood in the way of progress. Progress seemed to have passed them by. These Northern war resisters, sometimes called "Copperheads," were often arrested for having acted or spoken against the war. And they were attacked by neighbors who supported it.

The most bitter outburst of antiwar feeling came in 1863, when the Union began to enforce a *conscription* (draft) law. The South drafted soldiers almost from the start. But the North tried to fill the ranks by making patriotic appeals and offering **bounties**. Finally, however, a conscription act was passed. This act had a deeply unfair provision, which allowed a man to escape service by paying $300. This money would be given as a bounty to a substitute. Though many wealthy young men had enlisted, others were willing to buy their way out of duty and danger.

In New York City, this especially enraged the poorer people, among whom were many Irish immigrants. Though thousands of Irish

This photograph of soldiers of the 107th U.S. Colored Infantry was taken near Washington, D.C.

were fighting in Union armies, those who stayed at home to work were bitter. High wartime prices ate into their wages. Shabby living conditions sharpened their anger. Many came to feel that the war was being fought to free Blacks who would then compete with White laborers for jobs and status. So, when the draft calls were announced, savage rioting broke out. Blacks were special targets of mob rage. A Black orphanage was burned, and dozens of Blacks were lynched. Troops finally had to be called in to restore order. All the war-resistance movements took root among people who felt that the war gave them nothing, but instead took away their lives and taxes for remote purposes.

Questions for Discussion
1. Define *hoarding, profiteering, conscription, bounties.*
2. What advantages did the North have in fighting a modern war? Be specific.
3. What advantages did the South have?
4. What was the purpose of Lincoln's Emancipation Proclamation?

3. "War Is Hell"

The war was a great tidal wave, sweeping everything before it. And the verdict of victory or defeat was given on the battlefield. Halfway through the war, in the spring of 1863, General Robert E. Lee readied a new effort to swing that verdict in favor of the South.

In May 1863, Lee threw back a Union advance on Richmond at the Battle of Chancellorsville. The North's Army of the Potomac was

In July 1863, mobs in New York City rioted against the draft and looted and burned homes.

temporarily disorganized and demoralized. Lee also had suffered a loss when Stonewall Jackson was killed, accidentally shot by his own men. However, Lee decided to take advantage of the situation and move 80,000 men into Maryland and Pennsylvania. Perhaps that would convince the North that a military victory was impossible and force Northern leaders to ask for peace. So, late in June, the Army of Northern Virginia tramped along the roads running northward. And the Army of the Potomac moved alongside, keeping between the Confederates and Washington. On July 1, at the little crossroads town of Gettysburg, Pennsylvania, patrols of both armies met. Soon nearly 200,000 men were engaged in full battle.

The Union forces were pushed out of Gettysburg onto ridges and hills south and east of town. On July 2, Lee hurled attack after attack at their lines, waiting each time to see the Yankees reel back toward Philadelphia or Baltimore. Yet each thrust was beaten back in desperate fighting that cost some regiments up to eighty percent in casualties. On July 3 came the last all-out effort. A thunderous cannonade filled the hot sky with smoke puffs. Then General George Pickett's division stepped out to attack the center of the Union line. As the Southern troops charged across the several hundred yards of open ground between the armies, volley after volley ripped through their ranks. Only a handful finally made it to the Union lines. There was fierce hand-to-hand fighting. Then those Southerners not yet dead or wounded straggled back to their starting point. Finally, it was all over.

General Pickett's troops overrun an artillery battery at Gettysburg.

Lee had no strength to attack again. He stayed in position briefly while rescue parties went over the field, picking up groaning, wounded men. Then he retreated. The high tide of Confederate advance had been reached. By historical coincidence, just one day after Pickett's charge—Independence Day, 1863—the North broke the back of the Confederacy in the West, at Vicksburg on the Mississippi River. The capture of this key point ended a bitter and important campaign that had lasted nearly a year.

Grant Takes Vicksburg

In the autumn of 1862, Union forces seemed to have been stopped cold at Vicksburg. Cannons on high bluffs along the Mississippi blasted any ships moving past. They also protected the town from land assault from the North. The capture of Vicksburg would allow the Union forces to go downriver and cut the Confederacy in two. But as long as the town remained in Confederate hands, it was an important symbol of resistance that helped to build Southern morale.

Robert E. Lee confers with Stonewall Jackson at Chancellorsville, unaware that it was to be their last meeting.

After several unsuccessful attacks, General Ulysses S. Grant thought of a plan. Unlike McClellan who enjoyed the spit-and-polish of army life, Grant—though a West Point graduate—disliked soldiering. He had gone to West Point mainly to get a college education at government expense and repay it with time in the army. He had resigned in the 1850s, unable to support his family on army pay. And at the outbreak of war, he had returned to service.

Grant came from an Ohio farm. He had no fancy ways but good common sense. He could give commands but he did not strut. He usually appeared in a rumpled private's uniform with his starred shoulder straps of rank pinned to it. Yet this plain-looking "country cousin" had a mind for large-scale strategic thinking. He would take chances when necessary. However, he saw the military problem of the North clearly—how to make its superior power count.

In the spring of 1863, Grant knew that Union armies were attacking Vicksburg from the north side, because that position allowed them to protect their supply line to Memphis. Why not break that pattern and march the army down the west bank of the river, out of range of Vicksburg's guns? Let Union gunboats and transports dash past the sleeping city by night. Then let them ferry the troops across the Mississippi to swing around south and east of Vicksburg and come at it from its unprotected side facing away from the river. As for the supply line, it was not necessary. All the ammunition needed for a short campaign could be carried and food could come from the countryside.

This bold plan worked perfectly. Grant moved past Vicksburg on May 4. Three weeks later, he had won three battles and clamped a

Clara Barton organized supply and nursing services for sick and wounded Union troops during the Civil War. When the war ended, she was put in charge of a government-sponsored search for missing soldiers.

The Turning Point 1863–1864

Admiral David Porter's fleet runs the rebel blockade of the Mississippi River near Vicksburg.

siege line around the entire town. The defending Confederate garrison and townspeople held out for a month and a half, huddling in caves along the riverside to escape shelling. They ate mule meat when they were desperately hungry. Finally, they surrendered. And Grant became a new hero of the advancing North.

Sherman Marches to the Atlantic

Now Grant was called East to take over the Army of the Potomac, as well as the overall command of the war. He left General William Tecumseh Sherman, another Ohioan, in charge in the West. Sherman was also a former "regular" officer who had rejoined the army in 1861. He, too, saw that victory would come only when the North overpowered the South. Sherman did not see any romance in combat. "War is hell," he said bluntly. What he meant was that war was a brutal contest. To win meant not just battlefield victories but also the destruction of the enemy's resources and will to fight. This included harming civilians.

In May of 1864, Sherman moved with more than 100,000 troops out of southern Tennessee and into Georgia. Mile by mile, he used his superiority in numbers to outflank the Confederate army and force it

Above Left: Ulysses S. Grant meets with his chief of staff, General John Rawlins, in Cold Harbor, Virginia, in June 1864. Above Right: A grim and determined General William Tecumseh Sherman posed for this photograph dressed in his typical careless fashion.

to retreat toward Atlanta, the railroad hub of the South. That city fell in September. After resting his troops, Sherman began the war's most devastating operation. Like Grant, he would abandon his base of supplies and feed his armies off the land. Yet Sherman would do more. He would have scouting parties pick up every chicken, turkey, cow, ox, and horse in their path. They would burn every wagon, corncrib, barn, mill, warehouse, and shop that might be useful to any Confederates who followed them. They would pull up railroad tracks, heat them red hot, and twist them around telegraph poles. In Sherman's words, they would "make Georgia howl." Sherman did not hate Southern civilians, yet he believed that if their sufferings caused a quicker collapse of the Confederacy, the misery of the war would be over that much sooner. A few more hungry women and children would mean fewer dead heroes.

On December 22, 1864, Sherman's columns reached Savannah, Georgia, leaving a wide strip of destruction behind them. In February of 1865, he turned northward into the Carolinas. At Columbia, South Carolina's capital, a fire swept the town. It is still not known whether the fire was set by Sherman's troops or the retreating "rebs." But those gutted buildings were living proof of the White South's hatred for Sherman, long after Grant was forgiven.

A LETTER FROM THE FRONT

Camp before Petersburg, Va., August 1864

My dear family,

. . . Another quiet day but, as usual, the firing is now going on at the front. It always begins at dark and continues all night long. It is the last sound we hear on going to sleep and the first sound we hear on awaking in the morning. I think that there is more mining going on; it is to cover that, or prevent our pickets from communicating with the enemy. We will learn by & by.

The band of the 120th New York has just been here and give me a serenade. They play well. They played "Rally Round the Flag, Boys" splendidly. . . .

The dispatches from Mobile are cheering, and news from Sherman is quite good. Let us persevere and work on, hope, and pray, and all will be right. . . .

The explosion yesterday at City Point was a sad affair. Many lives were lost. It is not known, nor never will be, what caused the explosion. The report of a negro droping a shell is mear supposition. It was a boat load of shells that blew up, throwing a part of the vessel on to the land. The express office was blown to pieces. One man, a quartermaster's clerk, was standing there with $2000 in his hand, about to express it, when the explosion took place. He was killed and no money was found beside him. One of our Surgeons went down and was about to express $700. He was badly wounded. The money lost, &c. A large portion of the lifes lost were contrabands. . . .

Left: Sherman's men in Georgia pry loose railroad tracks that were heated, twisted to form "Sherman hairpins," and used to decorate tree trunks all the way to the sea. Above: In 1862, a refugee family flees from slavery across Northern lines.

In 1865, a fire in Union-occupied Columbia, South Carolina, destroyed two-thirds of the town.

Grant Pursues Lee

Meantime, in Virginia, Grant mapped out a final strategy. Up to 1864, the Army of the Potomac advanced, fought a battle, and then, if it did not win, went back into quarters to wait for the next effort, as eighteenth-century armies had done. But Grant had a different idea. On May 4, 1864, he moved south from a position near the old battlefield of Chancellorsville. Lee met him head-on in the three-day-long Battle of the Wilderness. At its end, both sides were battered and bloody. But Lee's army was unbroken, and Grant's casualties had been heavier. Yet instead of retiring to rest and regroup, Grant again moved his troops forward, around Lee's right flank. Lee dropped back and again met Grant. Once more the woods echoed with the thunder and shouting of combat. Still a third time, Grant circled to Lee's right, and Lee turned with him, keeping his back to Richmond. Then Grant's plan became clear. He would force Lee into constant action. Lee could not replace lost troops and equipment as readily as the Union armies. Ceaseless fighting would wear him down. Lincoln understood the idea. He telegraphed Grant: "Hold on with a bulldog grip, and chew and choke as much as possible." But the Union "bulldog" was chewed as

WILDERNESS ×
Appomattox ×
× PETERSBURG
Washington
Richmond
Raleigh
Columbia
Charleston
Mobile
New Orleans

North
South

The South Surrounded 1864–1865

well. Heavy casualties were the cost of Grant's plan, in spite of the fact that it was working.

The Siege of Petersburg

By July, Lee and Grant had circled around Richmond. And Grant had Lee pinned down at Petersburg, south of the Confederate capital. Lee could not move without leaving the city open to capture. And with Grant's army blocking his path, Lee could not receive supplies from the deep South. As Grant's troops steadily attacked Lee's lines, the Confederates responded by digging trenches and building "bomb-proof" forts. Union troops protected themselves from counterattack in the same way. The war became a dreary business. Men crouched in holes in the earth, battling heat, mud, insects, and sickness. Each day brought small engagements and mounting casualties. War in 1864 was a series of moments of pain and terror between long stretches of boredom.

Richmond Falls

However the end was inevitable. As spring thaws warmed the earth in March of 1865, Grant renewed his attacks and kept lengthening his front line by adding troops to its wings. Lee extended his line to meet these threats. But his much smaller force was being stretched

355

thin, and he knew one good blow would wipe him out. He could no longer save Richmond. The best he could do was try to slip away and save the army. On April 2, 1865, he gave notice to the Confederate government that the city must be abandoned. Fires lit the sky as the retreating army burned its remaining stores and supplies to keep them out of Yankee hands. Carriages full of worried officials with precious records jammed the streets. In the firelight, mobs of looters raced about with arms full of stolen food and clothing. And Confederate Richmond died in fire and brimstone. Soon Union troops—Blacks included—marched triumphantly down the streets, between ruins. The end was now near.

Lee Surrenders at Appomattox Courthouse

It came on April 9. Lee had tried to move westward to the safety of the mountains. But Union troops overtook and surrounded his tired survivers. To avoid further bloodshed, he sent a flag of **truce** to Grant to ask for terms of surrender. In a private house at Appomattox, he and Grant signed the surrender agreement. The Confederates were to be paroled—that is, allowed to go home in return for a promise not to take up arms again. They were given rations and were allowed to take their horses and mules with them for farmwork.

truce
an agreement by opposing sides to stop fighting for a while

Grant, the man who had been made into a giant by the war, acted like someone who knew how to bring real peace. And within a few weeks, all the other Confederate forces in the field surrendered. The dream of a slaveholding republic, supplying the world with cotton and an example of aristocratic virtue, was now over. The Union was saved. The personal anguish and joy of every American who fought on either side could never be recorded. "The real war," wrote the great poet Walt Whitman, "will never get in the books."

But if the human side of the war was hard to record, the results were not. The argument for secession died forever on the battlefield. Democracy and the Union survived the war, proving their inner strength to a watching world. Above all, the Civil War ended one era of race relations and began another. Slavery was gone. If Blacks were no longer slaves, they must be people, and as such, they are entitled to a full and equal share in the nation. The war and emancipation were the first steps on the road to that share. However, many hard journeys still lay ahead.

Questions for Discussion

1. Why was the Battle of Gettysburg a turning point in the war?
2. What was the strategic importance of Grant's capture of Vicksburg?
3. When did the truce come during the Civil War?

Chapter 15 Review

Summary Questions for Discussion

1. What was the strategy in the East? Why was the West such an important theater of war?
2. What advantages did the North have in the war?
3. How did each of the following affect the South's position during the war: Union damages, blockade, loss of crops?
4. What was Lincoln's main objective in the war? How did the war itself doom slavery?
5. How did conscription lead to riots?
6. Why was Vicksburg an important symbol of resistance for the Confederacy? What was Grant's plan to take Vicksburg? Why was his victory significant?
7. What did Sherman mean by the statement "War is hell."?
8. What was Grant's final strategy against Lee?
9. What were the terms of Lee's surrender to Grant?
10. Describe some results of the Civil War.

Word Study

Fill in each blank in the sentences that follow with the term below that is most appropriate.

logistics	conscription	bounties	profiteering
blockade	truce	hoarding	combat

1. An agreement by opposing sides to stop fighting for a while is a _____.
2. The draft or _____ is one method of recruiting an army.
3. _____ or payments for joining the service are another means of recruitment.
4. Once the fighting begins, someone must use _____ to bring soldiers, weapons, and supplies together at the right place and time.
5. The North closed the South's ports by means of a _____.
6. As the North began to take over the upper South, some people began _____ or piling up stocks for future use.
7. Food prices became very high when dealers engaged in _____.

Using Your Skills

1. Look at the painting of the first Battle of Bull Run on page 341 and the photograph of the after-effects of the Battle of Antietam on page 343. Compare the difference in attitude toward war expressed in the painting and the photograph.
2. Which pictures in the chapter can be used to show the advantages of the North over the South? State specifically why you chose each picture.
3. Look at any of the maps on the chapter and answer the following:
   a. Why did geography generally favor the North in the Civil War?
   b. Why was the West such an important theater of the war?
4. Refer to the map "The Turning Point 1863–64" (page 350). Why were the battles shown called turning points?
5. Refer to the map "The South Surrounded 1864–65" (page 355). What was the North's strategy in defeating the South? Why was it not necessary to occupy all the states of the South in order to achieve a surrender?

CHAPTER 16

The Reconstruction Period

Booker T. Washington was only 9 years old in 1865. Yet, he never forgot the day when he and the other slaves on James Burroughs' Virginia plantation were asked to gather at the master's house. There they were told, "You are all free. You can go where you please." The tears of joy shed by Washington's mother were among his sharpest memories of emancipation.

Not all slaveholders made such a ceremony of freeing their "property." In fact, many held onto the slaves until Union armies occupied their lands. But sooner or later freedom came. There was cheering in the slave quarters, for freedom is a great thing. But there was also fear. When freedom is new, it can be a frightening experience.

And for some 4 million ex-slaves, freedom was a new experience. American history before 1865 gave slaves no example to follow. Although the ex-slaves made up about one-tenth of the nation's population and nearly half the South's, they belonged to a race that almost every White American considered inferior. To improve their status, the slaves needed education, opportunities, and able leadership.

READING GUIDE

1. **How did Lincoln and Johnson plan to accomplish Reconstruction?**
2. **How did the aims of Johnson and those of the Radicals clash?**
3. **How did the Radicals finally achieve control?**
4. **What conditions led to the end of Radical Reconstruction?**
5. **How did the South develop a racial-caste system?**
6. **How did Black leaders view the condition of other Blacks?**

Charleston Square, South Carolina, after the Civil War.

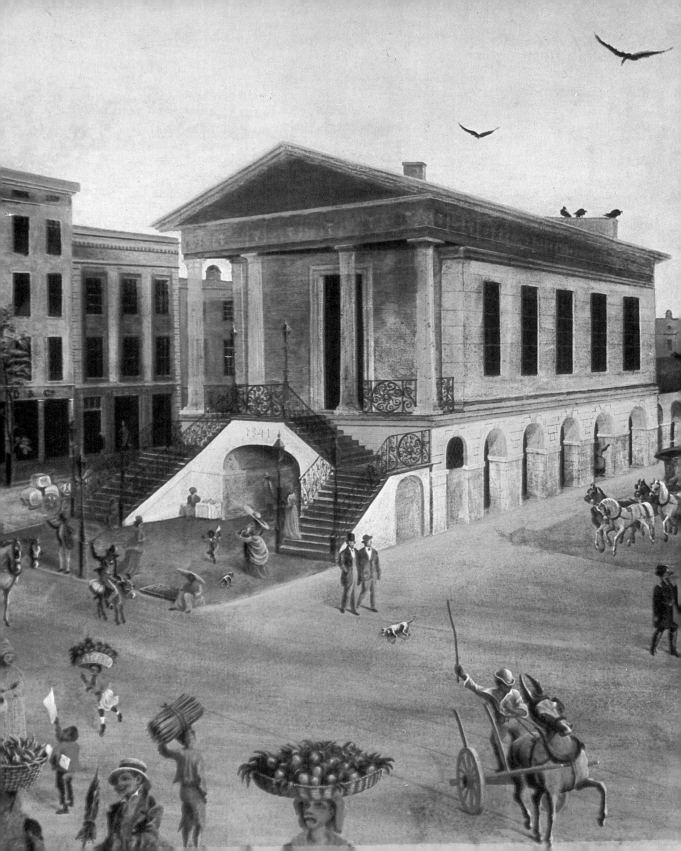

1. Reconstruction in the South

Reconstruction was the process of bringing the Confederate states back into the Union. It took over ten years to accomplish political reconstruction. It took even longer to achieve a healthy economy. Before the war was over, lines were being drawn over how to accomplish Reconstruction. Lincoln announced in his second inaugural address in March 1865, that Reconstruction should be achieved "with malice toward none and with charity toward all." His actions during the Civil War reflected this moderate approach.

Lincoln and other moderate Republicans held that the seceded states had never legally left the Union. Therefore, the restoration of normal relations with the federal government should be accomplished through a presidential pardon. On December 8, 1863, Lincoln issued his Proclamation of Amnesty and Reconstruction, called the *ten percent plan*. He offered amnesty and the restoration of property to any person who would take an oath of loyalty to the United States. High-ranking military and government officials of the Confederacy and those who had tried to return Black prisoners of war to slavery were excluded from this offer. In 1860, when ten percent of those eligible to vote in a state took the oath, that state could establish a constitution, elect officials, and send representatives to Congress. The House and the Senate kept their constitutional power to seat or reject elected representatives.

The proclamation was a lenient offer. Many Southerners who held office before the war were eligible for election. And the states were allowed to make any laws concerning freed slaves, short of enslaving them again. Political, social, and economic power would soon be returned to those who held it before the war.

Congress Objects

Congressional leaders had a different idea about the status of the Confederate states and the course of Reconstruction. They held that the Southern states had left the Union. The Constitution gave Congress the power to admit states. Therefore, Congress, not the President, was responsible for Reconstruction. The President's proclamation offended many members of Congress who thought that he was taking away their power.

In addition, the plans of a minority group of Congressional Radicals would be crushed if Lincoln's policies were adopted. This group, which included Thaddeus Stevens of Pennsylvania, Charles Sumner of Massachusetts, and Benjamin Wade of Ohio, wanted to accomplish certain goals through Reconstruction legislation. The Radicals planned to punish the rebellious states and grant civil and political rights to Blacks. They also wanted to increase the power of Congress and establish the supremacy of the Republican party.

In July 1864, Congress incorporated its ideas for Reconstruction into the Wade-Davis bill. Congress was to have jurisdiction over Reconstruction. A majority, not ten percent, of the voting population had to swear past and future loyalty to the Union before an acceptable state government could be established. The new state constitutions had to forbid slavery and prohibit former Confederate leaders from voting. The bill was passed on the last day of the Congressional session. But Lincoln let it die by exercising a **pocket veto**.

The cards were now on the table. The Radicals in Congress revealed their goals for a social revolution in the South. They would not be satisfied until they crushed the prewar aristocracy and granted political power to Blacks. By tying required oaths to professions of past loyalty, they sought to ban all who had helped the Confederacy from political participation. The Radicals wanted to make sure that no Southern state would be able to return Democratic members to Congress.

At the root of this program were several motives. Certain Radicals believed that if former Confederate leaders regained power, they would take away the rights of Blacks. Among the ranks of the Radicals were people who favored the high tariff and banking and railroad legislation passed by the Republicans during the war. If the South returned Democrats to Congress, legislation favoring Northeastern industrial interests could be overturned.

However, the election of 1864 showed that the people favored Lincoln and his policies. The Thirteenth Amendment abolishing slavery was a major issue during the campaign. After Lincoln was reelected, he used his prestige to obtain passage of the amendment.

Three months after the amendment was ratified, Lincoln was assassinated. His death on April 15, 1865, ended the era of moderate Reconstruction.

Andrew Johnson Becomes President

When Lincoln died, Andrew Johnson of Tennessee assumed the presidency. His background was similar to Lincoln's. He had been poor and was taught to read and write by his wife. Although a Southerner by birth, he had no liking for the wealthy planter class. Like Lincoln, he did not realize that more than emancipation was required to meet the needs of Blacks.

Johnson had neither the personal prestige nor the political pull of Lincoln. He had gained prominence as the successful military governor of Tennessee, whom Lincoln had appointed during the Civil War. The Republicans had chosen Johnson, a Democrat, as Vice President in order to stress unity. When he became President, Johnson lacked backing from either party. He had left the Democratic party. And the

Harriet W. Murray, a teacher working for the Freedman's Bureau, instructs two of her young pupils.

Radicals, who wanted control of the Republican party, were anxious to assert their leadership.

At first, the Radicals thought that Johnson would follow their lead. But shortly after he became President, Johnson made Lincoln's policy his own. He quickly recognized the "ten percent" governments in Louisiana, Texas, Arkansas, and Virginia. He appointed military governors in the remaining Confederate states. In May 1865, he issued a Proclamation of Amnesty similar to Lincoln's. In it, he offered amnesty to all but high-ranking Confederate military and civil officials and people whose assets were more than $20,000. These individuals had to apply to the President for amnesty. Johnson put a former Confederate officer in charge of processing applications for clemency. Soon many former highly placed rebels were pardoned and had their civil rights restored. By the end of 1865, nearly all the seceded states had organized new governments. Many officials in these states were ex-Confederates.

These first Reconstruction state governments passed laws in 1865 and 1866 to replace the slave codes. Ex-slaves were recognized as individuals in a legal sense. This status meant that their marriages were legal. They were given certain rights, such as making contracts, testifying for and against Blacks in court, and holding and transferring property. However, they were prohibited from serving on juries. Southern whites believed that Blacks would not work unless they were forced to. So the new Black Codes provided severe punishment for a Black who left his or her job for any reason without first getting a White person's permission. Vagrancy laws were strictly enforced. Anyone convicted of being idle could be put to work on state chain gangs or contracted out to planters. Blacks could not be employed as skilled workers if they were in competition with White workers. Nor was there any hint in the new Southern state constitutions that Blacks would ever be allowed to vote.

The North, however, tried to prepare Southern Blacks for life outside slavery. In 1865, a special organization, the Freedmen's Bureau, was set up by the federal government to accomplish this task. It was one of the nation's first **welfare agencies**. Freedmen's Bureau officials operated as health inspectors, judges, and school superintendents. They supervised the reopening of plantations and businesses. They also opened schools that were taught by volunteer teachers from the North, and gave food, clothing, and medical supplies to both Black and White refugees from the war's destruction. The Bureau made arrangements for landowners in need of workers to make contracts with ex-slaves. Such contracts usually provided for one year's work and wages.

White Southerners resented this "outside interference," especially

welfare agencies
special organizations of the government that act to improve the living conditions of people, especially those who are unfortunate or handicapped

when some Bureau officers expressed the feeling that Blacks should immediately be given all the rights that Whites possessed. When the White employer and the Black farmhand—formerly master and slave—disagreed about their bargain, the Black could appeal to the Freedmen's Bureau for judgment. The work of the Bureau clashed with the forces behind the Black Codes. Although the Bureau did not always take the ex-slaves' side, many Blacks believed that without it, they would be, as one group said, "sheep in the midst of wolves."

The Constitution Is Amended

A group of Radical Republicans in Congress watched Johnson's policies with dismay. When Congress convened in Washington in December 1865, it refused to seat Representatives and Senators from the newly-reconstructed Southern states. After excluding them, Congress passed a bill extending the life and jurisdiction of the Freedmen's Bureau. Congress also set up a joint committee to investigate conditions in the South. Although the committee was headed by a moderate Republican, several Radicals served on it.

The Radicals believed that the remaking of Southern society must be entrusted to loyal Union men in the South which generally meant Blacks. These Radical Republicans were not radical enough to take land outright from the ex-slaveholders and divide it among the freedmen. In 1866, it was considered an outrage to seize private property even from ex-rebels. Emancipation was as far as the North would go in the widespread taking of "property."

Between 1866 and 1870, the process of "radicalizing" the former Confederate states took place as the Radical Republicans moved against the Black Codes and other threats to Black rights. In March 1866, Congress passed a Civil Rights Act that prohibited the states from discriminating on the basis of color or race. President Johnson vetoed the bill because he thought it was unconstitutional. But the Radicals were able to muster a two-thirds vote to override the President's veto. Some moderate Republicans voted with the Radicals because they had been influenced by the findings of the Joint Committee on Reconstruction.

Congress wanted protection for Black rights. A law could be repealed or declared unconstitutional. The Radicals were able to get Congress to pass the Fourteenth Amendment and sent it to the states to be ratified. This amendment provided that every person born or naturalized in the United States was automatically a citizen of the United States and of the state in which that person lived. The amendment stated further that no state could limit the legal rights of any of its citizens or deny them the equal protection of the law. A Civil Rights Act of 1875—later declared unconstitutional—enforced the

A chaplain from the Freedman's Bureau presides over the marriage of a Black soldier in Vicksburg, Mississippi.

An American cartoon of 1880 compares the Reconstruction policies of Presidents Grant (left) and Hayes.

Fourteenth Amendment by setting penalties for denying any citizen equal treatment in public eating places, hotels, theaters, streetcars, and railroads.

However, the Fourteenth Amendment failed to specifically give Blacks the vote. Many Northern Republicans were at first unwilling to give Blacks the vote either in their own states or in the South. Finally, the desire to create a Black-based Republican party in the South overcame the prejudices of Northern Republicans who were not Radicals. So Northern Republicans agreed to the Fifteenth Amendment, ratified in 1870. This amendment specifically forbade any state to refuse suffrage to a United States citizen because of color. Congress enforced this amendment by passing two laws in 1871 that made it illegal to interfere with any citizen's right to vote.

The Radical Republicans acted with mixed motives. Some were truly interested in the rights of Blacks. Others were probably more interested in using Black voters to defeat political enemies in the North and South. Yet, in the Thirteenth, Fourteenth, and Fifteenth Amendments, the Radical Republicans had written into the Constitution an attack on **racism** and a promise of equality. Thereafter, the question was whether the nation as a whole would live up to the promise of equality, or try to make only the South obey it, or ignore it completely.

racism
the belief that one ethnic stock is superior to another and therefore entitled to favored treatment

Questions for Discussion

1. Define *welfare agency*, *Reconstruction*, *pocket veto*, *racism*.
2. What were the terms of the ten percent plan?
3. Why were Congressional members offended by Lincoln's ten percent plan?
4. What was accomplished by the passage of the Thirteenth Amendment? Fourteenth Amendment? Fifteenth Amendment?
5. How did Andrew Johnson's background compare to that of Abraham Lincoln's?
6. How did the Freedmen's Bureau try to prepare ex-slaves for their new lives?

2. The Struggle for Power

In the 1866 election campaign for Congress, President Johnson went to key cities to rally support for moderate candidates. However, he only succeeded in offending Northerners and turning them toward the Radicals. When the ballots were counted, the Radical Republicans had won control of Congress. The President lost prestige and with it the power to control the direction of Reconstruction.

Congress saw the vote as the people's approval of its policy of achieving an acceptable place in Southern life for freed Blacks. Legislation aimed at undoing Lincoln-Johnson Reconstruction was passed quickly. The First Reconstruction Act of March 2, 1867, declared illegal all but one of the newly reconstructed state governments. Tennessee was the one exception.

The South was divided into five military districts, each to be ruled by a general appointed by the President. Army commanders were ordered to enroll voters for new state constitutional conventions. Blacks were to be allowed both to vote for delegates to these conventions and to be selected as delegates. Most Southern White leaders were banned from voting and from holding office. After state constitutions were written, this new body of voters would elect state legislatures. When these lawmaking bodies ratified the Fourteenth Amendment, the states would then be readmitted to the Union. By June 1868, all the states—except Mississippi, Texas, and Virginia—had complied. In 1870, these states were required to ratify both the Fourteenth and the Fifteenth Amendments as conditions of readmission.

Congress was determined not only to reconstruct the South in its own way but to assert control over the federal government as well. Congress acted against the executive branch and Johnson, in particular, when it passed the Command of the Army Act in March 1867. This act required the President to issue orders to the army through the general of the army. Ulysses S. Grant, who held the position, was thought to be a Radical. According to the law, the President could not remove the general of the army without Senate approval. But through the Tenure of Office Act, Congress took away Johnson's power to control his Administration. The President was prohibited from removing federal officials, including his Cabinet, without Senate approval.

Congress also sought to protect its programs from adverse rulings by the Supreme Court. To this end, Congress passed a law that prohibited the President from appointing any members to the Supreme Court until the number of justices was reduced to six members through death or retirement. Another law was passed making it impossible to appeal to the Supreme Court in cases involving *habeas corpus*. In the case of *ex parte Milligan* (1866), the Supreme Court had stated that military rule was not allowed after civil courts were reinstated. It appeared that the First Reconstruction Act contradicted that ruling, because civil courts were operating in Southern states. When a case was brought to the Supreme Court testing the constitutionality of the First Reconstruction Act, the Court bowed to Congress and refused to hear it. In fact, throughout this period, the Supreme Court refused to rule on the constitutionality of Reconstruction measures.

Impeachment

Some Radicals believed that their program of Reconstruction would never be enforced while Johnson remained in office. The President had vetoed the Reconstruction Acts, the Command of the Army Act, and the Tenure of Office Act. Although Congress overrode his vetoes, the Radicals were convinced that Johnson would continue to oppose their programs for Reconstruction. Impeachment of Johnson, according to the law of succession then in force, would have allowed the president *pro tem* of the Senate to become President. Benjamin Wade, a Radical, held that position.

As the struggle over the course of Reconstruction grew, friction between the President and Congress increased. In 1867, the House Judiciary Committee conducted a year-long investigation but was unable to come up with charges for impeachment. Then, in February 1868, Johnson tested the constitutionality of the Tenure of Office Act. He demanded the resignation of the last Radical in his Cabinet, Secretary of War Edwin M. Stanton. The House reacted swiftly, passing a resolution calling for Johnson's impeachment.

The Committee of Reconstruction, headed by Thaddeus Stevens, drew up eleven articles of impeachment. Ten of these referred to the Tenure of Office Act. The other article accused the President of being "unmindful of the high duties of his office" and of trying to bring ridicule and contempt on the Congress. It cited incidents in which Johnson had raised his voice and uttered "loud threats and bitter menaces."

The major focus of the impeachment procedure was political. The Radicals wanted to remove Johnson because they believed that he was unfit to be President. Had they succeeded in convicting him, they would have set a precedent for removing "unpopular" Presidents. The vote in the Senate fell one vote short of the necessary two thirds. Thus, Johnson not only retained his office, but the system of checks and balances remained intact.

Questions for Discussion

1. What were the terms of the Reconstruction Act of 1867? What happened when the constitutionality of the Act was tested?
2. Which three states held out on ratifying the Fourteenth Amendment?
3. How did Congress strip Johnson of the control he had over his Administration?
4. How did the Supreme Court react to the constitutionality of Reconstruction measures?
5. On what grounds did Congress attempt to impeach Andrew Johnson?

3. The Election of 1868

The issue of Reconstruction continued to dominate the political scene. Shortly after Johnson's trial, the Republicans nominated Ulysses S. Grant for the Presidency. Grant was a Civil War military hero. Although he had no political experience, he was a popular figure. Although Johnson sought the nomination, the Democratic Party selected Horatio Seymour, a former governor of New York.

The Republicans wanted the foremost issue of the campaign to be Radical Reconstruction. So they dragged out all the supposed wrongs of the Democrats. They claimed that the Democrats were the party of rebellion, Black suppression, and financial ruin.

However, the Democrats wanted to turn attention away from the issues of the past. Instead, they stressed economic issues and proposed a policy of "cheap money." They hoped to win the Western farm vote by advocating the reissue of *greenbacks*. Greenbacks were paper money issued by the Union during the Civil War. Their value was less than gold. In 1866, the Republican Congress legislated the gradual withdrawal of greenbacks from circulation. Farmers, debtors, and some business people protested. The Democrats saw a chance to regain political support. They proposed that war bonds be redeemed in greenbacks unless the obligations called for repayment in gold or silver. Although they knew that creditors holding war bonds would not

HIRAM RHOADES REVELS

Hiram Revels was born of free parents in September of 1822 in Fayetteville, North Carolina. He was educated in a Quaker seminary in Indiana since, during this period, it was against the law for Blacks to get an education in the South. Revels went on to attend Knox College in Illinois. After his ordainment as minister in the African Methodist Episcopalian Church in 1845, he worked among Black people in the Middle West, Kentucky, and Tennessee.

Revels moved to Baltimore, Maryland. There, he served as a church pastor and a principal of a school for Blacks. After the start of the Civil War, he assisted in the organization of two volunteer Black regiments for service in the Union Army.

In 1863, Hiram Revels moved to St. Louis where he founded a school for freedmen and again assisted in the organization of another Black regiment to aid the Union forces. In 1864, he moved to Mississippi and served as a chaplain to a Black military unit. He organized several churches in Jackson, Mississippi. He finally settled in Natchez, Mississippi, to preach to a large congregation.

In 1868, Revels accepted a government appointment. In 1869, he was elected to the state Senate. Revels wanted to restore and maintain positive relations with White Southerners. In an effort to do this, he supported legislation that would have restored the power to vote and to hold office to disenfranchised White Southerners.

In January of 1870, Revels was elected to fill the unexpired term of Jefferson Davis and served in the United States Senate from February of 1870 until March of 1871. Thus, he became the first Black to hold a seat in the United States Congress. After leaving the Senate, Revels became the President of Alcorn Agricultural and Mechanical College, a newly opened Black institution near Lorman, Mississippi. He also served for a time as interim secretary of state in Mississippi. Shortly thereafter, he was dismissed from the presidency of Alcorn A&M by the governor.

In the years that followed, Revels was part of a group of politicians who helped overturn the Republican government of Mississippi. In a letter to President Grant, he claimed that too many of the Republican politicians elected to office were corrupt. He was rewarded for his activities by the Democratic governor, who in turn returned him to his presidency of Alcorn A&M. There he remained, developing the institution, until his retirement.

Hiram Rhoades Revels died on January 16, 1901, in Aberdeen, Mississippi, a man of the cloth, an acclaimed politician, a scholar, and a statesman.

favor this move, the Democrats did expect the measure to appeal to debtors.

The Republican candidate, Ulysses S. Grant, won the election. Considering the dullness of Seymour's campaign, Grant's victory was not impressive. He won 52.7 percent of the popular vote. Votes from the newly reconstructed states and newly freed Blacks gave him the edge over Seymour. This near miss encouraged Republicans to draw up the Fifteenth Amendment and urge its ratification.

"The Bottom on the Top"

In the period from 1868 to 1877, Radicals were in control, in most of the reconstructed states, at least part of the time. The Radical governments were made up of uneasy groups of *carpetbaggers*, *scalawags*, and Blacks.

The *carpetbaggers* were a group of Northerners who went to the South after the war. Some were crooked opportunists looking to make their fortunes. Still others were those who wanted to develop sound business opportunities. Some were humanitarians, eager to help the ex-slaves. But to White Southerners, all carpetbaggers represented the forces of alien rule.

Scalawags were Southerners who had not supported the rebellion. Like the carpetbaggers, their motives varied. Some welcomed Republican rule, because it offered a chance for industrial development of the South. Others saw an opportunity to gain political power.

The Southern Republican state governments gave Black Americans their first chance to share political power. Blacks worked with carpetbaggers, who usually held the most important positions, and scalawags. Although hundreds of Blacks sat in state legislatures, they formed majorities only in the lower houses of South Carolina and Mississippi and then only for a short time. Black legislators did not seek revenge against their former oppressors. Instead, they were ready to see to it that suffrage was rapidly restored.

Those Blacks who held office included both ex-slaves and educated Blacks who had never been enslaved. They performed their tasks of state government the way White officials did, some well and a few badly. And a few Black candidates were elected to and served in both houses of Congress.

Radical Control

Radical control brought unexpected social and political gains to many Southerners. Carpetbaggers added many democratic features to new Southern state constitutions. The Reconstruction Acts required adding a provision for Black suffrage to each new constitution. In addition, property qualifications for voting were eliminated for both Blacks and Whites. **Reapportionment** of congressional state legislative seats was begun to give representation to new Black citizens. Blacks and Whites now received free public education, despite strong opposition from many Southern Whites.

reapportionment
the way in which a state recreates its districts

Radical governments were conservative in their demands for economic benefits. There was no demand for property confiscation or for land redistribution. Sorely in need of land to raise food for themselves and their families, Blacks were urged to work and to save money for down payments.

These men were the first Blacks elected to Congress after the Civil War. Hiram R. Revels, seated at the far left, was the first Black Senator.

Yet Radical governments were not without faults. Some officials ran up very large state debts. They borrowed heavily to finance beneficial projects as well as questionable schemes. Welfare systems as well as the sale of bonds for the construction of railroads that were never built burdened the states. However, corruption was not limited to the South alone. The national government and the governments of many major cities were also riddled with scandals.

Questions for Discussion

1. Define *carpetbaggers, greenbacks, scalawags.*
2. In the election campaign of 1868, what were the wrongs of the Democrats?
3. List two factors that helped Grant gain the nomination.

4. Southerners Oppose Reconstruction

The presence of Blacks in seats of power was a sign that a social revolution was about to take place in the South. White Southerners, accustomed to dominating the region's life, would not accept this development. Nor were they willing to pay the higher taxes needed to support schools and other programs helpful to the new Black citizens. So they began to fight back.

One way in which Whites resisted was to campaign for Democrats pledged to restore "home rule." That meant White control of the states, although not necessarily barring all Blacks from government. When they could not persuade enough voters, some Southern Whites went outside the law. White election officials found ways to cheat

Blacks of the vote. For example, on election day, polling places were moved to new locations—revealed only to Whites. White votes were counted twice, while Black votes were not counted at all.

When cheating failed, force could be used instead. Many organizations of Whites took on fanciful names and set out to prevent Blacks from voting. The best known of these organizations was the Ku Klux Klan, founded in Tennessee in 1865. Its officials had such weird titles as "kleagles" and "wizards." Its members dressed in grotesque robes and hoods, which were supposed to frighten superstitious Blacks. These costumes also made the White wearers feel unique and concealed their identities. The Klan was not a harmless, secret club with passwords and special costumes. It was a **terrorist** group, whose purpose was to disenfranchise Blacks. The Klan whipped, burned, and shot Blacks who were bold enough to claim their constitutional rights.

terrorist
one who uses violence and scare tactics to achieve goals

The Klan's hate-filled propaganda dimmed the chances of cooperation between Blacks and Whites in rebuilding the South. Southern White moderates were embarrassed by the Klan. Even so, they did not attempt to break up the organization.

Congress responded to the violence by passing the Force Act of 1870 and the Ku Klux Klan Act of 1871. These acts gave the President power to suspend *habeas corpus*, to declare martial law, and to use troops to maintain order. Despite these powers, federal intervention in South Carolina in 1875 marked the last attempt by the national government to maintain order. Blacks fought back as best they could by forming organizations and defense associations. Gradually, however, Blacks lost ground, as they had at the time of the Black Codes in 1865. And the North failed to come to their aid.

The Ku Klux Klan organized as the "Invisible Empire of the South" and set out to restore social and political White supremacy. Members wore hoods and robes to keep their identities secret and to terrorize Blacks.

Corruption in Government

In 1868, when Grant was elected President, the power of the Radical Republicans was declining. Many Radicals no longer served in Congress. The power of the Republican Party was concentrated in state machines in the North. These political machines dominated the legislatures. Powerful bosses controlled the machines and made sure that payoffs and the sale of political offices were reserved for candidates who would do their bidding. In fact, Senators owed their election to this system.

Grant was the lamb in the lion's den. His inexperience in government made him easy prey for his dishonest associates. As a result, the spoils system flourished during his administrations. Politicians in positions of authority gave out appointments and favors to friends and party loyalists.

In fact, rivalry for the control of the spoils was so great that it divided the Republican Party. Senator James G. Blaine led the

In this 1868 drawing, Southern Blacks campaign for public office for the first time.

Half-Breeds. They were opposed by Senator Roscoe Conkling's faction, the *Stalwarts*. Conkling controlled patronage for the Federal Customshouse in New York City.

Many government scandals were fed by this atmosphere of corruption. The President was naive, and many of his associates lacked integrity. Two crooked financiers, Jay Gould and Jim Fisk, used their influence with the President to reap huge profits from gold speculation.

In 1869, Gould and Fisk plotted to buy up a major share of the gold in circulation—that is, "corner" the market. To do this, the two financiers had to get Grant to withhold gold from the banks. They succeeded by convincing him that this measure would help Western farmers. So once they learned through a dishonest assistant treasurer that the government gold sale would be halted, they bought up the available gold on the market. When Grant learned of their scheme, he authorized the Treasury to sell $4 million in gold. Gould and Fisk quickly sold their holdings but still realized an $11 million profit. The day of the sale (September 24, 1869) became known as Black Friday. And many speculators, lacking inside information, were ruined.

Hot on the heels of "Black Friday" came the Credit Mobilier scandal. A limited group of stockholders in the Union Pacific Railroad created the Credit Mobilier, a construction company. This company overcharged the railroad for work. The excess funds were pocketed by the company's founders. The plot was exposed in the *New York Sun* in 1872. Investigation by a congressional committee revealed that members of Congress and even Grant's Vice President were involved.

As the depth of corruption in Grant's administration was surfacing, a reform movement was developing in the Republican Party. By 1870, many Republicans demanded an end to Radical Reconstruction. They also urged tariff and civil service reform. In 1872, the Liberal Republicans, as the reformers were called, nominated for President the outspoken *New York Tribune* editor, Horace Greeley. Their aims were good, but their choice of a candidate was an unfortunate one. Greeley was a strong critic of the Democrats. But the Liberal Republicans needed the Democrats to elect Greeley. The Liberal Republicans succeeded in getting the Democratic party to nominate Greeley. However, Democratic voters did not support him. Grant swept all the Northern states and lost only six Southern states. Unfortunately, Grant's associates seemed to interpret the wide margin of victory as a go-ahead for even bolder abuses of power.

In the year after the election, Congress discredited itself. In March 1873, Congress doubled the President's salary to $50,000 and voted its own members a 50 percent pay raise (from $5,000 to $7,500). This increase was to be retroactive for two years. The legislation was

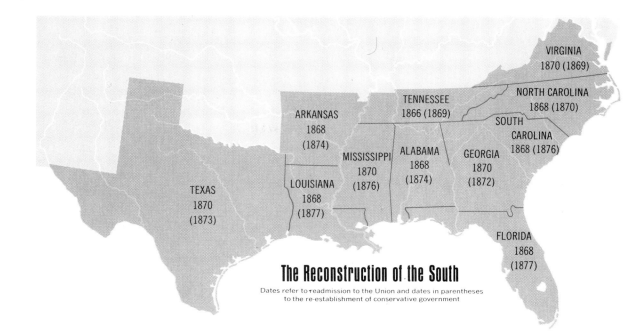

The Reconstruction of the South

Dates refer to readmission to the Union and dates in parentheses to the re-establishment of conservative government

aptly called the Salary Grab Act. And it took an outpouring of anger to repeal the raises for congressional members. However, the raises for the President and for Supreme Court judges remained in effect.

In 1875, Grant's Administration was rocked by yet another scandal. A conspiracy of St. Louis distillers and government officials, the "whiskey ring," had been defrauding the government of millions of dollars in tax revenue. The investigation, led by Secretary of the Treasury Benjamin H. Bristow, reached as far as Grant's private secretary, General Orville E. Babcock. Only Grant's intervention saved Babcock from being convicted with his coconspirators. Another Grant appointee, Secretary of War William W. Belknap, was impeached when it was discovered that he had received bribes from the sale of trading posts in American Indian territory.

Reconstruction Comes to an End

After a severe depression afflicted the nation in 1873, Republicans lost ground both in the North and in the South. Republicans were no longer willing to help Blacks. Northern industrialists considered commercial relations with conservative Southerners more beneficial to their interests than promoting equal opportunity for Blacks. So, one by one, the Southern states elected governments based on the principle of White supremacy. In 1876, only three states—Louisiana, Florida, and South Carolina—had Republican governments in which Blacks took part. The Northern public was also losing interest in changing the South.

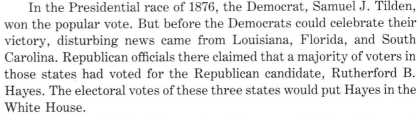

Above: In April 1877, federal troops leave New Orleans amidst cheers from local residents. Below: President Rutherford B. Hayes.

In the Presidential race of 1876, the Democrat, Samuel J. Tilden, won the popular vote. But before the Democrats could celebrate their victory, disturbing news came from Louisiana, Florida, and South Carolina. Republican officials there claimed that a majority of voters in those states had voted for the Republican candidate, Rutherford B. Hayes. The electoral votes of these three states would put Hayes in the White House.

"Fraud!" cried the Democrats. They argued that a fair count would give the three states to Tilden. Republicans answered that any fair Southern election—one in which Blacks were not afraid to vote—would yield a Republican victory.

Early in 1877, a special committee appointed by Congress with an eight-to-seven Republican majority began to investigate the election results in the three states. By a straight party-line vote, they awarded all the disputed electoral votes to Hayes. Finally, Inauguration Day approached. Would all members of Congress accept this report? Or would enraged Democrats refuse to recognize President Hayes? Would the election system break down? The country seemed to be headed for serious trouble.

Then, a behind-the-scenes deal was arranged. Congress awarded the disputed election to the Republicans. But in return, Hayes agreed to withdraw the last federal troops from the South. Without the support of these troops, the last Southern Radical governments were soon defeated.

But there was more to the Compromise of 1877 than troop withdrawal. Republicans in Congress also secretly promised to vote for federal gifts of land, loans, and *appropriations*—grants of money. These appropriations were to help the South build post offices, lighthouses, and railroads, to improve rivers and harbors, and to develop local mining and lumber industries. This program was in line with a Republican policy of encouraging economic growth through public aid to business. Unlike the prewar planter aristocracy, Democratic party leaders of the new South also approved this policy. The Southern social revolution ended mutual agreement between Northern and Southern politicians to help capitalists in both sections with their business enterprises. The nation was now in a mood for industrial and commercial expansion. In the public mind, protecting the rights of non-White minorities—whether Black, American Indian, or Oriental—ranked low on the list of important tasks.

Questions for Discussion

1. Define *terrorist, appropriations.*
2. What was meant by restoring home rule?
3. What circumstances prompted Congress to pass the Force Act of 1870?
4. What was "Black Friday"?
5. How did Grant succeed in getting reelected?
6. List the three southern states that had Blacks in government office in 1876.

5. The Birth of Jim Crow

Now it was the turn of White Southerners to call the tune in race relations. The return of the Democrats to full power did not throw all Blacks out of politics immediately. Some Southern leaders, mostly educated and responsible people, believed that there was room in honest governments for capable people of both races. However, some feared that *repression*—denial of rights—would give some Republicans an excuse to take action to reinstate the Reconstructionist political pattern. Therefore, small numbers of Blacks were allowed to vote and sit in state legislatures. Some were even appointed by Democrats to offices in state governments. However, those Blacks who "bucked the system" were kept in line by force and other means. For example, they might be arrested by the police for very small offenses. Or they might lose their jobs. Such repression was possible because both political and economic power was firmly in White hands.

After the Civil War, most landless Blacks became *sharecroppers.* A Black family lived on a portion of a former plantation. There they raised cotton, and gave a large share of the harvested crop to the landowner as rent for the land and as a fee for leasing tools, seeds, and work animals provided by the landowner. A single owner might have many such families working different parts of the land. The "croppers" got food and clothing on credit at a White-owned store. They were supposed to pay for these goods by selling their shares of the crops. But at the year's end, the money they got from these sales was usually not enough to pay what they owed. So they began each year deeper in debt to the storekeeper.

Though no longer slaves, many Blacks had to take jobs that were not much different from their chores as slaves. The woman below worked as a nurse for a wealthy Southern family.

The sharecroppers in these photos worked long hours on land owned by White men. For many Black farmers this was their only link to the land.

segregated
separated by race

There were some White sharecroppers and many independent White farmers. But for most Black farmers, sharecropping was the only way of staying on the land. Black sharecroppers tilled other people's soil with other people's tools. They rarely saw any cash. Their diet of fat meat and corn bread kept them undernourished. Their children received almost no education in the inferior, **segregated** schools provided for Blacks. The children had only one future— sharecropping or acting as servants to Whites. If Black sharecroppers protested, the planters might throw them off the land and merchants might refuse them credit. They had no money and held no power. Their conditions seemed little improved over those of slavery. In some ways, their lives might have been worse. Before their freedom, Blacks were chained to the land through slavery. Now, although they were supposed to be free, Blacks were chained to the land through sharecropping.

An Age of Violence

Violence has often been a means of settling arguments. In the pre-Civil War South, even plantation owners fought duels, though they were in violation of the law. But in the years after 1877, anti-Black violence had a special meaning. It enforced the unwritten law that Blacks must live as inferiors. Unwritten laws or customs can often be as powerful in regulating social behavior as legal codes.

Violence remained a basic method of enforcing White supremacy. In times of stress, when legal authorities are preoccupied or slow to act, it is all too common for people to take the law into their own hands.

Lynching was not a Southern invention. But in the postwar South, it was used primarily against Blacks. Thousands of Blacks accused of crimes ranging from insulting a White person to murder were lynched. Across the country between 1890 and 1920, 2523 Blacks were executed without trials. Despite the efforts of reformers, antilynching bills repeatedly failed to pass in Congress. Nevertheless, lynching eventually became a rarity.

Blacks and some poor Whites were subjected to other cruelties as well. Even when legally tried, those accused of crimes faced bitter experiences if convicted. They were often sent to work on chain gangs, roads, or in state-owned lumber camps, quarries, or farms. Sometimes, a state leased convicted criminals to private employers—that is, employers paid the state so much per day and worked the convicts as they pleased. In all cases, conditions were inhuman. Bad food, brutal punishment, and outright killings were common.

Segregation by Law

The South also turned to laws to enforce the *racial-caste system* that it shared with the rest of the nation. In a caste system, entire groups of people have an unchangeable status based on birth. In the South, a person's race largely determined his or her social status. No matter what individual Blacks did or did not do, they could not change their skin color. Racism condemned them to second-class status. Between 1877 and 1910, Southern lawmakers passed codes that required segregation in schools, restaurants, streetcars, railroads, and all other public gathering places. The unstated but clear purpose of these laws was to enforce the idea of Black inferiority. The all-Black facilities were always poorer and shabbier than those for Whites. Segregation laws received the unofficial name of Jim Crow, named after a minstrel show based on a slave of that name. Although Northern states did not pass segregation laws, most hotels, restaurants, and other such places either discouraged or refused to serve Black customers. Jim Crow did not live only in "Dixie."

Yet, segregation laws were not passed without arguments. Blacks reminded White lawmakers that during Reconstruction, they had shared public facilities without creating problems. In 1867, Black protests forced the city of New Orleans to give up Jim Crow streetcars. New Orleans maintained integrated schools until 1877. This was unusual, for the National Civil Rights Act of 1875 did not require desegregated education. In 1877, a group of Blacks told a Northern magazine writer, "We want to be treated like men . . . regardless of color." Some Southern Whites agreed. One Southern editor wrote that the South needed separate cars for "rowdy or

A drawing of Jim Crow, the exaggerated Black comic character upon which a minstrel act by "Daddy" Rice was based.

THE SHACKLE BROKEN — BY THE GENIUS OF FREEDOM.

HON. ROBERT. B. ELLIOTT,
of South Carolina.

Published in 1874, the above print, "The Shackle Broken," celebrated the abolition of slavery and the emancipation of slaves.

drunken white passengers" more than they needed Jim Crow cars.

However, by 1910, the segregationists had won. Soon White Southerners forgot how new Jim Crow laws were. They came to believe, and wrongly so, that segregation was part of an old Southern tradition instead of a practice that grew up after Reconstruction.

Late in the 1880s, White Southerners also tried to bury the Fifteenth Amendment. In the 1890s, a political party gained power and challenged the Democrats nationwide for about ten years. It was called the People's Party, or the *Populists*. Populists were mostly poor White farmers who, like Blacks, wanted better schools, fair wages for labor, higher prices for crops, and limits on high interest rates and freight charges. At first, it seemed that Black and White victims of poverty might work together as Populists. But after a time, that hope failed. Whites in both parties realized that Black voters might be able to bargain with both sides for support. And the prospect of Black influence disturbed Whites of all classes. Therefore, the aftermath of the Populist revolt consisted of a host of state laws that almost entirely eliminated Blacks from voting lists. Led by men such as South Carolina's one-eyed "Pitchfork Ben" Tillman, Southern states devised special poll taxes and literacy tests. These devices were used to bar Blacks, not Whites, from voting. "We have scratched our heads to find out how we could eliminate the last one of them," said Tillman. "We stuffed ballot boxes. We shot them. We are not ashamed of it." Soon, the last Black state legislators lost their seats.

Northern public opinion did not challenge these actions. The last hope for Blacks lay in the Supreme Court. But in the 1880s and 1890s, it too accepted disenfranchisement and segregation. In the Civil Rights cases of 1883, the Court decided that discrimination by individuals, such as restaurant owners, did not violate the Fourteenth Amendment. And in 1896, in *Plessy* v. *Ferguson*, it held that a Louisiana law requiring "separate but equal" accommodations on railroads did not deny Blacks equal protection of the law. The decision was used to justify "separate but equal" facilities from schools to graveyards. In fact, such accommodations were never equal. Moreover, as Justice John Marshall Harlan angrily declared in his **dissent**, "Our Constitution is colorblind." However, many years were to pass before a majority of the Court took this view.

As a justice of the Supreme Court, former slave owner John Harlan voted for Black rights.

dissent
an opinion which in whole or in part disagrees with the majority opinion (of the court)

Questions for Discussion

1. Define *repression, sharecroppers, segregated, racial-caste system, dissent.*
2. What was the unofficial name given to segregation?
3. Who were the Populists?
4. What was the basis of Justice John Marshall Harlan's dissent in *Plessy* v. *Ferguson?*

Northern Whites and a few Southerners had tried to remake the South's social system. But some Southern Whites tore up their work. During all this time, Blacks were not mere bystanders. They were trying to build their own futures. The small number of educated Black leaders explored and discussed several choices with their hard-pressed people. One choice was simply to leave the scene of distress. In fact, many Southern rural churches encouraged members of their congregations to move to the West. For example, in 1879 alone, some 40,000 Black Americans trekked westward, settling mainly in Kansas and Indiana. They did not find a land of plenty. Farmwork was dull and difficult. However, like those White Americans who moved to new frontiers, these Blacks hoped for better things to come.

Other Blacks became cowpunchers or members of the cavalry in wars with the American Indians. After their trail-riding and bugle-call days were over, they settled on the Great Plains.

Like Whites, Blacks also tried to escape to the cities. A growing number of Blacks migrated to the northernmost cities. Those Blacks who chose to stay in the South sought jobs other than farming. Young

6. The Search for New Answers

Blacks from the countryside began to leave home to seek their fortunes in Southern towns. They cooked, waited on tables, practiced trades, and drove wagons in Atlanta, Birmingham, St. Louis, New Orleans, and Memphis. A few got factory jobs. A few became members of a growing Black middle class. They became doctors, lawyers, and teachers. Some owned their own grocery stores, funeral parlors, barbershops, saloons, insurance companies, and other businesses, which served the Black community.

In 1900, over seventy-two American cities each had more than 5000 Black residents. Washington, Baltimore, and New Orleans each had more than 75,000. Like poor immigrants from Europe who were new to city life, many poor Blacks had a hard time finding jobs and decent housing, or staying healthy and out of trouble. So in 1910, concerned Blacks founded the National Urban League to help newcomers overcome the problems of city living. A new age in Black leadership was beginning.

The Rise of Black Leaders

Black community leaders needed education. In order to get fair treatment from the White world, they would have to use the same means that Whites used. They would have to publish newspapers, influence lawmakers, take legal action, and raise funds. Only educated Blacks could do such work. After 1865, these leaders came from two places—Black churches and Black colleges.

Black church members formed separate churches in far greater numbers than they had before the Civil War. Their purpose was to be independent of White control and to avoid the humiliation of being segregated within the churches by White fellow Christians. Hundreds of thousands of Black Baptists, African Methodists, and members of other religious groups gave the rituals of White Christianity a Black style. More important, Black ministers became experienced in organizing their members for common action.

Booker T. Washington as Educator

Black colleges such as Howard, Fisk, and Atlanta were founded during Reconstruction with funds from the Freedmen's Bureau and private donations. They were to Blacks what Harvard was to the little Massachusetts colony in 1636—a place to train future leaders. One such school was Virginia's Hampton Institute.

One day in the early 1870s, a dusty teenager showed up there and asked for admission. He was the person mentioned at the beginning of this chapter—Booker T. Washington. After emancipation, he had settled with his family in West Virginia where he worked in a coal mine and did odd jobs. After graduating from Hampton College, he was

inspired by the idea that rural southern Blacks should stay in the South and strive for economic independence instead of moving north to the cities. He believed that the path from slavery to independence lay through learning trades and modern farming methods.

In 1881, Washington, who had become a teacher, had a chance to try out his idea. He was put in charge of a new Black college in Alabama, Tuskegee Institute. In fifteen years of driving work, Washington made Tuskegee a model industrial and agricultural school. Proud of its young graduates, Washington planned an attack on the entire Black problem in the South.

Booker T. Washington as Politician

In September 1895, Washington was invited to speak at the Atlanta Cotton States Exposition, a fair held to show off Southern industrial progress. He used his remarks about Black business to make an offer to white Southerners. The principal of Tuskegee reasoned that the South needed a productive Black labor force, and that Blacks needed economic power. Therefore, he urged Whites to help with his programs of agricultural and vocational education. In return, he would urge Blacks to spend less time seeking social equality and political advancement and more time studying carpentry, book-keeping, stockbreeding, and other practical subjects.

To Black listeners in Atlanta, Washington said that they should "dignify and glorify common labor" and learn that "it is at the bottom

381

A photograph of the class of 1903 at the Tuskegee Institute for Negroes. Beginning with just four run-down buildings and only thirty students, the Institute by 1906 operated out of over 100 buildings and had an enrollment of 1,600 students.

of life we must begin and not at the top." Dignity and acceptance would eventually come to Blacks, as it would to any race with "anything to contribute to the markets of the world." To Whites, Washington said that Blacks, then one-third of the Southern populace, could be one-third of the South's prosperity instead of one-third of its ignorance and poverty. He added, "In all things that are purely social we can be as separate as the fingers, yet one as the hand in all things essential to mutual progress." To both races, he promised that his plan would bring a new heaven "into our beloved South."

In 1895 and thereafter, many Blacks sharply criticized this so-called Atlanta Compromise. But the White world was eager to hear and believe what Washington said. He became known among Whites as a leader of his race. In fact, rich Whites asked his opinion before donating to Black schools or charities. Republican Presidents sought his views on selecting Blacks to be named to the few federal jobs still open to them. Theodore Roosevelt made national headlines when he invited Washington to the White House to discuss matters and sat down to the family meal with him. Southerners raged at the breach of their racial "etiquette." However, Roosevelt had no intention of changing things in the South.

Washington was an early devoted promoter of Black capitalism. He held frequent meetings to encourage Black farmers to buy and improve land. He was also a leader in forming the National Negro Business League, which helped Black businesses get loans and acquire information vital to success.

Other Viewpoints in Black Leadership

White leaders listened to Booker T. Washington on racial matters in part because they liked his soft-spoken, peaceful approach. Actually, Washington worked indirectly against disenfranchisement and segregation laws. But he wanted those White people who dominated national life to support his program of upgrading Black economic status. In his mind, this was the best method in the long run to end Jim Crow. It was easier to get that support by avoiding anger or resentment.

William Du Bois (above) opposed Booker T. Washington's emphasis on vocational rather than academic training and his apparent willingness to wait for equal rights. Du Bois felt that Blacks must speak out constantly against discrimination and oppression.

However, Washington's style offended many Blacks. They considered Washington a man who flattered Whites and ignored injustices in order to build his own power. Their anger was sharpened by the increasing number of segregation laws and by a series of race riots in both the South and the North. In 1906, a race riot rocked Atlanta. Two years later, another exploded in Springfield, Illinois—Lincoln's home town!

A number of young Black thinkers publicly challenged Washington. One of the best known was William Edward Burghardt Du Bois. Born in 1868 in Massachusetts, Du Bois attended Fisk University and then did advanced studies at Harvard and in Europe. He became a pioneer in the field of **sociology**.

Du Bois thought that Washington was too concerned with money-making. In a book called *The Souls of Black Folk*, published in 1903, Du Bois argued that Blacks had gifts of what would now be called soul, which could not be measured in dollars. Later he wrote that the Black race, like all races, would be "saved by the exceptional men," philosophers, poets, and scientists. Black education should train thinkers, not only vegetable growers and bricklayers.

Du Bois and a number of other Black opponents of Washington's views met in 1905 on the Canadian side of Niagara Falls. There they could be sure of fair treatment in hotels and restaurants. They planned a public demonstration to demand "every single right that belongs to a freeborn American—political, civil, and social."

sociology
the scientific study of social behavior

Booker T. Washington's long-range hope was the Black's complete integration into American life. As seen in this photograph of an anniversary celebration at Tuskegee, he maintained close relationships with such public leaders as President Theodore Roosevelt.

Many members of the Black "Niagara Movement" helped found the National Association for the Advancement of Colored People (NAACP) in 1909. They were joined by a number of White men and women who felt that by participating, they were helping the United States. American democracy could not work unless all races shared its promises. The NAACP promised to work for change through lobbying and lawsuits. Because its members did not take on the outwardly-soothing tones of Booker T. Washington, the NAACP was considered radical at the time of its birth.

Fifty years after John Brown's raid, Blacks had made many strides forward. However, much remained to be done to improve the quality of American democracy.

Questions for Discussion

1. Define *sociology*.
2. What actions were taken by Blacks after the Civil War to shape their futures?
3. What institutions were the sources of Black community leadership after 1865?
4. How did Booker T. Washington's ideas about Black advancement differ from those of W. E. B. Du Bois?
5. Describe the "Atlanta Compromise" as stated by Booker T. Washington.

Chapter 16 Review

Summary Questions for Discussion

1. What was Lincoln's plan for Reconstruction? What plan followed?
2. What was the Freedmen's Bureau?
3. What rights were given to Blacks by the new Reconstruction governments?
4. What was the Fourteenth Amendment? How was the Civil Rights Act of 1875 tied to this amendment?
5. Why was the Fifteenth Amendment passed?
6. By what means were the Southern states readmitted to the Union?
7. Describe the circumstances that prompted the Compromise of 1877.
8. How did the lives of Black sharecroppers keep them segregated?
9. What groups made up the Populist Party?
10. What was the purpose of poll taxes and literacy tests?
11. What was the result of *Plessy* v. *Ferguson?*
12. What did Booker T. Washington do to foster his goals of Black advancement?
13. What were the views of W. E. B. Du Bois?
14. What was the purpose of the National Association for the Advancement of Colored People?

Word Study

In the sentences that follow, fill in each blank with the term that is most appropriate.

greenbacks   welfare agencies   dissent
poll taxes   Reconstruction   carpetbaggers
scalawags   sociology   repression

1. The Confederate states were brought back into the Union through the process called _____ .
2. Taxes on voting or _____ were instituted as a means of keeping Blacks from voting.
3. The Freedmen's Bureau was one the nation's first _____ .
4. The paper money that was issued during the Civil War was called _____ .
5. The groups of Northerners that went South after the Civil War were called _____ .
6. Southerners who did not support the rebellion were called _____ .
7. Justice Harlan Ferguson delivered a difference of opinion or _____ in the case of *Plessy* v. *Ferguson.*
8. W. E. B. Du Bois was a pioneer in the study of _____ .

Using Your Skills

1. "Despite a great many difficulties, Black Americans enjoyed more political and economic opportunity after the Civil War than before." Make a list of pictures from this chapter that would support this statement. Make another list that would contradict such a statement. Then in your own words, tell why you think the statement is basically true or false.
2. Examine the map "The Reconstruction of the South" on page 373. What four Southern states were the last to reestablish conservative governments? How did this affect the outcome of the election of 1876?

Unit 4 Review

Summary

In 1861 Civil War divided a nation that just eighty-five years before had united and successfully declared its independence.

Until 1830, sectional differences were worked out peacefully through compromise. This was possible because the sections remained roughly equal in wealth and population. However, as the balance shifted in favor of the Northeast and West, Southerners became uneasy. In addition, the institution of slavery, so essential to the South, became a political issue. The question of admitting new states to the Union centered around whether they would be free or slave. In 1854, the Kansas-Nebraska Act and the Dred Scott decision negated the Missouri Compromise. By 1858, Lincoln and Douglas were debating in Congress the rights of the federal government over the moral question of slavery. By the time John Brown led his raid on Harpers Ferry in 1859, the country had chosen sides. South Carolina led Southern states in secession. President Lincoln's attempts to restore the Union peacefully ended on April 12, when the firing on Ft. Sumter began.

The fighting continued for four years. The Civil War scarred farms and forests and stained the land with the blood of young soldiers. By the time Lee surrendered to Grant at Appomattox Courthouse, the Emancipation Proclamation had ended slavery in the seceded states of the South.

With the end of the war, the problem of rebuilding began. Reconstruction of the South lasted from 1865 to 1877. During this period, the Southern states were readmitted to the Union. And Black Americans began their struggle to gain a life of dignity as United States citizens. Many of the conflicts that began during this period remain unresolved to this day.

Summary Questions

1. What differences between the North, South, and West led to Civil War?

2. How did Southern and Northern politicians differ in their interpretation of the Constitution?

3. In what ways did the Civil War differ from previous wars in which the United States had fought? Why did the war last much longer than most people on both sides had expected in 1861?

4. List the advantages and disadvantages each side had in the Civil War.

5. What were the important turning points in the Civil War?

6. Did the war have the same economic effect in the South as in the North? Explain.

7. How did the Civil War contribute to sectional hatred even after the war ended?

8. Why did the Civil War and the amendments to the Constitution that immediately followed it fail to place Blacks on an equal footing with Whites?

9. In the period after Reconstruction, why did both White Northerners and Southerners favor policies that would ensure White supremacy?

10. Contrast the views of Booker T. Washington and W. E. B. Du Bois.

Developing Your Vocabulary

1. Popular sovereignty is a principle that the people (should, should not) have power in policy—making.

2. Gradualism is another term for (revolution, slow change).

3. Another term for the draft is (conscription, logistics).

4. A (truce, blockade) is a temporary agreement made by opposing forces to cease firing.

5. (Hoarding, Profiteering) is charging ex-

tremely high rates for goods that are in short supply.

6. A good military leader must be well versed in (logistics, racism).

7. (Pressure, Terrorist) groups usually use violence to achieve their ends.

8. A caste system will keep classes (segregated, integrated).

9. Poll taxes and literacy tests are used to (increase, decrease) the size of the electorate.

10. During Reconstruction, the Southern states (seceded from, were readmitted to) the Union.

11. The Populists advocated (reform, revolution).

12. Welfare agencies (would, would not) seek to give aid to sharecroppers.

13. To hoard is to (hide, sell) supplies.

14. (Repression, Secession) is the denial of one's civil rights.

15. To subsidize is to give (political, economic) aid.

Developing Your Skills

Mapping

1. On an outline map of the United States, indicate the states affected by the Missouri Compromise, the Compromise of 1850, and the Kansas-Nebraska Act.

Classifying and Comparing

2. Construct a chart comparing the North and South at the beginning of the Civil War. Include the following areas: population; industrial development; transportation; military advantages.

Comparing

3. Compare and contrast conditions in the South before and after the Civil War.

Organizing and Evaluating

4. Construct a chart listing the sucesses and failures of the Reconstruction Era.

Applying Understandings

5. Knowing the results of the Reconstruction era, what plan would you have come up with for Reconstruction?

Special Activities

1. Investigate the songs and poems written during the Civil War period. Prepare a report to the class on the circumstances that produced one or two of them.

2. Prepare a report on one of the following related to the Civil War Period: the *Merrimac* and the *Monitor;* the Trent Affair; the underground railroad; the Fugitive Slave Law, the Maximillian Affair, the Alabama Claims.

3. Individuals have always played an important role in history. Research and report to the class on the role of one of the following during the Civil War and Reconstruction Period: Clara Barton, Thaddeus Stevens, John Wilkes Booth, Frederick Douglass.

4. Lincoln revealed himself in many of his speeches and statements. Read each of the following and describe his outlook and character as revealed in each:

    a. "A House Divided" speech

    b. Emancipation Proclamation

    c. Gettysburg Address

    d. Second Inaugural Address

5. Read *John Brown's Body* by Stephen Vincent Benet. What was Benet's view of Lincoln? of John Brown? of slavery?

UNIT
5

The United States Becomes an Industrial Giant

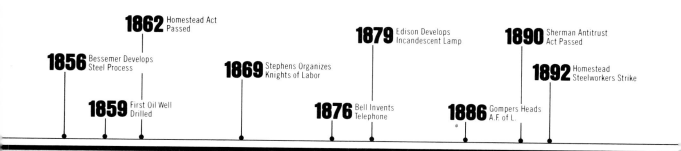

1862 Homestead Act Passed

1856 Bessemer Develops Steel Process

1859 First Oil Well Drilled

1869 Stephens Organizes Knights of Labor

1879 Edison Develops Incandescent Lamp

1876 Bell Invents Telephone

1886 Gompers Heads A.F. of L.

1890 Sherman Antitrust Act Passed

1892 Homestead Steelworkers Strike

CHAPTER 17
The Making of an Industrial Environment

CHAPTER 18
A Nation of Cities

CHAPTER 19
An Age of Reform

CHAPTER 20
A Nation of Immigrants

In 1870, the sons and daughters of farmers were leaving the plains and prairies to look for work in the cities. Thomas Jefferson had hoped that America would always be mostly a nation of small farmers. Few people could have forecast the tremendous impact that industrialization had on the nation.

1901 Teddy Roosevelt Becomes President

1909 Mass Production of Ford "Model T"

1903 Wright Brothers Airplane

1920 Urban Population Excedes Rural

In Chapter 17, there is a discussion of the forces that were turning the country into an industrial giant. The new kind of industrial city, which became the home of an increasing number of Americans, is the subject of Chapter 18. Industrialization and urbanization brought major changes to the way Americans were living. These changes, and the era of reform which sought to meet the challenge of change, are examined in Chapter 19. Finally, Chapter 20 presents an analysis of the large influx of immigrants during that time period.

Problems such as low farm prices, festering slums, dirty politics, and unsafe mines and mills demanded new solutions. "What is the responsibility of the government for the welfare of its citizens"? asked the reformers. As you shall see, both the reformers and opponents of reform had sure answers to this question.

CHAPTER 17

The Making of an Industrial Environment

In 1876, the Declaration of Independence was 100 years old. The United States gave itself a centennial birthday party with a mighty industrial fair in Philadelphia. In the city where the little united colonies had proclaimed their freedom, great buildings arose. One of these buildings, the Hall of Machinery, contained a gigantic steam engine. It powered thirteen acres of other machines for combing wool, spinning cotton, printing newspapers, sewing cloth, and doing many other kinds of work. Walt Whitman wrote of these inventions: "This, this and these, America, shall be *your* Pyramids." Americans saw these marvels as signs of their greatness as a people.

Yet, the centennial in 1876 was only one milestone on the long road to industrial independence. The streams of manufactured goods that began to flow from American factories around 1820 soon became torrents. By 1900, the United States was a leading world producer of steel, oil, and coal. All these materials were basic to modern industry. In addition, American-made clothing, machinery, foodstuffs, and other products traveled the world over. Africans and Asians wore garments of American cloth. Argentine farmers plowed with American plows. Japanese soldiers, after a victorious war over China, were given American-made watches as rewards for bravery.

Although the early factory system had caused some changes in the way Americans lived, it was the huge industrial growth after the Civil War that changed their surroundings almost completely. In 1860, Americans were largely a nation of farmers. Sixty years later, the majority of Americans lived in cities. In 1860, the United States was inhabited almost entirely by English-speaking peoples. But by 1910, hundreds of thousands of strangers from places as far away as China and Russia were familiar sights in Eastern and Western cities.

READING GUIDE

1. **What are the elements of industrialization?**
2. **How did industrialization change the United States and the way Americans lived?**

A busy Northern iron foundry in the 1860s, as painted by John Weir.

1. The Elements of Industrialization

John D. Rockefeller characterized the new captains of industry in his ruthless drive to monopolize any industry in which he was a competitor.

Many elements were responsible for this change from a frontier America to a world workshop. History, culture, and geography gave the United States a head start in three key areas: leadership, labor, and resources.

A new breed of strong, self-made people–those who did not inherit wealth or social position but earned success anyway–led the march of America toward industrial might. In a fast-growing country that preached equality, a clever, hard-working young person could succeed in business even without a family fortune as a start. Society encouraged young people to try to get ahead because there was a tradition in the nation of hard work and thrift. In addition, frontier America had long admired material growth and progress.

Industrial leaders such as oil refiner John D. Rockefeller or steel king Andrew Carnegie were not just ordinary business people. They were able to think big. And they planned huge business operations, certain that a growing nation would buy all they made. These leaders worshiped efficiency. They bought expensive machinery and paid high salaries to expert engineers just to cut a few cents off the cost of refining a barrel of oil or making a ton of steel. But those pennies, multiplied by millions of tons or barrels, added up to huge savings in manufacturing costs. And lower costs meant lower prices. Lower prices attracted more customers, which meant bigger sales and thus more profits.

The new captains of industry were often ruthless competitors—but only until they had eliminated competition. They believed it was wasteful for many small makers of the same product to fight each other for raw materials, workers, and customers. Their ideal was to achieve monopoly, or near-monopoly, with one company, or a few, dominating each industry.

These qualities and attitudes are shown best in the career of John D. Rockefeller. Rockefeller began as a Cleveland bookkeeper with a salary of $3.50 a week. Of this he saved enough to enter the grocery business. In 1863, he turned to oil refining. It was a risky enterprise. Prices rose and fell overnight. Rockefeller decided to take the lead in making the industry more efficient. First, he made his Standard Oil Company an outstanding refinery. One way to do this was to control all the ingredients of the finished product. Standard made its own oil barrels from Rockefeller-owned timber. It delivered oil products in Rockefeller-purchased wagons.

In 1870, Standard was refining 3000 barrels of oil a day. Now, Rockefeller met with other Cleveland refiners. He pointed out to them that as rivals, they competed in buying crude oil, refining machinery, and providing transportation. These factors drove their costs higher. Then they competed in selling the refined oil, driving down the prices they received. But if they combined, they could dictate their own terms to both their suppliers and customers. If they did not combine, Standard alone would undersell them and drive them out of business. Faced with such a choice, thirty-two independent refineries sold out to Rockefeller.

During the 1880s, Standard built or bought oil fields, tanks, pipelines, and warehouses all over the country. In 1886, its annual output was over 10 million barrels of refined oil. Standard, made up of many united companies, controlled each step in refining. Yet, while Rockefeller managed this huge empire, he would write to superintendents, asking them to account for a few barrel stoppers worth less than a penny each. These practices were part of what he called "better business prinicples."

The steel giant Andrew Carnegie illustrates the attitude many captains of industry held toward wealth and power. Carnegie was a frequent writer for magazines. One of his articles was entitled, "The Gospel of Wealth." A gospel is a statement of faith believed to be absolutely true. Carnegie's gospel stated that the very rich had a duty to use their wealth for the public good, rather than to leave it to their heirs. The rich should donate freely to such good works as libraries, hospitals, and universities. Thus, the fortunes made by the captains of industry would advance the whole human race.

Andrew Carnegie invested early in the steel industry and, by 1899, he controlled the bulk of United States steel production. He described his policy as "put your good eggs in one basket and then watch the basket."

PENNSYLVANIA RAILROAD VERSUS ROCKEFELLER

In the wars between the business tycoons of the 1870s and 1880s, bluffing was allowed. Millions of dollars were often spent with reckless generosity just to win a small point. In the 1880s, the Pennsylvania Railroad had a falling out with John D. Rockefeller over the price charged for hauling Standard Oil Company's products to eastern markets. Pennsylvania directors stuck to the high figure they named. Then, one day, with plenty of fanfare, work crews began to appear in southern Pennsylvania not far from the railroad lines, carrying grading and tunnelling and rail-laying equipment. The public announcement was made that Mr. Rockefeller was going to build another, competing railroad. His railroad would offer passengers much cheaper rates than the Pennsylvania Railroad. As a result the Pennsylvania Railroad would eventually run out of business. For many months, the war of words—and the construction—went on. The Pennsylvania management finally gave in and came to terms.

Meantime, the work crew had built a fine, partially graded roadbed, and tunnels. The crew then waited for rails and locomotives that never came. All the work and materials did not go to waste, however. In the 1930s, the first of the nation's modern superhighways was built: the Pennsylvania Turnpike—using much of the same route all the way from Philadelphia to Pittsburgh. Autos today are still speeding along a roadbed first surveyed and leveled as part of a clash of super corporations a century ago.

Many American millionaires who shared this idea gave away remarkable sums of money. Their skills and generosity benefited the nation. Yet, the gospel of wealth really said that a few great firms should rule the economy and a few rich people should improve society by granting gifts. These ideas were a far cry from the older American ideal of equal opportunity for all.

Labor for Hire

Another necessity for a huge increase in industrial production is a steady supply of labor. A great deal of rugged muscle power was needed to dig coal and iron ore from the earth, cut down trees for lumber, hammer steel rails into place, and dig foundation trenches for factories and city buildings. Also, once machines were placed in a factory, they needed hands to run them. However, many of those hands belonged to children.

The United States had two sources of labor. One was the countryside. From mountains and prairies, country boys and girls followed the lure of the city. They found jobs in heavy industry and in the offices, stores, and city services—such as police, fire, and sanitation departments—of the growing urban nation.

As the United States expanded industrially, women played a larger role in the labor force.

The second source of labor was immigration. America had a reputation as a land of freedom and opportunity. This paid off in economic terms because it attracted a mighty labor force. Between 1860 and 1920, nearly 30 million people migrated here from Europe and Asia. That number almost equaled the whole United States population in the year of Lincoln's election. Great numbers of these newcomers became industrial workers. The western section of the first transcontinental railroad, for example, was built by Chinese laborers.

Immigrant labor was both plentiful and cheap. So many people wanted jobs that they were willing to work long hours for low wages. Women and children of poor families did much of the work in the "light" industries that required little hauling and lifting.

Resources for Industry

The United States had a geographical advantage in becoming an industrial giant. There was a great abundance of resources in North America. The mountain ranges were vast storehouses of gold, silver,

In 1890, rich deposits of workable iron ore were discovered at the Mesabi Range in Minnesota. The range became the chief source of iron ore for steelmaking in the United States. The Mahoning mine in this 1899 photograph became the largest open-pit mine in the world.

Above: Pennsylvania coal miners prepare to descend for a day's work.

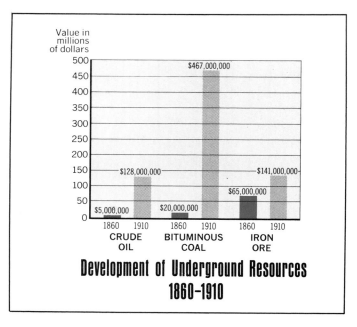

Value in millions of dollars

$467,000,000

$128,000,000

$141,000,000

$65,000,000

$5,000,000

$20,000,000

	1860	1910	1860	1910	1860	1910
	CRUDE OIL		BITUMINOUS COAL		IRON ORE	

Development of Underground Resources 1860–1910

lead, copper, coal, and other mineral treasures. The forests seemed limitless. Petroleum lay in huge natural underground reservoirs.

Coal and oil are essential to modern industry. They furnish industrial work-energy. As they are burned either in gasoline engines or in furnaces, they make steam that drives the generators that, in turn, make electricity. Steel is the basic building material of modern times.

Petroleum products were almost unknown in 1860. By 1910, production in all forms, of petroleum had soared from a few thousand to billions of gallons. This growth came even before widespread use of the gasoline engine. Most petroleum was refined into *lubricants*, which prevent moving machine parts from wearing each other out by friction. Petroleum was also refined into kerosene for heating and lighting purposes.

Before 1858, steel was costly and little was produced. People knew, however, that it was tougher and longer lasting than iron. In the 1850s, an Englishman and an American separately discovered processes for burning impurities out of molten iron by forcing a blast of air through it. The adding of other minerals completed the process. The resulting steel was both extremely strong and cheap to produce. Thereafter, American blast furnaces worked steadily. Huge new iron deposits were discovered. These deposits were mined by powerful steam shovels. As late as 1867, less than 23,000 tons of steel were produced. But by 1910, the United States led the world in millions of tons produced. The steel went into making rails, railroad cars, ships, armor plate, machinery, bridges, wire cables, and skyscrapers.

Revolution in Communications and Transportation

In the industrial environment, raw materials and finished goods moved back and forth over vast distances under the commands of the great managers. This movement would have been impossible without a huge transportation network.

The growth of railroads was the main development that made industrial miracles possible. Railroad mileage in the United States grew from some 30,000 in 1860 to over 350,000 in 1910. In this half-century of furious railroad construction, the attention-catching "spectaculars" were the five transcontinental lines completed between 1869 and 1893. Each of these lines had to be pushed through thousands of miles of barren or mountainous country. They were superb achievements of organization and engineering skill, like the globe-girdling airlines of today.

The real railroad revolution was in building the smaller lines in the East and South. These lines carried the everyday necessities produced by farm and factory to even the tiniest villages and towns. This made them an important part of the rapidly expanding economic system in the nation.

Communications also underwent a revolution. The telegraph dated from 1844. But after the Civil War, a set of new inventions

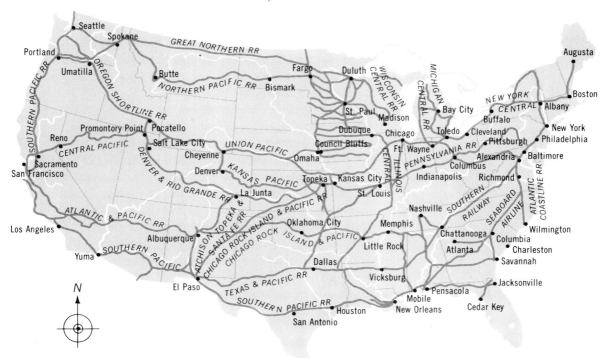

Transcontinental Railroads

The Atlantic telegraph cable, which seems so routine to us in this day of radio, was one of the marvels of the world. The cable was laid with enormous difficulty and at huge cost. A businessman originally from New England, Cyrus Field, was the guiding spirit. He put millions of dollars into the effort to develop insulated wire which would be resistant to salt water, biting fish, high water pressures, rocks, and extremely cold temperatures. These hazards could make the cable break or lose the power to transmit electrical signals over thousands of miles. He got the job done once, in 1858. Queen Victoria and President James Buchanan exchanged messages. But, thereafter, the cable snapped immediately, and it had to be started all over again. Victory finally came in 1866.

Alexander Graham Bell in 1892, at the New York end of the first telephone connection to Chicago.

greatly increased its speed and power of operation. In 1866, a telegraph cable was laid on the floor of the Atlantic Ocean. After that, Europe and America could communicate with each other at the speed of electricity. By 1910, early experiments in sending messages by radio waves instead of wires had been successful as well.

Many electrical inventions of this period were developed through the practical genius of Thomas Edison. In 1876 another genius, Alexander Graham Bell, worked out a device for changing voice sounds into electric currents and transmitting, or sending, them by wire. You know his invention today as the telephone. As early as 1900, more than a million telephones were in use in the United States.

Speedy communication allowed people to organize industries with nationwide and worldwide markets. The globe was shrinking. As it did, human behavior underwent change as well.

Mass Production Comes of Age

As we saw in Chapter 12, rapid production of goods by assembly-line methods was taking place as early as the 1840s. However, the quantity of goods produced increased enormously in the last half of the 1800s. The principles, though, remained the same. Machine-work replaced handwork as much as possible. Many identical, interchangeable parts were produced. These were put together to make a finished object on an assembly line. Yet, compared to the earlier models, the machines of the new age were like giants matched against dwarfs.

Thomas Alva Edison after seventy-two hours of continuous work improving his wax-cylinder phonograph in 1888.

For example, a cotton mill worker in 1840, working about fourteen hours a day, could make about 10,000 yards of cloth a year. In 1886, working ten hours a day, the worker could make 30,000 yards a year. In 1845, a Massachusetts bootmaker made about one and a half pairs of boots a day. By 1885, in many factories, that number was increased to seven pairs. A new kind of furnace for melting glass came into wide use in 1885. It let four workers produce a million square feet of glass in

This 1913 photograph shows one day's output of chassis for the Model T at the Highland Park Ford plant in Michigan. Largely as a result of Ford's efficient assembly line, the basic price of the finished Model T dropped from $950 in 1909 to $550 in 1913 to $290 in 1926.

eighteen days. The old furnace required twenty-eight workers laboring for a month to produce only 115,000 square feet of glass.

The man whose name became most closely associated with assembly-line production was Henry Ford. He was convinced that every American should be able to own an automobile. The trick was to produce a basic, unchanging model. In his Detroit plant, Ford created an assembly line that could roll out 1000 chassis a day for "Model T" Fords. By 1926, he had made 15 million Model T's. The price for the car was then under $300. More than any other auto manufacturer, Ford had put America on the road.

One result of the age of mass production was increased concentration of ownership. Only a few companies in each industry could really compete. Only a few could afford multimillion-dollar plants. Another result was that mass production spurred the search for millions of customers, to earn back the high costs of the machines. In that way, it encouraged the growth of new advertising and marketing practices. It reduced the workers to what one called "privates in the industrial army." Finally, mass production changed the look of the land itself and the lifestyles of people throughout the country.

Questions for Discussion

1. Define *lubricants*.
2. After the Civil War, how did industrial leaders change American industry?
3. How did John D. Rockefeller do away with competition in the oil industry?
4. How was mass production different before the Civil War?
5. What role did individuals play in transforming the United States into an industrial giant?

2. Industry Transforms the West and the South

After 1865, industrial plants were found mainly in the area east of the Mississippi. But much of the food for their workers, as well as the natural resources, came from the Far West, beyond the Mississippi and Missouri rivers. Between 1865 and 1900, farms, mining towns, and lumber camps replaced much of the open space that the mountain men had first mapped. Those who stood in the way were shoved aside. The Plains Indians were unfortunate enough to have been standing in the way.

Subduing the Plains Indians began when the great buffalo herds were destroyed. You have already seen how the tribes depended on the buffalo for the needs of life and how their culture rested on buffalo-hunting. However, when railroads brought Whites into the Plains in great numbers, the buffalo were doomed. White passengers shot them for sport from special trains. Hunters mowed them down for their bones and hides to sell to dealers in the form of fertilizers and robes. Before railroad days, the herds sometimes looked like great, moving brown rivers. But by 1882, a hunter, after witnessing the slaughter of a herd, wrote, "A man could have walked twenty miles upon their carcasses." Soon all but a handful of buffalo were gone.

For Plains Indians, this meant that they must either live on rations provided by the United States government or steal beef from White settlers. Sometimes, they did not have the first choice. The government agent sometimes cheated the American Indians by holding back food that he was supposed to give them. Instead, the agent would sell it to others for his own profit. Or, for a bribe, he might permit other Whites to sell the Indians unlawful guns and whiskey. So some hungry

Black workers remove the stems from tobacco in a mechanized cigarette factory.

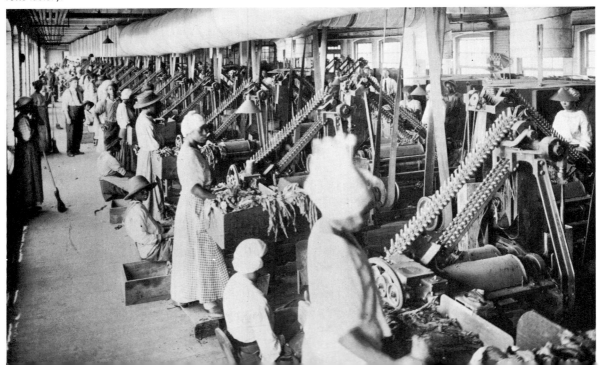

American Indians were forced to steal. Others became drunk and troublesome. It was clear that sooner or later there would be a clash between Whites and Indians. Finally, troops would move in, and a tribe would go on the warpath. Despite the well-publicized victory over General Custer at the Battle of the Little Big Horn, the end of these struggles was always the same. In time, the Indians would surrender to the better-armed White soldiers. As a result, they would walk the trail of captivity to the reservation.

In 1887, by passing a law known as the Dawes Act, the United States encouraged the division of tribal lands into individual farms. But most Indians did not want to give up their tribal way of life for the white man's pattern of owning individual property. So the Dawes Act began a long and sad history of governmental attempts to solve the Indian "problem." This problem had been created by the destruction of the Indians' livelihood and culture.

The Opening of the Plains: The Final Frontier

In the eyes of most Americans, farming was noble work that fed humanity and opened wild lands to progress. Despite such beliefs, individual farmers in the Far West were soon facing great hardships because agriculture was becoming big business. The nation wanted to see the unused lands of the West put to productive use. People rushed to take up land and make it pay profits in much the same way that they rushed to build railroads and steel mills.

In 1862, Congress passed the Homestead Act. This act gave a free farm to any adult male citizen who would claim the farm and actually

Although Nebraska was admitted to the Union in 1867, farmlands still lured pioneers. In 1886 this family arrived in central Nebraska's Custer County.

live on it for five years. By 1900, millions of hectares of public land had been given away. Yet, that was only a start. Another 128 million hectares (320 million acres) were given to the railroads and the states by the federal government. Much of this land was turned into the nearly 4.5 million farms added to the economy between 1860 and 1910. Yet, nothing seemed to satisfy the land hunger of Americans. In 1889, Oklahoma—once supposed to be preserved as Indian Territory—was opened to homesteading. Thousands of people crowded to the starting line on opening day. At the crack of a gun, they whipped their horses into a frantic race to be first at the choicest locations. Overnight, Oklahoma was populated and tent-and-shack towns were set up.

However, not all of the public domain went to the settler who wanted only a homestead. Land speculators and ranchers bought huge tracts from the states. In a number of cases, false homestead claims were put together to make giant-sized domains for single owners. Mining and lumbering companies also got huge shares as the public domain was carved up like a roast. A single company in Florida, for example, bought 800,000 hectares (2 million acres) of forest lands.

Before the Civil War, the Republican Party had demanded "free soil." Their idea was to save the Far West for family farms and not permit it to be turned into plantations. Yet, after the war, the single-family farmers in the Far West found that they were tiny beings in a world of landowning giants. These giants increasingly used machinery to replace the work once done by people and animals.

Farming Becomes a Big Industry

Just as invention increased the output of industrial workers, marvels of invention stood ready to help the farmer produce more. Machinery was creating an agricultural revolution. There were threshers, harvesters, combines, binders, cultivators, huskers, shellers, and other factory-built devices that made huge savings in human effort. A farmer of 1830 had to work sixty-one hours to harvest twenty bushels of grain by hand. In 1900, it took only three hours to do the same work. In 1850, a worker took twenty-one hours to harvest a ton of hay. Half a century later, the time was four hours. At first, the power for these machines came from farm work animals. Steam-driven equipment offered some improvement. In 1901, a gasoline engine powered the first tractor. Within forty years, mechanical inventions had driven the horse and the mule from all but the poorest farms.

Meanwhile, new and better seeds were being developed. Improvements in the breeding of cattle raised the quality of livestock. Research in agriculture was carried on in several places. The Department of Agriculture, which became a full-fledged Cabinet department in 1889, did scientific laboratory studies. Through officials known as county agents, this department spread word of the results to farmers. Agricultural colleges were beginning to open their doors. The Morrill Act of 1862 gave land grants to these colleges to further their work. Now farming was no longer a calling that depended entirely on the whims of nature for good harvests.

A steadily shrinking share of the whole United States population managed to keep feeding the country and other parts of the world as well. Wheat harvests rose to more than half a billion bushels each year.

Yet, all these mechanical improvements cost farmers a good deal. On the Plains, they needed barbed wire for fencing. Farmers paid out large sums of money for the great machines that helped them plant, tend, and harvest the crops, and for the special feeds that produced healthy hogs and fat chickens. In those parts of the West which were too dry, farmers needed to irrigate the land. They also paid the cost of building and running the railroads through the freight charges that came out of their pockets. The more crops they produced, however, the lower the prices they received. They were operating in a big-business economy. Success went to those who could make large

DULUTH IMPERIAL FLOUR

In this ad, the Duluth Imperial Flour Company used the ballooning craze to its advantage.

In 1902 this farmer in Washington used thirty-three horses to pull his wheat-harvesting machine.

investments in special equipment and who could combine with others to control the price of their products. Some farmers were able to become successful large-scale operators. But those with small holdings struggled constantly to keep out of debt. They were similar to the hand-loom weavers competing with textile factories in the East.

The Cattle Kingdom Becomes an Industry

In the Southwest, a thriving "cattle kingdom" rose. It, too, was part of an "industrial revolution" in food production. The cattle kingdom began because great natural resources were available. On the

Some farmers converted to steam power. These two steamers, pulling water wagons as well as plows, could run day and night and plow 50 to 60 acres a day.

grasslands still in the public domain, a skinny calf could grow into a fat beef animal. His owner would not have to pay anyone a cent for this—public-land prairie grass was free, like air and water.

After the Civil War, modern technology joined together with natural resources. At that time, railroads were built to points in Kansas and Missouri. Then it was possible for cowboys to drive their owners' herds northward over the cattle trails to the railhead towns like Dodge City. The herd would be sold to meat packers at a good profit to their owner. After a rail trip to the Chicago stockyards and processing plants the cattle would become steaks for meat-hungry Easterners. Americans now ate Texas red meat with their Minnesota white bread.

The workers in the cattle industry were quite special. Like the mountain men before them, the cowboys were colorful individuals. They did hard, dangerous, and often lonely work. Night and day, rain and shine, the cowboys ran risks from stampedes or accidents. For this grueling work, they received only small wages.

Yet, the cowboys work was done outdoors. The work constantly tested the cowboy. This work also allowed him to have individual freedom. There was no assembly-line method for roping a steer. Thousands of cowboys, Black and White, preferred their tough and carefree life to any other. In modern times, movies and television have made the cowboy—in his picturesque "ten-gallon" hat, chaps, and boots—as a symbol of honor and freedom.

However, the heyday of the cattle kingdom was short. The free-grazing lands became overcrowded. Owners were forced to move northward. But there, winter blizzards could wipe out herds left in the open all year. Soon ranchers realized that they would need to buy and fence land, build barns, buy feed, and take good care of their stock. This required capital. So, millionaires and corporations began to appear as important ranch owners in the cattle country. By 1910, even for those ranchers whose holdings were not large, ranching was basically a business. It still had some of the color of cowboy days, but it was clearly part of an industrial process for mass producing meat.

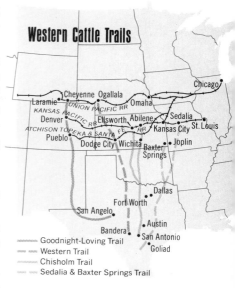

Oklahoma cowboys pause during a roundup in the 1890s.

The Growth of the Mining Industry

The mining frontier also gave way to a businesslike scene. The earliest miners in 1849 in California could work with simple tools like picks, shovels, and washbasins. A prospector who made a lucky find could become rich overnight. For this reason, new gold and silver discoveries always attracted hordes of footloose individuals with large hopes and small amounts of money for equipment. Each gold or silver "strike" pulled thousands to the new "diggings." Up to the end of the century, news of a "strike" started a rush. Thousands would be off to the Black Hills of South Dakota; to Denver or Leadville in Colorado; to Virginia City, Nevada; and even to Alaska in 1897.

However, it was soon necessary to go deeper into the earth for gold and silver. Mining was not only done for precious metals alone. Lead, copper, and other basic industrial metals were also dug out of the Western earth. To get at them, thousands of feet of shafts and tunnels had to be dug like honeycombs in the hearts of mountains. They had to be braced with timber and ventilated by machine-driven fans. In addition, the metals deeper in the earth were more firmly embedded in rocks or ores. *Smelters*—places that refined ore—were great factories for crushing and chemically treating these ores in order to extract their valuable contents. The costly processes of modern mining and refining gradually brought large corporations into this field and began to crowd out the lone-wolf types.

So the mining town—such as Lead, South Dakota; or Denver, Colorado; or Butte, Montana; or Bisbee, Arizona; or Boise, Idaho—became a part of the new western scene. Around these towns, the mountains still stood in purple majesty. Yet, in the streets, there was ugliness. Piles of *slag*—discarded rock—were visible. So were chim-

The Homestake Mine in Lead, South Dakota, photographed here in 1900, was one of the largest gold mines in the world. South Dakota led the nation in gold production after 1920.

neys that belched unpleasant-smelling smoke into the air. So were streams, discolored by refinery waste materials that were poured carelessly into them. So were ugly shacks in which the underpaid, hard-working miners lived. To improve their conditions, though, the miners soon formed unions and conducted strikes. Labor struggles became especially sharp in mining towns, where frontier violence was still a tradition. The result of producing copper, lead, iron, and precious metals for the new industrial and banking world was the creation of a West far different from the one that Lewis and Clark had gazed upon.

By the last years of the nineteenth century, people were beginning to realize how fast the West was changing. They worried about it for many reasons. If the West vanished, the American character, which was formed in a day of open land, might change.

The Beginnings of Conservation

Some far-sighted lawmakers began to worry that we might be using our natural resources so rapidly that they would disappear in a short time. So they pressed for national action to reserve oil and timberlands, to dam streams so that floods did not wash away good soil, and to do other things to manage the country's natural wealth. These were the founders of the *conservation* movement. Individuals and groups who simply wanted to save the great beauty of the American land for the future worked hand in hand with them.

Even before the 1890s, conservationists began to win some victories. Yellowstone National Park was created in March 1872. In 1890, Yosemite National Park was authorized by Congress. Thereafter, Presidents such as Theodore Roosevelt fought for and obtained the right to *set aside*—that is, keep from settlement or unrestricted commercial use—millions of acres of forest land. During Roosevelt's two terms of office, the number of national parks doubled. And in 1916, the National Park Service was created to operate these parks.

While conservationists worked at preserving the West, tourists came out in increasing numbers to look in awe at its marvels. The Grand Canyon and the auto were two wonders—one natural, the other manufactured. Could they live together?

As the frontier West disappeared, the imaginary West became more popular in books and on the stage. After about 1910, these were even popularized on movie screens. In the 1890s a popular entertainment was "Buffalo Bill's Wild West Show." Buffalo Bill was the nickname of William F. Cody. He had been an army scout and had taken care of horses for a freight-wagon company. He had served as a deadly buffalo hunter, providing meat for railway work gangs. A

Manufacturing, formerly scorned as unsuitable for a Southern gentleman, was recognized as a profitable investment around the turn of the century. This Birmingham, Alabama, tin factory employed thousands.

friend of his wrote a play called *Scouts of the Prairies*. Bill starred in it and liked it so much that he went into show business himself. He and his friends did roping, riding, and shooting tricks for cheering audiences.

Industry Begins to Build a New South

The hand of industry reached into the South to change its ways, too. After 1877, Southern leaders began to blame their section's poverty on the fact that they were too dependent on the cotton crop for wealth. They also felt that they were paying too much to Northern manufacturers for goods made from Southern raw materials. In the 1880s, a Southern editor, Henry W. Grady, used to make a speech about a Southern funeral that was held in a forest of pine trees near

TO MY OLD MASTER, COLONEL P. H. ANDERSON,

Big Spring, Tennessee. Sir: I got your letter, and was glad to find that you had not forgotten Jourdon, and that you wanted me to come back and live with you again, promising to do better for me than anybody else can. I have often felt uneasy about you. I thought the Yankees would have hung you long before this, for harboring Rebs they found at your house. I suppose they never heard about your going to Colonel Martin's to kill the Union soldier that was left by his company in their stable. Although you shot at me twice before I left you, I did not want to hear of your being hurt, and am glad you are still living. It would do me good to go back to the dear old home again, and see Miss Mary and Miss Martha and Allen, Esther, Green, and Lee. Give my love to them all, and tell them I hope we will meet in the better world, if not in this. I would have gone back to see you all when I was working in the Nashville Hospital, but one of the neighbors told me that Henry intended to shoot me if he ever got a chance. . . .

As to my freedom, which you say I can have, there is nothing to be gained on that score, as I got my free papers in 1864 from the Provost-Marshal-General of the Department of Nashville. Mandy says she would be afraid to go back without some proof that you were disposed to treat us justly and kindly; and we have concluded to test your sincerity by asking you to send us our wages for the time we served you. This will make us forget and forgive old scores, and rely on your justice and friendship in the future. I served you faithfully for thirty-two years, and Mandy twenty years. At twenty-five dollars a month for me, and two dollars a week for Mandy, our earnings would amount to eleven thousand six hundred and eighty dollars. Add to this the interest for the time our wages have been kept back, and deduct what you paid for our clothing, and three doctor's visits to me, and pulling a tooth for Mandy, and the balance will show what we are in justice entitled to. Please send the money by Adam's Express, in care of V. Winters, Esq., Dayton, Ohio. If you fail to pay us for faithful labors in the past, we can have little faith in your promises in the future. We trust the good Maker has opened your eyes to the wrongs which you and your fathers have done to me and my fathers, in making us toil for you for generations without recompense. Here I draw my wages every Saturday night; but in Tennessee there was never any pay-day for the Negroes any more than for the horses and cows. Surely there will be a day of reckoning for those who defraud the laborer of his hire. . . .

Say howdy to George Carter, and thank him for taking the pistol from you when you were shooting at me.

From your old servant,
Jourdon Anderson

iron deposits and good pasture land for sheep and cattle. The man, said Grady, was buried in a pine coffin from Cincinnati put together with nails made in Pittsburgh. He wore a coat from New York, shirt and pants from Chicago, and shoes from Boston. The South furnished nothing but the corpse and the hole in the ground.

People like Grady argued that the South should encourage the growth of industries. Southern factories would provide jobs for Southern workers. Their labor forces would eat food grown on Southern farms. The taxes their owners paid would build better schools and roads. The South would prosper like the thriving North.

Up to 1860, this argument had been rejected by Southern planters. But those in command of the "new South" were leading in a new direction. They encouraged factory and railroad-building, mining, lumbering, and steelmaking. Cigarette manufacturing became a major Southern industry. The number of cotton spinning and weaving mills in the Carolinas surged upward. By the turn of the century, Birmingham, Alabama—founded only in 1871—had become the "Pittsburgh of the South." And in Florida, Louisiana, and the Gulf States, Southerners worked at producing coal, oil, lumber, and other industrial products. The main cities in the South proudly held industrial fairs. They boasted of their electric lights, streetcars, and fine homes. Their newspapers no longer sneered at money-grubbing Yankees who lacked the grace of Dixieland. Instead, they crowed over the hustling spirit of Southern business people.

The South of slavery, religious revivals, Confederate flags, and mountain feuds became a land where factories were familiar. However, the expected prosperity did not come. Most major industries still remained outside the South or were owned by Northern business people. Moreover, in order to lure industrial capital southward, Southern states kept taxes low. They also encouraged the use of poorly paid labor of all ages and both sexes. Their police officials often helped employers to chase away organizers of labor unions, a practice not restricted to the South. Blacks, a big share of the Southern populace, got a tiny share of factory jobs.

The new South welcomed economic change. However, it remained conservative about social change. Thus, the South remained a section of special problems, even as it blended into the industrial environment.

Questions for Discussion

1. Define *smelters, slag, conservation.*
2. How did the destruction of the great buffalo herds affect the Plains Indians?
3. In what ways were the purposes of the Homestead and Dawes Acts similiar?
4. Why did both farming and ranching tend to become "big business"?
5. How was the West changed by the revolution in farming, ranching, and mining?
6. Why did industrialization fail to bring prosperity to the South?

Chapter 17 Review

Summary Questions for Discussion

1. What did Walt Whitman mean when he called America's inventions her pyramids?
2. How do John D. Rockefeller and Andrew Carnegie serve as examples of captains of industry?
3. What geographical advantages helped the United States become an industrial giant?
4. What was the role of the growth of railroads in industrialization? in the revolution in communications?
5. What were the results of the age of mass production?
6. What were the steps in the destruction of the Plains Indians?
7. What was the Dawes Act? How did the Indians react to it?
8. What was the Homestead Act? What were its effects?
9. Besides settlers, who else shared in the takeover of the public domain?
10. What advances and machines allowed for the revolution in agriculture?
11. How did the cattle industry use both technology and natural resources after the Civil War?
12. Why did the cowboy become a folk hero?
13. How and why did mining change from small to big business?
14. What were the goals of the founders of the conservation movement?
15. Even with industrialization, why did the South remain with special problems?

Word Study

Fill in each blank in the sentences that follow with the term below that is most appropriate.

industrialization   lubricants   slag   smelters   conservation

1. Great factories were built as _____ for refining ore.
2. Outside in the streets, ugly piles of _____ and discarded rock remained.
3. Machines ran smoother with _____.
4. The attempt by many people to preserve natural resources resulted in the founding of the _____ movement.

Using Your Skills

1. Compare the pictures in this chapter with those in Chapter 12. Then, using the pictures alone as evidence, comment on the following generalization: The industrial development that took place in the United States between 1865 and 1914 differs very little from the industrial development that took place in the United States between 1800 and 1860.

2. Study the maps that appear in this chapter. How does the map of transcontinental railroads help to explain why the era of the great drives on the Western cattle trails was so short-lived? How does it help to explain why the Indians who lived in the part of the United States shown on page 405 ceded more and more of their land to the government and were forced into reservations?

Graph Study

Why did steel, oil, and coal become the building blocks of modern industry? Look at the graph on page 396. If growth had remained constant, what would have been the figures for 1980?

CHAPTER 18

A Nation
of
Cities

In 1860, only one American in four lived in a place with a population of more than 2500. By 1910, the number of Americans living in cities increased to four out of every nine. By 1980, this figure had grown to seven out of ten. Most of these *urbanites* (city dwellers) lived in great metropolitan centers or their *suburbs*—little communities on the big town's outskirts.

The growth of a village of a few hundred people into a community of many thousands of families caused great changes in social behavior. Politically, for example, voters no longer had personal contact with every candidate. Therefore, they tended to vote more by party label than by "shopping" among office seekers. Economically, cities depended heavily on new inventions and gigantic construction projects to feed, house, and transport thousands of people each day. That meant a steady rise in the complexity and cost of local government. It spelled a need for more experts in office and for higher taxes.

However, a great bridge, power plant, or subway tunnel was more than a high-priced piece of engineering. It was a monument to human skills, as much as a cathedral or a pyramid. And a crowded city was more than population figures. Rather, it was a mixing bowl of many peoples with many different lifestyles. Despite its problems, metropolitan America was, and is, a great achievement of many different human beings working together.

READING GUIDE

1. **What attempts were made to make the growing cities healthy and safe places to live?**
2. **How did the lives of the poor, the middle class, and the wealthy differ?**
3. **How were education and culture affected by industrialization?**

A 1913 street scene—noisy crowds, rickety tenements, and a traffic jam.

1. Building the Modern Metropolis

The successful rise of the modern city was proof that people can sometimes use applied scientific knowledge to solve particular social problems. A growing urban population had to be housed within a fairly small area. A city of over a million people, such as Chicago in 1890, had a population equal to one-fourth of the whole United States in 1790! One way of housing a growing population was to expand upward—to stack people on top of each other in their homes and at their jobs.

So the *tenement* house was born. This was a dwelling that contained apartments for many families. A tenement building need not be unpleasant. Yet, in fast-growing cities in the late nineteenth century, profit-hungry builders were allowed to put up buildings several stories high on very small lots. This left no space between tenements for light and air. In addition, nothing stopped greedy landlords from putting many large families on each floor and providing only one water tap or one bathroom for all of them. The reporter and photographer Jacob Riis found 192 adults and children in one single New York tenement house! Dirt collected and disease bred in the narrow, dark, stuffy hallways. The danger of fire was great. Many cruel disasters encouraged some cities to pass laws to try to improve tenement-house conditions. However good or bad, the many-storied dwelling became a part of the urban scene.

In the 1880s, another important development took place. Architects learned how to construct a building around a steel framework

A print of the fireworks display that highlighted the opening of the Brooklyn Bridge on May 24, 1883.

that could rise to dizzying heights. Such "skyscrapers" appeared in Chicago as early as 1885. The Flatiron Building in New York, twenty stories high, was completed in 1902. At that time, it was the wonder of the city.

However, skyscrapers were too costly to be used profitably for housing. So they rose in the business districts and were used as offices. These skyscrapers depended on other inventions, too, such as electric elevators and powerful water pumps. Thanks to these developments, thousands of office workers did something miraculous as an everyday, unnoticed occurrence. They performed their jobs one-tenth of a mile or more straight up in the air!

Urban Transportation and Essential Services

Nineteenth-century engineers used steel, electricity, and steam to conquer great distances, as was the case with the Atlantic cable and the transcontinental railroad. They also employed the same resources to permit quick, safe movement of many thousands of people on short, frequent journeys to and from work.

For example, in 1883, the Brooklyn Bridge was completed. It was an iron bridge that hung from great towers by cables of twisted wire. this was the best and most secure kind of bridge yet made for handling floods of heavy traffic, while leaving room underneath for passing ships. The bridge was built by two great engineers, German-born John A. Roebling and his son, Washington Roebling. The father was killed and the son crippled in accidents that occurred during its construction. Today, the Brooklyn Bridge still stands and carries cars and trucks instead of horse-drawn wagons. It stands as a memorial to the Roeblings.

Another example of nineteenth-century engineering was the elevated railroad, or "el." The elevated railroad was first built in New York City in 1867. It was considered a fine invention, except by those underneath who were showered with cinders from its smokestacks. However, a solution to that problem came after 1888. In that year, in Richmond, Virginia, an inventor showed a practical way of running electrically powered cars over tracks in the street. By 1903, New York had converted its "el" to electric power. Like hundreds of other cities, New York also had fleets of electric street cars.

Besides reaching for the heavens, urbanites also dug down into the earth to make their new kind of life more efficient. First, engineers in big cities had to dig beneath the surface level to find space for the huge tunnels necessary to bring water to thousands of people and carry away waste products. Soon, it became clear that underground electric cables were necessary. With these cables, forests of poles and wires carrying current for telephones and electric lighting systems could be

Built in 1902, the Flatiron Building in New York was one of the country's first skyscrapers.

415

New York's Third Avenue "el," or elevated railroad, around 1880.

Sewer construction in Savannah, Georgia.

Below: A victim of urban poverty, this boy picks through a garbage can in search of valuables.

avoided. Poles with live wires were found to be very dangerous when knocked over by storms.

Soon, pipes for carrying steam and gas for cooking became part of the world beneath the streets, as well. New York went so far as to put a whole transportation network below ground. A private company completed the city's first subway system in 1904.

The Need for Urban Planning

In the early history of the United States, the growth of some towns had been planned. Puritan villages had grown in a pattern controlled by leaders of those close-knit communities. And Congress had hired Pierre L'Enfant to prepare a design for Washington, D.C. But the fast-growing industrial cities of the late nineteenth century were different. They had no single group of people with the power or wish to lay out a model city. Thus, the result was often disorderly, ugly urban areas where factories, cheap housing, stores, telephone poles, and car tracks were jammed into every inch of available space.

Nevertheless, there were some attempts made to change this picture. Several kinds of urban planning programs emerged. Some cities enacted laws that *zoned* their land, requiring factories and homes to be built in separate areas. Cities also provided *building codes*. Such laws were not always well enforced, but they were a beginning toward some regulation.

In addition, cities and corporations put up buildings for public use. These buildings were designed to lift spirits and express the outlook of the era. One example was the lofty Pennsylvania Railroad terminal in New York City. Its great interior spaces and steel columns honored the power of the railroads and industry in much the same way that a royal palace glorified a prince.

Finally, some cities even tackled the job of saving open space for recreation in natural surroundings. In the 1850s, for example, New York planned a "central park" in the middle of Manhattan. The task of design was given to a talented landscape architect, Frederick L. Olmsted, who, one observer said, "paints with lakes and wooded slopes." Olmsted tried to lay out a park that would give city dwellers "pleasurable and soothing relief" from buildings. Its many acres of ponds, hills, trees, and rocks still do exactly that. Among Olmsted's other accomplishments are the grounds of the nation's capitol, the park systems of Louisville, Boston, and Hartford, Belle Isle Park in Detroit, Prospect Park in Brooklyn, and the grounds of the University of California.

There were two parts to the new science of city planning. On the one hand, it aimed to make cities beautiful. On the other, city planners tried to foresee and provide for a city's future needs in housing and *public utilities*, such as mass transportation, power, and light.

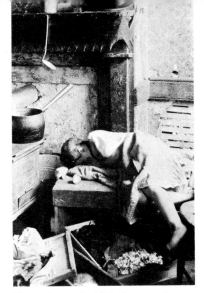

The exhausted child above rests after making artificial flowers. Photographer Lewis Hine urged child labor laws by concentrating on the plight of tenement children.

Questions for Discussion

1. Define *tenement, zoned, building codes, public utilities*.
2. What technological developments made tenement housing and skyscrapers possible?
3. What were the early attempts to solve the problems of transportation into the cities and within the cities themselves?
4. Why did industrialization lead to a need for urban planning?

2. The Gulf Between the Rich and the Poor

The city gave its inhabitants many varieties of life. Some of these scenes were educational and amusing. However, others were deeply shocking. For the city made the gap between the rich and the poor more visible than it had ever been in America. In Chicago, for example, there was a slum neighborhood known as the "Sands." It was in existence before the Great Fire of 1871. It was full of garbage heaps, saloons, and dark alleys where robbers lurked. Neglected and dirty children begged or wandered the streets. Old buildings where people lived were "damp, dark, ill-ventilated and had vermin-infested underground rooms" Yet, not far from the Sands was a stretch of Lake Michigan shorefront later known as the Gold Coast. Along its clean, well-lighted streets stood mansions such as that of Cyrus McCormick, the great reaper manufacturer. In the many rooms of these homes,

Jacob Riis, a Danish immigrant, was among the first to document life among the poor with photographs. He hoped that when Americans actually saw the miserable living conditions in a city slum, they would demand that something be done about it. His photographs, like the one above of an immigrant family in 1910, did much to stir the conscience of the nation.

servants carried out the wishes of people who surrounded themselves with fine furniture and priceless works of art. Every big city had—and still has—such contrasting districts.

In 1888, a book entitled *Looking Backward* by Edward Bellamy was published. Its hero falls into a deep sleep and awakens in the year 2000 to find a perfect world of equality and justice. In describing the society of his own time, he compared it to a coach. The masses of humanity dragged this coach, he says, up a hilly, sandy road. Their backs ached, their feet bled, they choked with dust. But hunger drove them on. A few fortunate people sat on top of the coach. In the city, those who pulled the coach and those who rode it were within easy view of each other.

The Urban Poor

The life of the urban poor was described by an immigrant, who used another grim image: "My people do not live in America. They live underneath America. America goes on over their heads." The sweatshop worker, the street vendor, and the unemployed clerk or factory hand all lived at a standard far below that of more well-to-do Americans. At least a poor family in a rural area had some homegrown

In the nineteenth century, wealthy families often commissioned grand family portraits. The William Astor family (above) struck a "casual" pose in formal dress for this 1875 portrait painted in their Fifth Avenue mansion. Not very many families could afford to keep up with the Astors.

food and the air and sunlight of the outdoors. Unfortunately, the slum dwellers and their children had neither. The child sleeping in the crowded tenement probably was one of the those of whom Jacob Riis wrote. Their "lullaby" was the squeak of the pump in the hall, the only source of water for many families. Deprived of proper air and nourishment, thousands fell victim to diseases such as tuberculosis, which affects the lungs. In fact, entire neighborhoods were known as "lung blocks." Rats and roaches carried other germs, which killed many young children before they reached school age.

The little boys and girls who did survive often had duties that cut their childhood brutally short. They took care of infant brothers and sisters, while both parents went in search of work. Or the children found jobs or sold flowers, matches, or other small items from sidewalk stands. They also delivered newspapers or shined shoes in order to add to the small family income. Whatever playtime they had, these children spent in the streets.

In the early 1900s, many brave men and women in slums held their families together and survived. Many tough-spirited youngsters rose from such an environment to success. But the discouragements were huge. Thousands were tempted to turn to alcohol or to crime in search

Beginning in 1884, the upper crust of Chicago society flocked to the annual running of the Derby. Held at an exclusive racing club, Washington Park, the event became far more social than sporting. The year of the painting above—1893—was also the year of the Columbian Exposition in Chicago, celebrating the 400th anniversary of Columbus' discovery of America. The elegant couple at the far lower right are spending an evening at an expensive New York cafe in 1905.

of some escape from the brutal facts of existence. A life of poverty was a grim training school. Its overall cost to society, because of the sickness and waste of life it created, was far too high.

The Pleasures of the Rich

The rich lived with a special glitter. Their money bought a great deal in the early twentieth century, when prices were low and taxes were light. So even millionaires who gave freely to charity had plenty left to spend on themselves. For example, they might live in seventy-two room mansions like that of banker Jay Cooke. They might travel by private railroad car or even own yachts, like J. P. Morgan's *Corsair*. The amusements of the very rich included the theater, the opera, driving, hunting, and occasionally gambling at the race track. Their meals were eight- or ten-course feasts that included soup, fish, poultry, roasts, vegetables, fruits, cheeses, puddings, cakes, and ice cream. And their children were educated at private schools or by tutors at home.

In 1873, the novelist Mark Twain, with Charles Dudley Warner,

wrote a book about such extravagance. The book is called *The Gilded Age*. In his book *Theory of the Leisure Class* (1899), a famous social scientist, Thorstein Veblen, referred to such spending as "conspicuous consumption." The meaning of this term is illustrated by the custom, called a *potlatch*, of some Pacific Coast Indians. A potlatch is a feast. At its end, the host gives away or else destroys as many valuable things as possible. This shows the guests how rich the host is. For America's wealthy classes, the period from 1870 to 1914 might be described as the "Age of the Big Potlatch."

The Growing Middle Class

The greatest number of urban Americans, however, did not live in slums or in mansions. They were members of the middle class. It is hard to say exactly who belonged to this class. The term *middle class* refers to those who are neither rich nor poor. In fact, this is the way most people think of themselves. It also has something to do with the ways one makes a living. People were apt to think of **white-collar workers** as middle class no matter what their income. However,

well-paid **blue-collar workers** living in spacious city apartments or in small houses in a factory town were members of the middle class as well.

Professionals and business people, such as doctors, store owners, and managers, set the basic tone of urban middle-class America. Some historians refer to them as the upper-middle class. They refer to low-paid white-collar workers and skilled industrial blue-collar workers as the lower-middle class. Around 1900 and thereafter, sizeable numbers of families of the upper-middle class, seeking space and cleanliness, began to move from cities into the suburbs.

Their homes were neat and roomy but not as grand as those of the rich. They kept the grounds outside neatly trimmed. Inside, there might be water colors painted by members of the family, a piano, and many lamps, rugs, small statues, and travel souvenirs.

Members of the middle class were extremely serious about doing socially approved things in order to set a proper example for others. Lower middle-class members worked especially hard at this. Since they did not have much money, they had to show by their behavior that they were not like the poor.

Middle-class citizens amused themselves in various ways. They might patronize the minstrel shows or the music hall but rarely attended the "highbrow" opera or ballet. Both the upper and lower middle-class members enjoyed professional baseball and outdoor excursions in the park or at the county fair. However, they avoided horse races. The well-off middle-class household had volumes of Shakespeare and the Bible on its bookshelves. But most of the family members did their major reading in the daily newspapers.

Middle-class Americans were proud of modern progress, especially that of the electric lights and the telephone. They took pride in their country and their religion. They were kindly, but had little room for understanding other lands, other cultures, and other classes. They belonged to an age when improvements in life seemed natural and expected, and problems were thought of as small and few.

A family picnic on a crowded New York beach around 1920.

Questions for Discussion

1. Define *white-collar worker*, *blue-collar worker*.
2. What did Thorstein Veblen mean by "conspicuous consumption"?
3. Who set the style of middle-class urban American life in the late nineteenth and early twentieth centuries? Why?

3. Popular Education

Although there were still limitations on free public education in the late 1800s, Americans took schooling seriously. Between 1870 and 1910, enrollments in public schools increased 240 percent. High school and college enrollments made similar gains. By 1900, most states and territories had followed Massachusetts' lead and had minimum attend-

422

ance requirements. However, many of these laws were very lenient and rarely enforced.

Before the Civil War, the spread of public education was linked to the need for an educated electorate. And after the war, the growth of cities, industrial expansion, and economic developments made the need for education even stronger.

Schools changed not only in quantity but also in quality. In the past, emphasis had been placed on memorizing and drill. With the aid of a paddle, children learned reading, writing, and arithmetic in their early years. Those who went on to high school took such courses as Latin, mathematics, and philosophy. But new ideas about the purpose and process of education were filtering into the schools.

John Dewey was one of the leading educational philosophers of the era. He felt that schools were an instrument of social reform. Students should be trained to channel their energy in a useful way. Only by doing and experiencing could children really learn.

Colonel Francis Parker, another reformer, insisted that classrooms should be free of rigid discipline. He, too, stressed active student participation. In addition, he introduced more geography and science into the elementary curriculum.

From Germany came the idea of kindergarten. In 1860, Elizabeth Peabody established the first English-speaking kindergarten in the United States. In 1873, the first public school kindergarten was established in St. Louis, Missouri.

Major changes, incorporating some of the new educational philosophies, were made in high school curriculums. A wide·variety of vocational courses was introduced. The job of training youngsters for a trade was now being performed by the public schools.

As discussed earlier, practical education on the college level was encouraged by the Morrill Land Grant Act of 1862. Land was set aside in each state to help finance agricultural and technical colleges. Within ten years, several states had established land-grant colleges.

Other colleges received the benefits of private **philanthropy**. Cornell University was financed through the land-grant system as well as by a hefty donation from Ezra Cornell, who made his fortune in the Western Union Telegraph Company. Two railroad tycoons endowed Vanderbilt University and Stanford University. The University of Chicago received millions from John D. Rockefeller, while the Carnegie Institute of Technology bore the name of its **benefactor.**

At Cornell University, the successful policy of admitting women did little to influence other schools in the Northeast, which admitted men only. Vassar, Smith, and Wellesley were established as independent colleges for women. Radcliffe and Barnard were set up as women's schools affiliated with male institutions, Harvard and Columbia.

An editor of a New York newspaper bicycling with his family through their neighborhood in 1891.

philanthropy
an active effort to promote human welfare

benefactor
one who gives a gift or charitable donation

423

As the needs of society changed, substantial reforms were made in college and university education. Before the Civil War, Greek and Latin studies were stressed. Then Charles W. Eliot, president of Harvard, introduced a more flexible curriculum. Students were given a wide variety of courses to choose from. Eliot also strengthened the requirements for professional study in law and medicine.

Literature

In the fifty years after the Civil War, literature mirrored the changes in society in various ways. In a time before television, movies, and radio, some books were simply meant to entertain, or to teach the lessons that society believed to be important. *"Dime novels,"* full of cowboy-and-Indian adventures, thrilled thousands of young readers, and, of course, justified the conquest of the West. In the novels of Horatio Alger, such as *Pluck and Luck* or *Ragged Dick*, some poor boy of good character, eager to work hard, turned a lucky break into a successful career. *Little Women*, by Louisa May Alcott, brought tears and smiles as it depicted a family with few worldly goods, but rich in love for each other and charitable deeds.

Walt Whitman, sometimes referred to as the "Good Gray Poet." In his poetry, Whitman praised the uniqueness of the individual while at the same time celebrating his own identity.

However, not all literature was "escapist." Surprisingly, few books touched on the issues of the Civil War or Reconstruction. Yet some of the wartime poetry of Walt Whitman celebrated the Union cause. Whitman's "O Captain, My Captain" was written as an ode to Lincoln after his death. Albion W. Tourgee, a Union officer and carpetbagger, wrote *A Fool's Errand*, praising the attempt to remake the South. He concluded, however, that for Blacks and Whites alike, the attempt proved fruitless. On the Southern side, Sidney Lanier wrote poetry praising the traditions of the region and the courage of his people. Later, Thomas Nelson Page, in such books as *In Ole Virginia*, furnished romantic tales of "good old times before the war." This went back to popular, sentimental, and anti-Black themes.

More and more after 1880, however, there was a tendency toward *realism*, which simply meant writing about everyday people in true-to-life situations. William Dean Howells, one of the noted realists, dealt with middle-class American families facing the changes brought on by industrialism and urbanization. His best-known work, *The Rise of Silas Lapham*, is about a likeable New Englander who has made money in business and tries to learn the rules of getting along in "high society." He is finally tempted by a crooked deal and turns it down, but not without some serious internal debate and family discussion.

Another form of realism was the *local color* movement. Stories in this movement depicted the special flavors and styles and *dialects* (speech patterns) of the old regional cultures that railroads, telegraphs, factories, and cities were wiping out. In New England, Sarah

Orne Jewett wrote stories of fisherfolk, farmers, widows, and other people struggling against declining opportunities. Some are in her book *The Country of the Pointed Firs*. In the South, George W. Cable composed beautiful stories of life in Louisiana. They were full of haunting echoes of a disappearing past touched by French and West Indian influences. His stories often contained themes that centered around family secrets linking the lives of Blacks and Whites. *Old Creole Days* is one of Cable's best-known collections.

Joel Chandler Harris, a White Georgian, is best remembered for his "Uncle Remus" stories. In them, he popularized Black folk tales from slavery days told to him by ex-slaves. He apparently was unaware of the hidden theme of rebelliousness in some of them. Paul Dunbar, the son of former slaves, also concentrated on "folk" literature. *Oak and Ivy* and *Majors and Minors* were two volumes of verse that brought him public notice.

In the Far West, Bret Harte wrote humorous stories of life in the hard-bitten California mining camps. They, too, were not offensive—rough miners appeared to have hearts of gold as well as pockets full of it—but they did have a tang of earthy American speech about them.

Around 1900, a few American writers adopted the style called *naturalism*. Naturalism is writing in which individuals are shown as subject to great biological or mechanical forces. Sometimes they are victims, sometimes masters, and sometimes neither. In Frank Norris's *The Octopus*, the railroad is the great "beast" whose tentacles economically crush helpless farmers. In Stephen Crane's *The Red Badge of Courage*, the hero is a Union private who runs away at his first taste of combat, but later returns to his unit and fights bravely. The "moral" is not the goodness of the cause, but that we must find courage within ourselves to deal with life as a never-ending struggle. This struggle is one in which we often do not know where we are fighting or exactly for what reason. Theodore Dreiser, in *Sister Carrie*, *The Titan*, and other novels, wrote of life in the big cities as a brutalizing struggle against poverty and greed. Winners and losers alike were as helpless to determine their fates as fish eating each other in a pond struggling to survive.

The very greatest writers, of course, combine elements of many styles with their own talent. Samuel Clemens, better known as Mark Twain, is one of the most important of these writers. His *Huckleberry Finn* is a classic that is realistic, romantic, full of local color, and even—almost to the end—a bit naturalistic. It touches on slavery and the hypocrisy with which it was protected. *Huckleberry Finn* focuses on how a vagabond White boy and a Black man become friends as "outsiders" but are always being parted by society. The book also centers on the dilemma of behaving easily and naturally as against

Samuel Clemens, better known as Mark Twain. Novelist and humorist, Twain, at his best, raised the lusty humor of the American frontier to a level of universal human appeal.

being "civilized." And as Huck and the runaway slave, Jim, float down the Mississippi, they meet a colorful array of characters from a fading Southern frontier society. These characters are always, in one way or another, trying to get a hold on Huck and Jim.

Henry James is another special case. His novels, such as *The Ambassadors*, *The Portrait of a Lady*, and *The Wings of the Dove*, deal with rich people, usually Americans in Europe (where James chose to live most of his adult life). The Americans are fascinated by the deep and complicated past that is reflected in European art and manners. But they find that it clashes with their own optimism, energy, and worship of freedom. On the other hand, the Europeans admire American vitality but feel that, without producing styles of art, belief, and behavior like those of older civilizations, American society may fall into mere worship of wealth and so decay. Or, at least, they think that American society offers little to help men and women deal with tragedy and complications in life. James expressed this meeting of old and new in rich, long, and subtle sentences full of symbols.

Therefore, in the long run, industrialism was a help to American literature. Industrialism made it possible for millions to read about their lives and their culture. And it furnished themes and issues from which other writers created a varied and rich diet of books—and more and more people, as the years went by, were sitting down to the feast.

Adult Education

A combination of interest in education and literature led to the flourishing of public libraries. Andrew Carnegie provided a major incentive. He offered to pay for the construction of libraries in towns and cities that would maintain them. In nearly forty years, he was responsible for the building of over 2500 libraries. Melvil Dewey then established the Dewey Decimal system of book classification, the American Library Association, and the first school of library science.

Newspapers also gained in popularity as the literacy rate improved. Joseph Pulitzer, a Jewish immigrant from Hungary, bought the St. Louis *Dispatch* and the *Post* in 1878. He combined the two papers soon afterwards as the St. Louis *Post-Dispatch*. This publication was to become one of the most influential news organs in the United States.

In 1883, Pulitzer added the New York *World* to his collection of newspapers. By playing up sensational journalism—a style characterized by large, screaming headlines, comic strips, and crime stories—Pulitzer turned the *World* into a profitable journal. By 1887, Pulitzer established the *Evening World*.

Publication of the *World* began with the sole intention of selling newspapers. In the years that followed, however, it established itself

NELLIE BLY

One of the first working women to make a name for herself in American public life was a Pennsylvanian named Elizabeth Cochrane. As a youngster, she showed a talent for writing. She did some articles for a hometown paper, and then, early in the 1880s, talked her way into a job on Joseph Pulitzer's lively *New York World*. She used as her pen name "Nellie Bly," after a sentimental song by Stephen Foster. But there was nothing flowery about Nellie. Her specialty was what we now would call "investigative journalism," done the hard way, from the inside. She would pretend to be insane and get herself locked up in an asylum. Then, when she was later released, she could expose conditions on the inside. She would pretend to be a shoplifter and get arrested. Afterwards she could tell Pulitzer's readers how badly New York's police treated women accused of crimes. Or she would assume a false identity and try to bribe a state lawmaker—and then show, on the front page, how sadly easy it sometimes was to bribe a lawmaker! Her most celebrated "stunt", involved a travel adventure. In 1887, Jules Verne's *Around the World in Eighty Days* had just been published. With the *World* steadily featuring her stories en route, Nellie (using only commercial transportation) did the trip in a few days less than it took Verne's fictional hero, Phineas Fogg. Later, Nellie retired from journalism to marry a man named Robert Seaman. When he died, she went back to reporting for a while in the 1920s. In 1922, she died, her journalistic triumphs forgotten.

as a responsible and politically independent paper of high standards.

Pulitzer was later responsible for the establishment of the Columbia School of Journalism in New York. He was also responsible for the Pulitzer Prizes, which have since been awarded annually for outstanding achievement in various literary categories.

Pulitzer's fiercest competitor, William Randolph Hearst, sought to outdo his rival in sensationalism. In short order, Hearst moved from a reporter's position with the New York *World* to become publisher of his father's *San Francisco Examiner* in 1887. In 1895, he purchased the New York *Morning Journal*. By lowering the price of the papers, encouraging more sensationalism, and running comic strips in color, Hearst boosted the circulation of the *Morning Journal*.

During the politically explosive years from 1896 to 1898, the *World* competed with William Randolph Hearst's *Evening Journal* in the area of sensational journalism. This form of sensationalism came to be known as *yellow journalism*. During those years, both papers contributed heavily to the public outcry for war against Spain.

In the years that followed, Hearst built a newspaper empire of over twenty papers. His publications were known for taking sides on controversial issues. Among them were reforms favoring an eight-hour day, and the popular election of United States senators.

In contrast, in 1896, Adolph Ochs bought *The New York Times*. He tried to win readership by developing comprehensive news coverage and a reputation for accuracy. Other American papers, such as the Baltimore *Sun* and the Chicago *Daily News*, rejected sensationalism also.

The newspaper industry capitalized on the technological progress of the era and on the methods of other industries. Improved newsprint, the Linotype machine, typewriters, telephones, and the telegraph all speeded up the news delivery process. Newspapers subscribed to news-gathering agencies like United Press and Associated Press. The newspaper industry eventually became big business, with the formation of newspaper chains owned or controlled by a few people.

When Congress lowered the postage rates on magazines, publishers met the public's increasing interest in magazines. Publishers introduced new magazines into a field previously dominated by the *Atlantic Monthly* and *Harpers*. Magazines of popular appeal, such as the *Ladies Home Journal, Cosmopolitan*, and the *Saturday Evening Post* were established. And political and social issues were treated in the *Nation*, the *Forum*, and the *Arena*.

The Chautauqua movement was another source of popular education and culture. Founded by the Reverend John H. Vincent and Lewis Miller, a manufacturer the Chautauqua movement was originally planned as a summer training program for Sunday-school teachers. Soon, more people were drawn to the programs presented in a large tent beside Lake Chautauqua in upper New York State. The movement became so popular that traveling Chautauqua speakers were soon bringing a week or two of learning to towns and villages throughout the country. Books and magazines were published to help people in self-education. Many early scholars, reformers, and politicians lectured at the Chautauquas. Later, lighter entertainment, such as music and humorists, was included. In fact, the Chautauquas were as welcome as the annual arrival of the traveling circus.

Questions for Discussion

1. Define *local color, yellow journalism, realism, naturalism.*
2. In what ways did education change in the late nineteenth and early twentieth centuries?
3. What were some of the subjects and themes of literature for this period?
4. How did the increased interest in education lead to the growth of libraries and to the publication of newspapers?
5. What were the Chautauquas?

Chapter 18 Review

Summary Questions for Discussion

1. What was good and bad about tenement housing?
2. How were steel, electricity, and steam used to conquer problems of transportation and communication?
3. What were the immediate and long-range purposes of urban planning?
4. Why was the gulf between the rich and poor more apparent in urban than in rural areas?
5. What did many of the urban poor do as a means of escape?
6. Describe the lifestyles of the urban rich.
7. Describe the values, amusements, and life-style of the middle class.
8. Around 1900, what prompted the movement of people to the suburbs?
9. How was public education viewed before and after the Civil War?
10. What was John Dewey's philosophy about education?
11. What changes were made in public education after the Civil War?
12. What topics were expressed in the post-Civil War literature?
13. What contributed to the growth of public libraries?
14. How did newspapers grow from merely news organs to swayers of public opinion? Include the roles of Joseph Pulitzer, William Randolph Hearst, and Arthur Ochs in your answer.
15. What contributed to the growth of the magazine industry?

Word Study

Fill in each blank in the sentences that follow with the term below that is most appropriate.

tenement   public utilities   blue-collar workers
building codes   white-collar workers   zoned

1. Small apartment buildings several stories high are called _____ houses.
2. Cities _____ their land, separating factories and homes.
3. Laws, or _____, were enacted requiring standards for construction.
4. Provisions were made for _____, or mass transportation, power, and light.
5. Manual laborers are classified as _____.
6. Office workers are classified as _____.

Using Your Skills

1. Look at the pictures of colonial cities such as Boston, Philadelphia, and Charleston in Chapter 4. Next, study the pictures of people and places in American cities that you found in this chapter. Then answer the following question, using only pictures as evidence. Were the cities of the late nineteenth and early twentieth centuries more like colonial cities of the 1700s or more like modern cities of the 1980s?
2. Construct a chart of personalities mentioned in this chapter who contributed to educational and literary advancements in the post-Civil War United States. Include their names, their work(s), their themes, or the effects of their actions.

CHAPTER 19

An Age
of Reform

On July 4, 1892, an exciting political convention met in Omaha, Nebraska. Its aim was to found a new national party. The delegates chosen to attend knew well that they had gathered on the anniversary of the birth of the United States as a free country. So, they deliberately adopted a *platform* (a statement of the goals and ideas of a political party), which they believed to be as revolutionary and as necessary as the Declaration of Independence. "We meet," it stated, "in the midst of a nation brought on the *verge* (edge) of moral, political and material ruin." The platform stated further that, "The fruits of the toil of millions are boldly stolen to build up colossal fortunes for a few." What had happened to produce such a platform full of angry accusations?

Those delegates at Omaha who were starting the People's Party, the *Populists*, had an answer. The nation had grown in wealth and productive power faster than it could handle the social problems created by this swift change. As one Populist writer expressed it, our science had gotten beyond our conscience.

Before the Civil War, the beginnings of industrialism had prodded the American conscience. The result was the formation of reform movements to make society more just. Then, with the coming of war, the slavery issue seemed to swallow all others. However, after 1865, a great spurt of industrialization and urbanization raised new and

READING GUIDE

1. **How did labor face the challenges of the new industrial age?**
2. **How did the cities combat corruption?**
3. **How were reform movements on the national level helped and hampered?**
4. **How did the farmers work for reform?**
5. **How were populism and progressivism reactions to the industrial boom?**

The power of big business was attacked in this 1889 cartoon by Joseph Keppler.

Above: Factories where workers toiled long hours for low wages under bad conditions were called sweatshops. This one employed men and women to make clothes. Above Right: This slum dweller is taking rags she has collected to a dealer who will pay her a few pennies.

difficult questions. Did a gigantic corporation—responsible for the economic health of a whole community—have the right to manage its "private" property without public regulation? How could there be equality among Americans when some were paupers and some multimillionaires? What was needed to provide government of the people, by the people, and for the people in the larger cities?

1. Labor Organizes

The march of industrial progress often left many people behind. Among these people were the laborers. In some ways, laborers were better off than their ancestors had been. Thanks to mass production, they ate better, dressed better, and had more physical comforts than the pioneers. Yet, the same mass-production system also created brutalizing working conditions.

Certain hard-driving manufacturers saw wages not as payment for the wealth created by the efforts of workers, but rather as a production cost. These manufacturers thought that wages, like all other production costs, must be cut to the bone in order to raise company profits. So, except in a few states that forbade such a practice, laborers worked twelve or fourteen hours a day. Even though the pace of work speeded up, pay was kept at rock-bottom levels. In addition, the growth of the railroad had put workers in every part of the country in competition with one another.

Women were paid less than men for the same work. And children were paid even less. As late as 1906, when some states already had passed laws prohibiting the employment of children under 14, nearly 2 million youngsters were still working for as little as twenty-five cents a day. A poet wrote, "We grind in our mills the bones of the little ones."

Finally, workers ran grave risks of industrial accidents and disease. They got tuberculosis in the foul air of sweatshops. They were slowly poisoned by chemical fumes, lost fingers and hands in unguarded machines, or were buried in collapsing mineshafts. It was clear that the worker was an unprotected soldier in a continual battle for survival.

These dangers were horribly illustrated by one episode that took place in New York City in 1911. The Triangle Waist Company, which occupied the top three floors of a ten-story building, caught fire. Its 500 screaming employees, mostly immigrant girls, tried to fight the blaze or flee. However, the single fire escape collapsed. Rotten water hoses burst. The company had spent nothing on safety equipment. So the girls, some burning like torches, flung themselves from the windows to the sidewalk far below. This disaster spurred the passage of laws requiring safe factories and providing for inspection and punishment of violators. Unfortunately, the laws came too late for 147 dead Triangle Waist Company victims.

Labor Leaders Seek Reform Through Unionization

Working men and women did not just wait for legislators to make things better. They organized to fight for their rights. Some joined unions, demanding better treatment and higher wages. Early unions were composed of workers in the same trade in the same city. Before the Civil War, some national unions were formed by uniting many such local groups into a single, nationwide body. Soon after 1865, labor leaders attempted a further step. They tried to link national unions together into a larger organization, "a union of unions." This large union would have as much power as huge corporations.

Right: Terence Powderly, head of the Knights of Labor, 1886. Left: New York City garment workers parade to recruit new members for their union.

In 1869, a garment worker, Uriah Stephens, founded a secret society—The Noble and Holy Order of the Knights of Labor. The union's secret rituals gave its members a sense of importance and shared responsibility. However, spreading the word about a society whose members were sworn to secrecy presented quite a problem. Terence V. Powderly succeeded Uriah Stephens as Grand Master Workman of the Knights in 1879. Within two years, the secrecy pact was abandoned, and the membership began to grow.

The Knights hoped to organize all working people in the United States. Unlike most unions, the Knights accepted Blacks. At the peak of its power, the union counted 70,000 Black members in segregated and integrated locals. Thus united, the Knights could demand political action to bring about fair play in industry through general reforms. The Knights favored such reforms as more free land for farmers and an increase in the supply of currency to make borrowing easier. Through such steps, the union thought that more Americans could go into business for themselves. The Knights even hoped to start their own factories. The workers in these factories would not be hired laborers slaving for capitalists. Instead, they would be craftspeople, cooperating in ownership and sharing the profits among themselves. These dreams of doing away with the wage system altogether ignored economic realities. The nation would not return to production in small shops and give up the efficiency of large-scale industry with a mass labor force of wage earners. Naturally, these ideas led to conflicts with management—and to strikes. In the 1880s, the Knights staged a number of successful strikes. Ultimately, organizational weaknesses and the rise of stronger unions led to the decline of the Knights.

Samuel Gompers was sharply opposed to the Knights' philosophy. By 1877, he was president of Local 144 of the Cigarmakers Union, where he fought for "trade unionism, pure and simple." Gompers wanted all unions to be composed of people sharing a special skill, even if that meant creating several such *craft unions* within one industry. In contrast, *industrial unions* bring together all workers in one industry. For example, the United Auto Workers Union today includes clerks in factories as well as people on the assembly line. Gompers believed that unions should use strikes and boycotts to force employers to grant increased wages, shorter hours, and safer working conditions. He called these reforms a fair share for labor, a "better tomorrow." But Gompers did not want unions to have political goals. Nor did he want unions to change the economic system. He only wanted to soften the harshness of employers.

In 1886, Gompers and others persuaded a number of craft unions to enter a new organization, the American Federation of Labor. Gompers became its first president. By 1892, unions whose combined

Left: Samuel Gompers traveled around the country helping to organize the AF of L. He posed for this photograph on a visit to strike-torn West Virginia coal mines. Under Gompers' leadership, the AF of L won wide acceptance among management as well as workers. During World War I, Gompers served on the Council of National Defense and was a frequent White House visitor. Right: A year before his death in 1924, Gompers posed outside the White House with the Prime Minister of New Zealand.

members totaled some 250,000 became affiliated with the AF of L. Until Gomper's death in 1924, he worked tirelessly. He wrote thousands of speeches and letters, helping to form new craft unions for the AF of L and to win public support for labor's demands.

Most labor unions in this era refused to accept Black members. Although the AF of L had originally admitted Blacks, the policy was changed when the membership objected. Only among the mine workers were Blacks unionized in significant numbers. The results were twofold. The strength of organized labor was weakened by the division. And Blacks were forced into the ranks of unskilled labor. It was not until after World War II that Black laborers became a major part of the industrial labor force.

The Strike as a Weapon

Gompers' "bread and butter" unionism included having the workers refuse to work until their demands were met. This tactic was the union's real power. However, striking was not always easy. In the early days of unions, strikes were often poorly planned. They were broken easily when workers grew hungry and returned to their jobs on the employer's terms. So it became necessary to plan carefully, collect dues, and build up treasuries before this weapon could be effective.

Also, employers were not always willing to wait for strikers to get tired and discouraged. Sometimes, they barred the strikers from returning—a practice called *lockout*—and gave their jobs to new people, who were known as *strikebreakers*. In turn, the strikers marched before the factories as pickets to bar the strikebreakers (whom they called "scabs") and to call public attention to their cause. Sometimes, pickets and scabs would clash, and violence would result. One such incident led to a tragedy and a violent national debate.

In 1886, during a strike at the McCormick Harvester plant in Chicago, police were on hand to protect the strikebreakers. When a fight erupted between pickets and the strikebreakers, the police opened fire and killed several workers. As a result, a mass protest meeting, announced in bilingual posters (German and English), was called in Haymarket Square. In Chicago at that time, there was a small group of anarchists. This particular group of anarchists believed that justice would be won only by destroying the government, beginning with the assassination of top officials. While the Haymarket meeting was in progress, someone—never found—threw a bomb. The bomb exploded in the midst of a squad of police. A number of them were killed. The police immediately arrested eight known anarchists and their sympathizers. They were accused of being responsible for the murders because of the ideas they expressed. The anarchists were hurriedly tried and convicted. Four were hanged. However, many leading Americans objected strongly to the idea that people should be executed simply for speaking out in favor of certain violent deeds, without any proof whatever that they actually committed a crime. The Haymarket riot and trial left the whole country angry, divided, and shaken.

In 1892, at Andrew Carnegie's Homestead steel plant near Pittsburgh, the workers refused to accept a wage cut. Predicting a walkout, the president of the Carnegie Steel Company hired 300 Pinkerton guards to protect the plant. The workers drove them away. The company then requested the state militia to maintain peace. By the time the workers returned to the plant five months later, the strike was lost. The attempted murder of the company president, Henry Clay Frick, by an anarchist turned public opinion against the strikers. The defeat was a significant setback for union organization in the steel industry.

Two years later, there was a railroad strike in Chicago, which brought the power of the federal government out against the unions. The employers of the Pullman Company walked out of work in a dispute over wage cuts and conditions in the "company town" in which they lived. With support from Eugene V. Debs and the American Railway Union, the strikers were able to stop most rail traffic on the Western railroads. They thought they would win their demands.

Twenty thousand hastily printed handbills announced the Haymarket protest rally in 1886. A bomb thrown at police during the rally by an unknown assailant resulted in what came to be known as the Haymarket Massacre.

However, the railroad managers, basing their arguments on the "restraint of trade" provisions of the Sherman Antitrust Act, got an **injunction** in federal courts forbidding the strike. But workers defied the injunction. Some of them, or possibly some hoodlums, set fire to millions of dollars' worth of railroad property. President Cleveland sent federal troops to Chicago to "keep order," which finally broke the strike. Debs was arrested and convicted of contempt of court. When the Supreme Court upheld that decision, organized labor was dealt a serious blow.

injunction
a court order prohibiting a specific course of action or demanding a certain action.

Industrialists now seemed to hold all the cards. In addition to the powerful weapon of an injunction, they had the money to pay for legal advice, favorable publicity, and lobbyists. In addition, politicians who lent a friendly ear to the employers were often assured of large campaign contributions.

The employers also had an arsenal of weapons against union organization. They hired private detectives to sneak into unions and pinpoint the leaders. Further, union organizers were fired and *blacklisted*, which meant that they could not get other jobs. Employers hired people of shady character to threaten employees who joined unions. In some industries, people applying for work had to sign "*yellow-dog contracts*," promises that they would not join a union. Many worried Americans saw strikes as a dangerous form of industrial warfare. They feared that capital and labor might eventually be locked in a new civil war. Workers would be on one side and police or troops on the other.

Despite these worries, only a handful out of many hundreds of strikes each year ended in bloodshed. Unions, especially those in the AF of L, continued to grow, reaching a membership of over 2.5 million by 1914. Though some employers continued to battle labor with lockouts and injunctions, a growing number found it sensible to accept the right of workers to bargain for better conditions through their unions. Samuel Gompers himself was invited to join the National Civic Federation. This organization of business people was devoted to promoting industrial peace through discussion and fair play.

The Labor Movement Splits

This change—the coming together of labor and employer—did not please everyone concerned with the welfare of workers. There were *socialists* who were convinced that a capitalist system would never divide the fruits of industry fairly among all members of society. Socialists argued that the basic means of production—factories, mines, and railroads—should be owned by the government. Government should also take responsibility for the distribution of wealth and for all large-scale economic decisions. Government should not allow the

Signs in photo:
TO WORK
THE WORKERS now divide up with the Shirkers — SOCIALISM will abolish the Dividing-up system

MAY I IS INTERNATIONAL LABOR DAY

WAR IN MEXICO IN COLORADO FOR THE ROCKEFELLER INTERESTS

The organizers of the IWW were far more radical than the AF of L. They were convinced that "The working class and the employing class have nothing in common." The IWW sponsored more than 150 strikes in its first fifteen years and as a result was nicknamed, the "I Won't Work" Party. In this photo, IWW members and supporters rally in New York City on May 1, 1914.

lure of profit to determine what was produced where, when, and by whom. The socialists hoped to persuade voters to elect them to office to carry out these reforms.

Other socialists fought the system by helping to form the "union of unions" in 1905, the Industrial Workers of the World. The IWW, or *Wobblies* as they were called, believed that workers should bring about socialism, but not through political action. All laborers, regardless of race, should belong to "One Big Union." When the proper time came, all could stop work together in a general strike that would completely tie up the nation. Then the working class could take the machines from the capitalist owners. The socialists said the capitalist owners "stole" most of the wealth or profit created by the factory workers. Until that time, there could only be war between the laboring and the owning classes. This radical view of how to make a good society became very visible in the IWW after 1908. However, it enjoyed little support among most Americans. But the IWW's spirited posters, songs, and slogans made converts among unskilled laborers. In addition, the IWW was successful in organizing certain workers, such as farmhands and lumberjacks, whom the AF of L had ignored.

Despite winning a few strikes, the IWW suffered from lack of a close organization. Considered un-American by some, the union lost support during the patriotic fervor of the World War I era. The 10 percent of American workers who were organized in the early 1900s clung to the AF of L. Both labor and management moved slowly and carefully toward industrial peace.

Questions for Discussion

1. Define *platform, craft unions, industrial unions, lockout, injunction, blacklisted, "yellow-dog contracts," socialists.*
2. Why was mass production both an advantage and a disadvantage to American workers?
3. How does the Triangle Fire illustrate the horrible conditions of the industrial worker?
4. How did the views of Uriah Stephens and Terence W. Powderly on the problems of labor differ from those of Samuel Gompers? How were they similar?
5. What methods were used by employers against labor unions?
6. Why did socialists, unlike other labor reform groups, reject capitalism?

2. Reform Comes to the City

In the growing cities of America, honest governments bent like overloaded bridges under new strains. One of these strains was caused by the huge profits made by those who got contracts and licenses to build public works. City governments were supposed to award these "plums" to the best and cheapest producers. However, the huge sums of money involved tempted some people to bribe officials. In return for these illegal payments, the right to build public works was awarded to a favored, dishonest few.

A second strain on honesty was due to the large increase in population. As mentioned earlier, voters rarely knew their officials in person. Therefore, they were unable to check up on them. A third strain arose because of the poverty and unfamiliarity with city life of both native and immigrant urban newcomers. These people welcomed any kind of help. The political machines took advantage of these developments to build power for themselves.

A political machine was usually organized as a political "club." This club employed workers in the neighborhoods. These workers gave poor voters free coal and food, helped them to find jobs and housing, and amused them with picnics and other entertainment. In return, votes were cast for political machine candidates without question. Therefore, the political machine could control elections and put its people in important offices. Then it could make deals with those willing to pay.

Political machines were controlled by a strong leader, or "boss." Mayors, city lawmakers, and judges were their puppets. An outstand-

Right: "Boss" Tweed and his Tweed Ring is estimated to have stolen between $20 and $200 million from New York City. For example, the city paid one of Tweed's friends $179,729.60 for three tables and forty chairs. Left: Thomas Nast, the staff artist of Harper's Weekly from 1862 to 1886, launched his attack on the Tweed Ring in 1869 with cartoons such as this one.

ing example of a boss was New York City's William Marcy Tweed. Tweed's base was a Democratic club known as Tammany Hall. Its mascot was a tiger. Between 1862 and 1871, Tammany's tiger ripped millions of dollars from New Yorkers. Tweed's people sold contracts for city work to companies which then overcharged the city treasury. Public taxes paid both bribe-givers and bribe-takers. Eventually, Tweed was exposed by newspapers and magazines. Finally, he was sent to jail.

Reformers Make Headway

"Boss" Tweed's conviction did not stop urban corruption. Machines and bosses appeared again, in New York as well as in other cities. The political machines helped handle problems of urban poverty and growth, which old-fashioned city governments often failed to do. The bosses knew how to speak and act plainly. Yet, these bosses were not Robin Hoods, taking from the rich and giving to the poor. Corruption raised the cost of government for everyone. It bred contempt for law and encouraged crime. Angry reformers began to insist that city dwellers deserved better urban rule.

There were several ways to reform cities. One was to spend money and energy to elect honest candidates. Victorious reformers could then arrest some of the more obvious machine lawbreakers. But no matter what reformers did, sooner or later the public would lose interest, and the bosses would return. It was clear that the basic causes of corruption had to be attacked first.

Therefore, reform mayors, such as Cleveland's mayor Tom Johnson (1901–1909) or Detroit's mayor Hazen Pingree (1889–1896), modernized city government in ways that cut the roots of machine power. They fought to have utility companies publicly owned or regulated, so that profiteers could not overcharge the cities. They tried to have city services run by experts who were selected by competitive examination. This principle of a professional civil service helped prevent the machine from filling public offices with its henchmen.

Along with this "scientific" or "progressive" urban reform, such mayors as Johnson and Pingree moved to improve the conditions of the poor. This meant that the bosses could no longer win elections by offering bread and coal to workers in exchange for their votes.

Jane Addams and the Settlement House

One way to help slum dwellers better their lives was the *settlement house*. This was a new kind of community center right in the slum. It offered services to the poor, especially immigrants. One of the first of these centers was Hull House, founded in Chicago in 1889 by Jane Addams. At Hull House, Addams conducted classes in sewing, child care, and English. Help for working mothers with babies was also available. There were free medical clinics, gymnasiums, and singing clubs to keep youngsters off the streets. The goal of the settlement house was to give charity as well as a helping hand to those who needed to adjust to American urban life.

The work of Jane Addams, however, was a threat to a local boss like Johnny Powers, leader of Chicago's tough Nineteenth Ward.

Left: This photograph of Jane Addams was taken around the time she founded Hull House at the age of 29. In addition to giving immediate help to the neighborhood, volunteers at Hull House led broader reform movements that got results: child-labor laws, a juvenile court, and a factory-inspection law. Jane Addams supported reform political candidates throughout the nation. She also worked for a lasting peace and remained against war even after the U.S. entered World War I. She was the second American to be awarded the Nobel Peace Prize. Right: A dentistry clinic at Hull House.

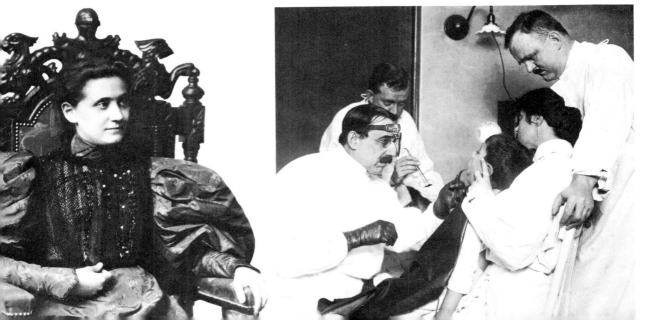

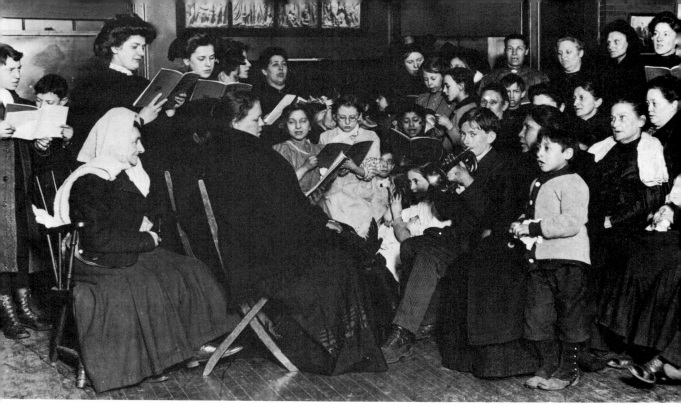

As hard as he tried to get rid of Hull House, Johnny Powers (next page) was unable to halt the settlement house's activities, such as its singing class (above).

Powers tried hard to get rid of Hull House. And Jane Addams tried to beat him at the polls. Both of these efforts failed. Yet, the struggle of the settlement house to survive was part of a widespread battle for urban betterment.

Questions for Discussion

1. List two strains on government honesty.
2. Identify William Marcy Tweed, Jane Addams.
3. What actions were taken by the reform mayors?

3. A Political Balancing Act

The era following the end of Reconstruction was marked by a political balancing act. Neither of the two major political parties was strong enough to take an unpopular stand on issues. Both parties counted on a coalition of opposing factions to carry elections. The Republicans took advantage of the Democrats' association with the South and secession. Years after the Civil War was over, the Republicans were still calling attention to this negative association. The Republicans attracted industrialists because of their support of "hard" money and a high tariff. The Republicans also controlled federal patronage for most of the era. Westerners favored the

Republicans as the party that supported the opening of the West for settlement. But Westerners also favored the Democratic policies of "cheap" money and a low tariff.

The Democrats depended on conflicting groups for political support. To counteract the Republican strength on the federal and state level, Democratic political machines appealed to the immigrants in the cities for votes. They also counted on the votes of the "Solid South." Once Reconstruction was over, the traditional powers in the South took over again. Blacks, and white Republicans were once more the minority at the polls.

Although the Republicans dominated the Presidency, elections were usually very close. In two instances, the Republican presidential candidate polled fewer votes than the Democratic candidate. However, the Republican became President because of the distribution of electoral votes. Presidential officeholders were not strong political figures.

In national elections, opposing groups within both major parties led to the nomination of bland, "compromise" candidates. From Hayes to Harrison, no President succeeded himself in office. However,

MOODY'S SUNDAY SCHOOL

Evangelism—the preaching of God's message—took on a special meaning in America's growing cities. Nobody in Chicago in the 1860s understood this special meaning better than Dwight L. Moody. Moody was a big-hearted, big-framed shoe salesman. When Moody was still in business (which he later left for fulltime evangelistic work), one of his weekend "recreations" was to go into one of Chicago's toughest slum districts, known as "The Sands." There, he would find the most desperate-looking young toughs he could locate. He would let them know that God loved them and wanted them to reform. He was not above getting their attention with candy. Once he got them to listen, he had amazing success.

He organized a Sunday school for these youths in an abandoned saloon. Every Sunday at dawn, Moody would enter the saloon and sweep it clear of the sawdust, cigar butts, and spilled beer before setting up desks and chairs. In time, Moody's classes of young exhoodlums became training grounds for many other evangelists and Christian workers.

Generally, Moody won his ways by persuasion. But there is one story of a time when an unruly newcomer was making life in the classroom a little too difficult. Moody directed his assistant to lead the scholars in a hymn—a good, loud, hymn. He then beckoned his problem-student into the cloakroom for a little private discussion. Muffled sounds of combat emerged—drowned out as the hymn swelled in fervor and volume. Finally, Moody emerged, red-faced and sweating, followed by a meek and, thereafter, very meek pupil. If asked, Moody would have given the credit to God and to the hymn.

443

An 1889 cartoon entitled "They All Do It—Cringing Before the Irish Vote and Support." The cartoon was a sly reference to the fact that politicians shortly after Reconstruction were forced to court any large voting group and offend no one.

Grover Cleveland, the only Democrat elected, did serve as the twenty-second and twenty-fourth President of the United States.

This lack of dynamic leadership was one reason why no party dared to ignore even a portion of its followers. At a time when neither party had stable political support, ignoring followers would have meant the loss of the election. The major parties failed to cope with the growing power of industrialists, the need for monetary and tariff reforms, the problems of labor, and the hardships of the farmers. To bring about needed changes, reformers struggled both within the parties and in third-party movements.

Rutherford B. Hayes

Widespread corruption on the national and local levels was revealed in the 1860s and 1870s. The major political parties responded to pressure from the public for reform. In the election of 1876, the Democrats nominated Samuel Tilden, who, as governor of New York, had contributed to "Boss" Tweed's downfall. Rutherford B. Hayes, also considered able and honest, won the Republican nomination. As you saw in Chapter 16, the election was disputed and finally resolved through a compromise. Hayes became President, but the Democrats still questioned his right to the position.

Hayes said that if he were elected, he would "show a *grit* that will astonish those who predict weakness." He set out quickly to end federal occupation of the South and to begin civil service reform.

Both measures made him unpopular with Senator Roscoe Conkling, the head of a political machine in New York. When Reconstruction ended, the Democrats took control of the South. The "Solid South" threatened Conkling's dream of total Republican control of the Congress. When Hayes removed Chester A. Arthur, a Conkling cohort, from a powerful position in the New York Customshouse, the President further separated the Stalwart faction of the Republican party. Hayes was trying to regain some of the Presidential power that Congress had assumed during Andrew Johnson's Administration.

Even though Hayes weakened the political machine, he still lacked the support of a united party. When Hayes refused to run in the 1880 election, the Republicans nominated and succeeded in electing James A. Garfield for President. Chester A. Arthur was chosen as his Vice President.

Garfield and Arthur

Garfield was in office only four months when a disappointed office seeker shot him on July 2, 1881. People were shocked that two Presidents had been assassinated in less than twenty years. By the time Chester A. Arthur was inaugurated, the country was ripe for reform. Although Arthur had been a product of the spoils system, he too sought reform.

Public support, along with the Democratic Congressional victories in the fall of 1882, helped secure the passage of the Pendleton Act of 1883. This law established the Civil Service Commission. Its members were appointed by the President. They were to draw up competitive examinations for people seeking jobs with the government. The law made it illegal to force federal employees to contribute to campaign funds. The Pendleton Act also made it illegal to fire federal employees for political reasons. This Act proved to be a major turning point in governmental reform.

Grover Cleveland

Chester A. Arthur failed to obtain the Republic nomination to run for a second term. His emphasis on reform had offended the Stalwarts. The Republicans nominated James Blaine, a leader of the Half-Breed faction of the party. Blaine's past record was tainted with corruption. In the end, the Democratic nominee, Grover Cleveland, won the election.

Grover Cleveland, like the Presidents before him, met with obstacles as he sought reform. There was a long tradition of Republican support for veterans' benefits. The Democratic President vetoed fraudulent pension bills passed by Congress. One act, the so-called pauper pension, would have given a pension to any needy veteran, regardless of disability. Cleveland vetoed private pension bills submitted by members of Congress for friends who were not entitled to a pension under any of the existing laws. He also extended the number of federal positions covered by civil service. Cleveland called for a lowering of the protective tariff. It was this issue that may have cost him reelection. Business and industry urged the defeat of people who sought to lower the protective tariff.

Harrison and the Republicans

In 1888, the Republicans regained control of the White House and Congress. They had waged a vigorous campaign against Cleveland's bid for reelection, making the high protective tariff the chief plank in their platform. The Republicans claimed that Cleveland's tariff reforms, if carried out, would ruin American industry and make American laborers even poorer. Although Cleveland had a majority of the popular vote, Harrison's electoral votes gave him the victory. Thus, civil service reform suffered a setback, as thousands of Democrats in federal jobs were replaced by Republicans. The Civil Service Commission still had limited powers at that time and could do nothing about it.

The coining of silver again, which had been stopped in 1873, became a big issue. Both Westerners who mined silver and farmers who wanted an inflated currency favored the unlimited coinage of silver. Easterners were in favor of a revision in tariff rates. In 1890, the Republicans in Congress who supported silver made a deal with the Easterners. As a result, two acts were passed at the same time. The McKinley Tariff, the highest tariff the United States had ever known, imposed a fifty-cent tax on all imported goods. As a result, almost all foreign imports were excluded. Also, the Sherman Silver Purchase Act allowed the treasury to purchase 126 million grams (4.5 million ounces) of silver a month with paper notes.

Following the long-standing pattern of Republican support, Congress passed legislation increasing pension benefits for Union veterans. The Sherman Antitrust Act, which outlawed "every combination . . . or conspiracy in restraint of trade" was also passed. The public assumed that this law would limit the abuses of monopolies. However, vague wording limited its effectiveness. Without any clear definition of the terms, the law was easily dodged in court. It was used more successfully against labor unions than big business. The Supreme Court weakened the law further when it decided, in *U.S.* v. *E. C. Knight Company* (1895), that a monopoly was illegal only if it were in "restraint of trade." The growth of trusts and monopolies flourished. However, the law did set the stage for more effective legislation in the future.

Questions for Discussion
1. Why is the era following Reconstruction called a balancing act?
2. What effect did the removal of Chester Arthur from his New York Customshouse position have on Hayes?
3. What was the effect of the Pendleton Act of 1883?

4. The Plight of Farmers

Hamlin Garland in his book, *Main Travelled Roads*, related the hardships and pain of farm life on the Plains. The last twenty years of the nineteenth century saw a decline in the quality of life for farm families.

Farmers had a weak position in the economy. They had no control over the prices they charged for their produce. So each farmer was in competition with every other farmer. The farmers increased production in an effort to maintain or raise their incomes. But this served only to lower the prices offered for their crops. The result was lower incomes. The overexpansion of Western farms after the Civil War damaged farmers in the East and South. But Western expansion coincided with a worldwide growth in agriculture. Neither the American market nor the world market could absorb the produce of the Western farmer. Therefore, prices dropped further.

Farmers were caught in a squeeze. Although they could not set the price for the products they sold, they did have to pay a price set by others for machinery and railroad transportation. Many farmers blamed their hardships on "hard" money policies, the high tariff favored by the industrialists, and unfair railroad practices. By the end of the century, the percentage of farmers who were tenants instead of owners had risen from 25 to 35 percent.

The Farmers Organize

In order to combat their problems, farmers began to organize. The first farm organization was the National Grange of the Patrons of Husbandry, or the Grange. It was founded in 1867 by Oliver Hudson Kelley.

Members of the Grange began to use their influence for political ends. In states such as Illinois, Iowa, and Kansas, farmers entered politics and struggled for favorable legislation. State laws were passed limiting warehouse charges and outlawing some of the worst abuses of the railroads.

In 1876, the Supreme Court had supported the state laws. In the case of *Munn* v. *Illinois*, the Court ruled in favor of regulation. However, in the *Wabash* case ten years later, the Court decided that states could not regulate rates on any rail traffic that started or ended in another state.

People were becoming fearful of the power of the railroads to a refund of part of a payment, as of taxes

control their welfare. **Rebates** to favored customers, such as Standard Oil, gave these industrialists advantages over others. Areas of the country where several railroads competed paid much lower rates than sections served by only one railroad. Sometimes, competing railroads would form a "pooling" arrangement, in which they agreed to keep the prices at a certain level. However, those farmers or manufacturers who had the misfortune to be served by only one railroad were forced to pay higher rates for a short haul than others paid for a long haul. In addition to resenting these abuses, many opponents of the railroads were uneasy about the power that the railroads had in obtaining special favors from Congress.

In 1887, during Cleveland's Administration, public opinion in favor of regulation was strong enough to obtain the passage of the Interstate Commerce Act. Although it outlawed the major abuses, this law had no means of forcing people to obey. And the Interstate Commerce Commission, created by the law, had little power. The Commission depended on the support of the courts. In most cases, the courts ruled in favor of the railroads. Yet, the law did represent a major step towards regulation of big business.

During the 1870s, other farmer alliances were organized. The Southern Alliance, the National Farmers' Alliance in the Northwest, and the Colored Farmers' Alliance met with the Knights of Labor and the Farmers' Mutual Benefit Association in December 1889. Although little cooperation developed from that meeting in St. Louis, the Northern and Southern Alliances did stress similar reform programs. When the farmers became convinced that neither political party was really listening, they merged their clubs into a new political party, the People's Party or the Populists.

Questions for Discussion
1. Why did farmers have a weak position in the economy?
2. Why were people fearful of the control railroads appeared to have over their welfare?

5. The Beginning of New Politics

Postwar economic changes raised new political issues. In the 1890s, national parties had to deal with problems created by the industrial boom and agricultural expansion of the 1870s and 1880s.

At the root of many of these problems was the difference between a corporation's legal form and its tremendous power. For example, the directors of a railroad company were only a few people with a few votes. By raising freight rates, however, they could wipe out the profits of thousands of farmers who used the road to ship grain to market. By giving one industrial shipper a special low price, they could help that shipper undersell competitors, thus driving them out of business. Also, by contributing to political campaigns, they could get favorable laws passed by grateful legislators. And by employing the most able and best paid lawyers, they stood a good chance of winning cases in court. What was true for railroads was true for other corporations doing essential jobs for whole communities, as well.

Competition among producers was supposed to keep prices down and quality up. Yet, around 1880, individual companies in the same industries began to combine, creating near-monopoly conditions. Customers then had no choice of which company to buy from and no power to influence company policy. The greatest of these combinations was John D. Rockefeller's strong, efficient Standard Oil Company. By 1882, Standard Oil had bought almost all of its competitors. Through a legal device known as a *trust*, Standard Oil ran many companies as a single organization. Like an octopus, it strangled opportunities for the few independent refiners still left in business. Soon trusts were formed in coal, steel, copper, sugar refining, meatpacking, and many other vital industries. Many people wondered how society could have any control over such "monsters." These monsters squeezed small producers out of business, set prices of needed goods, and made decisions deeply affecting the public. Yet, they were controlled by only a handful of wealthy directors who owned most of their stock. Slowly, Congress moved into action. However, many people, like the farmers and workers, could not wait for the legislators to make things better.

The Money Issue

Farmers as well as others who were often in debt traditionally favored "cheap" money. Plentiful supplies of money caused inflation of

Although the subject of many attacks like this 1904 cartoon, the Standard Oil Trust was one of many large trusts. Excluding railroads, in 1896 less than a dozen companies had over $10 million in assets; by 1903 there were over 300 such giants.

prices. If a farmer had borrowed money when produce brought a low price, and paid it back when produce was high, the farmer benefited. The farmer was paying back money that was cheaper in terms of goods than the money that was borrowed.

In 1792, the Mint Act called for the coinage of silver at a rate of sixteen to one with gold. However, few miners sold their silver to the government. They found that they could get more gold for their silver on the open market. Little silver was coined. Finally, in 1873, silver money was removed from the coinage list. Yet, at that time, no one really noticed.

When President Hayes came into office in 1877, he agreed with the measures taken by his predecessor, Grant. Grant had called for the redemption of greenbacks—the Civil War issue of paper money—with gold. As Hayes's Secretary of the Treasury prepared to carry out the law, the value of greenbacks rose. The farmers' position worsened. Now it took more produce to earn each dollar.

In the 1870s, Western mines began turning out great quantities of silver. This caused the price of silver on the open market to drop. When the miners turned to the government to purchase silver, they discovered that the law had been changed. Unpleasantly surprised, they howled about the "Crime of '73."

Farmers had flocked to the Greenback Party, which had been organized in 1876 to fight for "cheap" money. Now they joined forces with the silver miners to demand "free and unlimited coinage of silver at a ratio of 16 to 1." The farmers assumed that if the government took all the silver offered for sale and put the silver dollars into circulation, the country would have more and cheaper money.

In 1878, these combined forces had some limited success. The Bland-Allison Act was passed over President Hayes's veto. The Treasury Department was to buy no less than $2 million nor more than $4 million worth of silver each month. The ratio of silver to gold was set at sixteen to one.

During President Harrison's Administration, a political deal resulted in increased silver coinage. But the Sherman Silver Purchase Act did not result in increased silver prices. Nor did it result in inflated currency. Finally, the farmers and other cheap money supporters were goaded into action.

The Populist Crusade

The first sweeping political program for national reform came from the People's Party or Populists, founded in June 1890.

The problems of Populists were high prices for the things they bought, combined with low prices for the crops they sold. They blamed this squeeze on the power of organized wealth. A platform was drafted

Within the image:
- 16 to 1
- THE DAILY ILLUSTRATED HODGE-PODGE
- THE DAILY TOM-TOM
- THE MORNING BAZOO
- THE DAILY WINDGAUGE
- PRESS
- THE MORNING EXPECTORATOR
- J.S.Pughe

This Puck cartoon represents William Jennings Bryan and his supporters as fools and makes special fun of their demand for free coinage of silver at a ratio of 16-to-1 with gold.

that included broad reforms. First, the Populists wanted the government to increase the available money and credit by *coining*—that is, making into currency—more of the plentiful silver from Western mines. That would lower interest rates and raise the price of farm products. Next, the Populists wanted the government to limit the power of trusts to charge such high prices. As a first step, they called for government ownership of the railroads as well as the telephone and telegraph systems. They also wanted a *graduated income tax*. This is a tax on people's income that rises as income increases. They felt that this tax would distribute the nation's wealth more evenly. And the rich would be forced to pay a larger share of government costs.

Finally, Populists wanted to make certain that politicians listened to the people and not just to corporation lobbyists. So they urged the election of Senators directly by the people instead of by state legislatures, the secret ballot or other measure. They wanted to give voters more of a direct voice in government.

Cleveland's Second Administration

In 1892, the Populists won one million popular votes in the election that returned Grover Cleveland to the White House. They gained seats in Congress and in state legislatures. The major parties were alerted to the growing discontent of farmers and laborers.

Shortly after Cleveland's election, the country experienced a deep economic depression. The Populists blamed the "tight" money policy of the government. But the President blamed the depression on the Sherman Silver Purchase Act of 1890.

Since 1890, the Treasury had purchased more silver. But the price of silver continued to decline. So people began to demand gold instead of silver in exchange for silver bank notes. By the time Cleveland took office, the nation's gold reserves had sunk to $100 million. If this trend continued, the government would soon be unable to redeem bank notes with gold. Runaway inflation would result. So Cleveland urged Congress to repeal the Sherman Silver Purchase Act to stem the flow of gold. He then accepted the suggestion of financier J. P. Morgan to sell government bonds for gold to build up the reserve. When Morgan and other banking giants purchased these bonds, confidence was restored. Finally, the "Panic of 1893" was resolved.

Cleveland's solution to the crisis aroused opposition from the "cheap" money supporters. Cleveland fared little better in his struggle for a lowered tariff. Thus, those who had voted for the Democrats in 1892 because of the promise of a lower tariff felt betrayed.

The Election of 1896

As the election of 1896 approached, the issues of tariff, reform, and unemployment were overshadowed by the silver issue. The topic was no longer solely an issue of the Populists. The Republican Convention nominated William McKinley, who tried to avoid the issue. However, McKinley became the candidate of those favoring the gold standard. The Populists nominated the man already chosen by the Democrats, William Jennings Bryan of Nebraska. A spellbinding speaker, Bryan won the Democratic nomination with an emotion-charged speech in favor of coining more silver and denouncing the government's policy of using only gold as money. He concluded with a thundering cry, "You shall not crucify mankind upon a cross of gold!" In his campaign against the Republican candidate, William McKinley, Bryan chose to emphasize only this silver question. Since currency control was a complex economic question, Bryan's opponents were able to dismiss his simple ideas about economics as those of a windbag. By stressing the silver issue, Bryan lost the support of labor leaders, who were seeking wider reform. They feared that the inflation farmers sought would raise prices more than wages.

William Jennings Bryan in full oratorial flight. Bryan traveled 18,000 miles and gave more than 600 speeches in a losing cause.

Finally, in a close popular vote, Bryan was defeated by William McKinley. However, Bryan was to run twice more as a Democrat while the People's party faded away.

Yet, much of what the Populists hoped to achieve was accomplished anyway. Discoveries of large deposits of gold in Alaska, South Africa, and Australia increased money in circulation and increased inflation. Prices and crops improved. McKinley ran again in 1900, claiming "Republican prosperity." Many of the reforming ideas and the spirit of the People's party lived on in programs adopted by the Republicans.

New Political Parties Are Formed

In many states after 1900, a movement generally known as *progressivism* was born. Like the Populists, Progressives hoped to fit American democracy in to a modern age. But unlike Populists, Progressives believed that complicated national economic questions could not be settled directly by the people. Instead, they proposed that experts, responsible to publicly-chosen officials, should manage the business of society. Progressives would not have liked Bryan's statement that, "The people of Nebraska are for free silver and I am for free silver. I will look up the arguments later."

A typical Progressive governor was Robert La Follette of Wisconsin. During his term in office from 1901 to 1905, La Follette tried to make Wisconsin a "laboratory of democracy." He created special commissions to regulate railroads and utilities. Their members were often scholars from the faculty of the state university. Thus, LaFollette brought the best brains of the academic community into public service. He fought for fairer taxes and election laws. He led the legislature to the passage of laws providing safer factories, shorter working hours for women and children, and improved conservation of

The two faces of progressivism. Left: Robert La Follette believed in the basic soundness of the American economic and political machinery. He felt that reform and an informed public were what was needed to set the system right. Right: Eugene V. Debs, on the other hand, believed that real economic equality was not possible under the system of private ownership of productive property.

resources. La Follette believed that the American political and economic machinery was still basically sound. It needed only some reform and an informed public to make it work well.

Another reformer, Eugene V. Debs, did not share La Follette's faith in the capitalist system. Debs was an Indiana-born railroad worker and union leader. He was put in jail in 1894 for defying an antistrike injunction. There, he did much reading and became a socialist. As a socialist, he believed that real economic equality was not possible under a system of private ownership of productive property. Greed for larger profits would always rise above the spirit of community. The fruits of growth would not be shared. Only government ownership of factories, railroads, mines, and all industries would guarantee fair play. Debs's good humor and sense of brotherhood won him many supporters even among people who voted against him during his five unsuccessful tries for the Presidency.

Reform from the White House

The dawn of the twentieth century turned the average American's thoughts toward the future. The national mood for social improvement grew. But reform-minded Americans had blind spots. They overlooked the plight of minorities in the United States. As you shall see in Chapter 20, they welcomed the growth of an American empire as well as nativist attacks on immigrants of non-Anglo-Saxon stock.

However, Americans also listened when crusading newspaper and magazine reporters, known as *muckrakers* exposed corruption in government and business. Upton Sinclair' book, *The Jungle*, revealed the unsanitary conditions in the Chicago meatpacking industry. Ida M. Tarbell wrote *The History of the Standard Oil Company*, which told the story of its ruthless business methods. *McClure's* magazine offered outlets for writers such as Lincoln Steffens, Ray Stannard Baker, and William Allen White. People often voted for progressive mayors and governors who promised reform. In Theodore Roosevelt, they found such a President.

Roosevelt was no ordinary reformer. Born into a wealthy New York family, he had a keen mind, sharpened by a Harvard education. He read widely and wrote easily. He was also a naturalist, conservationist, outdoorsman, and athlete. He had even been a cowpuncher on his own western ranch. Before he was forty years old, Roosevelt was a combat hero of the Spanish-American War. He had done all this and still served in government jobs, from New York City Police Commissioner to Assistant Secretary of the Navy.

In 1900, Roosevelt was elected Vice-President with McKinley as President. Some big business representatives and party bosses were worried about what the energetic young reformer might be planning.

Voted into the Presidency as a reform candidate, Theodore Roosevelt's most notable achievements in office were the sponsorship of conservation of natural resources and of food-inspection and railway-rate legislation.

EDITORIAL COMMENT: OUR CHOICE

The following excerpt was taken from The Voice of the West, *a Black magazine in California in the year 1912. In this excerpt, the editor-in-chief of the paper, Rev. J. Gordon McPherson, endorsed Theodore Roosevelt for President.*

Before another issue of "The Voice of the West" shall come from the press, the National Republican convention at Chicago will have passed into history: the Republican standard bearers will be selected to lead the party on to victory, the contest for the presidential nomination will be settled, and we predict that our choice for the exalted position will be the nation's choice and Colonel Theodore Roosevelt, that peerless American, the Hero of San Juan Hill, the "Apostle of a Square Deal," and our own Hiram W. Johnson, "the Native Son," California's progressive governor, will be the Republican nominees for President and Vice President. The Black progressives throughout the country have every reason to congratulate themselves on having done their duty in helping to nominate these fearless leaders, but a nomination does not always mean an election, for the real fight will begin at the close of the Chicago convention.

And if the victory is to be complete, every progressive Republican must stand by his or her gun and be ready to respond to duty's call. The work of propaganda among the masses must go on; there must be no let up until victory shall be achieved at the polls and Theodore Roosevelt, our progressive leader, shall have triumphed.

To their horror, an assassin's bullet cut down McKinley in 1901 and Roosevelt did become the Chief Executive. However, the American public liked "Teddy," or "T.R." He was rich and educated, but could box, ride, and shoot. He was not a socialist, but he did say that trusts must be controlled by the national government to help people obtain a better life. In the early years of his administration, people were ready to support Roosevelt when he took on the giants of Wall Street.

Roosevelt used his position as President to put pressure on Congress for progressive federal legislation. Laws passed during his terms of office strengthened railroad regulation. The Interstate Commerce Act had been weakened by narrow Supreme Court interpretation of its provisions. The Elkins Act attacked the practice of rebates by making it illegal to charge any but the published rates. The Hepburn Act gave the commission the power to set rates. The Meat Inspection Act and the Pure Food and Drug Act provided for national inspection of meat and medicines to protect the consumer. Under the terms of the Forest Reserve Act passed in 1891, Roosevelt set aside almost 150 million acres of timberland. Gifford Pinchot, a professional conservationist, was put in charge of the national forests. The Justice Department was also given power to move against the trusts under the Sherman Act. And Roosevelt did not hesitate to threaten to use his authority to "bust the trusts." In reality, he did not "bust" many. Roosevelt wanted just enough reforms to head off more drastic changes by the "radicals."

Roosevelt was succeeded by William Howard Taft, a Republican who continued to support some reform measures. Taft supported the expansion of the jurisdiction of the Interstate Commerce Commission over telephone, telegraph, cable, and wireless companies. He also created a new Cabinet-level position for the Department of Labor. Taft sided with the conservative wing of the Republican party on tariff and conservation issues. As the 1912 election neared, the Republican party split. Theodore Roosevelt launched a new political party made up of the progressives. Now the Democrats saw their chance for victory.

The high tide of national progressivism came under Woodrow Wilson, a progressive Democrat elected in 1912. Under Wilson, the Clayton Antitrust Act was passed. This law made officers of corporations subject to prosecution if their companies violated terms of the law. Labor unions were not to be considered combinations in "restraint of trade." The Federal Trade Commission was created to protect the public from unfair business practices. The five-member commission could issue "cease-and-desist" orders against companies involved in unfair practices. A Federal Reserve System was established to provide some control over the nation's banks. The Underwood Tariff reduced rates more than any other law since the Civil War. Other laws between 1913 and 1916 restricted cheap labor, extended loans to farmers, improved the working conditions of merchant sailors, and provided an eight-hour-day for railroad workers. Meanwhile, the states finally ratified the Sixteenth and Seventeenth Amendments, providing for an income tax and the direct election of senators.

By 1916 progressivism was riding high. The way had been prepared through long years of patient work of early urban, state, and national crusaders. Then war clouds again filled the sky. Thus, the progressive movement took a back seat to preparation for yet another conflict. However, this time the conflict was across the Atlantic Ocean.

Questions for Discussion

1. Define *trust, coining, graduated income tax, progressivism, muckrakers, Wall Street.*
2. Why were most supporters of the Populists farmers and miners?
3. How did the Populist platform reflect a desire for government intervention in business?
4. How did the political ideas of Eugene Debs differ from those of Robert La Follette?
5. What reforms made during the presidency of Theodore Roosevelt entitle him to be called progressive?

Chapter 19 Review

1. List and describe the poor working conditions of the laborers.
2. What were the goals of the Knights of Labor? What were its successes? Why did it decline?
3. What were the goals and beliefs of Samuel Gompers? What organization did he found?
4. How were Blacks affected by the organization of labor unions?
5. How did employers react to strikes?
6. What caused the Haymarket riot? What resulted?
7. What advantages did the employers have over the workers and their unions?
8. How did the political machine control elections? Describe the techniques used by "Boss" Tweed and Tammany Hall.
9. What steps did President Hayes take to reform the political corruption of the time?
10. What problems did farmers face at the end of the nineteenth century?
11. What were the issues surrounding the question of railroad regulation?
12. What were the weaknesses of the Interstate Commerce Act?
13. Who was William Jennings Bryan?
14. How were Populists and Progressives similar? different?
15. What reforms did Robert La Follette introduce into the government of Wisconsin?

Word Study

Fill in each blank in the sentences that follow with the term below that is most appropriate.

coined	Populists	settlement house
craft union	yellow-dog contracts	graduated income tax
scabs	muckrakers	injunction
industrial unions	lockout	socialist

1. Workers who share a common skill organize into _____.
2. Workers who work in similar industries organize into _____.
3. Employers often used the _____ technique to prevent workers from returning to their jobs.
4. Striking workers were replaced by _____, who did not strike.
5. The courts sometimes issued orders demanding action, or an _____.
6. Employers often made new employees sign _____ or promises that they would not join unions.
7. The Wobblies believed in a _____ philosophy.
8. Jane Addams proposed the establishment of community centers called _____ as a means of reform.
9. A tax that rises as income rises is a _____.
10. Newspaper writers who exposed corruption were called _____.
11. When silver is turned into currency, it is said to be _____.

Using Your Skills

1. Look at the cartoon on page 431 What point does this cartoon try to make?
2. Look at the pictures on pages 432 through 442. Which of these pictures would most likely convince viewers that reform of labor practices was necessary? Why?
3. Consider Article I, Section 8 of the Constitution, enumerating the powers of Congress. In your own words, tell what powers Congress has to regulate business.

CHAPTER 20
A Nation of Immigrants

Thousands of newcomers to American cities were young men and women from the country. They were drawn by the bright lights, the hopes of quick fortunes, and the simple wish to change their lives. Thousands of other newcomers were European immigrants. From 1870 onward, the tide of migration rose.

The newcomers were attracted to America by many forces. For one, transportation in the Steam Age was quick and cheap. A ticket to the New World promised a new farm, a new job, and a new chance. But the lure of American opportunity was matched by the push of political and religious persecution at home. Russian Jews, German socialists, and Polish and Italian peasants were among those driven across the oceans by harsh laws and hard times in their native countries. By 1914, over 70 percent of the new arrivals came from southern and eastern Europe.

However, not all immigrants to America crossed the seas. Many came from Canada and other Western Hemisphere nations. Also, as the twentieth century began, there was a kind of "immigration" within the United States. Thousands of Blacks moved to the industrial cities of the South and the North in search of jobs.

In the 1880s, Americans welcomed the new arrivals. The inscription on the Statue of Liberty, built in New York harbor in 1886, said that the great copper figure lifted her lamp "beside the golden door" for "Huddled masses yearning to breathe free." Yet, at the same time, a law of 1882 barred Chinese laborers from entering the country. And later in 1907, Japanese immigrants were also denied entry. It was clear that America was placing restrictions on who could pass through the "golden door."

READING GUIDE

1. **What conditions in southern and eastern Europe led to mass emigration in the later nineteenth and early twentieth centuries?**
2. **How did the immigrants cope with the dramatic changes in their lives?**
3. **What questions did immigration raise for Americans?**

The first anxious moments of an immigrant family's landing in America.

1. Changes in European Society

In the years between 1882 and 1914, America experienced a new wave of immigration. These new immigrants no longer came from northern and western Europe in great numbers as they had fifty years earlier. Now, they came mainly from southern and eastern Europe.

This shift reflected the changes that were taking place in Europe at the time. The northern and western European countries had adjusted to the changes caused by land reform, a growing population, and the Industrial Revolution. Rapid industrialization in Germany and Scandinavia provided many jobs for unemployed farm workers. Germany and Sweden had begun to realize the economic and military value of their populations. Britain did not discourage **emigration,** but it directed the flow to its own lands and colonies. In addition, the original lure of plentiful, cheap farmland in America no longer beckoned as it once had.

emigration
leaving one's home or country to make a home in another place.

The End of Feudalism

During these years, southern and eastern Europe began to feel the effects of the social and economic upheavals that had rocked northern and western Europe fifty years earlier. In the late nineteenth century, feudalism came to an end when Russia freed its serfs. At first, the peasants were happy to be released from their obligations to work a set number of days on the land of the nobles. However, with the good came the bad. The peasants could no longer use the village pastures for their animals. Nor could they gather firewood from uncultivated land without paying a fee.

If peasant landholdings had been large enough and rich enough, they could have sold their crops and raised money. Instead, conditions were working against them. The population of Europe had increased rapidly since 1750. By 1915 it had tripled. Family land that had passed down to the oldest son for generations finally had to be split among several children. As a result, plots were no longer large enough to support the people living on them. So many people were forced to hire themselves out on another owner's land or to seek other means of survival.

Critical Conditions

In several areas of Europe, people were close to starvation. Meals consisted of bread, potatoes, and milk. Meat was a rarity. When harvests were bad, the strong ancestral bonds that tied peasants to their villages were being broken by the fear of famine. Men and women were forced to move out, seeking work and food elsewhere.

In some instances, American tariff policy aggravated these conditions. The McKinley Tariff of 1890, a high protective tariff, threatened the livelihood of many European workers who made

A group of Italian immigrants from the S.S. Princess Irene on their way to Ellis Island, where new arrivals were given medical and other tests for admission.

articles that were imported by the United States. As a result of this high tariff, many of these articles had no markets in the United States. For example, Czech artisans in glassmaking and textile industries emigrated to the United States in order to be protected by the tariff rather than hurt by it.

In the 1890s, the French government passed a tariff to protect French growers of *currants*—small seedless raisins—from foreign competition. The Greek economy had depended heavily on the export of its currant crop. Thus, Greek emigration to the United States resulted.

Southern Italians were affected by the wine tariff in France just as the Greeks were. At about the same time, the United States developed its own citrus industry and no longer imported oranges and lemons from Italy. The result was that many southern Italian workers were unable to earn enough to survive.

Political factors also encouraged Italian emigration. When Italy was united in the 1870s, northern and central Italy held most of the political power. Southern Italy and Sicily were burdened with taxes. These areas received little in return. There were also many absentee landlords who sought a quick profit from the land. These landlords were unwilling to pay for improvements that could make the land more productive.

Until the 1860s and 1870s, most of the countries in this region forbade their subjects to emigrate. Political reorganization in Austria-Hungary (1867), unification in Italy (1849–1870), and the effects of the Russo-Turkish War (1877–1878) finally loosened these restrictions.

Religious and Political Persecution

In the 1800s, the population of Russia included minorities of different national, cultural, and religious backgrounds. The Russian czars felt that if they did away with these differences, the people would be easier to control. They sought to carry out this aim through decrees. Austria-Hungary had a similarly mixed population, though their government was less harsh in its policies.

The Mennonites of German background were members of a special, very religious Christian sect. They were one of the first targets of the "Russification" decrees. Around 1870, they were stripped of their religious freedom and of their right to self-rule. They were also required to serve in the czar's army, which was in violation of their religious beliefs. Other Russians of German descent as well as the Poles and the Finns were discriminated against in the same manner. Poles especially fled in large numbers, seeking both freedom and jobs in the New World.

In addition, the Jews in Russia suffered harsh treatment. Czar Alexander II had attempted some reforms, but he was assassinated in 1881. After his death, the treatment of the Jews was more severe. They were forced to settle in the Pale of Settlement, a narrow strip of land on the western border of Russia. Jews could not conduct business on Christian or Jewish holidays. Nor were they allowed to move freely. Educational opportunities were also limited. Jews lived in fear of outbreaks of violence directed at them and their possessions. *Pogroms*—organized attacks against Jews—were encouraged by many government officials. In other areas of eastern Europe, Jews faced similar treatment. As a result, nearly one-third of the 8 million new settlers in the United States from Russia and Austria-Hungary were Jews. Many so-called Russian Jews were actually from Poland. Until 1920, Russia owned a large part of present-day Poland.

In the Ottoman Empire (ruled by Ottoman Turks) Christians were the victims of religious persecution. In 1870, Syrian Christians sought refuge in Egypt and India. As Turkey began to fear the rise of Armenian nationalism, thousands of Armenian Christians were massacred from 1894 to 1896. Massacres occured again in 1909 and in 1915. Those who escaped followed the Syrians into Egypt and India. In time, American Protestant missionaries encouraged Syrian and Armenian emigration to the United States. Syrians and Armenians joined the throngs gathered in the port cities waiting for new opportunity in America.

The Trip to the New World

The first adventurers in the new wave of immigration wrote home with news of life in the new world. These writers sometimes exaggerated their good fortune rather than admit that they were struggling. But these letters from America provided the motivation and often the means for others to venture out.

Agents from Western railroads, Western states, and steamship lines were often sent to Europe to recruit immigrants. These agents knew that larger populations would mean bigger profits on investments. The steamships that arrived in the ports of Europe were laden with wheat and cotton. The steamship companies knew that they could make money by loading up with passengers for the trip back to America. Their agents drummed up business by placing posters in gathering places and by greeting people outside churches. In fact, they painted a very rosy picture of life across the ocean.

The first portion of the immigrant journey was the trip by railroad to a port city on the Mediterranean, Baltic, or Adriatic Sea. The trip was slow and difficult. Many people traveled in windowless boxcars lined with benches. When they reached a port, they sometimes had to wait weeks, crammed in filthy boarding houses, until a ship sailed. Even though the ocean voyage took about ten days by steamship, there were no set dates for departure and arrival.

The majority of the "new" immigrants set out for New York, Boston, and other major cities. They had little money or education. Without the money to buy land, they had to find work. Money spelled to the "new" immigrants what land had meant to the "old" immigrants—security, power, and prestige.

In 1910, new arrivals in New York City—immigrants from overseas, Blacks from the South, and farmers lured by the big city—wait outside an employment agency for work.

463

Questions for Discussion
1. Define *currants*, *pogroms*.
2. Explain the difference between *immigration* and *emigration*.
3. What conditions in southern and eastern Europe brought immigrants to the United States?
4. Why were people sent to Europe to recruit immigrants?

2. A New Beginning

To the newcomers, the vision of the New York skyline and the Statue of Liberty was an awesome sight. As the ships prepared to dock, the immigrants' most pressing concern was whether or not they would be allowed to stay. Those who had traveled in the ship's best rooms were usually admitted directly from the ship after a brief visit from an immigration official and a public health doctor. Some poor families bought tickets for the best rooms on board for those members of their family who were the least likely to pass a careful medical examination.

Completing a long journey from the Old World, these immigrants get their first look at the Statue of Liberty as they enter New York Harbor.

However, for the majority of immigrants who sailed *steerage*, the cheapest and poorest accommodation, the process was different. These people were ferried to the examination center of Ellis Island in the New York harbor. There, the immigrants were examined by doctors to determine if they were physically and mentally fit. Not everyone was admitted. In 1903, a law was passed requiring steamships to return to Europe any persons who were denied entry into the United States, at the shipping line's expense. From then on, ship officials became more selective about recruiting passengers.

Once the immigrants passed the medical examinations, they were questioned through an interpreter about their plans and prospects. They had to assure the immigration officials that they would be able to support themselves. At the same time, however, they had to deny that they already had jobs. In 1885, Congress had passed the Contract Labor Act. This law forbade laborers from contracting their future labor in exchange for passage. Exceptions were made for professionals, skilled laborers, and domestic laborers. Unions thought that the coal mining interests were recruiting unskilled laborers from Italy and Slovakia as strikebreakers in Pennsylvania mines. Violation of the law could mean deportation. Congress had also passed a law in 1882, which excluded convicts and those likely to become "public charges." Instead, these people were returned to their homelands.

In spite of the restrictions and hardships, five out of six immigrants were admitted soon after they landed. Between 1890 and 1910, the population of the United States swelled from 63 million to 90 million, largely as a result of immigration.

Where They Settled

Where did the immigrants settle? There were Italians to be found in the wine-producing regions of California, Russo-Germans along the right-of-way of the Santa Fe railroad, and Czechs on farms in the Midwest. However, this was not the general rule. With the exceptions of the Jews, most of the immigrants had been farmers in Europe. They did not have money to buy land in America. Nor were most of them attracted by the lonely rural life in the wide-open Western states. Eighty percent of the new immigrants settled in the cities and industrial centers in the Northeastern quarter of the United States.

In the days before scheduled steamship travel, immigrants often took the first ship that had room for them—whether it docked in Boston or Baltimore. They then sent word back to the homeland to friends and relatives. This gave information to those immigrants who came later about where to go in order to be with people they knew. To be with others of their own origin, immigrants often took jobs in the

It was not unusual for immigrant families to work long into the night for a little extra money. This family, living in a New York tenement in 1912, earned income by making wreaths of artificial flowers.

same industries. As a result, many immigrants in America lived in clusters based on ethnic and national background.

The first homes of many Italian immigrants were the "Little Italies" of Mulberry Street in New York or The North End in Boston. The men worked on construction of subways and bridges. The women added to family income by using the dressmaking skills they had learned in their old villages. Other groups of Italians were found at work in the mines of Pennsylvania, in textile mills in New England, and in any other industry that required unskilled labor. The Finnish usually migrated to the iron and copper mines of the Midwest. Greeks and Syrians remained in the Eastern cities, where they worked as vendors or opened up restaurants. Bulgarians went to the steel towns of Illinois. The meat-packing industry in Chicago and the automobile industry in Detroit drew many Polish workers, as did the steel and textile mills. Some Poles and Italians were able to work as hired farmers, or even buy land of their own in rural New England. Some Italians migrated to California to work in agriculture there.

Jewish Immigration

Jewish immigration differed from that of other groups. Most Jews emigrated in family groups. And it was not unusual for three generations of a family to travel together. Unlike other eastern and southern Europeans, the Jews were usually town dwellers who had been engaged in trade. Therefore, when they arrived, they gravitated toward the big cities to use their trades. In this manner, many Jews became prominent in trades and in the garment industry.

For the immigrant who could not afford to open a shop, there was a pushcart. Piled high with an endless assortment of products, the cart served as the counter of a store without walls. In New York City, these vendors gathered on Hester Street. Some of these pushcarts were the forerunners of more conventional shops and businesses. It was on the street that the Jews purchased their provisions. It was also on the street that the laborer who was out of work looked for an employer.

About 10 percent of the Jewish immigrants came to the United States with skills in the "needle trade," or garment industry. In America, they worked in small factories, called sweat shops. These sweat shops were located in tenement buildings. The employer was a subcontractor for a manufacturer who supplied the precut fabrics to be sewn together. Men and women worked a sixty- to a hundred-hour week to earn less than $200 per year. Yet, it was the ambition of many to save enough money to set themselves up in business.

AN IMMIGRANT SEEKS ADVICE

The following letter is taken from Bintel Brief, *a collection of letters. Jewish immigrants in New York often wrote to their newspaper editors seeking advice on problems in their everyday lives.*

Dear Editor,

I am a newsboy, fourteen years old, and I sell the *Forverts* in the streets till late into the night. I come to you to ask your advice.

I was born in Russia and was twelve years old when I came to America with my dear mother. My sister, who was in the country before us, brought us over.

My sister worked and supported us. She didn't allow me to go to work but sent me to school. I went to school for two years and didn't miss a day, but then came the terrible fire at the Triangle shop, where she worked, and I lost my dear sister. My mother and I suffer terribly from the misfortune. I had to help my mother and after school hours I go out and sell newspapers.

I have to go to school three more years, and after that I want to go to college. But my mother doesn't want me to go to school because she thinks I should go to work. I tell her I will work days and study at night but she won't hear of it.

Since I read the *Forverts* to my mother every night and read your answers in the "Bintel Brief," I beg you to answer me and say a few words to her.

Your Reader,
The Newsboy

A Period of Adjustment

Immigrants faced many problems as they tried to adjust to life in America. They suffered uneasiness and loneliness because they were separated from familiar surroundings. In order to survive, it was necessary for them to learn a new language and new customs. They also had to master a new set of rules for dealing with every day life. Many suffered from what has since been termed "culture shock."

The influx of immigrants, which reached a peak of 1,285,000 in 1907, was too great a number for the public agencies to service. This meant that other alternatives had to be developed.

Thus, *mutual-aid societies* were set up to meet the immediate material needs of the immigrants. They provided help for the sick, food for the hungry, and burial expenses for the dead. They also filled the need for companionship.

As the government became better equipped to handle the welfare functions, these aid societies served other purposes. Some became self-improvement societies or trade organizations for skilled workers. One of the most outstanding was the Workmen's Circle in New York. Organized by two Jewish cloakmakers in 1892, it became a national agency by 1900. The Workmen's Circle stressed self-help and self-respect. It also encouraged loyalty to one's fellow worker—the backbone of a strong Jewish labor movement. Other societies became social clubs. They helped preserve the songs, dances, and crafts of the immigrants' native culture.

Opportunities for employment and land ownership grew in the West during the 1880s. As a result, many immigrants left the East in search of a better life. The photograph below shows a group of immigrants waiting in front of a Southern Pacific train at Mill City, Nevada, in 1886.

Immigrant culture was preserved in a variety of ways. Every group brought with them their own religion. Religion remained a great source of comfort. The immigrant press also served the function of maintaining immigrant culture. Papers by the hundreds were printed, with such varied names as *Az-Ember*, *Il Progresso*, *Atlantis*, *Arekag*, and the *Forward*.

Other Immigrants

A large percentage of the immigrants in the late nineteenth and early twentieth centuries were Polish, Italian, or Jewish who came over the Atlantic Ocean. Yet, French Canadians, Mexicans, Chinese, and Japanese were migrating to America as well.

The French Canadians came into the United States from Quebec. Many settled in New England, where they worked in the textile industry or took up farming. Unlike many groups that shed their more "foreign" characteristics, the French Canadians kept strong loyalties to their culture, language, and traditions. To this day, they have remained a distinct group.

Mexican immigration increased after restrictions were placed on European immigration. Eighty percent of the Mexican immigrants settled in the Southwest, where they joined other Spanish-speaking Americans who had lived there since the early days of exploration. The Mexicans worked on the American railroads and in copper, silver, and gold mines. Many Mexicans traveled throughout the West and South as migrant farm workers. This constant movement prevented many Mexican-American children from taking full advantage of public school education. This was one reason why the prospects of future generations were held down.

When East Meets West

While adventurous nineteenth-century Americans sought their fortunes in China, thousands of Chinese crossed the Pacific Ocean in the opposite direction for the same reason. Many came with the intention of returning to China once they made their fortunes. At first, they came to look for gold in California in 1849. Then many settled in the growing towns of the West. Few had the money to buy farms. Thus, many Chinese became cooks and launderers.

Beginning in 1868, Chinese laborers, willing to work for low wages, came in large numbers to help build the railroads in the West. In 1870, about 90 percent of agricultural labor in California was Chinese. Some moved eastward to settle in other American states. But the bulk of Chinese immigrants to the United States remained in the Pacific and Rocky Mountain states.

The Chinese gave American life a special flavor. Their homes and

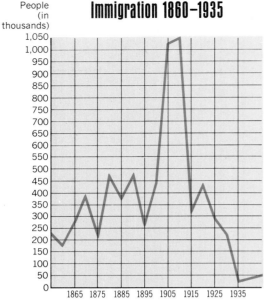

Immigration 1860–1935

People (in thousands)

1,050
1,000
950
900
850
800
750
700
650
600
550
500
450
400
350
300
250
200
150
100
50
0

1865 1875 1885 1895 1905 1915 1925 1935

This Puck cartoon from 1889 summed up a view held by many Americans of the time. This was that the one unmixable element in the national pot was the Irish.

shops brought exotic foods, incense, pictures, carvings, and other arts of a civilization thousands of years old to raw pioneer settlements. In spite of this, the Chinese people were not welcomed by Americans.

In part, the Chinese desire to live in neighborhoods of their own came from their strong sense of family and community. But the hostility of Americans also drove them together. Often White Americans scorned Oriental peoples and their cultures. The Chinese who worked for low wages, though they had no control over what they were paid, were accused of deliberately choosing a standard of living lower than that of Americans. Other racial accusations were also made. Their "odd" clothes, food, and religion were unjustly mocked. In 1877, anti-Chinese riots broke out in San Francisco. Workers, who were led to believe that their low wages were the direct result of Chinese competition, burned Chinese shops and beat and killed their owners.

A CHINESE IMMIGRATION STORY

A great influx of Chinese to the United States came about when four California merchants, Leland Stanford, Charles Crocker, Mark Hopkins, and Collis Huntington, were building the western section of the first transcontinental railroad. Their portion of the railroad was being pushed eastward from Sacramento across California's gold-rich mountains. As a result, the four merchants were having a hard time finding laborers. The tough, husky Americans who were in the track gangs consumed large quantities of hard-to-transport meat and whiskey. On Saturday nights, the consumption of this whiskey often led to fights, casualties, and desertions. Worst of all, when the line passed through mining-camp country, any rumor of a new strike in silver and gold caused hundreds to drop their tools and take off for the new "diggings" in search of fortune.

Crocker one day came up with the idea of using Chinese workers, who seemed to be plentiful in San Francisco. The others thought for a while, turning over in their minds the Chinese they had seen. Many were frail men and women who lived mostly on rice, vegetables, a little fish, and tea. They dressed in loose blue smocks and trousers and straw sunhats. No, the merchants said. Crocker's idea wouldn't work. They wondered how Crocker could imagine such people blasting rocks, swinging sledgehammers, hauling heavy rails, handling wheelbarrows full of earth.

"They built the Great Wall of China, didn't they?" was Crocker's retort. The others had not thought of it quite that way. They agreed to try the experiment. The Chinese people turned out to be superb, untiring workers. They were recruited by the thousands to drive the line eastward to its junction, at Promontory Point in Utah, with the Union Pacific coming west from Omaha.

Finally, Western states demanded that further Chinese immigrants be barred from settling there.

In 1882, Congress willingly passed a Chinese Exclusion Act, forbidding the immigration of Chinese laborers. Yet the Burlingame Treaty had given each nation's citizens the right to travel and to live freely in either country. President Arthur argued that the United States could not break its word and thus vetoed the measure. However, Congress repassed the Act over his veto. Now only Chinese business people, diplomats, and scholars could enter the United States. Court decisions denied all Chinese the right of naturalization. Never were the people of western nations so humiliated as the Chinese.

Around 1900, Japanese immigrants began to arrive in the West. They became farm workers and gardeners. Many soon owned their own farms and businesses. The same anti-Oriental feelings that barred Chinese were again aroused. Californians now demanded that the Japanese, like the Chinese, be excluded as "undesirable."

In October 1906, the San Francisco School Board passed a resolution calling for segregated schools for Oriental children. Angry demonstrations flared up in Japan, as the Japanese protested the humiliation of the Japanese people. President Roosevelt did not want to increase the rift between Japan and the United States that had resulted from the Treaty of Portsmouth (see Chapter 21). Promising that he would come to some agreement with the Japanese government, Roosevelt pressured the school board to revoke its resolution. The leaders of Japan prevented any further embarassment by signing a series of "Gentlemen's Agreements" with the United States in 1900 and again in 1907. Japan would not allow its laborers to emigrate to America, so no insulting anti-Japanese laws were necessary.

By 1910, it was clear that many Americans were willing to sell to Oriental customers and generously to provide schools, hospitals, missions, and charity to poverty stricken Orientals—provided that they stayed on their own side of the Pacific Ocean!

Education

Wide-scale efforts were made to attract immigrants to school. New teaching procedures were developed for instructing non-English-

Jewish immigrants also made their way to the New World. Many Jewish families settled on the Lower East Side of New York City. One of the main streets for Jewish merchants to sell their wares was Orchard Street, shown below.

speaking students. Posters, placards, and circulars advertised available classes. Information was circulated through employers, unions, and mutual-aid societies. Compulsory education laws were passed requiring attendance between certain ages and for a given length of time.

To the immigrant, public school education for their children was often a mixed blessing. Children who were in school could no longer work. They also became separated from their parents' culture. Friction often developed between the old and new cultures within families. Yet, for many people, education became the passport out of the **ghetto.**

ghetto
a section of a city in which members of a minority or ethnic group live especially due to social, legal, or economic pressure.

Questions for Discussion

1. Define *steerage, mutual-aid societies.*
2. Why were restrictions placed on immigration?
3. How and where did the immigrants make a living?
4. How did the immigrants cope with "culture shock"?
5. What role did mutual-aid societies play in the Americanization of immigrants?

3. Immigration Poses Questions

The growth of American cities seemed to multiply with the increase in the number of immigrants. Many Americans looked unfavorably on the changes brought about by this growth. Immigrants unfairly received the blame for the evils of urban growth and industrial expansion.

In addition to their other differences, the "new" immigrants were often of different religious faiths, either Catholic or Jewish. In fact, by the end of the nineteenth century, there were enough Catholic citizens to affect the outcome of elections. Fearing loss of their traditional political strength, a minority of the Protestants revived ill-feelings toward the Catholic immigrants. The rise of nativism was evident where immigrants were making progress and beginning to "crowd" into industry, politics, and society those who were already established.

In 1887, an anti-Catholic secret society, The American Protective Association, was founded. Claiming that the Pope was trying to take over America, their founders appealed to the fears of mostly the unemployed and uneducated. The society favored increasing the time before an immigrant could become a citizen and sought a drastic reduction in immigration. When an economic depression struck in the 1890s, membership in the American Protective Association soared. It seemed easier to blame someone, in this case the immigrant, for economic woes. However, as the economic picture improved, the short-lived popularity of this nativist association declined.

The Immigration Restriction League was another influential group. Founded in Boston in 1894, the League favored a literacy test to determine who should be allowed to enter the United States. Prospective immigrants would have to be able to read a passage in their own language in order to gain entry.

The campaign was supposedly aimed at accepting only high quality immigrants into the United States. In reality, the campaign was an attempt to keep southern and eastern Europeans out. Free education was not available in the countries of southern and eastern Europe. In addition, most of the newcomers came from rural backgrounds and did not have the opportunity to attend school. Bills based on literacy requirements were introduced into Congress many times during the administrations of Presidents Cleveland, Taft, and Wilson. But they were always vetoed by the Presidents. In 1917, during a wave of antiforeign feeling, Congress finally passed a literacy requirement over President Wilson's veto. This, in turn, started a trend of other restrictive measures.

Melting Pot or Salad Bowl

A number of ideas have been offered about what happens to an immigrant in the process of becoming an American. One theory that gained support was that of the "melting pot." Immigrants supposedly blended into American society, both changing it and being changed by it. The resulting product was a society with no cultural differences.

Henry Ford went as far as to introduce a "melting pot" ceremony. He had a huge pot constructed outside his factory. The immigrants were supposed to don their native clothing and approach the pot singing their native tunes. As they passed through the pot, they changed into American clothes and came out singing the "Star-Spangled Banner." At this point, they were truly Americans.

The melting pot theory put pressure on immigrants to shed any qualities that made them different. Americanization was not complete until all traces of immigrant heritage and culture were erased.

Some historians and sociologists then and now rejected the melting pot theory. Oscar Handlin, in his 1952 Pulitzer Prize winning book, *The Uprooted*, claimed that the newcomers would never totally fit into society. They would always retain some diversity. In 1915 Horace Kallen, a philosopher and educator, claimed that the melting pot idea was undemocratic. He felt that there should be cooperation among the different cultures. Kallen opposed a push for unity and spoke out in favor of diversity. Each group had a contribution to make to America. Carl Degler in *Out of Our Past* describes America not as a melting pot, but as a salad bowl. Rather than melting together and losing their differences, Degler suggested that all the parts remained

Views of life in the Chinese community of Virginia City, Nevada, in 1877.

AN OPEN LETTER TO MY BRETHREN

The following excerpt is taken from The Forum, *a Black newspaper of the early 1900s. The managing editor, Rev. J. Gordon McPherson, is trying to convince Blacks to move westward to California.*

"The Great State of California knows no man by reason of his birthplace, race, or color, or former condition of life—that stands with open arms to receive all who will accept a home in her broad lands." No words of mine can describe the variety and beauty of this, our Golden State. Every form of human industry awaits you; every facility for honorable employment can be attained. The farmer, the fisherman, the sailor, the miner, the mechanic of every description, the merchant, in all lines of trade, the minister and the doctor, as well as the lawyer, can all find ample means and opportunities to follow their chosen vocations in this State, unmolested. None live here but brave men and women, who have consecrated this State to

freedom, not only in letter but in fact, and moreover, by the practice here of those forces that tend to perpetuate the principles of freedom in its broadest sense. Here in the house and the Church, and the school all are one. Our motto is: "One God, one country, one flag, and one people," all known as American citizens.

Can anything in the South qualify you for citizenship! We know to the contrary. In the State of California it is different. There it is the internal and not the external qualifications of a man that recommend him to citizenship.

In the time of long suffering, people are too apt to forget their duty to themselves, their wives and their children, and allow the great opportunities of their lives to pass unnoticed. If we do not accept the glorious opportunities that this State offers us, and its manifold blessings, that we might secure and hand down to our children, and to our children's children, it is our own fault. . . .

what they were, yet contributed to the whole.

The immigrants who settled in America provided a significant amount of the backbreaking labor for the industrial expansion of the United States. In 1907, a Congressional committee studied the effect of immigrant labor on American industry. The committee discovered that in many of the basic, heavy industries, immigrant labor accounted for 60 percent of the work force. In addition, textiles were being produced in plants that had 70 percent foreign-born labor. Had it not been for the vast pool of foreign labor, American industry would not have expanded so quickly as it did.

Questions for Discussion

1. How and why did policies develop restricting immigration?
2. Explain the "melting pot" or "salad bowl" theory of immigration.
3. What is the relationship between immigration and the growth of American industry?

Chapter 20 Review

Summary Questions for Discussion

1. What problems were faced by newcomers to the United States?
2. Why did fewer people come from northern and western Europe between 1882 and 1914?
3. How did the end of feudalism provide a reason for immigration from southern and eastern Europe?
4. Describe living conditions in eastern Europe during 1882 and 1914.
5. What was the effect of Russification on Mennonites of German background? Jews?
6. Why did Syrians and Armenians come to the United States?
7. Describe the trip to the New World.
8. What was the Contract Labor Act of 1885? Why was the Contract Labor Act of 1885 passed?
9. Where did the new immigrants settle?
10. Why did immigrants tend to live in clusters?
11. What purpose was served by mutual-aid societies?
12. From where did non-European immigrants come? Why did they come to the United States?
13. Why were the Chinese not welcomed by many Americans? What actions were taken against them?
14. How did Americans react to Japanese immigration?
15. Why was education a mixed blessing for the immigrant?
16. What was the American Protective Association?
17. What other actions were taken to restrict immigration?
18. Describe the "melting pot" theory. Who rejected this theory? Why?
19. What did immigrants do to preserve their culture?
20. Why are Blacks also considered "immigrants" during this period?

Word Study

Fill in each blank in the sentences that follow with the term below that is most appropriate.

currants   steerage
pogroms   mutual-aid societies
emigration   ghettoes

1. Many immigrants came to the United States as cheaply as possible in _____.
2. Jews were forced out of Russia by organized attacks against them called _____.
3. Greeks left their homeland when the market for _____, or small seedless raisins, collapsed.
4. Those immigrants who were admitted to the United States were often helped by _____ which met their immediate material needs.
5. Many immigrants lived in _____ because of prejudice as well as the fact that they wanted to live near friends and relatives.

Unit 5 Review

Summary

Industrialization touched the life of every American and everyone who entered the United States. Industrialization had begun early in the nineteenth century. After the Civil War its impact grew by leaps and bounds.

The urban centers swelled with Americans and immigrants seeking jobs in the new factories. Immigration and the movement to the cities provided the labor for the new industry, but it also created problems. Housing, sanitation, education had to be provided for a swelling population. The enormous gap between rich and poor became more evident. A small group was controlling the social, economic, and political life of the majority.

Unions and reformers attempted to deal with the bad situations created by industrialization. Labor organized, but was met by the harsh weapons of the industrialist. Government reform was difficult to achieve because of the extensive corruption on all levels. Farmers were caught in the squeeze of paying high prices for machinery and transportation, but not receiving high prices for their produce. They, too, attempted to organize. The combined efforts of labor unions, the Grange, the muckrakers, the Populist, and the Progressives finally sparked the needed reforms.

Industrialization, urbanization, and immigration in the latter part of the nineteenth and early twentieth centuries went hand in hand. They greatly affected the business and labor organizations, the life styles, education, and culture of America. They created many successes, but they also created problems and challenges that still exist.

Summary Questions

1. What did the conservationists want to do besides save natural resources?
2. What are some of the factors that explain the changeover from a mainly rural to a mainly urban United States?
3. How did the growth of large cities tend to change government and other forms of social behavior?
4. What changes occurred in public education after the Civil War?
5. What were the effects of industrialization on the newspaper and magazine industries?
6. How did big-city political machines and newly arrived immigrants help each other?
7. How did reform mayors try to undercut the power of political machines?
8. Why did Samuel Gompers have greater success at forming a lasting national labor union than Terence V. Powderly?
9. What changes in European society led to mass immigration to the United States in the late nineteenth and early twentieth centuries?
10. Why were certain groups of immigrants faced with more opposition than others?

Developing Your Vocabulary

1. A person who practices conservation (destroys, preserves) natural resources.
2. (Lubricants, Smelters) are used to keep machines running smoothly.
3. (Smelters, Public utilities) are used for refining ore.
4. (Slag, Steerage) is the remains after ore has been refined.
5. (Americanization, Nativism) is the process by which a foreign-born person becomes part of the American culture.
6. Nativists (did, did not) believe in the equali-

ty of foreign and American born citizens.

7. A worker whose job involves manual labor is a (blue-collar worker, white-collar worker).

8. A person who works in an office is a (blue-collar worker, a white collar worker).

9. An area that is (zoned, blacklisted) is set aside for a certain type of building or activity.

10. Building codes establish (minimum, maximum) standards for new construction.

11. (Public utilities, Muckrakers) provide essential services such as water and electricity.

12. A (tenement, settlement house) is a low rental apartment building or rooming house.

13. A(n) (injunction, platform) is a statement of a political party's goals.

14. In a(n) (craft, industrial) union, all workers in an industry can belong, regardless of skill.

15. (Anarchists, Socialists) believe that all authority is evil.

Developing Your Skills

Critical thinking

1. List some positive effects of rapid industrialization. What are some of the negative effects?

2. How is the journey of Blacks to America different from the journey and settlement of immigrants described in this unit?

Comparing

3. Compare and contrast the organization, membership and aims of the (a) Knights of Labor (b) IWW, and the (c) AF of L.

4. Compare and contrast the motivation of immigrants to the United States in the late nineteenth and early twentieth centuries with that of immigrants during the seventeenth and eighteenth centuries. (Refer to earlier chapters.)

Drawing conclusions

5. Using the maps, pictures and graphs in the unit, explain how the geographical movements of Americans between 1860 and 1890 were influenced by industrialization.

Analyzing

6. Analyze from the material presented in the unit and your own experience, the effect of industrialization and immigration on education and literature in the United States.

Special Activities

1. Prepare a series of cartoons or drawings that trace the reasons why immigrants came to America and their problems upon arrival.

2. Read a biography of John D. Rockefeller or Andrew Carnegie. Present to the class a biographical sketch of the individual chosen including the techniques used to acquire his wealth and the philanthropic activities associated with him.

3. Read one of the works of literature described in Chapter 18. Report to the class by explaining the main points of view that the author is presenting and their relationship to this unit.

4. Prepare a three-person discussion for the class. Have one person represent a laborer, one person a union member trying to persuade the laborer to join a union, and one person an industrialist trying to persuade the laborer not to become a union member. The worker should make his or her choice and present reasons to the class.

UNIT 6

The United States Becomes a World Power

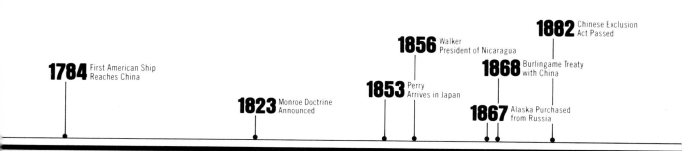

1784 First American Ship Reaches China

1823 Monroe Doctrine Announced

1853 Perry Arrives in Japan

1856 Walker President of Nicaragua

1867 Alaska Purchased from Russia

1868 Burlingame Treaty with China

1882 Chinese Exclusion Act Passed

CHAPTER 21
The United States in the Pacific

CHAPTER 22
The United States and Latin America

CHAPTER 23
World War I

Growing rapidly in size and wealth after independence from Britain, the United States soon became one of the world's most powerful nations. By the end of the nineteenth century, most of the other great nations were the hubs of immense empires that spread around the globe. Now Americans began to ask if the United States should have an empire too.

The stage for the American drama of expansionism in the 1800s extended to the borders of Canada and Mexico, from the Atlantic to the Pacific. Chapter 21 tells of how the limits of that stage were

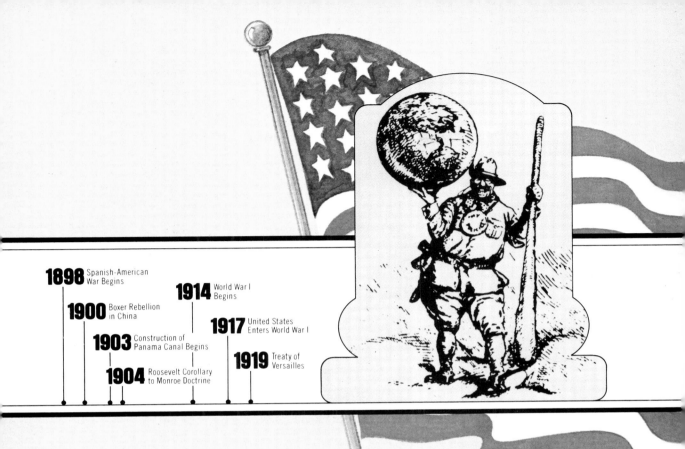

1898 Spanish-American War Begins

1900 Boxer Rebellion in China

1903 Construction of Panama Canal Begins

1904 Roosevelt Corollary to Monroe Doctrine

1914 World War I Begins

1917 United States Enters World War I

1919 Treaty of Versailles

stretched to islands in the Pacific, to Alaska, and to countries in the Far East. Chapter 22 describes the nation's growing involvement in the affairs of Caribbean islands and Latin American lands south of the Rio Grande. Chapter 23 discloses that even when Americans tried hard, they could not remain aloof from the affairs of the European countries from which most of their ancestors had come. Their involvement in a war that spread from Europe to the entire world renewed interest in a question that had concerned even Washington, Adams, and Jefferson: What should be America's role in the world?

CHAPTER 21

The United States in the Pacific

In August 1784, the Empress of China, a small merchant ship, entered the harbor in Canton, China, flying an unfamiliar banner at its masthead. Few Cantonese knew that it was the flag of the new country, the United States of America. Three years before the Constitution was written, the "red, white, and blue" had been carried into the far Pacific. By 1917, the United States was a major power in the Pacific world.

A number of forces kept pushing Americans to adventure beyond their borders. This process began while Americans were still British colonial subjects. Many were adventurous sailors and traders, who often traveled through strange waters to distant lands. When the United States, as a free nation, began to add new territory, its merchants grew ambitious for new markets. In addition, there was a strong American sense of religious mission, or special duty to benefit others. Many nineteenth-century Americans believed that God had chosen them to bring Christianity to the "heathens." Finally, as the United States industrialized, many of its citizens came to believe in a new version of this idea. For the good of humanity, "backward" peoples—who lacked railroads, telegraphs, factories, and other signs of "progress"—should be improved by "advanced" nations.

These forces at work led the United States and other strong, modernized countries to move toward *imperialism*—a policy of extending a nation's control over other peoples, either by actually taking over and ruling their territories or by making them economic dependents. The belief in Manifest Destiny, which led Americans across the continent, allowed them to go beyond the water's edge. Thus by 1917, the United States was a major power in the Pacific.

READING GUIDE

1. **How did the opening of new markets in the Pacific lead the United States to acquire land overseas?**
2. **What problems arose from acquiring these lands?**

This 1899 cartoon makes a strong case against imperialism by emphasizing the horrors of American policy in the Philippines.

1. The Beginnings of Imperialism

The voyage of the *Empress of China* was a huge success. The ship returned home with a cargo that earned a profit of $38,000, a large sum of money at that time. Soon, other ships were leaving Northeastern United States ports for China. Often, they went around Cape Horn and stopped on the Pacific Coast for furs. Then, partway across the Pacific, they would stop again at the Hawaiian Islands for fresh food and water. So Oregon, California, Hawaii, and China were linked together by American traders even before the first three areas belonged to the United States.

At first, American ships brought the Chinese furs and special plants, which were used to make medicines and perfumes. After industry came to New England, the cargoes were likely to be cotton cloth, hardware, and other manufactured goods. In exchange, tea, china, and silk were brought back to the ports of Boston and New York. The actual buying and selling was done by American business people who lived for a time in China. These people often learned Chinese manners, the language, and business customs.

However, it was clear that there were some drawbacks. The Chinese were unwilling to have foreigners in their country. They forced foreign merchants to trade only in one port, live in special neighborhoods, and deal only with a few specially chosen Chinese merchants. Western nations did not like these Chinese rules. So they used the modern weapons they had to force the Chinese to change. The Chinese did not have the weapons. Beginning in 1840, Great Britain fought the first of a series of small wars with China. After each war, the defeated Chinese emperor was forced to sign a treaty, opening up additional ports. As a result, rights for foreign powers were established in ports such as Shanghai, Canton, and Hong Kong. The

Chinese government also had to accept the presence of missionaries, who were trying to convert the Chinese people. Foreign governments also demanded the right of *extraterritoriality*. This meant that their citizens accused of committing crimes in China would be tried in special non-Chinese courts.

The United States did not join in these wars. Yet, America did share in the advantages gained through the fighting. In 1844, a United States diplomat, Caleb Cushing, negotiated a commercial treaty between the United States and China. In it, the United States received all the trading privileges enjoyed by the other nations in China. America acquired trading rights in five port cities. It also gained the right of residence in those cities, and extraterritoriality. Ten years later, the American navy took a hand in the process of "opening up the Orient."

Commodore Perry Opens Japan

Japan was even more isolated than China. From the 1600s to the 1800s, the *Shoguns*, those who ruled Japan, had limited western traders to contacts only through the port city of Nagasaki. With western merchants eager for enlarged Far Eastern trade—as they had been since the time of Columbus—some western country was bound to try to force open the door to Japan.

The United States became involved in trade with Japan through its busy whaling industry. American whaling vessels roamed the Pacific in pursuit of these great sea creatures, which provided valuable oil. Some of these ships were wrecked on the coasts of Japan. The survivors were imprisoned by the Japanese as foreign "invaders." In 1852, President Millard Fillmore sent a naval expedition under

From the time that trade with the West had begun in the sixteenth century, China tried to limit Western influence by confining merchants to certain areas. Contacts between Chinese and European public officials, such as the meeting in the picture on the opposite page, were polite, formal, and infrequent. The big break for English merchants came in 1842 when the Chinese were forced to sign a treaty opening two more ports. Similar treaties with other nations, including the United States, followed. By 1854, the busy port of Hong Kong, seen above, was jammed with clipper ships and side-wheel steamers.

485

The United States in the Pacific 1784-1917

█ United States Possessions

— Boundaries as of 1917

Kilometers
0   300   600   900   1200

0   200   400   600   800
Miles

Commodore Matthew C. Perry to "request " a treaty that would protect shipwrecked American sailors from being seized. But Fillmore also believed, as did his fellow members of the Whig Party, that a navy should not just fight battles. Rather, it should also help the nation's commerce to grow. So Perry was also to try to get one or more Japanese ports opened to American trade.

Perry conducted his assignment with great skill. He was told to be tough if necessary, but not to involve the United States in a war. In

July 1853, he sailed his ships boldly into forbidden Tokyo Bay and ignored Japanese orders to leave. He refused to see minor Japanese officials. Instead, he remained hidden in his cabin and sent word that he had a letter from the President to the Emperor. Perry would deliver it in person only to someone of the highest rank. Six tense days passed before this game of bluff finally worked.

A meeting was held between the Japanese and the Americans. The Americans displayed many gifts, including industrial products, tools, guns, a camera, and even a model steam train, which chugged around a circular track, carrying solemn Japanese nobles.

Perry left Japan to give the Japanese time to think over his offer. When he returned the following February, Japanese leaders were convinced of the advantages of commerce, industry—and most importantly, arms! So they signed a treaty opening two ports to Americans and admitting United States diplomatic officials into their country. This opened a long period of American-Japanese trade. It also marked a steady march by Japan toward modernization. Young America had helped to stimulate the growth of a new power in Asia.

This is a portrait of Commodore Perry by a Japanese artist.

Prophets of Imperialism

By the eve of the Civil War, the United States itself was becoming a power in the Pacific. America had treaties with China and Japan. And in Hawaii, an ideal stopping-off point for ships bound across the Pacific Ocean, American influence was growing swiftly. American

This watercolor shows Commodore Perry's fleet off present-day Yokohama. The note at left begins, "This morning I have seen for the first time the black ships of the barbarians."

Commodore Matthew C. Perry's negotiated treaty with Japan in 1853 opened two ports to American merchants and admitted United States diplomatic officials into Japan for the first time.

William H. Seward negotiated Russia's sale of Alaska to the United States in 1867 for $7.2 million.

missionaries had set up schools and were becoming educational advisers to the royalty of Hawaii. American business people had made Hawaii another frontier. They owned sugar plantations and trading firms. As a result, these Americans played a large role in directing the economic life of the Hawaiian Islands. They were Hawaiian citizens, but only in the way that early Texas settlers had been "Mexican" citizens.

Some Americans believed that Manifest Destiny called for American leadership in Asia as well as in North America. A few actually wanted to take over some Asian territory to provide *bases* for American naval and merchant vessels. These bases would be places to make repairs, to refuel, to get supplies, and to receive protection. On returning home, Commodore Perry urged that the United States take the island of Okinawa, annex Hawaii, and establish a **protectorate** over Formosa. His feelings were not shared by Congress. However, while many people favored some form of expansion, few would go so far as to advocate annexation of overseas territories.

Some expansionists urged that the United States treat Asian nations with the respect given to other governments. Townsend Harris, American consul general to Japan in 1858, worked hard for a trade agreement more favorable to the Japanese. He finally succeeded in getting it. Anson Burlingame, who became American minister to China in 1861, was anxious to prevent the great powers from carving up the lands of China among themselves. He was so good at presenting Chinese views to foreign diplomats that when the Emperor of China wished to send a mission to western nations in 1867, he asked Burlingame to head it. In 1868, Burlingame, accompanied by his staff, arranged a treaty between the United States and China. In it, each country allowed free entry to citizens of the other country.

People like Harris and Burlingame did not object to the growth of American influence in Asia. However, they did believe that trans-Pacific trade should achieve this result in a way that would help both Japan and China.

Seward Snags Alaska

The chief advocate of United States imperialism in the 1860s was Secretary of State William H. Seward. He was a lawyer from upstate New York who served as governor for one term before entering the Senate in 1849.

Seward was Secretary of State from 1861 to 1869. At the end of the Civil War, Seward saw his biggest task as one of helping American traders, bankers, and manufacturers bring progress to the nonindustrialized world. They were to do this by trading and using their goods and skills. Seward thought that this would require the peaceful

Left: Gold prospectors are shown crossing the Dyea Canyon in Alaska. The United States' purchase of Alaska paid off beyond all expectations when a wealth of gold and natural resources were discovered there in 1896. Right: In another Pacific acquisition, the United States annexed Hawaii in 1898. In this 1873 cartoon, Uncle Sam's growing interest in the Sandwich Islands, as the Hawiian Islands were then known, is shown.

American takeover of lands with good raw materials. These lands had customers for American products and had ports located along trade routes for American ships. At different times, Seward tried to get the Congress to buy Cuba, Puerto Rico, the Virgin Islands, Santo Domingo, and Hawaii. But he only won permission to annex the Midway Islands, two tiny dots of land west of Hawaii.

Seward did, however, score one huge success. In 1867, he learned that the Russians wanted to sell Alaska, their only North American colony. Its fur trade was no longer profitable. Besides, the czar feared that the weak Russian navy could not protect it in case of a war with their biggest rival at that time, Great Britain. So Seward quickly opened talks with the Russian ambassador. Finally, a price of $7.2 million was agreed upon.

Seward's real problem was to persuade Congress to vote the money to carry out the treaty. Most of Congress thought of Alaska as a "dreary waste of glaciers, icebergs, . . . and walruses." But Seward persisted and won. In 1896, long after his death, his faith was rewarded. Gold was found in the "dreary waste." This encouraged thousands of prospectors to rush there in search of fortune. In 1959, sixty-three years later, Alaska became a state, with untapped wealth in fish, lumber, coal, natural gas, oil, and other natural resources. In time, almost all the islands that Seward wanted became American-owned or American-dominated.

489

Island-Grabbing Across the Pacific

In the twenty-five years after Seward left office, the United States reached out for stepping stones across the Pacific Ocean. In 1878, the United States had signed a treaty with the native king of the Samoan Islands. This treaty gave Americans a naval base at Pago Pago. (In 1899, the United States annexed some of the islands, and Germany took the rest.) In 1887, Hawaii gave the United States exclusive trading privileges as well as the right to refuel and repair warships at Pearl Harbor. In the same year, White Hawaiian-born business people forced a new constitution on the authoritarian King Kalakaua. As a result of this so-called Bayonet Constitution, they acquired control of the government and extended the right to vote to White foreigners. Most of the native citizens were disenfranchised by property qualifications. By 1890, more than 90 percent of Hawaii's exports were sent to the United States.

In the early 1890s, the prosperous American sugar growers of Hawaii faced some hardships. Since 1875, their sugar had been admitted duty-free to the United States. Hawaiian producers faced little competition from sugar producers in Louisiana. However, in 1890, Congress lowered duties on Cuban sugar and also gave subsidies to American producers, in order to cut sugar prices. Such favoritism delivered a harsh blow to the Hawaiian planters. The price that they received for a ton of sugar dropped from $100 to $60. In addition, a new monarch, Queen Liliuokalani, took the throne and tried to reduce the influence of Americans in the government. This drew all the American business people in the islands together in resistance.

Early in 1893, the sugar planters staged a bloodless revolution. Help arrived when landing parties from a United States cruiser went ashore to "preserve order" and to keep Hawaiians loyal to the queen from interfering. Americans in Hawaii occupied government buildings, declared Liliuokalani deposed, and set up a temporary government. So, like the Austins and Houstons of Texas, the Americans in Hawaii asked the United States to annex them.

Their wishes were delayed, however, because a treaty was still under consideration in the Senate. Fierce argument was being waged over this annexation issue. Many Americans were opposed to the idea. They did not want to see an increase in military spending. They also feared that this would be the case if the United States began to expand overseas. Democrat Grover Cleveland opposed new territorial additions. Thus, when he assumed the office of President in 1893, he withdrew the treaty from the Senate. He sent a commission to Hawaii to investigate. The commission reported that American business people had created the revolution with the help of the American minister and marines. Cleveland even tried unsuccessfully to get

Queen Liliuokalani of Hawaii, who tried to assert native control of her homeland but was deposed by American sugar growers after just two years.

490

Louis Choris, a young Russian on a round-the-world voyage in 1816, painted the above watercolor of Honolulu.

Queen Liliuokalani restored as the leader of Hawaii. But Cleveland was forced to recognize the Republic of Hawaii with an American, Sanford B. Dole, named as its first president. Finally, the temporary government became a permanent one.

In 1898, developments in the Pacific increased the demand for annexation of the Hawaiian islands. The McKinley administration easily completed the work of annexation. By then, the United States, through war, had taken up the *white man's burden*—the idea that Whites had a duty to civilize "backward" peoples of other races.

Questions for Discussion

1. Define *imperialism*, *extraterritoriality*, *protectorate*, *white man's burden*.
2. How did the Chinese attempt to limit western imperialism?
3. How did the United States stimulate the growth of Japan?
4. Why did Seward want to purchase Alaska?
5. How did the United States acquire Hawaii? Why was there some opposition in the United States to this acquisition?

2. A New Global Power

After the war of 1812, America had expanded within its own continent. The question of slavery, the Civil War, and Reconstruction had absorbed the attention and energies of the nation. It was not until the last quarter of the nineteenth century that the United States was drawn into the game of international power politics. Americans began to realize that first England and then France, Germany, and Russia were carving territories for themselves out of the underdeveloped regions of Asia and Africa. Even as late as 1885, President Cleveland rejected any idea that America would become embroiled in foreign affairs.

By 1890, this policy of noninvolvement crumbled. At the same time, the American frontier closed, immigration swelled, and industrial development expanded. American business leaders and officials already had a great deal of influence in Asian countries. This was a kind of imperialism, limited to using economic and diplomatic pressure. Before the United States could become a full-fledged imperialist power—with colonies of its own or areas that it "protected" by actually ruling their peoples—Americans had to change some of their customary beliefs. One such deep-rooted attitude was a dislike of permanent large armies and navies.

Around 1890, this feeling began to undergo change, so far as the navy was concerned. Pressure mounted to build an up-to-date naval fleet. Some of that pressure came from *jingoism*—an exaggerated national pride that approves of tests of military strength. One jingoist was Josiah Strong, a Congregationalist minister, who urged the renewal of the nation through expansion. His views became popular through his book, *Our Country*, published in 1885. Another jingoist, professor John W. Burgess of Columbia University, proposed that certain nations, including the United States, were entrusted "with the mission of conducting the political civilization of the modern world."

Some pressure came from manufacturers who hoped to profit from building new warships. They realized that interest was developing in a better navy and merchant marine, which they hoped to capitalize on.

Much of the strength behind America's new global power was due to United States superiority. By 1904, when this photograph of Alfred T. Mahan was taken, his philosophy of the importance of sea power had won worldwide acceptance.

Others who encouraged imperialism were those business people who were beginning to worry about a hidden danger of industrial growth. What if the farms and factories in America produced too much for Americans to consume? Unsold goods would pile up. Factories would close down. Depression would grip the land. The United States had to be sure of having other markets. The country was already feeling the pinch of competition from other grain-exporting nations, such as Canada and Australia. Like other industrial nations, the United States also needed a supply of raw materials. Although America's need was not as great as that of some European countries, people in the United States were becoming aware that natural resources were limited. They were also realizing that the older powers were colonizing once again. Thus, for some, the answer was to enter the race before it was too late to catch up.

Building a Modern Navy

Trade on the high seas needed protection. This was the argument that Captain Alfred T. Mahan set forth in his book, *The Influence of Seapower on History* (1890). Captain Mahan claimed that, at different times, the leading powers in history—Spain, Holland, England—had owned great merchant fleets and unbeatable navies. The United States must have a strong navy if it were to rank as a leading power. According to Mahan, the United States had to secure overseas colonies as refueling ports and as sources of raw materials.

Pressure for a better navy had already resulted in Congress-appropriated money for naval construction. All during the 1880s, James G. Blaine and Mahan had pushed for expansion of the navy. And with the publication of Mahan's book, interest reached a new peak.

Benjamin Tracy, Secretary of the Navy, echoed Mahan's influential work when he said, "The sea will be the future seat of empire. And we shall rule it." Tracy spurred a program of construction that converted the navy from a group of aging wooden ships to a fast, powerfully armed force of armor-plated vessels. Only an industrial nation such as the United States, Great Britain, or Germany could afford to build and keep a modern fleet. These fleets demanded huge amounts of steel, complex machinery, coal, and oil. So when President Theodore Roosevelt sent the new United States fleet—painted white for peace—on a good-will cruise around the world in 1907, he was actually announcing that America had become a mighty military and industrial power.

United States naval superiority was first put to the test in 1898 when America's fleet, under the command of Admiral George Dewey (above) crushed the Spanish fleet at Manila Bay in the Philippine Islands.

Dewey, Manila, and the Philippines

Two years before the twentieth century began, the arguments for a big navy, overseas bases, and world leadership were put to an actual test. In April 1898, a crisis between the United States and Spain over the future of Cuba finally burst into war (see Chapter 22). Halfway around the world from Cuba, a small squadron of American warships

An artist's vision of the Battle of Manila Bay, the battle which struck a decisive blow against Spain's rule of the Philippines and paved the way for America's rule of the territory.

General Emilio Aguinaldo led the Filipinos against Spanish rule and then against American rule.

in Asian waters was already under secret orders from Theodore Roosevelt, who was at that time Assistant Secretary of the Navy. In the event of war with Spain, that squadron was to rush to Manila and attack the Spanish fleet in the Spanish-owned Philippine Islands. On May 1, only a week after Congress declared war, Admiral George Dewey carried out this mission with astounding success. In a short battle, the Spanish fleet was wiped out without any American losses.

Then a problem arose. In August, Spain surrendered. What should the United States do with the Philippines? After much soul-searching, President McKinley found an answer. He told of how he prayed in the White House at midnight for God's help. We could not, he said, give the Philippine Islands back to Spain without dishonor. We could not let commercial rivals, such as France or Germany, seize the Philippines. Nor could we leave the Philippine Islands alone, for they were "unfit for self-government . . . . There was nothing left . . . . but to take them all, and to educate the Filipinos, and uplift and Christianize them."

However, some Filipinos, led by General Emilio Aguinaldo, who had been fighting against the Spaniards, did not think themselves "unfit for self-government." They had welcomed liberation from Spain and therefore expected to become a free nation. So when they learned of American plans for annexation, they revolted. This added a new, unexpected look to the glories of empire. Suddenly, American soldiers were fighting in jungles and villages against Asians. They were battling guerrilla warriors who met superior weapons with cunning and courage and melted back among their own people when pursued. It was three years before the rebellion was broken. The horror stories that reached the United States about the conduct of American troops shocked the nation into a hot debate on what imperialism would actually do to American ideals.

The Anti-Imperialists Take a Stand

The election of 1900 was considered a test of public feeling on the issue of imperialism. A vote for McKinley, running for reelection, was supposedly a vote for empire. The arguments for empire in the Pacific were summed up vigorously by a young senator from Indiana, Albert J. Beveridge: "The Pacific is our ocean."

Voices of opposition were raised by a group of Americans, which included business people like Andrew Carnegie, authors like Mark Twain, and political leaders like former President Cleveland. These anti-imperialists argued that Americans were facing an impossible choice. They could not annex islands like the Philippines and admit them to the Union. Even anti-imperialists believed that "tropical people" were not ready for self-rule. Yet, to take in peoples without the promise of eventual statehood would deny the basic American promise of liberty and equality for all. Moreover, empire would force on the United States a huge army and navy. There would also be an "army" of colonial officials, tempted to corruption—super-bosses in the making. And the profits of empire would go to a few great organizers of trusts in hemp, sugar, tobacco, lumber, and other tropical products.

Strong opposition to the Spanish American War could also be found in the Black press. Black editors opposed the use of Black soldiers to kill Filipinos, who were fighting for their right to rule themselves. Newspapers decried the destruction of native populations that were supposedly receiving the "benefits" of civilization. How few people were left to enjoy them!

Anti-imperialists felt strongly that the war in the Philippines would betray everything for which the United States stood. "We have desolated homes and burned villages," said one, "and . . . we have created hatred of ourselves in the breasts of millions of people." The platform of an anti-imperialist league, organized in 1899, rang out, "We deny that the obligation of all citizens to support their Government in times of grave National peril applies to the present situation."

In the end, the anti-imperialists lost, and McKinley won the election. In the long run, neither the evils foreseen by the anti-imperialists nor the benefits promised by the imperialists came entirely to pass. After 1916, the United States allowed the Philippines to exercise greater self-government. Finally, in response to Filipino demands, Congress agreed to free the islands in 1946.

Spanish-American War in the Philippines, 1898

The Open Door Policy

In the early twentieth century, the policies of the major industrial nations toward China showed how it was possible to extend economic control over an area without actually occupying it. In 1899, England, Germany, Russia, and Japan (by then a powerful modern state, as well) were making demands that went well beyond the trading of former years. Each wanted special trading and military privileges at certain ports. And each wanted a particular Chinese region reserved for its own merchants to carry on profitable activities. Such a region was called a *sphere of influence.*

John Hay, then Secretary of State from 1898 to 1905, feared that the United States might be shut out of markets and investment opportunities in China. So he proposed that all major powers agree to an "Open Door" policy in their spheres. They should give business people of all countries equal rights. Hay also urged other nations not to cut up China by annexing their spheres. Since no nation was willing to disagree publicly, Hay announced that they all had agreed. The United States appeared as the defender of China's **territorial integrity.**

territorial integrity
the right of a nation to have its boundaries respected by all other nations

495

The Open Door Policy did allow that United States troops could be used in China when necessary. In 1900, a Chinese patriotic society known as the Boxers began a rebellion. Its members were young Chinese nationalists, tired of seeing the imperial rulers give in to the foreigners. They began to attack and kill western business people and their western employees, as well as missionaries and their Chinese converts. The Europeans fled to their embassies in Peking, where they were surrounded by the Boxers. An international force, including 2500 United States soldiers and marines, finally fought its way into Peking. The uprising then collapsed. And the territorial integrity of China seemed insured when the international force withdrew.

Nevertheless, China continued to suffer the fate of a weak power among strong ones. Rivalry between Russia and Japan over railroad and mining concessions in Manchuria led to the Russo-Japanese War of 1904–1905. This war threatened American business interests in China as well as the success of the Open Door policy.

Japan soundly defeated Russia in Manchuria. The Japanese then asked President Roosevelt to mediate a peace treaty. He agreed after getting Japan's assurance of support for the Open Door policy. Representatives of Japan and Russia met in Portsmouth, New Hampshire, in 1905. There, they worked out an agreement.

The Treaty of Portsmouth provided for the Russian evacuation of Manchuria and some small grants of territory to Japan. A huge cash payment sought by Japan for war damages was denied by Roosevelt. As a result of this denial, what appeared to be anti-American riots broke out in Tokyo. Although few Americans were injured, relations between the two countries were strained. In addition, the Gentleman's Agreements (see Chapter 20) made matters even worse. In 1908, the United States and Japan agreed to respect China's territorial integrity and to recognize each other's rights to do business in China. In the end, the engineers, bankers, and manufacturers of both nations continued to play a dominating role in Chinese life.

Questions for Discussion

1. Define *jingoism, sphere of influence, territorial integrity, imperialism, extraterritoriality.*
2. What role did industrialism play in imperialism?
3. Why was there an outcry around 1890 to create a large navy?
4. Why did a revolution break out in the Philippine Islands after the United States won them from Spain?
5. Why was the election of 1900 considered a test of public feeling on imperialism?
6. How would John Hay's Open Door policy protect the territorial integrity of China?

Chapter 21 Review

Summary Questions for Discussion

1. What factors caused American imperialism?

2. How did the Chinese react to foreigners? What rights did foreigners gain in China as a result of wars and treaties?

3. What were the purposes and results of Commodore Perry's trip to Japan?

4. Why did some Americans want to extend Manifest Destiny across the Pacific? What were the attitudes of Anson Burlingame and Townsend Harris?

5. What did William H. Seward see as his task, and what did he accomplish?

6. What was the role of each of the following in encouraging imperialism: the jingoists, the manufacturers, the business people, and the need for raw materials?

7. What did President McKinley decide to do with the Philippines? What were his reasons? How did the Filipinos react?

8. What was the "Open Door" policy proposed by John Hay?

9. What was the purpose of the Boxer Rebellion? What were its results?

10. What caused the Russo-Japanese War? What resulted? How did the war and the Gentlemen's Agreements affect Japanese-American relations?

Word Study

Fill in each blank in the sentences that follow with the term below that is most appropriate.

Open Door policy extraterritoriality white man's burden
imperialism   territorial integrity protectorate
jingoism   sphere of influence

1. The policy of extending a nation's control over other peoples is known as _____.

2. When a nation chooses to hold only partial control and set up a relationship of protection, this is known as a _____.

3. When a certain region of one nation is reserved solely for the merchants of another nation, this is said to be a _____

4. Often, imperialist nations protected their citizens abroad by demanding the right of _____, whereby their citizens would not be tried in another country's courts.

5. Imperialism often violated a nation's _____, or the right to have its boundaries respected.

6. An exaggerated national pride is known as _____

7. The philosophy known as the _____ was a belief that it was the duty of Whites to govern and to civilize the "backward" non-White populations of the world.

Using Your Skills

1. Study the possessions acquired by the United States on the map on page 486. Which major nations shown on the map might be concerned about the growth of American power in the Pacific? Why?

2. Compare the portrait of Commodore Perry (page 488) with the cartoon drawn by an unknown Japanese artist (page 487). What attitudes are expressed by the Japanese about Perry?

3. What ideas are expressed in the cartoons in this chapter? Which do you support? Give reasons for your answer.

CHAPTER 22

The United States and Latin America

United States interests abroad were not limited to the Asian mainland and the Pacific Basin. They also extended to the southern portion of the Americas. As early as 1820, President James Monroe spelled out a policy concerning this region. Between 1823 and 1898, the United States added the strength that allowed it to back up the Monroe Doctrine. Year by year, its stunning economic growth gave weight to the arguments of its diplomats. The building of a modern navy gave the United States supremacy on those waters once sailed by the New World explorers and sea fighters.

In 1900, a new era began. Now, other nations realized that the United States was an international giant. The United States government and its citizens used this might to get deeply involved in the affairs of other American nations. United States diplomats soon claimed to speak for the entire hemisphere. United States dollars, military troops, and cannons were major factors in the lives of its southern neighbors. Not until after World War I did the United States move toward more cooperative Latin American policies.

READING GUIDE

1. **How was the United States involved in Latin America prior to the Spanish-American War?**
2. **What was the significance of the Spanish-American War?**
3. **How did American involvement in Latin America expand in the early 1900s?**

The Battle of San Juan Hill, in which Whites and Blacks, regulars and Rough Riders fought side-by-side against the Spanish forces.

1. An Awakening Interest

In the early 1850s, Central America began to appeal to certain United States citizens. Some of these were wealthy business people, such as Cornelius Vanderbilt. He had hoped to build rail, steamboat, and canal lines across Central America to shorten the trip to the gold fields of California. Vanderbilt and others like him needed land and special legal rights. Most Central American rulers were willing to sell such rights and pocket the money themselves. They were often dictators with little popular support. Thus, they were in danger of being overthrown.

A second group of "Yankees" wanted to do more than just make deals with Central American rulers. These people wanted to replace the rulers. Many were Southerners who believed that Manifest Destiny made it easy, natural, and right for them to enter a Latin American nation with a few followers and seize control of it through skill and daring. A few were secretly encouraged by Southern politicians who saw an opportunity to add slave territory to the Union. Little bands of these adventurers, called *filibusters*, slipped out of the United States to make raids on Cuba, Mexico, and points south.

One of these raids was led by General Narciso Lopez, a Spanish general. He raised a troop of Spanish refugees and southern volun-

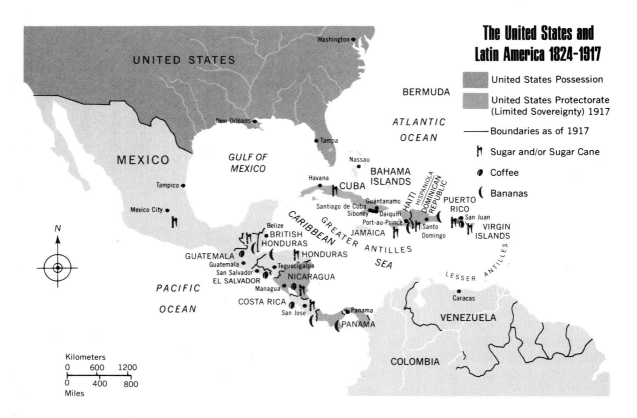

The United States and Latin America 1824-1917

United States Possession

United States Protectorate (Limited Sovereignty) 1917

Boundaries as of 1917

Sugar and/or Sugar Cane

Coffee

Bananas

teers to invade Cuba. However, their attempt to promote a rebellion failed. Lopez and several of his followers, including some Americans, were tried and executed. The Spanish consulate in New Orleans was damaged in riots spurred by the executions. The remaining American prisoners were released after the United States government paid for the damages to the consulate.

For a short time, the only successful filibuster was William Walker. Tennessee-born, Walker was trained in law and medicine but later became a New Orleans journalist. The doctor longed for greatness. In 1855, with the approval of Vanderbilt, Walker and some fifty "emigrants" sailed for Nicaragua. There, he joined and became the leader of a small guerilla force in revolt against the government. In four months, his troops captured the capital. Walker, who later made himself president of Nicaragua, had great visions of uniting the Central American states, introducing slavery, and digging a canal from the Atlantic to the Pacific.

His dream finally collapsed. Walker quarreled with Vanderbilt and seized the property of Vanderbilt's company in Nicaragua. Vanderbilt struck back by financing an invasion of Nicaragua by its neighbors. By April 1857, Walker was defeated and forced to return to New Orleans. On another invasion in 1860, he was captured and, at the age of 36, died before a firing squad.

William Walker's filibustering campaign in Nicaragua was not his first. In 1853, he led a force into Lower California, declared it independent from Mexico, and named himself president. Mexican troops forced him out, but his actions were so popular in the United States that a jury acquitted him of violating the neutrality laws.

A Growing Interest in Cuba

Other nations saw nothing romantic in the actions taken by Walker. They feared that such filibusters were the drum majors of a steady American march southward. Their fears seemed justified in 1854, when three American ambassadors in Europe met in the Belgian town of Ostend. There they were to draw up a secret report on Cuba for the Secretary of State. They suggested that if Spain refused to sell Cuba, the United States then would have the right, "by every law, human and divine," to seize that island. The report was leaked to the press and became known as the Ostend Manifesto. It created such an uproar that the Secretary of State was forced to announce that the United States had no intention of seizing Cuba.

Actually Cuba had tempted Americans long before 1854. Even John Quincy Adams had declared that a law of "political gravitation" would make it drop like an apple into the American basket as soon as its "unnatural" connection to the Spanish tree was broken.

After the Civil War, Americans revived their interest in Cuban harbors, mines, forests, ranches, and plantations. Secretary of State Seward tried to buy Cuba as well as other Caribbean islands. He failed in his attempt. Busy with Reconstruction and encouraging economic growth, Congress had no interest in island-grabbing. At that time, and in the 1880s, Americans were more concerned with adding markets than adding territory to the United States. James G. Blaine, Secretary of State from 1889 to 1892, urged tariff reductions on animal hides, sugar, and other products of Latin American countries if those countries would agree to buy more American-made goods.

Problems in Cuba

By 1868, Cuba and Puerto Rico were all that was left of the once-glorious Spanish empire in the New World. But years of poor management had caused bitter resentment among the Cubans, who largely lived in poverty. They rebelled. And for ten years, the Cubans struggled against the superior power of Spain. Finally, in 1878 Spain agreed to two major reforms. The people of Cuba were to be granted self-government, and slavery was to be abolished. But Spain delayed the end of slavery for ten more years. The promise of self-rule never came peaceably.

For a short time, economic progress forestalled the final, bitter confrontation. With the end of slavery in Cuba came major investments by European and American businesses. The sugar cane industry was modernized, and Cuba exported heavily to the United States. However, success was short-lived. Competition from sugar beet production in Europe began to drive down world sugar prices. Then in 1894, the United States imposed a high tariff on imported sugar. As Cubans faced a return to hopeless poverty, anger against Spain flared up again.

In 1895, the Cubans rebelled once more against Spain. Spain sent 200,000 soldiers, commanded by its best general. Yet they were unsuccessful in defeating the Cuban rebels. In waging their guerrilla war, the rebels ambushed Spanish troops, assassinated officials, and destroyed property. They burned plantations and American property in the hopes of attracting American intervention. Meanwhile, the Spaniards arrested and tortured suspected rebels. As a last resort, General Valeriano Weyler was sent to Cuba to act as military commander and governor. In February 1896, he ordered revolutionaries to be put in concentration camps. Many civilians were placed there as well.

Questions for Discussion

1. Why did some Latin American dictators cooperate with American investors in the development of Latin American resources?
2. What role did *filibusters* play in the affairs of Central American countries?
3. Why were Americans interested in Cuba? Why did we keep changing our policies in dealing with Cuba?

American newspapers reported the horrors of the Cuban revolution. Newspapers were becoming an important part of city life. For two cents, the average reader got local and world news, news of sports and theater, advertisements, cartoons, stories, and advice columns. As you saw in Chapter 18, the press had the power to shape public opinion. A number of editors ran exaggerated news stories. And this "yellow journalism" played a major role in determining foreign policy.

The *New York World*, published by Joseph Pulitzer, and the *New York Journal*, published by William Randolph Hearst, competed for sensational news by publishing stories of Cuban atrocities in blood-spattered detail. They ran cartoons showing the Spanish General Weyler as a butcher or a gorilla. They even staged "stunts." For example, the *Journal* sent a man to Havana to rescue an imprisoned 18-year-old female Cuban rebel. He rescued her by sawing through the bars of her cell and getting her out disguised as a man. Then he claimed to a record-breaking number of readers, "I have set free the beautiful captive of Monster Weyler."

Because of such stories and pressure from Cubans exiled in New York, a wave of enthusiasm for Cuban independence swept the country. Further enthusiam came from such people as Alfred T. Mahan, Henry Cabot Lodge, and Theodore Roosevelt. Coupled with the enthusiasm was the wish to test American fitness through battle.

2. The Spanish-American War

The 10th U.S. Cavalry embarking at Tampa, Florida, for Cuba in 1898.

President William McKinley, who, within two months after the sinking of the Maine, asked for a declaration of war against Spain.

However, not all Americans were in favor of war. As President Cleveland's term of office expired in 1896, he refused to be drawn into a war with Cuba.

The new President, William McKinley, was also opposed to war with Spain. He kept urging the Spanish government to grant Cuba self-rule, but he made no threats. He urged those eager for war to give Spain a chance to sort things out.

Even as McKinley was talking peace, events were getting out of hand. A private letter written by Dupuy de Lôme, the Spanish minister to the United States, was intercepted from the mail and printed in Hearst's *Journal*. In the letter, the minister characterized the American President as a "weak" and "a would-be politician." Although de Lôme immediately resigned, American pride still remained bruised.

On the night of February 15, 1898, while on a peaceful visit to the harbor of Havana, the United States battleship *Maine* exploded and sank, killing 260 sailors. To this day, no one is sure about what happened. The *Journal* and other jingoistic papers were quick to decide that the Spanish had planted an underwater mine to sink the ship. The war fever now became incurable. "Remember the *Maine*!" became a battle cry that drowned out the voices of caution and compromise.

War and Invasion

McKinley sent an **ultimatum** to Spain. In it, he demanded an end to the concentration camps and an immediate truce. On April 9, 1898, the Spanish government agreed to all of McKinley's demands. Unfortunately, this effort came too late. The hard-pressed McKinley had given in to the prowar hysteria. Two days later, he asked Congress for a declaration of war. It was easily passed. An amendment by Senator Henry Teller from Colorado was added. This amendment promised that the United States would not annex Cuba.

Thus, the United States began the war with high spirits but with little preparation. Volunteers rushed to enlist and were hastily sent to training camps in Florida. There, because no summer uniforms were ready, they sweltered in tropical heat in woolen shirts. In addition, some of their food was actually spoiled canned meat, which dishonest packers had sold to the government. The scandal of the "embalmed beef" helped to provide for federal meat inspection by law—but not until eight years later. At the end of June, there were barely enough ships to carry the attacking force to Siboney and Daiquiri, in Cuba. Almost no ships were available to follow with food and medical supplies. Siboney and Daiquiri had no wharves and warehouses. And the Americans were not equipped to build them. Despite it all, however, Americans moved inland from Daiquiri toward their objective, the capital city of Santiago. Fortunately for the United States, the Spaniards did not counterattack.

At sea, the picture was brighter. The naval building program of the 1890s proved valuable. Powerful American ships bottled up that part of the Spanish fleet in Santiago harbor. On July 3, Admiral Pascual de Cervera led his few cruisers and destroyers in an effort to break out. In a few hours, American guns turned every one of them into a flaming wreck. Four centuries of Spanish history in New World waters had finally come to an end.

The Battle for Santiago

Two days before this naval battle, American units on land had battled their way to the outskirts of Santiago, suffering heavy losses. Among the hard-hit outfits was a part of the First United States Volunteer Cavalry, nicknamed the "Rough Riders." They were proudly commanded by Colonel Leonard Wood and Lieutenant Colonel Theodore Roosevelt. The Rough Riders included the Negro Tenth Cavalry commanded by Lieutenant John J. Pershing. On July 1, 1898, the Americans charged a hotly defended Spanish position called Kettle Hill. Roosevelt spurred his horse up and down the battlefield, urging his soldiers on. When Kettle Hill had been secured, the infantry began the charge up nearby San Juan Hill. Roosevelt called on his soldiers,

The New York Journal *announced that Spain was suspected of being responsible for the sinking of the Maine.*

Gatling guns were used by these American forces to defend against Spanish attack in Cuba during the Spanish-American War.

who were cheering the San Juan Hill charge, to hit the next line of Spanish trenches.

On July 17, Santiago finally surrendered. An expeditionary force sent to Puerto Rico met with little resistance. However, the American army was in as much danger from victory as it would have been from defeat. Malaria, yellow fever, and other diseases swept the ranks. During the four months of combat, casualties totaled 379. But over 5000 died from diseases and other causes. Only the surrender of Spain on August 2, and the troops' return to the United States, prevented disaster.

This 1897 Puck cartoon was titled "Patient Waiters Are No Losers." A confident Uncle Sam expects Cuba, Canada, and Hawaii to fall into America's basket.

506

In the resulting peace treaty, Spain lost Cuba and gave the United States the Philippines for $20 million. The United States also received Puerto Rico and the Pacific island of Guam. American imperialism was truly on the rise.

Questions for Discussion

1. Define *ultimatum*.
2. What part did "yellow journalism" play in bringing the United States into war with Spain?
3. How did an early Spanish surrender prevent disaster for the American army in Cuba?

3. The Course of Empire

The question of the fate of Cuba and Puerto Rico was troublesome. Under the Teller Amendment, the United States had agreed not to annex Cuba. But after the war, enthusiasm for Cuban freedom cooled. Immediately following the Spanish defeat, Cuba was ruled by American military forces, although the Cubans had been fighting alongside the Americans to obtain Cuban independence.

Under General John R. Brooke, improvements were made in Cuban finances, education, sanitation, and health facilities. General Brooke worked actively to return control of Cuba to the Cubans. A majority of the members in Congress as well as many imperialists still wanted to maintain some control. They were afraid that if Americans withdrew hastily, American interests in the Caribbean Sea would be endangered by Cuban political and financial instability. General Brooke was replaced by General Leonard Wood, who favored the continued occupation of Cuba.

The question facing the United States now was how to protect Cuba from other foreign intervention without annexing it. Senator Orville Platt of Connecticut offered a solution in an amendment to a 1901 bill providing money for the army.

Under the Platt Amendment, Cuba had to sign a treaty with the United States, promising to make no agreements that would give any other nation control of its affairs. Cuba was not to borrow more money than it could quickly repay. If the United States thought it necessary, Cuba had to let United States forces land in order to protect life and property. And Cuba had to agree to lease land for naval bases to the United States.

Congress added that American military forces would not be removed until the provisions of the Platt Amendment were included in the Cuban constitution.

In the years that followed, the United States maintained interest in the internal affairs of Cuba. Three times American forces landed in Cuba to protect American property. In 1933, President Franklin D.

Left: Even before the United States had political influence in Latin America, it cast a long economic shadow across the land. In this photo, Latin American laborers are shown transporting freshly picked bananas for United Fruit. In return for their labor, the large American corporation provided schools, hospitals, homes, and a larger salary than they could have otherwise earned. Right: The United States often found itself on the brink of war over disputes with Latin American countries in the 1890s. In addition, Latin Americans resented the high American tariffs on their goods. This 1897 Puck cartoon suggests why the "Romance" between the United States and Latin America was in trouble.

commonwealth
a political unit having local self-government but voluntarily united with another country

Roosevelt sent an American ambassador to help mediate internal disputes. In 1934, a Cuban government favored by the United States negotiated the repeal of the Platt Amendment.

In the case of Puerto Rico, Americans were unwilling to set that island free. They were also unwilling to absorb its people into the United States as equal partners. In 1900, the Foraker Act provided for the establishment of a temporary civil government for the colony of Puerto Rico. The American President appointed the governor and the upper house of the legislature. The Puerto Rican people elected the lower house and a Resident Commissioner, who attended the United States House of Representatives.

The Jones Act of 1917 provided for American citizenship for Puerto Ricans. A bill of rights was established. And the people acquired the right to elect the upper house of the legislature. Finally, continued pressure from Puerto Ricans to control their own affairs led to the establishment of Puerto Rico as a self-governing **commonwealth** in 1952.

The Insular Cases

The acquisition of new territories presented new problems. Was the United States Constitution supposed to follow the flag? Were the people of Guam, the Philippines, Hawaii, Puerto Rico, and Alaska to enjoy the rights and privileges of American citizenship? The imperialists held that these rights were not automatically granted. When

508

William McKinley won a substantial victory over the anti-imperialist candidate, William Jennings Bryan, in the election of 1900, it seemed that the public agreed.

In the early 1900s, the Supreme Court added its vote for imperialism. In a series of cases called the Insular Cases, certain aspects of American foreign policy were established. In the 1901 case of *Downes* v. *Bidwell*, which originated in Puerto Rico, the Justices ruled that the Constitution did not automatically apply to inhabitants of annexed territory. The people were not necessarily granted the rights of citizenship. It was up to Congress to extend these privileges if it so decided. In a 1903 case originating in Hawaii, the Court decided that the laws of those islands could be followed instead of those of the American Constitution. Therefore, people in Hawaii could be denied trial by jury if their laws did not require it, because they were not entitled to the same rights as United States citizens.

Thus, a colonial foreign policy developed, based on the laws of Congress, Supreme Court decisions, and the support of public opinion. However, it was not long before most American territories were on the road to self-government or statehood.

The Panama Canal

After 1900, the United States had a giant's strength in the Caribbean Sea and began to use it. The first step was to bring part of the Isthmus of Panama—the narrow neck of land joining North and South America—under the Stars and Stripes in order to dig a canal through it. In 1850, the United States and Britain had agreed to have joint control over such a canal if it were built. By 1898, the United States had gained possessions that needed protection in both the Atlantic and Pacific Oceans. It became absolutely urgent that the American navy could move quickly from one ocean to the other. By then, British-American friendship was on a firmer footing. So in 1901, Britain gave the United States the right to build and control a canal. In return, the United States promised to allow ships of all nations to use the canal in peace and war.

Panama was then part of the Republic of Colombia. In January, 1903, the United States signed a treaty with Colombia, which put a 10-kilometer- (6-mile-)wide strip of the isthmus under American control. The United States agreed to pay $10 million immediately and make annual payments thereafter. For months, however, the Colombian government in Bogotá hesitated to sell this part of its territory. A French construction company had begun digging a canal during the 1880s. Their lease was due to expire and Colombia would own the equipment. They would then be in a better position to bargain with the United States. Roosevelt was furious.

Then some mysterious things happened. A small group of Panamanian nationalists, opposed to Colombian rule, made contact with individuals who had friends in the United States government. One person who made such a visit was Philippe Bunau-Varilla. Bunau-Varilla was a French engineer, deeply interested in completing the canal, which the French had begun and had abandoned. He was also a shareholder in the French company. He secretly visited the United States to solicit aid from the State Department.

In November, the rebels seized Panama City and proclaimed an independent republic. Two days later, an American cruiser, sent to the area by Roosevelt before the revolt, appeared at the nearby port of Colon. There, Colombian soldiers were preparing to land in hopes of crushing the uprising. The American cruiser had orders to protect American travelers in Panama by preventing fighting. Instead, the cruiser used the threat of its mighty guns to prevent the Colombians from retaking their own soil.

Helplessly, Colombia watched the United States recognize the Republic of Panama. Two weeks later, Bunau-Varilla went to the United States as ambassador from Panama. He signed a treaty giving the Americans control over a 16-kilometer- (10-mile-)wide zone across the isthmus.

Although the Panamanian national revolt was not started by Roosevelt, he clearly insured its success by his intervention. Later, Roosevelt would claim proudly, "I took the Canal Zone." This attitude on the part of an American President created many enemies for the United States in Latin America.

Building the canal was not an easy task. In 1889, French efforts under Ferdinand de Lesseps, the Suez Canal engineer, had ended in bankruptcy. But the Army Corps of Engineers, under Colonel George W. Goethals, took on the difficult jungle landscape with giant machines.

Meanwhile, American health officials, headed by Dr. Walter Reed, worked hard to battle diseases such as malaria, yellow fever, and bubonic plague. It was Dr. William C. Gorgas, Reed's associate, who discovered that spraying oil on breeding places of the mosquito would control the spread of yellow fever. In 1904, Gorgas was placed in charge of the sanitation program in Panama.

Expansion of the Monroe Doctrine

Americans did not protest European interference in Latin America in the era before the Civil War. On the occasions when Britain and France acted in the Western Hemisphere over nonpayment of debts, the United States claimed that it never meant to interfere with the legitimate activities of European powers. Gradually, however, Ameri-

510

Building the Panama Canal was a gigantic problem in engineering. The locks (above left) were arranged side-by-side in pairs for two-way traffic. The canal's opening sparked much interest worldwide. Panamanians (above right) were especially interested in this technological achievement on their own soil.

can attitudes changed. The United States began to look upon Latin America more and more as its particular sphere of influence. As Europe grabbed parts of Africa and other underdeveloped regions in Asia and the Middle East, the United States wanted to guard Latin America for its resources and markets.

The first test of the Monroe Doctrine came in the 1860s. Two groups in Mexico were engaged in a civil war. This war led to the destruction of foreign property. The United States, Britain, France, and Spain claimed damages. When Mexico, under President Benito Juarez, could not pay, Britain, France, and Spain sent troops to force payment. Britain and France withdrew after the debt was repaid. But the French ruler, Napoleon III, refused to pull out his troops. In addition, he installed Maximilian, a brother of the Austrian emperor (and a French ally), as a puppet ruler.

As the Civil War in the United States wound down, Americans pressured the government to do something about the French presence in Mexico. The United States prepared to send troops. But Napoleon III had already concluded that the venture in Mexico was too expensive to maintain. So the French troops were withdrawn by 1867. The result was that Americans and the rest of the world viewed the Monroe Doctrine with a growing respect.

Shortly thereafter, President Grant widened the provision of the Monroe Doctrine to include the principle of "no transfer." Grant was fearful that the Dominican Republic would be transferred from Spanish possession to ownership by some other European power. Although his plan to annex the Dominican Republic to the United States in 1869 did not win Senate approval, he declared that the "no-transfer" principle was part of the Monroe Doctrine.

The Venezuela Disputes

Venezuela was the site of two more conflicts that challenged the Monroe Doctrine. Since 1814, the boundary between British Guiana and Venezuela had been a source of dispute. Britain repeatedly moved the Guiana boundary onto territory claimed by Venezuela. Finally in 1882, Venezuela demanded that the dispute be submitted to a neutral party to determine the rightful line. Britain refused to submit the dispute to arbitration.

In 1895, Venezuela appealed to President Cleveland to invoke the Monroe Doctrine and protect Venezuelan territory. Secretary of State Olney sent a sharply worded statement to the Prime Minister of Britain. Olney claimed the United States' right to intervene in any issue concerning North or South America.

However, Britain rejected Olney's point of view. According to the British Prime Minister, the Monroe Doctrine was not international law. He also pointed out that the doctrine had not been violated. To this, he added that the United States had no right to intervene in the affairs of every country in the Western Hemisphere.

In spite of this, in a special message to Congress in December 1895, President Cleveland upheld the American interpretation of the Monroe Doctrine. He asked for funds to set up a commission to investigate the boundary issue. He proclaimed that the United States would "resist by every means in its power" the unlawful use of Venezuelan territory by Britain.

Britain was faced with a confrontation with the United States that could have meant war. At the same time, Britain was involved in a conflict with Germany over South Africa. So to avoid being embroiled in war with the United States, Britain gave in and agreed to arbitration. By acting in this manner Britain acknowledged the Monroe Doctrine. So once more, the principles of the Monroe Doctrine were strengthened.

Another Venezuelan dispute that tested the Monroe Doctrine occurred in 1902. Venezuela had failed to pay sums owed to several European nations. As punishment, British, German, and Italian naval forces blockaded Venezuelan ports.

At first, Theodore Roosevelt saw this as no threat, and he approved the action. The European nations had informed the United States of their plans before they carried them out. However, public opinion in the United States ran against the blockade. And Roosevelt finally urged arbitration to settle the dispute.

The Drago Doctrine and the Roosevelt Corollary

Latin Americans were disturbed about armed intrusion by European powers for the purpose of collecting debts. The blockade of

American companies built homes, such as the one above, in Latin America for American company managers and their families.

Venezuelan ports promoted action on the part of Luis M. Drago, the Foreign Minister of Argentina. In 1902, he proposed that the United States join Latin American countries in opposing the use of force to collect debts owed by Latin American governments. The Drago Doctrine won little support from Roosevelt, who wanted to maintain a position of authority over Latin America. Yet, many Latin American leaders as well as many United States citizens agreed with Drago.

In addition to this, in 1904, the Dominican Republic seemed about to go bankrupt. Roosevelt announced, "I have about the same desire to annex it as a gorged boa constrictor might have to swallow a porcupine wrong-end-to." He had no desire to see the little Caribbean country occupied by the nations to whom it owed money. But he did not want to annex it to the United States either. He announced to Congress a *corollary*, or an addition, to the Monroe Doctrine. Any Western Hemisphere nation that could keep order and pay its debts would not be interfered with. However, if any nation failed in these civilized responsibilities, the United States would act as an "international police force." It would be peacekeeper and bill collector for the Europeans. Roosevelt forced a special treaty on the Dominican Republic. Under that treaty, a United States official collected Dominican import duties, paid the republic's overdue bills with some of the revenue, and "gave" the rest back to the Dominican government.

American Influence Expands

Under the Roosevelt Corollary, the United States soon began to occupy other small neighbors. It assumed the right to supervise their tangled finances or protect lives and property during revolutions and civil wars. The protection tended to last a long time. During that time, the countries involved were, for all practical purposes, United States protectorates.

In 1912, marines landed in Nicaragua when the government of that Central American country was threatened by political rivals. Some marines remained until 1933, except for a brief withdrawal in 1925. This active intervention under President Taft marked an expansion of Roosevelt's policies of strategic and economic control of Latin America.

President Wilson pursued similar intervention policies. In 1914, France and Germany suggested that Haiti should be placed under international control because of its unstable financial condition. The United States tried to get Haiti to accept an arrangement similar to that imposed on Cuba by the Platt Amendment. Haiti refused. The following year, a revolt broke out in Haiti, The United States then landed marines to keep order. Under these conditions, the United States was able to conclude a treaty with Haiti, giving the United States major control over its affairs. The situation remained tense. Riots against the American troops broke out from time to time. The marines were removed in 1934, at which time Haiti resumed greater control over its financial affairs as well.

In 1916, the Dominican Republic announced its decision to repeal the protectorate set up by President Roosevelt. The United States answered by landing marines in the Dominican Republic. The forces remained for another eight years with the stated purpose of preparing the Dominican Republic for elections. After eight years, marines were withdrawn. This opened the way for Rafael Trujillo to establish his dictatorship.

During Wilson's administration, the United States took other steps toward protecting approaches to the Panama Canal and making the Caribbean "an American lake."

Fearing seizure of the Virgin Islands by Germany, the United States Congress approved their purchase from Denmark in 1917. To protect its interests, the United States also intervened in affairs in Nicaragua, Costa Rica, and Guatemala.

The United States defended this blunt use of its power as necessary to prevent Latin America from being divided—like Africa or parts of Asia—among European powers. Often leaders of Latin American countries asked for United States troops to protect their own power. Yet, because of these occupations, hatred for the "colossus

Left: Francisco "Pancho" Villa, third from the right, was considered something of a Robin Hood by his followers. He adopted his name, Francisco Villa, from a famous outlaw. Right: In March 1916, Brigadier General John J. Pershing led a large U.S. force into Mexico to find and punish Pancho Villa. Pershing did not get the cooperation he expected from Mexican government troops. In fact, clashes with them were nearly as frequent as those with the elusive Villistas. Eleven months and $130 million later, Pershing was ordered home.

(giant) of the North" remained a strong force in Latin American life even after the United States moved toward a more cooperative policy.

Mexican-American Relations

In 1911, the United States' relations with its closest southern neighbor, Mexico, took a turn for the worse. For some decades, Mexico had been ruled by the dictator, Porfirio Díaz. Díaz encouraged foreign investors to develop Mexican resources. By 1910, a billion United States dollars were invested in Mexican railroads, ranches, mines, and oil wells. Over 40,000 Americans lived and worked in Mexico. Yet, the average Mexican saw little of the profit made by this use of Mexico's natural wealth.

In 1911, a revolution broke out that overthrew Díaz. Several Mexican leaders, including Venustiano Carranza and Francisco "Pancho" Villa, fought among themselves to see who would replace Díaz. In February 1913, another dictator, Victoriano Huerta, gained control of the government. While these leaders and their armies fought for power, thousands of Mexicans and some foreign residents, including Americans, were killed and injured.

President Woodrow Wilson hoped to influence Mexican politics without large-scale American intervention. What he wanted was a government there that would be constitutional and democratic. At the same time, it had to be strong enough to protect life and property. He tried various methods to weaken Huerta, whose one-man government he did not approve of. In April 1914, a minor incident involving the arrest of some American sailors at Tampico led to strained relations between the United States and Mexico. A few weeks later, after being alerted that a German ship was delivering arms, Wilson ordered the bombardment and occupation of Vera Cruz by United States forces. Wilson did not want an all-out war with Mexico to develop. So he accepted the offer of Argentina, Brazil, and Chile—the so-called *ABC* powers—to arbitrate the dispute. War was just barely averted.

Wilson appeared to have scored some gain when Huerta was forced out and replaced by Carranza late in 1915. But Carranza could not control the turbulent Mexican revolution either. Wilson's hand was now forced by Pancho Villa. On March 9, 1916, Villa's troops—who had already murdered a number of Americans in Mexico—crossed into Columbus, New Mexico. There, they killed seventeen United States citizens.

The United States was outraged. The government mobilized a small army for an expedition to punish Villa. Under General John J. Pershing, they pursued Villa, intending to break up his force. Carranza was furious. He did not like Villa, but neither did he like an American invasion. Pershing's troops toiled through a hot, difficult campaign in rugged country. Yet his troops failed to capture Villa in any of his mountain hideouts.

The Mexican government continued to insist that Americans leave. But before a second war with Mexico could take place, other events changed the picture. By January 1917, the United States was dangerously close to war with Germany. So the troops were brought home to prepare for that conflict. Finally, the policing of Mexico was left to the Mexicans.

In 1917, the United States became involved in a war among the great powers of the world. Over a century had gone by since the end of the War of 1812, the last such war to involve Americans. The America of 1917 was no longer a little republic caught up in the clashes of giant European powers. It was no longer the country of 1823 that declared its separation from European affairs in the Monroe Doctrine. Instead, the United States now had far-flung strategic interests to guard. A hundred years before, most American problems were domestic in nature. Now a new period had begun, in which foreign developments were to become increasingly more important. As the twentieth century went forward, treaties, wars, and big military expenditures tended to take a prominent spot in the history of the United States.

Questions for Discussion

1. Define *commonwealth, corollary, arbitrate.*
2. After the Spanish-American War, how did the United States deal with Cuba and Puerto Rico?
3. How did Theodore Roosevelt insure the success of the Panamanian revolt from Colombia?
4. How did events in other areas of the world help to strengthen the Monroe Doctrine?
5. What was the immediate effect of the Roosevelt Corollary?
6. Why did American investment in Mexico lead to conflict?

Chapter 22 Review

Summary Questions for Discussion

1. What two groups of United States citizens were interested in Central America? Why?
2. What was the Ostend Manifesto?
3. Why was it necessary for Cubans to rebel two times against Spain?
4. What factors contributed to the growth of support for Cuban independence?
5. What resulted from the sinking of the battleship *Maine*?
6. What were the results of the Spanish-American War?
7. What was the purpose of the Platt Amendment of 1901? What were its provisions?
8. What was the Foraker Act? the Jones Act of 1917?
9. Why did the United States want to build a canal in the area of Panama?
10. What was the role of each of the following in the construction of the Panama Canal: Ferdinand de Lesseps, George W. Goethals, Walter Reed, and William C. Gorgas?
11. How was the Monroe Doctrine strengthened in the 1860s? What was Grant's principle of "no transfer"?
12. Why did the British acknowledge America's position on the Monroe Doctrine in Venezuela in 1895?
13. What was the effect of the Roosevelt Corollary in Nicaragua, Haiti, and the Dominican Republic?
14. What caused revolution in Mexico in 1911? What was President Wilson's goal there?
15. What was the purpose of Pershing's expedition into Mexico? Why was Carranza angered by this expedition? What put an end to the expedition?

Word Study

Fill in each blank in the sentences that follow with the term below that is most appropriate.

ultimatum   arbitrate   corollary   filibuster

1. If two parties cannot agree, an impartial third party is often sent in to _____.
2. One party may simply issue an _____, or list of demands, when that party is unwilling to compromise.
3. Even when compromise is reached, it is often necessary to add a _____ to further explain a decision.

Using Your Skills

1. Which pictures in this chapter would provide evidence for, and which would tend to disprove, the following hypothesis: "The United States has always followed a hands-off policy in Latin America"?
2. What reasons for building the Panama Canal did the United States have after 1900 that it did not have in 1890?
3. By the use of specific historical information, explain the meaning of the cartoons that appear in this chapter.
4. Examine the map on page 500. Why has the United States always been interested in who controls Latin America?

CHAPTER 23
World War I

On June 28, 1914, two pistol shots cracked loudly in a street in Sarajevo, a city in the province of Bosnia. The shots were fired by a young Serbian into the chests of Francis Ferdinand, the Austrian archduke, and his wife. The act was a protest against the condition of people living under Austro-Hungarian rule in Bosnia and Serbia. Few people in the United States had heard of Sarajevo, Bosnia, or Serbia. And few were even interested when the newspapers the next day reported the archduke's death. Yet, those shots changed the lives of Americans for all time, just as they changed the destiny of the whole world. The assassination triggered a world war, which became the biggest conflict in history up to then.

At its end, in November 1918, more than 8.5 million soldiers had died. Millions of civilians had also perished from disease, cold, and hunger. Billions of dollars' worth of farms, factories, homes, mines, and ships had been blown up. Three empires were overthrown by revolution. Riots and civil war threatened orderly government in the lands of the exhausted winners as well as in the defeated nations.

In 1914, Americans believed that the wars in Europe were not their affair. But the United States, with its industrial strength and worldwide trade, could not escape involvement. In 1917, America entered the war and shared in the bloodshed. In 1919, President Wilson took part in the peacemaking. After that, although the nation tried to withdraw from world affairs, it was never again possible for Americans to remain entirely uninterested in the fate of peoples around the globe.

READING GUIDE

1. Why did peace efforts fail to keep the world from war?
2. How did the United States meet the challenge of war?
3. Why was the peace uncertain?

This sheet music captures the spirit that many Americans took into World War I.

LET'S KEEP THE GLOW IN OLD GLORY
AND THE FREE IN FREEDOM TOO
Lyric by
Wilbur D. Nesbit
Music by
Robert Speroy
Frank K. Root & Co.
McKINLEY MUSIC CO. OWNERS
CHICAGO NEW YORK
Albert & Son, Australasian Agents, Sydney, Australia

1. Efforts for Peace

philanthropist
a person who puts forth an active effort to promote human welfare by giving gifts, especially large sums of money

disarmament
the reduction or abolition of military forces and weapons by a national government

Opposite page: The Hofbal—the dance given annually by Austrian Emperor Franz Joseph—in 1900.

Prior to 1914, many people had dreams about permanent peace and endless progress. Numerous attempts were made by private and public figures to turn these hopes into realities.

In the United States alone, sixty-three peace societies were organized to promote peace. Some were church-related, while others were supported by **philanthropists.** These societies were part of a worldwide effort to find alternatives to war. In Europe, Alfred Nobel, the inventor of dynamite, provided in his will for a prize to be given every five years to the person who had most advanced the cause of peace. One of its earliest recipients was the Baroness von Suttner, who founded the International Peace and Arbitration Association of London. Another early winner was Theodore Roosevelt. The Nobel Prize was awarded to him for the part he played in fostering the Treaty of Portsmouth.

Yet these moves toward peace would have meant little if powerful nations did not also promote mutual cooperation. In the late 1880s and early 1900s, many international conferences were held. The top priorities were to solve immediate problems the different nations faced and to set up mechanisms, other than war, for settling future international crises.

International Conferences

In 1889, Secretary of State Blaine's plan for an inter-American conference was realized. Delegates from the United States and seventeen Latin American countries met in Washington at the first International American Conference. They discussed common problems, and some progress was made. The International Bureau of American Republics, which held periodic meetings to discuss common interests and exchange information, was formed. In 1910, the organization changed its name to the Pan-American Union, which evolved into the Organization of American States (OAS) in 1948.

In 1899, the Russian czar called for an international assembly to discuss **disarmament,** limitations on methods of warfare, and arbitration. Twenty-six nations, including the United States, attended the conference held in The Hague in the Netherlands. One positive outcome of this conference was the establishment of the Permanent Court of International Arbitration. The purpose of this court was to encourage nations to use mediation or arbitration to settle international disputes. In the case of *mediation*, the nations involved in a dispute would ask a neutral individual or nation to suggest a solution. In cases resolved by *arbitration*, the disputing nations would agree in advance to accept the decision of the neutral party.

The Second Hague Conference was called by Czar Nicholas II in 1907. It had been originally suggested by Theodore Roosevelt before

the outbreak of the Russo-Japanese War. For this second meeting, forty-six nations met again in The Hague. The United States insisted on the inclusion of Latin American states in this meeting. But the Second Hague Conference ran into difficulties similar to those of the first conference. No nation wanted to lose its competitive edge or its right to independent action. Some progress was made with the acceptance of a revised version of the Drago Doctrine, which prevented countries from being invaded for failure to pay debts. Plans were made to hold another conference in 1916.

Meanwhile, the United States was expanding its participation in arbitration treaties. From 1908 to 1909, President Taft's Secretary of State, Elihu Root, negotiated agreements with twenty-five nations. In 1913, Wilson's Secretary of State, William Jennings Bryan, backed treaties calling for compulsory arbitration of international disputes. The United States and twenty-one nations concluded treaties calling for a "cooling off" period during conflicts. Nevertheless, counteracting influences pulled the world apart within a very short time.

The Great War Begins

With all these active efforts at international cooperation, why did one political murder start so much destruction? Part of the answer rests with the changes that were taking place in Europe at the time.

In the nineteenth century, two new national powers emerged— Germany and Italy. They wanted to close the gap between themselves and the older, established powers, such as Britain and France. Neither Germany nor Italy possessed the wealth of territory and markets that these other nations had. Most of the underdeveloped regions were already claimed by other nations. Any attempt to increase colonial holdings would bring nations into conflict with one another.

The growth of nationalism in Italy and Germany increased tension in Europe. France, which had lost the provinces of Alsace and Lorraine to Germany in 1871, looked for the day when they would be returned. Germany viewed Britain as a stumbling block to its territorial expansion and distrusted Russia. Russia sought ports that were ice-free. Certain Slavic groups wanted to rid themselves of Austro-Hungarian rule. As Turkish power in the Balkan peninsula decreased, many conflicting national interests rushed to fill the void.

The major powers in Europe wanted to maintain the balance of power that was being upset by imperialism and nationalism. Austria-Hungary, Russia, Germany, France, and Britain strengthened their positions in two ways. First, they had tried to outdo each other in building deadly military forces. France, Russia, Germany, and Austria-Hungary had huge land armies. Germany was also in an armaments race with England, one in which each nation tried to build

Czar Nicholas II of Russia and his son Alexis in 1913, four years before Nicholas, his wife, and their five children were executed during the Russian Revolution.

the biggest warships in the world. Secondly, in addition to raising walls of steel, the great powers formed alliances. Under these, if one member became involved in war, the others would have to go to that country's aid. This meant that the quarrel of one nation was sure to drag others into the conflict.

The alliance system was just a result of the way in which European countries had carried on their foreign affairs since early modern times. Kings and princes were accustomed both to fighting and to making bargains with each other. As they were often related by marriage, these were, in a way, family feuds and partnerships. The diplomats and generals who did the bargaining and fighting for royalty were a link to the feudal past. However, the alliance system was dangerously rigid.

How the system worked can be illustrated by what happened between June 28 and August 4, 1914. Immediately after the assassination of the archduke, Austria-Hungary sent a diplomatic note to Serbia with stiff demands. Serbia agreed to all of them, except those that threatened its independence. Austria was not satisfied with the Serbian reply and declared war. Russia, however, believed itself to be the protector of "brother" Slavs in Serbia. Thus, Russia declared war on Austria. Germany, allied to Austria, had to prove that it would also keep its word. Therefore, Germany declared war on Russia. Since Russia was allied with France and Great Britain, these two nations also joined in the combat. And so it went, until most nations of Europe and the world had lined up with either the Central Powers—chiefly Germany and Austria-Hungary—or the Allied Powers—chiefly Russia, France, and Great Britain.

Trench Warfare Leads to a Stalemate

Before 1914, the generals on both sides had planned and trained for fast, decisive drives that would destroy the enemy armies. However, their plans failed to work.

Russia launched an attack on Germany and Austria before preparation for war was complete. The Russian army had superiority in numbers but not in equipment or leadership. The huge Russian thrust into East Prussia ended in the last week of August, when the Germans almost wiped the Russians out at Tannenberg. Russia's allies were shocked at this devastating defeat.

In early September, a surprise German invasion into Northern France was turned back at the Battle of the Marne. The Germans had planned to march through Belgium, a neutral country, to the northern border of France. This was in violation of an international agreement. The Belgians fought back fiercely. Thus, they were able to delay the time it was supposed to take for the Germans to cross the country.

This delay allowed the French to move into position. And it also gave the British time to send troops to aid the French. The French formed a **defensive line at the Marne River and turned the Germans back in September, just outside Paris.**

Some military historians feel it was this failure at the Marne that ultimately led to the defeat of Germany. Eight weeks after the beginning of the war, each side had failed to strike a knockout blow.

By 1915, the war, especially on the Western Front, became a stalemate. Neither the Germans nor the French and English were able to make the winning move. Both sides had dug trenches along a line that extended 966 kilometers (600 miles) from the English channel to the Swiss border. For three years, Germans battled Allies from these trenches separated only by a narrow strip of land. Powerful artillery and machine guns made it impossible for even the bravest infantry charges to break through the lines. Great offensives by both sides bogged down in a few weeks. Casualties were in the hundreds of thousands. The "victors" in these battles captured only a few miles of scarred ground.

In the outlying areas of war, Japan took over German outposts in China and the Caroline and Marshall Islands. Japanese ships patrolled the Pacific sea lanes, helping the British destroy German shipping. In Africa, the German colonies of Togoland and the Cameroons fell to the Allies.

After the first few months of war, fields of dead lay on the European countryside. These are German soldiers killed at the First Battle of the Marne.

In the East, things fared better for the Central Powers. Turkey had entered the war on their side, cutting off Russia from Allied help by way of the Black Sea. Russia was not a major industrial power and could not stand the steady drain of continuous warfare. By 1916, Russian strength in numbers proved useless. Russian armies lacked ammunition, trucks, medicine, clothing, and food. A growing number of war-weary Russians blamed the czar for their predicament.

Then, in March 1917, a revolution overthrew the czar. In October of that year, the Bolsheviks, the founders of Russian **communism**, seized control of the revolution. Eager to get an exhausted nation out of the war, the new communist government signed the Treaty of Brest-Litovsk in March 1918. In it, Russia gave up a substantial portion of its land. Russia also lost one-third of its population and the majority of its coal and iron resources. Now Germany was virtually free to concentrate its efforts on the Western Front.

communism
an economic system based upon total government control of the means of production, distribution, and exchange of wealth

By early 1917, the war had become a monster, devouring millions of dollars and thousands of lives a day, with no end in sight. No victory could repay any nation for what it was losing. Yet, governments on both sides used propaganda to whip up feelings that identified the enemy with all that was evil. They had promised their suffering people victory. Now they could not consider a compromise peace. Thus, the slaughter went on and on.

Questions for Discussion
1. Define *philanthropist, disarmament, arbitration, communism.*
2. Prior to 1914, what actions were taken to insure permanent peace and unending progress?
3. Explain how the alliance system created world war rather than prevented it from occurring.
4. What was the course of the war on the Western Front?
5. Why did the war continue even after both sides knew they would gain little by a victory?

At first, most Americans hoped to stay neutral, despite generally pro-British sympathies among editors and other public opinion makers. However, from the beginning, the pro-British propaganda fell on the ears of many people willing to listen. Most Americans shared a common language and other strong ties with the British. Since war against Britain would involve war against Canada and France as well, many Americans considered the idea of war against the Allies unthinkable.

Britain, who controlled the Atlantic communication cables, took advantage of its superior capabilities to further anti-German sentiments. Thus, Americans quickly heard of the execution in Belgium of

2. The United States Enters the War

Edith Cavell, a British nurse convicted of helping Allied soldiers to escape. On the other hand, Americans were slow to hear of similar executions of German sympathizers by the French. British propaganda was increasingly successful as the war dragged on.

A more serious threat to neutrality existed than stories of war horrors. Neutrality was quickly endangered because of the new technology of war. Since the British surface fleet controlled the sea lanes, the British could stop neutral merchant ships. The German counterweapon was the newly invented submarine, or U-boat. Submarines attacked without warning from under the sea, leaving the crew and passengers of a torpedoed ship to their fate.

In May 1915, a U-boat torpedoed the unarmed British ocean liner *Lusitania*, killing 1198 people, 128 of whom were Americans. Horror swept the United States. Some Americans called for immediate war, while **pacifists** urged that the country keep cool.

President Wilson did not give in to the cry for war in 1915. Yet neither would he agree to prohibit trade or travel. The historic right of neutrals was to enjoy free commerce—except for guns, explosives, and other weapons—with all *belligerents* (warring parties). When the Allies began to run short of money in 1915, they asked President Wilson's permission to borrow from American banks. Secretary of State Bryan objected. He thought the act would place American neutrality in danger. In spite of that, Wilson decided to grant the request. The Central Powers would receive the same consideration. However, since the British blockade of Germany was completely effective, only the Allies could get supplies from the United States. American factories were kept busy with war orders as the Allies used the loans to finance the war. These Morgan loans, arranged by financier J. P. Morgan, amounted to over $2 billion by 1917. Thus, playing by the traditional rules of neutrality had made America the moneylender and arms-maker for one side only.

Still Wilson continued to protest the illegal blockade tactics of both Great Britain and Germany. But after the sinking of the *Lusitania*, he demanded that Germany end unrestricted submarine attacks. Wilson threatened to break off diplomatic relations with Germany after Americans aboard the French ship *Sussex* were killed. Fearing American intervention, the Germans agreed that no more merchant ships would be sunk without warning. This *Sussex* pledge also called for the United States to hold Britain accountable for breaking international law.

After Wilson's reelection in 1916, he tried, as he had before, to get the belligerents to compromise. The leaders of the warring nations were unwilling to accept "a peace without victory." And it was not long after that that the United States itself was caught up in the war.

Above: Two reactions to American involvement in World War I. Left: The Woman's Peace Party marched to cool the growing war fever in the country. Right: When the United States entered the war, journalist George Creel was appointed to head the Committee on Public Information. He recruited speakers, writers, artists, and filmmakers to mobilize public opinion against the enemy. This cartoon appeared in a Brooklyn magazine in 1917. Some individuals overreacted to the committee's message. Many loyal American citizens lost their jobs just because their names were German. School boards banned the teaching of German in public schools. Laws were passed officially changing the name of sauerkraut to "liberty cabbage."

In January 1917, the British intercepted and decoded a message from the German Foreign Secretary, Zimmermann, to the German Ambassador in Washington. The message called for the German Ambassador to promise Mexico help "to regain by conquest lost territory in Texas, Arizona, and New Mexico." In return, Mexico was to attack the United States if it entered the war against Germany.

This message was relayed to Wilson by the British. Before this, the Germans had been gambling that all-out submarine warfare would give them such a quick victory that it would not matter if the Americans entered the war. After the publication of the Zimmermann note and the resumption of unrestricted submarine attacks by the Germans, Wilson took the final step on April 2. He asked Congress for a declaration of war. He did not stress threatened American interests. Instead, he made the issue a moral and worldwide one. "The world," he said, "must be made safe for democracy." Inspired by Wilson's statement of idealism, Congress declared war by an overwhelming vote. So, under forests of waving flags, America said goodby to neutrality.

"Over There"

It was nearly fifteen months before Americans reached France in any great numbers. When Germans resumed unrestricted submarine warfare, they gambled that American help for the Allies would be too little, too late. When the United States entered the war, the entire armed forces numbered fewer than 500,000 people. Actually, by the fall of 1917, the first of more than 3 million draftees were being inducted.

The original plan of the Allied High Command was to use

American units as replacements for battered portions of British and French armies. The United States commander, tough General John J. Pershing, who had fought in Cuba and chased Villa in Mexico, insisted that a separate United States army be organized. Parts of this American Expeditionary Force (AEF) got their first taste of battle in 1918. In March 1918, the Germans launched a final all-out drive. By late May, they crunched to within 121 kilometers (75 miles) of Paris. As summer drew near, fresh soldiers in American uniforms poured into the trenches to relieve weary French warriors. On May 28, an American division took the village of Cantigny. In early June, Pershing assigned two other divisions to help the French drive the Germans back at Chateau-Thierry. One of these American divisions went on attacking through early July and took Vaux, Bouresches, and Belleau Woods.

The Germans launched two more great offensives to cross the Marne River. They were anxious now to end the war before American troop build-up in Europe would make it possible for the Allies to launch offensives. The French held on at the Second Battle of the Marne in July. Once again, they saved France. American help contributed to checking the last German drive.

By September, thirty-nine American divisions were in France. The AEF launched its first independent effort, a four-day assault that wiped out a German strong point around St. Mihiel. American land forces and pilots retrieved territory for France that had been held by the Germans since the early days of the war. Pershing thought that this victory did more than any other to revive French morale.

On September 26, the AEF began a massive offensive in the Argonne forest. Many of the German soldiers on the first defensive line were hardened veterans in bombproof shelters. They could not even imagine the zeal of the new troops. Many German leaders knew that the end was in sight. They could no longer muster the numbers needed to oppose the fresh American forces. Yet all through October, fierce fighting continued. The Americans and French inched their way through a forest held and reinforced by the enemy for four years. Meanwhile, the German line was collapsing under pressure from the British, Canadians, and Belgians elsewhere. Forty-seven days after the onslaught began, the Germans finally surrendered. In those six and one-half weeks, the United States force of 1 million had lost almost 50,000 killed in action and over 200,000 wounded.

Even in the short time that Americans saw action, they learned that twentieth-century warfare was not a matter of gallant charges up San Juan Hill. Rather, in 1918, it was crouching in trenches full of muddy water and swollen corpses. It was steady bombardment that broke one's nerves. It was a choking death by poison gas or

World War I

- Central Powers
- Allied Powers
- Furthest Military Penetration by Central Powers
- Neutral Countries
- German Submarine War Zone 1915
- × Battle Sites

Kilometers
0   400   800
0   250   500
Miles

N

NORWAY
SWEDEN
FINLAND
Petrograd
BALTIC SEA
DENMARK
RUSSIA
NORTH SEA
IRELAND
GREAT BRITAIN
NETHERLANDS
London
Ypres
BELGIUM
Cantigny
Chateau-Thierry
ARGONNE FOREST
Paris
BELLEAU WOOD
Saint Mihiel
EAST PRUSSIA
Tannenberg
Berlin
GERMANY
POLAND
Brest Litovsk
TREATY OF BREST LITOVSK 1918
Vienna
Budapest
ATLANTIC OCEAN
SWITZERLAND
AUSTRIA-HUNGARY
FRANCE
Caporetto
Trentino
BOSNIA
Sarajevo
Belgrade
SERBIA
ROMANIA
BLACK SEA
ITALY
Rome
BULGARIA
PORTUGAL
SPAIN
CORSICA
SARDINIA
ALBANIA
GREECE
Constantinople
Gallipoli
AEGEAN SEA
TURKEY
CYPRUS
SP. MOROCCO
MEDITERRANEAN SEA
SICILY
CRETE
MOROCCO
ALGERIA
TUNISIA

entrapment in the barbed wire strung between opposing trench lines. It was long lines of ambulances delivering the wounded to makeshift hospitals. In fact, Sherman's description of war as hell was fulfilled to the letter.

The Battle at Sea

Eight days after Wilson asked for a declaration of war, Admiral William S. Sims—Commander in Chief of United States Naval Forces

In this photograph taken early in the war, a French pilot and his spotter await combat over the Champagne front.

reconnaisance
an exploratory military survey of enemy territory

Chateau-Thierry, the scene of an important tactical and moral victory for the French and American forces against Germany's advance in 1918.

in Europe—called on Britain's First Sea Lord in London. German U-boats had been sinking ships at a faster rate than they could be replaced. Sims and the British leaders decided that armed escort ships were needed to accompany merchant ships traveling in convoys in order to subdue German attacks. This idea carried and proved to be the most successful strategy against U-boat attacks. The Allies laid out a barrier of mines across the North Sea from Norway to the Orkney Islands. This move made it hazardous for German ships to travel back and forth to and from Germany on the Atlantic Ocean.

As more ships became available, American contributions at sea increased rapidly. The American Navy transported nearly one-half of the American troops to Europe and provided at least 80 percent of the escort vessels. The effectiveness of the Anglo-American naval forces added pressure to the German High Seas Fleet.

New Engines of War

In all wars, every victim must suffer pain, fear, and grief alone. Yet, World War I, fought from 1914 to 1918, tended to make the process of fighting and dying more mechanical. Inventors, who hoped to end the stand-off between attack and defense, came up with new, scientific ways of destruction.

Aerial bombardment was one new horror. Early in the war, the Germans sent *dirigibles* to bomb London. These were cigar-shaped airships, kept aloft by lighter-than-air hydrogen gas. The "Zeppelins" (named for their inventor, Count Ferdinand von Zeppelin) had motors that made them self-propelled. They did not do much damage. But they did frighten the noncombatant populations, who suddenly found themselves in danger. Far more destructive was the development of long-range artillery.

Airplanes became steadily more deadly. In 1903, the Wright brothers' first plane just skimmed the ground for 37 meters (120 feet), carrying one person at about 56 kilometers (35 miles) per hour. By 1918, planes with two-person crews, machine guns, and bombs were flying 3 kilometers (2 miles) high at 153 kilometers (95 miles) per hour.

When the war began, air forces were geared toward **reconnaissance.** But by mid-1914, the French, Germans, and British all realized the need for fighting aircraft to protect their own "spy" flights and also to prevent the enemy from completing theirs. It was in World War I that the first *aces* emerged. These were pilots who became experts at sending their opponents to a fiery death.

Most pilots flew without parachutes, so their life expectancies were short. The British and French fliers bore the brunt of the assault on the Germans. However, Americans were represented. The Lafayette Escadrille was made up of American volunteers who served

In January 1916, the British tried out a secret weapon. When the new weapon was being shipped around England under cover, it was explained away as a water tank, and the name "tank" stuck. The weapon was first used in the Somme offensive nine months later.

with the French fliers a year before the United States entered the war. After war was declared, the American Army Air Force joined this new breed of warriors.

In May 1919, wartime aeronautical research and development led to the building of the first planes to fly the Atlantic. Other modern weapons included poison gas and tanks. In order to get better death-dealing machines, governments willingly paid the huge costs of these engineering marvels. They paid for the thousands of hours it took to prepare designs as well as for the numerous experiments and tests that were made.

At sea, destroyers and submarines hunted each other with torpedoes and depth bombs. Their crews, like those of other new war-machines, became dehumanized themselves. No longer did people battle face to face, like heroes of legend. They risked their lives bravely. But they fought from great distances and killed enemies—often innocent civilians—whom they never saw.

The Home Front

As the American Civil War showed, prolonged wars change societies in unexpected ways. Before April 1917, American foreign policy had been directed at such limited objectives as forcing the enemy to give up submarine blockades. Once Congress had declared war, official propaganda encouraged the idea that the enemy was not really human. A typical war editorial said that we were "dealing with madmen, whose sole purpose is to kill."

These attitudes stirred passions that made dissent almost impossible. A strong Espionage Act of 1917 and a Sedition Act of 1918 lashed out at those who were against the war. The Industrial Workers of the World (IWW) and the Socialists both had resisted the call to arms. They believed that the struggle was between the capitalists who controlled all the great powers and the workers who did the fighting, suffering, and dying, no matter which side won. Because of this opposition, IWW leader William Haywood and ninety-four of his supporters were arrested and jailed. As a result, their organization was crippled. Eugene V. Debs, the Socialist leader, was sentenced to federal prison for speeches against the draft. Even after the war was over, President Wilson refused to pardon him. Rose Patton Stokes, a New York socialite, was sentenced to ten years in prison because she "preached discontent with the government . . . ." Few people dared to protest this interference with freedom of speech. The Civil Liberties Bureau, the forerunner of the American Civil Liberties Union, tried but found it difficult to attract open supporters.

In addition, many Americans of German origin lived in the shadow of distrust. It was believed, quite falsely, that they would prove loyal to Germany rather than to the United States. Germans were not imprisoned. However, a tremendous wave of anti-German feeling swept the country. This feeling was encouraged by Hollywood movies, which portrayed German characters as vicious militarists or sinister spies. People with accents or German-sounding names were fired. And German literature was removed from some libraries.

The actual work of preparing for battle soon showed the importance of massive organization. In 1861, the North waited two years to draft soldiers. In 1917, the nation turned almost at once to this means of filling the ranks. Volunteering was encouraged by patriotic songs and posters. But the draft remained the basic recruiting policy. In the year and a half that the United States spent at war, about 4 million recruits were taken from every section, class, and trade, and put into uniform. About 2 million of them were sent overseas.

Raising a labor force was another great task. Women were urged to take factory and office jobs that had been closed to them before. The Wilson administration also took other steps to attract workers. One such move was to create a War Labor Board, with representatives from industry, unions, and government. It proposed standard working conditions at camps and bases and on other projects being built for the government. It *mediated*, or settled, disputes over wages and hours in critical industries. It also recognized the workers' right to organize. In return, Samuel Gompers, one of the Board members, gave the pledge of the AF of L not to strike during the war. Gompers was very pleased over what he believed to be a great gain. Capital and labor were

JOIN THE
ARMY AIR SERVICE
BE AN AMERICAN EAGLE!

CONSULT YOUR LOCAL DRAFT BOARD. READ THE ILLUSTRATED
BOOKLET AT ANY RECRUITING OFFICE, OR WRITE TO THE CHIEF
SIGNAL OFFICER OF THE ARMY, WASHINGTON, D.C.

REMEMBER!
THE FLAG OF LIBERTY
SUPPORT IT!

BUY
U.S.Government Bonds
3rd. LIBERTY LOAN

Left: This poster encouraged young men to join the struggling Army Air Service. Not until 1918 did the Army Air Service units see action. But during the last seven months of the war, American fliers made an important contribution to the Allied offensive. Right: Five massive Liberty and Victory Loan drives financed about two-thirds of the cost of the war. This poster was aimed at recent American immigrants. Directed by the advertising and entertainment industries, all the drives were huge successes. Persons who refused to buy were often publicly ridiculed and even assaulted.

wartime partners, pulling together. However, Gompers' critics reminded him that government—though its authority in this field was limited—held the reins.

Financing the war called for extraordinary measures too. The government borrowed money and raised certain taxes. Money was borrowed by selling war bonds. Through "Liberty Bond Drives" and "Victory Bond Drives," the government raised $21 billion. Excise taxes on train tickets, liquor, tobacco, and certain forms of recreation brought in even more money. Income taxes were raised as well.

The entertainment industry provided strong morale boosters for civilians and military alike. American songwriters wrote new tunes about war. Entertainers appeared at rallies encouraging the purchase of Liberty Bonds. They toured the country urging support for the American Red Cross. One actress raised $85,000 in a midday rally when the crowd learned that her fiancé had just been killed at the front.

Above: Two jobs in the war effort. Left: About a million women joined the labor force. The women in this photograph boxed munitions to be shipped overseas to soldiers in the trenches. Right: Of the 100,000 Black soldiers sent overseas, about 80,000 were assigned to segregated units that did the hard, dirty work behind the lines. The Secretary of War said the Army did not intend to settle the "so-called race question." A mayor warned Black troops leaving for France not to "get any new fangled ideas about democracy." Those who did reach the front—in segregated units—fought bravely. These men of the 369th Infantry were at the front for 191 days straight—longer than any other regiment.

Organizing Production for War

A major American contribution to the war was the power of its industry, agriculture, and financial institutions in supplying European needs for food, ships, and arms. The task of supplying gigantic armies and navies was so enormous that American machine-power was as welcome to the Allies in April 1917 as the promise of American fighting forces yet to come. President Wilson established the Council of National Defense to mobilize national resources.

Building war plants and shipyards was itself a long process. Congress provided for the Emergency Fleet Corporation to have widespread control of merchant shipping. Replacements had to be provided for the tonnage being sunk each month by German U-boats. The critical loss of cargo threatened to bring the Allies to the brink of disaster.

United States factories did not hit full productive stride until 1918. By then, the War Industries Board, under Bernard Baruch, had complete control over American industries that produced war materials. The Board decided who produced what, when, and where. It assigned responsibility for producing different items to various manufacturers. Ordinary peacetime production practically stopped as industries involved in wartime production received the supplies they needed first. Once underway, the war industries poured out floods of war material. As a single example, the nation produced forty-three airplanes in 1914—and 14,000 in 1918. Only 1800 planes were ready in time to be shipped to France before the fighting was over. The well-organized economy, assembly-line procedures, and round-the-clock work hours were responsible for these marvels.

The government took over the operation of the railroads when the systems failed under the pressure of troop movements and the shipment of war supplies. Lines were consolidated, equipment was standardized, and passenger traffic was discouraged.

The government also set limits on fuel and food consumption. Daylight savings time was introduced and "Fuelless Mondays" encouraged. Under Herbert Hoover, the Food Administration set high prices for farm products to encourage farmers to increase production. Americans were urged to reduce consumption as farmers worked their land to the limits. Record amounts of food were shipped to the Allies, as Americans voluntarily accepted "Wheatless Mondays," "Meatless Tuesdays," and "Porkless Thursdays."

More than 500 war agencies ran the industrial "front." Washington became the headquarters of a "super-trust," so full of business people that the Secretary of the Interior wrote to a friend, "It is easier to find a great cattle king or automobile manufacturer or a railroad president or a banker at the Shoreham (a Washington hotel) than it is to find him in his own town."

Clearly, a great change was taking place. Americans had rejected the arguments of Socialists who called for national ownership and economic planning. In 1914, through the Clayton Antitrust Act, Congress had approved a federal effort to keep competition alive in industry. Yet, just four years later, under the spur of war, the country accepted massive government regulation and combined efforts by companies which were rivals in peacetime.

Black Americans in World War I

About 371,000 Black soldiers served in World War I. Unfortunately, their contributions were stifled by restrictions based on prejudice. Even though these Blacks had combat training and requested combat duty, they were most often assigned to labor battalions. They cooked, cleaned, and served as orderlies. They also lived in segregated quarters and were restricted to segregated units.

Despite these handicaps, the Black 369th Regiment became the first Allied force to break through German lines at the Rhine River. Henry Johnson and Needham Roberts, both Blacks, became the first Americans to receive the French military honor—the *Croix de Guerre* (cross of war)—for bravery.

Questions for Discussion

1. Define *pacifist, belligerent, dirigible, reconnaissance.*
2. What factors led to the end of American neutrality?
3. What was the effect of the American entrance into World War I?

4. What was the role of the Anglo-American naval forces on the course of the war?
5. How did technology increase the horrors of World War I?
6. How did life in America change during the war?

3. An Uncertain Peace

On January 8, 1918, while American armies were still in training, Woodrow Wilson outlined fourteen points that he believed would end the system of armaments, alliances, national jealousies, and colonial economic rivalries that had brought on World War I. These points included an end to secret treaties, freedom of the seas, the lowering of international tariff barriers, disarmament, a fair adjustment of colonial claims with the interests of colonial peoples in mind, and self-determination for the national groups within the Turkish and Austro-Hungarian empires. Finally, there was to be a League of Nations to guarantee the freedom and boundaries of all nations. Wilson believed that acceptance of his program might actually make World War I the war to end all wars.

As reported in the international press, the Fourteen Points had a powerful impact, especially among the Germans. Many Germans realized that they were losing the war. They found Wilson's terms very attractive. The surrender terms were not as harsh as those that England or France had been demanding. Everyone knew that the old national order of 1914 was over. What should replace it? The Bolsheviks in Russia offered one choice—working-class revolution everywhere and international communism. Wilson promised something less drastic. He proposed an international society of nations under constitutional governments elected by all classes. These nations, he believed, would solve their disputes peacefully.

Assuming that Wilson spoke for the Allies, some German officials opened secret negotiations with him for peace. Wilson insisted that the German people first be freed of autocratic rule. In the first week of November, revolts broke out in Germany. On November 9, the Kaiser resigned and a German Republic was proclaimed. Its leaders asked for, and were granted, an armistice, which took effect at 11 a.m. on November 11, 1918. The next day, a war correspondent wrote, "Last night, for the first time since August in the first year of the war, there was no night of gunfire in the sky. . . The Fires of Hell had been put out." At the battle front and in cities, cheering thousands celebrated the end of the long plunge into the hell of total war.

Bolshevik
a member of the extremist wing of the Russian Social Democratic Party that seized power in Russia during the Revolution in 1917

Intervention in Russia

The **Bolsheviks**, who had taken over Russia, had renamed it "The Union of Soviet Socialist Republics," or, more simply, the Soviet

WOMEN IN WORLD WAR I

When the United States entered World War I, blue-collar jobs on the home front were suddenly opened up to women. During the war, women ran farms, worked in factories, and labored on the railroad. As Eleanor Flexner wrote in *Century of Struggle*, "They took jobs in blast furnaces, in the manufacture of steel plate, high explosives, armaments, machine tools, agricultural implements, electrical apparatus, railway, automobile, and airplane parts; they worked in brass and copper smelting and refining, in foundries, in oil refining, in the production of chemicals, fertilizers, and leather goods."

Women were supporting the war effort of their nation. And, in doing so, they were fighting another battle in their long, determined struggle for the right to vote.

In January, 1918, Woodrow Wilson appealed to the Senate on behalf of woman suffrage with these words: "We have made partners of the women in this war; shall we admit them only to a partnership of suffering and sacrifice and toil and not to a partnership of privilege and right? This war could not have been fought, either by the other nations engaged or by America, if it had not been for the services of the women—services rendered in every sphere—not merely in the fields of effort in which we have been accustomed to see them work, but wherever men have worked, and upon the very edges of the battle itself. . . ."

Wilson's plea was not enough to win a two-thirds majority. It was June, 1919, before the Nineteenth Amendment passed the Senate. And it was August 26, 1920, before the amendment was ratified. Women had won the vote. But, once the war was over, they lost their jobs. They had still not won equality.

Union. On March 3, 1918, the Soviets signed the Treaty of Brest Litovsk with Germany. In it, they gave up territory in the Baltic, Poland, and the Ukraine. On March 7, the British took over the Russian port of Murmansk. They hoped to encourage some Russian resistance to the Germans so that the Germans could not concentrate on the Western Front. But their major objective was to destroy the Bolshevik government. In Siberia, anti-Bolsheviks were aided in their resistance to the Communist government with help from British, French, American, and Japanese forces. Wilson resisted intervention but eventually sent troops to guard British supplies in the Arctic seaport of Archangel and to aid Czechs in Vladivostok. Even after the Armistice, military and financial support continued. There were American troops in northern Russia until 1919 and in Siberia until 1920. In 1922, Japanese troops were the last to leave. China took advantage of this situation and reclaimed Manchuria.

Many Russians began to distrust outsiders because of this interference. The fear of communism, in turn, caused the exclusion of the Soviet Union from the international community.

Woodrow Wilson and the Treaty of Versailles

Early in December 1918, a confident, smiling Wilson sailed for
Paris to take personal charge of the United States delegation at the
peace conference. In the streets of every European city he visited,
Wilson was welcomed with signs and cheering crowds. The people of
Europe believed that "Veelson," chief of the still fresh and powerful
United States, could really bring about the kind of world described in
his Fourteen Points.

But when the President met with the prime ministers of France,
Great Britain, and Italy at the Palace of Versailles, just outside Paris,
he received some rude shocks. For one thing, self-determination ran
head-on into secret wartime treaties that promised certain territories
to the winners, regardless of the nationality of their peoples. Moreover, many nationalities in Central Europe were still hopelessly
intermingled. So nations, such as Czechoslovakia and Poland, that had
been created or restored during the peace conference out of parts of
Germany and Austria-Hungary had their own unhappy minorities.

In addition, no agreement could be reached on tariff reduction.
There was no fair adjustment of the claims to German colonies.
Instead, these were simply divided among the winners. The British
would not promise freedom of the seas, and the French would not
disarm. Both countries still feared Germany too much to risk the
hard-won advantages of victory. Finally, France and England demanded harsh punishment for the beaten enemy. By the Treaty of
Versailles, which was finally accepted, Germany was branded as the
only nation responsible for the war and was forced to disarm almost

completely. Though stripped of its merchant marine and coal and iron lands, Germany was still ordered to pay heavy *reparations*—payments for damages—to its enemies. Poverty-stricken, the German people felt betrayed and bitter. As a result, the country soon became ripe for troublemakers.

Wilson was not at fault because the final treaty was so far from his hopes. He fought as best he could for his Fourteen Points. Nor was it a case of the diplomats of Europe being basically evil. The fact was that age-old social and national conflicts could not be solved by kind words and good will.

Wilson bargained away some of his Fourteen Points to keep one hope alive. The treaty created a League of Nations with headquarters in Switzerland. With this parliament of humankind in existence, Wilson believed that problems left by the treaty might be talked out instead of hammered out by war.

Woodrow Wilson—Statesman Defeated

The Treaty of Versailles was signed on June 28, 1919. Wilson immediately returned to the United States to ratify it and so accept membership in the League. However, he returned to an America in which opposition to the treaty had been hardening. Some Senators objected to Wilson's failure to consult them during the Versailles negotiations. Various nationality groups resented parts of the treaty that they thought unfair to citizens of their country. Progressives, who had hoped that Wilson was leading them to a more just world, were outraged at his seeming willingness to accept a brutal victor's peace. Finally, some voters believed that involvement in the League would drag the United States into future European power struggles, disguised as peacekeeping efforts. As one said, they did not want to "send our armed forces wherever and whenever a super government of foreigners sitting in Switzerland orders."

Some, though not all, of the opponents of the Treaty wanted the United States to follow a policy of isolationism. They believed that the United States could exert its greatest influence in the world by setting a good example of democracy at home. They would do this best by avoiding wars in Europe and the burdens of arms. Wilson's defenders argued that no nation was safe any longer without some international peacekeeping organization such as the League of Nations, any more than individuals were really safe without police and courts. Nonetheless, anti-League Senators, led by Henry Cabot Lodge (Chairman of the Senate Foreign Relations Committee), added reservations or limit-setting changes to the treaty. The most serious reservation denied any American "obligation" to protect member nations in the League unless Congress agreed.

In July 1919, American veterans marched through the Arc de Triomphe in Paris to celebrate peace.

Left: In September 1919, the English magazine Punch ran this cartoon showing President Wilson trying to drag a reluctant United States into the League of Nations. Right: "I know I'm at the end of my tether," said President Wilson, but "the trip is necessary to save the treaty." He was certain that his personal appeal would result in a public demand for Senate ratification.

Wilson could have accepted this language and gotten the treaty ratified. However, Lodge was a political enemy. And Wilson also felt that such limits were dishonorable. The United States must be forced, if need be, to enter the League as a full partner, with nothing held back. He decided to go over the Senate's head and to appeal directly to the American people to "see the thing through."

In September 1919, he began an extensive trip by train around the country. In three weeks, he traveled 9500 kilometers (6000 miles) and made thirty-seven speeches in twenty-nine cities. But the strain of overwork took its toll on the 62-year-old Wilson and led to tragedy. On September 25, at Pueblo, Colorado, Wilson became so ill that he had to be rushed back to Washington. A few days afterward, he suffered a paralytic stroke. For months he was too sick to conduct business or receive reports. Yet, he sent word to Democratic Senators not to give in by accepting the treaty with reservations. When it came to a vote, they loyally joined with those Senators who opposed the treaty in any form and defeated ratification. So ended Wilson's dream. And just twenty years later, war broke out again.

Questions for Discussion

1. Define *Bolshevik*, *reparations*.
2. How do the points outlined in Wilson's Fourteen Points coincide with his idea of "making the world safe for democracy."
3. Why was the Treaty of Versailles never signed by the United States?

Chapter 23 Review

Summary Questions for Discussion

1. What was the goal of the peace societies? From what groups did they get their support?
2. How did the major powers of Europe hope to maintain the balance of power?
3. Explain how the alliance system got the major powers of Europe involved in World War I.
4. How did Turkish entrance into the war aid the Central Powers?
5. What is unrestricted submarine warfare?
6. According to Wilson, why was the United States declaring war?
7. How did World War I change the nature of warfare?
8. Why did more women enter the labor force during World War I?
9. What handicaps were placed on Black American soldiers in World War I? What did Black soldiers accomplish?
10. What was the influence of the Bolshevik Revolution on the peace settlement?

Word Study

Fill in each blank in the sentences that follow with the term below that is most appropriate.

disarmament	arbitration	communism
pacifists	belligerents	dirigibles
reconnaissance	Bolshevik	reparations

1. Those who wish to stay out of war are known as _____.
2. An attempt to prevent two sides from fighting often involves _____, or bringing in a neutral party to settle the dispute.
3. Reduction of weapons, or _____, can help to limit warfare.
4. Those who fight are known as _____.
5. During a war, planes are often sent on _____ to gain information about troop positions and strategy.
6. In World War I, Germans sent cigar-shaped airships, or _____, to bomb London.
7. In November 1917, the _____ Revolution brought a new group to power in Russia. The new economic system, called _____, was instituted after the Revolution.

Using Your Skills

1. Which pictures in this chapter do you think support the following generalization: "World War I was a total war in which the efforts of citizens as well as soldiers were an essential part of the war effort"?
2. Look at the map on page 529. Find the boundary line set by the Treaty of Brest Litovsk. Whom did the treaty favor? Why?
3. Study the posters, headlines, and cartoons in this chapter. Explain the role propaganda played in World War I in relation to the rejection of the Treaty of Versailles.
4. Examine the map on page 529. List the Central Powers. Why were they so named? List the Allied Powers. Why was Russian withdrawal from the war effort a significant loss for the Allies?

Unit 6 Review

Summary

The United States became a global power as a result of events that occurred between 1870 and 1920. The rise of big business and the closing of the frontier left the United States ready to join the race for colonization.

At first, the United States was only interested in opening up new markets for trade. This course changed with the purchase of Alaska in 1867, followed by a period of island-grabbing in the Pacific.

United States expansion was not limited to the Orient. As early as 1850, business people had looked toward Latin America as an area for economic expansion. As a result of the Spanish-American War, the United States acquired the Philippines, Puerto Rico, and Guam. Cuba was not directly taken but the United States did become involved in its internal affairs.

However, with the outbreak of World War I in 1914, the United States was forced to turn its interests away from Latin America.

In the beginning, the United States attempted to remain neutral. Both British control of the seas and propaganda strengthened support for the Allies against the Central Powers. When Germany used unrestricted submarine warfare against the Allies and issued the Zimmermann note, President Wilson felt obligated to bring the United States into battle. Once the Americans entered the conflict, the tide began to turn. By November 11, 1918, Germany finally agreed to an armistice based on Wilson's Fourteen Points, which outlined a "peace without victory."

The result was the Treaty of Versailles, which was a compromise of Wilson's original goals. To disappoint Wilson even further, the Senate never accepted the Treaty. The United States, therefore, returned to a policy of isolationism. America had stepped into the world arena and promptly withdrew. And the treaty that the United States did not accept contained the seeds of future world conflict.

Summary Questions

1. What were the forces that led the United States to become a major power in the Pacific?
2. Why were the Chinese at a disadvantage in trying to keep foreigners out of their country?
3. State the arguments against imperialism.
4. What motivated United States interest in Latin America?
5. Why did the Spanish-American War occur even after Spain had agreed to President McKinley's ultimatum?

6. How was the Monroe Doctrine strengthened in the late nineteenth century?
7. How did the Roosevelt Corollary lead the United States to "police" Latin America?
8. Why did American relations with Mexico deteriorate in the early 1900s?
9. What did the events following the assassination of the Austrian archduke in June 1914 show about the ability of the alliance system to maintain peace?
10. Why did the Allied powers win World War I?

Developing Your Vocabulary

1. (Nationalism, Imperialism) is the policy of extending a nation's control over other peoples.
2. A colony that is protected and partially controlled by another country is called a (sphere of influence, protectorate).
3. The right of a nation to have its boundaries protected is known as the right of (extraterritoriality, territorial integrity).

4. Jingoism (would, would not) support an aggressive foreign policy.

5. When a nation is given political or economic control over a region of a certain nation, it is said to have a (sphere of influence, protectorate).

6. A final demand threatening serious penalties is known as an (ultimatum, arbitration).

7. A corollary is a(n) (amendment, deletion) to a document.

8. A third, neutral party is often called in to (confirm, arbitrate) a dispute.

9. Cigar-shaped aircraft such as the *Zeppelin* are called (gliders, dirigibles).

10. Disarmament is the (buildup, reduction) of military force and weaponry.

Developing Your Skills

Cause and Effect Relationship

1. For each of the following policies or actions, discuss one condition that led to the formulation of the policy or action and one effect of it on American foreign relations: the Open Door Policy, the Teller Amendment, the Platt Amendment, the Insular Cases, the Roosevelt Corollary.

Historical Analysis

2. Prepare a series of five newspaper headlines that you think would sum up the important events of World War I. Be prepared to justify your choice of events.

Analysis and Comparison

3. Analyze Seward's reasons for purchasing Alaska by comparing them with Jefferson's reasons for purchasing Louisiana. Were they similar? Give reasons for your answers.

Review and Analysis

4. Review the provisions of the Northwest Ordinance of 1787, which extended political equality to newly acquired territories of the United States. State the decisions of the Insular Cases. Why weren't the principles of the Northwest Ordinance extended to our overseas possessions?

Special Activities

1. Rudyard Kipling urged Anglo-Saxon nations to "Take up the White Man's Burden." Abraham Lincoln had stated, "No man is good enough to govern another without that man's consent." Discuss in class the meaning of these quotations. With which do you agree? Why? Which guided American foreign policy at the end of the nineteenth century? Why?

2. Study and report to the class the details surrounding the sinking of the *Maine* and its relationship to the Spanish-American War. Would twentieth-century communication and media systems have prevented war?

3. Investigate and prepare a report for the class on the Panama Canal. Include the French effort to dig the canal, why the route through Panama was chosen, the construction of the Canal, and its present status and importance.

4. Read Erich M. Remarque's book *All Quiet on the Western Front*, a German version of a common soldier's experiences and the horrors of trench warfare. Report your reactions to the class.

5. Write a newspaper account of the debate in the Senate over the ratification of the Treaty of Versailles.

UNIT 7

The Twenties and Thirties

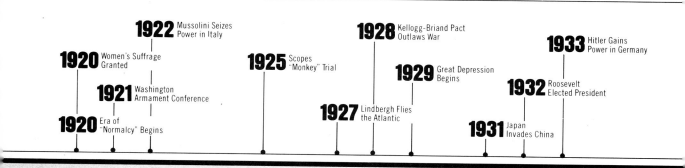

1920 Women's Suffrage Granted

1920 Era of "Normalcy" Begins

1921 Washington Armament Conference

1922 Mussolini Seizes Power in Italy

1925 Scopes "Monkey" Trial

1927 Lindbergh Flies the Atlantic

1928 Kellogg-Briand Pact Outlaws War

1929 Great Depression Begins

1931 Japan Invades China

1932 Roosevelt Elected President

1933 Hitler Gains Power in Germany

CHAPTER 24
The Golden and Not-So-Golden Twenties

CHAPTER 25
The Great Depression Tests American Democracy

CHAPTER 26
Between Two World Wars

Like a thunderbolt, the stock market crash of October 1929 ended a decade of sunny prosperity and began a decade of gloomy depression at home and growing turmoil in Europe and Asia. Prosperity was turned into poverty, gaiety into grimness. Unit VII gives us a picture of the contrasting halves of that period.

544

1935 Congress Passes
Social Security Act

1936 Spanish Civil
War Begins

1939 World War II
Begins

Chapter 24 presents a more detailed look at the way Americans worked and played during the 1920s. It also tells how Americans wrestled with questions of right and wrong in an era of rapid technological change. Chapter 25 describes the 1930s, the decade of the "Great Depression." What was happening in the rest of the world from 1920 to 1940, and how the country reacted to it, is the subject of Chapter 26. Though economic troubles at home continued to claim the attention of most people in the 1930s, fires of war began to sweep through Africa, Europe, and Asia. By the end of the decade, much of the world was at war.

CHAPTER 24

The Golden and Not-So-Golden Twenties

America became a modern-looking nation almost overnight. Highways, billboards, radios, and movies crowded the land. Automobiles were not new in 1920. After that year, however, they poured out of factories in such numbers that the automobile changed the look of the American countryside. Suburbs and advertising were unknown in 1910. Yet by 1925, all big cities seemed to be in a race to spread outward. Advertisements seemed to leap from every magazine page.

In everything from business and entertainment to family life, quick change was the rule of the day. Yet, a curious thing took place. The more things changed, the more some people lived in "old-fashioned" ways and defended time-honored beliefs. Any group of people faced with change feels some fright. So it was natural that some Americans in the 1920s tried to keep things as they had been. They attempted to shut the gates on immigration, or ban new ideas from the schools, or withdraw from the affairs of the world.

Yet these same people often enjoyed other aspects of progress. They were cautious about new social customs but loved new gadgets and wanted larger incomes. They cheered the growth of their communities. It was clear that not *all* change was a threat.

Meanwhile, other men and women of the 1920s accepted certain changing ideas. However, they feared that Americans were giving up former ideals in the rush to get rich. Reactions to life in the 1920s were varied. Yet almost everyone shared one special feeling. That feeling was a sense that they had crossed a dividing line that made their times unlike any ever before experienced by Americans.

READING GUIDE

1. In the 1920s why did some people welcome change while others opposed it?
2. What changes brought about in the 1920s proved to be most permanent?
3. What changes occurred in immigration policy during the 1920s?

The Golden Twenties, as depicted on the cover of Life *Magazine in 1926.*

1. "The Business of America Is Business"

President Warren G. Harding greets a young admirer.

It would be hard to find two people more different than Woodrow Wilson and Warren G. Harding, who succeeded Wilson as President in 1921. Wilson was an ex-professor, accustomed to lecturing others, especially on their duties. Harding was an easy-going, small-town newspaper owner, at ease bouncing a child or greeting a visiting baseball team. He had few strong ideas of his own on any issue and called only for a return to *normalcy*—a quiet pace after the Progressive and wartime crusades.

Although Harding himself was not politically corrupt, he appointed some friends who proved to be untrustworthy. They became known as the "Ohio Gang." Within eighteen months, the truth about the "Ohio Gang" was unfolding. And within twenty-seven months, Harding died—some felt as a result of strain and bitterness.

After Harding's death, investigations revealed that corruption was widespread. For example, Harding had appointed Charles Forbes as Director of the Veterans Bureau. Within a short time, Forbes diverted a substantial part of the $250 million budget spent by his agency to himself and his associates. When Forbes was finally convicted of taking bribes, he was fined and imprisoned.

People who applied to the Alien Property Custodian for the return of foreign-owned property seized by the United States during the war found that they had to pay someone off to get a settlement. It soon became public that a close friend of President Harding and the brother of the Attorney General were involved in this scandal.

The most famous scandal involved Secretary of the Interior Albert Fall. Fall persuaded the Secretary of the Navy, Edwin C. Denby, to secretly transfer control of the naval oil reserves from the Department of the Navy to the Department of the Interior. Secretary Fall soon began to argue that the government was losing money on the reserves because oil was leaking into neighboring wells. Fall therefore suggested that they be leased at a profit. In 1922, Fall leased reserves at Teapot Dome, Wyoming, and Elk Hills, California, to private speculators. This was done secretly and without any competitive bidding. At about the same time, Secretary Fall had become very rich. Investigations headed by Senator Thomas Walsh disclosed that Secretary Fall had been accepting bribes. He was finally convicted on these charges and imprisoned.

Senator Burton K. Wheeler investigated Harry Daugherty, Harding's close friend, political ally, and Attorney General. Daugherty managed to bank $75,000 while living in luxury and earning only $12,000 a year. The investigation led to a dead end. Daugherty convinced two juries that he was refusing to testify out of loyalty to the dead President. This line of defense kept him out of prison, but it did cast a deeper shadow over Harding's administration.

Coolidge Plays It "Cool"

Calvin Coolidge, Harding's Vice-President and successor, was not involved in these scandals. His fellow Americans viewed him as a healthy example of the simple life. Actually, Coolidge was a college graduate and a Massachusetts corporation lawyer before he entered politics. However, in an age when the Presidential "image" was becoming more important, it helped Coolidge to look and sound like a Vermont farmer who never wasted a word or a nickel. He was able to repair some of the damage done to the government by replacing Harding's dishonest appointees. And in 1924, he ran for reelection on the slogan, "Keep Cool with Coolidge." His opposition was divided between John W. Davis, a conservative nominated by a badly split Democratic Party, and Robert LaFollette, the candidate of a new third party that followed Progressive traditions. Coolidge won a decisive victory.

The slogans "Normalcy" and "Keeping Cool" meant a sharp departure from the Progressive policies of reforming and regulating the economy. Like President Wilson, Coolidge felt that the wartime level of taxation should be reduced. Wilson had wanted to reduce taxes on middle and low incomes to stimulate economic growth. Coolidge favored the plan of Secretary of the Treasury Mellon to lower taxes on the rich and cut corporation taxes to the bone to encourage investments. At the same time, Congress voted almost no funds to allow the government to enforce antitrust and other Progressive laws.

Both Harding and Coolidge had as their Secretary of Commerce Herbert Hoover, a brilliant engineer and organizer. Under Hoover,

President Calvin Coolidge (left) chats with Secretary of Commerce Herbert Hoover. Hoover was later to succeed Coolidge as President.

549

the Department of Commerce encouraged companies in the same industry to form "trade associations." These associations then provided the companies with information on markets, prices, new inventions, and sources of raw materials. In effect, this meant that the government was working for business. Efficiency in each industry increased. However, these trade associations also discouraged competition by independent outsiders.

The thinking behind such policies was that industrial prosperity would create wealth not just for business people but for all consumers—laborers, farmers, even the poor. As a result, no further national action to deal with social problems would be needed. As Coolidge himself said, "The business of America is business." However, not everyone agreed.

The Farm Crisis

The 1920s were not easy times for the farmers. They were faced with a post-war decrease in demand for agricultural products such as corn, wheat, and cotton. Many farmers had borrowed to buy more land and machinery during the peak-demand years of the war. Now they were threatened with **foreclosure** on their mortgages. Meanwhile, expenses were rising because of the growing use of gasoline-powered equipment. And overproduction, caused by improvements in machinery and insecticides, drove prices as well as income downward.

Worsening conditions caused rural members of both parties in Congress to form a "farm bloc." Their aim was to pass bills to aid the farmers. But Coolidge drew the line at any national action. Twice he vetoed versions of the McNary-Haugen bill, which called for the government to buy farm surpluses and sell them on the international market. Coolidge argued that the best solution would come from the farmers themselves—voluntary reduction of production—and not from the government.

America Becomes a Machine Civilization

The industrial machinery tuned to wartime pitch in 1918 soon began to produce civilian goods again. The boom of the 1920s differed from those of earlier times. In addition to **capital goods,** more and more **consumer goods** were being produced. These included not only everyday items, such as clothing and canned vegetables, but also a long list of new devices to save labor or increase personal pleasure. Toasters, radios, vacuum cleaners, and refrigerators were some of these products. Coal mining suffered because of overproduction, aging machinery, and competition from the oil industry. At the same time, newer industries, such as moviemaking, electric utilities, and aviation, were making eye-catching upward leaps.

foreclosure
a legal act that bars a person from redeeming his or her property, especially for nonpayment of loans taken out on property

capital goods
goods used in the production of other goods, such as steel girders and farm machines

consumer goods
things used directly by individuals

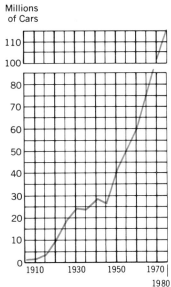

Registration of Passenger Cars 1910–1980

Millions of Cars

Left: In this 1904 ad appealing to the upper class, Ford promises an "8 actual horsepower" motor. Right: An indication of the dramatic rise in automobile purchasing in the United States between 1910 and 1970.

In order to sell new goods, especially luxuries, advertising itself became a big business. Its leaders claimed that their work was necessary to create the demand that kept factory wheels turning. Without "ads," said one man, the nation would have to "turn back the page to medieval times." For many, yesterday's luxury became today's necessity. Along with the rise of advertising as an encouragement to buying came the *installment plan*. This plan allowed customers to buy an item with a small down payment, but with a written promise to pay the rest later in weekly or monthly sums. Credit buying in weekly or monthly sums had been common in business and farming. But when used for more personal spending, it soon swayed the basic American ideas away from the value of thrift toward a new belief stressing consumption.

The manufacture of automobiles, a new industry, had the biggest effect on the economy. When cars first appeared in the 1890s, they were sold as luxuries. But by 1929, assembly-line procedures, easy credit, and advertising made the automobile commonplace. The manufacture of automobiles used up 20 percent of the steel, 80 percent of the rubber, and 90 percent of the oil produced in the United States each year. It also created millions of other jobs in the oil and highway industries.

The Growth of Suburbia

In addition to causing a huge economic impact, the automobile also had a revolutionary effect on society. A car gave anyone, regardless of

Cars crowd New York's Fifth Avenue in 1921.

class or background, a 64-kilometer- (40-mile-) an-hour magic-carpet ride to wherever he or she wished. It gave young people who were "keeping company" a chance to escape the supervision of older eyes. Thus, the automobile changed manners and morals by loosening family control over behavior. It also quickened the pace of American life by encouraging family travel. Soon the America of settled towns and time-honored habits became a land of "wheeled" wanderers.

The automobile also helped to put suburban living within the reach of the middle class. In the nineteenth century, only the well-off could afford to buy a "country retreat." But inexpensive automobiles allowed the middle class to seek fresh air and greenery for themselves and their children. Middle-income families no longer had to live near their jobs. Recognizing this, builders bought vacant lands near highways and put up new homes, spurring economic growth still further.

Because the homes of the new suburbia were low-priced for mass sale, they were built on small lots that pushed them close together. In addition, the cheapest way to build many houses was to make all features identical. As a result, many suburbs had a monotonous, crowded look. And cheap open land, needed for future growth, began to vanish under rows of houses.

Suburban growth deeply affected the future of urban centers. Big cities began to lose income for needed services. Former city taxpayers, after using city facilities while at work, now left the city for the

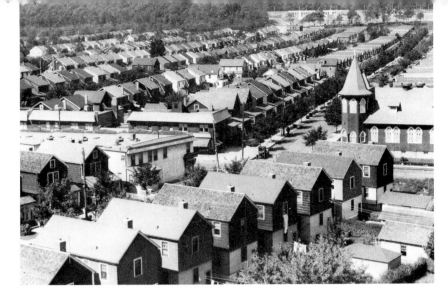

The new mobility brought on by automobiles also brought with it a boom in housing. Freed from the confines of the city, families moved to suburbs that sprouted up on the outskirts of urban areas. This photograph shows a typical Long Island, New York, suburb of the 1920s.

suburbs at sundown. The villages to which suburbanites rushed had their problems as well. Suburban communities could not build new schools, roads, and power and water systems fast enough to satisfy explosively growing needs.

Henry Ford and people like him started a cultural revolution. They were responsible for giving new forms to the American city, landscape, and family. As one Midwesterner said, the changes in America could be explained "in just four letters—A-U-T-O!"

Questions for Discussion

1. Define *foreclosure, capital goods, consumer goods, installment plan.*
2. What was the meaning of Coolidge's statement, "The business of America is business"?
3. What basic changes has the automobile made in the lifestyle of Americans?

While many city residents were moving to the suburbs, the steady march to urban areas still continued. By 1920, less than half of the American population lived in rural communities. As the ways of small-town America vanished, some Americans fought back against modernizing influences.

2. An Era of Reaction

Blacks Move to the City

Most Blacks who sought opportunities in the city faced the dim reality of living in overcrowded dwellings and accepting low-paying jobs. Black ghettos developed because when Blacks moved in, Whites moved out. A *ghetto* is a city slum where members of a minority group live. Slum conditions came about because landlords made little effort to maintain the property in which Black tenants lived. Unemployment, poverty, and crime became commonplace in the segregated portions of cities. Black people attempting to move out of the ghetto found that they were often barred from predominantly White areas.

White big-city dwellers objected to the growing number of Blacks in their midst. The summer of 1919 was hot with race riots. Between June and December, seventy-six Black people were lynched in some twenty-five riots. The worst riot occurred in Chicago. It began with an unimportant fight between White and Black youths on a bathing beach. Wild rumors that spread after the fight soon led to nearly a week of street battles between gangs of both races. Before the National Guard restored peace, fifteen Whites and twenty-three Blacks died. All in all, over 500 people were injured.

Frustrations caused by the conditions with which Blacks were forced to live brought about a new outspokenness and militancy. It was during this era that Marcus Garvey founded the Universal Negro Improvement Association in 1914. Garvey saw no end in sight to the injustices dealt by White America. So he pushed for the return of Blacks to Africa. He also sought to instill a new sense of pride and awareness in Blacks by stressing the accomplishments of members of

A major step into the modern age was the 1920 passage of the "Anthony Amendment." The Nineteenth Amendment was named after Susan B. Anthony, whose life was spent in tireless activity for women's suffrage. The partnership of Anthony and Elizabeth Cady Stanton was the movement's vital center from the 1850s through the turn of the century. Active into her nineties, always optimistic and forward-looking, Anthony inspired a younger generation of co-workers to continue the struggle. When she resigned as President of the National American Woman Suffrage Association in 1900, she designated Carrie Lane Chapman Catt, almost forty years younger, as her successor. Anthony died in 1906, fourteen years before her amendment became law.

554

Marcus Garvey (in plumed hat) leads a parade through Harlem in 1916. Garvey's oratory and natural leadership abilities drew thousands of American Blacks into the Universal Negro Improvement and Conservation Association, making it the first important U.S. Black nationalist movement.

their race. Many Black leaders, including W.E.B. Du Bois, disagreed with Garvey's "Back to Africa" movement. They believed that Blacks had been in America long enough to want to develop better conditions for themselves in America. They saw no point in running away. Garvey was eventually **deported** to Jamaica in 1925 on mail fraud charges. Without his leadership, the movement collapsed. Nevertheless, the heightened pride in Black identity continued.

Asa Phillip Randolph, another brilliant organizer, founded the Brotherhood of Sleeping Car Porters and Maids in 1925. This union attempted to obtain better wages and working conditions for Blacks who worked on Pullman cars. At the beginning, the union was strongly opposed by the Pullman Company on the grounds that it was radical. But with support from the NAACP, the union soon got the attention it deserved.

The New "Klan"

The most outspoken enemies of Blacks were members of the Ku Klux Klan, an organization which was revived in 1915. The new Klan, however, was not limited to the South. Nor were Blacks its only targets. Its slogan was "native, White, Protestant," By 1920, the Klan opposed Catholics, Jews, foreigners, and radicals, who, it said, were trying to "take over" America. The reborn organization quickly grew to a membership, estimated in 1923, of 5 million. It was a powerful political force in Texas, Louisiana, Oklahoma, Maine, Kansas, and Indiana. From 1920 to 1925, Klan political machines helped to elect or defeat governors and Congressmen. In 1928, the Democrats nominated Alfred E. Smith, a New York Catholic, for President. Klan

deported
sent out of the country by the government, especially because of unlawful presence or misbehavior according to the laws: said about an alien

Three generations of the Ku Klux Klan pose for this photo in 1925.

opposition was one of the reasons why seven Southern states broke their tradition of voting Democratic. Instead, these states voted for the Republican candidate, Herbert Hoover. This action guaranteed his election.

Though the Klan was strongest in rural areas, it did win recruits in big cities such as Washington, D.C. The Klan was probably guilty of terroristic acts against its "enemies," though its leaders always denied it. The Klan appealed not only to violence. It also gave some poorly educated men and women, who were fearful of change, a sense of superiority. However, in 1930, most Americans were not convinced that "Americanism" belonged to any one race, nationality, religion, or set of ideas. In addition, Klan leaders were found guilty of political corruption and murder. Thus, between 1923 and 1930, the Klan shrank to a tiny handful of followers.

The Golden Door Is Closed

There was still another reaction to the waves of change washing over America. The nation ended its historic practice of admitting almost unlimited numbers of European immigrants into the country. As you saw in earlier chapters, there had long been complaints against wide-open immigration. During World War I, suspicions of foreigners grew even stronger. Propaganda suggested that even innocent-looking neighbors might be German spies in disguise. After the Russian Revolution, it was easy to transfer these fears to possible Communist sympathizers. In 1919, a New York newspaper said, "All over the country, alien or foreign-born agitators are carrying on in many languages for the overthrow of the government."

red scare
the fear of communists. Communists are often referred to as reds.

A great **red scare** gripped the land. And this fear was increased by the actions of a few extremists. Bombs were sent through the mail to many prominent politicians and financiers. Only the alert action of a post office employee prevented most of the bombs from being delivered. The clerk, having just read about the recent wave of mail bombs, realized that he had just shelved sixteen similar packages for

Ellis Island, where incoming immigrants were processed before landing in New York Harbor.

insufficient postage. The police found that each package contained a bomb. On September 16, 1920, an explosion on Wall Street took thirty-eight lives, injured hundreds, and destroyed property worth millions of dollars.

Attorney General A. Mitchell Palmer launched a campaign against radicals and aliens. He had been provoked into acting when a bomb exploded at his home in the summer of 1919.

Beginning in November 1919, a series of raids known as the "Palmer Raids" began. The targets were the Bolsheviks, socialists, and anarchists. Because many of these people were recent immigrants, an unreasonable fear of foreigners arose. While the Palmer raids lasted, thousands of aliens were rounded up, many of them innocent people. Hundreds of others were deported, even in cases where there was no proof of wrongdoing. In fact, thousands of people were held in jail for months without trials.

Most Americans went along with these raids. Congress hammered out a new immigration policy, reflecting the negative feelings that some Americans had developed toward immigrants from southern and eastern Europe. Finally, in 1924, the policy became law. An immigration quota was set for each European country. Germany and Britain had large quotas. However, the allotments for countries such as Greece and Poland were extremely limited. In addition, all Asian immigration was ended.

Sacco and Vanzetti

Feelings of fear and hostility were obvious in the actions of the Ku Klux Klan and the restrictions on immigration. Many people came to believe that the same feelings determined the outcome of a trial that took place in 1921 in Dedham, Massachusetts.

On April 15, 1920, two murders were committed during a holdup at a factory in South Braintree, Massachusetts. Three weeks later, two Italian immigrants, Nicola Sacco and Bartolomeo Vanzetti, were arrested for these crimes. They were admitted anarchists. So after a trial before a judge who made no secret of his hatred of radicals, Sacco and Vanzetti were convicted.

For six years following the convictions, motions were made for a new trial. Arguments were based on the charges that Sacco and Vanzetti had not received a fair trial and that new evidence was available. A growing number of people, unknown and well-known, in this country and abroad, began to ask if it was the weight of evidence or the weight of prejudice that had convicted Sacco and Vanzetti. These efforts proved to be of no avail. Sacco and Vanzetti were executed in 1927.

Responding to pressure from Fundamentalist groups, the Tennessee legislature passed an anti-evolution law, certain the governor would veto it. He signed it, certain that school districts would ignore it. They did. But the American Civil Liberties Union wanted to test the law in court. John Scopes reluctantly agreed to deliberately break the law. The trial's most dramatic moment came when Clarence Darrow called the prosecutor, William Jennings Bryan (right), to the stand. Darrow's attack on Fundamentalist beliefs and the 100° heat combined to break Bryan; five days after the trial ended, he died.

For over fifty years, the controversy remained unsettled. If two innocent men were convicted, that crime was a greater one than the one they were accused of. Sacco and Vanzetti were pardoned by the governor of Massachusetts in 1978.

The Scopes Trial

Occasionally, a small incident in history is important because it stands for something much bigger. One such incident occurred in 1925 at a trial in the small town of Dayton, Tennessee. The trial became a famous event because it summed up the clash in the 1920s between the old and new points of view. The accused was a young biology teacher named John Scopes. He had broken a state law that forbade the teaching of Charles Darwin's 65-year-old theory of evolution.

One part of Darwin's theory held that people were animals who had evolved into their present form over millions of years. To *Fundamentalists*—Christians who read the Bible as a literal record of events—this idea was wicked. It seemed to be in direct conflict with the story of how God created human beings.

The issue was not simply what Scopes did. Supporters of the law believed that if the Bible could be questioned, then all religion, patriotism, family love—things that held society together—might also be fatally challenged. Surely, a free community had the right to protect itself against these poisonous ideas.

Opponents of the state law claimed that, if a majority anywhere could ban ideas that they disliked from schools, progress would end. Humanity, they said, had evolved from a primitive state only by questioning accepted wisdom. Free people needed free minds and free speech, which was protected by the Constitution.

The American Civil Liberties Union helped Scopes by hiring one of the country's foremost criminal lawyers, Clarence Darrow, to defend him. William Jennings Bryan, Democratic candidate for President in 1896, 1900, and 1908, volunteered to prosecute for the state.

Not only was Bryan himself a Fundamentalist, but he felt that he was defending the right of people to keep their world as it was and as they wished it to be.

The trial was a circus. The national press called it "monkey business" and made it a battle between "city slickers" and "hayseeds." Fundamentalism finally won an empty victory. Scopes was found guilty. However, as the years passed, the law was widely ignored.

Questions for Discussion

1. Define *ghetto, red scare, Fundamentalist.*
2. How did the post World War I period foster a growth in Black pride?
3. What conditions created the "red scare"?
4. Why did immigration policy change in the 1920s?
5. What circumstances surrounded the trial of Sacco and Vanzetti?

3. The Roaring Twenties

One of the strongest forces shaping life in the 1920s was Prohibition. In 1919, the Eighteenth Amendment was ratified. This amendment prohibited the manufacture, sale, and transportation of intoxicating liquor. It took effect one year after ratification. After a century of crusading against "demon rum," America had gone dry.

Many of those who supported the amendment had been Progressives. They thought that outlawing liquor would improve the quality of national life. As they pointed out, drunkenness cost society millions of dollars each year in accidents, crime, lost jobs, and broken homes.

However, times were changing in 1920. Many Americans, especially city dwellers, saw no harm in moderate drinking. They felt that

Left: Federal Prohibition agents pose with some captured distilling equipment. Right: Al Capone, who assumed control of Chicago's underworld in 1925. Capone was finally jailed in 1931 on charges of income tax evasion.

morality
judgments about right and wrong behavior

the government had no right to determine personal **morality**. So they ignored the law and bought illegal "booze" or made their own "home brew." This situation created problems. In rural areas, illegal liquor could be made in hidden distilleries. But city dwellers usually had to buy it. Their suppliers, known as *bootleggers*, most often smuggled in liquor from outside the country. Even frequent raids by police and Treasury agents failed to keep bootlegging from thriving.

But an illegal business lacks protection for both the buyer and seller. A bootlegger did not sue nonpaying customers in court. Instead, in extreme cases, bootleggers hired gunmen to "rub them out." Soon gangs of killers were fighting each other in the streets for control of the liquor business. Crime, like everything else in the 1920s, had become a big, well-organized business.

The best known gangster in the nation was Al Capone of Chicago. Using his many millions of dollars of illegal profit each year, Capone bribed officials to look the other way. His gunmen were the army of an "empire" of boats, trucks, warehouses, and *speakeasies*—nightclubs that sold drinks illegally. In fact, Capone himself avoided arrest.

"*Wets*" and "*drys*"—prohibition's enemies and supporters— blamed each other for its failures. Whoever was at fault, the amendment was impossible to enforce and the country tired of it. Finally, repeal of the Eighteenth Amendment was voted in 1933. Organized crime, however, continued.

Votes for Women

The 1920s began with votes for women. On August 26, 1920, the Nineteenth Amendment was signed into law. A long, intense effort was needed to achieve this victory. It had been seventy-two years since 1848, when Elizabeth Cady Stanton and Lucretia Mott held the first Women's Rights Convention in Seneca Falls, New York.

Susan B. Anthony had been the great nineteenth-century organizer of the movement for women's rights. The final "Winning Plan" was the work of her successor, Carrie Lane Chapman Catt. As president of the National American Woman Suffrage Association (NAWSA) from 1915 to 1920, Catt marshaled a force of two million women. She organized women to work in local political districts and also launched a nationwide campaign. This dual strategy worked. Victories for suffrage in state legislatures reinforced lobbying efforts in Washington. Finally, in June 1919, Congress passed the suffrage amendment. And, over the next fourteen months, it was ratified by the necessary thirty-six states.

As Catt observed, the suffrage struggle had been "a continuous, seemingly endless, chain of activity. Young suffragists . . . were not born when it began. Old suffragists . . . were dead when it ended."

Many suffragists wore "Votes for Women" buttons to demonstrate their support for the Susan B. Anthony Amendment.

Opposed to woman suffrage was what Catt labeled an "Unholy Alliance" of several interests. New England Republicans, who supported big business, united with Southern Democrats. Liquor brewers feared that women would always vote "dry." Political bosses feared that they would try to "clean up" politics. Business interests expected women to work against child labor and for better wages and working conditions. The suffragists themselves believed that women would form a political bloc for social reform.

To educate women for their new role, Catt converted NAWSA into the National League of Women Voters. Soon after women won the vote, some states passed minimum-wage, maximum-hour, and equal-pay laws. In many states, women gained the right to serve on juries. And, with a strong lobbying effort, women got the Sheppard-Towner bill through Congress. This bill appropriated over a million dollars a year to provide education in proper health care for mothers and infants.

But newly enfranchised women did not vote as a bloc. Instead, their votes tended to reflect the social and economic status of their families. In the main, women voted much as men did.

Meanwhile, the members of the National Women's Party were seeking more far-reaching change. In 1923, Alice Paul proposed the Equal Rights Amendment to the Constitution. Reformers feared that equal rights would mean the end of protective legislation for working women. Women's Party members felt this protection should be extended to working men. Over half a century later, the controversy over the proposed Equal Rights Amendment was still going on.

Left: Jazz played an important role in the Harlem Renaissance of the 1920s. Recognition of the artistry of jazz brought both Blacks and Whites uptown to listen to this exciting, vital music in night spots like the Cotton Club (above left). Right: Martha Graham, who departed from classical ballet to invent a new dance form, becoming a pioneer of modern dance.

One of the most popular musicians of this period was vocalist Ella Fitzgerald.

The New Woman

Women's work in World War I freed them from the long, narrow hobble skirt that hampered movement. Then, in the 1920s, young women bared their knees and bobbed their hair. They smoked, drank, and wore makeup. Their popular image was that of the *flapper*, the daring young woman who did as she pleased.

Behind this carefree image lay a different reality. The 1920s were not boom times for working women. Middle-class and upper-class women did enter white-collar jobs in increasing numbers, as typists, clerks, and secretaries. But over half the women in the workforce put in long hours of heavy work at the lowest level of pay. Many labored as domestics in private homes. Others could find industrial jobs only in the garment industry or in canning factories and textile mills. In the professions, women were channeled into teaching and nursing. Fewer women became doctors than in the decade before.

Even so, individual women showed that barriers could be broken. In 1926, Gertrude Ederle braved dangerous tidal currents to swim the English Channel. She broke all previous records set by men. In the 1920s Martha Graham dynamically freed the dance from the confines of classical ballet. In 1932, the pilot Amelia Earhart became the first woman to fly solo across the Atlantic. Most women of the time were still hobbled by custom and convention. But many young women had new heroes, new horizons, and a new sense of being free.

Harlem Renaissance

The 1920s saw a rebirth of culture in the Black community. The center of this cultural growth spurt was Harlem, the Black community in New York City. One of the sparks of this cultural revolution was

Alain Locke's book, *The New Negro*. Locke encouraged Blacks to be proud of their heritage and accomplishments. He believed that Blacks should stop apologizing to White America and should become assertive in order to gain full equality.

Jazz, with its roots in New Orleans, became very popular during this period. Great jazz musicians, such as Duke Ellington, Count Basie, Louis Armstrong, and Jelly Roll Morton, expressed the joys and sorrows of Black life through their music. Langston Hughes, Claude McKay, and Countee Cullen did the same with their literature. They hid nothing and spilled out verses and pages of bitterness laced with hope. This was the first time that the true emotions of American Blacks were put into novel form. The Renaissance instilled a new confidence in Black people. The works that came out of the period were valuable contributions to the American culture as well.

An Age of Hero Worship

One reason for the breakdown in older community standards was the rise of rapid mass communication. Local preachers, politicians, and editors had to compete for respectful attention with nationally known experts, who were interviewed on radio or in the big-city papers.

One definition of a *community* is a group of people who share something. Using that definition, the **mass media** were actually building a nationwide community. All Americans were coming to share in the news instantly reported over the airwaves, in print, or in newsreels. Journalism made millions of people "eyewitnesses" to events and "acquaintances" of newsmaking figures.

Since sensational news did not happen every day, the media created *celebrities*—people made famous through appearance in news columns. George Herman (Babe) Ruth played baseball from April to October. A super athlete, he was exciting to watch as his mighty swing drove the ball out of sight for yet another of his towering home runs. But the millions of words written about him were as sensational as his playing. He was the "Sultan of Swat," the "Bambino," the hero of youth.

Sports heroes grew so important that when a member of a minority group entered their ranks, it could affect the status of the whole group. Jesse Owens, a brilliant Black track star, won many gold medals for the United States team in the 1936 Olympics in Berlin. His tremendous official welcome home did not solve the problems of the Blacks in America. But his triumphs, like the victories of heavyweight champion Joe Louis, gave millions of ordinary Blacks and Whites a moment of common pride in the deeds of Black athletes.

The greatest hero of the 1920s was a young flier named Charles A. Lindbergh, son of a Swedish immigrant. On May 20, 1927, he took off

Babe Ruth swats one during his first season with the New York Yankees in 1920. He became one of the greatest drawing cards ever in American sports.

mass media
all the means of public communication that reach a large audience, such as newspapers, radio, and movies

Jesse Owens' 1936 Olympic victories forced the nation to recognize the abilities of a great Black athlete.

CHARLES LINDBERGH

Lindbergh's Unused "Cushion" The world called him "Lucky Lindy." And, of course, Charles Lindbergh *was* lucky that no tiny part of a plane or an engine snapped under strain. But Lindbergh was not one to rely on luck. Every last detail of his flight from New York to Paris was planned to a hair. He knew exactly how much gasoline *The Spirit of St. Louis* could carry. He knew how many miles his trusty little engine could wring out of every gallon and how many minutes it could keep firing. His technical knowledge enabled Lindbergh to believe in the future of flying. It was not all daredevil stunts. It was a matter of science and planning. Planes *could* fly the Atlantic.

How good was Lindbergh's planning? When Lindbergh finally crossed England on the last leg of his flight, he was so far ahead of his own schedule that he knew he could go on past Paris for another few hours. He toyed with the idea of setting an endurance and distance record as well as being first to solo across the Atlantic. Rome would be a perfect place to land.

But, then, he thought it out again. It would be night. No one was expecting him, he thought. And in those days, that meant that there might be no one who would turn on the lights of the landing field. Moreover, he was tired after flying more than thirty hours with no sleep for two nights. So he landed at the Paris airport. He was shocked by the crowds who streamed out to meet him. Lindbergh, however, did not forget to write in his story of the flight that he had enough gas left in his tank for that New York-to-Rome record he never set.

from New York, alone in a single-engine airplane, without a radio, for a nonstop flight across the Atlantic. A true pioneer of modern flight, Lindbergh landed in Paris thirty-three hours later. He discovered, much to his amazement, that he had become an international hero. The hearts of people throughout the world had been won by the courage of the shy, young, American aviator.

Questions for Discussion

1. Define *morality, mass media, speakeasy.*
2. How did the passage of the Eighteenth and Nineteenth Amendments reflect changing American attitudes?
3. What was one cause of the Harlem Renaissance?
4. How did mass media build a nationwide community?

Chapter 24 Review

Summary Questions for Discussion

1. What did President Warren G. Harding mean by a return to "normalcy"?
2. Scandal was widespread during Harding's administration. Identify and explain the role of each of the following in the corruption that existed. (a) the "Ohio Gang," (b) Charles Forbes, (c) the Alien Property Custodian, (d) Albert Fall, and (e) Harry Daugherty.
3. What image did Coolidge present to the American people?
4. How did Coolidge's policy of "Keeping Cool" give industry a lot of freedom?
5. (a) What did Herbert Hoover do as Secretary of Commerce to allow the government to work for business? (b) What was the thinking behind this policy?
6. As business was being favored in the 1920s, describe four problems that faced the farmers.
7. Why was the "farm bloc" formed?
8. Explain the effect of each of the following on the economy of the 1920s: (a) introduction of "labor-saving devices"; (b) advertising; (c) the installment plan; and (d) the manufacture of automobiles. Explain the revolutionary effect of the automobile in terms of (a) morals, (b) family life, (c) growth and character of suburbs, and (d) future of urban centers.
9. Explain the approach taken on the subject of Black pride by each of the following: (a) Marcus Garvey, (b) W.E.B. Du Bois, and (c) Asa Phillip Randolph.
10. What were the "Palmer Raids"?
11. How did the Immigration Law of 1924 reflect American feelings at that time?
12. How did the trial of Sacco and Vanzetti reflect the fear and hostility of the times?
13. What was the Eighteenth Amendment?
14. What was the effect of Prohibition on organized crime?
15. What was the Nineteenth Amendment?
16. Explain Carrie Chapman Catt's "Winning Plan" for woman suffrage.
17. What groups formed the "Unholy Alliance" opposing suffrage? Were their fears realized when women won the vote?
18. Describe the rebirth of Black culture in the 1920s.
19. What was the theme of Alain Locke's book, *The New Negro?*
20. How did the mass media expand the definition of *community*?

Word Study

Fill in the blank in the sentences that follow with the term below that is most appropriate.

consumer goods   red scare   foreclosure   morality
capital goods   mass media   deported   celebrity

1. Items that are most commonly found in the home are _____.
2. Farmers of the 1920s feared _____ when their expenses ran too high.
3. A supporter of heavy industry would support the production of _____.
4. An alien who fails to register runs the risk of being _____.
5. The Russian Revolution fostered in the United States a fear of Communists, or a _____.
6. Public awareness is increased through _____.
7. The government tried to regulate personal _____ by passing the Eighteenth Amendment.

CHAPTER 25

The Great Depression Tests American Democracy

The 1920s had been a time of optimism. It had been a period of a nation joyriding in new automobiles. The 1930s opened with a crash into despair. In 1930, the United States plunged into the deepest depression in its history. By the end of 1932, half the productive machinery in the nation was idle. Twelve million workers had no jobs. Hundreds of banks were closed. Depositors lost their lifetime savings forever. Farmers who could find no buyers for their crops saw their homes and lands taken for unpaid debts. City families huddled in shanties in vacant lots. Thousands trudged the roads in desperate search of jobs.

Though shocked and shaken by the economic collapse, the American people did not give up. They had believed that the business leaders of the twenties were magicians who brought progress with "the wave of a wand." Now, they realized that these "heroes" were human just like themselves.

America chose new political leadership and tackled some hard social questions. Such questions were: What is the responsibility of society to the helpless? How should wealth be distributed? What sacrifices are necessary to renew cities and save natural resources? How should the Constitutional balancing of individual rights, local government authority, and the federal government be changed to keep up with the times? Many voices gave conflicting, angry answers. There was tension as the country struggled back to its feet. At the end of the decade, a new world war broke out. Wartime prosperity returned to "cure" the depression—but left these big questions unanswered.

Those who lived through those years—your great grandparents and grandparents—remember them as full of argument and experiment. They were painful times—but exciting and challenging as well.

READING GUIDE

1. **What factors caused stock prices to fall so sharply?**
2. **What were the characteristics of the nation during the Depression?**
3. **What programs were established during the New Deal to help the nation recover?**

The sense of despair and frustration during the years of the Great Depression is depicted in Isaac Soyer's "Employment Agency."

1. Boom and Bust

Part of the boom of the 1920s was caused by real economic growth. Much of this growth was due to *speculation*. Speculation offers the opportunity to make quicker and higher profits. However, bigger losses can occur if the buyer guesses wrong.

As you saw in Unit 3, speculation in land and in the stocks of banks, railroads, and canals had long been part of the history of the nation. In the 1920s, people began speculating in industrial stocks as well. Speculation was not restricted to the business community above. In fact, hundreds of thousands of Americans from all walks of life made speculation a new kind of national pastime.

Shares of stock can be a reasonable, safe investment. They entitle their owner to *dividends*, which are a part of the profits. When buying stock, people hope that the value of each share will rise and that they will receive increased dividends. The rise in the value of a stock and the increased dividends are supposed to be based on a real increase in the value of the corporation due to higher production and profits.

In 1926, F. Scott Fitzgerald and his wife, Zelda, with their daughter, Scottie, return to America after two years in Europe. Through his novels and widely publicized social life, Fitzgerald emerged as a spokesman for, and typical product of, the Jazz Age—a term he coined to describe the twenties.

Around 1925, a wave of optimism swept the *stock market*, where shares are traded. Speculators, often buying on credit, began to pay higher and higher prices for certain stocks. The rise in the price of a stock was based not on the increased value of the corporation, but, rather, on the increased demand for the stock itself. Yet, the owners of these stocks were not worried. They believed that as long as stock prices were rising, they could always sell their stocks and make immediate profits without waiting for a single dividend. Like holders of banknotes in Jackson's time, they had fortunes—but only in "paper profits." Rising stock prices and dividends allowed thousands to live like the glittering, playful rich.

Everyone admired wealth. Even Calvin Coolidge, admired for his thrifty personal habits, did not discourage the big *"bull market"*—one in which everyone is buying and prices are rising. Democrats and Republicans alike approved of it. In 1929, John J. Raskob, Chairman of the Democratic National Committee, wrote an article claiming that anyone, by putting a few dollars a month into stocks, could have a handsome income in a few years. The title of his article was "Everybody Ought To Be Rich." Such statements encouraged people with modest incomes to borrow money to invest. This demand for stocks drove prices still higher. So more and more people crowded onto the get-rich-quick merry-go-round.

The Stock Market Crashes

In the election campaign of 1928, Herbert Hoover confidently told the country that, under Republican leadership, it would soon see the day "when poverty will be banished." Hoover won. Yet, just one year later, the boom collapsed, and poverty flooded the land.

While the bull market had been surging higher and higher, the prices received by farmers for their crops had been sinking steadily. More and more farm owners were unable to pay their bills. In addition, many industries were not thriving. Some were producing more than they could sell. And others were hurt by changes in technology. For example, coal mining had lost customers as gasoline and electric motors steadily replaced steam power. Although most workers' wages had risen, many workers—especially in the "sick" industries—were suffering cuts in their pay envelopes, long layoffs, or periods when there was no work at all. In "booming" 1929, 67 percent of all American families made $3000 a year or less. That sum left little extra to buy new goods, which would keep industry humming and, in turn, provide jobs for a growing population. A day was bound to come when the companies would run out of customers who could afford to buy their products. That day had finally arrived.

On October 24, 1929, a wave of selling swept the stock market. Unable to sell all their goods, corporations sought to sell stock to recover their losses. When there are few buyers and many sellers, prices can fall with alarming speed. This fall in prices cuts the value of stocks held by speculators. To ensure that they had enough to meet their debts, speculators frantically sold more stock. This sent prices tumbling still further. By October 29, entire fortunes had been virtually wiped out.

Questions for Discussion
1. Define *speculation, dividends, stock market, bull market.*
2. What caused the rise in stock prices around 1925?
3. How did John J. Raskob's article encourage people to buy stocks?
4. What conditions were farmers experiencing during the late 1920s?

2. A Nation Crippled and Desperate

In a modern economy, all groups rely closely on one another. What happens to one is soon felt by all. In good times, this can be a source of strength. A rise in wheat prices means that Kansas farmers buy more automobiles. This, in turn, opens up more jobs on the assembly line for Detroit workers. But during the Depression, this process worked in reverse. As companies laid off workers, families cut down on grocery buying. This cutback in spending caused farm prices to sink further. As jobless families drew all money out of banks, many of the banks closed their doors. Those who had not yet withdrawn their money lost it forever. Each closed factory was a blow to all the businesses that sold it raw materials and parts. Each family without a breadwinner bought less of everything, from food to telephone service. As citizens became unable to pay their property taxes, local governments had less to spend on relief. Eventually, all Americans, except a fortunate few, suffered from the crash.

Statistics recorded the decline. Motor vehicle output, the key element in Coolidge prosperity, sank from 4.5 million in 1929 to 1.1 million in 1932. In the same three-year period, new investments declined from $10 billion to $1 billion. And national income declined from $87 billion in 1929 to under $40 billion in 1933.

These statistics do not show the human pain of the Depression. There are no units to measure the bitterness of those standing in bread lines. In the North, whole families were trying to survive on $2 or $3 per week for food. Many areas, particularly in the South, had no relief at all. No adding machine can total the shame of people living in shanties in vacant lots—people who believed that poverty was not a misfortune, but a disgrace. Now it became their disgrace.

In 1932, perhaps 2 million homeless people were wandering the country. Some railroads finally gave up throwing illegal riders off the trains. Instead, they put on extra empty freight cars to accommodate them. A magazine article of 1932 told of "slow starvation" in Philadelphia. In St. Louis, people dug for food in garbage piles in the city dump. Families lived for days on stale bread or spoiled vegetables picked up around markets. State and city welfare agencies were

Bread lines, often sponsored by local charity organizations, kept many from starvation.

This photograph shows a typical family of a miner in Greenview, West Virginia, in the bituminous fields. The baby in the upper left hand corner, which looks three or four months old, is a year old.

overpowered. Their small sums of money could do very little for whole armies of needy citizens.

Depression in Rural Areas

Conditions were not much better outside the cities. Americans had once believed that farmers would never suffer from poverty because they could grow their own food, on their own land, with their own labor. But the industrial-age farmers of 1929 could not survive without equipment. They were in debt for various pieces of machinery, as well as for their land. And when they steadily lost income and could make no payments, they could be forced off their farms. As farm prices fell lower and lower, this became the fate of thousands of independent farmers, those whom Jefferson had once called "the chosen people of God."

An especially tragic fact was that in some places, crops brought in so little that growers could not afford to harvest or ship them. So, while city people starved, apples rotted on the ground in Oregon and mutton was fed to the buzzards in Montana. The nation became aware of the fact that poverty existed in the midst of plenty.

To make matters still worse, tremendous droughts hit the Great Plains in the early 1930s. Farmers watched helplessly as the dried-up soil was blown away by high winds. Huge "dust storms" blackened the skies. Week after week, "the sun blazed down on thousands of square miles once green but now discolored and grassless," as one observer recalled. Many families, "discouraged and beaten, began to load their few possessions into trucks or trailers and go east or west, anywhere to escape disaster."

Many farmers from Texas, Oklahoma, and Arkansas headed toward California to find work picking other farmers' crops. Some

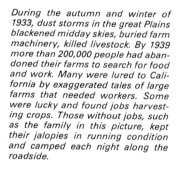

During the autumn and winter of 1933, dust storms in the great Plains blackened midday skies, buried farm machinery, killed livestock. By 1939 more than 200,000 people had abandoned their farms to search for food and work. Many were lured to California by exaggerated tales of large farms that needed workers. Some were lucky and found jobs harvesting crops. Those without jobs, such as the family in this picture, kept their jalopies in running condition and camped each night along the roadside.

California communities passed laws barring these American "immigrants." For these "Okies" and "Arkies," the end of the line was often a barren migrant labor camp. Here they ended the westward migration begun in hope by their pioneer grandparents. In 1939, John Steinbeck depicted their suffering in his novel *The Grapes of Wrath*.

Hoover and the Depression

No one could say that Hoover's response to the Depression was out of character with the man or with the Republican Party. In the 1920s, Republicans had repeatedly defeated legislation that would have involved the government more directly in the economy. Two such bills were the McNary-Haugen farm bill and the Muscle Shoals hydroelectric project.

Also, Hoover was convinced that political freedom depended on economic freedom. He did little to directly involve the federal government in relief programs. Instead, he sought the voluntary cooperation of business leaders to relieve the economic chaos. He asked industry to maintain levels of employment and salaries. He encouraged banks to form the National Credit Association to offer loans to banks and businesses on the brink of bankruptcy. He had the federal government coordinate the public-relief programs of private charities and state and local governments. He asked Congress to increase funds for public works, such as the Boulder Dam project, ultimately named for Hoover. He also asked for increased farm surplus buying as well as a tax cut.

In 1931, this man, who was once a near-millionaire, tried to earn a few pennies by selling apples.

In December 1931, Congress authorized the formation of the Reconstruction Finance Corporation (RFC) to lend money to banks, industries, railroads, and insurance companies. The following July, the Emergency Relief and Construction Act provided more funds and power for the Reconstruction Finance Corporation. The RFC could lend money to agricultural credit banks and to state and local governments that could not provide their own relief programs. The Home Loan Bank System received $125 million through the RFC to provide additional credit to banking institutions and savings and loan associations that held home mortgages. These agencies could then extend more credit to help prevent foreclosures.

Most of these programs, however, depended on money trickling from the top to the bottom. Hoover was condemned for his lack of pity for the distressed. This was not entirely fair. He was actually eager to relieve misery and spur recovery. However, it was true that Hoover favored neither a vigorous use of federal government power nor *deficit financing*—the spending of more money than is provided by taxation. Hoover felt that the special strength of America lay in the ability of its people to solve their own problems wisely and independently. Unfor-

573

tunately, the depth and extent of the Depression seemed to escape him.

Drift Toward Chaos

As distress clamped the land in its grip, some Americans seemed ready for strong action. Thousands of unemployed marched in protest through city streets. Farmers threatened to use force to prevent courts from seizing debtors' property. Visions of reenactments of Civil War draft riots and Shays' Rebellion disturbed many civic leaders, especially since Communists exploited the outraged feelings of Depression victims. It seemed possible that Communists and Socialists together would poll a huge vote in 1932.

Such talk alarmed the Hoover administration into reacting violently against a group known as "bonus marchers." After World War I, Congress had promised veterans a *bonus*—a special reward—payable in 1945. In 1932, unemployed veterans asked for immediate payment of this money. They said that it would help them through this crisis and that their spending would give business a lift. About 20,000 veterans, calling themselves the Bonus Expeditionary Force (BEF), came to Washington to petition Congress. On June 17, the Senate killed a bill that would have met the demands of the BEF. Most returned home when Congress rejected this appeal. But some 2000 veterans camped out in unsightly tents and shacks near the Capitol in Washington, D. C. Hoover refused to recommend early payment of the bonus and would not even meet delegates from the BEF. On July 28, 1932, frightened by rumors of a planned revolt, Hoover ordered the army to remove the threadbare lobbyists. With tear gas and bayonets, troops in full combat gear dispersed the unarmed veterans and set their camp ablaze. Two veterans were killed. Ironically, their bonuses could now be paid in full to their families.

Hoover's actions were interpreted by many as a sign of his indifference to the sufferings of the poor. What aid the federal government was providing came too late. The country demanded bolder steps. As a result of his inability to deal with the economic crisis, Hoover was defeated in the Presidential election in November. He carried only six states against his Democratic rival, Franklin D. Roosevelt. The Socialist and Communist parties combined won even fewer votes than the Socialists alone had in 1920. Americans were now ready for a change. They wanted what Roosevelt called "a New Deal," not a brand-new political system.

Questions for Discussion

1. Define *deficit financing, bonus.*
2. Under what conditions did families live during the Depression?

3. Why do hard times in industry cause hard times in rural areas?
4. What is meant by the statement "poverty existed in the midst of plenty"?
5. Why did Hoover react so violently to the bonus marchers?

3. The New Deal

Franklin D. Roosevelt was a good symbolic choice to lead a nation that needed courage to fight its way out of despair. He himself had battled back from a crippling attack of polio in 1921. Though bound to a wheelchair and leg braces for the rest of his life, he gamely refused to quit politics. Instead, he won election as governor of New York in 1928 and 1930. In 1932, he went from there to the White House.

In 1933, Roosevelt judged that the country wanted a strong President to get things moving and to break the grip of terror. "The only thing we have to fear," he said in his inaugural address, "is fear itself . . . This Nation asks for action, and action now."

"Action now" was what the nation got. Roosevelt was given sweeping emergency powers. Almost immediately he declared a "bank holiday" to give government examiners a chance to eliminate unsound banks and to restore faith in the value of the dollar. Then he brought a stream of special advisers to Washington. Most were young university professors. Therefore, they were nicknamed the "Brain Trust." In the first hundred days of the New Deal, lights burned late as the Brain Trust boldly planned war on the Depression. At first, Congress enacted almost everything the reformers proposed.

The immediate goal of 1933 planning was to get people back to work. Early programs bore down on this task and spent freely to

Below Left: Franklin D. Roosevelt seeks votes for New Deal Congressional candidates in 1938. Below Right: This 1934 cartoon shows Dr. Braintrust tatooing Uncle Sam with the Initials of New Deal programs. Above: WPA employees were paid more than they could get on relief but far less than workers with jobs in private industry.

achieve it. One measure set up a Public Works Administration (PWA). The PWA was funded with $3.3 billion for immediate work on projects such as constructing roads, bridges, tunnels, post offices, and government office buildings. A Federal Emergency Relief Administration (FERA) got $5 billion to help feed and house the jobless. In his first morning of work, its director, Harry L. Hopkins, authorized the spending of several million dollars. A Civilian Conservation Corps (CCC) swiftly put thousands of young men to work in national and state forests. These men, between the ages of 18 and 25, were given the task of planting trees, fighting fires, and building dams. In theory, many of these programs were similar to Hoover's plans. However, they were much larger in scale.

When the PWA, FERA, CCC, and other New Deal "alphabet agencies" came under attack, they were brilliantly defended by a man with another well-known set of initials—FDR. When he grinned at crowds or addressed them on the air as "my friends" and spoke of "your government," they believed he meant it. As his wife Eleanor Roosevelt said, "There was a real dialogue between Franklin and the people."

The painting below, "Building of a Dam" by William Gropper, is part of a mural contracted by the WPA. Critics charged the WPA with inefficiency, extravagance, and political corruption. Supporters claimed that the WPA eased the unemployment crisis and produced results that benefited the entire nation.

The New Deal in the Cities

Between 1934 and 1938, the New Deal settled down to making long-range changes in American life. New and lasting relationships were created between the federal government and local governments, and directly between the federal government and the people. A completely new view of public responsibility for social needs was formed. Its results could actually be seen in the changing American landscape.

A new look came to the cities of the nation as the PWA built libraries, hospitals, schools, and government office buildings. Yet, by 1935, unemployment was still very high. Some New Dealers found the PWA pattern too slow to help. Under the PWA system, cities and states proposed improvements. Then, if the government approved, private companies were awarded contracts and hired workers.

A new approach was tried by the creation of the Works Progress Administration (WPA). Despite the similar initials, WPA worked differently from PWA. It put people on relief directly to work as employees of the federal government. Between 1935 and its end in 1943, the WPA spent $11 billion on over a million projects, employing a total of 8.5 million workers.

In the frontier nation, artistic activities had been considered leisure-time frills, less important than the work of helping the country grow by farming or business enterprise. Thus, there was resistance to the idea of supporting the arts with government funds. Nevertheless, from 1935 to 1938, the WPA was permitted to sponsor music, art, drama, and writing projects.

Another New Deal experiment was the entry of the federal government into the housing business. An act of 1937 created a United States Housing Authority (USHA), which lent money to low-income communities for the construction of housing projects. Housing projects were supposed to be temporary dwellings for families that had been living in slum areas. These families could not yet afford to move to privately owned apartment houses where rents had to be high enough to return profits to the owners. The projects begun by USHA did not meet growing low-cost housing needs. Nevertheless, they were further signs of a growing partnership between Washington and metropolitan regions. As a result of this growing partnership, federal money devoted to social planning and improvement became a large part of the income of every big city.

Farmers, too, received the attention of the New Deal. Farmers' purchasing power had decreased during the 1920s, because prices for farm products had dropped. This prevented farmers from buying enough manufactured goods to keep industries going. President Roosevelt felt that if the farmers' income was raised, the whole economy would benefit. Industry would have to increase production to meet the new demand for goods, and more workers would be needed.

In 1933, Congress passed the Agricultural Adjustment Act to provide a way to raise farm income. Farmers were encouraged to withhold parts of their croplands from the cultivation of certain basic products, such as wheat, corn, tobacco, and cotton. According to the theory of supply and demand, a smaller available amount of the product would make the price rise. Farmers would receive more money for the crops that they sold. The law provided that they would also receive a cash payment from the government for each acre of land that they had withheld from production. The money for this payment came from a tax levied on the companies that processed the food for market—packers, canners, millers, and the like.

This policy was severely criticized for a variety of reasons, not the least of which was anger at the idea of decreasing food supplies amid widespread hunger. Then in 1936, in a 6-3 decision, the Supreme Court declared the processing taxes unconstitutional. This nullified the entire Agricultural Adjustment Act.

Rather than leave farmers without aid, Congress finally replaced the unconstitutional law with the Agricultural Adjustment Act of 1938. Payments for withdrawing land from cultivation were replaced with payments for growing soil-conserving crops such as clover. Any surpluses were stored by the government for use during years when crops were smaller. And the tax on food processors was replaced with direct payments from the government.

Large farm owners who grew basic agricultural products benefited the most from these laws. Nonetheless, it was not until World War II that farming achieved a true economic recovery. How effective the legislation was in improving the economy as a whole is hard to

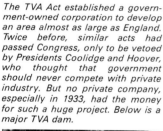

The TVA Act established a government-owned corporation to develop an area almost as large as England. Twice before, similar acts had passed Congress, only to be vetoed by Presidents Coolidge and Hoover, who thought that government should never compete with private industry. But no private company, especially in 1933, had the money for such a huge project. Below is a major TVA dam.

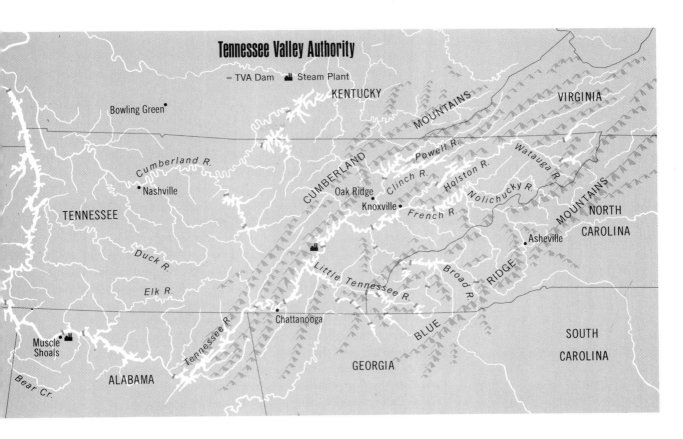

Tennessee Valley Authority

— TVA Dam ⬛ Steam Plant

KENTUCKY

VIRGINIA

Bowling Green

CUMBERLAND MOUNTAINS

Cumberland R.

Nashville

Powell R.

Clinch R.

Oak Ridge

Knoxville

French R.

Holston R.

Watauga R.

Nolichucky R.

TENNESSEE

CUMBERLAND

Asheville

NORTH CAROLINA

Duck R.

Little Tennessee R.

Broad R.

BLUE RIDGE MOUNTAINS

Elk R.

Tennessee R.

Chattanooga

Muscle Shoals

SOUTH CAROLINA

Bear Cr.

ALABAMA

GEORGIA

BLUE

---

determine. But with the New Deal, the federal government had assumed responsibilities for agriculture that have continued to the present day.

The Tennessee Valley Authority

The most spectacular New Deal achievement was the creation of the Tennessee Valley Authority (TVA) in 1933. It carried Senator George W. Norris's idea of government production of hydroelectric power beyond his wildest dreams. The mission of TVA was to remake an entire mountain region, covering parts of several states, over many years. First, it built a string of dams on the rampaging Tennessee River. These harnessed the rapids and controlled floods by storing excess water in rainy seasons and releasing it in dry periods. The tamed river and its tributaries formed an inland waterway connecting the valley with the Great Lakes and the Ohio and Mississippi river systems. With such good water transportation available, industry was encouraged to move into the fast-changing area.

Water, roaring through gates in the dams, turned turbine wheels to generate hydroelectric power. This power was sold at low cost. Soon lights twinkled and news broadcasts crackled in once-lonesome mountain towns and farmhouses that had never before enjoyed the benefits of electricity. TVA also manufactured chemical fertilizers, sold them cheaply, and offered instruction on their use.

Over a twenty-year period, the income of the region increased nearly 200 percent. The change in outlook was more far-reaching than dollars and cents. An Alabama editor rejoiced that his people had "caught the vision of their own powers." And one of the first directors of TVA, David Lilienthal, said simply, "Democracy is on the march in this valley."

The 1942 photograph above shows men at work on a TVA dam site.

The New Deal and Organized Labor

The American labor movement also scored important gains under the New Deal. In the 1920s, there had been little progress. Many employers had fought hard and fiercely with "union-busting" tactics. They had fired union organizers, forced workers to join company unions controlled by management, and hired toughs to beat and threaten would-be strikers into surrender.

Labor unions had not considered Roosevelt an especially friendly figure in 1932. But they soon recognized the open good wishes of members of his administration, such as Frances Perkins, Secretary of Labor and the first woman to be a Cabinet member.

The New Deal concern for labor was demonstrated in the provisions of the National Industrial Recovery Act of 1933 (NIRA). The NIRA was designed to revive American industry by doing away with competition. By suspending antitrust laws, the federal government was now licensed to determine production quotas, prices, and fair business codes for many industries. It also set up a labor code that prohibited child labor, set a minimum wage, and established maximum hours in certain industries. It further guaranteed labor the right to organize and bargain collectively with management.

In 1935, when the NIRA was declared unconstitutional, Congress quickly passed the National Labor Relations Act. Often called the Wagner Act after its sponsor, Robert F. Wagner, the NIRA forbade certain unfair labor practices. These included most company activities designed to interfere with union organization. Workers could ask for an election to choose a union. And unions could negotiate for many benefits, including the *closed shop*, or the right to insist that only union laborers be hired. Or the workers might try for a *union shop*, under which anyone could be hired by the employer but would then have to join the union representing that shop. A National Labor Relations Board (NLRB) was set up to supervise elections and to hear complaints. The NLRB could demand an injunction to force an end to unfair dealings by employers. For years, workers had bitterly felt that

Frances Perkins, Secretary of Labor during Roosevelt's entire Presidency, won the respect of union members across the country. Here, she is greeted by Pittsburgh steel-workers.

judges were allies of "the bosses". Now the shoe was on the other foot.

Though the NLRB was supposed to be a neutral umpire, many of its early decisions favored the union at the expense of the employer. Complaints were widespread that the Wagner Act tipped the balance of power too far in the direction of labor.

Whether or not such charges were justified, labor was at least getting much needed support from the federal government. This encouraged unions to undertake vigorous organizing campaigns. A split over tactics in 1935 led to the birth of a new national body, the Congress of Industrial Organizations (CIO). The AF of L was built around craft unions of workers sharing a particular skill. On the other hand, the basic unit of the CIO was the industrial union of all workers in a given industry. After twenty years of rivalry about which form of organization would triumph, the AF of L and CIO merged in 1955. By then, some 16 million workers were enrolled in the unions controlled by the AFL-CIO.

In 1938, the New Deal finalized its position on wages and hours with the Fair Labor Standards Act. It provided, in Roosevelt's words,

Mary McLeod Bethune, pictured here, was the director of the Division of Negro Affairs in the New Deal's national administration.

"a floor below which wages shall not fall, and a ceiling beyond which the hours of industrial labor shall not rise."

The New Deal and Minorities

Franklin D. Roosevelt was perhaps more aware of the needs of minority groups than any President before him. Roosevelt was the first President to bring people who would defend the needs and rights of Black people to the executive branch of the federal government. Harold Ickes, Rexford Tugwell, Harry Hopkins, and first lady Eleanor Roosevelt were among those near the President who urged bringing the fullness of American life to all. Prominent Black leaders, such as Mary McLeod Bethune, Ralph Bunche, and Robert C. Weaver served as advisers to President Roosevelt.

Most New Deal measures were not aimed specifically at helping minority groups or those who were normally unemployed. Programs to prevent mortgage foreclosures or offer home-business loans benefited only middle-class workers. Some laws even hurt poor people. Acreage taken out of cultivation according to the provisions of the Agricultural Adjustment Act of 1933 was often land used by tenant farmers and sharecroppers. These people were faced with the choice of becoming migrant laborers or joining the swollen ranks of the urban unemployed. The minimum wage law did not cover many industries that employed minorities. As a result, as few as one out of every seven Black workers was earning even a minimum wage.

Nonetheless, minorities were helped by some New Deal programs. Black workers received jobs through the WPA and PWA. Many Black youths obtained jobs through the CCC, though the number of jobs was not in proportion to their numbers in the population. In 1937, the Bankhead-Jones Act set up the Farm Security Administration (FSA). The FSA supervised conditions in migrant camps and retrained some families for industrial work in the cities. It lent tenant farmers money to buy their own land and helped them to organize cooperative groups to buy low-cost electric power, machinery, supplies, and the services of doctors and dentists. The Resettlement Administration bought low-quality farm land and resettled its inhabitants on more productive land.

The already unsatisfactory position of American Indians was worsened by the Depression. With little land or education and few job skills, many American Indians lived in poverty. John Collier, Secretary of the Indian Defense Association, tried to help. He called for preservation of American Indian culture and encouraged establishment of tribal self-government. Some attempts were also made to improve business opportunities and the education of American Indian youths. Unfortunately, these measures accomplished little.

Mexican-Americans, who made up a large portion of migrant farm labor, were virtually passed over by New Deal programs. They lived on the brink of starvation, working for pitiful wages and crisscrossing the country in search of crops to pick. The attempts of the Farm Security Administration to improve living conditions in migrant labor camps were not enough to prevent a desperate situation.

Minority groups during the 1930s still had a long road to equal opportunity ahead of them. In 1941, at the urging of A. Philip Randolph, Roosevelt issued an executive order that barred discrimination based on race or religion in government defense industries. Like any New Deal effort to help minorities, this was a small step. But it was a significant one. The federal government was now beginning to demonstrate concern for social conditions.

Frustrated by the Supreme Court declaring major New Deal legislation unconstitutional, FDR announced—on February 5, 1937—his plan to reorganize the federal judiciary. During the five months of bitter debate that followed, FDR was accused of corrupting the Constitution and trying to destroy judicial independence. These two cartoons comment on this situation.

The New Deal—A Watershed in History

Sometimes, the New Deal simply brought Progressivism up to date. Many of the laws it proposed added to the list of measures taken early in the century to limit the power of great corporations and to make sure that they kept the public's health and safety in mind.

Banking and the stock market were placed under strict supervision. The Glass-Steagall Act of 1933 placed tighter controls on national banks. It also established the Federal Deposit Insurance Corporation (FDIC), which insured deposits in member banks. The Securities and Exchange Commission was established to eliminate abuses in the stock markets.

New federal agencies were created, and old ones were strengthened to regulate the aviation, radio, electric power, natural gas, shipping, and trucking industries.

Another type of New Deal legislation tried new social experiments. Some won acceptance, while others were later dropped. An example of a New Deal experiment that became permanent is the Social Security Act of 1935. A payroll tax is collected from employers and employees. That money is used to provide pensions for workers who reach retirement age. It is also used as financial help for widows, orphans, the blind, and other needy people. Parts of the law also encouraged states to create similar funds to pay benefits to workers during jobless periods. Some European nations already had similar

Most members of the upper class thought that FDR—who was himself upper class—had betrayed them. This 1938 cartoon expressing that view was captioned, "Mother, Wilfred wrote a dirty word!"

plans. For Americans, however, the Social Security Act was a break with the past. The tradition of an era of plenty had been to leave this planning entirely to individuals. Yet, the majority accepted the argument that in a modern, interdependent society, where misfortune could strike people through no fault of their own, some provision on a larger scale had to be made. Today, the Social Security program is in its fifth decade of operation.

Reform movements in American politics often have short lives. In 1936, Roosevelt won an overwhelming victory at the polls. He got the electoral vote of all but two states—Maine and Vermont. Yet, in the next two years, he could not prevent rising resistance in the courts and Congress in opposition to his further New Deal measures. The difficulty with the Supreme Court was particularly annoying. The justices had been appointed by previous (Republican) administrations and tended to brand much of the New Deal as "unconstitutional." So early in 1937, Roosevelt submitted a measure calling for an enlargement of the Supreme Court. He hoped to appoint justices who would be more sympathetic to New Deal measures than the "nine old men" who had killed the National Industrial Recovery Act and the Agricultural Adjustment Administration. The public was outraged by what seemed to be an attempt to "pack" the Court with judges friendly to the President. People saw this as potentially destroying the balance of power between the branches of the federal government. So in the end, FDR's plan was beaten soundly in Congress.

In the following year, while other "Roosevelt inspired" bills failed to be passed by a Congress with a mind of its own, the President decided to challenge some of his conservative Congressional opponents. During the spring of 1938, he called for Democratic voters in primary elections to defeat certain *incumbents*—office-holding members of Congress—who stood in the way of further New Deal developments. Despite his plea, the same citizens who had elected FDR in 1936 returned his opponents to office in 1938. To make matters worse, the economy slumped and unemployment again shot up in that year.

By 1939, however, the political climate in one world began to change. Europe went to war that September. Even earlier, however, military orders from European governments began to set American factory wheels in motion. Congress also voted for a large expansion of the United States naval and air forces in preparation for the coming crisis. So the beginning of an era of war and global responsibility restored prosperity and changed the issues of the day.

To this day, no one knows for sure whether the New Deal by itself would have succeeded in curing the Depression or what would have happened after 1938 if the war had not come. As events developed, however, the need for a huge government and long-range economic and social planning remained. Presidents who came later continued to meet this need. Even though the New Deal of 1933 to 1937 may have ended, the nation never returned to a "normalcy" like that of the 1920s. The 1890s marked the closing of the frontier. The 1930s marked a great dividing line in the history of the nation.

Questions for Discussion

1. Define *closed shop, union shop, incumbent.*
2. What was the purpose of Roosevelt's "bank holiday"?
3. What was Roosevelt's "Brain Trust"?
4. How were minorities affected by New Deal measures?
5. What was the purpose of the Agricultural Adjustment Act?
6. In what ways was the New Deal a continuation of Progressivism?
7. What effect did the coming of World War II have on the Great Depression?

Chapter 25 Review

Summary Questions for Discussion

1. How did speculation lead to the collapse of the stock market?
2. Why was there no money to spend after the stock market crash?
3. List five examples of the human pain and suffering of the Depression.
4. What were the results of Hoover's actions against the bonus marchers?
5. Why was the Tennessee Valley Authority (TVA) considered "the most spectacular New Deal achievement"?
6. List and explain specific examples of important gains made by the American labor movement during the New Deal.
7. Although FDR was more aware of minority groups than his predecessors, explain how New Deal measures were not actually aimed at helping minority groups or hard-core unemployed.
8. How were American Indians and Mexican-Americans affected by the New Deal?
9. How was the Social Security Act of 1935 a break with the past for Americans?
10. How did the Democratic voters react in the primary elections of 1938?

Word Study

In the sentences that follow, fill in each blank with the term below that is most appropriate.

speculation	stocks	stock market
dividends	relief	national income
deficit financing	bonus	closed shop
union shop	subsidies	incumbent
payroll taxes	primary election	bull market

1. People often become involved in a business transaction known as _____, hoping for large profits even though there are large risks involved.
2. Shares of ownership in a company are called _____.
3. Stocks and bonds are bought and sold in the _____.
4. When a company shares its profits with its investors, the investors receive _____.
5. Governments give _____ to those in poverty or in need.
6. The _____ of a country is its total net earnings from the production of goods and services.
7. If a government spends more money than it receives from taxes, it is involved in _____.
8. Something given in addition to what is usual is a(n) _____.
9. In a _____, union membership is required for continued employment but not for hiring.
10. In a _____, union membership is required for hiring.
11. The government gives _____ to help or encourage private, agricultural, or industrial undertakings.
12. A person who is already in a political office and is seeking reelection is a(n) _____.
13. The money collected from _____ is used to provide pensions for workers who reach retirement age, as well as to provide financial help for widows, orphans, the blind, and other needy people.
14. An election held to nominate a candidate of a political party for office is called a(n) _____.

Between Two World Wars

In 1919, when the Treaty of Versailles was defeated in the Senate, it seemed that the United States would reject any role in the postwar affairs of the world. Although the United States might disband its army and reduce its navy, the economic factors that had already drawn the country into the network of international relations continued to limit any American desire to withdraw.

Postwar America was rich, and Europe was poor. The world needed—and got—American loans and American goods. The Republican leadership of the 1920s was aware that foreign investments would be jeopardized by a war. So the Harding and Coolidge administrations arranged disarmament and antiwar treaties among the great powers. Yet, they gave no pledge of using American might to guarantee these agreements.

This attitude matched their policies at home. Government should help business—but limit the active use of its own power as much as possible. According to historians, the 1920s was an era of "isolationism." But isolation did not seem to stop American diplomatic activities designed to protect investments and markets.

Until about 1930, this diplomacy worked rather well. When world prosperity collapsed, international stability crashed with it. Strong new leaders, especially in Italy and Germany, challenged the Treaty of Versailles. This treaty had left France and Great Britain as the dominant powers in Europe. And Japan drove toward establishing a commanding position in the Pacific that would bar Western powers from a share in the wealth of Asia.

Now the United States was forced to make a choice. America could wait out events and make new "deals" to preserve stability. Or the United States could defend the existing order, but at the risk of war. These were the hard, hotly debated choices that existed in the stormy 1930s.

READING GUIDE

1. **What efforts were made to maintain peace?**
2. **What was the status of the United States-Latin American relations just before the outbreak of World War II?**
3. **What were some of the extreme political changes taking place in Europe and Asia just before war broke out?**

This World War I anniversary poster argues against American isolationism.

THE ISOLATIONIST
"AM I MY BROTHER'S KEEPER?"

AMERICA WILL NEVER ACCEPT
THE CURSE OF CAIN!

Shown here, the League of Nations flag, which incorporated the flags of all member countries.

1. The Legend of Isolation

The Treaty of Versailles did not bring real peace to the world. Instead, it provided a short rest between battles while nations rearmed and realigned. President Wilson had warned that a treaty that was aimed at punishing the losers would "leave a sting, a resentment, a bitter memory upon which the terms of peace would rest, not permanently, but only as upon quicksand." Unfortunately, he was right. The hatred created by the peace settlement was to become the backdrop for another, even more devastating, world war.

The United States came out of World War I with a desire for a new world order in which peace would be kept. At the same time, America had no desire to become involved in preventing world conflict. From this line of thinking came several ambitious, if impractical, measures. These measures were aimed at keeping the peace while avoiding involvement in worsening Far Eastern and European affairs.

Americans took part in conferences called by certain nonpolitical bodies under the League of Nations. There were also permanent American observers in Geneva to serve as eyes and ears for the United

States government. The failure of the United States to join the League of Nations meant that American voices did not ring out in the debates at Geneva. Nor did the American flag appear along with those of other nations as part of the standard of the League of Nations.

In July 1921, President Harding called for a conference of nine nations—all with colonial holdings—to meet the following year in Washington. The first subject for discussion was naval disarmament. Fleets of mighty battleships then were like the bombers and **ballistic missiles** of today. Only great nations could afford them, and even they groaned under the heavy cost. The United States itself could not slim its federal budget without reducing its navy. So when the sessions opened, the United States Secretary of State, Charles Evans Hughes, surprised everyone. Not only did he propose limits on future naval shipbuilding, but he also urged that the United States, Great Britain, and Japan actually scrap a total of over a million tons of warships. Two historians noted that Hughes, in a few words, "proceeded to sink more ships than all the admirals in the history of the world." Eventually, a Five-Power Treaty was signed, setting quotas of naval strength for the naval "Big Three" (The United States, Britain, and Japan) and for France and Italy, as well.

ballistic missile
a particular kind of self-propelled missile used in warfare

Whether America should join the League of Nations became an issue in the 1920 Presidential election. Democratic candidate James Cox favored American membership. Republican candidate Warren Harding's campaign slogan was "America first!" However, since Harding also spoke vaguely of favoring an "association of nations," the candidates' positions were not as clearly defined as the cartoon indicates.

COX OR HARDING

LEAGUE OF NATIONS

AMERICA FIRST HARDING

JAS KROINER

REPRODUCED FROM "THE WORLD"
THE LEADING COX ORGAN

"UNDER WHICH FLAG?"

FROM "HARVEY'S WEEKLY"
SUPPORTER OF HARDING

The Washington Conference also tried to "freeze" the balance of power in Asia. The United States, Britain, Japan, and France (which governed Indochina as a colony) agreed to recognize the boundaries of each others' possessions in the Pacific. All nine nations present pledged to continue the Open Door policy in China and to continue to guarantee Chinese territorial integrity.

The United States had made no commitment to enforce these Washington agreements for dividing seapower and sharing Asian raw materials and markets. The world was to rely on good faith and public opinion as its peacekeeping forces. Yet, American sponsorship of the conference, like its taking part in some of the League's work for international welfare, was a long way from a policy of "isolationism."

American Business Goes Overseas

Meanwhile, American dollars marched abroad. World War I created a basic change in the position of the United States. It became a *creditor nation*. Once, young America had borrowed money from European bankers to build railroads and canals. Now, American financiers were moneylenders to the world. They made their loans by buying the bonds of foreign companies and local governments. A *bond* is a written promise to pay back a loan at the end of a set time, usually within twenty or more years. Meanwhile, the bondholder receives interest each year. By the mid-1920s, American bond purchases had provided funds to build railroads in Poland, housing developments in

American companies trying to attract foreign markets used tested advertising techniques, such as this ad for cameras.

No. 1.
PRIX FR. 6.50

No. 2.
PRIX FR. 12.50

LES "BROWNIE" KODAKS

Fonctionnement Démontré en Quelques Minutes. GRATUITEMENT.
SE CHARGENT EN PLEIN JOUR.
Un Enfant peut faire des Jolies Photographies avec un Brownie

Austria, and public utilities in Tokyo. American dollars were also helping to drill oil wells in Arabia and to open rubber plantations in Malaya. Soon, world prosperity rested in good part on billions of dollars in American loans overseas. That same prosperity helped American industry, as well. It made it possible for the people of other countries to purchase an increasing amount of goods made in American factories.

The Department of Commerce busily encouraged overseas investments. Secretary Hoover proudly described the Department's agents in fifty-seven foreign offices as "hounds for foreign sales." European farmers plowed their acres with American tractors. Asian workers rode to their jobs on American-made bicycles or streetcars. Latin American secretaries pounded out their letters on American typewriters. Children everywhere cheered the heroes of American movies.

Sometimes, American companies built plants abroad to take advantage of low foreign taxes and cheap foreign labor. These investments also put money, in the form of wages and payments to suppliers, into the world economy. Despite this help, foreigners did not earn enough through sales of their own goods to other countries to pay for what they bought from the United States. In addition, high American protective tariffs tended to keep foreign products off American shelves. Congress, however, was not aware that these tariffs were becoming a serious international problem.

War Debts and Reparations

The United States had lent over $10 billion to European countries to finance World War I. As early as December 1918, proposals were being made to cancel these war debts.

The countries of Europe resented having to repay the loans. They claimed that this money was actually a contribution to the war effort made by the United States before it got involved militarily. Europe had used the money to buy supplies from American businesses, which had benefited from the transactions. In addition, high protective tariffs were making it impossible for European countries to raise the money to repay the debts. Most of their gold had been spent in the early days of the war. What was left was needed for currency stabilization. France had an added objection. The loans made by the French to the United States during the American Revolution had never been repaid.

Under Presidents Wilson, Harding, and Coolidge, the United States remained steadfast in its demand for repayment. In 1925, worsening financial conditions in Europe forced the United States to give in a little. However, even drastic reductions of principal and interest did not remove the growing anti-American feelings in Europe.

By 1933, only Finland had paid its debt in full. The failure of Europe to pay its war debts reinforced the American desire for isolation. It also helped explain the reluctance of Americans to become involved in another European war.

By 1923, Germany was having severe economic problems. The value of the German mark had sunk very low. The mark that had been valued at nine-to-the-dollar in 1919 was 4-million-to-the-dollar by 1923. So President Coolidge appointed Charles G. Dawes as head of a commission to investigate German finances.

The Search for Peace

The United States had a stake in keeping the world prosperous. This meant keeping the world peaceful. Only nations that were productive and safe could offer good markets in the long run.

The realization that profits and peace might be linked helped to strengthen the *pacifist movement* in the United States. Pacifist organizations had existed since the early days of American reform movements. Their members held many different views. Some were Christians whose reading of the Bible told them that killing another person was never justified. Some were nonreligious believers in human reason. These people simply saw war as an insane way to "solve" problems. Socialists held that wars only enriched capitalists who produced the weapons at the expense of the workers who did the

A number of events in the 1920s seemed to indicate that nations really wanted to insure world peace. Below Left: On January 17, 1929, President Calvin Coolidge signed the Kellogg-Briand Pact, committing the United States to the peaceful settlement of disputes. By 1934, some sixty-four nations had agreed to the privisions of the pact. Below Right: The Women's International League for Peace and Freedom produced this broadside during the 1920s as part of their campaign against an international arms race.

SECURITY?

ARMAMENTS DO NOT GIVE SECURITY

JEANNETTE RANKIN

Jeannette Rankin (1880-1973) was the first woman ever elected to the United States Congress. She was also the only Member of Congress to vote against the nation's entry into both world wars.

Three years before the Nineteenth Amendment was ratified, Rankin went to Congress as a Republican Representative from Montana. Montana women had won the vote in 1914. Rankin had led the successful statewide campaign for suffrage.

Jeannette Rankin was highly visible when she took her seat in the House of Representatives on April 2, 1917. She was one woman surrounded by 421 men. And she was not only a suffragist. She was also a pacifist. She believed that war was wrong. Only three days after she entered Congress, Rankin cast her vote against the entry of the United States into World War I. Forty-nine men voted with her, but critics singled her out for attack. Many said that, in taking her stand, she had committed "political suicide." She failed in her bid for a Senate seat the following year.

A quarter of a century later, Rankin was back in Congress, serving a second term. She had won election in 1940 running as an isolationist. It was December 8, 1941—the day after the Japanese attacked Pearl Harbor. This time, Rankin was greeted with hisses when she cast the only vote against America's entry into World War II.

Rankin never stopped working for women's rights and for world peace. On January 15, 1968, when she was eighty-seven, she led five thousand women—the Jeannette Rankin Brigade—in a protest demonstration against the War in Vietnam.

fighting. After World War I, pacifism became a nationwide movement. Many distinguished business and educational leaders joined such groups as the American Committee for the Outlawry of War. They urged the United States to take the lead in banishing armed conflict from the world. In 1928, they won a victory.

Secretary of State Frank Kellogg had received a proposal from the French for an agreement that the United States and France would never go to war against each other. Kellogg did not wish to commit the United States to a treaty with France. Neither did he wish to offend Paris with a refusal. He saw a way to solve his problem and please the pacifists at the same time. Therefore, he suggested to the French foreign minister, Aristide Briand, that they sign a treaty that would condemn and give up war as a way of settling disputes. France and the United States would then invite all the great powers to join them.

Neither France nor any other nation could well refuse. It would be like refusing to condemn sin! So on August 27, 1928, fifteen nations signed the Kellogg-Briand pact. The next year, Kellogg, who private-

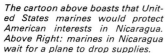

The cartoon above boasts that United States marines would protect American interests in Nicaragua. Above Right: marines in Nicaragua wait for a plane to drop supplies.

ly thought many pacifists were unrealistic "fools," received the Nobel Peace Prize. Eventually, more than sixty nations signed this pact.

Of course, nothing, could force nations to obey the treaty. Yet, it was historically important that antiwar feeling all over the world was strong enough to compel governments to bow in that direction.

Questions for Discussion
1. Define *ballistic missile, creditor nation, bond.*
2. Which policies after World War I showed that the United States was not strictly following a policy of isolationism?
3. In what ways are world prosperity and world peace linked?

2. The United States and Latin America

At the beginning of the 1920s, United States marines still occupied Nicaragua, the Dominican Republic, and Haiti. However, the Republicans soon began to move away from the pattern of using United States armed forces in Latin American nations. In 1923, Secretary Hughes said that he hoped to keep the peace of the hemisphere "not by arms but by mutual respect and good will."

The change came partly because of the growing dislike of war. It also was due to the changing beliefs of progressive business people. They now felt that it was better to have solidly established governments in the Americas—even if they were sometimes unfriendly—than constant "brushfires" of revolution to be stamped out by United States troops.

In 1924, the new policy was first applied when the marines were withdrawn from the Dominican Republic. The next year, the marines

596

pulled out of Nicaragua as well. However, in 1927, a revolt against Nicaraguan dictator Adolfo Diaz brought the "leathernecks" pouring down the gangplanks once more. This time, however, Henry L. Stimson, a distinguished corporate attorney and public servant, was sent down as a "troubleshooter." He talked things over with both sides and got the parties to agree to free elections supervised by the United States. In return, the "rebels" were to lay down their arms and Diaz was to complete his term of office. The marines stayed on duty until 1933, however, to handle the guerrilla fighters of one leader, Augusto Sandino, who refused to enter this agreement.

The United States also began to try to develop a better understanding with Puerto Rico. The inhabitants of this island territory, although not at their request, had been made citizens of the United States one month before United States entry into World War I. Before the Puerto Ricans had a chance to benefit from citizenship, they supplied 120,000 draftees, $12 million for Liberty Bonds, and support for the Red Cross. After such loyal support during the war, Puerto Ricans were disappointed with Harding's appointment of E. Mont Reily as governor in 1921. Mont Reily replaced competent judges and officials with his untrained, overpaid friends. Finally, under threat of a Congressional investigation, the governor resigned. The new appointment of Horace M. Towner as governor relieved some of the ill feeling that had developed. In the years to follow, this experience goaded the Puerto Ricans into demanding greater control over their own affairs.

In Mexico, in 1927, President Plutarco Calles demanded that American companies owning oil wells and mines in his country return these valuable subsoil properties to the Mexican people. Many of the owners, who had paid heavily for developing their holdings, were outraged. They joined Secretary Kellogg in denouncing Calles as a "Bolshevik." But Coolidge once again kept cool. He sent Dwight W. Morrow, a partner in the mighty J.P. Morgan banking house, to Mexico City as United States ambassador. Morrow took great pains to be friendly and made no threats. He even got Charles Lindbergh to fly down for a goodwill visit to show how much Americans thought of Mexico. Morrow, meanwhile, worked out a compromise with Calles.

The improvement in relations with Mexico was an important benefit for the United States. During World War I, Germany had offered Mexico the states of Texas, Arizona, and New Mexico. In addition, they offered a large financial settlement in an effort to gain Mexican support against the United States. Although privately sympathetic to Germany, Mexico remained officially neutral. But by the time World War II began, Mexico offered support to the United States, cooperated fully in its defense, and declared war on the Axis powers.

Presidents Hoover and Roosevelt each tried to change the image of the United States in Latin America. Hoover took a pre-inaugural tour of Central America and South America (above left). Although Hoover coined the term "Good Neighbor Policy," it was Roosevelt who captured the imagination of Latin Americans. When he visited Argentina in 1936, he was hailed as "el gran democrate." A song in praise of Roosevelt was set to a Latin American beat (above right).

The Good Neighbor Policy

Herbert Hoover continued this new look in hemisphere diplomacy. Immediately after his election, he embarked on a goodwill tour of Latin American nations. His Secretary of State, Henry L. Stimson, made it clear that the Monroe Doctrine would no longer be used to justify the invasion of other American republics. The Roosevelt administration took up in 1933 where Hoover and Stimson left off.

In his inaugural address, FDR spoke of his wish to "dedicate this Nation to the policy of the good neighbor." He was speaking of American relations with all countries. But his words were taken to refer especially to southern neighbors. He and his Secretary of State, Cordell Hull, soon backed friendly words with deeds. Between 1933 and 1936, the United States withdrew all forces from Haiti and Nicaragua. They also renounced treaty rights to intervene in Cuba and Panama. In addition, a program of economic development was begun in Puerto Rico. However, no significant strides toward autonomy were made until after World War II. Finally, in 1938, the United States signed a treaty with Mexico. In this treaty, the United States accepted the *expropriation*—seizure of property—of American companies in return for agreed sums of money, known as *compensation*.

Meanwhile, in 1934, Congress passed the Trade Agreements Act, which amended the Tariff Act of 1930. This act allowed the President to negotiate individual trade agreements with other countries and to lower tariffs on a *reciprocal* basis—that is, favor-for-favor. For example, if Argentina would agree to lower its duties on American flour, the United States would reduce the tariff against Argentine beef. Though this program was worldwide, it was especially helpful to

Latin American countries, who depended heavily on a strong trade with the United States.

The change in United States hemispheric policies did not end all Latin American problems. The poverty, illiteracy, and tyranny that remained still threatened the well-being of Latin America. These problems were still too often ignored by the rich United States. Yet, there had been a start toward economic and social assistance.

Questions for Discussion

1. Define *expropriation*, *reciprocal*, *compensation*.
2. What changes were made in United States foreign policy in Latin America in the 1920s? Why?
3. What was the purpose of the Trade Agreements Act?

3. The Gathering Storm

When Woodrow Wilson dreamed of the League of Nations, he hoped that its member states would all be like the most progressive Allied countries. They would have elected governments and guarantees of individual freedom. More importantly, they would recognize the time-honored rules of international trade and borrowing. They would keep treaty promises. And they would respect the rights of other governments, like law-abiding citizens in a community of nations.

However, in the fourteen years after 1919, new political systems arose which violated all these principles. The first such system was Russian communism. Taking advantage of a badly weakened wartime

Russian citizens in Petrograd in 1917 watch as soldiers set fire to the monarchist royal insignia ripped down from shops and buildings. The Bolshevik Revolution had begun, and by 1922 Russia had become the Union of Soviet Socialist Republics.

In a nearly bloodless takeover, the Bolsheviks ended Russia's experiment in democracy and named Vladimir Ilyich (Nikolai) Lenin (above) to head the government. He was convinced that his program of "bread, peace, land" would solve the country's problems. The words on the poster reflect Lenin's dedication to worldwide communist revolution: "There is a spectre haunting Europe, the spectre of Communism."

monarchy, the Bolshevik faction of the Russian Social Democratic Party had seized power in October 1917. Under Leon Trotsky and Nikolai Lenin, who soon took dictatorial control, they executed the czar and his family. They then made overwhelming changes in Russian life. The Bolsheviks also took steps that badly shook the foundations of European diplomacy. First, Bolsheviks proclaimed that Russia was now the "homeland" of worldwide communist revolution. Communist Russia would encourage and help workers in all capitalist countries to overthrow their rulers. Thus, the Bolsheviks automatically made Russia the enemy of noncommunist governments everywhere. Next, they declared that they would keep no treaties and repay no loans made by the czarist government. The "capitalist" governments believed that the Bolsheviks were declaring themselves to be outlaws. They responded by trying to help anti-Bolshevik "White" Russians to overthrow the "Reds." But, by 1921, the Bolsheviks had won their bloody civil war at a tremendous cost in suffering in their own land. Americans contributed to famine relief for the Russians. However, the

United States did not officially recognize the new government until 1933.

Gradually and suspiciously, Russia—renamed in 1922 the Union of Soviet Socialist Republics—and the other powers reestablished contact. Lenin was succeeded in 1924 by Joseph Stalin, a brutal tyrant. Nonetheless, Stalin was willing to put off international revolution and make deals with other nations in order to strengthen Russia. Even then, the Soviet Union was a disturbing force in Europe.

The Rise of the Dictators

Democratic government also collapsed in Italy. That country suffered deeply from postwar unemployment and unsolved social problems. Numerous leaders, including the Communists, came to power, each with "miracle cures." One leader, Benito Mussolini, had his followers organized into a party that he named *Fascist*. In 1922, Mussolini led thousands of Fascists in a march on Rome and frightened the Italian king into naming him prime minister. Soon, he seized dictatorial powers. He became an international figure when he began to argue that Italy was "cheated" out of its share of the colonial wealth of the world by France and Great Britain. Someday, he said, Italy must conquer what rightly belonged to it.

Then trouble brewed in Germany. The Republic established after the kaiser fled in 1918 was in constant trouble. Communists tried to

In January 1936, Benito Mussolini— also known as Il Duce, or leader— reviewed some of the 250,000 men he sent to conquer Ethiopia.

Hitler assumed the title Fuhrer and made effective use of mass media and mass rallies to spread his message, inspire loyalty, and to create an appetite for war. Above: he arrives at Nuremberg in September 1934.

overthrow the Republic in 1919. At the other extreme, certain parties of Germans, bitter in defeat, charged that the Republic was too soft on Bolsheviks and other radicals. They felt that Germany must return to its military tradition and honor. One such group was the National Socialist German Workers' Party (abbreviated to Nazi) led by Adolf Hitler. Hitler shrieked his message to thousands of hysterical followers at huge rallies. Germany, he charged, had been "stabbed in the back" in 1918 by Bolsheviks and Jews. Both must be driven out of German life and replaced by clean-cut members of the "pure" German race.

When the German economy collapsed, poverty drove many people to seek extreme remedies for extreme distress. Thus, in 1932, thousands of people voted for the Nazis. In January 1933, Hitler finally became chancellor. At once, he began to jail and execute his rivals. He also announced plans to tear up the Treaty of Versailles, rebuild the army, and unite all Germans in Europe under one flag. Now there were two dictator-controlled nations—Germany and Italy—ready to use armies to change the map of Europe and Africa. However before Mussolini marched or Hitler came to power, the first shots against world order were fired halfway around the globe, in Asia.

Japan Invades China

In the 1920s, Japan faced a growing economic crisis. Its population of 80 million was rapidly increasing. Yet, its total land area was no bigger than California. Japan had taken giant steps in industrialization. However, Japan still needed huge stocks of raw materials and millions of overseas customers in order to keep its machines working and its people employed. Since Japan was poor in raw materials, its business leaders were tempted by nearby China. China had great untapped resources in addition to millions of potential consumers for Japanese goods. In their eyes, China was in their economic "front yard" as surely as Latin America was economically tied to the United States.

Japan's ambitions to make China an economic colony ran head-on into obstacles. Since the middle of the nineteenth century, China had been subject to the demands of many foreign powers, including the United States. In the first Sino-Japanese War (1894–1895), China had lost territory to Japan, including Korea and Formosa (now Taiwan). These humiliations fostered the development of a revolutionary spirit in China. There was a wave of Chinese nationalism that led to boycotts and demands for the withdrawal of all foreigners from Chinese soil.

In addition, European and American businesses in China would not give up their privileges. A naval armaments race ensued in the Pacific that began to look alarmingly like the beginnings of war. A series of treaties forced Japan to recognize that, at least on paper, Europe and the United States defended their own interests in the Far East. The Lansing-Ishii Agreement in 1917 between the United States

Five months after Japanese troops invaded the northern Chinese province of Manchuria in 1931, they had established control. Conquering the rest of China proved more difficult, even though China was in the midst of a civil war between the nationalists led by Chiang Kai-Shek and the Communists led by Mao Tse-tung. But each side fought the Japanese, often using guerilla tactics. The Japanese attacked Shanghai in 1932. Six months later, their officers, seen at right, were wearing bullet-proof vests to protect them from sniper fire.

The Japanese soldiers at right are prodding captured Chinese guerrillas with bayonets.

and Japan reaffirmed the Open Door policy in China. Yet, it did allow that Japan had special interest in parts of China bordering on Japanese territory. The Washington Conference of 1922 and the London Naval Treaty of 1930 limited Japanese arms buildup by declaring a "naval holiday" of ten years during which no new warships would be built.

Japan could meet these apparent obstacles to expansion in the Far East in two ways. It could try to negotiate new treaties concerning China with other powers. Or it could follow the advice of its militarists who argued that Japanese troops should simply smash into China and take it over.

By 1931, the militarists had won strong influence in Japanese affairs. That September, they struck. A train carrying Japanese soldiers was blown up by a bomb in Mukden in the rich Chinese province of Manchuria. Using this incident as an excuse to "restore order," the Imperial Japanese Army quickly and efficiently overran Manchuria.

They set up their own rule, renamed the region Manchukuo, and annexed it to Japan. China was virtually powerless to prevent the land from being carved up into little pieces. Further, the nationalism of the 1900s had given birth to two opposing forces that were trying to rid China of the remains of the Manchu dynasty and foreign domination. A civil war between these two factions—the Nationalists and the Communists—left the country at the mercy of the Japanese.

The United States Secretary of State, Henry L. Stimson, saw that the entire balance of power in Asia was in danger if Japan got away with its aggression. He tried to get the United States and the League of Nations to join in some kind of punishment, such as an embargo. But neither the League nor President Hoover would risk war with Japan. The best Stimson could do was to refuse diplomatic recognition of Manchukuo. It was clear that the structure of world peace had begun to topple.

The End of Peace in Europe

Now the peace in Europe collapsed in six whirlwind years. In 1933, Germany quit the League. In 1935, it began to rearm, in violation of the Treaty of Versailles. And in 1936, Germany marched into the Rhineland, an area that was supposed to remain "neutralized" under the treaty. In 1938, the Nazis invaded and annexed Austria and then seized parts of Czechoslovakia. In 1939, Hitler swallowed the rest of Czechoslovakia and made it clear that Poland was the next country due to have its German minority "liberated" through conquest. All these victories came without one shot being fired. Unprepared Britain and France kept backing down rather than face Hitler's huge forces of infantry, tanks, and bombers.

Meanwhile, in 1935, Italy overran the brave, but almost totally unarmed warriors of Ethiopia, in East Africa. In 1937 and 1938, Japan seized all the helpless coastal provinces of China. China's "Open Door" was now closed.

A few people outside of Germany, Italy, and Japan admired these acts of aggression. Some thought well of fascism's energy and power, compared to the slow-moving democracies. A number of strong anticommunists believed that Hitler would save Europe from communist Russia. Still others felt that Germany and Italy had been harshly treated by the Treaty of Versailles and had fair claims in Europe.

However, most of the world was disgusted by Nazism. Under Hitler's flag, ugly things became official German policy, such as **anti-Semitism**, and the crushing of truth, free thought, and justice. Yet Hitler and his "bullies" were winning. Was a world ruled by aggressors a nightmare about to come true?

anti-Semitism
prejudice against, and persecution of, Jews

American feelings came to a boil during the Spanish Civil War. In 1936, General Francisco Franco led the Spanish army in a revolt against the "Loyalists" who had established a Republic of Spain in 1931. Germany and Italy at once supported Franco with "volunteers"—actually, well-armed air and ground forces. The Loyalists—whose government included Communists—received some outmoded equipment from the Soviet Union, which had little to spare.

Many strongly anticommunist Americans sympathized with Franco's rebels. Yet thousands believed that aggression must be checked in Spain in order to preserve freedom everywhere. American Communists and noncommunists alike joined the International Brigades,

Robert Capra's photograph of a Loyalist soldier at the instant of death captures the grim reality of the Spanish Civil War.

volunteers for the Loyalists from all over the world. Before Franco's final victory in 1939, hundreds of these young volunteers found graves in Spanish earth.

Isolationism Abandoned

It was a strange fact that just when aggressors were tearing up treaties, Americans finally reached a mood of real isolationism. The depression cut foreign trade and investments and forced the United States to be concerned above all with its own problems. In the 1930s, Americans came to realize the important part arms sales and loans to the Allies had played in ending American neutrality between 1913 and 1917. A congressional investigating committee under Senator Gerald P. Hye concluded that "the lure of the profits" in munitions shipments was a root cause of American involvement in war.

Wilsonian idealism was forgotten. The depression generation did not want a rerun of "America's Road to War." Congress, therefore, passed three Neutrality Acts between 1935 and 1937. Under them, if war—or civil war—broke out anywhere, Americans were barred from selling or delivering arms or lending money to the belligerents.

By 1936, even Roosevelt seemed to have given in to the pacifist mood. He said that the United States would avoid any political commitments that might involve it in a foreign war. The United States would also avoid connection with the political actions of the League of Nations. Not everyone believed that Roosevelt really held these views. However, when war broke out in Spain, he turned to Congress to impose an arms embargo.

President Roosevelt had good reason to reevaluate his foreign policy by 1937. Hitler and Mussolini were becoming bolder in Europe. And matters in the Far East were getting worse as well. While attacking China, the Japanese were making a deliberate effort to drive American and European religious, educational, medical, and social activities out of China. American churches, schools, and hospitals were frequently "accidentally" bombed. Comments were actually made that the most dangerous place to be during an air raid was in an American mission. The military leaders in Japan were also drawing closer to Hitler and Mussolini. So Roosevelt began to look for ways to strengthen the United States in case of war.

By 1938, with the stamping of German boots shaking Europe, the Neutrality Acts were under attack. One argument against them was that in a world being shrunk by rapid transportation, no nation could afford to ignore the breakdown of peace anywhere. To ex-Secretary of State Stimson, isolation was "a fantastic impossibility." And Secretary Hull voiced a second argument against the laws. Since aggressors had a head start in the arms race, Great Britain and France—in case of war—could only catch up by importing from the United States. An embargo on both sides, Hull said, would therefore play "into the hands of those nations which have taken the lead in building up their fighting powers."

Despite such pleas, isolationist feelings remained strong. In 1938, a Gallup poll indicated that 70 percent of American voters who had an opinion on isolationism favored complete withdrawal from China of United States civilian interests and the Pacific fleet. But in one swift year, starting in the summer of 1939, the picture changed dramatically. That spring, Great Britain and France decided that they had to make a stand. They promised Poland aid if it were attacked. In August, Hitler and Stalin, supposedly the deadliest of enemies, astonished the world by signing a *nonaggression pact*. Under this pact, Germany and Russia agreed not to go to war against each other. Now Germany was temporarily safe against a war on two fronts. Thus, on September 1, Germany threw a bruising attack at Poland. Two days later, the French and British declared war on Germany. However, they had to stand by powerlessly as the German *blitzkrieg*—lightning war—overpowered the Poles in twenty-one days. Three weeks after the German attack, Russia drove into Poland from the east.

Then the German armies turned to the west. In a ten-week period from April to mid-June 1940, waves of Nazi armor rolled over Denmark, Norway, Holland, Belgium, and France. The British army in France barely escaped capture at Dunkirk, on the coast of France. They fled back to England, leaving most of their equipment behind.

Now the United States faced a critical choice. Most Americans wanted a British victory—but still hoped to stay neutral. Yet, without a great deal of American help, Britain was certain to lose. Most Americans also did not want the burden of building up costly armed forces. However, an unprepared America would be in serious trouble in a world threatened by war.

On August 14, 1936, President Roosevelt made a campaign speech at Chautauqua, New York. He spoke of the danger of being drawn into war and declared "I hate war." The Chicago Tribune cartoon above questioned the sincerity of Roosevelt's speech. Notice the comparison to Woodrow Wilson's 1916 campaign slogan—"He kept us out of war."

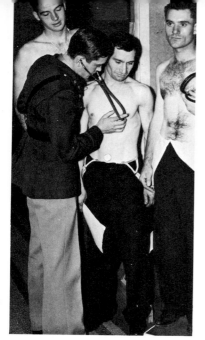

In September 1940, as the Senate debated the nation's first peacetime draft law, mothers of draft-age men lobbied against the bill by staging a "Death Watch" in the Senate reception room (above right). Above Left: two of Chicago's first draftees received their physicals on November 18, 1940.

Cartoonists pictured President Roosevelt as talking peace but planning war. In 1939, FDR asked Congress to change the neutrality laws to allow American help to flow to France and England. In the autumn of 1940, he ran successfully for a third term of office. During the election campaign, FDR stood firmly behind legislation that provided for the first peacetime *conscription*—mandatory enlistment for service in the armed forces—law in the history of the nation. The draft was strongly opposed by many, especially American mothers of draft-age young men. However, Roosevelt used his popularity to carry the nation toward a wartime footing. Originally meant to run for only one year, the draft law was renewed late in 1941 by only a one-vote majority in Congress. No one knew then that the nation had less than three months of peace left.

Questions for Discussion

1. Define *Fascist, anti-Semitism, blitzkrieg*.
2. How did communist views come into conflict with the European capitalist views of economics and international relations?
3. How did the goals of the Fascists in Italy and the Nazis in Germany pose threats to world peace?
4. How did the militarists in Japan influence foreign policy in the 1930s?
5. How did United States policy on neutrality change between 1935 and 1941?

Chapter 26 Review

1. What was the name of the treaty ending World War I? What was President Wilson's warning concerning that treaty?
2. What was the significance of the Kellogg-Briand Pact?
3. Why did United States foreign policy change during the 1920s?
4. Give specific examples of President Roosevelt's "Good Neighbor Policy" in Latin America.
5. What obstacles stood in the way of Japanese ambitions in China?
6. What resulted from Japan's attack on Manchuria in 1931?
7. What acts of aggression were taken by Germany, and Italy between 1933 and 1938?
8. What part did Americans play in the Spanish Civil War?
9. What was the purpose of the Neutrality Acts of 1935 and 1937?
10. Why did President Roosevelt have good reason to reevaluate his foreign policy in 1937?

Word Study

In the sentences that follow fill in each blank with the term below that is most appropriate.

ballistic missile	Fascists	aggression	reciprocal	conscription
bonds	anti-Semitism	creditor nation	militarist	
compensation	financiers	expropriation	blitzkrieg	

1. A type of weapon that is used in modern warfare is a(n) _____.
2. A(n) _____ is owed money by another nation.
3. Drafting citizens for military service is known as _____.
4. People bought _____ as a means of investment in order to gain interest on their monies.
5. Government seizure of property is known as _____.
6. A(n) _____ agreement involves mutual agreement by two parties.
7. Payment for a loss, debt, or service is known as _____.
8. The centralized, autocratic rule under Benito Mussolini in Italy was set up by _____.
9. A(n) _____ supports or favors a warlike national policy.
10. Invasion is a form of _____ by one nation against another.
11. One term for prejudice against and persecution of Jews is _____.
12. Hitler's lightning-type warfare was known as _____.

Using Your Skills

1. Look at the cartoon concerning the League of Nations on page 591. Explain how the cartoon expresses American action and world opinion.
2. Examine the pictures on page 608. Why were these women staging a "Death Watch"? What are advantages of a peace-time draft? What are the disadvantages?
3. Construct a chronology or time line of all the events between 1920 and 1939 that could be included under the heading "Steps Leading to World War II."

Unit 7 Review

Summary

America emerged from World War I unlike anything it had been before. "Change" was the word for the 1920s. Some welcomed it while others opposed it. As the decade began, half the American people won the right to vote.

Business people prospered while farmers suffered. President Coolidge's Puritanism called for "keeping cool." However, technology gave America the automobile, radio, the movies, the suburbs, and other "hot" new items. Some Americans tried to keep all that was new to themselves. Immigration was curtailed, new ideas were banned in schools, and America returned to a policy of isolationism. The 1920s were like no times before. Very few could foresee the crash that would end this glittering decade.

The 1930s were characterized by despair. Americans and all their political, social, and economic institutions were put to the test. Could capitalism and democracy survive? Pain and suffering were everywhere. Franklin D. Roosevelt assumed leadership. He called for "action now" and instituted a "New Deal." "Alphabet agencies," fireside chats, relief, reform, recovery—these would all bring America out of the Great Depression, or so he hoped.

American foreign policy, at this time, also underwent change. After World War I, the United States Senate defeated the Treaty of Versailles. Thus, the 1920s was to be an era of isolationism. Economics, however, kept American interest in the world in the forefront. American loans and goods were exported, and the profits imported. Diplomatic activities abroad were designed to protect United States investments and markets.

During the 1930s, activities throughout the world caused the United States to reexamine its diplomacy. World prosperity collapsed. Italy and Germany ignored the Treaty of Versailles. Japan sought domination of the Pacific. The worldwide threat of dictatorships made external security as critical a problem as the restoration of prosperity. The maintenance of neutrality as well as security became questionable. The United States was able to avoid war in the 1930s. But, too soon, the question of war or peace was answered for the United States.

Summary Questions

1. How were Blacks, immigrants, and women affected by the changes of the 1920s?

2. How did the roles of the three branches of government change during the New Deal?

3. Why was the United States policy of isolationism after World War I considered a "legend"?

4. How were the actions of the rising dictators in Russia, Italy, and Germany similar? different?

Developing Your Vocabulary

1. The farmers of the 1920s feared (foreclosure, deportation) when expenses ran too high.

2. An alien who fails to register can be (demoted, deported).

3. When a person buys a share of a corporation, he or she purchases a (stock, dividend).

4. In a (closed shop, union shop), only union members can be hired.

5. Elections held to choose party nominees are called (primary, secondary) elections.

Developing Your Skills

Historical Interpretation

1. Draw a cartoon representing one of the following:

  (a) the attitude in the 1920s toward big business and farmers;

  (b) the effects of the automobile;

  (c) the social climate of the 1920s.

Historical Analysis

2. Write a news story describing the events indicated by one of the following headlines:

  (a) "The United States is the only nation that ever drove to the poorhouse in an automobile."—Will Rogers.

  (b) The 1920s—a decade that carried within itself the seeds of its own destruction.

  (c) The forgotten person at the bottom of the economic pyramid—the focus of the New Deal.

3. Write a newspaper or magazine ad supporting the pacifist views between World War I and World War II.

Critical Thinking

4. Look at the pictures in this unit depicting the 1920s. Which are the most similar to today? the most dissimilar? Why?

Chronology

5. Construct a chronology of events in American foreign policy between World War I and World War II. Explain how the events supported the stated and unstated policies of the United States.

6. Show how New Deal laws still affect us today.

Special Activities

1. Blacks of both sexes and women of all races have had to struggle to gain rights held by other citizens. Make a chart that historically traces the acquisition of rights for each group. Compare and contrast the movements.

2. For each of the following periods—1789–1870, 1880–1910, and 1920–1940, make a chart showing

  (a) the number of immigrants who came to the United States,

  (b) where they came from, and

  (c) why they came.

3. Investigate the crime wave that accompanied Prohibition. Center your report on Al Capone and Chicago gangsters.

4. Attitudes toward women in business have changed a great deal in the past sixty years. In the 1920s, many jobs were considered to be "for men only." Make a list of jobs that were held by males in the 1920s that today are also held by females.

5. Investigate how a broker's business and the Stock Exchange operate. Prepare a report for the class including the following terms: buying on margin, selling short, brokers' loans, mutual funds, blue chip stocks, preferred and common stocks, Dow Jones averages, New York Stock Exchange, and American Stock Exchange.

6. Every age has its critics, poets, and novelists. Choose a work of literature from the 1920s or 1930s. What is the major theme? What historical events encouraged the writer to present this theme?

UNIT
8
A Changing Society in a Changing World

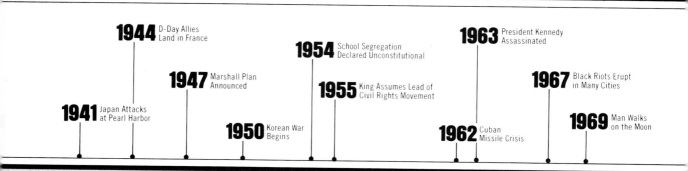

1944 D-Day Allies Land in France

1954 School Segregation Declared Unconstitutional

1963 President Kennedy Assassinated

1947 Marshall Plan Announced

1967 Black Riots Erupt in Many Cities

1941 Japan Attacks at Pearl Harbor

1955 King Assumes Lead of Civil Rights Movement

1950 Korean War Begins

1962 Cuban Missile Crisis

1969 Man Walks on the Moon

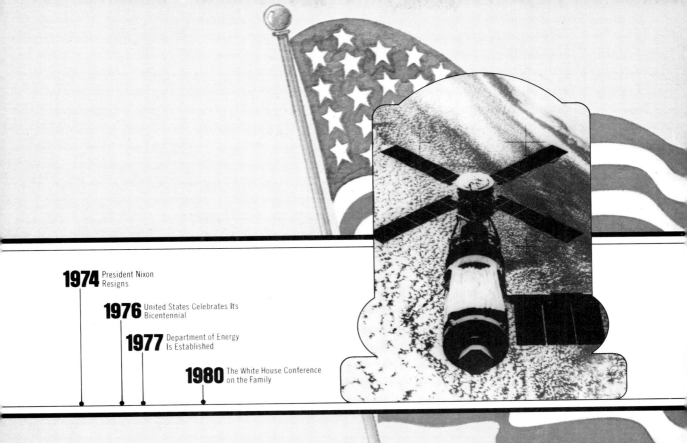

1974 President Nixon
Resigns

1976 United States Celebrates Its
Bicentennial

1977 Department of Energy
Is Established

1980 The White House Conference
on the Family

The period of history beginning with World War II brought change that was very far-reaching. Many Americans began to wonder if the nation was going to be overwhelmed by it. Much of this change was caused by an explosion of technology.

In Chapter 27, you will study World War II, the most technological—and most terrifying—of modern wars. World War II ended with the dropping of a weapon of unheard of destructive power—the atomic bomb. Even after the war ended, the mushroom-shaped cloud caused by the bomb seemed to be ever present.

The United States and its relationship with the world immediately after World War II is the subject of Chapter 28.

The focus of Chapter 29 is the fifties, the beginning of a new era in American history. The turmoil and frustrations of the sixties are discussed in Chapter 30. In Chapter 31, the domestic and international events of the seventies are examined. Finally, Chapter 32 provides a look at where America stood at the beginning of the eighties.

CHAPTER 27
World War II

World War II was more than a large-scale replay of World War I. While World War I had changed the world from what it was in the past, World War II seemed almost to wipe it out. The use of far-ranging aerial bombardment killed millions of civilians. For six years, bombs smashed cities into junk piles. Many of these cities had been the proud achievements of many centuries of European civilization.

The war also set free revolutionary forces of nationalism in both Asia and Africa. After 1945, a weakened Europe could no longer check a rush toward independence by its possessions. Thus, 500 years of world mastery by European colonial empires finally came to an end.

The war ended with the blazing explosion of the atomic bomb in the skies over Japan. As an official United States document said, it was "the most terrible weapon ever known in human history, one bomb of which could destroy a whole city." This destructive power opened an era of international relations unlike any yet known.

In one sense, World War II was a triumph for the United States. The nation had been divided and crippled by the Great Depression of 1933. Only ten years later, the United States was able to perform miracles of production for one unifying purpose—to give the best to its armed forces. Yet, the victory of 1945 over the Axis powers— Germany, Italy, and Japan—left the United States the only powerful and still unscarred nation on the entire globe. As a result, there was no escape, as in 1919, from the heartaching burden of preventing chaos in the world. There was no chance even to pretend that the United States could return to a simple, isolated past.

READING GUIDE

1. **What series of events led to the entry of the United States into battle?**
2. **How did life in Europe differ from life in the United States during the war years?**
3. **How were the Germans finally forced to surrender?**
4. **How did Japan lose its chance to be the dominating power in Asia?**

This World War II poster urges civilians to support their fighting men.

OUR FIGHTERS

DESERVE OUR BEST

1. The Storm Breaks

After the shattering Nazi victories of 1940, the United States moved swiftly to arm itself. Congress passed both a multibillion-dollar program for building up American armed forces and a peacetime draft act. Meanwhile, the situation was critical for Britain. British cities staggered under daily pounding by waves of Nazi bombers. Submarines feasted like sharks on the merchant ships whose cargoes kept the island kingdom from starvation.

Roosevelt was convinced that a British collapse would be a disaster. While American public opinion had moved away from the isolationism of the Neutrality Acts, Americans were not yet ready for combat. Therefore, Roosevelt had to devise steps short of war to help the hard-pressed British fighting under Prime Minister Winston Churchill's leadership. In January 1941, the President proposed a dramatic new idea called lend-lease. He explained it with a little story. If a man's house were afire and he needed a hose, said FDR, any good neighbor would lend him one. All the neighbor would expect was the return of the hose or a replacement when the fire was put out. Roosevelt wanted congressional authority to produce $7 billion worth of military hardware to lend the British as their "hose." It could be repaid in arms or other goods at the end of the war. After sharp debate, Congress enacted lend-lease in March. The United States was now a nonbelligerent partner of Great Britain. In time, lend-lease aid went to Russia, China, and other Allies, as well.

The headlines of 1941 blared forth one shock after another. In April and May, Hitler conquered Yugoslavia and Greece. In June, he tore up his pact with Stalin and attacked Russia. As Hitler's power grew, American neutrality wore thinner. In August, Roosevelt and Churchill signed the Atlantic Charter, agreeing on the kind of world they hoped for after "the final destruction of Nazi tyranny." Then, since it was pointless to manufacture lend-lease goods only to have them sunk at sea, the United States moved to help the thinly stretched British navy to guard the Atlantic supply line. American warships began to conduct submarine-spotting patrols in the North Atlantic. After some of them were fired on, American ships received orders to "shoot on sight" any German or Italian undersea craft. November 1941 found the United States in an undeclared naval war with Germany. Suddenly, lightning struck halfway around the world, on an island in the Pacific.

Pearl Harbor and War with Japan

Defeat in 1940 stripped Hitler's enemies of the power to protect their overseas possessions. Japanese expansionists looked hungrily at French Indochina, British-ruled Malaya and Burma, and the Dutch East Indies (see the map on page 632). Each of these areas was rich in rubber, tin, oil, or other materials sorely needed by the industrial economy of Japan.

Only the United States stood in the way. The United States was strongly pressing Tokyo to get out of China, threatening an embargo on vital industrial materials to Japan. Even the few remaining propeace moderates in the Japanese government, however, could not support a pullout from China. Such an action would be considered a disgraceful surrender.

The impatient Japanese generals were ready to move. In July 1941, Japan occupied French Indochina. The United States struck back with an embargo on gasoline, copper, and scrap iron. The Japanese moderates begged their government for a final chance to negotiate a Pacific settlement. The moderates got their chance—with conditions. A surprise attack against the Americans would be readied—and put into execution if talks produced no results by December 1.

On November 26, Washington informed the Japanese ambassadors that the United States had not changed its stand. There would be no Pacific pact or lifting of the boycott until Japanese troops withdrew from both Indochina and China. To the United States, this was part of its historic support of a free China. To the Japanese, it was a demand: "Surrender, or be destroyed economically." Secret orders sent Japanese carriers steaming to a point north of Hawaii.

At 7:55 A.M. on Sunday, December 7, 1941, Japanese planes caught the American base at Pearl Harbor unprepared. Within 2 hours, columns of oily smoke marked the graves of three battleships, many smaller ships, 188 aircraft, and nearly 2400 soldiers and sailors. The

The sinking of the U.S.S. Arizona *at Pearl Harbor on December 7, 1941.*

next day, an angry President Roosevelt, denouncing Japan's sneak attack, got a declaration of war from Congress. Japan's allies, Germany and Italy, then declared war on the United States. Once more the United States was actively involved in battle.

In the overall picture of the war, the Japanese attack on Pearl Harbor proved to be a serious mistake. It replaced American isolationism with a strong determination to destroy Japan. When the United States entered into full-fledged battle, its military advantage was in doubt. At that time, the United States was not counting heavily on the Pacific fleet in case of war. Even before the attack, the fleet was too weak to hold back Japanese aggression. In effect, the attack forced the United States into the European conflict as well. Now, the United States was involved in a difficult two-front war. In the long run, this had a decisive effect on world history. In declaring war on the United States, Hitler brought the full weight of American power against him. Thus, in a way, he was guaranteeing his own defeat.

Questions for Discussion
1. Why did the United States give aid to Britain?
2. Why can it be said that by November 1941, the United States was in an undeclared war with Germany?
3. Why did the Japanese attack Pearl Harbor?

2. Mobilization for Victory

When Japan attacked Pearl Harbor, the United States was more prepared for battle than it had been in 1917. Yet, if the Allies were to win the war, the nation still had to undergo drastic changes.

Industry had to be organized to produce planes, tanks, and merchant ships vital to the war effort. At first, businesses were afraid to expand because of their experiences during the "boom-and-bust" of the twenties. However, by 1942, production picked up. In some essential industries, the government actually paid for the expansion by building plants at public expense. After the war, these plants were turned over to the private firms that ran them.

One stumbling block to industrial expansion was the shortage of raw materials. President Roosevelt's War Production Board adopted a plan to control the flow of steel, copper, and aluminum. This plan would enable the government to obtain the most from what was available and to minimize delays in production. In time, it even became necessary to stop or limit production of some consumer items. For example, nylon for stockings ended up in parachutes. Steel for refrigerators and cars was used for planes and tanks.

As the war progressed, the speed and efficiency of production improved. Businesses shared plans and and patents. Cooperation and standardization made production simpler. For example, guns that had been produced with loving care by the Colt military supply experts were now being mass-produced by the Saginaw Steering Gear Division of General Motors. At Ford, Chrysler, and General Motors, assembly lines that had been turning out the latest in motor cars were now churning out the latest in airplane motors and tanks.

Outstanding achievements were made in other industries as well. In 1939, airplane production in the United States was an infant industry. Yet, by August 1945, it employed 12.4 percent of all manufacturing employees.

In the early days of the war, German U-boats were sinking cargo ships faster than they could be produced. Henry J. Kaiser, an American industrialist, took over production of the *Liberty Ship*, a cumbersome, dependable cargo vessel. Realizing that many of the ships might be sunk before they ever needed repairs, Kaiser cut corners and used mass-production techniques. Delivery time was reduced from 244 days to an average of 42 days. In one instance, one of Kaiser's shipyards actually delivered a ship in 14 days.

During wartime, unemployment became a thing of the past. Of the 34 million men required to register for the draft, 10 million were inducted into the armed forces. Only 6000 men refused to register or when registered, refused to serve in any capacity. Minorities and women, the skilled and the unskilled, the young and the old were all drawn into the labor pool. Nothing like this on this scale had ever happened before.

The War and Social Justice

In one way, there was more home-front unity in World War II than in 1918. There were almost no antiwar radicals. It was also taken for granted that all but a tiny minority of German-Americans were loyal. Much of this good feeling was generated by the end of the Great Depression. In spite of the war, people who had suffered severe economic hardship saw a chance to improve their lives.

There was one glaring exception. On the West Coast, 110,000 Americans of Japanese birth or descent made their homes. During the early months of 1942, Japan was winning the opening battles of the war. Fears were expressed that a Japanese force might land on the United States Pacific Coast and that Japanese descendants living there would support Japan. Nothing whatever in the past behavior of Japanese-Americans supported such a belief. Behind it was a long history of prejudice against Asians.

In April 1942, with strong support from the local authorities, the army ordered all West Coast Japanese to prepare in 48 hours for removal to "relocation centers." These centers were similar to prison

By nightfall on December 7, 1941, the FBI had arrested some 1300 "potentially dangerous" Japanese aliens in California. By spring of 1942, the civil liberties of all Japanese-Americans living on the West Coast had been suspended. Beginning in April, nearly 110,000 Japanese-Americans—half of them under 20—were ordered to relocation centers. From there they were moved to barracks surrounded by barbed wire.

In all, 8000 Japanese-Americans joined the armed services despite the loss of their civil liberties at home. The 442nd Combat Team posed for this photograph in 1944, while receiving citations for bravery.

camps. Forced to sell their homes and property at once, for whatever price offered, the Japanese-Americans obeyed. It is important to note that neither the 264,000 German aliens nor the 599,000 Italian aliens living in the United States were subject to a similar policy.

By August 1942, there were 109,650 Japanese-Americans assembled, awaiting the completion of ten internment camps located in desolate, isolated areas of the country. Anyone who had at least one great-grandparent who was Japanese was interned. When the government realized that the system was unworkable, some Japanese-Americans were allowed to leave the camps to attend school or obtain jobs in other parts of the country.

Despite this bitter experience, almost all the Japanese in America expressed only a desire to prove their loyalty. Moreover, 8000 *Nisei*—children born in the United States of Japanese parentage—enlisted in the armed forces, such as the infantry of the much decorated 442nd Regimental Combat Team.

Other home-front non-White minorities had both good and bad experiences. Blacks found some industrial jobs open to them that had heretofore been closed. In 1943, only 3 percent of the workers in war industries were Black. By 1945, that figure was increased to 8 percent. The number of Blacks hired by the federal government tripled. In 1943, the War Labor Board outlawed differences in wages based on race. And the National Labor Relations Board refused to certify unions that excluded minorities.

Many barriers still remained. Blacks remained in segregated units in the armed forces. As minorities moved into wartime boom towns to take advantage of new opportunities, overcrowding resulted in tension

and violence. In Detroit, a major center of the defense industry, an interracial fight in a crowded park on a hot June Sunday in 1943 led to a riot that left 38 dead and 500 wounded. In Los Angeles, in a 1943 outbreak, Mexican-American civilian youths were beaten by mobs (including off-duty servicemen). Racial conflicts continued under the surface of wartime unity.

Stories of these racial incidents upset other cities that also had minority populations. Cities established interracial councils. They became concerned about race relations. Problems of housing, jobs, and education were not solved; but at least they were recognized as problems. Publication of *Brothers Under the Skin* by Carey McWilliam and *The American Dilemma* by Gunnar Myrdal indicated that America was undergoing a change in its race relations. The minority races were also strengthening their position for the future by the economic gains of war prosperity.

Women were also faced with opportunities as well as discrimination during World War II. At first, war industries were reluctant to hire women. However, the shortage of male workers made it necessary. Women working at the same jobs as men were rarely paid the same wages. In addition, their chances for promotion remained slim. One-third of the manufacturing work force was made up of women. Many of them gave up their jobs reluctantly when the men returned from overseas. The organized women's liberation movement was yet to come.

Women also had to overcome prejudice against their inclusion in the armed forces. Almost 100,000 women enlisted during World War II, but they were *not* treated as the equals of men. For example, over 1000 women served as Women's Airforce Service Pilots (WASPs). They flew every plane in the American arsenal from the B-20 Superfortress to the P-51 Mustang fighter. They flew test flights and

Above: The United States Army recruited women workers with posters like this one. The millions of women who flocked to defense plants inspired the popular song, "Rosie the Riveter." Above Right: These pilots were members of a group of WASPs who delivered B-17 Fortresses to bases around the country. Right: WACs in training march along Daytona Beach, Florida.

ferried planes around the country for less pay and with less chance of advancement than men. For years, Congress refused to recognize the contributions of these women in military service. Finally, in a bill signed by President Carter in 1977—more than thirty years after the end of the war—women pilots of World War II were granted veteran status and benefits.

The Arsenal of Democracy

War is a mighty machine that speeds up social changes. Since the end of the nineteenth century, the United States had been moving rapidly in new directions. People were leaving farms for cities. An economy based on many small, competing companies was shifting to one of large, powerful corporations regulated by a large, powerful government. A society based on thrift, hard work, family unity, and community loyalty was adjusting to an age of mass marketing, movement, and high spending.

From 1942 through 1945, these movements increased in force. As in World War I, wartime government agencies, staffed by business people and their lawyers, managed the economy. They assigned raw materials and production tasks to factories. They rationed civilian goods, such as tires, gasoline, and meat. And, for the first time in history, these agencies set ceilings on how high wages and prices could go. While much of this activity was bogged down by inefficiency, people put up with it because of their loyalty to the war effort.

Now the movement to the cities became a stampede. In West Coast shipyards, (Midwestern tank and airplane factories, and Southwestern refineries and munitions plants,) an industrial army fought the battle of production in round-the-clock shifts. Housing problems became critical. Ugly rows of boxlike "homes," boarding houses, and trailer camps sprang up. Like the swollen towns around army camps, these areas were full of a quickly moving population, cheap stores, and places of entertainment.

All of this change shook up families and communities. Children changed schools many times. Religious ties were weakened as people moved in and out overnight. A wartime factory town had no local customs.

President Roosevelt signs the "G.I. Bill of Rights" for veterans' aid at the White House, June 22, 1944.

In a sense, this new way of life was similar to life on the frontier. But there were differences. The old frontier drew families together for protection. But wartime living tended to scatter them. Father might be overseas and Mother in a factory. The children stayed with relatives too old to work or with sitters. The millions of women who answered the national call in industrial jobs were an advance guard of liberated women. Yet, the change pulled up an important social anchor. The question of how family duties were to be shared between working husbands and wives remained unanswered. It was one of many that would linger to become important in postwar America.

America Prospers While Europe Burns

In one way, America did not change during the war, compared to the European nations. While the fighting battered European lands like some gigantic wrecking machine, the United States remained untouched, a healthy giant among wounded victims.

From the summer of 1940, Nazi bombers pounded British cities and factories. The English struck back with air raids on Nazi-occupied Europe. Later, their planes were joined by those of the Americans. By 1944, as many as a thousand bombers a night rained explosives on all the elements of industrial civilization—dams, electric plants, highways, rail lines, power lines, mines, shipyards, and oil refineries. In eastern Europe, land and air battles between Russians and Germans scorched the earth and destroyed thousands of villages.

Workers place the deck on a freighter hull. When that task was finished, the freighter would be launched and completed in the water so that a new hull could be started in its place. During the war, American shipyards set amazing production records— 6500 naval vessels, 64,500 landing craft, and 5400 cargo ships.

Germany's invasion of Russia in June 1941 completely surprised the Red Army. By the end of September, it had suffered 2.5 million casualties. The German policy toward the civilian population was to offer a choice—enslavement or annihilation. A German photographer took this picture. The burning cottage is probably the home of a Russian peasant who resisted the Nazis.

Throughout Europe, war production was kept up only by starving the civilian economy. Fuel, food, power—all were severely *rationed*, that is, the government decided how much of certain goods a citizen was to have. People had books of stamps entitling them to buy only a certain *ration*, or portion. Needy families shivered in unheated, unlit, half-ruined apartment buildings. They ate dried vegetables and coarse bread. They drank substitute coffee. They got only a few ounces of meat, butter, or sugar each week. Few ever saw eggs, milk, or fresh fruits. Many survived only by stealing, by using the **black market**, or by selling themselves for any purpose to occupying armies. This was the world that European teenagers grew up in from 1939 to 1945.

black market
illegal trade in goods or services that violates official regulations

In contrast, America flourished. Between 1940 and 1945 the United States turned out nearly 300,000 planes, over 64,000 landing craft, 5000 cargo ships, and 102,000 tanks and self-propelled guns. Yet, in no war year was even half the total national production devoted to war goods. A fair amount of consumer goods was still available. American cities were whole and thriving.

Despite rationing and some discomfort, American civilians found the war a time of jobs, savings (in the form of war bonds), and future hopes. By 1945, Americans were the rich relatives of the rest of the world. This fact shaped American feelings toward other peoples in a special way.

Questions for Discussion

1. Define *Nisei*, *rationed*.
2. What were the effects of World War II on the economic life of the United States?
3. What were the effects of World War II on social justice for Blacks, women, and other minorities?
4. How were families and family life affected by World War II?
5. Why was there such a sharp contrast between life in America and life in Europe from 1939 to 1945?

The actual fighting raged in two theaters of operations—Europe and the Pacific. In both, the military story for the United States, Britain, Russia, China, and the other nations allied with the United States was one of struggling along a comeback road from defeat.

In September 1942, Germany had reached its greatest expansion (see map on p. 626). Hitler's divisions were attacking Stalingrad (now Volgograd), deep in Russia. Some divisions were moving southward around the eastern end of the Black Sea, toward the rich oil fields of the Middle East. Other German troops had gone to Libya, in North Africa, to take over the fighting from the Italians there. Under the

3. Victory in Europe

brilliant General Erwin Rommel, their Afrika Korps launched an early 1942 offensive that carried its tanks streaking across desert sands into Egypt. Only one more push seemed necessary to take the Germans beyond the ancient pyramids, which had looked down on so many other conquerors. Then Rommel would be able to cut the Suez Canal and pinch off a vital supply route of the British empire.

In October, the tide began to turn. The Russians held on at Stalingrad. They even counterattacked and surrounded the enemy. The Russian troops, who were better equipped to cope with the cold, cut off the German supplies. Low on gas for their tanks and food for themselves, the entire Nazi force at Stalingrad surrendered in

World War II in Europe

- Allied and Allied-Controlled Nations
- Axis Nations
- Furthest Extent of Axis Occupation (November 1942)
- Neutral Nations
- ← Allied Offensives

Dates indicate occupation by the Axis powers

In October 1942, the British launch an offensive against Rommel in North Africa.

January 1943. Meanwhile, the British in Egypt launched a huge offensive at El Alamein on October 23. Two weeks later, a great fleet landed British and American forces in French Morocco and Algeria. The pro-German French government in these provinces quickly surrendered. Rommel was squeezed between forces advancing into Tunisia from two directions. His supplies were cut off by Allied control of the air over the Mediterranean Sea. In June 1943, Rommel's battered force—its tanks and planes useless from lack of gas—gave up. For the second time in four months, a whole German army was defeated.

The victory was important to bolster morale and to strengthen the Allied military position. With this second major defeat, the German army could no longer make up the loss of soldiers. Britain could now maintain its control over the Mediterranean Sea and the Suez Canal. As a result, the Allies were in a position to launch an assault on Sicily that would take some of the pressure off England and Russia.

In July 1943, Allied armies landed in Sicily. By August 17, the entire island was captured by the Allies. In September, the Allied forces attacked the mainland and began a long, bitter fight up the Italian peninsula. By then, Mussolini had been forced out of office. Shortly thereafter, the Italians gladly surrendered. The first enemy was now out of the war. Germany still dug in and stubbornly defended mountain strongholds such as Monte Cassino. Hitler had ordered his army to put up a bitter struggle for every yard of territory. The Allies inched forward. By June 1944, the Americans had taken Rome.

The Great Invasion Begins

The Nazi empire began to crumble. Aided by a stream of American lend-lease supplies, the Russians pushed the Germans back along a thousand-mile-long front in the biggest battles of the war,

The United States Fifth Army liberates Rome on June 4, 1944.

General Dwight D. Eisenhower (above) became Supreme Commander of Allied Forces in January 1944. He supervised the planning of Operation Overlord, the largest amphibious operation in history. On D-Day, 176,000 troops and 4000 landing craft, aided by 600 warships and 11,000 planes, headed for 5 separate points along the Normandy coastline. A little more than a month later, General George S. Patton (above right), a tank commander with a reputation for ruthless efficiency, was pushing his Third Army across western Europe at a record-setting 40 miles a day.

involving millions of troops. By the end of 1944, the Russians had liberated most of their country and were in Poland, Rumania, Czechoslovakia, Hungary, and even the eastern part of Germany itself.

Germany bled from many wounds. It had to pour reinforcements into Italy, which, after surrendering, had turned around and declared war on Germany. In the occupied countries, fierce attacks by underground resistance fighters blew up trains and supply dumps and pinned down thousands of troops on guard duty. Allied air raids grew greater daily. Unable to replace vital losses, the Germans concentrated their airplanes over Germany for a fierce defense of their home skies. The price for this move was loss of air control everywhere else. This became a key element in the plans of the Allied high command to end the war by invading western Europe and striking directly at the Nazi heartland.

All through the spring of 1944, an army of more than 2.5 million, with a crushing weight of supplies, was concentrated in England. Day after day, the Allied forces trained for an attack on the heavy fortifications along the French coastline across the English Channel. The Germans were aware that an invasion would be launched. However, they were unable to determine the exact date or location. The commander of this force—consisting of Americans, British, Poles, Free French, and soldiers from every country conquered by Nazis and from British Commonwealth nations—was General Dwight D. Eisenhower.

D-Day, the secret day chosen for the assault, was set for June 6, 1944, on the beaches at Normandy. By chance, the leader of the

German army, General Rommel, had chosen to be in Germany that day to celebrate his wife's birthday. Thus, he was twenty-four hours late responding to the attack. In the early morning hours, Allied commanders gave their tense troops final instructions. Then thousands of planes roared out to smash German positions and every possible route of reinforcements. Paratroopers dropped in to seize key bridges and crossroads behind the German lines. As dawn lightened the sky, an *armada* (fleet) of fighting ships and landing craft, under an umbrella of fighters, crossed the English Channel. Troops poured ashore. In the teeth of savage machine gun and artillery fire, they fought their way inland past barbed-wire obstacles and land mines. By nightfall, 2000 had paid with their lives to establish a beachhead. But the walls of Hitler's fortress were finally penetrated.

The Road to Victory

The British and Americans poured supplies into the area they controlled, then broke out explosively in a massive assault. While Allied truck convoys steadily fed gasoline and ammunition to advancing armored columns, German supplies and reinforcements were blasted off the roads by unceasing aerial assault. By August 25, 1944, Paris had been freed. Ten days earlier, another Allied landing had been made. This time, the Allies landed on the Mediterranean coastline of France. By November, German columns were reeling backward toward their own frontiers, and all France was liberated.

In December, the Germans struck back with a vicious counteroffensive in Belgium. The "bulge" they drove into American lines gave the battle its name. But this last desperate thrust ran out of steam. The Germans were tough, veteran fighters, and they were well led. But now they were up against equally good soldiers who had overwhelming superiority in weapons. In March 1945, the Allies crossed the Rhine and the invasion of Germany from the west had begun. On April 25, the Americans met the Russians advancing from the east. American tanks were rolling into Austria and Czechoslovakia as well as into Germany. The Red Army was fighting its way into Berlin. Block by block, the Russians leveled the city to rubble.

In his underground headquarters in Berlin, Hitler finally realized that the end had come. On April 30, he committed suicide. Loyal followers burned his body. One after another, Nazi generals surrendered their exhausted forces. The final, unconditional surrender of all remaining German forces took place on May 8, which thus became V-E Day (Victory in Europe).

All over Europe, millions celebrated the end of Hitler's rule. The Nazis had imprisoned, starved, and tortured millions of their enemies both inside and outside Germany. Moreover, Hitler had planned the

In April 1945, American tanks enter gutted Magdeburg, Germany.

Crowds gather to celebrate in the streets of New York on V-E Day, May 8, 1945.

systematic extermination, primarily by gassing, of all European Jews and other people he felt were undesirable. The task was almost completed when advancing Allied armies liberated Hitler's "death camps." Over six million people had been put to death. Thus, the twentieth century saw an unbelievably brutal revival of *genocide*—the deliberately planned destruction of an entire people. It was for this reason in particular that some of the leading Nazis were tried as "war criminals" at Nuremberg in 1946. They were found guilty, and many of them were executed.

Questions for Discussion

1. Define *genocide*.
2. What battles were turning points in the war in Europe?
3. Why was the Normandy invasion a significant action on the part of the Allies?
4. Describe Allied actions from D-Day to V-E Day.

The war in the Pacific, like the war in Europe and Africa, began with enemy triumphs (see the map on p. 632). The Japanese battle plan had been to strike quickly and to paralyze the American fleet. After that, they could overrun the weak defenses of the Philippines, the Dutch East Indies, Malaya, and Burma. In the first six months of the war with Japan, this timetable worked brilliantly.

Japanese *amphibious* (land and sea) forces, supported by waves of fighters and bombers, overran Guam and the Wake Islands and landed in the Philippines—all in the first week of their attack. Soon Japanese tanks rolled through Manila. Four months later, hollow-eyed, starving American and Filipino defense forces surrendered first at Bataan and later at Corregidor. Their commander, General Douglas MacArthur, was not captured. He was ordered to escape to Australia and to take charge of all Allied forces in the Southwest Pacific. He did so, darting through enemy-infested waters in a small torpedo-boat and vowing, "I shall return."

At the time, it did not look as if he would. The Japanese astonished the world with their speed and skill. By mid-February 1942, they captured all Malaya, including the great British fortress of Singapore. They occupied Burma and cut off China from the world except by a perilous air route over the towering Himalaya Mountains. They took the Dutch East Indies by the end of April with only light casualties.

Now Japan was in a commanding position. Japan could, if it chose, appeal for the friendship of the Asian peoples in what it called its "co-prosperity sphere." If Japan could hold out, negotiate peace terms with weary Allies, and then share the fruits of its industry with those who supplied its raw materials, it might become the champion of a powerful "Asia for Asians" movement.

Instead, Japanese militarists fumbled this chance. They treated their possessions harshly and exploited the local peoples like any other imperialists. Movements for national independence in each Japanese-occupied land became anti-Japanese as well as anti-European. Moreover, the Japanese army and navy reached too far. They landed on islands off the northwest coast of Australia to cut off that island continent from help and possibly soften it for invasion. But this stretched their seaborne supply lines dangerously thin.

Carrier War in the Pacific

In fact, the downfall of Japan came through a new kind of warfare. Instead of capturing territory or destroying its mainland armies, the American navy attacked Japan's lines of communication, thousands of miles long. The key was control of the air. Surface ships could not survive aerial attack without protecting planes of their own. Aircraft carriers, not battleships, were now the rulers of the sea. Naval battles

4. Victory in the Pacific

On February 29, 1944, in the midst of his struggle to return to the Philippines, General Douglas MacArthur views the results of heavy naval bombardment.

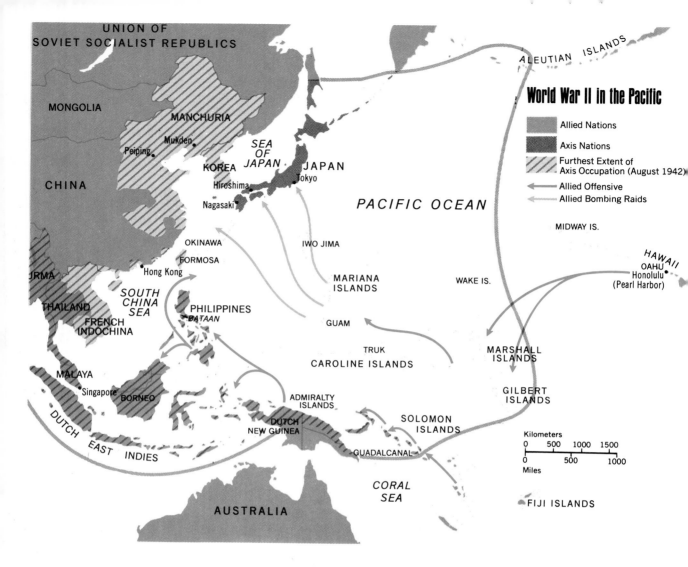

World War II in the Pacific

Allied Nations

Axis Nations

Furthest Extent of
Axis Occupation (August 1942)

Allied Offensive

Allied Bombing Raids

could be fought by forces hundreds of miles apart, sending out planes
to destroy each other's floating airbases. In carrier warfare, the
United States was bound to win. Its shipyards poured out more than
two dozen full-sized carriers and over seventy smaller "escort"
carriers. As a result, a two-part strategy took shape.

First, the American navy had to win mastery of the air. An early
test of American carrier strength came in a sea fight near Midway
Island in June 1942. This battle turned the tide of the war in the
Pacific. A huge Japanese fleet moved out to capture Midway. But
American planes found and sank the four Japanese carriers in the
striking force. The invasion armada, thereupon, turned back, without
having fired one single shot at a United States surface vessel.

American success at Midway established, once and for all, the importance of carrier warfare in World War II. The defeat of the Japanese at Midway destroyed any hopes Japan had of wiping out the United States Pacific fleet and moving farther east. Now Japan would have to look elsewhere for conquests. Japan did not feel strong enough to attack Russia. Nor was it inclined to attack India. The most vital link left was the southern Solomon Islands. If Japan controlled these islands, it would be within striking distance of the United States supply lines to Australia. It was in Australia that General MacArthur was staging a military build-up of soldiers and equipment so that he could fulfill his promise to return to the Philippines.

The second part of America's Pacific strategy was a campaign of "island hopping." The first success came at the end of 1942. At about the same time the Russians were holding on at Stalingrad and the Allies were regaining North Africa, a fierce struggle took place for Guadalcanal, the southernmost island of the Solomon Islands. The jungle battle for control of the island and its airstrip lasted eight months. Six separate naval battles took place. The losses on both sides were heavy. In one tragic incident, for example, five brothers went down on the same ship. But by February, the Allies had given the Japanese their first land defeat in the war.

Lieutenant Commander William Draper, a navy combat artist, painted these planes bombing Japanese-held islands in the Pacific in March 1944. The planes were flying in support of General MacArthur's invasion force.

Another William Draper painting, "Planes Return." This picture portrays the recovery of a strike force in May 1944.

On Guadalcanal, the marines and soldiers had gained valuable experience in island hopping. An island would be seized and developed as a base from which bombers and submarines could assault Japanese merchant vessels and strong points. Meanwhile, strength would be built up to take another island closer to Japan. Eventually, Japan itself would be brought under air attack. Many of its island outposts, as well as its armies on the Asian mainland, could be ignored or "bypassed." They would be starved out as Japanese ships were sent to the bottom.

This was not an easy technique. The land and climate were unfamiliar. The heat was oppressive. Frequently, there were drenching rains. Snakes and bugs were everywhere. Except for the Philippine Islands, occupied in October 1944, all the islands assailed were small. And all were bitterly and bravely defended. The enemy followed a code of conduct that was alien to Allied troops. The military code of the Japanese discouraged surrender. To die in the service of the Emperor, whom the Japanese considered a god, was an honor. As a result, the Japanese often fought down to the last soldier. Many deliberately carried out attacks that were suicidal. Thousands of soldiers and marines died in assaults on dots of coral on the map. Nevertheless, by the spring of 1945, Americans had taken Iwo Jima and Okinawa. They were now within fighter-plane range of Japan and able to protect fleets of B-29 Superfortresses. These flew from the Marianas to drop millions of tons of explosives on the Japanese main islands. Meanwhile, submarines, produced in great quantities by American shipyards, steadily destroyed Japan's merchant marine, whose cargo was crucial to the war effort in Japan.

The Atomic Age Begins

July 1945 finally saw the end at hand. Japanese factories were crippled, its cities gutted, and hundreds of thousands of its civilians dead as a result of great bombing raids. But the final blow to Japan did more than end the long struggle. It opened a new era of fear for humanity.

In 1945, only a handful of Americans knew that the United States had worked for more than three years on a terrifying new weapon. This was a bomb that produced an explosion powerful enough to wipe out an entire city in one blast.

The possibility of creating such a bomb had first been brought to American attention in 1939 by several distinguished European scientists who were refugees from Fascism and Nazism. The Italian Enrico Fermi; the Hungarians Leo Szilard, Eugene Wigner, and Edward Teller; and the German Albert Einstein had all learned of experiments in atom-splitting. They realized that the process had military possibilities and dreaded the thought of Hitler's scientists giving Germany this weapon. During the war, some of these men, along with American scientists, worked at top-secret factories. Two billion dollars were spent on research experiments to assemble this bomb that would work by *nuclear fission*, or atom-splitting. On July 16, 1945, one atomic bomb was prepared and ready to test in New Mexico. It exploded with a searing blast of fire "brighter than a thousand suns," as one observer recalled. The United States had two more such atom bombs ready. Each had the power of 20,000 tons of TNT. By comparison, the most powerful ordinary bombs then in use contained only one or, at most, two tons of this explosive.

On April 12, 1945, President Roosevelt (reelected a fourth time in 1944) suddenly died. His successor, Harry S Truman, was told of the research for the A-bomb. He was advised by his military leaders to use it to frighten Japan into immediate surrender. Otherwise, his advisors argued, it would be necessary to invade Japan, causing countless casualties on both sides. But some scientists who had developed the bomb thought that such an appalling weapon should not be used if the Japanese could be brought to their knees by continuing the air and sea blockade. Truman was meeting with Russian and English leaders at Potsdam (near Berlin) when he received word that the bomb was ready. The Allied leaders closed their conference with an ultimatum to Japan to surrender or be totally destroyed. The Japanese government refused.

On August 6, 1945, a B-29 dropped an A-bomb over Hiroshima, an industrial town with a population of about 350,000. A mushroom-shaped cloud shot 40,000 feet into the air. Beneath it, a fireball killed 70,000 people in a few seconds and turned what was once a thriving

Fifteen seconds after the first successful detonation of an atom bomb, in New Mexico, this awesome sight filled the predawn sky. The bomb had been dropped from a tower. After the blast, all that remained was a crater 1200 feet wide and 25 feet deep at the center. There was nothing in it except little green glass beads, which had been formed out of the sand by the fantastic heat from the explosion.

This photograph of Hiroshima gives some idea of the terrible physical destruction caused by the A-bomb. Nearly 60 percent of the city's total area all but disappeared. Some 40,000 buildings simply vanished.

city into a charred wasteland. Later, as many as 100,000 more Japanese—the exact number is uncertain—died of illness from the deadly radiation that followed the explosion. On August 8, Russia hurried to join the kill by declaring war on Japan. Still the Japanese refused to surrender. They vowed to fight to the last mountaintop. So, on August 9, a second A-bomb was dropped on Nagasaki, killing an estimated 50,000 more Japanese. Finally, the Imperial Government asked for peace terms. On September 2, Japanese officials signed a document of surrender aboard an American battleship in Tokyo Bay.

The cruelest and costliest war in history was over. Amid the triumph, however, there was now cause for concern. The A-bomb had opened a frightening possibility—that nations might go on to develop weapons powerful enough to destroy their own species. The fireballs in the skies over Hiroshima and Nagasaki might stand for the dawn of a new day when people might be forced to build a peaceful world. Or the bombs might symbolize the final blaze that would wipe out humanity altogether.

Questions for Discussion
1. Define *amphibious, nuclear fission*.
2. How did Japan destroy its own chances of conquest in Asia?
3. Why was the Battle of Midway an important battle in the war in the Pacific?
4. Why did President Truman agree to use the atomic bomb?

Chapter 27 Review

Summary Questions for Discussion

1. What actions did the United States take after 1940 to arm itself?
2. How did Roosevelt give aid to Britain without participating in the combat?
3. Why was Japan interested in French Indo-China, British-ruled Malaya, Burma, and the Dutch East Indies?
4. What prompted the Japanese attack on Pearl Harbor? Why was the attack a serious mistake?
5. What effect did World War II have on the (a) expansion of industry, (b) government control of industry, (c) production of consumer goods, (d) speed and efficiency of production, and (e) unemployment?
6. Why were Japanese-Americans relocated to internment camps in 1942?
7. How did Blacks benefit from World War II? What were some negative effects for other minorities?
8. List examples of the opportunities and the discrimination that women experienced during World War II.
9. Which was the first of the Axis powers to fall? When?
10. Why can it be said that by 1944 "Germany bled from many wounds"?
11. What was the effect of D-Day?
12. What was the battle of the "bulge"?
13. What is V-E day? When did it occur?
14. What happened at the Nuremberg trials?
15. What was the Japanese battle plan in World War II?
16. Identify General Douglas MacArthur.
17. How did carrier warfare give the United States an advantage? What was its effect at the Battle of Midway?
18. Why was "island hopping" a difficult strategy?
19. What arguments convinced President Truman that he should use the atomic bomb against Japan?
20. When and where was the first atomic bomb dropped? Why was it necessary to drop the second bomb? Where was that bomb dropped?

Word Study

In the sentences that follow, fill in each blank with the term that is most appropriate.

Nisei   genocide   amphibious   rationed

1. Children born in the United States of Japanese parentage are known as _____.
2. A craft that can operate on land and sea is said to be _____.
3. Hitler practiced _____ in an attempt to systematically wipe out the Jews.
4. Goods are _____ when the government decides how much the public can have.

Using Your Skills

1. Look through the pictures in this chapter as well as those in Chapter 15, *The Civil War*, and in Chapter 23, *World War I*. In what ways were each of these wars alike? In what ways were they different?
2. Look at the map on page 626. Why was the Battle of El Alamein of great importance? What prevented Hitler from defeating England as easily as he had Belgium, Holland, and France? Why was Hitler's attack on Russia ill-conceived?
3. Look at the map on page 632. Why was it difficult and costly for the Allies to defeat Japan?
4. Which pictures in this chapter could be used to support the generalization that, "During World War II, America prospered while Europe burned."

CHAPTER 28

Emerging into a New World 1945–1952

In 1945, the United States took on the role of world leader. The end of World War II left the nation an unharmed giant with a responsibility for using its strength wisely. Most Americans also realized that from then on, they would be affected by almost everything that happened on this globe.

In the last week of April 1945, two tanks halted, facing each other. These tanks were deep in wartime Germany. Their grinning crews climbed out and shook hands for photographers. One tank was Russian, the other American. The armies of these two Allied powers had united to split the Nazi empire. World War II was almost over.

Just three years later, American planes were flying food and supplies into Berlin over the Russian sector of Germany. The land route was cut off by the Russians. Stalin was trying to force the United States to abandon Berlin. He wanted the United States to accept the permanent division of Germany.

What had happened to the relationship between Russia and the United States? First, the wartime alliance between the West and Russia broke up right after the fighting stopped. The Russian dictator, Joseph Stalin, began expanding Russian power. He claimed that he only wanted protection against future invasions. The United States saw Stalin's policies as a threat to free peoples everywhere. President Harry S Truman fought back by giving economic and military aid to many European countries. America rearmed and formed anticommunist alliances across the globe. Soon, both superpowers were deep in an arms race that threatened humanity with destruction.

Domestic affairs in the United States were not peaceful either. Readjustments to a peacetime economy and to a changing world put strains on the nation. There were strikes, and shortages, and fears came to the surface.

READING GUIDE

1. **What were the characteristics of post-World War II America?**
2. **Why was the United Nations founded?**
3. **How was the United States affected by the Cold War?**

An aerial view of the United Nations Building from the East River, New York City.

1. The Search for Domestic Tranquility

No one was more stunned by the death of Franklin D. Roosevelt on April 12, 1945, than the man who took his place. Vice-President Harry S Truman had been chosen more for his ability to balance the Democratic ticket than for what was thought to be his potential as a President. Truman was from an agricultural Midwestern state, Missouri. He was 61 years old and down-to-earth in character. Even so, he was not politically naive.

Truman had spent twelve years in state politics. There, he had learned the ins and outs of the party organization before he was elected to the United States Senate. During his years in the Senate, he gained more political experience and developed a wider view of the world. He balanced friendship with Southern Democrats with support of farmers, labor union members, and Blacks. His work as chairman of a Senate committee investigating national defense contracts saved the government millions of dollars. Truman soon achieved a nationwide reputation for hard work and honesty.

Truman needed all of his political know-how and support for the job ahead of him. He had inherited enormous problems. The war in Europe and the Pacific had to be ended. In addition, he had to carry out Roosevelt's plan for the establishment of the United Nations. He had to lead the country through its adjustment from war to peace. Finally, it was his responsibility to guide the relief program for war-torn countries.

Demobilization

demobilization
the discharging of troops from military service

As the war wound down, the first concern of many Americans was the **demobilization** of the armed forces. Immediately after V-E Day, the discharge of military personnel began. In late June 1945, the first large group of veterans pulled into the New York harbor aboard the *Queen Mary*. Thousands more followed. The trickle became a stream as the rapid collapse of Japan made it possible to reduce the armed forces even further.

With so many veterans returning from the war, military and national leaders soon became concerned about the strength of the armed forces in the United States. They reacted by reducing the number of soldiers discharged. This slowdown was met with an outcry from the public and near mutiny on the part of those in the military. Mothers sent baby bootees to members of Congress with notes that read, "I want my Daddy home." "Wanna-Go-Home" riots broke out in American military bases throughout Europe and Asia. Within one year after the end of the war, Congress finally gave in to the pressure. The demobilization process picked up speed once more.

In many ways, the United States had prepared well for its returning veterans. In 1944, Congress passed the Servicemen's

Readjustment Act, also known as the G.I. Bill of Rights. By 1950, veterans' hospitals served an average of 108,000 patients daily. Thousands of service men and women were helped by the hospitals' rehabilitation programs. Loans and grants were made available to those who wanted to go to school or to buy their own businesses, homes, or farms. Under Truman, the Veterans' Administration spent $13.5 billion for the education and training of veterans and self-help programs. Over $16 million in loan programs were provided as well. There was to be no repeat of the difficulties facing many veterans after World War I.

The Postwar Economy

In many ways, the years that followed World War II were unlike the years that followed World War I. For one thing, the economic picture after World War II was a brighter one. Returning veterans had little difficulty finding work. Thus, employment remained high. Farm income, which was usually most sensitive to economic swings, also maintained its wartime gains.

There were a number of reasons for the improved economic situation. The public had learned habits of thrift during the Depression. As wartime wages increased, people found that they were able to open savings accounts and invest in war bonds. The American people saved over $140 billion during the war. Afterward, they were anxious to spend their savings on consumer goods that had been unavailable during the war. Aid programs for war-torn countries assured a continuing demand for American exports. Also, private investment and government spending boosted the domestic economy.

Soldiers, glad to be home from Luzon and other Pacific Island conflicts, wave from the deck of a returning troopship.

However, one major problem remained—inflation. Wartime controls on prices, wages, and rents were still being enforced one year after the end of World War II. However, businesses wanted to resume regular consumer production. The demand for cars, appliances, and living quarters exceeded the supply. Landlords and industrialists were unhappy because controls limited their profits. Consumers were angry when controls were lifted because prices rose and forced them to pay higher prices for limited quantities of goods.

Truman was in a political bind. There was no way to resolve the problem of prices and production without turning the country against him. If price controls remained in effect, there would be less incentive for producers to get their products that were in demand to the market-place. This would lead to high unemployment and to shortages. The public would be angered. In turn, if price controls were removed, the products would be available. However, prices would still soar because of the great demand for them. In this case, too, the public would react with anger.

Truman finally decided to allow a gradual loosening of controls. Prices started to move in an upward spiral. Congress failed to pass effective replacement laws for expiring controls. By January 1948, prices were at least 47 percent higher than they had been eighteen months before. The public was both angered and confused.

However, the question of price controls was a reflection of yet a deeper controversy. Even as the country entered the twentieth century, lines were being drawn to define the level and type of government intervention that would be allowed. Liberals favored government involvement as a means of social change and distribution of wealth. Conservatives viewed increased government involvement as a step toward socialism and the destruction of private initiative.

This same basic controversy affected Truman's efforts to deal with organized labor. During the war, unions had gained political and economic strength. When the war ended, they started flexing their muscles.

Labor

One week after the bombing of Pearl Harbor, President Roosevelt asked labor to honor a no-strike pledge until the war was over. With few exceptions, this pledge was kept. Blue-collar workers made the production miracle of the war years possible by putting in long hours, working **swing shifts**, and investing in war bonds. But by V-J Day (August 14, 1945), their accumulated grievances were unbearable. Within a year, 4.6 million workers had gone on strike, spurred by fears of inflation, unemployment, and a postwar depression.

swing shifts
work shifts in industry from mid-afternoon until midnight

Basically, President Truman was sympathetic to the situation of labor. He believed that industry could meet demands for wage increases without increasing prices. Manufacturers held firm to their belief that wages could rise only if prices rose as well. The result was a series of battles in which labor and management tried to outmaneuver one another. Prices and wages reached extremely high levels.

The United States was now a world leader. America had to show the world that a democratic society could maintain a healthy economy. President Truman was concerned about the effect the strikes would have on the nation.

In two instances, Truman felt that strikes were endangering both the good of the nation and the progress of European recovery. So he acted immediately. When John L. Lewis, head of the United Mineworkers, pulled the miners out of the coal mines in April 1946, the government took over the mines. Over Lewis's objections, the miners went back to work. In the final settlement, the union got most of its demands. The price of victory, however, was a rise in anti-union sentiment.

Miners watch for the latest developments in the miners' strike of 1946.

The second instance involved the railroads. When the nation was faced with a total railroad strike, President Truman seized the railroads to force the workers back to work. In defiance of government orders, the workers refused. So Truman went before Congress to ask for the authority to draft all railway workers into the Army. News of the settlement of the strike came as Truman was addressing Congress. Truman did not have to carry out his threat. But in the process, he lost the support of many liberals as well as union leaders.

At the peak of the controversy over price controls and labor demands, the people went to the polls in 1946 to elect the members of the Eightieth Congress. They elected a Republican majority to Congress. The new members rode into office on a wave of anti-union, anti-inflation sentiment.

The Eightieth Congress

When Truman became President, no one was quite sure what his domestic programs would be. In a message to Congress in September 1945, Truman called for a long list of reforms. He favored a higher minimum wage, unemployment compensation, and the extension of social security coverage. He wanted the federal government to pass full employment legislation and make the Fair Employment Practices Committee a permanent one. He favored public housing, continued support for farm programs, limited tax cuts, and regional development of natural resources. In all, Truman's program was one that favored the growth of the federal government.

The members of the Eightieth Congress looked upon the election results as a rejection of Truman's leadership. They were confident that the people wanted less government, not more. Thus, many of

Truman's proposals were rejected on these grounds. In fact, in several instances, his vetoes were overridden.

One of the first plans of the new Congress was to curb union strength. Many people felt that the National Labor Relations Act of 1935 had upset the balance of power between labor and management. So, in June 1947, Congress drafted the Taft-Hartley Act to readjust that balance.

The Taft-Hartley Act outlawed the closed shop and the **secondary boycott**. This act gave the government the power to invoke an 80-day injunction against strikes that might affect national health or safety. It also prohibited, among other things, political contributions by unions, **featherbedding**, and excessive dues.

Truman vetoed the Taft-Hartley bill. In doing so, he stated that "it would contribute neither to industrial peace, nor to economic stability and progress." Labor, which had turned against Truman after the miners' strike and the railroad strike, now returned to his camp. Meanwhile, Congress overrode Truman's veto.

Another stumbling block for Truman was civil rights legislation. On December 5, 1946, Truman had appointed a committee to study the question of civil rights. In 1947, the committee issued its report, "To Secure These Rights." Truman asked Congress to pass several measures based on that report. He wanted an antilynching bill, elimination of the poll tax, a permanent civil rights commission, and federal guarantees of fair employment practices. A coalition of Republicans and Southern Democrats stalled the legislation. Truman tried to do what he could without their support. He speeded up the desegregation of the armed forces and forbade discrimination in federal employment.

In spite of their differences, the President and the Congress were able to agree on some issues. In July 1947, the legislature authorized a commission to study the reorganization of the executive branch. Truman appointed Herbert Hoover to head the committee. After exhaustive studies, the Hoover Commission issued reports for streamlining the government. Most of these revisions were accepted. At about the same time, Congress passed the Presidential Succession Act of 1947, which limited how many terms one President could serve. Another important act made possible the Truman Doctrine and the Marshall Plan (which will be discussed later in this chapter). In the end, however, the lawmakers failed to act on most of Truman's domestic programs.

The Fair Deal *

Truman won the 1948 election with a campaign that put down a "do-nothing" Congress. Major questions remained unresolved. Truman was sure that Congress would not act on any of his domestic programs. He therefore called Congress back into session to "prove" to the American people, before the election, how ineffective the Republicans were. The Congress reconvened on the day turnips are traditionally planted in Missouri. That Congress was thus dubbed "the turnip Congress." As Truman predicted, the problems remained unsolved. This gave Truman his campaign issue.

In an election that defied the experts and the pollsters, Truman defeated Thomas E. Dewey. In fact, Truman himself was the only person who thought he would win. One newspaper had even printed that Dewey won before the results were all in. Truman had won the support of labor because of his veto of the Taft-Hartley Act. He had also won the support of Blacks because of his stand on civil rights. Catholics and Jews voted for him because he favored a liberal immigration policy. And farmers approved his position on farm issues. Truman had the edge he needed to win.

The Eighty-first Congress, elected at the same time, supported many of Truman's programs for a "fair deal" for every American. Many changes, however, could not be made. Truman did not have Roosevelt's ability to stir popular support or to pressure Congress. In addition, many conservatives remained in the powerful committees in Congress. Concern, also, about the Cold War and communism took attention away from reform.

President Harry S Truman (left) with Vice President Alben William Barkley.

Questions for Discussion

1. Define *demobilization, swing shifts, secondary boycott, featherbedding.*
2. How did the Truman administration convert the United States from a wartime society to a peacetime society?
3. How did the problems of prices and production put Truman in a political bind?
4. Why did the end of the war bring labor problems for Truman?
5. Why did Truman veto the Taft-Hartley Act?
6. How does the Eightieth Congress represent the difficulties of a Democratic President working with a Republican Congress?

2. The Illusive Peace

While the United States demobilized over 9 million men and women, Russia maintained an armed force of 10 million. This fact gave cause for a great deal of uneasiness. The spread of Russian-directed communism could not be ignored. So Congress reintroduced the draft in June 1948, a draft that had ended only eighteen months before. Throughout Europe and Asia, the United States became engaged in a new struggle that people did not yet fully understand.

The Foundation of the United Nations

Before the end of World War II, the "Big Three" powers—the United States, Russia, and Great Britain—had hammered out plans not only for the war, but also for the peace. In the Atlantic Treaty of 1942, the United States and Great Britain had expressed a desire to establish a "system of general security." The following year at the Moscow Conference of Foreign Ministers, the great powers accepted the idea of a United Nations organization.

Within the next two years, other conferences were also held. The ideas for a world organization finally took shape. At the Yalta Conference in 1945, the last conference Roosevelt attended, the United States, Britain, and Russia agreed that "a general international organization to maintain peace and security" would be formed. They discussed in detail which nations should be admitted. They also decided how much veto power the members could exercise.

Before his death, Roosevelt had sent out invitations to a conference to be held in San Francisco. He invited the countries that had declared war on Germany and Japan before March 1945 to send delegates. The purpose of this conference was to draft a charter for the new organization. Roosevelt chose an American delegation that included prominent members of Congress from both political parties. Roosevelt did this because he was determined to avoid the political rivalries that had doomed the United States entry into the League of Nations after World War I. As it turned out, President Truman, in office less than two weeks, headed the delegation.

From the outset of the conference, it was obvious that agreements would be hard to reach. In fact, it took three days just to decide who would chair the proceedings. Fearing undue influence of the United States, the Russians objected to the usual procedure of allowing the host country to appoint a chairperson. Many other compromises were necessary before the **Charter** was finally presented for ratification.

charter
a document outlining the principles, functions, and structure of an organization

On October 24, 1945, the United Nations became an official organization when its charter was ratified. The Charter of the United Nations provided for a General Assembly made up of all members. This body would investigate, debate, and recommend. The Security Council was to consist of five permanent and six elected members. Only the Council was given the power to act in international disputes. However, a veto by any of the permanent members—the United States, Britain, Russia, France, and China—would prevent any action. As the Cold War developed, the Russians frequently used their veto power.

Yet, some reason for hope still remained. The United Nations in its first years did score some successes. It served as a forum for many ideas. It also helped reduce tension in several international crises.

Delegates from 50 nations attended the United Nations Conference on International Organization in San Francisco on April 25, 1945. At this conference, the United Nations Charter was drafted and ultimately approved.

The United Nations and the Middle East

The strength of the United Nations was put to two very early tests. These tests involved the Middle Eastern countries of Iran and Palestine.

During World War II, Russian troops were stationed in Iran to prevent Nazi takeover in that area. By December 1945, when British and United States support troops were withdrawing, the Russian troops were not. In a demand sent to the Security Council early in 1946, the United States called for the immediate withdrawal of these troops. Shortly thereafter, Iran announced that the Russian troops had finally withdrawn.

In the second situation, in Palestine, the problem was different. After World War I, the League of Nations had granted Britain a *mandate*, or control, over Palestine. In the years following World War I, Britain allowed Jewish immigrants to settle in Palestine. This site had been the ancient Jewish homeland. Hitler's persecution of the Jews caused an increase in immigration to this area. Tensions sprouted between the Arabs who were already in Palestine and the Jews who were now coming in greater numbers.

As World War II ended, there were those who believed that the time had come to reestablish a Jewish homeland in the Middle East. Britain turned the question over to the General Assembly of the United Nations. The United Nations proposed to divide Palestine into two states. One would be Jewish, the other Arab. In April 1948, the British mandate ended. Israel immediately declared its independence. Within eleven minutes, the United States recognized the state of Israel.

Almost as quickly, neighboring Arab countries went to war with Israel. But they were unable to overwhelm the new nation. Immediately, the United Nations began negotiations. Finally, the UN mediator, Ralph Bunche, was able to get the warring parties to call a cease-fire. The United Nations also set up emergency relief services for the Palestinians who fled from Israel during the hostilities. Many Palestinian refugees were refused admittance by other Arab countries. Others chose to remain in refugee camps as a symbol of resistance. This area was to remain a source of world tension for years to come.

The Clash of the Superpowers

Russian control of much of eastern Europe was another source of postwar conflict. In 1944, Russia had seized the small Baltic nations of Estonia, Latvia, and Lithuania. By 1946, it had taken parts of Poland and East Prussia. By 1948, Russia controlled most of the East European countries. In the countries occupied by Russian troops, puppet communist regimes were set up, which were controlled from Moscow. In these *satellite nations* —countries under the domination or influence of others—all those who did not put Russian interests first were suppressed.

The British and American governments became convinced that the Soviet Union was doing more than just acting like a great power influencing other countries. They decided that the Russians wanted what Winston Churchill had called "the indefinite expansion of their power." Many Americans who had been sympathetic to Russia during

In 1945, Germany was divided into four sectors—American, British, French, and Russian. Berlin, inside the Russian sector, was divided similarly. Russia closed Allied access routes to Berlin in June 1948. In response, President Truman ordered an airlift of supplies to the city. Over 2 million tons were flown in before the blockade ended in May 1949.

Suspicion of Russian support for a communist insurrection against the Greek government in 1947 caused the United States to respond with $400 million in military aid. That aid included supplies such as the jeep shown in the above photograph.

the war began to share this view. They believed Churchill's warning that an "iron curtain" was coming down over the European continent.

It was also suspected that Russia was sending soldiers from Yugoslavia and Albania to support a communist guerrilla uprising against the Greek government. In March 1947, President Truman decided that the moment had come for action. He believed that if Greece fell, the Communists would soon threaten neighboring Turkey. So Truman asked Congress for $400 million in military aid for Greece and Turkey. Truman claimed that dictatorial governments forced upon free peoples weakened peace everywhere. This in turn weakened American security. Congress granted Truman his request. The United States was now pledged to defend anticommunist nations against attack or communist-led revolutions. This policy became known as the *Truman Doctrine*. It was based on the belief that communism could not be eliminated. However, it could be contained in those countries where it was already established. Even then, some people foresaw that the policy of **containment** could involve the United States in wars to defend friendly governments against communists. Russia would be able to pick the time and the place.

containment
the policy of restricting the territorial growth or strategic power of a hostile nation

The Marshall Plan

The Marshall Plan was a successful outgrowth of the Truman Doctrine. At first, the United States did not realize how badly Europe

George Marshall, Secretary of State under President Truman, was the architect of the Marshall Plan.

had been damaged by the war. Americans were more concerned with finding jobs and settling down. They had not really been touched by the reality that Europeans were dying from starvation and lack of shelter. Everywhere communists were taking advantage of the widespread misery in Europe.

A government official who had spent weeks traveling in Europe made a dramatic report to the President. Soon all Americans were aware of the desperate conditions in Europe. In June 1947, Secretary of State George Marshall suggested that the United States offer Europe a comprehensive aid program. The United States would give money, machinery, and supplies to any country that agreed to participate in the program. The plan, which was not anticommunist oriented, was also offered to the Soviet Union. But the Russians denounced it as another act of imperialism by the Americans. American opponents of the Marshall Plan argued that the United States could not afford such a charitable plan.

Within weeks, applications for aid came from European countries. Within months after the plan's passage by congress in early 1948, malnutrition had been significantly reduced and many industries were back in operation. The plan was a tremendous success.

During Truman's first administration, world leadership had passed from the dying British Empire to the United States. The Truman Doctrine and the Marshall Plan held off the immediate collapse of the surviving democracies in Europe. But American actions strengthened communist resistance. The policy of containment now faced many severe tests.

Questions for Discussion
1. Define *mandate, charter, satellite, containment.*
2. What actions were taken in the creation of the United Nations to avoid the mistakes that were made in the creation of the League of Nations?
3. How did the Truman Doctrine institute the American policy of containment?

3. The Cold War

One of the first challenges to the policy of containment came in Europe. After the war, Germany and its capital city were divided among Britain, the United States, Russia, and France. Each country was to administer its sector until all of them together reached a decision on the future of Germany. The Russians tested the American will to support a free Germany. In 1948, they cut off land routes through the Russian-occupied zone that supplied Berlin. Instead of abandoning the city, the United States used airplanes to bring in supplies.

HARRY S TRUMAN

A History Lesson from Missouri Not much was known about the personality of Vice President Harry S Truman when he took office in April of 1945. Only later did the world find out that he was a man with strong views and one who did not budge if he was sure he was right.

But the White House staff found out early that Truman was very well read in the history of his country. One day Truman walked into a White House room, and looked at a rug into which was woven the Great Seal of the United States. (You can see the Seal on the back of a dollar bill.) The new President looked at the picture depicting an eagle holding the arrows of war and the olive branch of peace in its two claws.

"It's wrong," he snapped. The eagle's head was facing the arrows, and not the olive branch. "Fix it," he ordered. There were smiles. How did a former Missouri businessman, without higher education, know what the original design of the Great Seal was? And it did matter? But Harry Truman believed that everything about the White House should be as nearly perfect as it was possible to make it.

The rug was fixed.

Day and night, American planes flew the airplanes over Russian-occupied territory. Their destination was an airfield in Berlin. Their cargo was 2.5 million tons of food, fuel, and raw materials. By May 1949, eleven months later, the warehouses in West Berlin were crammed with supplies. Stalin finally put a stop to the blockade.

The Soviet blockade of Berlin and the communist opposition to the Marshall Plan spurred other European countries into action. These countries felt the need for a common defense against the Russian threat. In April 1949, nine European nations joined the United States, Canada, and Iceland to form an economic and military alliance. This alliance was called the North Atlantic Treaty Organization (NATO). The membership was later expanded to fifteen countries.

That summer, the British, French, and American zones of Germany combined to form the Federal Republic of Germany (West Germany). Soviet authorities then set up the communist-controlled German Democratic Republic in their zone (East Germany). After recovering from its war damage, West Germany also joined NATO. East Germany became part of the alliance system of the Soviet Union. The split in Germany symbolized the division of Europe into eastern and western camps.

President Truman's belief that communism could be contained, but not eliminated, was the basis for the policy that became known as the Truman Doctrine.

Civil War in China

In Asia, things did not go well for the Truman Doctrine of defending nations against communist-led revolutions. A civil war in China ended with a communist victory in 1949. This victory overturned nearly half a century of American policy. The United States

Under the leadership of Mao Tsetung (left), state-controlled communes in mainland China nearly tripled food production by 1958. Russian technology spurred the growth of industry (right).

had always tried to keep a friendly Chinese government in power. This was the idea behind the Open Door policy. Moreover, the United States had, in large part, fought Japan to prevent Japanese control of the Chinese land, people, and economy.

During the 1930s, China had actually become divided between two governments. Chiang Kai-shek, the dictatorial leader of the Nationalist Party, united the leaders of many provinces to fight the Japanese after 1937. But he could not always count on the support of the people. Many of his followers were loyal to him only because he did not investigate their corrupt deeds. Meanwhile, the Chinese Communists had won control of the northeastern provinces of the country. They were dictatorial, disciplined, and dedicated. Until 1945, the Communists and Chiang Kai-shek fought Japan together. Now the country was at war within itself.

After 1945, both Nationalist and Communist groups claimed the right to govern all China. The United States sent one of its ablest soldiers, General George C. Marshall, to try to work out an agreement between them. Marshall failed. War broke out early in 1947. It soon became clear that Chiang Kai-shek was losing. The United States believed that nothing could save Chiang except American troops and supplies. Unwilling to enter the fight, the United States watched as Chiang was driven back. By 1949, he was forced to flee to the island of Taiwan (Formosa) off the southern coast of China. There were now two Chinese governments—the Communist People's Republic of China on the mainland and the Republic of China on Taiwan. The United States continued to recognize Chiang's government as the official government of all China.

The Chinese Communists soon began a program of industrial development and mass propaganda. At first, the communist takeover of mainland China was thought to be a victory for Russia. But the Chinese Communists soon showed that they were more interested in their own national welfare than in Soviet needs. Though at first they accepted much-needed Russian help, by the late 1960s, they had broken with Russia. That opened the way for new developments in Chinese-American relations in the 1970s.

The Korean War

In 1950, another part of Asia exploded. From 1910 to 1945, Japan had controlled Korea. Russia's last-minute declaration of war against Japan in World War II gave Russia the right to invade Korea. Since 1945, Korea had been occupied by both Russian and American troops, in a pattern similar to the Russian-American occupation of Germany. As in Germany, two separate governments had been established. The government in the North was supported by Stalin and Mao Tse-tung, the Chinese Communist leader. The government in the South, under Syngman Rhee, was set up under United Nations observation. When both Russia and the United States withdrew their armies, the dividing line between the two armies became the boundary between two hostile Korean nations. Suddenly, on June 25, 1950, forces of the Communist Republic of North Korea smashed across the border, the 38th parallel, and invaded South Korea. It was assumed these troops had been encouraged and armed by Stalin.

Within two days, President Truman ordered American troops into Korea. He also asked for an emergency session of the United Nations Security Council. Russia boycotted the session. When the Security Council voted to send a peacekeeping force to Korea, Russia thus could not object. The United Nations force was placed under the command of

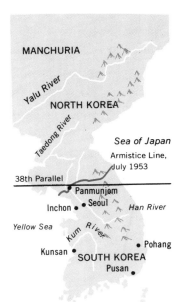

The Korean War

Below Left: American troops in combat in Korea. Below Right: General MacArthur assures President Truman that the Chinese will not enter the Korean War.

653

General Douglas MacArthur. Over 90 percent of the troops were American and South Korean. For this reason, the Korean War is often thought of as an American conflict. However, soldiers from over one dozen countries—including Australia, New Zealand, the United Kingdom, and Canada—participated.

At first, the North Koreans, with their Russian equipment, nearly pushed the Americans and South Koreans into the sea. The combined force managed to hold the port of Pusan until MacArthur was able to muster air and naval forces. On September 25, 1950, he used this support to launch an amphibious attack on Inchon, a coastal port near the South Korean capital of Seoul. The attack was well thought out and well executed. MacArthur met with success. From that point on, General MacArthur and his troops turned the tide and sent the Communist forces reeling back across the 38th parallel. They pressed on into North Korea to "punish the aggressors." The Chinese Communists warned that they would not stand for United Nations forces approaching their border with North Korea. General Mac-Arthur told President Truman that the Chinese would not attack and that, if they did, the Chinese would be defeated. With this assurance, President Truman gave General MacArthur approval to bring troops to the Yalu River, the border with China. In mid-October, MacArthur's troops were within a few miles of the Chinese border. In late November 1950, the Chinese Communist troops entered the battle. In MacArthur's report he said, "We face an entirely new war." Mao Tse-tung's "volunteer" troops, equipped with Russian tanks and planes, drove hard through the harsh terrain and the bitter cold winter. Stories came back to the United States about the treacherous conditions and the torture of United Nations prisoners.

For the American people, this was a shocking experience. A second shock came when the United States did not at once launch air attacks on enemy bases and supply routes inside China. This had been the desire of General MacArthur. He believed that in war, there was "no substitute for victory." He proposed bombing Chinese industrial cities, blockading the Chinese coast, and supporting a Nationalist Chinese invasion of Communist China. President Truman, however, announced that, "our goal is not war but peace." He and the **Joint Chiefs of Staff** feared that such action might provoke Russia into starting an atomic war in defense of its communist ally. MacArthur challenged President Truman's authority. He had been ordered not to make any statements that conflicted with UN policy. Yet, he publicly criticized the President's decision not to invade or attack China. As a result, Truman fired General MacArthur on April 11, 1951. He replaced him with General Matthew Ridgway. Ridgway was able to drive the enemy back across the 38th parallel.

Joint Chiefs of Staff
the Chiefs of Staff of the army, the air force, and the navy who serve as the major military advisory body to the President

654

General MacArthur receives a hero's welcome in New York following his dismissal by President Truman early in 1951.

MacArthur returned to the United States where he was greeted with a hero's welcome. Throughout the country and before Congress, he defended his position. Average citizens and prominent officials were outraged at Truman's action—at first. The Chiefs of Staff, whom Truman had consulted, made their feelings public. They said that if the United States got involved in war with China, the United States would spend its strength and leave Russia unharmed. One adviser said that it was "the wrong war, at the wrong place, at the wrong time, and with the wrong enemy." In the end, enthusiasm for MacArthur's position waned.

So the war surged back and forth. Neither side could win without the risk of starting a third world war. It was now clear to both sides that the best way out was to work out a settlement calling for a return to the division of Korea before 1950. In June 1951, the Communists agreed to discuss an armistice. Only a very popular American could sponsor a "no-win" standoff without facing charges of a "sellout" to the Communists. Such a man was Dwight D. Eisenhower, elected President in November 1952. Eisenhower visited Korea, then approved peace talks that lasted two years. During that time, Stalin died. His successor, Georgi Malenkov, seemed to favor some peace proposals. A breakthrough developed when an agreement was reached to exchange sick and wounded prisoners. Further discussions led to an armistice, finally signed on July 27, 1953. When the time came to exchange all prisoners, 23 percent refused to return to North Korea. Only 3 percent refused to return to South Korea.

Left: Korean refugees fleeing from the enemy pass by American infantrymen who are on their way into battle. Right: President-elect Eisenhower, who had promised during the campaign to visit Korea and end the war, tours battlefield sites with General James Fry in December 1952.

In this new kind of war, 33,000 Americans died. Many Americans were disappointed that the United States had not scored a decisive victory. However, the communist invasion had been stopped. Korea remained divided, like Germany, into communist and noncommunist countries. American troops remained in Korea to help guard the border between the two nations.

The Cold War at Home

During this period, the fear of communism in the United States increased. Soviet relations with the United States and the Korean War were among the causing factors. Many Americans wondered if the Communist Party was a political party or a foreign conspiracy. Certain real events led some people to imagine the worst.

From Canada came a report of a spy ring. Several well-known scientists and a member of Parliament were feeding atomic secrets to the Russians. This news, coupled with a leak of confidential information to one publication, jangled official nerves. In 1947, President Truman ordered an investigation of the loyalty of all federal employees. Within four years, over 3 million civil servants were investigated. Two thousand resigned, and 212 were dismissed as security risks.

Meanwhile, the House Un-American Activities Committee was conducting sensational investigations. It claimed that the nation was riddled with **subversives**—in unions, schools, and the entertainment industry. So many reckless charges were made that some people felt that the committee itself was un-American. But the committee did uncover some disturbing evidence.

subversives
those who attempt to overthrow or cause the destruction of an established government

In a hearing before the committee, Whitaker Chambers, a former Soviet agent, told his story. He claimed that Alger Hiss, a former State Department employee, had given him documents to send to Russia. Hiss denied all the charges. The evidence seemed to outweigh his defense. After two trials, Hiss was finally found guilty of perjury—lying under oath—and sentenced to five years in prison.

A more serious case of espionage was uncovered by the FBI, working with Canadian and British agencies. After four years of investigation, Dr. Klaus Fuchs, an atomic scientist, was arrested in England for involvement in a Canadian spy ring and linked to Julius and Ethel Rosenberg, two Americans. The Rosenbergs were arrested and convicted of passing atomic secrets to the Russians. They, too, insisted that they were innocent, but on March 29, 1951, they were sentenced to death, a sentence thought by some to be excessively harsh in peacetime. The Rosenbergs were executed on June 19, 1953.

Events such as these provided an opportunity for Senator Joseph McCarthy of Wisconsin to ride the wave of anticommunist feeling. McCarthy made outrageous claims about the number of communists working in the State Department. He led a widely publicized hunt for subversives. Many people lost their jobs and were subject to public disapproval. But no communists or spies were found. McCarthy finally went too far. He questioned the integrity of the Secretary of the Army and some army officers. He also accused certain Senators of being too

THE ARMY-McCARTHY HEARINGS

For four years, Wisconsin Senator Joseph McCarthy made headlines with his largely unsupported claims that various public figures were communists. In 1954, he finally went too far. In attacking the Army, McCarthy found an opponent that would not be bullied.

The Army countered McCarthy's charges of harboring communists with charges of its own. It alleged that the Senator and his aides had sought special treatment in the army for a member of their staff. The televised investigation of these charges lasted thirty-five days. The drama of the hearings riveted the eyes of the nation to the television screen. Television was to play a large part in the downfall of McCarthy and his "witchhunts."

For the first time, McCarthy's bullying tactics failed him. He had met his match in chief Army counsel Joseph Welch, whose softspoken, often humorously-expressed questions cut through McCarthy's ravings and cries for "point of order." Before 20 million Americans, McCarthy became not a hero, but a pathetic figure who had for too long used his position to ruin the lives of innocent Americans.

Senator Joseph McCarthy (left) with two of his top aides, counsel Roy Cohn (standing, center) and Francis Carr (right, background).

easy on communists. The Senate then publicly criticized and investigated his unfounded charges. McCarthy was finally discredited, and, in 1954, stripped of his power by the Senate.

Fear of aliens accompanied the fear of communists. In June 1952, over President Truman's veto, Congress passed the McCarran-Walter Act. This law kept the discriminatory national-origin quotas of 1924. Measures to screen out subversives were added. However, the ban against Asians and Pacific peoples was lifted.

The years following World War II were a troubled time for the United States and for the world. When the United States acquired the leadership of the free world, it acquired many world problems as well. When the 1952 election was held, Americans sought relief. They looked to a war hero—Dwight D. Eisenhower—as a kindly, reassuring leader who would make everything right.

Questions for Discussion

1. Define *Joint Chiefs of Staff, subversives.*
2. How did the Berlin airlift represent a United States victory in the Cold War?
3. In 1949, after the creation of two Chinese governments, why did the United States choose to recognize the Republic of China on Taiwan?
4. Why did Truman recall General Douglas MacArthur during the Korean War?
5. Was the Korean War a success or failure in America's policy of containment?
6. How did the Cold War manifest itself in the United States?

Chapter 28 Review

Summary Questions for Discussion

1. What problems did Truman inherit?
2. Why was demobilization slowed up? How did the public react? What was the result?
3. Why didn't the United States return to a policy of isolationism after World War II?
4. What is the role of the General Assembly of the United Nations? Of the Security Council?
5. Describe the situations and the successful role played by the United Nations in Iran and Palestine in the late 1940s.
6. What prompted Truman to issue the Truman Doctrine?
7. Why was the Marshall Plan instituted?
8. Why was the economic situation after World War II better than it was after World War I?
9. What caused the problem of inflation after World War II?
10. What were President Truman's beliefs concerning labor?
11. How did Truman react to strikes by miners and railway workers?
12. What provisions of the Taft-Hartley Act were passed?
13. What civil rights legislation did Truman support? What was the result in Congress? What actions did Truman take?
14. Who supported Truman's election in 1948? Why?
15. How did Russia test American support of Berlin?
16. Why was NATO formed?
17. How did the communist victory in China in 1949 overturn half a century of American policy?
18. How was the United Nations able to send forces into South Korea without the Soviet Union vetoing it?
19. What were the results of the Korean War?
20. Identify Senator Joseph McCarthy. Describe his activities.

Word Study

Fill in each blank in the sentences that follow with the term below that is most appropriate.

demobilization   closed shop   secondary boycott
swing shifts   Joint Chiefs of Staff subversives
featherbedding   containment

1. The discharging of the personnel in the armed forces is known as _____.
2. American foreign policy aimed at limiting communism to areas where it already exists is known as _____.
3. In order to increase production and the effective use of the labor force, industries often employ _____.
4. In a _____, an effort is made to persuade the public not to buy the products of a company that supplies materials to a plant whose workers are on strike.
5. The practice whereby unions force employers to hire more workers than necessary to do a particular job is know as _____.
6. The _____ are the overall commanders of the United States armed forces.
7. Senator Joseph McCarthy sought to uncover and punish _____, who he felt were undermining the United States.

Using Your Skills

Refer to the map "The Korean War" on page 653. Where was the Armistice line drawn in 1953? Why is a peace drawn on an arbitrary line?

CHAPTER 29

An Intermission of Stability: The Fifties

Americans tend to look back on the fifties as a simpler time. For many, the fifties was an era of calm, growth, and prosperity.

Politically, the fifties was typified in mood by President Dwight D. Eisenhower. Ike set the pace for the era with his slow, deliberate style, conservative outlook, and lack of emphasis on ideology.

Economically, the fifties was a time of great advancement for many Americans. Consumer demand skyrocketed, the housing industry flourished, and foreign trade increased dramatically. America was entering an age of a new kind of wealth. By the end of the decade, the majority of American households had at least one car, a television set, a washing machine, and a refrigerator. The use of credit cards was strongly encouraged. Many people used this system of *deferred payment*—payment withheld for or until a certain time—to live out wild buying fantasies.

Culturally, the nation experienced a boom such as it had never experienced before. Mass production put art and literature within the grasp of almost everyone. Television made news, sports, and cultural events immediately available to the entire country.

Although the prevailing mood of the nation was calm throughout the fifties, the decade was not without its problems. Racial discrimination continued to set White against Black. The concept of desegregation remained little more than a dream until the sixties. The Korean War had everyone concerned and uneasy. Americans were worried that a failure in Korea would encourage the expansion of communism.

For many Americans, the decade of the fifties was a brief pause between the terror of World War II and the anxious tension of the Cold War. For many others, it was an era of intense struggle.

READING GUIDE

1. **How did Eisenhower view the role of government?**
2. **What forces were changing American life?**
3. **In what ways was Eisenhower's foreign policy a continuation of Truman's foreign policy?**
4. **How was American determination to contain communism tested in President John F. Kennedy's administration?**

Norman Rockwell's "After the Prom" typifies one view of the fifties in the United States as a decade of simplicity and innocence.

Norman Rockwell

1. The Return of the Republicans

In November, 1952, Republicans had cause to celebrate. Dwight D. Eisenhower had defeated the Democratic candidate, Adlai Stevenson. The election of Eisenhower brought the first Republican administration in twenty years.

Each President has come into office with an idea of what his role will be. In turn, each President has imprinted his own style on the office. Eisenhower was no different. He believed that Roosevelt and Truman had seized too much power from Congress. Thus, Eisenhower planned to "reestablish" the balance between the executive and the legislative branches of government. He expected Congress to form its own programs without White House pressure and intervention. He expected his staff to do the same. Eisenhower's years of Army training had taught him how to delegate authority. The members of his Cabinet were supposed to make plans and carry them out without bothering him with day-to-day details. Eisenhower saw his role as one of promoting cooperation and harmony between the branches of government.

As a result, Eisenhower's appointees had a great deal of power and influence. For the most part, they were people who had been successful in big business. The President had a high opinion of business people. Three members of his Cabinet had formerly been with the General Motors Corporation. Charles E. Wilson was named Secretary of Defense. Arthur Summerfield was appointed Postmaster General. Douglas Mackay was appointed Secretary of the Interior. The Secretary of State was John Foster Dulles, a corporate lawyer who specialized in international law. George Humphrey, Secretary of the

Dwight D. Eisenhower's election to the Presidency in 1952 inaugurated a new era of stability and progress in America. Under the Eisenhower administration, the national economy expanded and business prospered. Significant gains were made toward integrating the nation, and programs were set up to provide greater funding for public education.

Treasury, was successful in the steel and coal industries. Oveta Culp Hobby, publisher of the *Houston Post*, headed the newly created Department of Health, Education and Welfare. Many people were concerned that Eisenhower's Cabinet represented only big business interests. In time, it became evident that certain administration decisions and appointments favored big business.

The same election that brought Eisenhower into office also returned Joseph McCarthy to the Senate. But people still remembered McCarthy for the years of false accusations and twisted testimony. He was now surrounded by an atmosphere of suspicion. No longer could people be sure that they would be judged solely by what they did. Loyalty was now being determined on the basis of a person's friends, associates, and ideas.

Some Supreme Court decisions supported these feelings. Others counterbalanced them. In a series of decisions handed down by the Court during the early fifties, several abuses were prevented. The State Department was prevented from denying passports at will. The NAACP was protected from having to disclose its membership and activities. In addition, a state attorney general was denied the right to spy on college professors.

During Eisenhower's administration, there was an unusual blend of liberal and conservative action in each branch of government. On April 11, 1953, the Department of Health, Education and Welfare was created. Oveta Culp Hobby was sworn in as its first Secretary. The President was trying to show an interest in human rights while at the same time favoring states' rights and economic conservatism.

As Secretary of State in the Eisenhower Cabinet, John Foster Dulles was a major force in American foreign policy from 1953 to 1959. Truman had believed in the policy of containment. Dulles took a hard-line approach to American involvement in world affairs; he advocated a policy of "liberation" of communist-held territories. He also believed that the United States had committed itself to hold West Berlin from the communists—by force, if necessary.

Economics and Economies

One major goal of Eisenhower's administration was to balance the budget. For years, Republicans had found fault with the rising national debt. Now that they were in power, they hoped to get rid of some expensive government programs. Some Republicans even hoped to sweep away the results of the New Deal and the Fair Deal. As Eisenhower put it, he was looking for things that the government could stop doing rather than for things it could start doing.

The Republicans found that it was easier to preach decreased spending than to practice it. In the twenty years that the Republicans had been out of power, the world had changed. Few politicians would talk seriously about doing away with social security, federal responsibility for full employment, or government regulation of business.

Many items on the federal budget could not be greatly reduced or eliminated. Payments of interest on debts and veterans benefits were required by law. Only so much could be saved by reusing paper clips and shortening coffee breaks. The Republicans decreased federal employment by 200,000 workers. But 2.2 million people still remained on the federal payroll.

The major outlay of the federal budget was for military defense and foreign aid. Any attempt to cut spending in these areas usually brought cries from the Democrats about weakening national security. In the early years of the Eisenhower administration, it was possible to decrease defense spending. An armistice was reached in Korea. In the years that followed, however, defense spending rose again. The development of new weapons and increased foreign aid were responsible for this rise. The administration stressed the development of nuclear weapons over conventional ones.

The Eisenhower administration was also faced with problems of inflation and recession. When inflation became a serious problem, the Secretary of the Treasury took steps to make it harder for private borrowers to obtain loans. Tax cuts were made, and social security benefits were raised. Both Eisenhower and his Cabinet favored waiting out the recession. They depended on private industry to return prosperity by increasing spending and investment.

In 1958, a more serious economic recession endangered "Eisenhower prosperity." The President again favored a moderate approach. Despite demands for a tax cut that would increase a budget deficit, Eisenhower held firm. He did use other means for easing the economic slowdown. He increased spending for the interstate highway system, college dormitory construction, and urban renewal. Federal defense contracts were awarded to areas where unemployment was most severe. Eisenhower also asked Americans to spend more money. The results of these measures were temporarily successful.

One nagging problem that undermined Eisenhower's attempts to achieve a balanced budget was the farm surplus. Even when the nation

In response to soaring dairy prices brought on by government stockpiling of farm surpluses, consumers rebelled. Boycotts were suggested by owners of small groceries as well as by their customers.

was prosperous, farm income was falling. The farm population decreased each year. But each year farming output rose. The Truman administration had used price supports to keep farm income up.

Eisenhower recognized the need to help the farmers. At first, he favored high price supports for farm products. But the Secretary of Agriculture, Ezra Taft Benson, convinced him that this policy encouraged overproduction. The government had to pay for the storage of surpluses. Benson recommended flexible price supports and incentives for producing products such as wool and milk. Still, the farmers' share of the national income continued to fall. In 1956, Congress set up the "soil bank" program. This program authorized payments to farmers for taking acreage out of production. Instead of producing crops, the farmers could plant trees on the land or build dams and reservoirs. Other programs were put into affect to get rid of the surplus. Excess food was used for school lunch programs and for disaster relief. Some surpluses were traded for goods that the United States needed from abroad.

However, none of these measures curbed the declining farm income and growing surpluses. The more measures that were tried, the more bountiful was the harvest. Despite everything, Eisenhower's administration increased aid to farmers sixfold between 1952 and 1956.

Eisenhower's economic policy reflected his respect for private industry and a balanced budget. His efforts to reduce federal spending and cut taxes pleased big business. For most of his eight years in office, the national economy expanded and businesses thrived. Yet, Eisenhower balanced the budget only three times. Toward the end of the fifties, the economy began to slow down. Unfortunately, Eisenhower did nothing to launch major programs to counteract growing unemployment and an increasing rate of inflation.

Questions for Discussion

1. Define *deferred payment*.
2. How did Eisenhower view his role as President? What effect did this have on his selection of appointees?
3. How did President Eisenhower show an interest in human rights?
4. In what ways did Eisenhower's economic policies reflect his respect for private industry and a balanced budget?

2. The Changing Scene

When President Eisenhower took the oath of office, civil rights for Black people had not progressed in over fifty years. President Truman had tried to make some changes. However, many of his plans had been stopped by a conservative Congress. Had the civil-rights movement been left up to Eisenhower and Congress, another fifty years could have passed without any significant changes. But new demands were beginning to stir among American Blacks.

What had prompted this new attitude? When Blacks returned from the war, they encountered many of the same prejudices at home that they had fought against for others abroad. They realized that drastic changes were necessary in order to achieve a decent standard of living. Conditions in the North were not much better than in the South. Discrimination in housing and employment still played a major role in frustrating many.

Some Blacks reached new heights in education and employment after the war. Their numbers were insignificant when compared to the vast number of Blacks who remained poor and shut off from equal opportunity.

On May 17, 1954, a milestone was reached in the attack on racial discrimination. On that day, the Supreme Court ruled, in the case of *Brown* v. *Board of Education of Topeka*, on a suit brought by some Black Kansas citizens against segregated schools. The high court unanimously overturned the 1896 doctrine of *Plessy* v. *Ferguson*. That doctrine had defended "separate but equal" public facilities. Now the nine justices said that a segregated education was unequal by its nature. It was also a violation of the Fourteenth Amendment. The following year, the Supreme Court ordered seventeen states to desegregate their schools "with all deliberate speed."

Some states complied. Others resisted. One district even went to the extreme of closing down its public schools rather than desegregate them.

In September 1957, a federal court ordered Little Rock, Arkansas, to admit nine Black students to Central High School. But the governor of Arkansas, Orval Faubus, decided to buck the order and prevent the entry of the students. He summoned the National Guard and stationed them around the school to prevent the students from entering.

Eisenhower, who was vacationing in Newport, Rhode Island, summoned Faubus to a conference. After the discussion, Faubus continued to resist. Finally, a federal court issued an order that prevented Faubus from barring the students. In addition, Eisenhower had to federalize the National Guard and send federal troops to protect the Black students when they finally gained entry.

This new attitude became more apparent when Rosa Parks, a Black woman returning home after work, refused to give up her seat on a bus to a White passenger. The year was 1955. Rosa Parks was arrested and fined $10 for violating the segregation laws of Montgomery, Alabama. The Blacks of that city joined in a common cause—to

When Arkansas Governor Orval Faubus called out the National Guard to block Black students from entering a previously segregated high school, a tense confrontation between the state and the federal government was set up.

After a federal court ordered the National Guardsmen removed from Central High School in Little Rock, hostile mobs of Whites resisted the attempts of Black students to enter the school. President Eisenhower then ordered troops to the school again to prevent violence and to allow the Black students to attend.

fight these laws. For a year, they boycotted the public transportation system in Montgomery. The boycott was so effective that the bus company had to raise its rates for the other riders to keep from going bankrupt. In 1956, a federal district court declared the bus segregation laws of Alabama unconstitutional.

Out of this protest, Dr. Martin Luther King, Jr., emerged as a leader in the struggle for equal rights. The son of a leading Atlanta minister, he was the pastor of a Baptist church in Montgomery. Dr. King taught his followers that the best weapon to use against discrimination was nonviolent demonstration. In September 1957,

King, along with Bayard Rustin and others, organized the Southern Christian Leadership Conference (SCLC). They hoped to achieve full rights for Blacks as well as integration in all aspects of their lives. By the end of the 1950s, it was clear that integration was an idea whose time had come.

The Baby Boom and Education

The system of education in the United States faced many strains during the fifties due to causes beyond its control. In 1947, the birthrate had been 25.8 births per thousand. This compared with 16.6 per thousand in 1933. The large baby population was ready for kindergarten in 1952. But was kindergarten ready for it? Throughout the country, the growth of the suburbs was spreading out a population that would need new schools.

After World War II, many people came to realize the value of higher education. The G.I. Bill, prosperity, new pressures for women's rights, and the civil-rights movement increased the demand for education. In 1900, only 11 percent of 14- to 17-year-olds were enrolled in full-time high schools. By 1940, the percentage was up to 73 percent. College enrollment expanded at the same time. By the postwar years, 2.4 million students enrolled in colleges and universities that had an enrollment of 1.4 million students before the war.

Schools and universities had to compete with private industry for qualified teachers. But public education could rarely pay the high salaries that industry paid. Thus, the schools lost out because qualified people usually went for the better-paying jobs. While colleges and universities were struggling over what to teach and how to get the money to do it, the Russians launched a satellite—Sputnik I—in October 1957. Suddenly attention turned toward American education. Was a weak education system the cause of the United States' failure to launch the first satellite?

Parents and educators alike were jolted by John Gunther's book *Inside Russia Today*. Gunther reported that Russian students attended school six hours a day, six days a week. They were assigned four hours of homework a day during their last two years in school. In addition, emphasis was placed on science and technology. For example, while only 50 percent of American students had any physics education, Russian students were required to have five years of physics, six years of biology, and four years of chemistry.

Even before the Russian space success, Eisenhower had tried to develop a program of federal aid to education. Now he had an excellent case. Though large-scale aid to elementary education did not develop until the Johnson administration, Eisenhower was able to get some money for higher education. Congress and the public agreed that it was necessary for national security. In September 1958, Congress passed the National Defense Education Act. This law set up a $295 million loan fund for college students. Federal matching grants were provided to states that spent money for laboratory equipment and texts for mathematics, science, and modern language education. To meet the increased demand for college instructors, fellowships were provided for those going into college teaching.

Meanwhile, something else was happening that was to affect education in the United States. People of all economic classes were watching television—in mansions, development homes, mobile trailers, and tenements. Television was here to stay.

The Cultural Explosion

One of the most significant trends of the fifties was the mass production of culture. This was due in large part to advancements in technology. Never before had the arts been so available to so many Americans.

The most widely acclaimed development of the cultural explosion was the arrival of television. A minor statistic in Baltimore in May 1950 signaled a major change in American homes. For the first time, evening television viewers in one community outnumbered the radio listeners. Although early televisions had only tiny screens and poor reception, television sets developed rapidly as a means of mass communication.

In its infancy, all television was locally produced. By September 1951, however, that was changed. The first coast-to-coast broadcast was made via cable and microwave. Soon thousands of relay stations were built. Now, the switch from radio to television went into high gear. People were buying televisions at a rate of 20,000 a day. By the end of the decade, 46 million sets had been purchased.

At its best, television served as an excellent news medium, presented high-quality dramas and fun-filled comedies, and even provided some much-needed educational programming. Nightly, Americans watched commentator Edward R. Murrow, comedians Milton Berle, Sid Caesar, Ernie Kovacs, and Lucille Ball, talk show hosts Steve Allen and Jack Parr, and Burr Tillstrom's marvelous puppet show, *Kukla*, *Fran*, and *Ollie*.

There were some negative aspects to television as well. Minorities were usually not represented. When they did appear, they were portrayed in stereotyped roles as domestics or people with little or no sense. With the televised Estes Kefauver crime hearings and the Army-McCarthy hearings came the realization that television could break or make its subjects. To this day, debate over the social and cultural value of television continues.

One of the first television stars was comedian Milton Berle, affectionately known as "Uncle Miltie." In the photograph below, Berle parodies Charles Laughton's portrayal of Captain Bligh in the film "Mutiny on the Bounty."

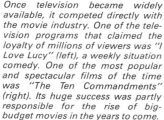
Once television became widely available, it competed directly with the movie industry. One of the television programs that claimed the loyalty of millions of viewers was "I Love Lucy" (left), a weekly situation comedy. One of the most popular and spectacular films of the time was "The Ten Commandments" (right). Its huge success was partly responsible for the rise of big-budget movies in the years to come.

The film industry suffered as a result of the introduction of television. Large sums of money were pumped into Hollywood spectaculars, such as *Cleopatra, Ben-Hur,* and *The Ten Command-ments,* to lure customers away from their television sets and back into the movie theaters. On Broadway, *My Fair Lady* continued the trend toward big-budget musicals and was the single biggest stage hit of the fifties. Other smash hits included *The Sound of Music, The King and I, The Music Man,* and *West Side Story.* One new concept in theater was the development of off-Broadway productions. Off-Broadway meant that the budget for a production was drastically scaled down. This reduced the ticket price for more adventurous presentations.

Another cultural area that experienced massive growth in the fifties was literature. This was due primarily to the mass production of the paperback book. This meant that there was a cost savings in manufacturing as well as a price savings for the reader. By the middle of the decade, paperbacks could be purchased in drugstores and supermarkets, as well as in bookstores all over the country.

"Sensational" fiction, often referred to as "pulp," was most popular. Serious literary works also flourished in the fifties. The questions of personal identity and the awareness that American society was no longer diverse, gave rise to literary efforts by such respected writers as J. D. Salinger, Saul Bellow, Henry Miller, Ralph Ellison, James Baldwin, Richard Wright, and Norman Mailer.

The music industry experienced a revolutionary transformation as well. This change was spurred on by the price-reducing introduction of the 45 r.p.m. single record and the twelve-inch long-playing album. Record sales soared from the thousands to the the millions.

Records became big business. So did recording stars. As the fifties passed, the smooth stylings of Lena Horne, Perry Como, Harry Belafonte, Eddie Fisher, Peggy Lee, and Julie London gave way to a loud new sound called *rock and roll*. This was a frenzied mixture of country and western music along with rhythm and blues. Rock and roll was driven by the talent and personality of performers such as Elvis Presley, Buddy Holly, Chuck Berry, Jerry Lee Lewis, and Little Richard.

Jazz also underwent numerous changes in the fifties. Influenced by such great and innovative talents as Duke Ellington, Charlie Parker, Charles Mingus, Miles Davis, and Thelonious Monk, jazz branched out into new variations and greater public acceptance. The distinctive singing styles of Billie Holliday, Ella Fitzgerald, Sarah Vaughan, and Abby Lincoln set new standards of excellence by which future jazz vocalists would be judged.

As did the decades preceding it, the fifties saw trends, innovations, and commercial gains in the arts which would now become a part of American life.

The Highway Boom

The flight to the suburbs that began shortly after World War II continued during the fifties. This move was encouraged by a combination of forces. Cities had become crowded during the war, as industry expanded to produce war materials. After the war came prosperity and the baby boom. The G.I. Bill made it possible for thousands of veterans to get home mortgages. At the same time, urban renewal projects were not very successful. Many people felt that they wanted to leave the cities and find nice, quiet neighborhoods in which to live. All these pressures and dreams would have meant little if the automobile had not existed.

The automobile was the ticket to suburbia. Homes, shopping centers, schools, and churches no longer had to be within walking distance. Detroit, which had geared up for war production, switched back to automobiles. In 1950, a record 8 million cars and trucks were produced. Each year that followed, production remained near 7 million. By the late 1950s, there was at least one car or truck in use for every household in the country.

The Highway Act of 1956 indirectly encouraged the growth of the auto industry and all the profit-making businesses that depended on that industry. This act provided for the construction of 41,000 miles of interstate highway systems. As a result of these roads, there was an increase in housing developments, motels, fast-food chains, billboards,

During the fifties, many urban residents fled the cramped, often decaying conditions of the central city (as seen in this photograph of Detroit) for the new, more spacious environments of the suburbs.

671

and litter. Public transportation and inner cities began to decline. Some cities, such as Los Angeles, became almost totally dependent on private transportation. Two thirds of central Los Angeles was covered with cement for driving or parking. A new word—smog—was coined for air that could be seen, but barely breathed. And every once in a while, someone would stop to wonder if all this was progress.

Questions for Discussion

1. How did *Brown* v. *Board of Education of Topeka* affect the idea of "separate but equal"?
2. How was desegregation aided or hindered by each of the following: the Supreme Court; Governor Orval Faubus; Rosa Parks; and Dr. Martin Luther King, Jr.?
3. What changes in American education were necessary as a result of the post-World War II baby boom, the increased demand for education, and Sputnik I?
4. What are the advantages of increased mass communication such as television, newspapers, and paperback books?
5. After World War I, the automobile put America on wheels. What effects did it have after World War II?

3. Republican Foreign Policy

During the 1952 campaign, the Republicans tried to blame world turmoil on the Democratic foreign policy. Here the Republicans found a weak spot. The hope for peace that followed World War II had been shattered. Americans had seen world communism spread. They were in a war that the United States was not winning. And they were learning a hard lesson. The United States could not impose its will on the course of history.

Eisenhower would not sharply criticize the policies of Roosevelt and Truman. He had too much experience in NATO to join the most conservative wing of the Republican Party. Nevertheless, he had made the twofold promise to reduce federal spending while making the United States stronger militarily. This required a departure from the Truman plan for an expensive ground force. In his State of the Union message in January 1954, Eisenhower explained the "New Look" in national defense. The United States would place emphasis on the development of nuclear weapons to be carried by the Air Force.

At first, this change in emphasis seemed to signal a bolder stand on foreign policy. Secretary of State John Foster Dulles announced that the United States would rely less on a country's local defenses. The backbone of the foreign policy would be "the deterrent of massive retaliatory power." He implied that no nation would dare to provoke the United States if faced with such a huge striking force.

If followed to its logical conclusion, this policy of massive retaliation could escalate into a nuclear war. Throughout Eisenhower's administration, crises developed in every corner of the globe. But the difference between the Eisenhower and Truman administrations existed more in words than in deeds. The United States still tried to encircle communist countries with a network of alliances. It still offered military and economic aid to countries in danger from internal revolutionary forces. It still tried to develop a posture of strength to woo the emerging nations in Africa, Asia, and Latin America. Though an armistice was reached in Korea and American ground troops were not engaged in war, only a kind of peace existed during the Eisenhower administration. Two great powers—the United States and Russia—were engaged in a race to build the most effective means of destruction.

In the decade of the fifties, the people of the world no longer could hide from the ravages of war. Everyone everywhere knew that they could be destroyed without seeing the enemy or even the weapon. In one decade, progress in hydrogen bombs, missiles and antimissiles, rockets, and nuclear submarines had made air, land, sea, and space vulnerable. Genetic experts warned that not only a political system but also the whole ecological system was at stake. The radiation from nuclear weapons could have terrible effects on living things. Even testing nuclear weapons in the atmosphere could be hazardous. Many feared that somewhere in the world a conflict might become a war that would destroy the human race.

The Beginnings of Vietnam

Since the 1860s, Vietnam had been part of the French colonial empire. During World War II, the Japanese occupied that region. National feeling spurred a movement by the Vietnamese to throw off both the Japanese and the French. Ho Chi Minh emerged as the popular leader. Both a nationalist and a communist, he saw the chance to reestablish Vietnamese independence after World War II. He asked for recognition of Vietnamese independence from the anti-Axis powers. At first, the United States remained neutral. It did not support Ho Chi Minh. Nor did it support the French puppet government of the Emperor Bao Dai.

At about the same time, China fell to the Communists. The Republicans blamed President Truman for failing to contain communism. Stung by criticism, Truman and his advisers hastened to support the French regime in Vietnam. At first, the United States offered money to help the French. By 1954, millions of dollars were being spent in support of the French army. In spite of this, in May 1954, the Vietnamese overwhelmed the French.

In March 1954, the French make a stalwart, but futile, effort to defend the key northern outpost of Dien Bien Phu. The fortress fell in May, overrun by 20,000 communist troops. The loss signalled the end of French involvement in Vietnam.

The United States began to act as a buffer against a communist takeover in Vietnam. Ten years later, the caption to this 1964 cartoon would read, "What's so funny, monsieur? I'm only trying to find my way."

At this time, a conference was in progress in Geneva. The foreign ministers of the "Big Four"—the United States, Russia, Great Britain, and France—had invited interested countries to attend the conference to discuss Indochina (Vietnam, Laos, and Cambodia) and Korea. After the French defeat, the Big Four decided to divide Vietnam into two parts. The North would be administered by Ho Chi Minh. The South would be led by the Emperor Bao Dai. Free elections were to be held in 1956 to determine who would rule all of Vietnam.

The United States was not happy about the Geneva settlement. However, the United States government promised not to interfere with the agreement. Meanwhile, the United States began a policy to prevent further communist expansion. The Southeast Asia Treaty Organization (SEATO) was established on September 8, 1954. The United States, Britain, France, the Philippines, Australia, New Zealand, Thailand, and Pakistan formed this pact. An attack on one was considered an attack on all. The guarantee was extended to include Laos, Cambodia, and the southern portion of Vietnam. But SEATO was weak. It lacked the unified military organization of NATO. Only two Southeast Asian countries—Thailand and the Philippines—were actual members. SEATO failed to win the support of India, Burma, Ceylon, or Indonesia. In case of attack, the agreement to defend was in reality an agreement to advise.

The United States gave economic aid to support the southern portion of Vietnam. Unfortunately, the man that the Emperor appointed as his Premier, Ngo Dinh Diem, was not a democratic ruler. He delayed holding elections and failed to win the popular support of the peasants. Finally, Ho Chi Minh began aiding the Communists and anti-Diem rebels in the South.

By then, Eisenhower was committed to keeping the Communists from taking over Vietnam. He explained that Southeast Asia was like a row of dominoes. If one country fell, the other countries were bound to follow. When Eisenhower left office, John F. Kennedy inherited these unsettled problems in Asia.

Crisis in Hungary

For all too brief a period in 1955, there seemed to be a lessening of tension in world affairs. Stalin was dead. The immediate danger of a Chinese Communist attack on Formosa had passed. There was a truce in Korea and a compromise in Vietnam. The major nations had gathered in Geneva to hold discussions on a note of hope. Talks centered around the problems of German unification, peaceful use of the atom, and disarmament. Nothing developed to sustain the hope raised in Geneva. A treaty banning nuclear tests in the atmosphere was out of reach.

Within months, the Cold War was as bitter as ever. Encouraged by Dulles' strong talk about rolling back the Iron Curtain, Hungarian patriots turned on their Russian oppressors on October 23, 1956. Four days of violent fighting went on between Soviet troops and Hungarian patriots. Finally, the Soviets called back their troops. This led the Hungarians to believe that they were on their way to doing away with the one-party dictatorship.

In reality, they had been tricked. On November 4, Soviet troops began a massive attack on Budapest that resulted in a brutal end to the struggle for freedom. While the whole world looked on in horror, the Hungarian resistance was crushed. Eisenhower could not act without risking a confrontation with Russia.

A new Soviet-controlled Hungarian government was established. Hundreds of rebels were imprisoned or deported to Russia. Those who could fled to Austria.

Crisis in the Middle East

At the same time, one of the many underlying conflicts in the Middle East erupted. Egypt's leader, Gamal Abdel Nasser, seized the Suez Canal. The canal was on Egyptian territory. However, it was owned and operated by British and French investors. Faced with being cut off from their Middle East oil supplies, France and Britain attacked Egypt with paratroopers. They were joined by Israeli forces.

Unfortunately for the Western alliance, the United States was stunned by the attack. Only a week earlier, Eisenhower had said that he was against the use of force as a means of settling international disputes. He called on the United Nations to condemn France and Britain. Faced with worldwide opposition, America's European allies gave in and finally withdrew. This signaled the end of allied power in the Middle East. Now the United States alone carried the weight of Western interests and Israeli security in the Middle East.

Eisenhower had to provide for this new national responsibility. In 1957, he asked Congress for the authority to give economic and military aid to any Middle Eastern country threatened by a communist

The Middle East remained a hot spot in the fifties. In 1958, the United States sent Marines into Lebanon to support a pro-Western government against rebels.

takeover. But the conditions in the Middle East were far different from those in the European countries that had benefited from NATO and the Truman Doctrine. Anti-American sentiment remained, strengthened by anti-Israeli sentiment. The following year, Eisenhower successfully defended the independence of pro-Western Lebanon. However, there were few bright spots for American diplomacy in the Middle East.

Latin America

Another unpleasant shock jolted the United States, this time in Latin America. During the past years, Latin American friendship had been taken for granted. Distracted by European and Asian problems, the United States had ignored the economic needs of its southern neighbors.

In 1950, Guatemala elected President Jacobo Arbenz Guzman, who granted local Communists a role in Guatemalan affairs. Secretary Dulles was shaken into action. He demanded a resolution condemning communism from a reluctant Interamerican Conference. The United States also sent arms to support anti-Arbenz forces located in Nicaragua and Honduras. The government was overthrown by a military coup. It was finally replaced with a conservative anticommunist leader. After that, economic and military aid was given to Latin American countries that proclaimed anticommunist feeling. Unfortunately, the military aid often kept in power those dictators who received it. America appeared to be blocking social progress.

Unaware of the rising anti-American sentiments in Latin America, Vice-President Nixon set out on a "good will' tour in 1958. He was greeted with jeers. Local citizens threw rotten vegetables and rocks at his motorcade. Nixon himself felt that though the Communists encouraged the rioting, they succeeded because of real economic problems. It was clear now that the United States must give serious thought to revising its Latin American policy.

Both Eisenhower and Congress listened to Nixon's view of the causes of unrest in Latin America. Billions of dollars in aid and investment poured into Latin American republics. The United States cooperated in improving agriculture, education, and health facilities in many areas. In 1960, Eisenhower was greeted warmly when he toured Latin America.

However, the problems in Latin America were far from over. On January 1, 1959, Fidel Castro overthrew the dictator of Cuba, Fulgencio Batista. At first, Americans supported Castro. They believed that he would establish a constitutional, democratic government. But within six months, this illusion ended. Castro was drawing closer to the communist bloc. He condemned the United States, declared himself to be a Communist, and seized three American-and British-owned oil refineries in Cuba after they refused to process two barge-loads of Soviet oil. Two weeks before President Eisenhower left office, the United States broke off diplomatic relations with Cuba.

Questions for Discussion

1. How did Eisenhower's foreign policy affect the future of the arms race? of the world?
2. How effective was the SEATO alliance?
3. What role did the Truman and Eisenhower administrations play in the developments in Vietnam after World War II?
4. What effects did Eisenhower's action during the seizure of the Suez Canal have on future relations with the Middle East?
5. How was the United States forced to change its foreign policy in Guatemala and Cuba in the 1950s?

4. The New Frontier and the World

In a close contest in 1960, John F. Kennedy defeated Richard M. Nixon for the Presidency. In victory, Kennedy won the right to shape a domestic policy and a foreign policy to fit a changing world. He brought to the Presidency a style and an enthusiasm that won the support of a wide range of people. In his Inaugural Address, Kennedy called for "a grand and global alliance" to fight against poverty, disease, and war.

President Kennedy understood the changes that had taken place in the postwar world. He realized that these changes would affect what America could do and how it could do it. For the first time, Asian and

The inauguration of John F. Kennedy on January 20, 1961, in Washington, D.C. In the spirit that was to characterize his administration, Kennedy urged his fellow Americans to "ask not what your country can do for you—ask what you can do for your country."

African countries held the majority in the United Nations. Prosperous European states were in a position to challenge American leadership. In addition, more than half the population in the world was uninterested in allying itself with either side in the Cold War.

Kennedy hoped to strike a different chord. One exceptional attempt was the creation of the Peace Corps in March 1961. The President carried out an idea that had formed while he was campaigning. He asked for a group of volunteers to serve—expenses paid—as instructors and helpers in underdeveloped countries. These volunteers would share their knowledge and experience with the people of the host country. The program was an outstanding success. In addition, it symbolized the dedication of the United States to the cause of humanity.

Another goal of the new administration was to build on Eisenhower's improved Latin American policy. Dubbed the Alliance for Progress, Kennedy's plan was an updated Marshall Plan. Private and government sources in the United States, Latin America, Japan, and Western Europe would provide support for the $100 billion program. It was hoped that these funds would improve social and economic conditions in poor Latin American countries.

The Alliance for Progress never reached its goals. There was a wide gap between the rich and the poor in Latin America. Much of the money was pumped into private business interests and military aid. Congress finally reduced its Alliance budget. The goal of political stability replaced the goal of social and economic change. In the end, the United States eventually dealt with Latin American nations on a one-to-one basis.

The course of friendship with nations in Africa was not an easy one either. The Congo was torn between the forces of Patrice Lumumba, favored by Russia, and the forces of Moise Tshombe, favored by the West. When the United Nations intervened to help establish a neutral government, the Russians refused to give money to support the United Nations mission in the Congo. The United States made up the difference to keep the world organization from going bankrupt. President Kennedy's dealings with underdeveloped nations had not always been so cautious.

Problems in Cuba

When Kennedy took office, there already existed an ill-planned scheme to invade Cuba. In April 1961, the President permitted a United States Central Intelligence Agency (CIA) attempt to overthrow Castro. This was to be accomplished by training and landing in the Bay of Pigs a force of Cuban anti-Castro, anticommunist exiles. The CIA expected a general revolt to follow. Instead, many of the

In October, 1962 President Kennedy appeared on television to announce that American ships would set up a partial blockade of Cuba to intercept any shipment of Soviet missiles to the island.

MISSILE ERECTOR

CABLE

MISSILE SHELTER TENT

TRACKED PRIME MOVERS

FUEL TANK TRAILERS

A spy-plane photograph shows one of the controversial missile sites under construction in Cuba.

invaders were quickly captured and killed. The American role in the affair was revealed. Many Americans objected to this act of clumsy aggression.

Khrushchev may have thought that Kennedy, having gambled and failed in Cuba, would be unwilling to face a new showdown there. So in the summer of 1962, Russia began to ship Soviet medium and long-range missiles to that island. When American spy planes took photos of the missile sites, Kennedy met the situation head on. On October 22, 1962, he gravely announced to the world a partial blockade of Cuba by American ships. Russian vessels carrying missiles to Cuba would be turned back. The Organization of American States (OAS) backed the American position. The United States had to present its case in the United Nations. For a few tense days, everyone waited to see how the Russians would respond. Would an angry shot in Cuban waters be the signal for a nuclear exchange? Finally, Khrushchev backed down and agreed to remove the missiles.

Kennedy And Khrushchev

Shortly after the bungled Bay of Pigs invasion, President Kennedy and Soviet Premier Khrushchev met in Vienna. That meeting was difficult and unsuccessful. Khrushchev threatened to make a treaty

679

The Berlin Wall was built to keep citizens of East Berlin from leaving. The British sector is to the right of the wall, and the Brandenberg Gate is in the background.

with East Germany that would endanger West Berlin. He also rejected a second United States offer to negotiate a test-ban treaty. Kennedy, in turn, warned that the United States would not turn its back on West Berlin.

The failure of the Vienna summit meeting to achieve any notable agreements increased world tension. A buildup of defense budgets and personnel occurred in both the East and West. The uncertainty over the future of Berlin led to a massive exit of East Berliners into West Berlin.

On August 12, 1961, the East Germans began to close off access to West Berlin. What started as a barricade became a 40-kilometer (25-mile) cement-block wall between East and West Berlin. President Kennedy moved armed forces into West Berlin. He sent General Lucius Clay and Vice-President Lyndon Johnson on a symbolic visit. The crisis finally came to a halt on October 17 when the Russians backed down. They realized that the Western powers were not about to compromise the safety and freedom of West Berlin. The wall remained; so did America's resolve to stand by its ally. Fast on the heels of this crisis came the Cuban missile crisis. Again, the United States drew a line and stood by it.

The United States and Russia were too often coming to the brink of war. The world faced the possibility of nuclear disaster. In the summer of 1961, the Russians resumed atmospheric testing of nuclear bombs. In 1962, the United States also resumed nuclear testing.

In June 1963, President Kennedy offered a "strategy of peace." He pledged that the United States would not carry out any more nuclear tests in the atmosphere if other countries would not. He appealed to Russia to consider its common goals with the United States. The time was ripe, and the Russians were willing. By the end of the year, a limited test-ban treaty was signed by ninety-nine nations. The notable exceptions were France and China, who were both eager to enter the "nuclear club."

The New Frontier at Home

No one had to look very far to find the roots of Kennedy's "New Frontier." Many of the features of the President's program had first been put before the Republican Eightieth Congress. Some parts fared better the second time around. But there was still a coalition of Southern Democrats and conservative Republicans blocking action.

The issues that met with the greatest opposition were the questions of medical care for the aged, civil rights, and federal aid to education and mass transportation. Congress did approve a higher minimum wage, better social security benefits, aid to housing, and a training program for unemployed workers. Congress also supported a spending program aimed at reversing an economic downswing.

Once in office, Kennedy found that he had to take a stand on civil rights. He acknowledged support of the *Brown* vs. *Board of Education* decision. Federal troops were ready to enforce integration. Kennedy also set up a Committee on Equal Economic Opportunity and drew many Blacks into government service. The administration took great pains to enforce the voting rights provisions in the 1957 and 1960 civil rights laws.

John F. Kennedy's brother Robert F. Kennedy was the United States Attorney General. Under Robert's leadership, the Department of Justice actively pursued cases of discrimination and violation of voting rights. In 1961, Robert Kennedy sent federal marshals to protect *freedom riders*. The *freedom riders* were White and Black students who were challenging segregated waiting rooms in the interstate bus systems. Most important, in 1962, Kennedy sent federal marshals to enforce a court order requiring the University of Mississippi to admit its first Black student, James Meredith. In many other instances, the White House and the Department of Justice put pressure on public officials to protect the rights of all citizens. During the Kennedy years, civil rights picked up a momentum that it had not had since Reconstruction.

Many conflicts were coming to a head. As the sixties began, President Kennedy had made major decisions that would change American priorities. People and materials were committed to a war of

James Meredith becomes the first Black to graduate from the University of Mississippi.

THE DEATH OF A PRESIDENT

"President John Fitzgerald Kennedy died at approximately one o'clock." With those words, the worst fears of a nation were realized. At 12:30 P.M. on November 22, 1963, a short burst of gunfire directed at a downtown Dallas motorcade ended the life of John Kennedy. The controversy surrounding the President's death has never been stilled.

What began as a routine campaign stump through Texas ended in Dallas, with bullets fired from the sixth-floor window of the Texas Public School Depository. In six seconds, the firing was over. President Kennedy was fatally wounded in the head. Texas Governor John Connally was shot in the chest, wrist, and thigh.

The succession of events was rapid. At 1:33 P.M., a press aide announced to a stunned nation that its President was dead. At 1:45 P.M., a "hot suspect," Lee Harvey Oswald, was arrested. At 3:38 P.M., Lyndon Baines Johnson was sworn in as President.

As Kennedy's body lay in state in the East Room of the White House, words of sympathy and regret poured in from all over the world. The American people watched their televisions as tens of thousands of mourners filed past his flag-draped casket.

Before much could be learned from Lee Harvey Oswald, he, too, was gunned down. As Dallas police moved Oswald from their city prison to a county jail, a club owner named Jack Ruby pushed his way through the crowd. At a close range, he shot Oswald in the abdomen, ending the life of Kennedy's alleged assassin. Ruby later died in prison, of cancer.

A government-appointed commission determined that the Kennedy assassination was the work of one man. However, theories of conspiracies, communist-inspired or right-wing ultraconservative, have never been completely discounted.

questionable motives ten thousand miles away in Asia. Billions of dollars were committed to putting an American on the moon. When President Kennedy was shot in Dallas on November 22, 1963, disturbing undercurrents were already in motion.

Questions for Discussion

1. Define *freedom riders*.
2. What role did each of the following play in President Kennedy's foreign policy: the Peace Corps; the Alliance for Progress; aid to the United Nations?
3. How did President Kennedy react to Russia sending missiles to Cuba?
4. What developments occurred between Kennedy and Khrushchev concerning Berlin and a test-ban treaty?
5. Why can it be said that during the Kennedy years, the executive branch took the lead in the fight for civil rights?

Chapter 29 Review

Summary Questions for Discussion

1. What was President Eisenhower's view of the Roosevelt and Truman administrations? How did this affect his plan during his administration?
2. How did people react to the return of Joseph McCarthy?
3. What was the major goal of Eisenhower's administration?
4. How did Eisenhower deal with inflation? What was the result?
5. What means did Eisenhower use in 1958 to ease the economic slowdown? Were they successful?
6. How did Eisenhower attempt to deal with the problem of farm surplus?
7. Describe the condition of Blacks after World War II.
8. The Supreme Court decision in the case of *Brown* v. *Board of Education of Topeka* is considered a landmark decision. (a) What previous decision did it overturn? (b) What was its ruling in 1954? (c) How quickly was it implemented?
9. What happened in Little Rock, Arkansas, when a federal court ordered desegregation? What action did Eisenhower take? What was its effect?
10. Identify Rosa Parks.
11. Identify Dr. Martin Luther King, Jr. What weapons did he use against discrimination?
12. Explain the influence of each of the following on the United States system of education in the fifties: (a) the birthrate after World War II; (b) competition with private industry; (c) launching of Sputnik I; and (d) information about education in Russia.
13. What were the positive aspects of the introduction of television? The negative aspects?
14. How were the media areas of literature, music, and film changed during the 1950s?
15. What encouraged the American flight to the suburbs? What were the results?
16. What was Eisenhower's "New Look" in national defense? What did it imply?
17. How did the Eisenhower administration deal with crises around the world?
18. In relation to Vietnam, explain the significance of: (a) Ho Chi Minh; (b) Bao Dai; (c) the Geneva Conference; and (d) SEATO.
19. How did the Soviets trick the Hungarians in 1956? What was the result?
20. What caused the Suez Crisis? What action did Eisenhower take? What was the result?
21. Explain the changes that occurred in United States-Latin American policy in Guatemala and Cuba in the 1950s.
22. What changes had occurred in the postwar world that affected President Kennedy's administration?
23. What was the purpose of Kennedy's Peace Corps?
24. Was the Alliance for Progress effective?
25. What was the Bay of Pigs crisis?
26. Why was there a confrontation between Khrushchev and Kennedy? What was the result?
27. What actions did Kennedy take in response to the construction of the Berlin Wall?
28. Identify the limited test-ban treaty of 1963.
29. Show how President Kennedy's actions on civil rights differed from those of his predecessors.

Using Your Skills

1. Look at the cartoon on page 674. Identify the characters. What clues did you use? What message is the cartoon conveying? What emotions does the cartoon convey?
2. Which pictures in this chapter represent the cultural aspects of the fifties?

CHAPTER 30

The Turbulent Sixties

The relative calm that characterized the fifties was shattered in the sixties. Crises erupted with sudden, volcanic fury. It was a decade of chaos, anger, and protests.

Blacks and Whites marched, lobbied, and sat in together in an attempt to integrate a racially segregated society. As frustrations reached a peak, ghettos exploded in riots. The gentle strains of "We Shall Overcome" were being joined by new cries of "Burn, Baby, Burn."

As protests against American domestic policies grew, so too did opposition to the "undeclared war" in Vietnam. As the war escalated under the presidency of Lyndon Johnson, so too did the demand for its end. The loudest cries came from college students. They saw the war as immoral and economically motivated.

In addition, America was forced to face the reality of other issues—equal rights for all Americans, environmental safeguards, and economic opportunity. Women served notice that they would no longer be treated as second-class citizens. By the dawn of the seventies, "women's liberation" became a household expression.

Protest sparked the unpredictability of the sixties. But prosperity supplied the stability upon which all else was supported. America experienced an unprecedented period of prosperity in the fifties that carried over to the sixties. This was due in large part to the postwar revolution in science and technology. Many economists referred to the period as "an economy of abundance."

To a great number of Americans, the sixties represented "the good life." For many, the decade meant a confirmation of their dreams of economic well-being. For others, it was a time of "doing your own thing"—a time to experiment with new ideas and lifestyles.

READING GUIDE

1. **How did President Johnson try to meet the needs of the poor?**
2. **Why did the Vietnam War create conflicts in America?**
3. **How have demands for equality by minority groups changed American life?**

Right: November 1969—some 400,000 demonstrators ask for "Peace Now."

1. The Torch Is Passed

On November 22, 1963, President John F. Kennedy was assassinated in Dallas. On that day, the Presidency passed to Lyndon Johnson. President Johnson was following a well-liked, appealing President Kennedy into office. Johnson had to win the loyalty of the Kennedy appointees and the American people. The grief that many people felt undoubtedly made Johnson's task much harder.

Lyndon Johnson's background differed greatly from that of his predecessor. President Kennedy, educated at the finest schools, including Harvard, came from a wealthy Massachusetts family. His father had served the country as Ambassador to Britain. On the other hand, President Johnson was the son of a Texas farmer. He attended a state teachers college. Johnson's "folksy ways" contrasted with the polished, youthful style that the Kennedys brought to the White House.

President Johnson came to the presidency with a great deal of experience. He arrived in Washington in 1931 as the secretary to a wealthy Texas member of Congress. He later served in President Franklin D. Roosevelt's National Youth Administration. Between 1937 and 1949, Johnson served as a member of the House of Representatives. After his election to the Senate, he became a powerful legislative leader. He served as Senate majority leader from 1953 until he was elected Vice-President in 1960.

From a position of power in the Congress, Johnson went to the relatively obscure position of Vice-President. In some ways, this was a letdown. President Kennedy's brother, Robert Kennedy, and other Democratic liberals had opposed adding Johnson to the ticket. When Robert became John Kennedy's closest and most trusted adviser, Johnson was excluded from the inner circle of influence. Few doubted that Johnson was waiting for a chance at the top spot.

When he rose to that position, Johnson was faced with the pressure of time. There was only a year until the next Presidential election. He had to forge an alliance with Kennedy supporters so that they would continue to serve under him. He also had to reinforce the Democratic ties with Blacks and labor. In addition, he had to prove his strength as an executive leader.

Unfinished Business

Shortly after President Johnson took office, he addressed the Congress. He explained that he wanted to carry out the programs that had been started by John Kennedy. Many American people supported measures that were *logjammed* (deadlocked) in Congress. Thus, the President felt assured of popular support for his requests.

Congress began to take action on bills that had been logjammed in committees. Some believed that the action taken by Congress was a

President John F. Kennedy in the motorcade in Dallas shortly before his assassination.

tribute to the slain President. But others gave credit to Johnson's legislative experience. Within a month after Johnson's rise to the Presidency, Congress voted a $1.2 billion bill to support college construction projects. President Johnson also obtained quick passage of an urban mass-transit bill and a wilderness protection act.

There were other matters that Johnson considered vital. President Kennedy had been plagued with a declining economy and rising unemployment. Kennedy's request for a tax cut to boost the economy had been blocked by conservative members of Congress. President Johnson presented Congress with a much smaller budget than Kennedy had been expected to ask for. Johnson also used such symbolic gestures as cutting off unnecessary lights in the White House to give the impression of responsible management. As a result, in February 1964, Congress passed an $11.5 billion tax cut. *Take-home pay*—or a person's salary after taxes—rose. Consumer spending increased. Industrial production expanded. In 1964, the **gross national product** (GNP) was up $38 billion over the previous year.

There was still another, more important, piece of unfinished business that needed attention. President Johnson was the first President from the South since Andrew Johnson a century before. Some people thought that Lyndon Johnson would stall civil rights legislation. Instead, he urged Congress to pass the civil rights bill as a memorial to President Kennedy. In June 1963, President Kennedy had sent to Congress the strongest civil rights bill ever proposed by a

gross national product (GNP)
the total value of goods and services produced by a nation during a specified time period, usually one year

President Lyndon B. Johnson hands a commemorative pen to Dr. Martin Luther King, Jr. after signing the historic Civil Rights Act of 1964.

President. In August, 200,000 demonstrators peacefully marched on Washington in a powerful plea for Congressional action. When Johnson became President, that bill was still stalled in committee.

In the past, the Southern bloc of Senators had staged **filibusters** to talk any civil rights bills to death. President Johnson knew that this could happen again. So he turned to Senator Hubert Humphrey to usher the civil rights bill through the Senate. Humphrey needed the support of some Republicans in order to get the required two-thirds vote to stop a filibuster. Once the bill had the support of Republican Senator Everett Dirksen from Illinois, it was possible to break an 83-day filibuster. This filibuster was the longest in the history of the Senate. On July 10, 1964, the historic Civil Rights Act of 1964 was finally signed. The new law prohibited discrimination in public accommodations. It gave the Attorney General the power to bring suits on behalf of those seeking integrated schools. It strengthened voting rights and prohibited discrimination in labor unions and businesses. Also, the act gave the federal government the power to withhold funds from state-run projects where there was evidence of discrimination.

President Johnson was not content merely to carry out President Kennedy's plans. In his State of the Union address on January 8, 1964, he announced that his administration was declaring "unconditional war on poverty in America." In a speech given shortly thereafter, he dubbed his program the "Great Society . . . a place where the city . . . serves not only the needs of the body and the demands of commerce, but the desire for beauty and the hunger for community. . . . It is a place where (people) are more concerned with the quality of their goals than the quantity of their goods." Starting with the

Economic Opportunity Act of 1964, Congress funded several antipoverty programs over the following two years. For example, the Head Start program gave preschool instruction to underprivileged children. Upward Bound was a program that encouraged bright underprivileged students to attend college. The Job Corps and the Neighborhood Youth Corps were designed to help unemployed youths. Volunteers in Service to America (VISTA) was a domestic peace corp. President Johnson hoped that his triumphs—the antipoverty programs, the tax cut, and the civil rights bill—would provide him with a strong enough political base to be retained as President in the next election.

The 1964 Election

Up until the 1964 election, the Republicans usually chose a "middle-of-the-road" candidate to oppose the more liberal Democrats. When the Republicans gathered in the Cow Palace in San Francisco in 1964, they seemed determined to try to turn back the clock. They nominated Senator Barry Goldwater, a self-proclaimed conservative. He favored returning regulatory powers to the states and reducing the operations of the TVA. In foreign affairs, Goldwater favored taking a strong stand against the Soviet Union. He also wanted to drive Castro out of Cuba and send more military aid to South Vietnam. The Senator chose William E. Miller as his running mate. Miller opposed federal aid to education, antipoverty programs, Medicare, public power, and subsidies to agriculture. The Republican ticket of Goldwater and Miller seemed determined to rid America of anything that smacked of liberalism.

The Democratic Convention, held in Atlantic City in August, 1964, nominated Lyndon B. Johnson for President. To President Johnson's right that evening were his wife, Lady Bird Johnson, Secretary of Defense Robert S. MacNamara, and Attorney General Robert F. Kennedy.

Lyndon Johnson was determined too. He was not content just to win the election. Having been President without being elected to the position, he wanted to achieve the greatest possible majority of votes. He wanted to rid himself of the Kennedy shadow by winning the White House on his own. A landslide victory was what Johnson felt he needed to consolidate his power.

The Democrats took advantage of the feeling some people had that Goldwater was an extremist. Goldwater had accepted the support of extremely conservative organizations. Also, some people felt that he would be too willing to use nuclear weapons. Goldwater referred to Russia as "the enemy," thereby implying that conflict with Russia was inevitable. In domestic affairs, Goldwater had voted against the Civil Rights Act of 1964 and the welfare programs of Kennedy and Johnson. His views were so far from the mainstream of American political thought that it was estimated he lost a million votes every time he made a major speech.

Johnson campaigned on his record. The success of his programs in Congress helped his campaign. While Goldwater was preaching war, Johnson was claiming that he would keep Americans out of war. For anyone voting on that issue alone, Johnson appeared to be the right choice. However, many Americans became disillusioned shortly after Johnson's overwhelming victory, when he stepped up military participation in Vietnam.

The Great Society

Johnson was elected with the landslide he felt he needed. Now he could bargain with Congress from a position of strength. In addition, the Democratic majority in Congress presented him with a definite advantage. Opposition seemed to melt away. In 1965 Congress passed, and Johnson signed into law, eighty-nine bills. Among them were a wide range of liberal measures aimed at promoting the "Great Society."

Johnson managed to overcome two nagging questions about aid to education. One was the question of separation of church and state. Aid was given to underprivileged students whether they attended public or private schools. It was provided in such a way as to sidestep the religious issue. The second difficulty concerned a fear of federal intervention in education. Direct federal aid was provided mainly to schools that served the poor. The massive aid to elementary and higher education was a departure from federal policy.

Medicare became law in 1965. Administered by the Social Security Administration, it provided low-cost medical insurance for those over 65. A far-reaching feature was a provision for **grants-in-aid** to states that set up *medicaid programs*. These programs provided payments

grants-in-aid
grants or subsidies for public funds paid by a central or local government in aid of a public undertaking

Central business districts, like the one at the left, are often sites of new commercial building or reconstruction by government and business. But high construction costs have slowed the building of new urban housing. Too often, older housing decays (right), and middle income families move to the suburbs in search of a better environment.

to the poor for certain medical bills. During Johnson's administration, payment for health-related services rose from $4 billion to $14 billion.

In two other acts that were passed, Congress gave help to such widely different locales as mountain hamlets and inner cities. The Appalachian Regional Development Act provided funds for highway development, health centers, and resources development. This aid was for the poverty-stricken mountain region that runs south from Pennsylvania into Alabama and Georgia. Second, the Omnibus Housing Act (1965) designated funds for low-income housing and urban renewal. On September 9, 1965, Congress created the Department of Housing and Urban Development (HUD) to deal with the problems of the cities. In January 1966, Robert C. Weaver was sworn in as the first head of this new Cabinet-level department.

Meanwhile, Congress was acting on a bill to protect the voting rights of Black citizens. Even the provisions of the Civil Rights Act of 1964 were still not strong enough to prevent interference with voter registration. Various groups had tried to register Black voters in Southern states. Often violence broke out. Official protection was minimal.

In March 1965, the Rev. Martin Luther King, Jr. led thousands of marchers from Selma to Montgomery, Alabama, dramatizing a voter-registration drive and objecting to harassment of Blacks.

In March 1965, Alabama state troopers set upon Dr. Martin Luther King, Jr., and over 400 demonstrators seeking voting rights in Selma, Alabama. Having witnessed the scene on national television, the public was outraged. Two days later, three White ministers who came to support Dr. King were attacked by a White mob. One of the ministers, the Rev. James Reeb, died of his injuries. Later, the mother of five children, Viola Liuzzo, was killed as she helped the demonstrators.

President Johnson went before Congress and denounced the denial of basic civil rights. In an emotional plea he declared: "Their cause must be our cause too. Because it is not just Negroes, but really it is all of us who must overcome the crippling legacy of bigotry and injustice. And we shall overcome." A bill was passed that called for federal voting registrars in all districts where Blacks were under-enrolled. President Johnson signed the Voting Rights Act into law on August 6, 1965.

The cooperation between the President and Congress put many measures into action. By upholding these laws, the Supreme Court took an equally strong stand for human rights. The Voting Rights Act of 1965 suspended literacy and other voter tests. It also authorized federal supervision of voter registration in southern districts where fewer than half of voting age residents were registered. This act also struck down the poll tax in local elections.

But throughout the country, North and South, civil rights laws were not enough to soothe the hard feelings caused by poverty and prejudice. In August 1965, the Watts district of Los Angeles was the scene of a violent riot. Thirty-four people died as a result. Millions of dollars worth of property was destroyed. In the summer of 1966, Chicago, Cleveland, and San Francisco were scenes of similar incidents. Much of Newark, New Jersey, was devastated by flames in 1967. But the worst of the violent rioting took place soon after that in Detroit, Michigan.

On April 4, 1968, an assassin shot and killed Dr. Martin Luther King, Jr., as he stood on a Memphis, Tennessee, motel balcony. Rioting in over 100 cities and suburbs across the country followed.

Looking back, some people feel that Johnson's administration did more to change the scope of the federal government than any other Presidential administration. His programs were concerned with many different human activities. Yet, unrest and discontent, which had been postponed by hope, were unleashed during his administration.

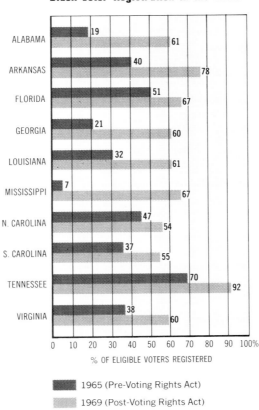

Black Voter Registration in the South

	1965 (Pre-Voting Rights Act)	1969 (Post-Voting Rights Act)
ALABAMA	19	61
ARKANSAS	40	78
FLORIDA	51	67
GEORGIA	21	60
LOUISIANA	32	61
MISSISSIPPI	7	67
N. CAROLINA	47	54
S. CAROLINA	37	55
TENNESSEE	70	92
VIRGINIA	38	60

0 10 20 30 40 50 60 70 80 90 100%

% OF ELIGIBLE VOTERS REGISTERED

■ 1965 (Pre-Voting Rights Act)
■ 1969 (Post-Voting Rights Act)

Johnson's Foreign Policy

Though Johnson favored a liberal domestic policy, he took a tough stand on foreign affairs. Many of those who praised his programs at home questioned the wisdom of his foreign policy.

In 1964, an American flag was hung outside of a school in Panama. This act touched off an anti-American riot. Sovereignty—American or Panamanian—was the issue. It was a sign of the deep resentment Panamanians felt about the presence of Americans in the Canal Zone. Panamanian President Roberto F. Chiari broke off diplomatic relations with the United States. He demanded a revision of the Panama Canal Treaty.

President Johnson refused. Instead, Johnson offered to "discuss" but not to "negotiate." Some feared that Johnson was undoing hard-won gains in United States-Latin American relations. So after four months, Johnson agreed to "review" the treaty. Eventually, a treaty was worked out that was more satisfactory to Panama. Hard feelings still remained. Some twenty years later, during President Carter's administration, a new treaty was approved over strong Senate opposition. The provisions included the return of the Canal Zone and the Canal to Panamanian ownership and control by the end of the twentieth century.

Far more damaging to Johnson's image as a moderate in foreign affairs was his reaction to a crisis in the Dominican Republic. Events in that country were unsettled by the assassination of the dictator, Rafael Trujillo Molina, in 1961. By 1963, a civil war had broken out between two groups seeking control of the country. Fearing communist influence among the rebels, Johnson sent over 21,000 marines to help stabilize matters. The marines set up a neutral zone between the rebels and the military **junta.** Not since 1925 had the United States sent armed forces into a nation in the Caribbean Sea.

junta
a group of persons controlling a government, especially after a revolutionary seizure of power

This action was widely criticized. Many American liberals felt that the United States should not have intervened in a civil war. They felt that Johnson had returned to the old way in which the United States had treated Latin America. Eventually, the United States was able to get the Organization of American States (OAS) to help mediate the crisis in the Dominican Republic. Both sides finally accepted a cease-fire. The military junta and the rebels agreed on a compromise government. When free elections were held in 1966, Johnson was sure that the measures he had employed had been successful.

When a crisis developed in the Middle East, Johnson's activities were more restrained. In 1967, tensions flared in that area of the world. President Gamal Abdel Nasser of Egypt demanded the removal of United Nations forces that separated the Egyptians and the Israelis. He also called for the closure of the Gulf of Aqaba to Israeli ships. Nasser's wishes were granted. Egyptian forces moved close to the border of Israel. The Israelis now felt threatened and let down by the United Nations.

President Johnson hoped to prevent hostilities through diplomacy. Israel was afraid to wait. So on June 5, the Israelis attacked the Egyptian forces. In what became known as the Six Day War, Israel defeated the Egyptians and extended its boundaries into Arab land. On June 10, the United Nations Security Council, with Russian and American support, declared a cease-fire. Since that time, several high-level diplomatic efforts have been made to resolve problems in the Middle East. An adequate settlement of both Palestinian and Israeli claims to the same land was a problem that would confront the world for years to come.

Questions for Discussion

1. Define *logjammed, gross national product, filibuster, grants-in-aid, junta.*
2. In which areas did President Lyndon B. Johnson direct his first actions?
3. Why was it surprising to many that Johnson would push for a civil rights program?
4. How did the Johnson administration change the federal government?
5. How was Johnson's diplomacy tested in Panama, the Dominican Republic, and the Middle East?
6. Why did so much civil unrest occur during this period despite the attempts to correct social injustice?

Gamal Abdel Nasser, President of Egypt at the time of the Six Day War with Israel.

Prior to President Kennedy's administration, American involvement in the Vietnam War had been minor. However, after the Bay of Pigs invasion and the 1961 Berlin crisis, President Kennedy felt that he had to take a strong stand on Vietnam. The South Vietnamese communist forces were scoring measurable gains over the South Vietnamese government. The government, headed by President Ngo Dinh Diem, was very unpopular. Buddhists, who made up most of the population, feared the Catholic government.

The United States government was in an awkward position. It wanted to prevent South Vietnam from falling into the hands of the Communists. However, to do this, the United States felt that it had to support a pro-American government. Between 1961 and 1963, the number of advisers in Vietnam increased in number from 2000 to 16,000. In early 1963, President Diem was overthrown and murdered in a military coup. The United States hoped the new government

2. The Fork in the Road

Left: Premier Ngo Dinh Diem was the first elected leader of the Republic of South Vietnam. His suppression of opposition parties, censorship of the press, and hostility toward Buddhism made him many enemies. He was killed in a takeover by military forces in November 1963. Right: Ho Chi Minh founded the Communist Party of Vietnam in 1930. He later fought the French, the Japanese, and—after World War II—the French once again as leader of the nationalist movement in Vietnam. In 1954, he became the first President of North Vietnam, and held that position until his death in 1969.

Vietcong
a member of the Vietnamese communist movement supported by North Vietnam who engaged in guerrilla warfare

coalition
a temporary alliance of distinctly different parties, persons, or states in an effort to promote a joint action

would be more popular. Meanwhile, in late 1963, President Kennedy was assassinated.

With the death of both leaders, there was the possibility of a change in strategy. The **Vietcong**, outnumbered six-to-one by the South Vietnamese military, controlled more than one half of the land. They offered to negotiate for a cease-fire and a **coalition** government. President Johnson believed this would result in a takeover by the Communists. In turn, he offered the South Vietnamese government "American personnel and material as needed to assist you in achieving victory."

American Involvement Increases

At this point, President Johnson had a choice between two opinions concerning the conflict. He could have viewed the Vietnam conflict as a civil war in which a more popular, smaller force was defeating a less popular, better equipped, larger force. If this were the case, the United States should reconsider its military presence.

The other opinion was that the Vietnam conflict was the result of a communist plot. The Vietcong were the agents not only of Hanoi in North Vietnam, but also of Peking in Red China and Moscow in the Soviet Union. In this case, the United States would be helping South Vietnam defend itself against outside aggressors. This belief won the support of the American government. With the acceptance of this point of view came the justification for increased military aid, American combat troops, and attacks on North Vietnam. The United

States government also believed that it would not take long to win the war. Plans for deeper intervention by the United States in the Vietnam conflict were put off until after the election. By then, events had occurred that changed the course of the war.

In the Gulf of Tonkin off the coast of North Vietnam, there was an incident involving an exchange of fire between American ships and North Vietnamese PT boats. According to government sources, the North Vietnamese had attacked two American destroyers on August 2, 1964. The North Vietnamese had assumed that the destroyers were a part of a South Vietnamese force that had just raided North Vietnamese islands. Doubt now exists that the North Vietnamese attacked the ships without cause, if at all. At the time, however, that was the accepted notion. On August 4, President Johnson announced that two American ships had been attacked. Three days later, in what became known as the Gulf of Tonkin Resolution, Congress gave the President the authority "to take all measures necessary . . . to prevent further aggression."

The immediate increase of American activity in South Vietnam and against North Vietnam was held in check by the American political scene. The year 1964 was an election year. The Republican candidate, Barry Goldwater, called for attacks on North Vietnam. He even proposed the use of nuclear weapons and commitment to total victory. President Johnson wanted to appear as the "moderate" candidate. Thus, he played down the involvement of the United States.

Down the Wrong Road

After President Johnson won the election, his military advisers began making plans to bomb North Vietnam. Meanwhile, things were going from bad to worse in the South Vietnamese government. Coups, attempted coups, demonstrations, and protests resulted in the rise to power of General Nguyen Van Thieu and Air Marshall Nguyen Cao Ky. These leaders were unwilling to compromise with the Vietcong.

On February 7, 1965, the Vietcong killed eight Americans in a raid on an American military advisers' compound. On February 8, American planes raided a North Vietnamese barracks. Shortly thereafter, the American military stopped claiming that air attacks were in answer to specific Vietcong attacks.

Thus, the buildup of formal military forces began. By April, United States military support forces, Marine combat forces, and ground troops were being used in the war. Bombing raids on North Vietnam increased. The American government believed that it could weaken North Vietnam. The United States felt that Ho Chi Minh would be forced to allow the independence of South Vietnam with a noncommunist government.

The Vietnam War

However, as President Johnson increased American ground forces to nearly 20,000, North Vietnam kept matching the buildup. From July of 1965 to October of 1967, an additional 300,000 American troops were involved in the war. In all, 40 percent of the American combat force, 50 percent of American tactical air power, and 33 percent of American tactical naval power were committed to the Vietnam conflict. In spite of these forces, the morale of the enemy was not broken. If anything, each increase in American force seemed to strengthen the North Vietnamese will to fight. In May 1965, the Vietcong summer offensive began. The United States was unable to stop the flow of supplies and troops now coming from the North. In addition to that, the South Vietnamese government was unable to win the support of the peasant population.

In June 1965, United States troops engaged in their first major "search-and-destroy mission." This became the typical operation of the war. In these missions aimed at getting rid of the Vietcong, many civilians were killed. The war seemed to be destroying South Vietnam—both the countryside and the people.

The Growing Protest

Even before President Johnson ordered the bombing of North Vietnam and the huge troop buildup, a core of antiwar protestors existed. Part of the vote that President Johnson received in 1964 was a protest vote against the warlike attitude of Barry Goldwater. So when the bombing of North Vietnam began in 1965, many *doves* (those who were against the war) became angry demonstrators.

By mid-1965, various groups were forming to protest American activities. The members of these groups came from many different backgrounds. Some college and university professors began "teach-ins" to explain the history of the Vietnam War and the American intervention in Vietnam. Young men who were eligible for the draft protested in various ways. Some burned their draft cards. Others ran away to Canada and Sweden. Still others accepted jail sentences rather than enter a war they believed to be unjust.

At first, these groups were noisy yet small. But the war dragged on. As the costs in lives and materials rose more and more, people in government, public, and private life began to voice serious doubts.

Meanwhile, *hawks* (those who favored the war) were urging a bolder stand in Vietnam, even to the extent of using nuclear weapons. The administration insisted that the war was a scheme of Russia and China to take over Southeast Asia. President Johnson's closest advisers were convinced that North Vietnam could be beaten into submission. Thus, bombing raids were continued. Occasionally, the bombing would be temporarily halted to encourage peace talks.

Civilians suffered the most in the Vietnam War. Both sides committed crimes against noncombatant men, women, and children. One such tragedy took place in January 1968, when a huge Vietcong assault killed many civilians and created 350,000 refugees, like the ones in this photo fleeing the city of Hue.

However, as each side became firmer in its demands, the bombing was resumed.

By 1967, the protests were becoming larger, louder, and longer. People such as Dr. Martin Luther King, Jr.; Dr. Benjamin Spock (author of a famous book on child care); Rev. William Sloane Coffin (the chaplain of Yale University); and Senators William Fulbright, George McGovern, Eugene McCarthy, and Robert Kennedy became outspoken opponents of the war. It was clear that the Vietnam War was tearing the nation apart.

For months the administration conducted programs to win the loyalty of South Vietnamese peasants. They claimed that these programs were successful. In January 1968, the Tet offensive made a mockery of these claims. Ignoring the week-long truce proclaimed for Tet (the Lunar New Year), the Vietcong made massive attacks on thirty targets in South Vietnam. They even took over a portion of the United States Embassy compound in the South Vietnamese capital of Saigon.

Several realities began to surface. For one, the Vietcong were still a military power and would remain so for some time to come. Also, some of the South Vietnamese people were helping the Vietcong. Then too, the bombing was not putting a halt to the war. As a result, President Johnson was in trouble politically. So, on March 31, 1968, he announced a cutback in bombing along with his decision not to seek reelection. Thus, Johnson's political career became yet another victim of the war.

Questions for Discussion
1. Define *Vietcong, coalition, doves, hawks.*
2. How and why did the United States become involved in Vietnam?
3. What caused the American involvement in Vietnam to change from advisory to military?
4. Why was the United States unable to defeat the Communist forces in North Vietnam?

3. Groups in Motion

Before Johnson made his announcements, two Democrats had already begun the race for the Presidential nomination. Senator Eugene McCarthy and Senator Robert Kennedy ran against each other in the Democratic Presidential primaries. Kennedy won every primary he entered except the one in Oregon. On June 5, 1968, the night of his victory in the California primary, Sirhan Sirhan, a young Jordanian immigrant, shot and killed him. Only a few weeks earlier, Dr. Martin Luther King, Jr., had met with the same fate. These examples of violence and unrest served to stun and frighten many people in America and around the world.

Yet, more shocks were still to come. The Democratic Convention was held in Chicago from August 26–29, 1968. Inside the convention hall, there was a mass of confusion. The order of business was interrupted by such acts as California and New York delegates chanting, "We shall overcome."

The events that took place outside the convention hall were even more astonishing. Thousands of demonstrators gathered in Chicago to voice their protest against the war. Mayor Richard Daley of Chicago summoned the police. They were given orders to disperse crowds and prevent any demonstration. The result was a brutal clash between demonstrators and police. As Americans tuned in on their television sets, they witnessed firsthand a violent attack by police on everyone in sight—demonstrators, onlookers, passersby, and even people sitting in restaurants.

It was one of the most shocking scenes that had ever been shown on the screen. And that night, Hubert Humphrey won the Democratic nomination for President.

THE LOGAN ACT

Fonda, Clark, and Hayden Visit Hanoi In the late stages of the war in Vietnam, three Americans—Jane Fonda, Ramsey Clark, and Tom Hayden—made a visit to Hanoi. Their purpose was to see for themselves how "the other side" was doing. They also wanted to find out directly what the North Vietnamese government's viewpoints and demands were. All three were strong opponents of the war. They claimed that their trip was needed to cut through the propaganda screen that they believed was set up by the United States. Various North Vietnamese officials welcomed and interviewed them.

In the United States, supporters of the war were outraged. Some suggested that the three had violated the Logan Act and should be prosecuted. The *Logan Act* provided that no American citizen might enter diplomatic negotiations with a foreign government unless given official authority by the United States government. The Act was also about 169 years old at that time!

The Logan Act was named for an American Quaker, George Logan. Logan was disturbed in 1798 by the fact that the United States seemed to be drifting into a war with France. Selling off some of his land to pay his own expenses, he sailed off to Paris. There he held a number of conversations with the French government. He was told unofficially that the French would welcome a special American envoy to deal with the question of American rights to trade in nonmilitary goods with the enemies of France. President John Adams later sent such an emissary, though the arrangement was in the making before Logan's arrival. All the same, Logan had helped to cool off an explosive situation.

But when he arrived home, Logan discovered that the Federalists in Congress, eager to fight the French, were furious. They succeeded in getting the Logan Act passed. The law was designed to make sure that no pacifist would dare to try such a mission again. Congress felt that great confusion would result if a government spoke with several people—especially those who were not officials—on foreign affairs.

Nothing actually happened to Logan as a result. The act was passed after he had made his effort. In fact, he was later elected to the United States Senate.

However, the law named for him still remained on the books—unused—but always ready to be invoked, at least in theory. The Logan Act was not used against the three who visited Hanoi. But the fact that it was mentioned shows how long and loud an echo Logan's journey left behind.

1968 Election

In the 1968 Presidential election, Hubert Humphrey opposed Richard M. Nixon. Nixon had been selected on the first ballot at the Republican Convention. Two minor parties of opposing views also selected candidates. George Wallace, ex-Governor of Alabama, was chosen by the American Independent Party, which he had founded. The Peace and Freedom Party chose Black Panther leader Eldridge Cleaver. Of the two, only George Wallace presented a serious threat to the two-party system.

The last major candidate to enter the Presidential campaign in 1968, Vice President Hubert H. Humphrey won the Democratic Party's nomination.

Richard M. Nixon, who had been Vice President under Dwight D. Eisenhower, was the Republican candidate in 1968. He won the Presidency in a dramatically close election.

During the campaign, Vice-President Humphrey was plagued by his identification with President Johnson's administration. His public appearances were disrupted by hecklers. They saw Humphrey as a representative of the Vietnam War and the repression of antiwar demonstrators. It was not until the end of the campaign that he broke away from President Johnson and called for an end to the bombing in Vietnam. On what became a second issue of the campaign—the problem of street crime—he called for "order and justice." He also stressed a need for an end to discrimination.

Richard M. Nixon, the Republican candidate, stressed a "law and order" theme. To many people, this meant that demonstrators would be kept in line. To others, it meant that they could put to rest their fears of unrest in the cities. People also felt that a call for law and order would mean a tighter rein on crime. Nixon claimed he had a plan for peace in Vietnam, but he could not yet disclose it. His campaign was well organized. Nixon planned his major appearances so that the television networks would have time to prepare the news for the evening programs. His major problem seemed to be Wallace's candidacy. By appealing for a strong stand on law and order as Nixon did, Wallace drew more votes away from Nixon than from Humphrey.

In spite of some late support, Humphrey could not overcome Nixon's lead. Nixon polled 43.4 percent of the popular vote to Humphrey's 42.7 percent. Wallace received 13.5 percent with a strong showing in the Deep South. The election seemed to indicate a voter reaction to the war and the social unrest that was rocking the nation.

Richard M. Nixon was elected to the Presidency at a time when American society was in a state of change. The turmoil of the sixties had shaken people up. They were no longer sure what they believed in. During the sixties and early seventies, many groups were searching for self-respect and self-identity.

The Continuing Black Struggle

In earlier times, Blacks had tried to change their circumstances. Several movements developed for Blacks to separate themselves from Whites to avoid the effects of racism. One such program was the "Back-to-Africa" movement led by Marcus Garvey in the 1920s. Though the plans went awry and Garvey was convicted of mail fraud and deported to Jamaica, he had awakened a spirit of Black pride.

In the 1930s, a group known as the Nation of Islam was founded in Detroit, Michigan. In 1934, Elijah Poole, who changed his name to Elijah Muhammad, took over as leader. He preached a message of hope to Black urban dwellers. His group, known as the Black Muslims, urged their followers to adopt strict rules of personal behavior. Liquor, tobacco, and drug use were forbidden. Blacks were urged to open their own businesses and patronize Black-owned industries. During the mid 1960s, the Black Muslims were the largest and the most powerful economic Black group in the United States.

Malcolm Little, renamed Malcolm X, became one of the best known Black Muslims. At one time deeply involved in crime, he became an extraordinary convert. At first he bitterly preached hatred of Whites and the separation of races. He believed that this was the only way the White and Black races could coexist. Eventually, his thinking on this issue changed. As a result of this change in philosophy, Malcolm X left the Black Muslims and formed his own organization. For this group, he adopted a theme of Black unity and preached that unity among Blacks would be the key to a better life in the United States. Assassinated in 1965, he left behind two influential works, *The Autobiography of Malcom X* and *Malcolm X Speaks*.

Though relatively few people joined these movements, their effects were still very noticeable. More militant Blacks began to feel that Dr. Martin Luther King's methods of getting equal rights were too slow. Thus, the Black civil rights movement took a more radical twist.

In 1966, Stokely Carmichael of the Student Nonviolent Coordinating Committee (SNCC) challenged Dr. King's theme of nonviolence with a new slogan—"Black Power." Carmichael advocated meeting violence with violence. He believed that Blacks would never gain their rights unless they became economically independent of Whites. He realized that Blacks had to become politically powerful as well.

Between 1965 and 1970, other Black militants began to gain prominence. It was during this period that Huey Newton, Eldridge Cleaver, and Bobby Seale organized the Black Panther Party. This group advocated using any means necessary to protect Black Americans against racism. Even though they initiated many valuable social programs, such as free lunch for young school children, these Black leaders were most often noted for the antagonism they aroused, especially among police. A handful of militants even talked openly of guerrilla warfare against their oppressors.

On college campuses and in high schools, Black students demanded courses in Black art, literature, and history. They also demanded more Black instructors. In the cities and towns, Blacks were seeking local control over school boards and social programs. In politics, moderate Black leaders were seeking political offices. They all knew that changes were needed. The question was how to cause these changes.

Malcolm X split away from the Black Muslims in 1964 and founded his own movement. He preached unity among Blacks, but no longer advocated the separation of Blacks and Whites. In 1965, Malcolm X was assassinated as he spoke at a gathering in New York.

Student Protest

Many people associate the 1960s with scenes of campuses in revolt. Marches, boycotts, picket lines, mass meetings, building takeovers, and even explosions astounded the public. These protestors were often at the best schools. More often than not, they were the sons and daughters of upper-middle-class New Deal liberals.

These student activists had a number of gripes. Like other groups during the sixties, the students wanted more control over their lives as students. They wanted changes in the curriculum and in dormitory living conditions. They wanted to do away with rules that limited their independence.

Students and faculties were among the first to protest against the Vietnam War. Many students were able to put off military service because of draft deferments. But many young males were required to participate in the Reserve Officer Training Corps (ROTC) during their freshman year. Students picketed the offices of the ROTC on campus and heckled army and navy recruiters. Students and faculties succeeded in reducing military activities on campuses.

In 1970, a demonstration against the invasion of Cambodia by American troops resulted in a bitter confrontation between the National Guard in Ohio and Kent State University students. Four students were shot and killed on the University campus. In the protest that followed, over 400 campuses were shut down by students. In another violent confrontation, "hardhats" at a New York City construction site beat up antiwar protestors.

Consciousness Raised

By the 1960s, so many groups were struggling for recognition and for a share of the good things of life that one writer spoke of the period as an "equality revolution." The battle took many forms and involved all kinds of people who believed that they lacked power. In addition to Blacks, among these were other non-Whites, voteless young people, the poor, and the aged. And much was heard from a "minority" that was not a minority—women.

Women became more militant. An important leader, Betty Friedan, wrote *The Feminine Mystique*. She believes that women should not measure their success in terms of a husband and children. Women should be free to seek educations, find careers, and insist on an equal opportunity to succeed in business or in the professions. They should be able to have both a family and a career if they choose to do so. To promote these ideas, Betty Friedan founded the National Organization for Women (NOW). NOW and groups like it conducted campaigns for many goals. One very important area of concern was that of jobs. Feminists took legal action to prevent employers from considering only men for certain jobs, such as airline pilot or civil engineer. In growing numbers, they won admission to law, medicine, and other professions. Court action opened many new doors. In 1970, racetracks were forced

With the publication of her book, The Feminine Mystique, *in 1963, Betty Friedan became a major figure in the struggle for women's rights. She founded the National Organization for Women and served as its president from 1966 to 1970.*

to hire the first female jockeys. In 1973, Little League teams had to admit girls to baseball tryouts.

In 1972, Gloria Steinem, another outspoken champion of women's rights, founded *Ms.* magazine. This national magazine became a voice of the women's movement. As a result of this effort and other similar feminist efforts, leading publications have changed the type of articles they feature in recognition of the new role of women.

Women's organizations wanted all people to recognize the contributions of women to every field of human striving. They urged that people of both sexes be unrestricted in their activities. Individuals should cook or build bridges not on the basis of what was thought proper for a man or woman but of what each person could do best. As a step toward this goal, women's groups sought the passage of the Equal Rights Amendment (ERA). The ERA, passed by Congress in 1972 and presented to the states for ratification, is intended to protect the rights of women. It provides that, "Equality of rights under the law shall not be denied or abridged by the United States or by any State on account of sex."

Other Groups Struggle for Equality

American Indians also demanded fair treatment. The average income of American Indians is one half that of Blacks. They are the poorest Americans. In an effort to improve their condition, American Indians called for a return to tribal councils for decisions about life on the reservation. In addition, they asked for fair settlements for land taken by the government. In a series of demonstrations throughout the sixties, they challenged the White establishment. In 1973, the Sioux at Wounded Knee, South Dakota, seized part of the town. They

Emerging as the most militant group for the radical reform of federal-Indian relations, the American Indian Movement (AIM) spearheaded the Sioux occupation of the village of Wounded Knee, South Dakota, in 1973. The occupation challenged the locally elected Oglala Sioux government and demanded general reform in Indian tribal government.

A passionate believer in nonviolence, Cesar Chavez led nationwide boycotts of grapes and lettuce in the sixties and seventies in efforts to attain union representation for non-union farm workers.

barrio
an Hispanic neighborhood or ghetto. *Barrio* is a Spanish word meaning district.

Ethnic pride is often demonstrated in festivals and celebrations. Top Left: Dancing at a Polish party in Minnesota. Top Right: A West-Indian Day parade in Brooklyn. Bottom Left: A celebration of the Chinese New Year. Bottom Right: Children at a parade honoring the 25th anniversary of the founding of Israel.

held off United States marshals for ten weeks (February 27–May 8) before giving up. Even then, they surrendered only after their demands for negotiations were met.

East Los Angeles, a **barrio**, was the scene of rioting and demonstration in the sixties and early seventies. Mexican-Americans protested against the Vietnam War, poverty, poor housing, and inferior schools. They were also concerned that the heritage of Mexican-Americans was not being taught. Thus, they organized throughout the American Southwest. They worked toward such goals as the use of both Spanish and English in the classrooms of the public schools. Bilingual classrooms would permit Mexican-American children, who might not hear much English at home, to have more of a learning advantage in school.

The work of Cesar Chavez brought new pride to Mexican-Americans and changed the lives of thousands of farm workers. In 1965, a new union of almost entirely Mexican-American grape pickers struck against working conditions in California. Their leader, Cesar Chavez, urged a nationwide boycott of California-grown grapes. Many important public figures supported him. Thus, by 1970, the grape growers gave in and recognized the union.

The struggle was not over, but at least it had begun. Later, Chavez began another national boycott, this time against California growers of lettuce who did not employ members of the United Farm Workers union.

A New Pride in an Old Heritage

In appealing for national sympathy for the farm workers, Chavez did not play down their Mexican background. The strikers' slogan, *Viva La Huelga* (Hurrah for the Strike), was printed in Spanish everywhere. This illustrated a new attitude of American minorities that was part of the equality revolution. It showed itself in many noticeable ways. One way was a new interest by American Blacks in their African background. For example, natural hairstyles became more common and accepted. And African clothing and ornaments became quite fashionable.

When Blacks, American Indians, Puerto Ricans, and other non-White groups proudly displayed the special ways of life of their ancestors, they were involved in a change. For many years, the model held up to minorities was that of the melting pot. Their members might rise in life as they gained in education and income. As they did so, they were expected to give up their "foreign" foods, styles, ideas, and customs. Successful Americans were alike! Now, what racial and national minorities were saying was that they objected to such a definition of "Americanism."

Puerto Ricans living in New York celebrate Puerto Rican Day with a parade up Fifth Avenue.

Non-White pride of heritage reawakened a similar spirit in those descended from European immigrants. In big cities, Americans of Polish, Irish, and Italian backgrounds marched along in holiday parades honoring Casimir Pulaski, a Pole who fought in the American Revolution, St. Patrick, or Columbus. Italian-Americans, like American Jews, organized groups to put pressure on filmmakers and broadcasters to avoid unfavorable stereotypes of their people. A common name for these people who were not of English descent was "White ethnics."

There was value for many Whites and non-Whites in seeking an independent cultural identity. However, some Americans, including some minority group members, were disturbed. They believed that the special strength of the United States lay in keeping different peoples working peaceably within the same political and social system. They argued that a degree of conformity was a price worth paying for so rare an achievement. Cultural separateness, they feared, would make ordinary political disagreements far too bitter. This question was to become one of the issues of the seventies, as America tried to resolve the problems of the sixties.

Questions for Discussion

1. Define *barrio*.
2. What groups and actions sought to give Blacks greater prestige and identity?
3. Who took part in the "equality revolution" in the 1960s?
4. What groups would be considered "White ethnics"?

Chapter 30 Review

Summary Questions for Discussion

1. How did President Johnson overcome the obstacles of passing the Civil Rights Act of 1964? What were its provisions?
2. What actions did Johnson take to combat poverty?
3. Who were the Republican candidates in the Presidential election of 1964? What was their platform?
4. How did Johnson's programs under his Great Society affect the following: education, medical programs, aid to the poor, housing, and voting rights of Blacks?
5. What negative actions resulted from the poverty and prejudice that existed in the mid-1960s?
6. How did Johnson deal with problems in Panama? When were they resolved?
7. How had Johnson hoped to prevent the Six Day War?
8. List the events that led President Johnson to offer the South Vietnamese government American personnel and material.
9. What events or conditions prompted the Gulf of Tonkin Resolution? What were its provisions?
10. Why did American involvement in the Vietnamese conflict increase between 1965 and 1967?
11. What was the significance of the Tet offensive?
12. What was the role of each of the following in the development of Black pride and awareness: Elijah Muhammad, Malcolm X, Stokely Carmichael, Huey Newton, and Eldridge Cleaver?
13. What changes were sought by Blacks during the 1960s?
14. What victories have been won by feminists?
15. What demands were made in the 1960s by the following groups: American Indians? Mexican-Americans?
16. How did various groups renew pride in their old heritage?

Word Study

Fill in each blank in the sentences that follow with the term below that is most appropriate.

doves   Vietcong   logjammed   filibuster

barrio   grants-in-aid   hawks

1. When bills are stuck in Congress and are prevented from becoming law, they are said to be _____.
2. During a _____, Senators try to "talk a bill to death."
3. A method whereby the federal government assists states in the establishment of certain programs is referred to as _____.
4. The South Vietnamese guerrilla force that opposed the Saigon government was known as the _____.
5. People who oppose war and often demonstrate against it are called _____.
6. Strong supporters of war are called _____.
7. Mexican-Americans often live in a _____, or a ghetto-type area.

Using Your Skills

Study the graph, Black Voter Registration in the South, on page 693. Which state's political life would you expect to be most changed as a result of the 1965 Voting Rights Acts? Why? Which of the states do you think would be least affected? Why?

CHAPTER 31
Issues of the Seventies

On July 4, 1976, tall colonial-style ships sailed into New York harbor. Fireworks crackled and sparkled from coast to coast. "Minutemen" paraded in communities all over the country. Red, white, and blue flags waved in the air. The United States was at the height of a grand celebration—its 200th birthday. Despite the glory of the bicentennial year, many Americans felt disillusioned by recent events in their country.

Government officials in the highest positions had abused the power entrusted to them. Powerful persons in the Nixon administration were involved in serious crimes and had violated their oaths of office. This affair, known as the Watergate scandal, shook the faith of the American people in their elected officials.

Both American experience in Vietnam and the Arab oil embargo raised questions about the role of the United States in world affairs. The old alliances and loyalties of the post-World War II years were weakening. In addition, unstable conditions in the Middle East were threatening to draw the East and the West into another major conflict.

The economy, which had experienced a boom during the sixties, became troublesome during the seventies. In fact, for two years—from 1973 to 1975—the country experienced the worst economic *recession* since the Great Depression. Recession occurs when there is a slowdown of economic activity marked by a decrease in employment, profits, production, prices, and sales. Economic recovery was greeted with feelings of gloom, because no one was sure it would last.

Many people realized that the past approaches to social problems had failed to produce peaceful race relations. These measures had also failed substantially to reduce crime and poverty. Indeed, the decade of the seventies was a time of serious reflection.

READING GUIDE

1. **How did Nixon's administration reflect a break with the past?**
2. **Why did people lose faith in the government?**
3. **In what ways were President Ford's policies similar to Nixon's?**
4. **How did President Carter's policies compare with those of his predecessors?**

A spectacular fireworks display highlights the July 4, 1976 celebration of America's bicentennial year as a nation.

1. Nixon at the Helm

During the seventies, Americans paid the price for the economic boom of the sixties. This price was severe inflation. As you have learned, inflation exists when the costs of goods and services increase without an increase in production. This condition leads to a decrease in buying power. Economists debated the exact causes of inflation. However, they did agree on some factors that proved influential. Heavy government spending on military goods and services and on welfare programs put more money into circulation without increasing productivity. People relied heavily on credit to buy items for which they did not have cash. In addition, an increase of money in circulation without an increase in goods and services led to price rises. Productiv-

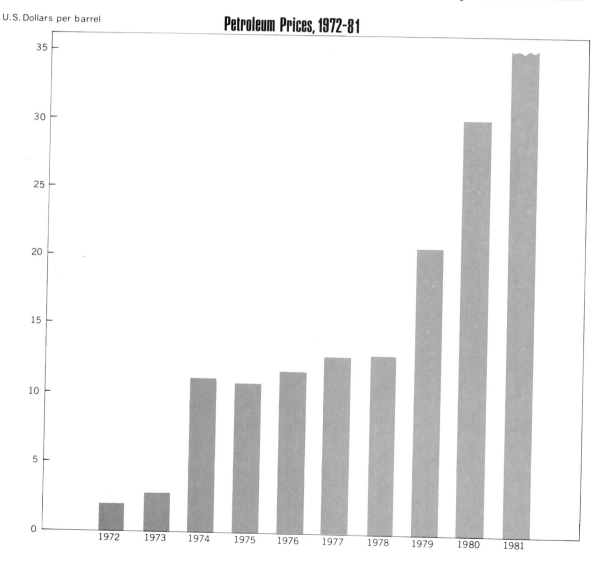

U.S. Dollars per barrel

Petroleum Prices, 1972-81

ity was affected unfavorably by the failure of businesses to replace worn-out factory equipment with more efficient machines. Workers were also at fault. They were not putting forth all their efforts to get jobs done. Finally, the cost of energy kept getting higher and higher each time there was trouble in oil-exporting countries.

Whatever the causes of inflation, the results were clear. As prices rose, workers demanded raises to maintain their standard of living. Higher wage costs in turn forced employers to raise prices again. And so this "upward spiral" continued. There was a limit to how high wages could be raised. Continued inflation would shrink the value of money to such an extent that simple necessities would cost huge sums. As a result, the whole country would collapse.

There was no one villain to be blamed for inflation. Each time manufacturers raised their prices, they could argue that the costs of labor, materials, and distribution methods had gone up. People living on *fixed incomes* were among those hardest hit by inflation. These people include the elderly living on pensions and widows and orphans living on insurance payments. These people will have no increase or decrease in the amount of money they can spend, even if prices rise or fall. The unemployed—whose numbers increased drastically at this time—were helpless victims as well.

Nixon inherited these economic woes from the Johnson administration. As the Vietnam War wound down, the state of the economy became a major issue. Nixon tried to attack inflation by adopting the policies of the Federal Reserve System—raising interest rates, thereby encouraging saving instead of spending.

With an election coming up, Nixon "stole" the economic program of the Democrats. In a television speech, he revealed his new economic policy. He called for a ninety-day wage, price, and rent freeze—a measure long favored by the Democrats. In Phase II of his program, the freeze was to be lifted. A Pay Board and Price Commission, however, were to be given authority to rule on wage and price increases.

Nixon also announced that the dollar would no longer be converted to gold at $35 per ounce on the world market. The value of the dollar would rise or fall based on the decisions of foreign buyers. Because foreign buyers preferred to invest in such stable economies as the Federal Republic of Germany and Japan, the dollar was expected to decrease in value compared to the German mark and the Japanese yen. Thus, Nixon's decision actually had the effect of *devaluating* the dollar. The prices of American export goods were lowered in terms of foreign currencies. However, foreign imports cost more. Nixon hoped that this measure would encourage exports, reduce imports, and thus improve the United States **balance of payments.**

The Rate of Inflation 1940-1979

The Dollar's Purchasing Power

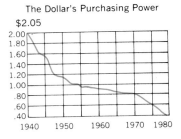

Consumer Price Index

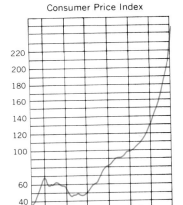

The top chart illustrates the purchasing power of the dollar, using 1955 as the year in which the dollar was worth 100 cents. At that value, the dollar in 1955 could buy $2.05 worth of goods in 1940, but only $0.40 worth of goods in 1980. The second chart concerns the Consumer Price Index. Goods that could be purchased for $100 in 1960 would have cost $40 in 1913 and $200 in 1981, with the price continuing to rise. These charts thus show the effects of inflation on the purchasing power of the dollar and its subsequent effect on consumer prices.

balance of payments
a summary of the international transactions of a country or region over a period of time. This summary includes service transactions and gold movements.

United States Foreign Trade
1910-1978

Billions
of dollars

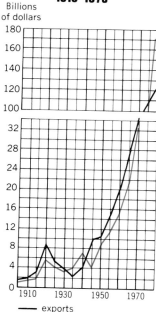

— exports
— imports
(includes merchandise, gold,
and silver)

After President Nixon broke the $35 conversion rate between gold and the dollar, the price of gold soared in the next ten years to over $600 an ounce. Above: The chart shows that U.S. trade with the world has increased sharply since World War II. However, look at the charts on page 713. Although the number of dollars is increasing rapidly, the value of dollars is decreasing rapidly.

2. Groping for Peace

For a while, an economic upturn and a moderating rate of inflation coincided with Phase II of Nixon's plan. During 1973, however, the continually rising price of oil and other scarce raw materials served to fuel worldwide inflation.

Questions for Discussion

1. Define *fixed incomes, devaluating, recession, balance of payments.*
2. Why did Nixon's attempt to solve the economic woes of the nation fail?

In 1971, the Chinese and United States governments realized that the time had come to normalize relations. For more than twenty years, the United States had refused to recognize the government of mainland China, favoring instead the Nationalist Chinese government of Taiwan. There were several reasons for the change in attitude. There was a flicker of hope for settling the Vietnam conflict. The two communist giants, China and the Soviet Union, were at odds with one another. Japan had become an economic power in Asia. Japan and other nations were no longer willing to keep the People's Republic of China isolated.

Late in 1971, a smiling President Nixon sprang a surprise on a nationwide television audience. He announced that his assistant for national security affairs, Henry Kissinger, had gone to Peking, China. Kissinger's mission was to open avenues of communication with the leaders of the People's Republic of China. The success of his mission prompted the Chinese to invite Nixon to visit their capital early in

1972. Nixon's reputation as an anticommunist calmed the fears of some Americans who believed that United States recognition of China would encourage the People's Republic of China to seize Nationalist China. At the end of his visit in February 1972, President Nixon and Premier Chou En-lai issued the Shanghai Communiqué. Both leaders expressed their desire to "reduce the danger of military conflict."

Although that visit produced no formal agreement for an exchange of ambassadors, it did prepare the way for diplomatic, cultural, and trade exchanges. After twenty-three years of opposition to Chinese communism, the United States sought to achieve peace in Asia with the cooperation of the People's Republic of China.

Detente Between East and West

After a series of atomic tests following World War II, many scientists and government officials became concerned about the effects of unleashing airborne radioactivity on the world. In the years after the war, controlling the spread of this nuclear technology proved to be impossible. The United States and the Soviet Union dominated the field of nuclear weapons. But other nations, such as the United Kingdom, France, China, and India, also possessed nuclear weapons.

As world tensions deepened, some countries made efforts to control the spread and use of nuclear weapons. The Limited Test Ban Treaty and the Nonproliferation Treaty of the sixties were two notable successes. The Limited Test Ban Treaty was signed in August 1963 by the United States, the Soviet Union, and Great Britain. These nations promised not to test nuclear weapons in outer space, in the atmosphere, or under water. However, they could test underground. The

Nonproliferation Treaty prohibited the spread of nuclear weapons, established safeguard procedures, and insured that all nations could have access to nuclear energy in the name of peace.

Nevertheless, by 1969, the United States and the Soviet Union were spending $130 billion a year for defense. Both superpowers finally realized the advantages of slowing down the arms race and of reducing tensions between them. In 1967, President Johnson suggested joint negotiations. He scheduled a **summit meeting** to take place before the 1968 election. But the Soviet Union invaded Czechoslovakia that year, and the meeting was cancelled.

President Nixon proposed negotiating arms limitations with Moscow. However, he and Kissinger believed that these negotiations should be linked to other issues, in particular, that of Vietnam. In November 1969, The United States and the Soviet Union began the first in a series of strategic arms limitation talks (SALT). These talks resulted in agreements signed by President Nixon and Premier

summit meeting
a conference of the top leaders of governments

Europe 1970

Warsaw Pact Nations

North Atlantic Treaty Organization
(Also included: United States and Canada)

Not members of either alliance

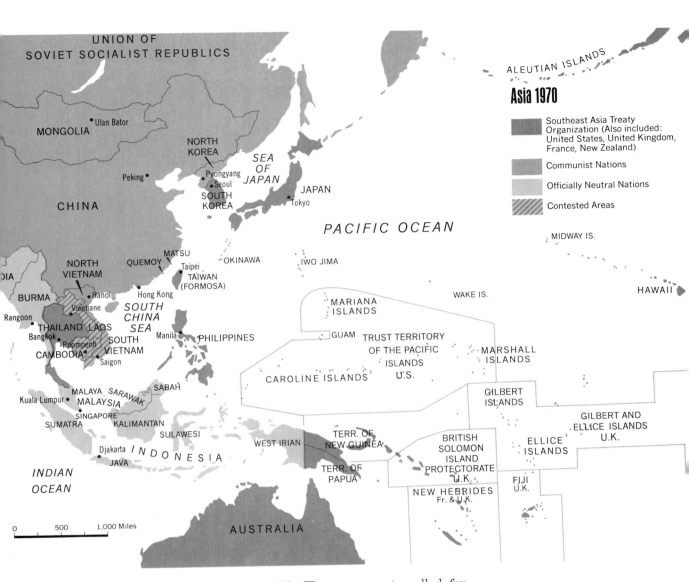

Asia 1970

- Southeast Asia Treaty Organization (Also included: United States, United Kingdom, France, New Zealand)
- Communist Nations
- Officially Neutral Nations
- Contested Areas

Brezhnev in Moscow on May 26, 1972. The agreements called for limiting **antiballistic missile** sites as well as limiting the production of missiles and warheads. United States representatives believed that they had also secured a promise of Soviet help in ending the Vietnam conflict. In March 1973, a second round of talks, aimed at extending arms limitations, began in Geneva.

While the SALT talks were in progress, the two nations discussed other approaches toward mutual cooperation. For example, the United States and the Soviet Union agreed to undertake joint scientific projects, to exchange information, and to begin trading with one another.

antiballistic missile
a missile whose purpose is to intercept and destroy ballistic missiles. It is a very powerful defensive weapon.

717

Upon reaching an agreement with the North Vietnamese on a cease fire in January 1973, the United States began to withdraw its troops. Here, U.S. Marines at Da Nang, South Vietnam, board a transport ship for home.

Withdrawal from Vietnam

In the summer of 1972, after the Moscow summit, Secretary of State Kissinger assured the world that negotiations were progressing at the Paris peace talks. However, those talks broke down in October. One month later, the Presidential elections were held. Nixon won an overwhelming victory over George McGovern, the Democratic antiwar candidate. Encouraged by his political victory, Nixon ordered massive bombing raids on the North Vietnamese cities of Haiphong and Hanoi. These raids were not confined to military targets alone.

Finally, in January 1973, Kissinger and Le Duc Tho, the North Vietnamese negotiator, reached an agreement on a cease-fire. United States troops were to be withdrawn. In addition, American prisoners of war were to be released. After ten years of military involvement, the United States was finally withdrawing from Vietnam.

That same year, Congress acted to limit American involvement in any more "Vietnams" by passing the War Powers Act. This act was designed to limit the power of the President to wage an undeclared war. It required the President to report to Congress within forty-eight hours of sending American troops to foreign soil. The troops could not remain beyond sixty days without congressional approval. Nixon vetoed this bill, but his veto was overridden.

The Middle East

During Nixon's administration, American attention turned once more to the Middle East. In the six years since their stinging defeat in the Six-Day War in 1967, Egypt and Syria had rebuilt their forces with the aid of Soviet arms. They vowed that they would recapture their lands, which were now occupied by Israeli troops. In addition, the Palestinian Arabs demanded a state of their own along with the destruction of Israel. From bases in Jordan and Lebanon, Palestinian commandos conducted terrorist raids on Israeli border settlements. Palestinian hijackers seized American and European aircraft and demanded the end of Jewish immigration to Israel. They also demanded the release of those Arab prisoners convicted of terrorist activities. Israel struck back, launching attacks on Palestinian bases.

In October 1973, Egypt and Syria launched an attack on Israel. In support of Egypt and Syria, the Arab nations used what became known as "the oil weapon." They refused to ship oil to any nation that supported Israel. This embargo caused a worldwide crisis. How did this happen?

In 1960, the nations that export oil formed OPEC, the Organization of Oil Exporting Countries. They did this so that they would have some strength in dealing with the international oil companies that produced and shipped their oil. Until 1973, few people knew much about OPEC. Then in that year, OPEC quadrupled prices and cut off oil to the United States and most of Western Europe.

In this view of a closed session of an OPEC meeting in 1968, representatives of member countries prepare to vote on the next rise in the price of crude oil.

719

The crisis was eased when Secretary of State Kissinger arranged a truce between the warring parties. Kissinger, flying back and forth between Egypt and Israel, engaged in what was called *shuttle diplomacy*. In his meetings with Egyptian President Anwar Sadat and Israeli Prime Minister Golda Meir, Kissinger negotiated a pullback of Israeli forces from the area of the Suez Canal. Despite the attempts of the Palestinian Liberation Organization (PLO) to disrupt the peace mission, Israel and Syria also signed an agreement. Thus, the Arabs ended the oil embargo.

Questions for Discussion

1. Define *summit meeting, antiballistic missile.*
2. How did the passage of the War Powers Act reflect the American attitude toward war and the Vietnam conflict?
3. What actions on the part of the Nixon administration helped to ease the tensions between the free world and the communist world?
4. What was the role of Kissinger's "shuttle diplomacy"?

3. The Runaway Presidency

The military and economic growth of modern America has allowed an increase in presidential power. As foreign affairs became more important, the President, as commander in chief of the armed forces, sometimes acted without congressional approval. In 1940, Franklin D. Roosevelt traded fifty destroyers to Great Britain for the right to lease West India bases. And Presidents before him sent marines to foreign lands without formal declarations of war, as Presidents after him did in Korea and Vietnam. President Nixon had ordered the bombing of Cambodia in 1969 without even informing Congress or the public. Presidents have open channels to many necessary sources of information that other people do not have. They alone hold the responsibility to authorize the use of nuclear weapons. In addition, Presidents overshadow Congress in dealing with foreign leaders.

As a result of the great expansion of the federal government's role in regulating the economy, Presidents have also obtained many powers at home. They appoint members of dozens of agencies that regulate railroads, banks, broadcasting networks, and other vital parts of national life. They also have emergency powers to raise and lower tariffs and to distribute energy supplies. By the decade of the seventies, a feeling had developed that the presidency had become dangerously strong.

The extent of that danger was made public by the Watergate scandal. In 1972, Richard M. Nixon won reelection by a landslide. During the campaign, several men were arrested for breaking into the national headquarters of the Democratic party in the Watergate Hotel in Washington, D.C. These "burglars" broke in to plant illegal listening devices on telephones. In 1973, it was revealed that the burglars had actually been working for the Committee to Reelect the President— Nixon's campaign organization. Bit by bit, the full story was uncovered by law-enforcement officials, news media, and congressional investigators. The President and his chief White House aids had tried to hide the truth. They had encouraged those who participated in the scandal to lie. They had also made every effort to stop the congressional investigations. They even went so far as to pay "hush money" to the burglars to keep them quiet about who had hired them. As the story slowly unfolded, it was further revealed that a secret, White House-directed group (the "plumbers") had been formed. It was the job of the plumbers to spy on federal appointees who "leaked" information to the public that President Nixon wanted kept secret.

Discovery of these unlawful activities brought into play the basic Constitutional system of checks and balances. The Supreme Court ordered the President to give up tape recordings, secretly made in his office, that provided much of the case against him. In addition, Congress began the process of impeachment. In the face of growing evidence against him, on August 9, 1974, Richard Nixon resigned. Ordinarily, Spiro T. Agnew, the Vice President chosen in 1972, would have succeeded Nixon. But ten months before, in yet another scandal that shook the nation, Agnew had resigned. He had been charged with accepting illegal payments from business representatives for favors granted. Under the Twenty-fifth Amendment, the President, with the approval of Congress, fills a vacancy in the vice-presidency. So after Agnew's departure, Nixon had named Gerald R. Ford of Michigan. Ford had been the Republican Minority Leader of the House of Representatives. His image was one of great honesty.

Money and Political Honesty

The Watergate scandal showed that Presidential secrecy made it hard to control that office of government. It also illustrated the problem of political contributions. The unlawful White House activities had been financed by surplus campaign contributions made to Nixon. Only he and his associates knew how much money had been collected and where it went. There were other charges—not fully proven—against Nixon. Among these were charges that he had performed political favors for large contributors. These were favors such as raising government-support prices for milk after the dairy industry made a pledge to contribute a large sum. Even if untrue, the stories reminded Americans that Presidents should not be indebted to powerful interest groups and wealthy corporations. Indebtedness could only lead to corruption.

On October 10, 1973 Vice President Spiro Agnew resigned from public office following his plea of nolo contendere, or "no contest," to a charge of income-tax evasion. Agnew steadfastly maintained his innocence, yet he accepted a plea bargain in return for a dropped charge. As part of the plea bargain, publication of grand jury criminal information against him cited instances of acceptance of payoffs from construction company executives. The payoffs had occurred while Agnew was governor of Maryland and Vice President under Richard Nixon.

721

Huge sums of money are necessary to pay for the mounting costs of campaigning. Presidential candidates spend a great deal of money to round up convention votes for the nomination as well as for the election campaign itself. Jet travel, polling, nationwide campaign work, and above all, television commercials, are very costly. A serious presidential candidate needs millions of dollars. A person needing so much money may be forced to listen to the views of those who provide those funds.

So to prevent corrupt deals between big donors and Presidents, Congress passed a Campaign Reform Act in 1974. Contributions to presidential campaigns are limited. A great deal of the money for campaigning comes from *public financing*. This money comes from a special checkoff box on the federal income-tax form. On line 8, each taxpayer has the option of checking off whether or not $1 of his or her tax money is to go to the campaign funds.

The reform act left unanswered another question raised by some critics of the broadcasting industry. These critics claim that the networks and network commentators have too much power. Thus, they can shape public attitudes about candidates and issues. In other words, they feel that the networks are "marketing" or selling the candidates of their own choice. The networks, though, answer that they merely report, but do not make the news.

The Watergate affair made everyone—politicians and voters alike—more sensitive to morality in politics. It also led to a new problem. For the first time in its history, the United States had as its executive leaders a President and a Vice President who were not elected by the people. Scandals had forced Nixon and Agnew from office.

Ford wanted as his nominee for Vice President, Nelson Rockefeller, former governor of New York and one of the descendants and heirs of John D. Rockefeller. The Senate held hearings to approve Rockefeller's appointment. However, testimony revealed that, as governor, Rockefeller often gave expensive gifts and loans to political associates. Those who opposed his nomination charged that he was guilty of exercising improper influence. Rockefeller held that such gifts were made to encourage capable people to remain in low-paying public offices. Eventually, Rockefeller was confirmed. But the hearings showed that people were now studying the role of money in our political system with increasing seriousness and caution.

Questions for Discussion

1. Define *public financing*.
2. How did the Watergate scandal demonstrate the danger of the growth in strength of Presidential powers?

3. Why do some people think that the heavy use of television in political campaigns can hurt our political system?
4. After Watergate, how was the concern for morality in politics demonstrated?

Gerald Ford, the first appointed President in United States history, was determined to restore confidence in government. As they watched the dramatic unraveling of the Watergate cover-up, the American people had lost a great deal of faith in the system. President Nixon, who had received 97 percent of the electoral vote in the 1972 election, had been forced from office less than two years after receiving that extraordinary vote of confidence. Gerald Ford believed that the Watergate era had to be ended in order to resolve the crisis of leadership. Amid cries of outrage and protest, President Ford granted a pardon to former President Nixon. Ford did so in spite of the fact that Nixon had not actually been convicted of any crimes.

President Ford brought to the presidency skills that had enabled him to win election to the House of Representatives for twenty-five years. He was honest, open, and even–tempered. Experience as minority leader of the House had given him the chance to develop ways of working out compromises that provided something for everyone. Most of Ford's programs were continuations of Nixon's domestic and foreign policies.

Ford and the Nation

By the summer of 1974, inflation was dangerously high. Yet measures to cool down inflation (such as credit restrictions) threatened to chill business into a recession with high unemployment. Thus, dealing with this problem was a high-priority matter. A month after

President Gerald Ford posing with his family in the Oval Room of the White House shortly after being sworn in on August 9, 1974.

he took office, Ford held a White House conference on the economy. The conference brought together 800 political, labor, and business leaders. Drawing on the information provided by the participants, Ford shaped his economic policy. In October, he presented his program to a joint session of Congress. Ford stated that a sound economy without inflation was the goal of his administration. He called for a decrease in government spending and a **surtax** on corporate income and middle-and-upper-level personal incomes. The President sported a "WIN" button, symbolizing the motto of his program, "Whip Inflation Now." Ford failed, however, to win congressional support.

surtax
an additional tax on something already taxed

The November 1974 election, the first Congressional contest since the Watergate scandal, resulted in substantial Democratic gains. This result posed a problem for the Republican President. When unemployment deepened in 1975, Ford requested a tax cut tied to a decrease in government spending. Congress passed the tax cut. However, the Congress offered no assurance that spending would be limited. Although the economy improved in 1976, continued high unemployment threatened Ford's chances for election.

Another serious problem was the worsening energy crisis. In September 1974, the World Energy Conference opened in Detroit, Michigan. Thousands of energy experts from around the world gathered to study the rising costs as well as the environmental and economic impact of energy. On the national level, Ford established the Energy Resources Council to shape energy policy. He created the Energy Research and Development Administration (ERDA) as a replacement for the Atomic Energy Commission (AEC). Ford favored voluntary conservation. He rejected suggestions that gasoline be taxed heavily to reduce its use.

As the media began to focus less attention on the Watergate scandal, the activities of two government agencies provoked new publicity damaging to public confidence. In 1974, Attorney General William B. Saxbe revealed that from 1956 to 1971, the Federal Bureau of Investigation (FBI) had illegally gathered information on certain radical political groups. In many instances, agents, posing as protesters, had tried to disrupt their activities.

Even more damaging to public faith in government were revelations that concerned the Central Intelligence Agency (CIA). Investigations revealed that the CIA had contributed millions of dollars to the forces that overthrew Salvador Allende Gossens, the popularly elected president of Chile. The CIA had also considered assassinating certain foreign leaders, such as Fidel Castro of Cuba.

The agency had also violated its charter. The National Security Act of 1947 limited the CIA to foreign operations. Investigations showed that agents had conducted spy operations in the United States.

Despite his election by democratic process, Chilean President Salvador Allende Gossens was overthrown in a coup staged by the Chilean military with the help of the CIA. The economy of Chile had been destabilized. While the country exploded in angry strikes for higher pay and better working conditions, the military took over in a bloody struggle during which Allende was murdered.

They had opened mail and installed wiretaps. Agency officials had planted undercover agents and ordered illegal searches of the headquarters of protesters. Files were compiled on 10,000 Americans, particularly on those who were outspoken critics of government policies. These findings raised once again the question of how to resolve the conflict between the need to maintain national security and the right of the people to those freedoms guaranteed in the First Amendment. By 1980, however, there was a movement to reestablish the role of the CIA. People realized that an intelligence agency was essential to national security.

Ford and the World

When he retained Henry Kissinger as Secretary of State, President Ford signaled that his foreign policy would be similar to that of President Nixon. Early in his administration, Ford went to the Soviet Union and met with Soviet Premier Brezhnev. They agreed to negotiate an agreement on limiting offensive nuclear weapons.

In 1975, President Ford visited the People's Republic of China. When he returned, he announced his "Pacific Doctrine." This was a continuation of Nixon's Far East policies. Ford called for maintaining close friendship with Japan, the establishment of a balance of power in the Pacific based on American strength, and the normalization of relations with the People's Republic of China.

In September 1975, Egypt and Israel signed an *accord* (a settlement of issues between nations) in Geneva despite hostile political pressures in both countries. This accord was a result of the continuing "shuttle diplomacy" of Secretary Kissinger. In an effort to promote peace, the United States had pledged military and economic assistance to Israel. Many problems remained unresolved, however. Israel still occupied land that it had taken in the Six-Day War. And the Palestinians were still without a homeland.

The Vietnam conflict continued to affect the United States. Shortly after Saigon fell to the Communists in April 1975, Cambodia and Laos came under communist control. The United States merchant ship *Mayaguez* was seized by the new communist government in Cambodia. President Ford reacted quickly. He used armed forces to recapture the ship and free the crew. But thirty-nine Americans died in the rescue. Some believed that not enough warning time was given to the Cambodians for a peaceful release of captives.

While Ford was in office, Soviet and Cuban influence became more threatening in Africa. There was an increase of Soviet arms shipments to African nations. Cuba sent troops and advisers to assist revolutionary forces in several African nations, such as Angola and Ethiopia. The United States was also concerned about the serious consequences of continuing minority White rule in South Africa. It was feared that the result would be more revolutions, creating fresh trouble spots.

In 1976, President Ford sent Secretary of State Kissinger to Rhodesia to encourage negotiated settlements in that country as well as in Namibia (Southwest Africa). Kissinger was unable to achieve this goal. However, the efforts of Ford's administration showed a change in the official American attitude toward Africa. The United States government was beginning to lean toward majority Black rule.

Questions for Discussion

1. Define *surtax*.
2. How were President Ford's programs a continuation of Nixon's programs?
3. How did the actions of the FBI and CIA bring out the question of national security versus individual freedoms?
4. How did Ford make use of techniques of foreign policy that had been used by Nixon?

5. Carter Arrives

On November 2, 1976, Jimmy Carter defeated Gerald Ford and became the thirty-ninth President of the United States. Until he declared his candidacy, few people outside Georgia knew who Jimmy Carter was. He had served in the Georgia legislature and as governor of that state. Carter ran for the office of President at a time when the American people seemed to have lost faith in politics and national government. He gained support by reminding his audiences that he was an engineer, a farmer, and a Washington outsider. President Ford tried to overcome his association with Nixon. Ford ran on his record, and Carter ran on his promises. President Ford emphasized his years of experience in Washington. Jimmy Carter claimed that he, as an outsider, could renew the faith of the American people in their government.

President Jimmy Carter had been unable to resolve numerous domestic and foreign policy problems that plagued his administration, and was faced with plunging popularity in public-opinion polls. Consequently, he declared in a 1979 speech with Vice President Walter Mondale at his side that the American people were suffering from a "crisis of confidence" in their leaders and their government.

The election was close. Only 54 percent of the electorate voted. Carter edged Ford in the popular vote, winning 40.8 million to 39.1 million for Ford.

For six months after he entered office, public opinion polls showed that President Carter was held in high esteem. However, his popularity began to decline, especially since he found it very difficult to carry out his campaign promises. In addition, he did not know how to work well with Congress, and many people thought his foreign policy was little more than a series of blunders. The number of people who thought that President Carter was doing a good job decreased sharply during his administration.

Carter and the Economy

Like those before him, President Carter was unable to find a quick cure for the economic problems that had taken years to develop. As inflation soared, so did the criticism of Carter's plan to curtail it. He had hoped that by spending money, he would stimulate the economy and ease unemployment.

Although he had proposed programs that required additional government spending, Carter vetoed bills passed by Congress that he deemed inflationary. He urged Congress and the public to refrain from the spending that would increase inflation.

In October 1978, President Carter announced his economic program before a nationwide television audience. He called for voluntary wage and price guidelines. He appealed to labor to accept a limit of 7 percent annual increase in wages and fringe benefits. Carter also pledged that he would cut the federal budget and place a partial freeze on federal hiring. The instability of the economy affected the foreign exchange rate of the nation. American tourists were shocked to see how little the dollar was worth abroad. At home, Americans saw the price of foreign goods rise as the value of the dollar declined. Speculation in the gold and **commodities markets** reflected growing anxiety over the effects of inflation. As the nation moved into the eighties, the long-anticipated recession resulting from these policies seemed to have begun.

Energy Woes

The energy crisis, heightened by OPEC price increases, led President Carter to establish the Department of Energy in 1977. He also proposed a national energy plan. This plan called for a mixture of remedies, including import restrictions, government investment in synthetic fuel plants, an end to certain price controls on oil, and special fees. All of these regulations were designed to discourage oil use by raising prices. Congress and the American people were slow to respond to what the President termed "the moral equivalent of war"—energy independence. In many instances, members of Congress delayed, debated, and substituted their plans for those proposed by the President. In the end, President Carter was unable to get enough votes in Congress to carry out all of his energy policies, although important parts were made into law.

Many people who once considered nuclear energy an answer to the energy problem began to view it with increasing doubt and caution. An accident at the Three Mile Island power plant in Pennsylvania in March 1979 raised difficult questions about the safety of nuclear plants. Defenders of nuclear energy pointed out that the industry had

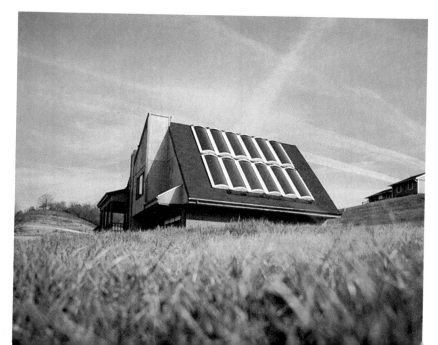

As concern heightened over skyrocketing fuel prices, many Americans began to show more interest in the possibilities of solar and wind energy. This house has been outfitted with panels on the roof which absorb the rays of the sun to heat the home.

While the debate over the safety of nuclear energy raged on, an accident at the Three Mile Island nuclear facility in Harrisburg, Pennsylvania, turned the argument from speculation to reality. Radioactive particles released from the plant caused concern for the safety of Pennsylvania's citizens. Radioactive particles were discovered in the air, in the water, and on the grass, trees, and bushes miles from the plant. Particles were even found in the milk of cows that had eaten the grass on which radioactive materials had fallen. Although there were no immediate effects from the radioactivity, no one can be sure of the long-term effects.

a very good safety record. Nuclear power provides a small percent of the energy needs of the nation. Many people questioned whether the benefits were worth the risks.

A recent study by the coal-producing and exporting nations suggested that coal could fill the oil gap. Because of air pollution and other harmful effects, the widespread use of coal would raise once again the question of benefits versus risks.

People continued to look to scientists and technicians to come up with a solution. Even if the sun or wind proved to be the answer, it would take a great deal of time for solar or wind technologies to be developed. By the end of the seventies, people were beginning to realize that no solution would be easy or cheap.

Bakke and Beyond

On June 28, 1978, the Supreme Court announced a decision that had far-reaching implications. Its immediate effect was to secure the admission to medical school of a 38-year-old White engineer, Allan Bakke. The decision affected college admissions policies based on racial quotas and raised questions about all **affirmative action** programs.

Allan Bakke claimed that he had been a victim of *reverse discrimination*. Reverse discrimination occurs when people who are not normally singled out are treated differently. The medical school of the University of California at Davis had denied him admission. Instead, it accepted minority students, some of whom had lower admissions test scores than those of Bakke. The university had set aside sixteen places in each entry class for Black, Chicano, and Asian

affirmative action
programs in which special efforts are made to recruit minority groups. It is an attempt to provide benefits for groups that have heretofore been discriminated against.

729

students. Bakke claimed that because he was White, he was rejected under this quota system.

By a 5 to 4 vote, the Supreme Court delcared that Bakke had been unfairly denied entry. Because that medical school had never discriminated against minority applicants, it could not admit such applicants under a system of racial preference. This case was not the setback for civil rights that some people feared. The court had ruled that admissions directors could legally include race as a factor in considering which applicants to admit.

To help clear up any confusion caused by the decision, the federal government issued guidelines to colleges and universities in 1979. College and universities were encouraged to recruit students from minority communities, to offer tutoring to disadvantaged students, and to consider factors other than academic achievement in admitting applicants. All of this was an attempt to make up for handicaps imposed by past discrimination and to give minority applicants a truly equal opportunity to compete. Many agreed that this was actually the long-run target.

The direction of affirmative action programs in industry and education is still being formed on a case-by-case basis. For example, in June 1979, the Supreme Court decided against a White employee who claimed that he was a victim of reverse discrimination. Brian Weber brought a lawsuit against the Kaiser Aluminum and Chemical Corporation. Weber claimed that the company violated Title VII of the 1964 Civil Rights Act, which prohibits discrimination based on race. For a training program, the company had chosen two Black workers with less time on the job than Weber had. The court declared that Title VII was specifically designed to improve opportunities for Blacks. In this case, the Court declared that racial preference was legal. In addition, in June 1980, the Supreme Court upheld the constitutionality of a law passed by Congress. This law required the awarding of 10 percent of federal contracts to minority building contractors. In this case, the court declared that the racial quota system established by Congress was constitutional, because minority contractors had been the victims of racial discrimination.

Carter and Foreign Affairs

Designing a foreign policy that would work in a rapidly changing world posed a major challenge for the Carter administration. The President stressed action on behalf of human rights as a keystone of American foreign policy. But some nations reacted negatively, especially in Latin America.

President Carter made it clear that the United States would tie its aid to the human rights records of each Latin American country.

Before a meeting of the United Nations, he declared that "no member of the United Nations can claim that mistreatment of its citizens is solely its own business." The United States followed through by cutting aid to Argentina and Uruguay. These countries responded by refusing all United States aid. Several Latin American countries voiced their objections to what they considered interference with their internal affairs.

Most Latin American leaders were pleased with the steps taken by the United States to transfer the Panama Canal and the Canal Zone to Panama. For thirteen years, under four presidents, negotiations over this issue had produced no results. In the summer of 1977, two agreements were finally reached. Panama was to assume increasing responsibility for the maintenance and operation of the canal. By the year 2000, it would assume full control. The United States would continue to protect the canal and its neutrality. In case of war, ships of the United States would be granted preference. The treaties went into effect in 1978, after the Panamanian people approved them in a national referendum and the United States Senate ratified them.

In keeping with his theme of human rights, President Carter strongly supported Soviet **dissidents**. This undermined the spirit of cooperation that had led to the SALT I agreement. However, in 1977, after the original agreement ended, both the United States and the Soviet Union informally agreed to maintain the levels of nuclear armaments specified in the agreement.

dissident
an individual who strongly disagrees with the established policies of a government

Although the SALT II agreement was signed in June 1979, approval by the Senate seemed uncertain. When the Soviet Union invaded Afghanistan at the beginning of 1980, SALT II was withdrawn from the Senate agenda by the President. The presence of Soviet troops in Cuba and Cuban troops in East Africa also caused an

Since arriving in the United States after being exiled from the Soviet Union in 1974, Nobel prize-winning author and social critic Aleksandr I. Solzhenitsyn has continued to speak out against the Soviet regime and in support of Soviet dissidents.

731

In 1980, the workers in Poland forced the government, by prolonged strikes, to recognize a trade union that is independent of the Communist Party. A leader during the strikes, Lech Walesa, pictured above, was chosen to head the union. Since this union represented a loosening of communist control over the country, the Soviet Union massed troops along the Polish border, threatening to invade. In response, the United States warned that an invasion of Poland would mean an end to detente between the two world powers.

uneasiness between the two superpowers. The argument against SALT II was that arms limitation should be linked to more peaceful Soviet behavior in the world. But without some formal understanding, the United States and the Soviet Union might be tempted to begin an unlimited arms build-up.

President Carter's decision to recognize the People's Republic of China was greeted with mixed reactions. In August 1977, Secretary of State Cyrus Vance undertook delicate negotiations in Peking. The United States was willing to establish diplomatic relations with the People's Republic of China. However, the question of continued United States recognition of the Nationalist Government in Taiwan remained troublesome. Secretary of State Vance was also aware of the possible effect on United States-Soviet relations if the United States established diplomatic relations with Peking. China accused the Carter administration of retreating from the position taken by President Ford in 1975. Difficult negotiations continued until an agreement was finally reached.

President Carter announced on nationwide television that the United States was ending diplomatic relations and the 1954 defense treaty with Taiwan. On January 1, 1979, the United States and the People's Republic of China established diplomatic relations and exchanged ambassadors. Thus, the United States acknowledged the necessity of adopting a realistic foreign policy.

Not everyone was pleased with this turn of events. Anti-American demonstrations broke out in Taiwan shortly after Carter's announcement. Fifteen members of Congress filed a suit claiming that congressional approval was necessary before a treaty could be revoked. Carter assured the country that the United States would maintain "cultural, commercial, and other unofficial relations" with Taiwan. It would also sell to Taiwan "selective defensive weaponry." Although United States armed forces left Taiwan, many civilians still remained.

One of the main objectives of President Carter's foreign policy was the development of a framework for achieving peace in the Middle East. When Egyptian President Anwar Sadat journeyed to Jerusalem to meet with Israeli Prime Minister Menachem Begin, a major stalemate was broken. But when the talks appeared to be heading for danger, Carter stepped in. He held an historic summit meeting at Camp David, the presidential retreat in Maryland. For nearly two weeks, the three leaders thrashed out a settlement that offered hope of peace. On March 26, 1979, Begin and Sadat, with Carter as witness, signed a peace treaty in Washington, D.C. Israel agreed to withdraw to the pre-1948 Egypt-Palestine border. In turn, Egypt became the first Arab country to recognize the existence of the state of Israel.

THE SPACE PROGRAM

The United States launched the first of a series of scientific satellites on January 31, 1958—Explorer I. In December 1958, the first commercial satellite—Project Score—was launched. In February 1959, the first weather satellite—Vanguard II—was launched.

Early in 1959, the United States launched a probe, Pioneer IV. It passed the moon, went into orbit around the sun, and became one of the first artificial planetoids.

In the early 1960s, human beings began to travel to space. On May 5, 1961, Alan B. Shepard, Jr., rocketed to a height of 187.5 kilometers (116½ miles) in a flight 480 kilometers (300 miles) long. John H. Glenn, Jr., was the first American astronaut to orbit the earth, making three revolutions on February 20, 1962, in Friendship VII.

The first American man-in-space project was the Mercury program. The first Mercury flight was in April 1961 and the last in May 1963. The next steps into space were the Gemini and Apollo programs. The first manned flight in the Gemini program was made in March 1965 and the last in November 1966. The first manned Apollo flight was made in October 1968.

The first people to set foot on the moon were astronauts Neil A. Armstrong and Edwin E. Aldrin, Jr. Their Apollo II Lunar Module landed on the moon on July 20, 1969.

In 1975, the United States and Russia undertook their first joint space mission—the Apollo-Soyuz Test Project. On July 17, a three-man United States Apollo spacecraft docked with a two-man Russian Soyuz craft. Crew members conducted experiments for two days before carrying out separation maneuvers. In November of that same year, the United States and Russia conducted another joint space mission. An unmanned Soviet Vostok satellite carried five United States biological experiments around the earth for approximately nineteen days.

Interest in the space program began to decline during the 1970s. Funds for the programs were also shrinking as competition for dollars increased. With the funds remaining, work was begun on the United States Space Shuttle. This is a spacecraft designed to take off like a rocket and land like an airplane. The space shuttle was expected to begin carrying astronauts and materials back and forth between Earth and an orbiting space station in the 1980s. Scientists also planned to use the shuttle to launch, repair, and recover various types of unmanned satellites.

The European Space Agency (ESA) is assisting the United States in its work on the space shuttle. Other foreign countries cooperate with the United States in order to make the exploration of space a truly international effort.

The historic Middle East peace talks held at Camp David, Maryland produced the framework through which a state of peace between Egypt and Israel was developed. The three major political figures involved in these talks were Egyptian President Anwar Sadat (left), American President Jimmy Carter (center), and Israeli Prime Minister Menachem Begin (right).

The Palestinian question remained unsettled, although the PLO had gained more international support for its cause. Egypt and Israel had not resolved questions about Israeli settlements on the West Bank and in the Gaza Strip.

For a time, agreement seemed close at hand. But the May 26, 1980, deadline for resolving the question of Palestinian autonomy passed without settlement being reached.

From time to time during Carter's administration, relations with West European countries were strained. European leaders were no longer willing to follow the lead of the United States in conducting their relations with the rest of the world. European leaders maintained that the United States undertook actions and changed policies without consulting them and still expected to receive their support. They were further concerned about the tougher position that the United States was taking toward the Soviet Union. Nevertheless, strong ties were maintained, based primarily on mutual defense interests and similar economic and political goals.

Questions for Discussion

1. Define *commodities market, affirmative action, reverse discrimination, dissidents.*
2. What obstacles did President Carter face in his attempts to solve the economic and energy problems facing the nation in the 1970s?
3. How was affirmative action affected by the Bakke decision? By other Supreme Court decisions?
4. How did Carter's emphasis on human rights affect his foreign policy?
5. What changes in American foreign policy were effected by President Carter?

Chapter 31 Review

Summary Questions for Discussion

1. What factors contributed to the inflation that occurred in the 1970s? What were the results?
2. What resulted from the Shanghai Communiqué?
3. What resulted from the SALT talks in 1972? In what other areas did the United States and the Soviet Union agree to cooperate?
4. How and when did the United States withdraw from Vietnam?
5. What is OPEC? How could they use their economic power as a weapon? How was one such conflict resolved?
6. What was the Watergate scandal during the Nixon administration?
7. How was Gerald Ford different from any President who preceded him? What was his background?
8. What actions did Ford take to curb inflation and recession? Why did he meet with limited success?
9. What activities of the FBI and CIA were revealed during Ford's administration?
10. What were the bases of Carter's successful bid for the Presidency?
11. What was Carter's economic program?

Word Study

Fill in each blank in the sentences that follow with the term below that is most appropriate.

recession   reverse discrimination   dissidents
summit meeting   devaluating   fixed incomes
affirmative action   surtax   antiballistic missile

1. During _____, there is a slowdown of economic activity marked by a decrease in employment, profits, production, prices, and sales.
2. People who live on _____ are faced with the problem of having no increase or decrease in the amount of money they are able to spend.
3. _____ diminishes the worth of currency.
4. A meeting of top leaders of governments is known as a _____ .
5. A very powerful defensive weapon that intercepts and destroys certain missiles is called an _____ .
6. A _____ is an additional tax on something already taxed.
7. _____ is an attempt to provide benefits for groups that have heretofore been discriminated against.
8. _____ occurs when people who are not normally singled out are now treated differently.
9. Persons who strongly disagree with established policies of a government are referred to as _____ .

Using Your Skills

1. Study the map of Europe on page 716. List the members of NATO and the Warsaw Pact. Do you feel these alliances are necessary in the eighties? Give reasons to support your answer.
2. Study the map of Asia on page 717. Which areas were part of the concerns of the foreign policies of President Nixon? Ford? Carter? Why? Which areas do you think will be part of the problems of the eighties?

CHAPTER 32
Issues for the Eighties

There will be many challenges during the decade of the eighties. Among them will be problems of the environment, energy, world peace, equal rights, opportunities within our country, and human rights around the world. But the United States has vast natural resources, the world's largest economy, a stable government, and an educated and talented population with which to meet these challenges.

Energy will be a problem for the United States and the world throughout the eighties. The United States imports almost half the petroleum used to run automobiles and trucks, to heat buildings and homes, and to generate electricity. Yet, much of the imported oil comes from the Middle East, a part of the world that is not stable.

People are more aware today that our earthly home is small and fragile. We must take steps to protect it from all kinds of pollution.

In many areas of the world, the decade of the eighties promises to be one of turmoil. In the Middle East, Southeast Asia, Central America, and Southern Africa, groups of people are fighting one another. Each serious outbreak raises the possibility of a confrontation between the United States and the Soviet Union.

Minorities and women have become vocal and visible in the eighties. Their quest for equal rights has awakened others to support their own cause. Hospital patients, schoolchildren, the disabled, and the handicapped have obtained some rights as well. And the elderly have become a political force to be reckoned with.

Although there are many serious problems facing people everywhere, there is still the hope that ways can be found to solve those problems that can be solved and to live with those that seem to resist solutions.

READING GUIDE

1. **How will changes in population affect American life in the eighties?**
2. **What major issues will affect world affairs in the immediate future?**
3. **What trends will influence Americans in the eighties?**

An Indiana oil refinery stands silhouetted against the sunrise. The availability and price of oil will be a major concern in the 1980s.

1. Shifting Population

In the decade of the eighties, population shifts will continue to impact on the American way of life. In the 1870s, Americans began to move to the cities in record numbers. Half a century later, in the 1920s, the automobile spurred the growth of the suburbs. After World War II, the movement to the suburbs resembled a stampede. Most suburbs used to be populated largely or entirely by Whites. Suburban homes were too costly for most non-White Americans. In fact, many real-estate developers refused to sell houses to non-Whites.

After 1945, while the suburbs were growing, the inner cities were undergoing decay and renewal. The decay affected old neighborhoods abandoned by those who moved to suburbia. Newcomers to the city took their places. Like the immigrants who flocked to the cities early in the twentieth century, these newcomers were often poor. Many were non-White. In many places, the parts of the city they lived in became slums when landlords did not maintain their buildings. Tenant complaints about broken windows, peeling paint, and inadequate electric, plumbing, and heating systems went unanswered.

Other parts of the inner city prospered. Business corporations headquartered in downtown areas spent vast sums to build steel, chrome, and glass skyscrapers. In 1947, the federal government began a program of urban renewal. It gave financial help to city governments and private builders to replace decayed neighborhoods. Among the projects were shopping plazas and cultural centers containing theaters and museums. Private homes and public housing developments for poor and middle-income people were also planned.

However, such help did not solve the basic urban housing problem. It often destroyed low-income housing, which was not replaced. It encouraged the building of expressways to carry automobiles from the suburbs into the business and shopping districts. The cities were becoming divided. On the one hand, there were the attractive areas where well-to-do people did business and sought entertainment. And then there were the decaying slums where the poor lived. City governments could not halt the process of decay without new powers and more money. They obtained neither. In fact, the 1980 census showed that the large cities were losing population. Because of this loss, the number of representatives in Congress from cities will be reduced, as will the money given to cities in aid.

During the seventies, a number of elements affected the flow of people to and from the cities. Black people speeded up their migration to the suburbs that began in the sixties. Some old residential sections of cities were renovated and became the homes of well-to-do Americans who returned to the conveniences of city life. Many people moved to semirural areas beyond the suburbs where housing was less expensive and other central-city problems were left behind. This

trend, combined with shifts of population to the South and the West, drew people away from the Northeastern **megalopolis**. Projections indicate that during the eighties, California, Florida, and Texas will experience the greatest increase in population. New York could perhaps experience the largest decline. The 1980 census has shown that small cities, towns, and rural areas will continue to grow in population while population the larger cities and their older suburbs will decline.

Demographic Projections

Shifts in population are expected to be accompanied by substantial changes in the makeup of the population. By the end of the decade, the median age of Americans will reach 32.5 years. This projection means that half the population is expected to be younger than 32.5 years, and half is expected to be older. This aging trend is expected to continue into the twenty-first century. Some people refer to this as the "graying of America."

As the population gets older, social and economic challenges will arise. As the number of teenagers declines, there could be a decrease in some kinds of unemployment and crime. But there will be a need to provide jobs for the expanding young adult population (ages 21 to 35). With the rising expectations of women and minorities, there will be strong competition to secure professional and management positions.

megalopolis
area of several large cities and their surrounding areas close enough to be considered as a single urban complex

Also, the average size of families is expected to decline. But the number of households will increase as the children of the "baby boom" become adults. This could raise the demand for housing, particularly in the **sun belt.**

The percentage of Americans 65 and over will also increase. This trend could affect a number of areas. The demand for improved health care and for greater government funds to subsidize such care will increase. People who are working will find an even greater percentage of their income going into the Social Security system to meet the needs of the elderly.

Challenge of Refugees

The refugee fleets from Cuba in 1980 posed serious challenges to the immigration policy of the United States. Each year, 4 million people apply for visas to immigrate to the United States. Many applications are rejected. The United States limits immigration to a set number each year. However, the government is more flexible about admitting applicants who request *political asylum.* People who ask for political asylum are seeking refuge from another government.

After the fall of the South Vietnamese government, thousands of Vietnamese left their country. Many of the early refugees were members of the well-to-do and educated middle class. Individuals, charitable organizations, and communities were quite moved by humanitarian concerns, thus sponsoring additional refugees. Some Cambodians and Laotians fled as their countries fell to the Communists. Before long, many people were streaming onto unseaworthy, ill-supplied boats to escape the new regimes. These "boat people," as they were called, joined the ranks of displaced persons. The United States continued to accept Southeast Asian emigrants, considering them political refugees who had fled repressive regimes. Although there were some incidents of conflict, many Americans seemed to be sympathetic to these newcomers.

Cuban refugees wave from the deck of an American trawler as they near the shore of Key West, Florida.

Vietnamese refugee children and their families huddle aboard their sinking boat while awaiting rescue. Displaced and unwanted, these and other so-called "boat people" would remain at sea until a country allowed them entrance. Many died before ever seeing land.

Thousands of other immigrants face a hostile environment. The Immigration and Naturalization Service estimates that the number of illegal aliens residing in the United States exceeds 8 million. Many came to the United States from Mexico and other Latin American countries. Relations between the United States and Mexico have been strained by American efforts to restrict the flow of illegal aliens from Mexico. That country has a rapidly increasing population, a high rate of unemployment, and a high incidence of poverty. Therefore, Mexico views this exodus as a necessary safety valve. In time, Mexico may tie its oil exports to the United States to the resolution of the legal status of its emigrants. That is, Mexico will export more oil for a more generous treatment of Mexicans who migrate to the United States.

The difficulty of deciding which refugees to admit was shown in the reaction of the United States to Haitian and Cuban emigrants. The solution to the problem seemed to hinge on whether those seeking entry to the United States sought economic opportunity or political freedom.

The Immigration Service claims that many Haitians have come to the United States on rickety boats in search of jobs. Thus, Haitians are considered the victims of poverty, not of political persecution. Haitians have filed a class-action suit in a federal court in Miami. The Haitians claim that they are indeed political refugees. They maintain that the government of Jean-Claude Duvalier is one of the most repressive in the Caribbean.

In 1980, Castro allowed thousands of people to leave Cuba. The United States reopened the refugee centers that had processed Southeast Asian refugees. The overall effects of the massive influx of Cuban refugees was troublesome to the United States. Yet the Immigration Service did not question the rights of these people, since they came from a communist country.

Crowds of people jam a state labor office to collect unemployment checks and to look for work.

At the beginning of the 1980s, the unemployment rate in the United States was increasing. Budget cuts were affecting many social programs. Thus, the United States immigration policy again became a sensitive issue. How could America open its doors to poverty-stricken immigrants when it was having problems helping its own poor? Shortly after the wave of Cuban refugees arrived in Miami, riots broke out in the Black community. They were touched off by the acquittal of four White police officers who had been charged with beating a Black man to death. Some people believe that deep-rooted frustration over unemployment fueled the expressions of outrage. Blacks claimed that many jobs formerly available to them were being taken by Cuban immigrants. As they have done in other times of distress, Americans were questioning unrestrained immigration that seemed to lessen opportunities for those who were born in the United States.

Questions for Discussion

1. Define *megalopolis, political asylum, sun belt.*
2. How did the growth of suburbs cause problems for inner cities?
3. Why were city governments unable to solve the problems they faced after 1945?
4. What are the effects of the "graying of America"?
5. Why is American immigration policy a problem in the eighties?

2. The World Framework

After World War II, foreign policymakers looked at the world as two camps, communist and noncommunist. Foreign policy seemed to be based on the theory, "if you're not for us, you're against us." This view led the United States to react to local conflicts as aspects of the

Cold War and not as expressions of national or regional problems, which might have been the case. The United States saw the victory of communism in China as the extension of the Cold War into Asia. American actions in Korea and Vietnam were designed to prevent communism from spreading throughout the region.

Like other world views, this one seems to be undergoing a transformation. Some signs of change were visible in the seventies. For example, **détente** and the establishment of diplomatic relations with the People's Republic of China were two signs of changing attitudes.

détente
a relaxation of strained relations or tensions, as between nations

There are a number of strategies that the United States is developing to protect its own interests. President Carter pledged to defend the independence of Persian Gulf countries in order to assure the flow of oil. The United States is also developing a *rapid-deployment force*. This force of over a hundred thousand troops will be equipped with many high-speed cargo planes. These planes are capable of carrying vast amounts of equipment and numbers of people to remote areas. Ships with the necessary equipment to support a Marine Corps *amphibious force* (assault troops that land on shore from seaborne transports) will be ready to be sent to a troubled area. The rapid-deployment force has been designed to move into an area very quickly and to be able to begin fighting as soon as it arrives. At the same time, the United States is establishing military bases in the Persian Gulf area.

The Persian Gulf area will continue to be a trouble spot during the eighties. In 1979, Islamic militants in Iran, supporting Ayatollah Khomeini, overthrew the government of the Shah, or emperor, of Iran. Since then, Islamic leaders have sought to spread their revolution throughout the region. This has gained them the enmity of many governments of nearby countries. Hostility toward the Shah, a staunch ally of the United States, spread when the United States admitted the exiled Shah into its borders for medical treatment. In retaliation, Iranian militants seized the United States embassy in Teheran and held hostage its diplomatic and military staff.

During the 1980s, it became harder than ever to make foreign policy. Without exception, all nations agreed that the militants who had violated the centuries-old rules of diplomatic immunity were in the wrong. But what could be done? The United States had the power to take military action, such as bombing Iranian oilfields. But that would probably lead to the death of the hostages. In addition, it would stop the flow of vital oil entirely. It could also cause the Moslem world to turn against the United States, which would be a serious diplomatic disadvantage. Or the United States might even provoke Soviet intervention to "protect" Iran. However, this could escalate a small

The Ayatollah Khomeini, the Iranian Moslem instrumental in the overthrow of the Shah. From his home-in-exile, Paris, Khomeini directed opposition groups seeking the overthrow of the Iranian monarchy. Once the Shah had fled, Khomeini returned to assume the leadership of Iran's.

The former Shah of Iran, Mohammed Reza Pahlevi. The focus of violent demonstrations by Muslim extremists and leftists who objected to his secret police, Savak, and his attempts to modernize Iran, Pahlevi was overthrown in 1979. He had been the country's ruler since 1941.

affair into a threat of world war and possible annihilation. The United States could—and did—attempt economic sanctions against Iran, such as a suspension of trade and travel. To be effective, though, that required the cooperation of other nations. Even the allies were unwilling to take on the economic burdens of such a policy. President Carter could also try a rescue attempt. And he did so. But it failed. Or he could, as the militants demanded, apologize for past United States support of the Shah. However, that would have destroyed him politically at home. In short, every choice had heavy costs. No answer was simple. The only thing to do was to hold a consistent overall policy—to insist on getting the hostages back unharmed—and then try a variety of ways to enforce it and hope for the best. That was a long way from the days of "gunboat diplomacy," but it seemed the only way.

The shock waves produced by the Islamic revolution in Iran were felt not only in Washington but in Moscow as well. Then the Soviet leaders sent their armed forces into Afghanistan. Since Afghanistan was their neighboring country and had a regime that they supported, it is possible the Soviets feared the revolution would spill into Afghanistan. After suppressing widespread resistance, the Soviets secured the communist puppet government. Many members of the United Nations condemned this action. The United States reacted by halting talks on Salt II. The President also secured a partial boycott of the 1980 summer Olympic games in Moscow. The Soviets still seemed determined to hold onto Afghanistan, a state very close to the Persian Gulf.

The United States is continuing to work toward a settlement of the Arab-Israeli conflicts. It is clear that without a solution to the Palestinian question, there can be little hope of lasting peace.

There are indications that the United States is developing a more realistic policy toward **third-world nations**. The fear that political instability would lead to communist takeovers caused the United States to support some repressive regimes. It appears that the United States is becoming more sensitive to the needs of third-world countries. The bases for this view include (1) cutbacks in aid because of violations of human rights, (2) the Panama Canal treaties, (3) the United States efforts at the United Nations to develop a new economic order, (4) the support for a Black majority government in Rhodesia, and (5) the immediate recognition of the government of Zimbabwe.

In recent years, the political activities of some *multinational corporations* have provoked congressional inquiries. Multinational corporations are large companies that do business in many different countries.

Corporations have always been involved in international business. For example, the development of the United States was affected by such trading companies as the Hudson's Bay Company and the Virginia Company. In the nineteenth century, American companies, such as United Fruit, set up plantations in Central America. During the early twentieth century, Coca-Cola, Singer, Woolworth, and Exxon and other oil companies were among the many corporations that extended their operations abroad.

In the 1960s, the multinational corporation, with its home office in one country and a network of offices in many host countries, became the dominant feature of international business. The majority of these corporations are based in the United States. With increasingly improved communications and jet plane transportation, it has become possible for corporate leaders to keep track of developments throughout the world. During the 1970s, Japanese and European multinational corporations grew and made significant inroads into some fields once dominated by American multinationals.

Many nations are wary of foreign corporations that propose to invest in their economies. For one thing, some companies have exploited the raw materials of foreign nations. Others have transferred profits earned in one country to another country to avoid paying taxes. Some companies have gone as far as to interfere with the political life of a country. Multinationals may succeed in raising living standards by making investments that the host country cannot afford to undertake. However, corporate decisions made in one country may not be in agreement with the political and social goals of the host country.

third-world nations
a group of nations, especially in Africa and Asia, that are not aligned with either the communist or the noncommunist blocs. The term is also used to refer to the underdeveloped nations of the world.

The 1970s saw increased foreign investment in the United States, which continues today. Here, a Japanese builder studies a construction project in California.

In this area, the outlook for the eighties suggests some encouraging trends and some trends that may prove troublesome. With the increasing development of European and Japanese multinationals, the cry of "American imperialism" has been softened. The increase in the number of multinational corporations has enabled host countries to turn down one company's terms and seek better terms from another.

Another concern over the operations of multinationals is their relationship with the governments of host countries. Because multinationals have been more eager to invest in nations with stable governments, there is the suspicion that they may encourage the repression of opposition groups. Cleverly timed announcements of more or less investments in a country may also affect elections in host countries. During the eighties, the influence of the multinationals will be watched, as countries struggle to combat the inflation and unemployment that have affected the lives of people throughout the world.

Questions for Discussion

1. Define *détente, amphibious force, rapid-deployment force, third-world nations, multinational corporations.*
2. How has the United States changed its policy toward third-world nations?
3. What are some of the positive and negative effects of multinational corporations?

3. Trends in the Eighties

The trend of politics during the eighties can be gleaned from the 1980 presidential campaign. Even before campaigning began, President Carter reacted to slipping popularity polls by hiring a public-relations expert. When Ronald Reagan became dissatisfied with his showing in the early primaries, he fired his campaign manager and hired another. When John Anderson realized that he could not outpoll Reagan in the Republican primaries, he ran as an independent.

The 1980 campaign reflected the change in attitude toward campaigns, elections, and political parties. Since the fifties, candidates have been forming their own campaign committees and developing their own campaign strategies. The development of television as the primary medium of campaigning may be responsible for this. In the past, candidates counted on their political parties to get voters to the polls. Now, they depend on professional imagemakers to help them convince television viewers to vote for them. Another change that has affected the power of political parties is the growth of primaries. (Sixteen primaries were held in 1952. Thirty-six primaries were held in 1980.) In 1980, more and more states changed to the primary system of choosing delegates to the Presidential nominating convention. The

The 1980 Presidential election saw three major candidates compete for the office. From left to right: Jimmy Carter, encumbent President, Democratic Party; Ronald Reagan, Republican Party; and John Anderson, Independent Party.

power to name delegates to the nominating convention has shifted from party bosses to party voters. This is true even though the number of voters loyal to a party has decreased by 20 percent since 1952. According to survey researchers, the percentage of people who consider themselves independents has increased during the past forty years, rising rapidly between 1964 (23 percent) and 1978 (37 percent).

What political trends will candidates have to deal with? One trend may be the continuing *apathy* or *disaffection* of voters. Apathy suggests laziness or indifference. But in fact, many voters just do not like the choices presented. They have also come to feel that their votes do not make a difference. The percentage of voters turning out for presidential and congressional elections has dropped considerably since 1960. So, politicians will not only have to deal with a number of traditional special-interest groups, such as labor unions, but with one-issue groups as well, such as the Right to Life movement. The Republican party can no longer automatically count on the loyalty of college-educated voters. Nor can the Democratic party automatically count on the traditional support of Catholics, Jews, and labor union members. In addition to these considerations, Blacks, Hispanics, and women have begun to demand recognition of their needs in return for their votes.

Campaign costs will continue to increase over the high levels of 1980. Candidates will continue to use computers to analyze public opinion and the impact of issues on their campaigns. Television advertising will probably account for one half of the campaign budget, as media experts package and present what a majority of the public tells them it wants.

With a crushing victory over incumbent President Jimmy Carter, President-elect Ronald Reagan and a new, Republican-controlled Senate swept into office on January 20, 1981.

The 1980 Election

Throughout the 1980 Presidential campaign, Americans had complained that they did not like the choice given them by the major parties. In newspaper editorials, magazine articles, and television interviews, people said that they did not think President Carter was equal to the job, but that Ronald Reagan frightened them. Reagan, they thought, was too conservative and might get the country into war. Right up to election day, the polls showed the two candidates running very close. A distant third was John Anderson, the Independent candidate.

On election day the American people made their choice. They wanted a change in Washington. Ronald Reagan won 51 percent of the popular vote to President Carter's 41 percent. However, Reagan won 483 votes in the electoral college to Carter's 49. Carter carried only five states and the District of Columbia. He was the first Democrat since Grover Cleveland, in 1888, to be voted out of office. The Republicans also got control of the Senate, and picked up thirty-three seats in the House.

In the transition period between the election and inauguration, Ronald Reagan began reassuring the American people. He picked conservative, but moderate people for his cabinet. He put together groups of experts to propose ways to bring the economic problems of the nation under control. He began talking about cutting federal spending, cutting taxes, and providing more incentives for business.

The Economy and the Environment

Can the United States afford programs designed to protect the environment? Can it afford to postpone such programs? In the seventies, pollution of the environment became an important issue. In 1970, Americans celebrated the first Earth Day and the passage of the National Environmental Policy Act. The Environmental Protection Agency (EPA) was created to enforce standards for pollution control. During the next decade, however, inflation and recession threatened to undermine some of the arguments advanced by environmentalists (people concerned about the environment).

Environmentalists were among the first to call for protection of national resources. Their arguments convinced legislators to investigate threats to the environment and to pass suitable legislation to protect the land, water, and air.

A major cause of poor air quality was exhaust from cars, buses, and trucks. Thus, Congress required manufacturers to make design changes to control such pollutants. Emission-control devices contributed to the sharply rising cost of cars. They also caused cars to use more fuel. At the beginning of the eighties, the automobile industry was in trouble. Sales fell because Americans wanted more fuel-efficient cars. In order to help the industry, the government eased some pollution standards. The air, however, was cleaner in 1980 than it had been in 1970.

The control of pollution is not a simple matter. Here is an example of how antipollution and economic policies can become entangled. Smokestacks belching clouds of fumes and smoke fouled the air in

The dumping of chemical wastes in the area around the Love Canal in Niagra Falls, New York, resulted in the pollution of the area's water supply. When many residents of the area became ill, their angry protests convinced the state and federal governments to buy up their property and condemn the land. Pictured here is one street of boarded up homes in the Love Canal area.

industrial regions. The Environmental Protection Agency established standards for industrial emissions. Higher stacks, scrubbers, and chemical separators were required to cut down on dust and the chemical sulfur dioxide. In one case, the Tennessee Valley Authority (TVA) was required to use low sulfur coal from the East in its coal-fired generating plants to cut down on sulfur dioxide emissions. But the Council on Wages and Prices determined that the measure was inflationary. Armed with this information, some industrial users of TVA power filed a suit, hoping to nullify the EPA ruling. American groups were beginning to question the costs of some of these regulations.

In 1978, the government established the Regulatory Analysis Review Group to analyze the costs of regulation. Because of inflation and the lack of money to invest in new factories, there will be an even greater need to determine which regulations are worthwhile and which may be harmful.

Americans want clean air and clear sparkling rivers. In order to achieve that, everyone will have to pay for them. The cost may well result in higher prices and fewer jobs. Economic growth may be reduced if funds reserved for capital investment to increase productivity are used instead to pay for equipment to meet environmental standards. In the 1980s, people will have to answer this question: Can the United States afford economic growth and a clean environment, or must the country make a choice?

Technology and Science

In recent years, scientific knowledge has increased tremendously. As a wealthy nation possessing the universities and laboratories to train thousands of research scientists, the United States has made many contributions to the "information explosion."

For example, some advances in medicine have freed people from the age-old grip of pain and early death caused by disease. There are new vaccines and *antibiotics*—drugs that destroy germs but do not harm other organisms essential to life. Such "miracle medicines" have made death caused by infection from wounds and injuries rare. They have almost wiped out former "automatic" killers such as diphtheria, polio, and smallpox. Progress in finding ways of controlling cancer has been significant as well.

Science has also helped increase food production. Scientists have sought to develop more productive, disease-resistant strains of grains and vegetables. They have carried out experiments in *hydroponics*—the growing of plants in nutrient-rich water—as well as in *aquaculture*—raising fish in a controlled environment. Scientists are trying to win a race against the clock. It is estimated that at least one

Pollution takes many forms. Above: Workers clean up after an oil leak off Santa Barbara, California. Left: Many factories release smoke and gases that poison the air.

eighth of the world's 4 billion people are undernourished or starving. By the year 2000, the population of the earth could reach 6 billion. If scientists lose the race to develop other sources of foods, the number of undernourished or starving people may increase.

During the eighties, the United States space program will center on the manned space shuttle. Seats on the first thirty-seven flights of the four-shuttle fleet have already been reserved by interested individuals and countries. The shuttle is designed to carry satellites and cargo into space. Then it will return to Earth and be launched again. By the late 1980s, space shuttles may even be carrying equipment for construction projects in space.

The use of commercial satellites for television and advanced communications will expand as the shuttle makes launching them more economical. Scientists also hope to explore new areas of the universe by using a space telescope, which is expected to be launched in the mid-1980s. Efforts to contact *extraterrestrial life* (out of this world), should it exist anywhere in the universe, will continue.

The decade of the eighties will also be the age of the computer. Computers and electronic devices will become routine equipment in homes, cars, and offices. (They are already found in some late-model cars.) Computers are now being used to help predict weather, earthquakes, and the paths of tornadoes. They have made possible the storage and retrieval of vast amounts of information. They are being installed to maximize the flow of air, rail, and water traffic and to minimize delays and fuel waste. They are used to keep inventory and keep track of profit and loss. In the future, their applications to communications will shrink the world even further.

Scientific research has contributed greatly to the rising quality of life in America. The field of food production has especially benefitted from breakthroughs in science and technology. In the above photograph, a laboratory technician experiments with a fungus that has been found to turn cellulose (a nonedible material used in the production of newspaper) into glucose (sugar).

The Future of the Family

The exceptionally large turnout for preliminary meetings of the 1980 White House Conference on the Family indicated that people were concerned about the future of the family.

The difficulty encountered by conference delegates in defining the word *family* reflects the fact that lifestyles and family situations have changed. The birth rate has declined steadily. In addition, the divorce rate has reached new heights. More and more married women are working, some out of necessity and some for self-fulfillment. It is estimated that 45 percent of the babies born in 1978 will at some time in their childhood live in a one-parent household.

Rapid changes are not limited to the family. The world in which the family must function is also undergoing a period of instability. People are concerned with what they see as signs of the declining ability of the family to cope with change. Spouse desertions, child and wife/husband abuse, and alcohol and drug abuse seem to reflect failures on the part of family members to deal with their interpersonal problems.

Within limits, the government is seeking direction on how it may help families. The government requires environmental impact statements before it approves certain projects. Perhaps the time has come to require a "family impact statement" to prevent the government from adding greater strains to family living. Some tax policies penalize married couples. Some aspects of the Medicare system make it easier to put the elderly into institutions than to obtain allowances for care that could help families keep the elderly at home. Further, the current system of welfare payments seems to undermine the soundness of the family. For example, a woman will receive less welfare money if it is known that her husband lives with her, even if he is unemployed and poor. Yet, Americans still appear determined to strengthen the vital institution of the family.

The Future of Our Energy Resources

Of greatest concern for the eighties and beyond will be energy—energy to heat our homes, to light our cities, and to run our cars.

As we near the end of the twentieth century, two facts are clear. One is that our dependence upon petroleum must ultimately cease. The supply is not endless, and the demand for oil worldwide will eventually overtake it. The other fact is that alternative sources of energy must be developed.

Because petroleum supplies are not bottomless, fuel conservation is also necessary. Conserving fuel means being more energy-efficient, and saving energy is a job in which all of us must share responsibility.

In the meantime, new energy sources are being developed. Already government research has rediscovered the benefits of natural gas and coal. Ways to produce nuclear energy are constantly being refined. Research is also underway to explore the possible uses of other fossil fuels, such as oil sand and oil shale, and of renewable energy sources, such as hydroelectricity, solar energy, and wind power.

Questions for Discussion

1. Define *apathy, antibiotics, hydroponics, aquaculture, extraterrestrial, family.*
2. How did the 1980 Presidential election reflect changes in American society?
3. What is the role of television in the politics of the 1980s?
4. How has the economy affected the protection of the environment?

5. In what ways are scientists and technologists working to improve life in the future?
6. How does the family of the 1980s differ from the family of the 1880s?
7. What must be done for us to insure energy for the future?

Prospects for the Future

The eighties are merely proving a lesson that Americans have been learning since the beginning of this century. The world is getting smaller and more interdependent. Economic, social, and political problems are deeply entangled with each other. Technology is not the answer to every dilemma. And no one nation or people can have its way forever.

Americans are bound up in the fate of the whole human race. In the long run, starvation or revolution halfway around the world will have some effect on us. All peoples are tightly connected to each other. Thus, in this country a failure to help any one group escape the grip of poverty sooner or later, one way or another, brings about social costs that have to be shared among all. The technology that people once thought would go on forever providing jobs and wealth, works serious changes in our lives and on the environment. Therefore, costs against these gains must be weighed. The people of the United States no longer have a limitless gift of natural resources, protection from danger by broad oceans, and a universal faith in tomorrow.

That, however, is looking at the mud, and not at the sky. The people of America are still a large, diverse people who operate what is now one of the world's oldest democracies with more success than one realizes, especially when things go wrong. There is not a dissident in a totalitarian country who would not change systems with the people of the United States. There is hardly a person in the impoverished regions of the world who would not live a better life in the United States. This is not to say that the people of America should, therefore, bask in self-satisfaction. There is still hard work for Americans and sacrifices to make, so that they can keep what they have, and improve it. Americans have to change many of their ideas about what people are entitled to as individuals and as a nation.

America, fortunately, has many things going for it—inherited things. There is the productive machinery that was built over the centuries, the energy and skills of people of every race, rich traditions, and nationwide organizations that give Americans a common culture. These are good birthrights. If Americans continue to believe as their forebears did, that America offers fine prospects, then there is every reason to expect that today's Americans will build an even greater future.

Chapter 32 Review

Summary Questions for Discussion

1. Between 1945 and 1980, why did sections of the inner cities undergo decay?
2. What are the projections concerning the character of the population of the 1980s? How will it affect jobs, housing, health care, and social security?
3. Why and from where have refugees come to the United States during the 1970s and 1980s?
4. What problems have resulted from the influx of refugees?
5. Why is the Persian Gulf a trouble spot for the 1980s? What events have occurred there?
6. What actions on the part of the United States have indicated a more realistic policy toward third-world nations?
7. How did the 1980 campaign reflect the change in attitude toward campaigns, elections, and political parties.
8. What actions resulted from environmentalists seeking to protect the environment?
9. What scientific advances have been made in the areas of disease control, food production, space travel and exploration, and computer science?
10. What problems are faced by the American family in the 1980s?

Word Study

Fill in each blank in the sentences that follow with the term below that is most appropriate.

megalopolis
aquaculture
rapid-deployment force
third world

multinational
corporations
apathy
political asylum

family
détente
hydroponics

1. A _____ encompasses a large region including several large cities and their surrounding areas.
2. Many refugees seek _____ to rid themselves of harsh governmental control in their native country.
3. A friendly understanding between nations, such as the United States and the Soviet Union during the 1970s, is known as _____.
4. The development of a _____ is designed to allow for the protection of areas without American defense bases.
5. In the Cold War, the forces of democracy and the forces of communism have sought to lure the members of the _____ or underdeveloped or neutral nations—mainly of Asia and Africa—onto their side.
6. Corporations that have their home offices in one country and a network of branch offices in many host countries are known as _____.
7. Widespread disinterest is referred to as _____.
8. The growing of plants in nutrient-rich water is known as _____.
9. In _____, fish are raised in a controlled environment.
10. A _____ is a group of closely related individuals, the nature of which is changing in the 1980s.

Using Your Skills

Examine the photographs in this chapter. Then examine the photographs in this week's newspapers. Clip out the photos in the newspaper that can be considered updates for topics discussed and illustrated in Chapter 32.

Unit 8 Review

Summary

World War II brought Americans out of the Great Depression. But its conclusion unleashed an all-powerful problem. Humankind was capable of destructive power of a magnitude never before imagined. The United States and the Soviet Union had become superpowers, around whom global policy would be shaped. Domestically, the United States faced the strains of readjusting to a peacetime economy.

The fifties proved to be the calm before the storm. Prosperity prevailed for most. The generation that emerged was exposed to more art, music, literature, and culture than ever before. Racial discrimination and the Korean War marred the decade. However, most people were optimistic. Political leaders and institutions were trusted. The sixties were to change all this.

The sixties were noisy, turbulent, bloody, unpredictable, and disillusioning. Americans grew up. Men went to the moon. Soldiers died in Vietnam. The assassination of a President, a Senator, and a great Black leader stunned Americans and the world. Change occurred in the perception of women's rights, race, sex, government, and the limits of our military power. The country was held together by an economy of abundance. However, this too was to change in the seventies.

During the decade of the seventies, the United States withdrew into itself. It was shaken by failure, dishonesty, and corruption in government. It had failed in Vietnam, a President had resigned, and science and technology were not making the problems go away. Despite the celebration of the bicentennial, strong currents indicated that people had little faith in government. The problems of the seventies are the legacy for the eighties.

Foremost in the minds of Americans in the eighties is energy. Where are we going to find the energy to power our industrial environment? Our population will be older. How do we meet its needs? What will be the role of women and other minorities? Of science and technology? Of the family? These are overwhelming challenges that must be met in the 1980s.

Summary Questions

1. In what ways did the United States join the war against the Axis powers even before it formally declared war on them?

2. Why did the United States declaration of war against Japan lead to the declaration of war against Germany and Italy?

3. Contrast the lives of civilians on the home front in the United States and in Europe.

4. What were the immediate and long-range effects of the dropping of the atomic bomb?

5. What immediate domestic problems awaited Truman at the end of World War II? How did he deal with them?

6. How is the United Nations different from its predecessor, the League of Nations?

7. What was the policy of "containment"?

8. What is the Cold War?

9. How have American relations with China changed since Truman's recognition of the Republic of China in 1949?

10. Why was the decision in *Brown* vs. *Board of Education of Topeka* so important to Blacks?

11. What forces were at work during the 1950s that changed American life?

12. In what way was Eisenhower's foreign policy a continuation of Truman's foreign policy?

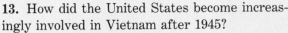

13. How did the United States become increasingly involved in Vietnam after 1945?

14. How did President Johnson continue the domestic policies of President Kennedy?

15. Who were some of the leaders in the movement to obtain justice and equality for minorities in the United States in the 1960s?

16. What goals have feminists worked for in recent years?

17. What events helped bring about friendlier relations between the Soviet Union and the United States in the late 1960s and 1970s?

18. Why did the Watergate scandal result in a reexamination of the growing powers of the presidency and political honesty?

19. How did the election of Jimmy Carter reflect American attitudes in the 1970s?

20. How will the American role and attitudes in the world scene be affected by third-world nations and multinational corporations?

Developing Your Vocabulary

Choose the correct term to complete the following sentences.

1. (Genocide, Pluralism) allows many religious and ethnic groups to live together peacefully.

2. (Swing shifts, Secondary boycotts) are used to increase production and employment.

3. The practice of hiring more workers than are necessary to do a particular job is referred to as (filibuster, featherbedding).

4. Dissidents are (satisfied, dissatisfied) with the policies of their government.

5. Federal assistance to states for specific programs is known as (surtax, grants-in-aid).

6. (Affirmative action, Reverse discrimination) is aimed at aiding minorities who have been the object of prejudicial actions.

7. Apathy is widespread (interest, disinterest) in events.

8. Devaluation (increases, decreases) the worth of currency.

9. During a recession, there is (an increase, a slowdown) in economic activity.

10. (Megalopolises, Suburbs) consist of several large cities and their surrounding areas.

Developing Your Skills

Evaluation and Synthesis

1. Write five newspaper headlines that you think would sum up the important events of the 1960s.

2. Which of the methods used by members of minority groups to gan equality and justice were most effective? Defend your answer.

Critical Thinking

3. Debate: "Science and technology—a blessing to humankind."

Comparing and applying information

4. Compare American immigration policies of the 1970s and 1980s with those studied earlier.

Presidents of the United States

1789	George Washington, *Virginia*		1881	James A. Garfield, *Ohio, Republican*
1797	John Adams, *Massachusetts, Federalist*		1881	Chester A. Arthur, *New York, Republican*
1801	Thomas Jefferson, *Virginia, Democratic-Republican*		1885	Grover Cleveland, *New York, Democratic*
1809	James Madison, *Virginia, Democratic-Republican*		1889	Benjamin Harrison, *Indiana, Republican*
1817	James Monroe, *Virginia, Democratic-Republican*		1893	Grover Cleveland, *New York, Democratic*
1825	John Quincy Adams, *Mass., Democratic-Republican*		1897	William McKinley, *Ohio, Republican*
1829	Andrew Jackson, *Tennessee, Democratic*		1901	Theodore Roosevelt, *New York, Republican*

1789   **George Washington,** *Virginia*
1797   **John Adams,** *Massachusetts, Federalist*
1801   **Thomas Jefferson,** *Virginia, Democratic-Republican*
1809   **James Madison,** *Virginia, Democratic-Republican*
1817   **James Monroe,** *Virginia, Democratic-Republican*
1825   **John Quincy Adams,** *Mass., Democratic-Republican*
1829   **Andrew Jackson,** *Tennessee, Democratic*
1837   **Martin Van Buren,** *New York, Democratic*
1841   **William H. Harrison,** *Ohio, Whig*
1841   **John Tyler,** *Virginia, Whig*
1845   **James K. Polk,** *Tennessee, Democratic*
1849   **Zachary Taylor,** *Louisiana, Whig*
1850   **Millard Fillmore,** *New York, Whig*
1853   **Franklin Pierce,** *New Hampshire, Democratic*
1857   **James Buchanan,** *Pennsylvania, Democratic*
1861   **Abraham Lincoln,** *Illinois, Republican*
1865   **Andrew Johnson,** *Tennessee, Republican*
1869   **Ulysses S. Grant,** *Illinois, Republican*
1877   **Rutherford B. Hayes,** *Ohio, Republican*

1881   **James A. Garfield,** *Ohio, Republican*
1881   **Chester A. Arthur,** *New York, Republican*
1885   **Grover Cleveland,** *New York, Democratic*
1889   **Benjamin Harrison,** *Indiana, Republican*
1893   **Grover Cleveland,** *New York, Democratic*
1897   **William McKinley,** *Ohio, Republican*
1901   **Theodore Roosevelt,** *New York, Republican*
1909   **William Howard Taft,** *Ohio, Republican*
1913   **Woodrow Wilson,** *New Jersey, Democratic*
1921   **Warren G. Harding,** *Ohio, Republican*
1923   **Calvin Coolidge,** *Massachusetts, Republican*
1929   **Herbert Hoover,** *California, Republican*
1933   **Franklin D. Roosevelt,** *New York, Democratic*
1945   **Harry S Truman,** *Missouri, Democratic*
1953   **Dwight D. Eisenhower,** *New York, Republican*
1961   **John F. Kennedy,** *Massachusetts, Democratic*
1963   **Lyndon B. Johnson,** *Texas, Democratic*
1969   **Richard M. Nixon,** *New York, Republican*
1974   **Gerald R. Ford,** *Michigan, Republican*
1976   **James E. Carter,** *Georgia, Democratic*
1980   **Ronald W. Reagan,** *California, Republican*

Constitution of the United States

We the people of the United States, in Order to form a more perfect Union, establish Justice, insure domestic Tranquility, provide for the common defence, promote the general Welfare, and secure the Blessings of Liberty to ourselves and our Posterity, do ordain and establish this CONSTITUTION for the United States of America.

Article I (LEGISLATURE)

Section 1. All legislative Powers herein granted shall be vested in a Congress of the United States, which shall consist of a Senate and House of Representatives.

(House of Representatives)

Section 2. The House of Representatives shall be composed of Members chosen every second Year by the People of the several States, and the Electors in each State shall have the Qualifications requisite for Electors of the most numerous Branch of the State Legislature.

(Qualifications for Representatives)

No Person shall be a Representative who shall not have attained to the Age of twenty-five Years, and been seven Years a Citizen of the United States, and who shall not, when elected, be an Inhabitant of that State in which he shall be chosen.

(Method of Apportionment)

Representatives and direct Taxes shall be apportioned among the several States which may be included within this Union, according to their respective Numbers, which shall be determined by adding to the whole Number of free Persons, including those bound to Service for a Term of Years, and excluding Indians not taxed, three fifths of all other Persons. The actual Enumeration shall be made within three Years after the first Meeting of the Congress of the United States, and within every subsequent Term of ten Years, in such Manner as they shall by Law direct. The Number of Representatives shall not exceed one for every thirty Thousand, but each state shall have at Least one Representative; and until such enumeration shall be made, the State of New Hampshire shall be entitled to chuse three, Massachusetts eight, Rhode-Island and Providence Plantations one, Connecticut five, New York six, New Jersey four, Pennsylvania eight, Delaware one, Maryland six, Virginia ten, North Carolina five, South Carolina five, and Georgia three.

(Vacancies)

When vacancies happen in the Representation from any State, the Executive Authority thereof shall issue Writs of Election to fill such Vacancies.

(Rules of the House Impeachment)

The House of Representatives shall chuse their Speaker and other Officers; and shall have the sole Power of Impeachment.

(Senators)

Section 3. The Senate of the United States shall be composed of two Senators from each State, chosen by the Legislature thereof, for six Years; and each Senator shall have one Vote.

Immediately after they shall be assembled in Consequence of the first Election, they shall be divided as equally as may be into three Classes. The Seats of the Senators of the first Class shall be vacated at the Expiration of the second Year, of the second Class at the Expiration of the fourth Year, and of the third Class at the Expiration of the sixth Year, so that one-third may be chosen every second Year; and if Vacancies happen by Resignation, or otherwise, during the Recess of the Legislature, of any State, the Executive thereof may make temporary Appointments until the next Meeting of the Legislature, which shall then fill such Vacancies.

(Qualifications of Senators)

No person shall be a Senator who shall not have attained to the Age of thirty Years, and been nine Years a Citizen of the United States, and who shall not, when elected, be an Inhabitant of that State in which he shall be chosen.

(Vice President)

The Vice President of the United States shall be President of the Senate, but shall have no vote, unless they be equally divided.

The Senate shall chuse their other Officers, and also a President pro tempore, in the absence of the Vice President, or when he shall exercise the Office of the President of the United States.

(Impeachments)

The Senate shall have the sole Power to try all Impeachments. When sitting for that purpose, they shall be on Oath or Affirmation. When the President of the United States is tried, the Chief Justice shall preside: And no person shall be convicted without the Concurrence of two thirds of the Members present.

Judgment in Cases of Impeachment shall not extend further than to removal from Office, and disqualification to hold and enjoy any Office of honor, Trust, or Profit under the United States: but the Party convicted shall nevertheless be liable and subject to Indictment, Trial, Judgment, and Punishment, according to Law.

(Elections)

Section 4. The Times, Places and Manner of holding Elections for Senators and Representatives, shall be prescribed in each state by the Legislature thereof: but the Congress may at any time by Law make or alter such Regulations, except as to the Places of Chusing Senators.

(Sessions)

The Congress shall assemble at least once in every Year, and such Meeting shall be on the first Monday in December, unless they shall by Law appoint a different Day.

(Proceeding of the House and the Senate)

Section 5. Each House shall be the Judge of the Elections, Returns and Qualifications of its own Members, and a Majority of each shall constitute a Quorum to do Business; but a smaller number may adjourn from day to day, and may be authorized to compel the Attendance of absent Members, in such Manner, and under such Penalties, as each House may provide.

Each house may determine the Rules of its Proceedings, punish its Members for disorderly Behavior, and, with the Concurrence of two thirds, expel a Member.

Each House shall keep a Journal of its Proceedings, and from time to time publish the same, excepting such Parts as may in their Judgment require Secrecy; and the Yeas and Nays of the Members of either House on any question shall, at the Desire of one fifth of those Present, be entered on the Journal.

Neither House, during the Session of Congress, shall, without the Consent of the other, adjourn for more than three days, nor to any other Place than that in which the two Houses shall be sitting.

(Members' Compensation and Privileges)

Section 6. The Senators and Representatives shall receive a Compensation for their Services, to be ascertained by Law, and paid out of the Treasury of the United States. They shall in all Cases, except Treason, Felony, and Breach of the Peace, be privileged from Arrest during their Attendance at the Session of their respective Houses, and in going to and returning from the same; and for any Speech or Debate in either House, they shall not be questioned in any other Place.

No Senator or Representative shall, during the Time for which he was elected, be appointed to any civil Office under the Authority of the United States, which shall have been created, or the Emoluments whereof shall have been increased, during such time; and no Person holding any Office under the United States shall be a Member of either House during his continuance in Office.

(Money Bills)

Section 7. All Bills for raising Revenue shall originate in the House of Representatives; but the Senate may propose or concur with Amendments as on other bills.

(Presidential Veto and Congressional Power to Override)

Every Bill which shall have passed the House of Representatives and the Senate, shall, before it become a Law, be presented to the President of the United States; If he approve he shall sign it, but if not he shall return it, with his Objections, to that House in which it shall have originated, who shall enter the Objections at large on their Journal, and proceed to reconsider it. If after such Reconsideration two thirds of that House shall agree to pass the bill, it shall be sent, together with the objections, to the other House, by which it shall likewise be reconsidered, and if approved by two thirds of that House, it shall become a Law. But in all such Cases the Votes of both Houses shall be determined by Yeas and Nays, and the Names of the Persons voting for and against the Bill shall be entered on the Journal or each House respectively. If any Bill shall not be returned by the President within ten Days (Sundays excepted) after it shall have been presented to him, the Same shall be a Law, in like Manner as if he had signed it, unless the Congress by their Adjournment prevent its Return, in which Case it shall not be a Law.

Every Order, Resolution, or Vote to which the Concurrence of the Senate and House of Representatives may be necessary (except on a question of Adjournment) shall be presented to the President of the United States; and before the Same shall take Effect, shall be approved by him, or being disapproved by him, shall be repassed by two thirds of the Senate and House of Representatives, according to the Rules and Limitations prescribed in the Case of a Bill.

(Congressional Powers)

Section 8. The Congress shall have Power To lay and collect Taxes, Duties, Imposts and Excises, to pay the Debts and provide for the common Defence and general Welfare of the United States; but all Duties, Imposts and Excises shall be uniform throughout the United States;

To borrow money on the credit of the United States;

To regulate Commerce with foreign Nations, and among the several States, and with the Indian Tribes;

To establish an uniform Rule of Naturalization, and uniform Laws on the subject of Bankruptcies throughout the United States;

To coin Money, regulate the Value thereof, and of foreign Coin, and fix the Standard of Weights and Measures;

To provide for the Punishment of counterfeiting the Securities and current Coin of the United States;

To establish Post Offices and post Roads;

To promote the Progress of Science and useful Arts, by securing for limited Times to Authors and Inventors the exclusive Right to their respective Writings and Discoveries;

To constitute Tribunals inferior to the Supreme Court;

To define and punish Piracies and Felonies committed on the high Seas, and Offenses against the Law of Nations;

To declare War, grant Letters of Marque and Reprisal, and make Rules concerning Captures on Land and Water;

To raise and support Armies, but no Appropriation of Money to that Use shall be for a longer Term than two Years;

To provide and maintain a Navy;

To make Rules for the Government and Regulation of the land and naval forces;

To provide for calling forth the Militia to execute the Laws of the Union, suppress Insurrections and repel Invasions;

To provide for organizing, arming, and disciplining the Militia, and for governing such Part of them as may be employed in the Service of the United States, reserving to the States respectively, the Appointment of the Officers, and the Authority of training the Militia according to the discipline prescribed by Congress;

To exercise exclusive Legislation in all Cases whatsoever, over such District (not exceeding ten Miles square) as may, by Cession of particular States, and the acceptance of Congress, become the Seat of Government of the United States, and to exercise like Authority over all Places purchased by the Consent of the Legislature of the State in which the Same shall be, for the Erection of Forts, Magazines, Arsenals, dock-Yards, and other needful Buildings;– And

To make all Laws which shall be necessary and proper for carrying into Execution the foregoing Powers, and all other Powers vested by this Constitution in the Government of the United States, or in any Department or Officer thereof.

(Limits on Congressional Power)

Section 9. The Migration or Importation of such Persons as any of the States now existing shall think proper to admit, shall not be prohibited by the Congress prior to the Year one thousand eight hundred and eight, but a tax or duty may be imposed on such Importation, not exceeding ten dollars for each Person.

The privilege of the Writ of Habeas Corpus shall not be suspended, unless when in Cases of Rebellion or Invasion the public Safety may require it.

No Bill of Attainder or ex post facto Law shall be passed.

No capitation, or other direct, Tax shall be laid

unless in Proportion to the Census or Enumeration herein before directed to be taken.

No Tax or Duty shall be laid on Articles exported from any State.

No Preference shall be given by any Regulation of Revenue to the Ports of one State over those of another: nor shall Vessels bound to, or from, one State, be obliged to enter, clear, or pay Duties in another.

No Money shall be drawn from the Treasury, but in Consequence of Appropriations made by Law; and a regular Statement and Account of the Receipts and Expenditures of all public Money shall be published from time to time.

No Title of Nobility shall be granted by the United States: And no Person holding any Office of Profit or Trust under them, shall, without the Consent of the Congress, accept of any present, Emolument, Office, or Title, of any kind whatever, from any King, Prince, or foreign State.

(Limits on Powers of the States)

Section 10.   No State shall enter into any Treaty, Alliance, or Confederation; grant Letters of Marque and Reprisal; coin Money; emit Bills of Credit; make any Thing but gold and silver Coin a Tender in Payment of Debts; pass any Bill of Attainder, ex post facto Law, or Law impairing the Obligation of Contracts, or grant any Title of Nobility.

No State shall, without the Consent of the Congress, lay any Imposts or Duties on Imports or Exports, except what may be absolutely necessary for executing its inspection Laws: and the net Produce of all Duties and Imposts, laid by any State on Imports or Exports, shall be for the Use of the Treasury of the United States; and all such Laws shall be subject to the Revision and Control of the Congress.

No State shall, without the Consent of Congress, lay any duty of Tonnage, keep Troops, or Ships of War in time of Peace, enter into any Agreement or Compact with another State, or with a foreign Power, or engage in War, unless actually invaded, or in such imminent Danger as will not admit of delay.

Article II   (EXECUTIVE)

(President)

Section 1.   The executive Power shall be vested in a President of the United States of America. He shall hold his Office during the Term of four years,

and, together with the Vice President, chosen for the same Term, be elected, as follows:

(Election of President)

Each State shall appoint, in such Manner as the Legislature thereof may direct, a Number of Electors, equal to the whole Number of Senators and Representatives to which the State may be entitled in the Congress: but no Senator or Representative, or Person holding an Office of Trust or Profit under the United States, shall be appointed an Elector.

(Electors)

The Electors shall meet in their respective States, and vote by Ballot for two persons, of whom one at least shall not be an Inhabitant of the same State with themselves. And they shall make a List of all the Persons voted for, and of the Number of Votes for each; which List they shall sign and certify, and transmit sealed to the Seat of the Government of the United States, directed to the President of the Senate. The President of the Senate shall, in the Presence of the Senate and House of Representatives, open all the Certificates, and the Votes shall then be counted. The Person having the greatest Number of Votes shall be the President, if such Number be a Majority of the whole Number of Electors appointed; and if there be more than one who have such Majority, and have an equal Number of Votes, then the House of Representatives shall immediately chuse by Ballot one of them for President; and if no Person have a Majority, then from the five highest on the List the said House shall in like Manner chuse the President. But in chusing the President, the Votes shall be taken by States, the Representation from each State having one Vote; a quorum for this Purpose shall consist of a Member or Members from two-thirds of the States, and a Majority of all the States shall be necessary to a Choice. In every Case, after the Choice of the President, the Person having the greatest Number of Votes of the Electors shall be the Vice President. But if there should remain two or more who have equal votes, the Senate shall chuse from them by Ballot the Vice President.

The Congress may determine the Time of chusing the Electors, and the Day on which they shall give their Votes; which Day shall be the same throughout the United States.

(Qualifications of President)

No person except a natural-born Citizen, or a Citizen of the United States, at the time of the

Adoption of this Constitution, shall be eligible to the Office of President; neither shall any Person be eligible to that Office who shall not have attained to the Age of thirty-five years, and been fourteen Years a Resident within the United States.

(Succession to the Presidency)

In Case of the Removal of the President from Office, or of his Death, Resignation, or Inability to discharge the Powers and Duties of the said Office, the same shall devolve on the Vice President, and the Congress may by Law provide for the Case of Removal, Death, Resignation, or Inability, both of the President and Vice President, delcaring what Officer shall then act as President, and such Officer shall act accordingly, until the disability be removed, or a President shall be elected.

(Compensation)

The President shall, at stated Times, receive for his Services a Compensation, which shall neither be increased nor diminished during the Period for which he shall have been elected, and he shall not receive within that Period any other Emolument from the United States, or any of them.

(Oath of Office)

Before he enters on the execution of his Office, he shall take the following Oath or Affirmation:–"I do solemnly swear (or affirm) that I will faithfully execute the Office of President of the United States, and will, to the best of my Ability, preserve, protect, and defend the Constitution of the United States."

(Powers of the President)

Section 2. The President shall be Commander in Chief of the Army and Navy of the United States, and of the Militia of the several States, when called into the actual Service of the United States; he may require the Opinion, in writing, of the principal Officer in each of the executive Departments, upon any subject relating to the Duties of their respective Offices, and he shall have Power to Grant Reprieves and Pardons for Offenses against the United States, except in Cases of Impeachment.

(Making of Treaties)

He shall have Power, by and with the Advice and Consent of the Senate, to make Treaties, provided two thirds of the Senators present concur; and he shall nominate, and by and with the Advice and Consent of the Senate, shall appoint Ambassadors, other public Ministers and Consuls, Judges of the supreme Court, and all other Officers of the United States, whose Appointments are not herein other-

wise provided for, and which shall be established by Law: but the Congress may by Law vest the Appointment of such inferior Officers, as they think proper, in the President alone, in the Courts of Law, or in the Heads of Departments.

(Vacancies)

The President shall have Power to fill up all Vacancies that may happen during the Recess of the Senate, by granting Commissions which shall expire at the End of their next Session.

(Additional Duties and Powers)

Section 3. He shall from time to time give to the Congress Information of the State of the Union, and recommend to their Consideration such Measures as he shall judge necessary and expedient; he may, on extraordinary occasions, convene both Houses, or either of them, and in Case of Disagreement between them, with respect to the Time of Adjournment, he may adjourn them to such Time as he shall think proper; he shall receive Ambassadors and other public Ministers; he shall take Care that the Laws be faithfully executed, and shall Commission all the Officers of the United States.

(Impeachment)

Section 4. The President, Vice President and all civil Officers of the United States, shall be removed from Office on Impeachment for, and Conviction of, Treason, Bribery, or other high Crimes and Misdemeanors.

Article III (JUDICIARY)

(Courts, Judges, Compensation)

Section 1. The judicial Power of the United States, shall be vested in one supreme Court, and in such inferior Courts as the Congress may from time to time ordain and establish. The Judges, both of the supreme and inferior Courts, shall hold their Offices during good Behaviour, and shall, at stated Times, receive for their Services, a Compensation, which shall not be diminished during their Continuance in Office.

(Jurisdiction)

Section 2. The judicial Power shall extend to all Cases, in Law and Equity, arising under this Constitution, the Laws of the United States, and treaties made, or which shall be made, under their Authority:–to all Cases affecting ambassadors, other public ministers and consuls;–to all cases of admiralty and maritime Jurisdiction;–to Controversies to which the

United States shall be a Party;–to Controversies between two or more States;–between a State and Citizens of another State;–between Citizens of different States,–between Citizens of the same State claiming Lands under Grants of different States, and between a State, or the Citizens thereof, and foreign States, Citizens or Subjects.

In all Cases affecting Ambassadors, other public Ministers and Consuls, and those in which a State shall be Party, the supreme Court shall have original Jurisdiction. In all the other Cases before mentioned, the supreme Court shall have appellate Jurisdiction, both as to Law and Fact, with such Exceptions, and under such Regulations as the Congress shall make.

(Trial by Jury)

The trial of all Crimes, except in Cases of Impeachment, shall be by Jury; and such Trial shall be held in the State where the said Crimes shall have been committed; but when not committed within any State, the Trial shall be at such Place or Places as the Congress may by Law have directed.

(Treason)

Section 3. Treason against the United States, shall consist only in levying War against them, or in adhering to their Enemies, giving them Aid and Comfort. No Person shall be convicted of Treason unless on the Testimony of two Witnesses to the same overt Act, or on Confession in open Court.

The Congress shall have power to declare the Punishment of Treason, but no Attainder of Treason shall work Corruption of Blood, or Forfeiture except during the Life of the Person attainted.

Article IV   (FEDERAL SYSTEM)

Section 1. Full Faith and Credit shall be given in each State to the public Acts, Records, and judicial Proceedings of every other State. And the Congress may by general Laws prescribe the Manner in which such Acts, Records, and Proceedings shall be proved, and the Effect thereof.

(Privileges and Immunities of Citizens)

Section 2. The Citizens of each State shall be entitled to all Privileges and Immunities of Citizens in the several states.

A Person charged in any State with Treason, Felony, or other Crime, who shall flee from Justice, and be found in another State, shall on demand of the executive Authority of the State from which he fled,

be delivered up, to be removed to the State having Jurisdiction of the crime.

No Person held to Service or Labour in one State, under the Laws thereof, escaping into another, shall, in Consequence of any Law or Regulation therein, be discharged from such Service or Labour, but shall be delivered up on Claim of the Party to whom such Service or Labour may be due.

(Admission and Formation of New States; Governing of Territories)

Section 3. New States may be admitted by the Congress into this Union; but no new State shall be formed or erected within the Jurisdiction of any other State; nor any State be formed by the Junction of two or more States, or parts of States, without the Consent of the Legislatures of the States concerned as well as of the Congress.

The Congress shall have Power to dispose of and make all needful Rules and Regulations respecting the Territory or other Property belonging to the United States; and nothing in this Constitution shall be so construed as to Prejudice any Claims of the United States, or of any particular State.

(Federal Protection of the States)

Section 4. The United States shall guarantee to every State in this Union a Republican Form of Government, and shall protect each of them against Invasion; and on Application of the Legislature, or of the Executive (when the Legislature cannot be convened) against domestic Violence.

Article V   (AMENDMENTS)

The Congress, whenever two-thirds of both Houses shall deem it necessary, shall propose Amendments to this Constitution, or, on the Application of the Legislatures of two-thirds of the several States, shall call a Convention for proposing Amendments, which, in either Case, shall be valid to all Intents and Purposes, as part of this Constitution, when ratified by the Legislatures of three-fourths of the several States, or by Conventions in three-fourths thereof, as the one or the other Mode of Ratification may be proposed by the Congress; Provided that no Amendment which may be made prior to the Year One thousand eight hundred and eight shall in any Manner affect the first and fourth Clauses in the Ninth Section of the first Article; and that no State, without its Consent, shall be deprived of its equal Suffrage in the Senate.

Article VI

All Debts contracted and Engagements entered into, before the Adoption of this Constitution, shall be as valid against the United States under this Constitution, as under the Confederation.

This Constitution, and the Laws of the United States which shall be made in Pursuance thereof; and all Treaties made, or which shall be made, under the Authority of the United States, shall be the supreme Law of the Land; and the Judges in every State shall be bound thereby, any Thing in the Constitution or Laws of any State to the Contrary notwithstanding.

The Senators and Representatives before mentioned, and the Members of the several State Legislatures, and all executive and judicial Officers, both of the United States and of the several States, shall be bound by Oath or Affirmation to support this Constitution; but no religious Test shall ever be required as a qualification to any Office or public Trust under the United States.

Article VII (RATIFICATION)

The Ratification of the Conventions of nine States shall be sufficient for the Establishment of this Constitution between the States so ratifying the same.

Done in Convention by the Unanimous Consent of the States present the Seventeenth Day of September in the Year of our Lord one thousand seven hundred and Eighty seven, and of the Independence of the United States of America the Twelfth. In Witness whereof We have hereunto subscribed our Names.

Articles in Addition to, and Amendment of, the Constitution of the United States of America, Proposed by Congress, and Ratified by the Legislatures of the Several States, Pursuant to the Fifth Article of the Original Constitution.

Amendment I [1791] (FREEDOMS)

(Speech, Press, Assembly, and Petition)

Congress shall make no law respecting an establishment of religion, or prohibiting the free exercise thereof; or abridging the freedom of speech, or of the press; or the right of the people peaceably to assemble, and to petition the Government for a redress of grievances.

Amendment II [1791] (RIGHT TO BEAR ARMS)

A well regulated Militia, being necessary to the security of a free State, the right of the people to keep and bear Arms shall not be infringed.

Amendment III [1791] (QUARTERING OF SOLDIERS)

No soldier shall, in time of peace, be quartered in any house, without the consent of the Owner, nor in time of war, but in a manner to be prescribed by law.

Amendment IV [1791] (FREEDOM OF PERSONS

(Warrants, Searches, and Seizures)

The right of the people to be secure in their persons, houses, papers, and effects, against unreasonable searches and seizures, shall not be violated, and no Warrants shall issue, but upon probable cause, supported by Oath or affirmation, and particularly describing the place to be searched, and the persons or things to be seized.

Amendment V [1791] (CAPITAL CRIMES)

(Protection of the Accused; Compensation)

No person shall be held to answer for a capital or otherwise infamous crime, unless on a presentment or indictment of a Grand Jury, except in cases arising in the land or naval forces, or in the Militia, when in actual service in time of War or public danger; nor shall any person be subject for the same offence to be twice put in jeopardy of life or limb; nor shall be compelled in any criminal case to be a witness against himself, nor be deprived of life, liberty, or property, without due process of law; nor shall private property be taken for public use, without just compensation.

Amendment VI [1791] (TRIAL BY JURY)

(Accusation, Witnesses, Counsel)

In all criminal prosecutions, the accused shall enjoy the right to a speedy and public trial, by an impartial jury of the State and district wherein the crime shall have been committed, which district shall have been previously ascertained by law, and to be informed of the nature and cause of the accusation; to be confronted with the witnesses against him; to have compulsory process for obtaining witnesses in his favor, and to have the Assistance of Counsel for his defence.

Amendment VII [1791] (CIVIL LAW)

In suits at common law, where the value in controversy shall exceed twenty dollars, the right of trial by jury shall be preserved, and no fact tried by a jury, shall be otherwise reexamined in any Court of the United States, than according to the rules of the common law.

Amendment VIII [1791] (BAILS, FINES, AND PUNISHMENTS)

Excessive bail shall not be required, nor excessive fines imposed, nor cruel and unusual punishments inflicted.

Amendment IX [1791] (RIGHTS RETAINED BY THE PEOPLE)

The enumeration in the Constitution, of certain rights, shall not be construed to deny or disparage others retained by the people.

Amendment X [1791] (RIGHTS RESERVED TO THE STATES)

The powers not delegated to the United States by the Constitution, nor prohibited by it to the States, are reserved to the States respectively, or to the people.

Amendment XI [1798] (JURISDICTIONAL LIMITS)

The Judicial power of the United States shall not be construed to extend to any suit in law or equity, commenced or prosecuted against one of the United States by Citizens of another State, or by Citizens or Subjects of any Foreign State.

Amendment XII [1804] (ELECTORAL COLLEGE)

The Electors shall meet in their respective States and vote by ballot for President and Vice President, one of whom, at least, shall not be an inhabitant of the same State with themselves; they shall name in their ballots the person voted for as President, and in distinct ballots the person voted for as Vice President, and they shall make distinct lists of all persons voted for as President, and of all persons voted for as Vice President, and of the number of votes for each, which lists they shall sign and certify, and transmit sealed to the seat of the government of the United States, directed to the President of the Senate;–The President of the Senate shall, in the presence of the Senate and House of Representatives, open all the certificates and the votes shall then be counted;–The person having the greatest number of votes for President, shall be the President, if such number be a majority of the whole number of Electors appointed; and if no person have such majority, then from the persons having the highest numbers not exceeding three on the list of those voted for as President, the House of Representatives shall choose immediately, by ballot, the President. But in choosing the President, the votes shall be taken by states, the representation from each state having one vote; a quorum for this purpose shall consist of a member or members from two-thirds of the states, and a majority of all the states shall be necessary to a choice. And if the House of Representatives shall not choose a President whenever the right of choice shall devolve upon them, before the fourth day of March next following, then the Vice President shall act as President, as in the case of the death or other constitutional disability of the President.–The person having the greatest number of votes as Vice President, shall be the Vice President, if such number be a majority of the whole number of Electors appointed, and if no person have a majority, then from the two highest numbers on the list, the Senate shall choose the Vice President; a quorum for the purpose shall consist of two-thirds of the whole number of Senators, and a majority of the whole number shall be necessary to a choice. But no person constitutionally ineligible to the office of President shall be eligible to that of Vice President of the United States.

Amendment XIII [1865] (ABOLITION OF SLAVERY)

Section 1. Neither slavery nor involuntary servitude, except as a punishment for crime whereof the party shall have been duly convicted, shall exist within the United States, or any place subject to their jurisdiction.

Section 2. Congress shall have power to enforce this article by appropriate legislation.

Amendment XIV [1868] (CITIZENSHIP)

(Due Process of Law)

Section 1. All persons born or naturalized in the United States, and subject to the jurisdiction thereof, are citizens of the United States and of the State wherein they reside. No State shall make or enforce any law which shall abridge the privileges or immunities of citizens of the United States; nor shall any State deprive any person of life, liberty, or property, without due process of law; nor deny to any person within its jurisdiction the equal protection of the laws.

(Apportionment: Right to Vote)

Section 2. Representatives shall be apportioned among the several States according to their respective numbers, counting the whole number of persons in each State, excluding Indians not taxed. But when the right to vote at any election for the choice of electors for President and Vice President of the United States, Representatives in Congress, the Executive and Judicial officers of a State, or the members of the Legislature thereof, is denied to any of the male inhabitants of such State, being twenty-one years of age, and citizens of the United States, or in any way abridged, except for participation in rebellion, or other crime, the basis of representation therein shall be reduced in the proportion which the number of such male citizens shall bear to the whole number of male citizens twenty-one years of age in such State.

(Disqualification for Office)

Section 3. No person shall be a Senator or Representative in Congress, or elector of President and Vice President, or hold any office, civil or military, under the United States, or under any State, who, having previously taken an oath, as a member of Congress, or as an officer of the United States, or as a member of any State legislature, or as an executive or judicial officer of any State, to support the Constitution of the United States, shall have engaged in insurrection or rebellion against the same, or given aid or comfort to the enemies thereof. But Congress may by a vote of two-thirds of each House, remove such disability.

(Public Debt)

Section 4. The validity of the public debt of the United States, authorized by law, including debts incurred for payment of pensions and bounties for services in suppressing insurrection or rebellion, shall not be questioned. But neither the United States nor any State shall assume or pay any debt or obligation incurred in aid of insurrection or rebellion against the United States, or any claim for the loss or emancipation of any slave: but all such debts, obligations, and claims shall be held illegal and void.

Section 5. The Congress shall have the power

to enforce, by appropriate legislation, the provisions of this article.

Amendment XV [1870] (RIGHT TO VOTE)

Section 1. The right of citizens of the United States to vote shall not be denied or abridged by the United States or by any State on account of race, color or previous condition of servitude.

Section 2. The Congress shall have power to enforce this article by appropriate legislation.

Amendment XVI [1913] (INCOME TAX)

The Congress shall have power to lay and collect taxes on incomes, from whatever source derived, without apportionment among the several States, and without regard to any census or enumeration.

Amendment XVII [1913] (SENATORS)

(Election)

The Senate of the United States shall be composed of two Senators from each State, elected by the people thereof, for six years; and each Senator shall have one vote. The electors in each State shall have the qualifications requisite for electors of the most numerous branch of the State legislatures.

(Vacancies)

When vacancies happen in the representation of any State in the Senate, the executive authority of such State shall issue writs of election to fill such vacancies: *Provided,* That the legislature of any State may empower the executive thereof to make temporary appointments until the people fill the vacancies by election as the legislature may direct.

This amendment shall not be so construed as to affect the election or term of any Senator chosen before it becomes valid as part of the Constitution.

Amendment XVIII [1919] (PROHIBITION)

Section 1. After one year from the ratification of this article the manufacture, sale, or transportation of intoxicating liquors within, the importation thereof into, or the exportation thereof from the United States and all territory subject to the jurisdiction thereof for beverage purposes is hereby prohibited.

Section 2. The Congress and the several States shall have concurrent power to enforce this article by appropriate legislation.

Section 3. This article shall be inoperative

unless it shall have been ratified as an amendment to the Constitution by the legislatures of the several States, as provided in the Constitution, within seven years from the date of the submission hereof to the States by the Congress.

Amendment XIX [1920] (FEMALE SUFFRAGE)

The right of citizens of the United States to vote shall not be denied or abridged by the United States or by any State on account of sex.

Congress shall have power to enforce this article by appropriate legislation.

Amendment XX [1933] (TERMS OF OFFICE)

Section 1. The terms of the President and Vice President shall end at noon on the 20th day of January, and the terms of Senators and Representatives at noon on the 3d day of January, of the years in which such terms would have ended if this article had not been ratified; and the terms of their successors shall then begin.

Section 2. The Congress shall assemble at least once in every year, and such meeting shall begin at noon on the 3d day of January, unless they shall by law appoint a different day.

(Succession)

Section 3. If, at the time fixed for the beginning of the term of the President, the President elect shall have died, the Vice President elect shall become President. If a President shall not have been chosen before the time fixed for the beginning of his term, or if the President elect shall have failed to qualify, then the Vice President elect shall act as President until a President shall have qualified; and the Congress may by law provide for the case wherein neither a President elect nor a Vice President elect shall have qualified, declaring who shall then act as President, or the manner in which one who is to act shall be selected, and such person shall act accordingly until a President or Vice President shall have qualified.

Section 4. The Congress may by law provide for the case of the death of any of the persons from whom the House of Representatives may choose a President whenever the right of choice shall have devolved upon them, and for the case of the death of any of the persons from whom the Senate may choose a Vice President whenever the right of choice shall have devolved upon them.

Section 5. Sections 1 and 2 shall take effect on the 15th day of October following the ratification of this article.

Section 6. This article shall be inoperative unless it shall have been ratified as an amendment to the Constitution by the legislatures of three-fourths of the several States within seven years from the date of its submission.

Amendment XXI [1933] (REPEAL OF PROHIBITION)

Section 1. The eighteenth article of amendment to the Constitution of the United States is hereby repealed.

Section 2. The transportation or importation into any State, Territory, or possession of the United States for delivery or use therein of intoxicating liquors, in violation of the laws thereof, is hereby prohibited.

Section 3. This article shall be inoperative unless it shall have been ratified as an amendment to the Constitution by conventions in the several States, as provided in the Constitution, within seven years from the date of the submission hereof to the States by the Congress.

Amendment XXII [1951] (TERM OF PRESIDENT)

No person shall be elected to the office of the President more than twice, and no person who has held the office of President, or acted as President, for more than two years of a term to which some other person was elected President shall be elected to the office of the President more than once.

But this Article shall not apply to any person holding the office of President when this Article was proposed by the Congress, and shall not prevent any person who may be holding the office of President, or acting as President, during the term within which this Article becomes operative from holding the office of President or acting as President during the remainder of such term.

Amendment XXIII [1961] (WASHINGTON, D.C.)

(Enfranchisement of Voters in Federal Elections)

Section 1. The District constituting the seat of Government of the United States shall appoint in such manner as the Congress may direct:

A number of electors of President and Vice President equal to the whole number of Senators and Representatives in Congress to which the District would be entitled if it were a State, but in no event more than the least populous State; they shall be in addition to those appointed by the States, but they shall be considered, for the purposes of the election of President and Vice President, to be electors appointed by a State; and they shall meet in the District and perform such duties as provided by the twelfth article of amendment.

Section 2. The Congress shall have power to enforce this article by appropriate legislation.

Amendment XXIV [1964]   (POLL TAX)

Section 1. The right of citizens of the United States to vote in any primary or other election for President or Vice President, for electors for President or Vice President, or for Senator or Representative in Congress, shall not be denied or abridged by the United States or any State by reason of failure to pay any poll tax or other tax.

Section 2. The Congress shall have the power to enforce this article by appropriate legislation.

Amendment XXV [1967]   (SUCCESSION)

Section 1. In case of the removal of the President from office or his death or resignation, the Vice President shall become President.

Section 2. Whenever there is a vacancy in the office of the Vice President, the President shall nominate a Vice President who shall take the office upon confirmation by a majority vote of both houses of Congress.

Section 3. Whenever the President transmits to the President pro tempore of the Senate and the Speaker of the House of Representatives his written declaration that he is unable to discharge the powers and duties of his office, and until he transmits to them a written declaration to the contrary, such powers and duties shall be discharged by the Vice President as Acting President.

Section 4. Whenever the Vice President and a majority of either the principal officers of the executive departments, or of such other body as Congress may by law provide, transmit to the President pro tempore of the Senate and the Speaker of the House of Representatives their written declaration that the President is unable to discharge the powers and duties of his office, the Vice President shall immediately assume the powers and duties of the office as Acting President.

Thereafter, when the President transmits to the President pro tempore of the Senate and the Speaker of the House of Representatives his written declaration that no inability exists, he shall resume the powers and duties of his office unless the Vice President and a majority of either the principal officers of the executive departments, or of such other body as Congress may by law provide, transmit within four days to the President pro tempore of the Senate and the Speaker of the House of Representatives their written declaration that the President is unable to discharge the powers and duties of his office. Thereupon Congress shall decide the issue, assembling within 48 hours for that purpose if not in session. If the Congress, within 21 days after receipt of the latter written declaration, or, if Congress is not in session, within 21 days after Congress is required to assemble, determines by two-thirds vote of both houses that the President is unable to discharge the powers and duties of his office, the Vice President shall continue to discharge the same as Acting President; otherwise, the President shall resume the power and duties of his office.

Amendment XXVI [1971]   (VOTING AT AGE 18)

Section 1. The right of citizens of the United States, who are eighteen years of age or older, to vote shall not be denied or abridged by the United States or any State on account of age.

Section 2. The Congress shall have power to enforce this article by appropriate legislation.

Glossary

abolitionist a person who works to do away with slavery forever

affirmative action favorable treatment for members of groups that have been discriminated against

alien a person who is visiting or living in a country but who is not a citizen

alliance a formal association for the purpose of mutual help

amendment a change in or addition to a law or any written material

amphibious able to operate on land and water

amphibious force assault troops that land on a shore from seaborne transports

anarchy a condition in which there is no government whatever

annexation incorporation of a territory within the domain of another state or country

anthropologist a scientist who studies human cultures and their development

antiballistic missile a weapon of war designed to intercept and destroy a ballistic missile in flight

antibiotics drugs that destroy germs without harming the patient

anti-Semitism prejudice and hostility directed against Jews

apathy lack of interest

apprenticeship a period of time spent learning a trade by being employed as helper to a skilled worker

appropriation a sum of money earmarked for a specific purpose

aquaculture the use of a controlled environment for care and feeding of fish intended for human consumption

arbitration the use of a neutral party to settle a dispute

aristocracy a political system in which power is held by hereditary nobles

armada a fleet of fighting ships and landing craft

autonomy the right or power of self-government

balance of payments the difference between the estimated values of imports and exports of a country or region in a given period, including movements of money and services as well as goods

ballistic missile a particular kind of long-range self-propelled missile used in warfare

Barbary States the former name of the North African states of Tripoli, Algiers, Tunis, and Morocco

barrio a section of a city inhabited by Spanish-speaking people; a Hispanic ghetto

barter economy an economic system based on exchanging goods for goods

belligerent a party in a war

benefactor one who gives a gift or charitable donation

black codes special laws that apply to Blacks only

blacklisted having one's name on a list of persons to be denied employment or to be treated unfavorably in any way

black market trade in goods or services that violates official regulations

blitzkrieg a sudden, massive military attack planned to result in speedy victory

blue-collar worker one who wears work clothes on the job; usually, one who does manual labor

Bolshevik a member of the party that seized power in Russia during the Revolution in 1917

bond a written promise to pay back a loan at the end of a set time

bonus a special reward or payment in addition to what is usual

booster someone who is active in publicizing the good features of a locality

bootlegger a person who makes a business of supplying liquor illegally

bounty a payment to individuals made by a government to encourage enlistment or some other activity

boycott to protest by refusing to have anything to do with a certain product or service

building codes regulations that govern the types of buildings and the standards of construction permitted in a city or region

bull market a market in which prices are rising and many people are buying

capital the money and equipment needed to produce goods

capital goods any of the equipment and plant used to produce goods; the basic economic building blocks, such as steel girders and farm machines

capitalist a person who is the owner or part owner of a business that sells products for profit

carpetbagger a Northerner in the South after the Civil War, especially those with certain motives such as private gain

caucus a meeting of members of local and national legislatures

centralized government a government in which power is held by one central authority

charter a document outlining the principles, functions, and structure of an organization

closed shop a place of employment where all employees are union members

coalition a temporary alliance of independent groups, persons, or states for the purpose of promoting a joint action

coffle a line of animals or people tied together, such as African villagers when taken captive for the slave trade

coining the process of turning a metal into currency

colony a permanent settlement of pioneers, or colonists, from another land

commodities market a market in which contracts are sold for future delivery of specific goods at a price agreed upon at the time the contract is sold

commonwealth a political unit that has local self-government and is voluntarily united with another country

communism an economic system based on total control by government of the means of production, distribution, and exchange of wealth

compensation a payment intended to make up for something taken away, lost, or damaged

compulsory forced; unavoidable

conciliation an effort to bring about goodwill in place of hostility

confederacy a league

confirm to approve

confrontation a head-on meeting of opponents

conquistador Spaniard who conquered and pillaged the wealth of Mexico and Peru in the sixteenth century

conscription a call-up for compulsory military service

conservation an effort to preserve natural resources and a favorable environment for future generations

consumer goods things used directly to serve personal needs

containment a policy of restricting the territorial growth or strategic power of an aggressive nation

corollary an addition to a statement that follows logically from the statement itself

cowry shell a type of seashell used as money in parts of Africa and southern Asia

craft union a union of workers with common or related skills

creditor nation a nation whose loans to other countries are greater than its debts

culture shared ways of living and thinking that characterize a people and are passed on from generation to generation

currant a small seedless raisin

deferred payment payment delayed by agreement with the vendor until a specified time after goods or services have been delivered

deficit financing the spending of more money by a government than is acquired by taxation

demobilization the discharging of troops from military service

democracy a system of government where rule is by consent of the people

Democratic-Republicans a political party, consisting mostly of farmers, workers, and small merchants, who were supporters of Thomas Jefferson in opposition to the pro-Hamiltonian Federalists

deport to send out of the country, especially to send an alien back to his or her own country because of unlawful presence or misbehavior according to the laws of the host country

depose to remove from a position of power

détente a relaxation of tensions or strained relations, as between nations

devaluating decreasing in value, as the currency of one country in relation to that of others

dictator a ruler who has total authority without limits or checks by others, usually having obtained it by force

diplomacy the art of conducting relations between nations

diplomatic immunity special treatment, including freedom from arrest, given by a government to the members of the diplomatic corps of a foreign country

dirigible a cigar-shaped airship that is filled with lighter-than-air gas to keep it aloft and is equipped with engines to drive it in the desired direction

disarmament the reduction or abolition of military weapons and forces

disenfranchise to deprive of the right to vote

dissent an opinion that disagrees in whole or in part with the opinion of the majority

dissenter one who opposes generally accepted beliefs and practices

dissident a person who strongly disagrees with the policies of a government

dividends the part of the profits of a company that are paid out to the shareholders

dove a person who opposes war, particularly one who was against American involvement in Vietnam

duty a tax, especially a tax on imports

economy a system of production and distribution of goods

emancipated freed from domination or hurtful influence

embargo an official order forbidding trade with another country

emigration the act of leaving one's country to make a home in another place

empire territories scattered over a large area and ruled by a single authority

empresario a type of land agent in Texas to whom the Mexican government gave large grants of land along with the responsibility for colonizing them

environment the sum of all the conditions surrounding an individual or a community

envoy a person chosen to represent a government in its dealings with another country

established church a church that is supported by tax money and is regarded as part of the official organization of a country

evangelism the attempt to spread a religion as widely as possible by preaching

excise tax a tax levied on the production, sale, or consumption of a product within a country

expropriation seizure of property by a government

extended family a group of more or less closely related people, often living close to each other, and possibly including several generations of brothers and sisters and cousins, their relatives by marriage or adoption, and servants

extraterrestrial away from the earth

extraterritoriality the right to have citizens abroad tried by special courts set up by their own government

factor an agent who carries out business transactions on behalf of an individual or company

family a group of individuals who are closely related to each other, especially a father and mother and their children living in one household

Fascist a follower of the Italian dictator Benito Mussolini

featherbedding the practice of requiring an employer to hire more workers than necessary or to limit production according to a union rule or safety statute

federalism a principle of government in which power is distributed among a number of territorial units and a central authority

Federalist a follower of Alexander Hamilton in his support of ratification of the Constitution

feminist one who actively supports equal political, economic, and social treatment of the sexes

filibuster (1) a type of small band of adventurers from the United States that made raids in the 1850s into Cuba, Mexico, and points south (2) a tactic used by Senators to delay or prevent passage of a bill by nonstop talking during debate on the bill

fixed income an income that remains the same while the cost of goods and services changes

foreclosure a legal action that bars a person from redeeming his or her property, usually for nonpayment of loans taken out on property

franchise the right to vote

freedom riders students, both Black and White, who challenged racial segregation in interstate bus systems

Fundamentalist a Christian who regards the Bible as a factual record of events

genocide deliberate destruction of an entire ethnic group or nation

ghetto a section of a city or an area where members of a minority or ethnic group live because of social, legal, or economic pressure

gradualism the belief that desirable changes in society are best brought about slowly

graduated income tax a tax on income in which the tax rate rises as the amount of income rises

grant-in-aid (plural **grants-in-aid**) a subsidy or payment from public funds covering part of the cost of a public undertaking or a personal program of education or the like

greenback paper money issued by the Union during the Civil War

gross national product (GNP) the total value of goods produced and services paid for within a nation during a specified time, usually one year

guerrilla warfare irregular warfare by independent bands, often using hit-and-run tactics

habeas corpus an order requiring that a detained person be brought before a court to decide the legality of his or her detention

hawk a person who favors a warlike government policy

hoarding piling up stocks of goods far beyond immediate needs in the expectation that they will later be in short supply

humanitarianism the belief that all people are entitled to live without being subjected to avoidable pain and suffering

hydroponics the cultivation of plants in water containing added nutrients

hygiene the maintenance of cleanliness and practices that promote health and prevent disease

ideology a set of principles underlying a system or theory of government

immigration entry into a country by an alien who intends to remain

impeach to charge a public official with misconduct in office

imperialism a policy of extending a nation's control over other peoples

impressment forcible seizure of persons for the armed forces or public service

incumbent one who holds office

indentured servant a person bound by legal contract to work for another person for a fixed number of years

industrial union a union of the workers in a single industry or numerous related industries

inflation an increase in the cost of goods and services without an increase in production, leading to a decrease in buying power

injunction a court order prohibiting a specific course of action or demanding a certain action

installment plan a merchandising plan whereby customers obtain an article for a small down payment and a written promise to pay the rest, plus interest, in weekly or monthly sums

institution an established practice or organization of a society

interdependent having each individual or part dependent on others

interest the fee collected for a loan

jingoism an exaggerated national pride that favors tests of military might

Joint Chiefs of Staff the heads of the Army, the Navy, and the Air Force, who act together as military advisors of the President

judicial review a determination by the courts as to whether a given law or executive action is in agreement with the Constitution

junta a group in control of a government, particularly after a forcible seizure of power

laissez faire a policy of letting business run the economy without government intervention

land speculator a dealer in land who buys large tracts and parcels it out to sell at a profit

legal tender money that is officially recognized as acceptable for the payment of debts

legislature a lawmaking assembly

lobbying the practice of attempting to influence members of a legislature on behalf of some special interest

local color details in a story or report that illustrate unique characteristics of a particular region

lockout an employer's tactic barring striking employees from returning to work until they agree to certain concessions

logistics the military science of bringing together soldiers, weapons, and supplies at the right time and place

logjammed deadlocked

lubricant a substance that reduces friction between the moving parts of a machine, thereby conserving energy and lessening wear and tear on the machine

lynching execution carried out by a mob without a legal trial

maize Indian corn

majority a number more than half the total number of members of a collection, as of votes in an election

mandate an authority conferred by the League of Nations to manage the affairs of a territory

manumitted freed from slavery

market economy an economic system in which people work for wages and pay for goods with money

maroon a fugitive Black slave of the West Indies or Guinea in the seventeenth and eighteenth centuries, or a descendant of such a slave

martyr one who sacrifices his or her life in supporting a strongly held belief

mass media (singular **mass medium**) the channels of public communication that reach a very large audience, such as television, radio, and newspapers

mass production the technique of using interchangeable parts and assembly lines to manufacture goods in large quantities at low cost

mediate to act as go-between in settling a dispute

mediation the settlement of a dispute by having both sides submit proposals to a third party

megalopolis an area in which the outskirts or suburbs of several large cities overlap to create a single urban complex

mercenary a professional soldier who fights for hire

middle class the middle stratum of society, consisting of people who are neither poor nor rich

militiaman a citizen who serves as a soldier in an emergency

minuteman a colonial militiaman who drilled with others locally to prepare for action at a minute's notice

missionary a person sent to do religious work in a foreign country

moderate a person who believes in and works for slow, orderly change

monarchy government by a single all-powerful leader

monopoly sole control of an industry or a service by one business group without competition from others

morality a sense of what is right; a system of distinguishing right and wrong

muckraker a writer who investigates and calls attention to corruption in government and business

multinational corporation a corporation having a network of branch offices in many host countries

mutual-aid society a type of self-help association formed around 1900 to meet the needs of immigrants

nationalism intense patriotism
nativism a dislike of anything foreign
naturalism a way of writing that stresses the effect of the natural world on the course of people's lives
naturalized having become a citizen by following a legal procedure

neutrality a policy of not taking sides
Nisei children born in the United States of Japanese parents
nomadic wandering; without a fixed abode
nonaggression pact an agreement between nations that they will not attack each other
normalcy a steady, quiet operation of business and government
nuclear fission splitting of the nucleus of atoms with the release of immense energy
nullification a process whereby a state declares a federal law null and void in that state

oarlock a small stirrup for holding an oar in position for rowing a boat
ordinance a regulation or law

pacifist one who believes that war and violence should not be used to settle disputes
pacifist movement the combined actions and statements of people who are opposed to war
patronage the power to base appointments to government jobs on considerations other than just merit
philanthropist one who promotes human welfare by giving gifts, especially money, to help specific movements or causes
philanthropy an effort to promote human welfare
piety devotion to religious duties
pillage to loot or plunder
platform a statement of the goals and ideals of a political party
pocket veto a President's indirect rejection of a bill by holding it unsigned until after the adjournment of Congress
pogrom an organized violent attack against the persons and property of Jews
polarization movement away from moderate positions toward two conflicting extreme views
political asylum the acceptance by one country of refugees who have fled their native country to avoid political persecution
political system the way a country is ruled
polygamy the practice of having several wives
popular sovereignty the principle that people should have a decisive voice in governmental decisions

Populists a nationwide political party in the 1890s that sought reforms that would benefit the common people

precedent an example from the past; in law, a judicial decision that may be used as a model in later cases

prejudice a hostile opinion or judgment formed without regard to the facts

presidential elector one of the officials chosen by the states to choose the first President

presidio a military garrison maintained by Spain in the New World

pressure group a group organized to influence public opinion and governmental policy on a particular issue

primer a reader used by beginners in schools

privateer a privately owned armed ship authorized to cruise against the commerce or warships of an enemy

profiteering charging very high prices for goods that are scarce

progressivism a political movement that proposed to give the task of managing the business of society to experts responsible to elected officials

propaganda the circulation of information aimed at arousing strong emotion for one side of an issue

proprietary colony a colony formed when a ruler grants a large tract of land and the authority to govern it to a proprietor

protectorate a relationship of protection and partial control by a superior power over a dependent country or region

public domain land owned by the government and open to free use by the community at large

public financing the voluntary assignment by taxpayers of a small portion of their income tax toward meeting part of the cost of presidential campaigns

public utility a business organization that supplies the public with essential service, such as transport or electricity

public works works constructed for public use or enjoyment, especially when financed and owned by the government, such as school buildings and highways

racial-caste system a social system in which a person's status is unchangeably fixed by visible racial characteristics, such as skin color

racism the belief that one ethnic stock is superior to another and therefore entitled to favored treatment

radical one who believes in and works for thoroughgoing changes in society

rancho the estate of a large landowner in Texas

rapid-deployment force troops and equipment transported by a fleet of high-speed cargo planes that can reach remote areas quickly

ration a fixed allowance of a scarce commodity granted to an individual

realism the accurate description of people, things, and events in true-to-life situations

reapportionment the redistribution by a state of legislative representation in accordance with shifts in population

rebate a refund of part of a payment, as of taxes

recession a slowdown of economic activity characterized by a decrease in employment, profits, production, and sales

reciprocal returning favor for favor

reconciliation the settling of differences and the resumption of friendly relations

reconnaissance an exploratory survey of enemy territory

Reconstruction the process of bringing the Confederate states back into the Union after the Civil War

red scare a widespread wave of fear of communists and communism

regalia special dress and finery for special occasions

reparations payments demanded of the loser in a war, in compensation for damage done

repression denial of rights

residual powers powers kept by the states and the people by virtue of not being expressly given to the central authority by the Constitution

revenue the income of government

reverse discrimination discrimination affecting people not normally singled out for special treatment

revolution a sudden major change

royal colony a colony ruled by monarchs and ministers of another country

satellite a country that is dominated or controlled by another more powerful country

scalawag a White Southerner who had not supported the Confederacy and who welcomed Republican rule during Reconstruction

seasoned accustomed to working as a slave on a plantation

secession withdrawal from the Union

secondary boycott a gesture of labor solidarity in which the members of a union refuse to purchase or handle products of a company whose workers are on strike

Secretary the head of an executive department of the federal government and a member of the President's cabinet

sedition extreme criticism of a government of a kind that encourages riot or rebellion

segregated separated by race

self-sufficient able to provide for oneself without assistance; independent

Senatorial courtesy the Presidential practice of consulting with a state's Senators before making appointments in that state

serf a person bound to a particular piece of land and transferred with it to a new owner

set aside to designate an area of public land in which settlement and commercial use will be restricted

settlement house a community center that offers services to the poor, especially immigrants, in a slum

sharecropper a member of a landless family in the South who lived and grew crops on a landowner's plantation and returned a large share of the income to the landowner

Shogun one of a succession of military governors who ruled Japan from the 1600s to the 1860s

slag waste material remaining after metal has been extracted from ore

smelter a factory for refining ore

socialist one who favors government ownership of the means of production and a fair division of products among all the members of society

society a group of people bound by common ways of thinking and day-to-day living

sociology the scientific study of social behavior

sovereign fully independent and self-governing

speakeasy a nightclub that sells alcoholic beverages illegally

speculation the taking of business or financial risks in the hope of making a large profit

sphere of influence a specific area in which one foreign power claims exclusive military and trading privileges in a country under foreign domination

spoils system the practice of replacing government officials with followers of the victors in an election

squatter a settler who clears and farms land without having legal ownership

staple crop a farm product produced in large quantity to satisfy a general demand, such as cotton or wheat

status rank or social position

steerage the cheapest and poorest passenger accommodations on a ship

stock market a market dealing in shares of certain companies; a market where stocks and bonds are traded

strategy an overall plan for winning a war or any kind of contest

strikebreaker a worker hired to take the place of a striking worker

subjugate to force to submit to control or servitude

subsidize to support with financial help

suburb a small community on the outskirts of a larger one

subversive a person inside a country who attempts to overthrow or cause the destruction of the established system of government

suffrage the right to vote

summit meeting a conference of the top leaders of governments

sun belt the southern part of the United States, including California, Arizona, Nevada, New Mexico, Texas, and states of the Deep South

sunshine patriot one who gives loyal support to a country's struggles only so long as things go well

surtax an additional tax on something already taxed

swing shift the work shift in industry from midafternoon to midnight

take-home pay a person's wages or salary after taxes and other deductions

technology the application of scientific knowledge to useful purposes

temperance abstinence or strict control of the drinking of alcohol

tenement a small apartment building containing quarters for many families, especially one that is crowded and poorly constructed

tepee an American Indian dwelling made of three or more poles lashed together at the top and covered with skins

territorial integrity the right of a nation to have its boundaries respected by all other nations

terrorist one who uses violence and scare tactics to weaken opposition

theocracy a political system ruled by religious leaders

theocratic society a society governed by officials believed to have divine guidance

third-world nations a group of nations, especially in Africa and Asia, that are not aligned with either communist or noncommunist nations; the nations that are not industrially developed

title legal ownership

topography the physical or natural features of a region

tributary a stream that flows into a larger stream, river, or lake

tribute payment demanded of subjects by a ruler or conqueror

truce a temporary cease-fire agreement between opposing forces

trust a combination of individual companies under a central management

ultimatum a final statement threatening serious penalties if certain specified terms are not accepted

unanimous having the agreement and consent of all

Union the United States as a whole, or the states that did not secede in 1861

union shop a shop in which union membership is required for continued employment but not for hiring

urban pertaining to city life; having to do with cities or towns

urbanites city dwellers

utopia an imaginary land where social conditions are perfect

vassal a person in a subordinate position who owes service and obedience to a protector or ruler

verge edge; borderline

veto the rejection by a President of a law approved by Congress

Vietcong (plural **Vietcong**) a member of the guerrilla forces of the Vietnamese communist movement supported by North Vietnam

vigilantes unofficial police who also act as self-appointed judges and jurors

Wall Street a street in the financial district in New York City which has become a symbol of financial power and capitalism

welfare agency a government organization or office that acts to improve the living conditions of people, especially those who are unfortunate or handicapped

wet a person who is in favor of and supports the sale and consumption of alcoholic beverages

white-collar worker a worker who dresses in business clothes on the job and does not do manual work

white man's burden the idea that Whites have a duty to govern and civilize "backward" people of other races

white supremacy the control of political, social, and economic life by Whites

wickiup a dwelling made of saplings and brush by American Indians

yellow-dog contract a promise not to join a union, required by an employer as a condition of employment

yellow journalism the use of sensational stories to sell newspapers

zone to divide an area into parts, or zones, that are restricted to specific activities, types of building or services

Index

Throughout the Index **boldfaced** page references indicate pictures or captions.

Cooke, Jay, 420
Coolidge, Calvin, as President, 549–550
Cooper, James Fenimore, 280
Copley, John, **80**
"Copperheads," 346
Corbin, Margaret, 134–135
Cornell, Ezra, 423
Cornish, Samuel, 322
Cornwallis, Charles, 135–137, **142,** 150
  and Yorktown, 153–154
Coronado, Francisco de, 48
Cortes, Hernando, 34–**36**
Cotton gin, 248, 264, 272
Council of Censors, 166
Council of National Defense, 534
Crane, Stephen, 425
Crawford, William, 283–284
Credit Mobilier scandal, 372
Crockett, Davy, **295**
Croix de Guerre, 535
Crow, Jim, 375–379
Cuba, 489, 493–494
  American interests in, 501–502, 507–508
  and arms support in Africa, 726
  and Bay of Pigs, 676
  and Castro, 674–675
  filibuster raids on, 500–501
  and "Ostend Manifesto," 330
  and Spanish-American War, 503–507
  Spanish conquest of, 34
Cullen, Countee, 563
Cumberland Road, 242
Currency Act (1764), 110
Cushing, Caleb, 485
Custer, George A., 401
Czar Alexander II, 462
Czar Nicholas II, 520
Czechoslovakia, 538
  invasion of Soviet Union, 716
  Nazi invasion, 605
  in World War II, 628

DaGama, Vasco, 32
Daiquiri, 504–505
Daley, Richard, 700
Dallas, Alexander J., 299
Darrow, Clarence, 558
Dartmouth vs. Woodward, 289
Darwin, Charles, 558
Daugherty, Harry, 548
Davis, Jefferson, 329, 335, 338
Davis, Miles, 671
Dawes, Charles G., 594
Dawes, William, 114, 117
Dawes Act, 401
D-Day, 628–629
Deane, Silas, 124
Debs, Eugene V., 436, **453–454,** 532
Declaration of Independence, 68, 125–130,
  162, 167, 184, 200, 212, 234
Declaratory Act of 1766, 108, 110
Deerfield Massacre, **102–103**
Defense spending, 716
Degler, Carl, 474
De Grasse, François, 153–154
De La Vérendrye, Pierre, 26, 48
De Leon, Juan Ponce, 34
De Lesseps, Ferdinand, 510
De Lôme, Dupuy, 504

De Magallanes, Fernando (*see* Magellan,
  Fernando)
Demobilization, defined, 640
Democracy:
  and the Constitution, 192–194
  among First Americans, 20
  rise of, 280–284
Democratic Party, beginning of, 289
Democratic-Republicans, 204, 217, 219
  and Thomas Jefferson, 215–218
  and XYZ Affair, 216–217
Democrats, 299, 329–330
  election of 1868, 367–368
  during Reconstruction, 445
De Narvaez, Panfilo, 4
Denby, Edwin C., 548
Department of Agriculture, 403
Department of Energy, 728
Department of Health, Education and Wel-
  fare, 663
Department of Housing and Urban Develop-
  ment (HUD), 691
Department of Labor, 456
Department of State, creation of, 206
Department of the Treasury:
  and Alexander Hamilton, 206–208
  creation of, 206
Department of War, creation of, 206
Depression, the Great, 566–586
  and Cleveland's administration, 451–452
  and President Hoover, 573–574
  Roosevelt and the New Deal, 574–586
  in rural areas, 571–573
  stock market crash, 568–569
Desegregation, school, 666
De Soto, Hernando, 46
Detente, 743
De Thulstrup, Thur, **338**
Detroit, 693
  British occupation of, 158
  in War of 1812, 228
DeVaca, Cabeza, 46
Dewey, George, 494
Dewey, John, 423
Dewey, Melvil, 426
Dewey, Thomas E., 645
Dewey Decimal system, 426
Dias, Bartholomew, 31
Diaz, Adolfo, 597
Diaz, Porfirio, 515
Dickens, Charles, 236
Dickinson, John, 122
  and Articles of Confederation, 167–169
Dictators, rise of, 601–602
Diem, Ngo Dinh, 680, 695
"Dime novels," 424
Dirksen, Everett, 688
District of Columbia, 210
  and slaves, 328
Dix, Dorothea Lynde, 278
Dogon tribe, **59**
Dole, Sanford B., 491
Dom Affonso, King of the Congo, 69
Dominican Republic, 511, 513, 596
  and Johnson foreign policy, 694
Doolittle, Amos, **115**
Douglas, Lewis, 345
Douglas, Stephen A., 327, 330
  (*See also* Lincoln-Douglas debates)
Douglass, Frederick, 322–**323**
Downes vs. Bidwell, 509

Draft, the, 608
  protests, 698
  (*See also* Conscription)
Drago, Luis M., 513
Drago Doctrine, 512–513, 522
Drake, Sir Francis, 48
Dred Scott decision, 332, 386
Dreiser, Theodore, 425
DuBois, William Edward Burghardt, 383,
  555
Dulles, John Foster, 662, 672
Dunbar, Paul, 425
Dunkards, 84
Dunkirk, 607
Dunn, Harvey, 238
Durang, Ferdinand, 228
Dust storms, 572
Dutch West India Company, 43–44, **46**
Duvalier, Jean-Claude, 741

Earhart, Amelia, **561**
Earth Day, 749
Economic Opportunity Act of 1964, 689
Economy:
  barter, 29
  market, 29
Edison, Thomas Alva, 398
Education:
  adult, 426–428
  in Aztec society, 12
  and the baby boom, 668–669
  for free Blacks, 278
  higher, 423
    for Blacks, 380–384
  for immigrants, 472–473
  public, 277–278, 422–423
  and rise of Black leaders, 380
  for women, 278
Edwards, Jonathan, 74, 77
Egypt, 52
  attack on Israel, 719
  and Six-Day War, 695
  in World War II, 626–627
Egypt-Israel peace treaty, 733
Einstein, Albert, 635
Eisenhower, Dwight D., 628
  as President, 655, 658, 660, 662–665
  and federal aid to education, 669–669
  and foreign policy, 672–673
  and Latin America, 674–675
El Alamein, 627
"Elastic clause," 208, 290
Electors, 216
  presidential, 281
Eliot, Charles W., 424
Eliot, John, 78, 90
Elkins Act, 455
Ellicott, Andrew, 211
Ellington, Duke, 563, 671
Ellison, Ralph, 670
Emancipation Proclamation, 345–346, 386
Embargo Act of 1807, 224
Emergency Fleet Corporation, 534
Emergency Relief and Construction Act,
  573
Emerson, Ralph Waldo, 280, 322
Emigrants:
  Cuban, 741
  Haitian, 741

779

Gold standard, 452
Goldwater, Barry, 689–690, 697
Gompers, Samuel, 434–435, 437
    in World War I, 532–533
Good Neighbor Policy, 598
Gorgas, William C., 510
"Gospel of Wealth, The" (Carnegie), 393
Gossens, Salvador Allende, 724
Gould, Jay, 372
Government:
    in colonial New England, 77
    in the colonies, 91–94
        (See also Continental Congress)
    of the Incas, 7–10
    of new-formed states, 162–163
Grady, Henry W., 408–410
Graham, Martha, 562
Grand Canyon, 48, 407
Grange (see National Grange of the Patrons
    of Husbandry)
Grant, Ulysses S., 350–352, 354–356, 365,
    511
    as President, 368
        and greenback issue, 450
        and Reconstruction, 364, 369–373
Graves, Thomas, 154
Great Lakes, 15, 44, 104, 258
    in War of 1812, 228
Great Plains:
    droughts in, 572
    and westward Indian movement, 250–252
Great Salt Lake, 253
    exploration of, 255
    and Mormons, 258
Greeley, Horace, 372
Greenback Party, 450
Greenbacks, 367, 450
Greene, Nathanael, 134, 152–153
Grenville, George, 107
Gross National Product (GNP), 688
Guadalcanal, 633–634
Guam:
    acquisition of, 507
    in World War II, 631
Guatemala, 13, 514, 674
Guerrilla warfare, 151
Guilford Courthouse, 153
Gulf of Aqaba, 694
Gulf of Tonkin, 697
Gunther, John, 668

Habeas corpus, writ of, 366, 371
Hague, the, 520, 522
Haiti, 514, 596
    slave revolt in, 63–64
    U.S. withdrawal, 598
Hakluyt, Richard, 42
Haley, Alex, 97
Hamilton, Alexander, 178, 181
    and Federalists, 214–218
    and national banking system, 206
    as Secretary of the Treasury, 206–208
Hamilton, Henry, 146
Handlin, Oscar, 474
Hanoi, 696, 718
Hanson, John, 168
Harding, Warren G., as President, 548,
    591
Harlan, John Marshall, 379
Harlem Renaissance, 562–563
Harmar, Josiah, 244

Harpers Ferry, 334
Harris, Joel Chandler, 425, 488
Harrison, Benjamin:
    as President, 446
    and silver coinage, 450
Harte, Bret, 425
Hartford Convention, 281
Hawaii, 171, 484
    annexation of, 490–491
    early American interests, 487–488
Hawthorne, Nathaniel, 280
Hay, John, 495
Hayde, Tom, 701
Hayes, Rutherford B., 443
    and greenback issue, 450
    as President, 374, 444–445, 364
Haymarket Massacre, 436
Hayne, Robert, 286, 321
Hays, Mary Ludwig (see Pitcher, Molly)
Haywood, William, 532
Head Start program, 689
Hearst, William Randolph, 427, 503
Helsinki Agreement, 736
Henry, Patrick, 109–111, 114, 181, 186
Henry the Navigator (see Prince Henry of
    Portugal)
Hepburn Act, 455
Herman, George (see Babe Ruth)
Hessians, 133, 140
Highway Act of 1956, 671
Himalaya Mountains, 631
Hine, H.G., 252
Hine, Lewis, 417
Hiroshima, 635–636
Hispaniola, 33–34, 63
Hiss, Alger, 657
Hitler, Adolf, 602, 606–607, 616, 627, 629–
    630
Hoban, James, 212
Hobby, Oveta Culp, 663
Ho Chi Minh, 673, 680, 697
Holiday, Billie, 671
Holland, 26, 39, 607
    exploration and colonization, 44–45
    and slave trade, 59
Holmes, Oliver Wendell, 280
"Holy Alliance," 260
Home Loan Bank System, 573
Homer, Winslow, 274
Homestead Act, 401–402
Hoover, Herbert, 556, 568
    and the Depression, 573–574
    as President, 535
    as Secretary of Commerce, 549
Hoover Commission, 644
Hopkins, Harry, 582
Horne, Lena, 671
House Judiciary Committee, 366
House of Burgesses, 93
House of Commons, 110
House of Representatives, 193
    first speaker, 200
    and impeachment, 195
    and Jefferson-Burr decision, 218
    role of, 206
House Un-American Activities Committee,
    656–657
Houston, Sam, 296–299
Howe, Julia Ward, 340
Howe, Samuel Gridley, 278
Howe, William, 133–135, 142

Howells, William Dean, 424
Hudson, Henry, 39, 44
Hudson Bay, 42
Huerta, Victoriano, 515
Hughes, Charles Evans, 591
Hughes, Langston, 563
Hull, Cordell, 598, 607
Hull, William, 228
Hull House, 441–442
Humanitarianism, 278–279
Humphrey, George, 662
Humphrey, Hubert, 688, 700
    and 1968 election, 701–702
Hungary:
    and Russian suppression, 681
    in World War II, 628
Hutchinson, Anne, 77
Hydroponics, 751
Hye, Gerald P., 606

Ickes, Harold, 582
Immigrants, 275–276
    Armenian, 462
    arrival and processing of, 458–460, 464–
        465
    Bulgarian, 466
    Catholic, 473
    Chinese, 458, 469–471
    Czechoslovakian, 461, 465
    and education, 472–473
    Finnish, 466
    French Canadians, 469
    German, 458
    Greek, 461, 466, 557
    Irish, 89
    Italian, 458, 461, 465–466, 469
    Japanese, 458, 469, 471–472, 557
    Jewish, 465, 469, 472
        (See also Immigration, Jewish)
    Mexicans, 469, 741
    in Northeast, 317
    Polish, 458, 462, 466, 469, 557
    problems of, 468–469
    Russian Jews, 458, 462
    settling of, 465–466, 469
    Sicilian, 461
    Syrian, 462, 466
    in West, 319
Immigration:
    fears and problems of, 473–474
    Jewish, 466–467
    and labor, 395
    and literacy requirement, 474
    quotas, 557
    reasons for, 460–462
Immigration and Naturalization Service,
    741
Immigration Restriction League, 474
Imperialism:
    beginnings of, 484–491
    defined, 482
    prophets of, 487–488
    and Spanish-American War, 506–507
    and U.S. as global power, 492–496
Implied powers, doctrine of, 290
Impressment, 223–224
Inca Indians, 7–10
    Spanish conquest of, 35–36
Indentured servants, 81
    in Middle Colonies, 82

King, Rufus, 282
King George's War, 104
Kissinger, Henry, 714
  and Arab oil embargo, 720
  and Ford administration, 725–726
  and Vietnam cease-fire, 717–718
Knights of Labor, Noble and Holy Order of the, **433**–434, 448
Know-Nothing Party, 276, 331
Korean War, 653–656
Kosciusko, Thaddeus, **144**–145
Ku Klux Klan, 371, 555–557
Ky, Nguyer Caor, 697

Labor:
  migrant, 583
  and the New Deal, 580–582
  and post-World War II economy, 642–643
  sources of, 394–395
Labor movement:
  beginnings of, 274–275
  organization of, 432–439
    (*See also* Unions)
  split in, 437–439
  and women, 432–433
Lafayette, Marquis de, 145
Lafayette Escadrille, 530–531
Lafitte, Jean, 230
LaFollette, Robert, 453–454, 549
Lake Champlain, 116, **118**, 138
  in War of 1812, 229
Lake Erie:
  and the Erie Canal, 266
  in War of 1812, 227
Lake of the Woods, 231, 259
Lanier, Sidney, 424
Lansing-Ishii Agreement, 603
Laos, 680
  and communist control, 726
LaSalle, Robert de, 44, 48
Latin America:
  and Eisenhower administration, 674–675
  and Good Neighbor policy, 598
  U.S. interests in, 498–516, 596–597
    Cuba, 500–502, 507–508
    Mexican interests, 515–516
    Panama Canal, 509–510
    Spanish-American War, 503–507
    Venezuela, 512
Latrobe, Benjamin, 212
League of Five Nations, 22, 43–44
  (*See also* Iroquois confederacy)
League of Nations, 536, 539–540, 590–591, 599
League of Six Nations, 22
  (*See also* Iroquois confederacy)
League of the Iroquois, 20
  (*See also* Iroquois confederacy)
Le Duc Tho, 718
Lee, Jason, 255
Lee, Richard Henry, 125
Lee, Robert E., 342, 347–349, 354–356
Legislatures, colonial, 93–94
Lend-lease aid in World War II, 617
L'Enfant, Pierre Charles, 210, **212**, 416
Lenin, Nikolai, 600
Lewis, Meriwether, **220**
Lexington, 114–115, 117, 123
Liberia and free Blacks, 321
Liberty bell, **130**

Liberty Bonds, 533, 597
Libraries, public, 426
Lilienthal, David, 580
Liliuokalani, Queen, 490–491
Limited Test Ban Treaty, 715
Lincoln, Abraham:
  and justice of Mexican War, 303–304
  opposition to American Party, 331
  as President, 335–336
    assassination of, 361
    and ten percent plan, 360
    (*See also* Lincoln-Douglas debates)
Lincoln, Benjamin, 149–150
Lincoln-Douglas debates, 332–334
Lincoln University, 278
Lindbergh, Charles A., 563–564, 597
Lindeux, Robert, **251**
Literature, American, 424–426
  in the Fifties, 670
  growth of, 279–280
Little Big Horn, battle of, 401
Little Richard, 671
Little Rock, 191, 666
Liuzzo, Viola, 692
Livingston, Robert, 267–268, 290
Locke, Alain, 562
Locke, John, 128–129
Lockout, 436
Lockport, **266**
Lodge, Henry Cabot, 503, 539–540
Logan, George, 701
Logan Act, 701
London Company, 41
London Naval Treaty of 1930, 604
"Lone Star Republic," 297
  (*See also* Texas)
Longfellow, Henry Wadsworth, 22, 280
Lopez, Narciso, 500
Lord Inca, 9–10, 35
Louis, Joe, 563
Louis XIV, King of France, 48, 144, 212
Louisiana, 48
  acquisition by Spain, 106
  and Spanish claims, 158
Louisiana Purchase, 220–221
Louisiana Territory, 44, 220–221, 232
L'Ouverture, Pierre Toussaint, 64, 220
Lowell, James Russell, 280
Lumumba, Patrice, 676
Lundy, Benjamin, 321
Lynching, 377
Lyon, Mary, 278

MacArthur, Douglas, 631, 633
  and the Korean War, 654–656
McCarran-Walter Act, 658
McCarthy, Eugene, 699
McCarthy, Joseph, 657, 663
McClellan, George B., 342
McCormick, Cyrus, 417
McCormick Harvester plant strike, 436
McCulloch vs. Maryland, 290
McGovern, George, 699, 718
McGuffey, William Holmes, 277
McKay, Claude, 563
Mackay, Douglas, 662
McKinley, William, 452–454, 509
  and Philippine Islands, 494–495
  and war with Spain, 504
McKinley Tariff of 1890, 446, 460–461

McNary-Haugen bill, 550, 573
McPherson, J. Gordon, 455, 476
McWilliams, Carey, 621
Madison, James, 162, 164, 193
  and the Bill of Rights, 186–188
  and Constitutional Convention, 181
  as President, 225–229, 242, 258
  as Secretary of State, 225
Magellan, Ferdinand, 38
Mahan, Alfred T., 492–493, 503
Mailer, Norman, 670
Malcolm X, 703
Malenkov, Georgi, 655
Manchukuo, 604
Manchuria, 496, 537
  Japanese invasion of, 604
Manhattan Island, 132–133, **316**
Manifest Destiny, 292, 294, 304–308, 481, 488
  and Latin America, 500
Manila, 494·
  in World War II, 631
Mann, Horace, 277
Mansa Musa, 52
Marbury, William, 188
Marbury vs. Madison, 188
Marion, Francis, 151
Marne, battles of the, 523–524, 528
Maroon, 64
Marquette, Jacques, 44, 48
Marshall, George, 650, 652
Marshall, James and discovery of gold, 306–307
Marshall, John, 188, **196**, 289–290
Marshall Plan, 644, 649–650, 676
Maryland:
  and Articles of Confederation, 169
  colonial, 82, 84
  and slavery, 65
  Tories in, 131
Mason, George, 86
Massachusetts, 41–42
  colonial, 74, 77–79, 83
    and American militia, 116
    education in, 90
    government, 93
    and "Intolerable Acts," 112
  and constitutional convention, 163
  and public education, 277
  and slavery, 164
  state constitution of, 164
  Tories in, 131
  town meetings, 124
Massachusetts Bay Colony, 42
Massachusetts Supreme Court and labor unions, 274
Mass production, 398–399
  concept of, 272
Mather, Cotton, 77
Mather, Richard, 74
Mayaguez, 726
Meat Inspection Act, 455
Medicare, 690
Meir, Golda, 720
Melville, Herman, 280
Mennonites, 84, 462
Meredith, James, 679
Mexican War, 254, 299–305, 326
Mexican-Americans:
  and migrant labor, 583
  and racial conflict, 621

Photo Credits

000304

FROM SEA TO SHINING SEA

8 th grade

$22.00